THE ORIGINS OF THE URBAN CRISIS

PRINCETON STUDIES IN AMERICAN POLITICS:
HISTORICAL, INTERNATIONAL, AND COMPARATIVE PERSPECTIVES

SERIES EDITORS
IRA KATZNELSON, MARTIN SHEFTER, THEDA SKOCPOL

A list of titles in this series appears at the back of the book

THE ORIGINS OF THE URBAN CRISIS

RACE AND INEQUALITY
IN POSTWAR DETROIT

With a new preface by the author

Thomas J. Sugrue

PRINCETON UNIVERSITY PRESS   PRINCETON AND OXFORD

Copyright © 1996, 2005 by Princeton University Press
Published by Princeton University Press, 41 William Street,
Princeton, New Jersey 08540
In the United Kingdom: Princeton University Press, 3 Market Place,
Woodstock, Oxfordshire OX20 1SY

First edition, 1996

First paperback printing, 1998

First Princeton Classic Edition, with a new preface by the author, 2005

Library of Congress Cataloging-in-Publication Data

Sugrue, Thomas J., 1962–
The origins of the urban crisis : race and inequality in postwar Detroit :
with a new preface by the author / Thomas J. Sugrue.— 1st Princeton Classic ed.
p.   cm. — (Princeton classic editions) (Princeton studies in American politics)
Includes bibliographical references and index.
ISBN-13: 978-0-691-12186-4 (pbk. : alk. paper)
ISBN-10: 0-691-12186-9 (pbk. : alk. paper)
1. African Americans—Michigan—Detroit—Social conditions—20th century.
2. African Americans—Michigan—Detroit—Economic conditions—20th century.
3. Racism—Michigan—Detroit—History—20th century. 4. Poverty—Michigan—
Detroit—History—20th century. 5. Detroit (Mich.)—Economic conditions—20th century.
6. Detroit (Mich.)—Social conditions—20th century. 7. Detroit (Mich.)—Race relations.
I. Title. II. Series. III. Series: Princeton studies in American politics
F574.D49N4835   2005
305.8′00977434—dc22   2005047695

British Library Cataloging-in-Publication Data is available

This book has been composed in Bitstream Caledonia

Printed on acid-free paper. ∞

pup.princeton.edu

Printed in the United States of America

10 9 8 7 6 5 4 3 2 1

For Dana and My Parents

Contents

Appendixes

Illustrations _____

Figures

Maps

Tables

P.1 Abandoned and collapsed houses, like this one near my father's childhood home on Detroit's West Side, are a common sight in Detroit in the early twenty-first century. As working-class poor neighborhoods continue to suffer population loss and disinvestment, their landscapes are pockmarked by decrepit buildings and vacant lots.

Preface to the Princeton Classic Edition ——————

A FEW SUMMERS AGO, I spent a humid afternoon driving through the neighborhoods where my parents had grown up on Detroit's West Side. My tour took me to the intersection of Chalfonte and Santa Rosa, an unassuming corner in a quiet neighborhood of working-class homes where my father had spent much of his childhood. My grandparents' house is still standing, but they would not recognize the neighborhood around it. My father and his brother and sisters used to run across the alley to play at their Aunt Margaret's house. Only faint brick and cement traces of that long-ago demolished house remain—the hint of a foundation, pieces of the cement walkway. Aunt Margaret's house exists intact only in yellowing family photographs. Parts of the neighborhood have reverted to nature. By mid-summer, waist-high grass and weeds obscure the many vacant lots where twenties-era wood-frame bungalows and simple brick and shingle homes like Aunt Margaret's once stood. Just a few blocks away, a little house, very much like my father's (fig. P.1) had collapsed into a pile of shingles and splinters. However grim the vista, many longtime homeowners have created little oases amidst the rubble and ruin. Postage stamp–sized, neatly cut lawns, bordered by zinnias and impatiens, stood out amidst the overgrown lots. A group of boys played hoops underneath a backboard nailed to a telephone pole—a small pocket of vitality in what was otherwise a dreary place.

The neighborhood around Santa Rosa Drive is, in many ways, a typical blue-collar Detroit neighborhood, a microcosm of the city's twentieth-century history. In the years following World War II, when my father was a teenager, manufacturing jobs were plentiful in the city. Along Lyndon Street, just a few blocks from my father's house, was a row of small factories that fabricated parts and supplies for the automobile industry. Livernois and Wyoming Avenues, the major thoroughfares that bounded the neighborhood on the east and west, provided easy access to the big West Side General Motors plants and, further to the south, to the massive Ford River Rouge complex and the myriad steel mills and chemical plants along the Detroit River. A short drive or bus ride to the east led to the archipelago of Dodge and Chrysler plants near Highland Park and Hamtramck. My grand-

I am indebted to my colleagues, friends, readers, and critics who have offered astute comments and asked hard questions about *The Origins of the Urban Crisis* over the last eight years. I am particularly grateful to the dozens of scholars, teachers and writers, activists, and policymakers who have invited me to speak about this book and have generously taken time to give me tours of their own cities. Thanks also to Dana Barron, committed urbanite and sharp critic, for her comments on this preface, and to Liz Moselle for her useful suggestions.

parents' neighborhood was also home to carpenters, ironworkers, cement masons, and other tradesmen (all of them men, nearly all of them white). Construction was booming in Detroit's peripheral neighborhoods and its nearby suburbs. Only a few miles to the north and west, thousands of new houses were under construction in sprawling suburbs like Oak Park, Southfield, Redford, and Livonia. Developers broke ground on the first suburban shopping centers and office parks just about the time that my father graduated from high school.

By the summer of 2002, Detroit's postwar boom was a distant memory. Most of the little factories along Lyndon had closed. Even in rush hour, all six lanes of once-busy Livernois Avenue were almost empty, allowing me to drive slowly past the bricked-over storefronts and vacant lots in this once-thriving neighborhood business district. Ravaged by industrial decline, racial conflict, and disinvestment, Detroit had lost nearly half of its population since 1950. Most of the factories that had provided many of my grandparents' neighbors with stable jobs and union-negotiated wages and benefits were shuttered or demolished or running with small, rump workforces. Old Dodge Main had been torn down, the West Side Fleetwood plant was long closed, and even the gargantuan Ford River Rouge plant now ran with a few thousand workers, a mere fraction of the 90,000 it had employed during World War II.

The neighborhood around Chalfonte and Santa Rosa had also changed profoundly over the last half of the twentieth century. Until 1963, all of the neighborhood's residents had been white. When I visited, the neighborhood's residents were almost all people of color. Detroit's often violent history of racial conflict over housing had played out with particular force in my grandparents' old neighborhood. In 1949, area residents (including one of my father's older cousins and my grandmother's twin brother) had formed a neighborhood association to stem the movement of "the colored" into their neighborhood. Their efforts were, for a time, successful. Blacks moved into neighborhoods to the south and east, but the threat of harassment was an effective deterrent to "race mixing" in the area around Santa Rosa and Chalfonte. An intrepid black family moved onto Chalfonte briefly in 1955, but protests and violence drove them out. As the neighborhood's white population aged and as many white families trekked to Detroit's booming suburbs, resistance to blacks weakened. After one last burst of antiblack violence, the remaining whites left in droves. By 1970, the surrounding neighborhood residents were overwhelmingly African American. Aunt Margaret, the last family member to move from the neighborhood, befriended some of her new neighbors, but watched with sadness as many of the nearby houses—not built to last the ages and now mostly a half-century old—rapidly deteriorated. Many properties had been converted into rentals; others suffered the ravages of their residents' poverty (old houses, especially cheap ones, often required costly repairs). Exacerbating the situation was the persistence of redlining. Banks and mortgage firms were notoriously reluctant to invest in older, urban neighborhoods with large minority populations. As Detroit continued to hemorrhage jobs, population, and tax dollars (a process that had begun in the 1950s), city services deteriorated, schools suffered, and neighborhood residents joined in the litany of complaints about inadequate police protection, irregular trash pickup, lack of snowplowing in the winter, and infrequent bus service.[1]

Data from the 2000 U.S. census provide a more complete picture of the economic and demographic transformation of the little slice of Detroit's West Side where my father grew up. In 2000, the neighborhood was 99 percent African American. Twelve percent of area adults were unemployed, and many more had joined the ranks of what economists called "disappointed job seekers," who were no longer counted as unemployed because they had given up looking for work. The median income in the census tract around Santa Rosa was $23,848 (nearly $20,000 less than the national median household income in 2000). About one-quarter of all households in the neighborhood earned less than $10,000 per year. Altogether, 36 percent of families with children under the age of eighteen lived beneath the poverty line. And, as a stark reminder of the chronic health problems that afflict many working-class and poor people, 35 percent of area residents between ages twenty-one and sixty-four were disabled. The area around Chalfonte and Santa Rosa was by no means one of Detroit's poorest neighborhoods—many census tracts had poverty rates of 60, 70, even 80 percent and many had lower household incomes. If the census were to take place today, after several years of recession (remember that the 2000 census data were gathered amidst the longest economic boom in the last fifty years), the situation would probably be much worse.[2]

The fate of my grandparents' neighborhood is grimly familiar to anyone who has spent time in a major American city. Despite more than half a century of civil rights activism and changing racial attitudes, American cities (particularly the old industrial centers of the Northeast and Midwest) remain deeply divided by race. Poverty rates among people of color in major American cities are staggeringly high. Vast tracts of urban land lie pockmarked with boarded-up buildings, abandoned houses, and rubble-strewn lots. At the same time, hundreds of thousands of acres of marshland, meadow, farm, and forest on the periphery of major metropolitan areas get gobbled up each year for vast tracts of new housing, shopping malls, and office parks. City governments struggle with shrinking tax bases and ever-increasing demands on public services, while wealthy suburban municipalities enjoy strong property tax revenues, excellent public services, and superb schools. The causes and remedies of persistent metropolitan inequalities continue to vex policymakers and to generate intense debate among scholars, activists, and the general public.

These inequalities—and a host of deeply held misunderstandings about their causes—led me to write *The Origins of the Urban Crisis*. The book explains the transformation of American cities—through a case study of Detroit—as the result of a combination of three forces that occurred simultaneously. Any one of them would have had devastating consequences, but the combined effect of all three reshaped American cities in ways that still affect us today. First was the flight of jobs, particularly the relatively well-paying, secure, and mostly unionized industrial jobs that dominated the postwar urban economy. Second was the persistence of workplace discrimination, despite remarkable legal and political gains accomplished by the struggle for black civil rights. The third was intractable racial segregation in housing, segregation that led to the uneven distribution of power and resources in metropolitan areas, leaving some places behind while others thrived. Sociologist Charles Tilly describes "resource hoarding" as one of the major contributors to historical inequalities—and the story of American metropolitan areas, like Detroit, is a history of the ways that whites, through the combined advantages of race and residence, were able to hoard political and economic resources—jobs, public services, education, and other goods—to their own advantage at the expense of the urban poor.[3] *Origins* uncovered a largely hidden, forgotten history of actions by policymakers, large corporations, small businesses (particularly realtors), and ordinary citizens that created and reinforced racial and class inequalities and perpetuated the political marginalization of African Americans in modern American life.

The transformation of Detroit was not the "natural" inevitable consequence of market forces at work. At a political moment when Americans have a deep faith in the market—a faith that has strengthened since I wrote *Origins*—it is difficult for many readers to see that racialized inequality is, at core, a political problem. Still widespread is the assumption that blacks and whites live apart solely because of personal choice, not because of the enduring effects of public policies that have encouraged racial segregation. Deeply rooted is the belief that unemployment and poverty are the fault of poor people and their deviant attitudes and behaviors, not the consequence of macroeconomic changes that have gutted urban labor markets. In the year that *Origins* was first published, Congress passed a "welfare reform" act that was premised on a fundamentally individualistic understanding of the causes of poverty. The assumptions that shaped the Personal Responsibility and Work Opportunity Reconciliation Act of 1996 were belied by the previous fifty years of the history of racial discrimination, segregation, and job flight that I chronicled. The fate of Detroit and other cities like it, I argued, was not primarily the result of the supposedly pathological behaviors of the poor, the lack of a work ethic among African Americans, or the breakdown of the "traditional" nuclear family in inner cities. While many historians and other social scientists have continued to chip away at explanations of poverty that give primacy to culture and behavior, influential conservative scholars, backed by well-funded think tanks and foundations, have continued to ignore or downplay the political and economic causes of impoverishment. Instead, they have resuscitated theories about racial differences in culture, values, and even intelligence. Those arguments—however discredited by rigorous scholarly research—continue to appeal to those who believe that the causes and solutions of social problems start and end with poor people themselves.[4]

Origins was my effort to challenge the stale thinking about the causes of race and class inequalities in modern America. It was also part of a scholarly project to open up a rich, historical understanding of the racial dynamics, economic changes, and political processes that remade America in the mid-twentieth century. When *Origins* was first published, the literature on post–World War II American history was thin. I situated the history of race and the transformation of postwar urban America in the context of dramatically changing racial attitudes and practices; in the emergence of new forms of capital mobility; and in the strange career of New Deal liberalism that simultaneously empowered African Americans while perpetuating race-based inequalities in American life. Each of these topics has now generated a large and incredibly rich scholarly literature—some of which builds on *Origins*, some of which pushes beyond it, and some of which sets forth important new directions for the field.

At the core of *Origins* is a reappraisal of liberalism and a discussion of the rise of grassroots conservatism. Challenging the conventional wisdom that the New Deal had unraveled because of the supposed "excesses" of 1960s liberalism, black power, and identity politics, I argued that grassroots conservatism, particularly around civil rights and racial equality, was deeply rooted in the North. I also argued, building on the cutting-edge work of scholars of American political development, that racial inequalities were a constitutive part of the New Deal's "rights revolution." Recent work by political scientists and political sociologists on welfare, fair employment practices and workplace discrimination policy, affirmative action, and political ideology has provided an even richer, more comprehensive picture of the ways that federal policies reinforced racial inequalities, even at the zenith of liberalism.[5] A slew of local case studies have shown that the patterns of racial politics and policymaking that shaped postwar Detroit were common to metropolitan areas throughout the country. Studies of housing policy and grassroots politics in cities as diverse as Baltimore, Brooklyn, Lancaster, Milwaukee, Chicago, Philadelphia, and St. Louis have demonstrated convincingly that white racial conservatism or indifference hamstrung the struggle for racial equality well before the tumult of the 1960s.[6] Even in multiethnic and multiracial metropolitan areas like Los Angeles and Oakland and the East Bay, black-white divisions remained a persistent element of post–New Deal politics.[7] The postwar urban South, widely treated as exceptional by popular analysts and many historians, also shares much in common with the urban North. The process of the "southernization" of the North, driven by black and white migration to places like Detroit, Pittsburgh, and Chicago, was countered by a "northernization" of the South, particularly in the 1950s and 1960s, as northern migrants reshaped southern metropolitan politics and southerners began to embrace the northern rhetoric of de facto racial segregation. Postwar Charlotte and Atlanta have much more in common with postwar Detroit than I ever could have imagined when I wrote Origins.[8]

Tying together the history of these diverse places was a shifting but ever-persistent ideology of whiteness. Origins also built on a then-new, now well-established, literature on racial identities. The early 1990s witnessed a burgeoning interest in the cultural construction of "whiteness," with scholars taking a racial marker that had largely been taken for granted and probing its creation and permutations. With the exception of Arnold Hirsch's work on Chicago, however, most scholars of whiteness then (and now) paid little attention to the material origins and political and economic advantages of whiteness. Rather, whiteness scholars—reflecting the influence of literary studies—spent a disproportionate amount of time on cultural phenomena such as minstrelsy, novels, music, art, even skiing, with relatively little attention paid to political institutions, markets, and public policies that, more than anything else, manufactured and replicated white racial privilege. Origins was an attempt to bridge the cultural and the structural—to start with the important questions asked by whiteness scholars, but to provide a more rigorous account of the mechanisms that perpetuated racial difference in ideology and in experience. Urban inequality, I argued, is the result of the mapping of understandings of racial differences onto the geography of a city—and of the power of categories of racial difference to create racial hierarchies that shaped housing patterns, workplace practices, private investment, and the public policies that reinforced them. Above all, I contended racial inequalities persist because of the mutually reinforcing processes of ideology and political economy, of identity and self-interest. [9]

Origins is also an account of postwar American political economy, of the ways that corporations, aided by state and federal policies, reorganized capital and workplaces. Above all, it argues that the process of capital mobility and urban devastation began amidst the post–World War II economic boom. When I wrote Origins, most popular and scholarly analyses of deindustrialization focused on the 1970s, in particular the oil shocks, the rise of international competition in industries which America had long dominated, and globalization, as corporations roamed the globe in search of cheap labor. A spate of recent historical scholarship on the industrial transformation of twentieth-century America (a subfield that has taken off in recent years) bears out my argument about the crucial role that capital flight and the introduction of labor-saving technologies played in the devastation of urban America well before the 1970s. The process of deindustrialization began as early as the 1920s in cities dominated by the textile industry, intensified in the post–World War II years, and took a new form in the wake of the economic crises of the 1970s. Cities dominated by a single industry—like Detroit, Pittsburgh, and Gary—reeled when their key industries began to close plants and relocate to other regions. But the process of deindustrialization was equally damaging in cities like Philadelphia, Oakland, and Chicago, which had diverse economic bases. The ostensibly "new" globalization of capital seen in the late 1990s and the early part of the twenty-first century is part of the same process that I described ravaging mid-twentieth-century Detroit, even if American corporate tax and trade policies have made it easier for companies to ignore national boundaries and for capital to migrate long distances.[10]

The flip side of urban deindustrialization, disinvestment, and depopulation was the process of suburbanization. One of the greatest migrations of the twentieth century was the movement of whites from central cities to suburbs. From the opening of "greenfield" factories to the rise of corporate "campuses" to the proliferation of shopping malls, suburbs have attracted a lion's share of postwar private and public sector investment. While *Origins* does not discuss suburbanization in any detail, a host of new studies have pushed its analysis of race, politics, and economics beyond city limits. Suburbanization exacerbated the impact of boundary drawing and neighborhood defensiveness that shaped the postwar city. In fact, suburban governments often acted as super-neighborhood associations, using their governmental powers to enforce zoning laws that relentlessly excluded low- and moderate-income "outsiders," disproportionately people of color. They fiercely resisted intergovernmental cooperation, staunchly defended the age-old principle of local control, and relied on local taxes to fund local public works, social services, and de facto private schools. Even as African Americans began, in increasing numbers, to make their way to the suburbs, they largely remained confined to racially segregated communities. Remembering the history of white hostility and racial violence that shaped the postwar city, many blacks avoided working-class white suburbs (in Detroit, those included Wayne, Westland, East Detroit/Eastpointe, Warren, and Hazel Park, among others). In wealthier suburbs, where upwardly mobile blacks moved (such as Southfield, a middle- and upper-middle-class postwar suburb north of Detroit), whites, especially those with children, steadily moved out and few new whites moved in.[11]

To a great extent in postwar America, geography is destiny. Access to goods and resources—public services, education, and jobs—depends upon place of residence. In modern America, where you live determines to a great extent the quality of your schools, your roads, your access to employment, and how much you pay for these benefits in the form of taxes. The best new histories of suburbia have focused on the ways that racial exclusion, politics, and taxation have reinforced the patterns of racial inequality that I describe in *Origins*. As capital relocated to suburban and exurban places that were overwhelmingly white, cities saw their tax bases depleted by job loss, shrinkage of property tax revenues, and rising social service expenditures. Suburbs and exurbs, by contrast, availed themselves of wealthier taxpayers and the property taxes generated by shopping malls, office campuses, and industrial parks. City governments found themselves burdened with an aging infrastructure, an increasingly impoverished population, and fewer resources than ever to pay for infrastructure repairs, education, or social services. The result was a reallocation of political power and public resources to the increasingly privatized, exclusionary world of white suburbia.[12]

Origins examines the ways that Detroit's policymakers and politicians responded to urban change. Equally important was the role of activists and citizens who resisted racial segregation, who challenged runaway jobs, and who fought for the city's dispossessed. I explored the role of Detroit's branch of the NAACP (the largest local chapter in the country in the 1940s), the Urban League, and neighborhood activists like Burneice Avery, who challenged racial inequities in housing and employment. I also uncovered the history of trade unionists and working-class activists who struggled against workplace discrimination and deindustrialization. But because of my emphasis on racial politics and economics, these grassroots struggles were not the primary focus of *Origins*. I argued that the history of resistance to oppression must begin with a clear-eyed understanding of power—who wields it, and its impact on ordinary people. That is not to deny the importance of oppositional politics. In many respects, *Origins* laid the groundwork for the next stage of research: how did urban residents challenge racial inequality? Within the constraints of multiple, reinforcing racial and economic inequalities, what worked and what did not?

The triumphs and failures of the northern black freedom struggle—the central theme in my current research—is the next frontier for postwar urban, labor, social, and political historians. Some of the most exciting work in recent American history focuses on the grassroots activists—black and white—who struggled against the odds to undermine racial injustice in the North. Northern activists fought workplace discrimination and pushed for inclusion in union leadership; open housing advocates challenged unequal housing, while black residents of public housing projects fought valiantly against official neglect; boycotters and litigators challenged separate and un-

equal education throughout the North; advocates of black self-determination formed cooperative stores and pushed for community-controlled economic development; civil rights and neighborhood groups rallied against
police brutality; welfare recipients demanded an end to punitive and stigma-
tizing regulations; and black political activists (with some white allies) ran for
elected office and pushed to redefine urban liberalism in their own terms.
To be sure, all of these activists wielded the weapons of the weak. They
struggled for rights, justice, and power on a terrain that was shaped by the
larger structural forces that I describe. But they also provided an alternative
vision for urban change that ultimately influenced public policies from affirmative action to antipoverty efforts to educational reform, even if they
struggled against the odds in a political climate that grew increasingly hostile to their demands.[13]

The summer that I visited my father's childhood neighborhood, I took a tour
of downtown Detroit and some surrounding neighborhoods with a friend
who is a real booster of the city. Detroit has lagged a little behind some of its
Rustbelt counterparts, but in recent years the Motor City has built glitzy
gambling emporia, two new downtown stadiums, a new opera house, and
new riverfront parks. Formerly grim inner-city neighborhoods, particularly
around Wayne State University and the Detroit Institute of Arts, have witnessed modest gentrification and a profusion of upscale bars, restaurants,
and even a quaint bed-and-breakfast. Several downtown blocks have
sprouted art galleries and trendy watering holes. A few of the empty downtown skyscrapers that photographer and critic Camilo José Vergara once
suggested be turned into an "American acropolis," where visitors could con-
template the ruins of a once-grand civilization, have been converted into
artists' lofts and luxury apartments.[14] Detroit's avant-garde music scene continues to find creative, adaptive reuses for old factory buildings and warehouses throughout the city. And private developers (usually with public subsidies) have built new housing on Detroit's East Side and on riverfront
brownfields.
    In recent years, many Rustbelt cities, including Detroit, have turned to
arts and culture, entertainment, and tourism to revitalize their economies.
They have spent hundreds of millions of dollars in subsidies and tax abatements for entertainment venues, conference centers, and hotels in an attempt to lure free-spending, out-of-town visitors to their downtowns.
Atlantic City rebuilt its sagging boardwalk and built windowless casinos
connected to giant parking garages to buffer gamblers from the city's increasingly black, impoverished population. Detroit has placed its bet on
gambling; Pittsburgh and Philadelphia will soon open downtown slots par-
lors; and many other cities have opened riverboat casinos to attract tourists
and their dollars. Nearly every Rustbelt city has gussied up its downtown

shopping districts (some more successfully than others) to draw suburbanites downtown. Baltimore built a much-celebrated "festival marketplace" in
its Inner Harbor area (though similar efforts have largely failed elsewhere).
Cleveland (viciously dubbed "the Mistake by the Lake" by urban detractors)
put its hopes on waterfront attractions like nightclubs and the Rock and Roll
Hall of Fame. Even bleak Camden, New Jersey, has lured tourists to its
postindustrial waterfront by building a state-of-the-art aquarium and children's park. Philadelphia, Pittsburgh, Cleveland, Baltimore, Chicago, Detroit, and Washington, D.C.—among others—provided lavish subsidies for
new urban stadiums and sports arenas. Even if, in nearly every case, their
costs outweighed their benefits, stadium builders and many fans celebrated
the intimacy, postmodern style, and symbolism of their new coliseums.[15]

Skeptics of showy downtown redevelopment schemes have promoted
community-based economic development as an alternative. Beginning in
the 1970s, as the federal government began its long, steady withdrawal from
urban spending, small-scale community groups were left with the task of
rebuilding their neighborhoods, scrambling for dwindling community economic development block grants, foundation dollars, and charitable contributions. Against sometimes formidable odds, they have constructed new
housing, built community centers, and even attracted supermarkets back to
neighborhoods that chain stores long ago abandoned. Cities have also joined
in public-private partnerships to encourage the redevelopment of middle-
class housing in inner-city neighborhoods. Cleveland's Hough neighborhood, devastated by 1960s riots, now has gated condominium complexes;
North Philadelphia has blocks of affordable housing; and the South Bronx,
once an international symbol of America's urban woes, has sprung forth hundreds of new, single-family homes. Community developers in Detroit also
have some proud accomplishments. A community development corporation
spearheaded by the Greater Hartford Baptist Church brought a K-Mart to
Detroit's West Side and another nonprofit developer attracted a Farmer
Jack supermarket and several chain stores to a stretch of Woodward Avenue
that had long been devoid of retail. And public-private partnerships have
brought affordable and market-rate housing to the area around Detroit's
medical center.[16]

More so than in my lifetime, Detroiters are bullish about the future of
their city, even if they realize that it has a long, long way to go. They are not
alone in their optimism. In the last decade, I have spent time in hip neighborhoods along the Milwaukee, Baltimore, and Cleveland waterfronts; in
the revived cultural district in Newark's once-forlorn downtown; in the
beautiful late-nineteenth-century neighborhoods of St. Louis and Buffalo,
where preservationists and young people are restoring grand, old homes;
and in the edgy, bohemian enclaves of Chicago's West Side. Every city is
hoping that the expansion of a diverse, youthful "creative class" will be its

ticket to revival. I have visited innovative community economic development projects in formerly bombed-out neighborhoods in Boston, the Bronx,
Brooklyn, Cleveland, and Newark. In my own adopted hometown, Philadelphia, Center City has been flooded with yuppies and empty nesters who are
moving into converted lofts and luxury apartments. The neighborhood
around the University of Pennsylvania, which had witnessed serious disinvestment and depopulation beginning in the 1950s, now has restored Victo-
rian houses that cost more than their suburban counterparts. New affordable
townhomes are springing up in North Philadelphia brownfields. My own
neighborhood in northwest Philadelphia, long a haven of racial diversity, has
a livelier business district than it has had in decades. I can now walk from my
house to get a hand-pulled microbrew at our once-shabby corner bar or
listen to a Brazilian or zydeco band play at our local nightspot. Nearly every
city has a trendy "gayborhood," hip artists' colonies and loft districts, and
funky enclaves where young people sip lattes and buy vintage clothing.
Urban places that were once written off as dead are now buzzing with life.
Could the "urban crisis" be over?[17]

It is dangerous to let our optimism about urban revitalization obscure the
grim realities that still face most urban residents, particularly people of
color. Acres of rundown houses, abandoned factories, vacant lots, and shuttered stores stand untended in the shadow of revitalized downtowns and hip
urban enclaves. There has been very little "trickle down" from downtown
revitalization and neighborhood gentrification to the long-term poor, the
urban working class, and minorities. An influx of coffee shops, bistros, art
galleries, and upscale boutiques have made parts of many cities increasingly
appealing for the privileged, but they have not, in any significant way, altered the everyday misery and impoverishment that characterize many
urban neighborhoods. Redevelopment projects—those that have attracted
the lion's share of tax subsidies and public investment—have left places like
Santa Rosa and Chalfonte untouched. Neighborhood shopping districts,
particularly in African American sections of cities, are dominated by pawn
shops, check cashing agencies, liquor and beer stores, and cheap clothing
sellers. Full-service supermarkets are still scarce and quality clothes, with
the exception of sneakers, are hard to find. Little city, state, or federal money
goes into fixing up rundown neighborhood shopping districts. And despite
some conspicuous successes—often against formidable odds—community
development corporations have made only a small dent in the urban economies and housing markets. Local nonprofits have the will but ultimately not
the capacity to stem the larger processes of capital flight that have devastated the city.

As with all urban transformations, the question is, Who benefited and who
lost? Chalfonte and Santa Rosa—and their counterparts throughout urban
America—stand largely untouched by reinvestment, gentrification, and

urban boom. Downtown festival marketplaces and shopping malls provide amenities largely for suburbanites and tourists. Art galleries, hip bistros, and coffeehouses are wonderful refuges from the bland uniformity of suburban shopping malls. For people with means, today's revitalized urban neighborhoods have a lot to offer. New businesses also contribute much-needed revenue to city tax coffers. Over time, perhaps, they will generate even more investment in central cities. For now, however, racial and class inequalities have persisted—even hardened—in most Rustbelt metropolitan areas. Most people of color have remained on the margins of downtown booms, still segregated by race, still facing the consequences of disinvestment and job flight, still suffering from decades of cuts in urban funding and public services. Detroit residents have, by and large, been disappointed in the relatively few new jobs produced by the city's casinos. Making fudge in Baltimore's Inner Harbor, cleaning hotel rooms in Center City Philadelphia, or selling beer and gourmet sandwiches in Chicago's new Comiskey Park might create a congenial atmosphere for suburban visitors but seldom offers living wages or job security. The noteworthy exception to the loss of remunerative jobs in central cities—only partially studied by historians—has been the expansion of "meds and eds" and government employment. In this sector, public spending and urban reinvestment has brought real benefits to many urban residents. Hospitals and universities, buoyed by large-scale federal expenditures and often unionized, proved to be the only reliable source of job growth in northern cities in the wake of deindustrialization. City government employment, often forced open by civil rights activism in a story that still needs to be told, became an increasingly important employment niche for minority workers left behind in the postindustrial economy. Still, meds, eds, and government jobs are particularly vulnerable to state and federal budget cutting. Urban hospitals are jeopardized by the unavailability of health insurance, an influx of impoverished patients, skyrocketing malpractice and equipment costs, and by the gradual suburbanization of health care. City governments have been cutting jobs under fiscal pressures. Universities have increasingly outsourced employment, and those that are publicly funded also face serious budget cutbacks.[18]

American cities have long reflected the hopes as well as the failures of the society at large. From the mid-twentieth century to the present, American society has been characterized by a widening gap between rich and poor, between communities of privilege and those of poverty. Despite a rhetoric about race relations that is more civil than it was in 1950, racial divisions by income, wealth, education, employment, health, and political power remain deeply entrenched. Whether the course that American cities take in the next decades is a continuation or a departure from the current patterns of inequality, segregation, and disinvestment remains to be seen. What is clear is that urban America continues to be shaped by processes that have their origins deep in the mid-twentieth century. Coming to grips with that history is not a mere academic exercise. History is a process, ongoing, that at once opens up possibilities and constrains our choices in the present. To come to grips with the problems and promises of our cities, we must grapple with the past as a means to engaging with the present.

　　　　　　　　　　　　　　　　—Mount Airy, Philadelphia, January 2005

Notes

1. For my discussion of this neighborhood and its fate (I refer to it as the De Witt-Clinton area on the Wyoming Corridor), see below, pages 22, 235–40, 246–47, 254–56. On my relatives' participation in the Greater Detroit Homeowners' Association, Unit No. 2, in the late 1940s and early 1950s, see references below to [Matthew] Twomey on p. 211 and James Sugrue, p. 340, note 9.

2. Data for tract 5364, Detroit, Michigan, from 2000 U.S. Census, Summary File SF-2, Tables DP-2 and QT-P3, Summary File SF-3, Table DP-3. Available at www.census.gov. For an excellent summary of demographic and economic changes in Detroit, see Reynolds Farley, Sheldon Danziger, and Harry J. Holzer, *Detroit Divided* (New York: Russell Sage Foundation, 2000).

3. Charles Tilly, *Durable Inequality* (Berkeley: University of California Press, 1998).

4. Thomas Frank, *One Market Under God: Extreme Capitalism, Market Populism, and the End of Economic Democracy* (New York: Doubleday, 2000); Public Law 104–193, 22 August 1996, 110 *Stat.* 2105. Michael B. Katz, *The Price of Citizenship: Redefining the American Welfare State* (New York: Metropolitan Books, 2001). The most influential conservative book on race is Stephan Thernstrom and Abigail Thernstrom, *America in Black and White: One Nation, Indivisible* (New York: Simon and Schuster, 1997). The most influential conservative tract on race and intelligence is Richard J. Herrnstein and Charles Murray, *The Bell Curve: Intelligence and Class Structure in American Life* (New York: Free Press, 1996). For a powerful rejoinder to racial conservatives of all stripes, see Michael K. Brown et al., *Whitewashing Race: The Myth of a Color-Blind Society* (Berkeley: University of California Press, 2003).

5. Robert C. Lieberman, *Shifting the Color Line: Race and the American Welfare State* (Cambridge: Harvard University Press, 1998); Michael K. Brown, *Race, Money, and the American Welfare State* (Ithaca, N.Y.: Cornell University Press, 1998); Anthony S. Chen, "From Fair Employment to Equal Opportunity Employment and Beyond: Affirmative Action and Civil Rights Politics in the New Deal Order, 1941–1972" (Ph.D. diss., University of California, Berkeley, 2002); Philip A. Klinkner with Rogers M. Smith, *The Unsteady March: The Rise and Decline of Racial Equality in America* (Chicago: University of Chicago Press, 1999); John David Skrentny, *The Ironies of Affirmative Action* (Chicago: University of Chicago Press, 1996); Paul Frymer, "Race, Labor, and the Twentieth-Century American State," *Politics and Society* 32 (2004): 475–509.

6. Kenneth D. Durr, *Behind the Backlash: White Working-Class Politics in Baltimore, 1940–1980* (Chapel Hill: University of North Carolina Press, 2003); Wendell

Pritchett, *Brownsville, Brooklyn: Blacks, Jews, and the Changing Face of the Ghetto* (Chicago: University of Chicago Press, 2002); articles by Raymond A. Mohl, Roger Biles, Wendy Plotkin, Amanda Irene Seligman, and D. Bradford Hunt in special issue on race and housing, *Journal of the Illinois State Historical Society* 94 (2001): 8–123; James Wolfinger, "The Rise and Fall of the Roosevelt Coalition: Race, Labor, and Politics in Philadelphia, 1932–1955" (Ph.D. diss., Northwestern University, 2003); David Schuyler, *A City Transformed: Redevelopment, Race, and Suburbanization in Lancaster, 1940–1980* (University Park: Penn State University Press, 2002); John Bauman et al., eds., *From Tenements to the Taylor Homes: In Search of an Urban Housing Policy in Twentieth-Century America* (University Park: Penn State University Press, 2000); see more generally, Steven Grant Meyer, *As Long as They Don't Move Next Door: Segregation and Racial Conflict in American Neighborhoods* (Lanham, Md.: Rowman and Littlefield, 2000).

7. Robert Self, *American Babylon: Race and the Struggle for Postwar Oakland* (Princeton, N.J.: Princeton University Press, 2003); Shirley Ann Wilson Moore, *To Place Our Deeds: The African American Community in Richmond, California, 1910–1963* (Berkeley: University of California Press, 2000); Becky Nicolaides, *My Blue Heaven: Life and Politics in the Working-Class Suburbs of Los Angeles, 1920–1965* (Chicago: University of Chicago Press, 2002); Josh Sides, *L.A. City Limits: African American Los Angeles from the Great Depression to the Present* (Berkeley: University of California Press, 2003); Deirdre L. Sullivan, "Letting Down the Bars: Race, Space, and Democracy in San Francisco, 1936–1964" (Ph.D. diss., University of Pennsylvania, 2003).

8. Kevin Kruse, *White Flight: Atlanta and the Making of Modern Conservatism* (Princeton, N.J.: Princeton University Press, forthcoming); Matthew Lassiter, "The Suburban Origins of 'Color-Blind' Conservatism: Middle-Class Consciousness in the Charlotte Busing Crisis," *Journal of Urban History* (May 2004): 549–82, and Lassiter, *The Silent Majority: Suburban Politics in the Sunbelt South* (Princeton, N.J.: Princeton University Press, forthcoming); James N. Gregory, *The Southern Diaspora: How Two Great Migrations Transformed Race, Region, and American Politics* (Chapel Hill: University of North Carolina Press, 2005); James N. Gregory, "Southernizing the American Working Class: Post-War Episodes of Regional and Class Transformation," *Labor History* 39 (May 1998): 135–54, with responses by Thomas J. Sugrue, Grace Elizabeth Hale, Alex Lichtenstein, and James Gregory, pp. 155–68.

9. For critical overviews of whiteness scholarship, see Eric Arnesen, "Whiteness in the Historian's Imagination," *International Labor and Working-Class History* 60 (Fall 2001): 3–32, with responses by James R. Barrett, David Brody, Barbara J. Fields, Eric Foner, Victoria Hattam, Adolph Reed, Jr., and Eric Arnesen, pp. 33–92; and Peter Kolchin, "Whiteness Studies: The New History of Race in America," *Journal of American History* 89 (2002): 154–73. Arnold Hirsch, *Making the Second Ghetto: Race and Housing in Chicago, 1940–1960*, repr. ed. (Chicago: University of Chicago Press, 1998); George Lipsitz, *The Possessive Investment in Whiteness: How White People Profit from Identity Politics* (Philadelphia: Temple University Press, 1998); Karen Brodkin, *How the Jews Became White Folks and What That Says about Race in America* (New Brunswick, N.J.: Rutgers University Press, 1998). Two exemplary recent studies of whiteness are John Hartigan, Jr., *Racial Situations: Class Predicaments of Whiteness in Detroit* (Princeton, N.J.: Princeton University Press, 1999)

and Thomas A. Guglielmo, *White on Arrival: Italians, Race, Color, and Power in Chicago, 1890–1945* (New York: Oxford University Press, 2003).

10. Ruth Milkman, *Farewell to the Factory: Auto Workers in the Late Twentieth Century* (Berkeley: University of California Press, 1997); Jefferson Cowie, *Capital Moves: RCA's Seventy-Year Quest for Cheap Labor* (Ithaca, N.Y.: Cornell University Press, 1999); Jefferson Cowie and Joseph Heathcott, eds., *Beyond the Ruins: The Meanings of Deindustrialization* (Ithaca, N.Y.: Cornell University Press, 2003); Guian McKee, "Urban Deindustrialization and Local Public Policy: Industrial Renewal in Philadelphia, 1953–1976," *Journal of Policy History* 16 (2004): 66–98; Joseph Heathcott and Máire Agnes Murphy, "Corridors of Flight, Zones of Renewal: Industry, Planning, and Policy in the Making of Metropolitan St. Louis, 1940–1980," *Journal of Urban History* 31 (2005): 151–89; Sherry Lee Linkon and John Russo, *Steeltown U.S.A.: Work and Memory in Youngstown* (Lawrence: University Press of Kansas, 2002). Judith Stein, *Running Steel, Running America: Race, Economic Policy, and the Decline of Liberalism* (Chapel Hill: University of North Carolina Press, 1998) offers an important discussion of economic and trade policy, but a problematic treatment of race and civil rights politics.

11. Andrew Wiese, *Places of Their Own: African American Suburbanization in the Twentieth Century* (Chicago: University of Chicago Press, 2004); Thomas J. Sugrue, "Black Suburbanization," in Kwame Anthony Appiah and Henry Louis Gates, Jr., eds., *Encarta Africana 2000*, CD-ROM encyclopedia (Redmond, Wash.: Microsoft, 1999). For an optimistic view of black suburbanization, see Thernstrom and Thernstrom, *America in Black and White*, 211–13.

12. See, among others, Lizabeth Cohen, *A Consumers' Republic: The Politics of Mass Consumption in Postwar America* (New York: Knopf, 2003); Nicolaides, *My Blue Heaven*; Self, *American Babylon*; Margaret Pugh O'Mara, *Cities of Knowledge: Cold War Science and the Search for the Next Silicon Valley* (Princeton, N.J.: Princeton University Press, 2005); David Freund, "Making it Home: Race, Development, and the Politics of Place in Suburban Detroit, 1940–1967" (Ph.D. diss., University of Michigan, 1999); Stephanie Dyer, "Markets in the Meadows: Department Stores and Shopping Centers in the Decentralization of Philadelphia, 1920–1980" (Ph.D. diss., University of Pennsylvania, 2000); Peter Siskind, "Growth and Its Discontents: Localism, Protest, and the Politics of Development on the Postwar Northeast Corridor" (Ph.D. diss. University of Pennsylvania, 2002); Kevin Kruse and Thomas J. Sugrue, eds., *The New Suburban History* (Chicago: University of Chicago Press, forthcoming). Lisa McGirr, *Suburban Warriors: The Origins of the New American Right* (Princeton, N.J.: Princeton University Press, 2001), an otherwise excellent book on Orange County, California, inexplicably ignores racial politics.

13. Eric Arnesen, *Brotherhoods of Color: Black Railroad Workers and the Struggle for Equality* (Cambridge: Harvard University Press, 2001); Bruce Nelson, *Divided We Stand: American Workers and the Struggle for Black Equality* (Princeton, N.J.: Princeton University Press, 2001); Roger Horowitz, *"Negro and White, Unite and Fight!": A Social History of Industrial Unionism in Meatpacking, 1930–90* (Urbana: University of Illinois Press, 1997); Rick Halpern, *Down on the Killing Floor: Black and White Workers in Chicago's Packinghouses, 1904–54* (Urbana: University of Illinois Press, 1998); Ruth Needleman, *Black Freedom Fighters in Steel: The Struggle for Democratic Unionism* (Ithaca, N.Y.: ILR Press, 2003); Self, *American Babylon*;

Martha Biondi, *To Stand and Fight: The Struggle for Civil Rights in Postwar New York City* (Cambridge: Harvard University Press, 2003); Matthew Countryman, *Up South: The Civil Rights and Black Power Movements in Philadelphia* (Philadelphia: University of Pennsylvania Press, 2005); Richard B. Pierce, *Polite Protest: The Political Economy of Race in Indianapolis* (Bloomington: Indiana University Press, 2005); Jack Dougherty, *More Than One Struggle: The Evolution of Black School Reform in Milwaukee* (Chapel Hill: University of North Carolina Press, 2004); Rhonda Y. Williams, *The Politics of Public Housing: Black Women's Struggles against Urban Inequality* (New York: Oxford University Press, 2004); Felicia Kornbluh, *A Right to Welfare? Poor Women, Professionals, and Poverty Programs, 1935–1975* (Philadelphia: University of Pennsylvania Press, forthcoming); Suzanne E. Smith, *Dancing in the Streets: Motown and the Cultural Politics of Detroit* (Cambridge: Harvard University Press, 1999); Sidney Fine, *"Expanding the Frontiers of Civil Rights": Michigan, 1948–1968* (Detroit: Wayne State University Press, 2000); Victoria W. Wolcott, *Remaking Respectability: African American Women in Interwar Detroit* (Chapel Hill: University of North Carolina Press, 2001); Kevin Boyle, *Arc of Justice: A Saga of Race, Civil Rights, and Murder in the Jazz Age* (New York: Henry Holt, 2004); Heather Ann Thompson, *Whose Detroit? Politics, Labor, and Race in a Modern American City* (Ithaca, N.Y.: Cornell University Press, 2001); Jeanne F. Theoharis and Komozi Woodard, eds., *Freedom North: Black Freedom Struggles Outside the South, 1940–1980* (New York: Palgrave, 2003).

14. Camilo José Vergara, *The New American Ghetto* (New Brunswick, N.J.: Rutgers University Press, 1995), 215–25.

15. Bryant Simon, *Boardwalk of Dreams: Atlantic City and the Fate of Urban America* (New York: Oxford University Press, 2004); Alison Isenberg, *Downtown America: A History of the Place and the People Who Made It* (Chicago: University of Chicago Press, 2004); Howard Gillette, *Camden after the Fall: Decline and Renewal in a Post-Industrial City* (Philadelphia: University of Pennsylvania Press, forthcoming).

16. Alexander von Hoffman, *House by House, Block by Block: The Rebirth of America's Urban Neighborhoods* (New York: Oxford University Press, 2002); Alice O'Connor, "Swimming against the Tide: A Brief History of Federal Policy in Poor Communities," in Ronald F. Ferguson and William T. Dickens, eds., *Urban Problems and Community Development* (Washington, D.C.: The Brookings Institution, 1999), 108–13; Thomas J. Sugrue, "Carter's Urban Policy Crisis," in Gary M. Fink and Hugh Davis Graham, eds., *The Carter Presidency: Policy Choices in the Post–New Deal Era* (Lawrence: University Press of Kansas, 1998), 137–57; June Manning Thomas, *Redevelopment and Race: Planning a Finer City in Postwar Detroit* (Baltimore: Johns Hopkins University Press, 1997).

17. Eugenie Ladner Birch, "Having a Longer View on Downtown Living," *Journal of the American Planning Association* 68 (1): 5–21 offers an excellent survey of population trends and growth patterns in new downtowns. Richard Florida, *The Rise of the Creative Class and How It's Transforming Work, Leisure, Community and Everyday Life* (New York: Basic Books, 2002) has been an influential guide for urban planners and policymakers.

18. On the importance of "meds and eds," see especially Daniel Gitterman, Joanne Spetz, and Matthew Fellowes, "The Other Side of the Ledger: Federal

Health Spending in Metropolitan Economies" (discussion paper, Brookings Institution Metropolitan Policy Program, September 2004, http://www.brook.edu/metro/pubs/20040917_gitterman.htm). On race and city government employment, see Francis P. Ryan, "Everyone Royalty: AFSCME, Municipal Workers, and Urban Power in Philadelphia, 1921–1983" (Ph.D. diss., University of Pennsylvania, 2003). On the struggles of meds and eds in central cities, see O'Mara, *Cities of Knowledge*.

Acknowledgments ─────────────────────────

THIS BOOK has deep roots in the academy, in friendships, and in family. Over the past two decades, I had the good fortune to have as my teachers a remarkable group of historians who have offered me models of humane and serious scholarship: Gerald F. Moynahan, James P. Shenton, Alden T. Vaughan, Kenneth T. Jackson, Leonard Wallock, David Rothman, Jay M. Winter, Gareth Stedman Jones, Bernard Bailyn, Ernest May, and the late Nathan I. Huggins. Special thanks to Stephan Thernstrom and Barbara Gutmann Rosenkrantz who shepherded this project through its first incarnation as a dissertation. Their suggestions (even when I ignored them) and faith in my work made this book possible.

A number of friends have sustained me throughout this project, especially Eric Arnesen, Brian Balogh, Annamaria Basile, Sue Beale, Rosemary Byrne, Steve Conn, Sarah De Lone (and her friends in the UAW Legal Department), Harlan Eplan, Florence Farrell, Karen Farris, Tom Fennell, Beth Fordham-Meier, Rachelle Friedman, Tim Gilfoyle, Dan Gitterman, Greg Goldman, Kurt Hack, Sally Hadden, Diedra Harris-Kelley, Liz Hersh, Jana Hollingsworth, Tom Jackson, Felicia Kornbluh, Joseph Kearney, Jennifer Laszlo, Abby Letcher, Cecelia Lynch, Debi Maughan, Steve Maughan, Mark Meier, Sylvie Murray, Mike Neus, John Logan Nichols, Alice O'Connor, Kevin O'Rourke, Max Page, Susan Schulten, Tom Schwartz, Tony Simonelli, John Skrentny, Jeannie Sowers, Gene Sperling, Marc Stein, Mark Stern, Monica Tetzlaff, Tom Warnke, and Rebecca Zeigler. My friends and students in Lowell House diverted me with countless hours of dining table conversation and camaraderie. John Simmons and the members of Painters' District Council 35 brought me out of the ivory tower to places like Dorchester, Roxbury, South Boston, Fall River, and Lynn, and reminded me that politics can be empowering. When I was in Michigan doing research, Ken Horn introduced me to an Ann Arbor I did not know and drank a lot of coffee with me. Lars Waldorf deserves special mention for his inestimable contributions to my intellectual growth and personal sanity. His combination of rigorous analysis and political engagement continues to inspire and challenge me.

When I was just beginning this project, I had the good fortune to meet Michael B. Katz, who expressed a great deal of faith (which I hope is warranted) in a young, unknown historian. Michael also brought me into a group of scholars whose work and ideas have been very influential for mine—The Social Science Research Science Council's working group on history and the urban "underclass." Two lively meetings of the authors of *The "Underclass"*

Debate: Views from History gave me the invaluable opportunity to air my ideas as they developed, to discuss a lot of important work in progress, and to build some enduring friendships. Michael also read the entire manuscript and offered valuable suggestions and advice.

A number of other friends have also read drafts of this book in their entirety and pushed me to rethink many of my assumptions. Special thanks to Eric Arnesen (who offered an extraordinary set of comments and filled my mailbox right up until the last minute with photocopied newspaper clippings), Dana Barron, Peter Coclanis, Lizabeth Cohen, Gerald Gamm (and his Urban Politics students), Gary Gerstle, Jim Grossman, Ira Katznelson, Robin Kelley, and Robert Lieberman. Other sections of the book have benefited from the astute comments of Jo Ann Argersinger, David Bartelt, Kevin Boyle, Alan Brinkley, Rick Halpern, Arnold Hirsch, Alison Isenberg, Michael Kazin, Phil Klinkner, Dan Letwin, Nelson Lichtenstein, John McGreevy, James Morone, Bruce Nelson, Alice O'Connor, James T. Patterson, Adolph Reed, Marshall Stevenson, and Roger Wilkins. Several audiences have listened carefully to parts of this manuscript, and I am deeply indebted to those whose collegiality and astute criticism have assisted my work. Thanks to participants in lively discussions at the Chicago Seminar on the City at the Chicago Historical Society, the Columbia Seminar on the City, the PARSS Seminar on Work and Welfare and the Urban Studies Seminar at the University of Pennsylvania, the Charles Colver Lecture at Brown University, the Labor History Seminar at Pennsylvania State University, the German Historical Institute Conference on Race and Ethnicity, and the Research-in-Progress Seminar at The Brookings Institution. Thanks also to the interested audiences and commentators at meetings of the American Historical Assocation, the Organization of American Historians, the Social Science History Association, the UNESCO Program for Comparative Research on Poverty, the American Political Science Association, the SSRC Conference on Persistent Urban Poverty, and the North American Labor History Conference. I cannot imagine a better editorial staff than at Princeton University Press. Not one, but two talented editors, Brigitta van Rheinberg and Lauren Osborne, have offered guidance and support as my project has worked its way from concept to book. And my lengthy manuscript benefited greatly from the keen eye of copy editor Gavin Lewis.

Every historian owes a great debt to archivists and librarians, as do I. The excellent staff at the Archives of Labor and Urban Affairs at Wayne State University, especially Ray Boryczka and Tom Featherstone, answered my countless annoying inquiries with cheerful dispatch and provided a comfortable home away from home. The archivists at the Bentley Historical Library at the University of Michigan deserve special praise. They were not only courteous and helpful, but unfailingly generous with their time and resources. I am especially grateful to the Bentley staff for offering me access to the library's collection of fragile and still unprocessed Detroit neighborhood newspapers. I have great admiration for the staff of the Burton Historical Collections of the Detroit Public Library, who serve an enormous number of patrons in a magnificent civic institution in dire need of adequate funding. Roman Godzak of the Archives of the Archdiocese of Detroit helped me track down some crucial sources. The staffs of the National Archives and Library of Congress and the librarians at The Brookings Institution, the Pattee Library at Penn State, the Purdy-Kresge Library at Wayne State, and the Moorland-Spingarn Research Center at Howard University also offered invaluable assistance.

The generous financial support of several organizations made this project possible. My research and writing was assisted by the Social Science Research Council Dissertation Research Fellowship on the Urban Underclass through funding provided by the Rockefeller Foundation. The Harvard University History Department and the Charles Warren Center for American History at Harvard provided travel grants. The Josephine de Karman Fellowship Trust helped defray my expenses as well. My research at the Walter P. Reuther Library at Wayne State University was supported by a Henry Kaiser Family Research Fellowship. The Bentley Historical Library of the University of Michigan generously awarded me a Bordin-Gillette Research Travel Fellowship. The reproduction of photographs in this book was subsidized by a grant from the University Seminars at Columbia University.

The Brookings Institution offered me a year-long Research Fellowship, an office, and a year of undivided time to think over and write much of this book. The camaraderie of my Brookings colleagues Keith Banting, Bruce Bimber, Julie Drucker, David Fagelson, Bob Katzmann, Philip Klinkner, Jessica Korn, Tom Mann, Bert Rockman, and Kent Weaver made a year of writing productive, intellectually challenging, and fun. I owe special thanks to Sarah Gorham and Todd Quinn who provided valuable research assistance when I was in a real pinch, and to Susan Stewart, who administered my fellowship and helped in countless ways.

I am honored to be a part of the History Department at the University of Pennsylvania, where I have a remarkable group of supportive and interesting colleagues whose healthy aversion to meetings has given me much more time to research and write than I could have hoped for. I have learned a great deal from my undergraduates and from the stimulating comments and skepticism of my graduate students. The intellectual and social camaraderie of our graduate program has been especially enriching. The University of Pennsylvania has also provided research travel grants and energetic student research assistants who helped me with this project, especially Brad Rosenberg, Regan Otto, Marc Isser, David Mays, Charles Stewart, and Jeff Reiser. Brad and Jeff deserve special mention for their countless hours of labor helping me prepare my maps.

Finally, I would like to thank my family. Tom and Sharon Sugrue instilled in me a passion for learning, and inspired me with their humane spirit. Their inquisitiveness, their boundless energy, and their unwavering love have nurtured and sustained me. Long after I had grown up and they thought I had left home for good, they put me up (and put up with me) in several long research trips to Michigan. Their influence on me has been immeasurable. My aunt Jane Sugrue Ryan has been my intellectual role model and political comrade for as long as I can remember. My sisters, Peggy and Patty, co-conspirators with Bill Mackie and Maureen McDonnell, have always bolstered me with their humor and never failed to put me in my place. The extended Barron family, especially Michael and Susan Barron, continues to welcome and encourage me.

Above all, I wish to thank Dana Barron. She has helped me find the right words and offered inspiration and support that go beyond words.

—Mount Airy, Philadelphia, October 1995

THE ORIGINS OF THE URBAN CRISIS

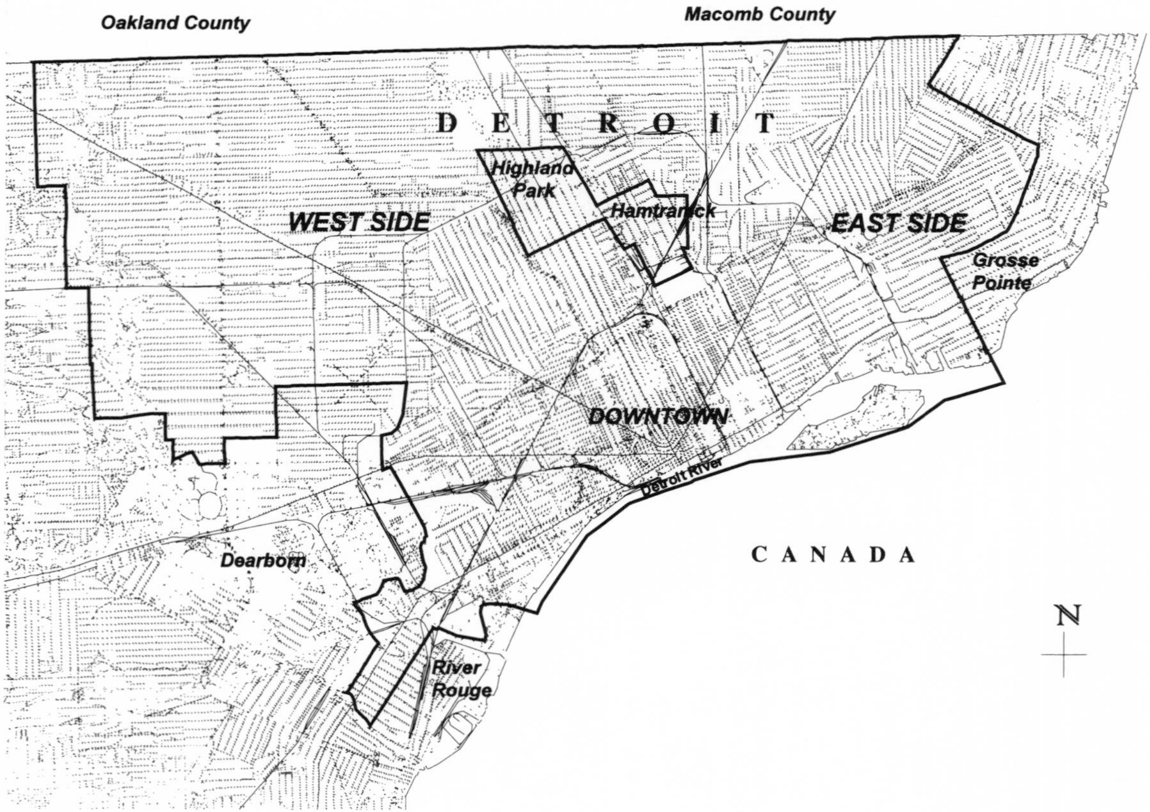

Map I.1. Detroit, 1940

Introduction _____

THE STORY I tell is one of a city transformed. In the 1940s, Detroit was America's "arsenal of democracy," one of the nation's fastest growing boomtowns and home to the highest-paid blue-collar workers in the United States. Today, the city is plagued by joblessness, concentrated poverty, physical decay, and racial isolation. Since 1950, Detroit has lost nearly a million people and hundreds of thousands of jobs. Vast areas of the city, once teeming with life, now stand abandoned. Prairie grass and flocks of pheasants have reclaimed what was, only fifty years ago, the most densely populated section of the city. Factories that once provided tens of thousands of jobs now stand as hollow shells, windows broken, mute testimony to a lost industrial past. Whole rows of small shops and stores are boarded up or burned out. Over ten thousand houses are uninhabited; over sixty thousand lots lie empty, marring almost every city neighborhood. Whole sections of the city are eerily apocalyptic. Over a third of the city's residents live beneath the poverty line, many concentrated in neighborhoods where a majority of their neighbors are also poor. A visit to the city's welfare offices, hospitals, and jails provides abundant evidence of the terrible costs of the city's persistent unemployment and poverty.[1]

Detroit's journey from urban heyday to urban crisis has been mirrored in other cities across the nation. Scenes of devastation and poverty are disturbingly familiar to anyone who has traveled through the streets of America's Rust Belt, the northeastern and midwestern cities that formed the backbone of American industrial might a half-century ago. The urban crisis is jarringly visible in the the shattered storefronts and fire-scarred apartments of Chicago's South and West Sides; the rubble-strewn lots of New York's Brownsville, Bedford-Stuyvesant, and South Bronx; the surreal vistas of abandoned factories along the waterfronts and railways of Cleveland, Gary, Philadelphia, Pittsburgh, and Saint Louis; the boarded-up and graffiti-covered houses of Camden, Baltimore, and Newark. Rates of poverty among black residents of these cities all range from 25 to 40 percent. With a few exceptions, all have witnessed a tremendous loss in manufacturing jobs and the emergence of a low-wage service sector. Almost all of these cities, as Douglas Massey and Nancy Denton have argued, "have large ghettos characterized by extreme segregation and spatial isolation." The faces that appear in the rundown houses, homeless shelters, and social agencies in these urban wastelands are predictably familiar. Almost all are people of color.[2]

Central-city residence, race, joblessness, and poverty have become inextricably intertwined in postindustrial urban America. In the post–World

War II period, patterns of class and racial segregation in large northern cities have persisted and hardened. Poor people have become increasingly isolated in neighborhoods with large numbers of other poor people. A grow-ing number of urban residents, especially young African Americans, find themselves detached from the mainstream economy, often outside the labor market altogether. Unemployment and poverty are certainly not new fea-tures of American urban life. The bleak depictions of life in turn-of-the-century America offered by observers such as Jacob Riis and Robert Hunter offer powerful reminders of a troubled past. But the forms and distribution of postindustrial urban poverty are novel. In previous periods of American history, poverty and unemployment were endemic, but poor people did not experience the same degree of segregation and isolation as exists today. And in the past, most poor people were active, if irregular, participants in the labor market.[3]

Why the transformation of Detroit and other major Northern cities from magnets of opportunity to reservations for the poor? What was it that turned America's former industrial centers into economic backwaters, abandoned by manufacturers? What explains the high rates of joblessness among the urban poor? Why has discrimination by race persisted in both urban neigh-borhoods and workplaces? What explains the emergence of persistent, con-centrated, racialized poverty in Rust Belt cities? Explanations abound for these questions, particularly in the large literature on the urban "under-class," the most influential body of scholarship to emerge on urban problems in twenty-five years. The "underclass" debate has moved in three—some-times overlapping—directions. The first, and most influential, focuses on the behavior and values of the poor, and the role of federal social programs in fostering a culture of joblessness and dependency in inner cities. A variant, going back to the work of Daniel Patrick Moynihan and E. Franklin Frazier, emphasizes the role of family structure and unwed pregnancy in perpetuat-ing inequality.[4] A second offers structural explanations for inequality and urban poverty. Proponents of structural explanations tend to divide among those who point to the effects of economic restructuring (following William Julius Wilson) and those who emphasize the continuing significance of racial discrimination (following Gary Orfield and Douglas Massey).[5] A third expla-nation focuses on politics, emphasizing the marginalization of cities in Amer-ican social policy, particularly in the aftermath of the urban unrest and racial conflict of the 1960s. The "excesses" of Black Power and the rise of affirma-tive action fueled white suburbanization and justified a newfound white backlash against the urban poor. Implicit in this analysis is a contrast be-tween the booming postwar years and the troubled post-1960s years, urban heyday versus urban crisis.[6]

Recent scholarship has identified important elements of the contempo-rary urban crisis. But what is largely missing from the "underclass" debate is the perspective of history. My examination of Detroit in the quarter-century after World War II suggests that the origins of the urban crisis are much earlier than social scientists have recognized, its roots deeper, more tangled, and perhaps more intractable. No one social program or policy, no single force, whether housing segregation, social welfare programs, or deindustrialization, could have driven Detroit and other cities like it from their positions of economic and political dominance; there is no simple explanation for the inequality and marginality that beset the urban poor. It is only through the complex and interwoven histories of race, residence, and work in the postwar era that the state of today's cities and their impoverished residents can be fully understood and confronted.[7]

This book is a guide to the contested terrain of the postwar city, an examination of the unresolved dilemmas of housing, segregation, industrial relations, racial discrimination, and deindustrialization. I argue that the coincidence and mutual reinforcement of race, economics, and politics in a particular historical moment, the period from the 1940s to the 1960s, set the stage for the fiscal, social, and economic crises that confront urban America today. My analysis of Detroit builds on the insights of those who offer structural explanations of urban inequality. But, both in its focus on a multiplicity of structural forces, and in its location of the origins of the urban crisis in the 1940s and 1950s, my analysis diverges from much of the current literature on the "underclass." There are, of course, other approaches to the history of inequality, race, and poverty, such as the study of family structure and family strategies. The emphasis in this book on economic and spatial structures is not meant as an alternative to these approaches, but instead as a context in which they can be best understood. Economic and racial inequality constrain individual and family choices. They set the limits of human agency. Within the bounds of the possible, individuals and families resist, adapt, or succumb.

Detroit's postwar urban crisis emerged as the consequence of two of the most important, interrelated, and unresolved problems in American history: that capitalism generates economic inequality and that African Americans have disproportionately borne the impact of that inequality. The patterns of race and class inequality are by no means fixed and unchanging in American history. Detroit's racial and economic crisis emerged in a particular context—mid-twentieth-century America. Shifts at the national level in economics, race relations, and politics interacted with local forces to cause the urban crisis. In the aftermath of World War II, the post-Reconstruction racial order was in flux. Newly resurgent racial liberals and radicals battled with deeply entrenched racial conservatives over fundamental questions of rights and equality. At the same time, the national economy underwent a period of extraordinary dynamism and growth, fueling unprecedented prosperity, but also unleashing what economist Joseph Schumpeter called the forces of "creative destruction." Northern industrial cities like Detroit were overwhelmed by the combination of racial strife and economic restructuring. Their impact played out in urban streets and workplaces. The labor and housing markets of the postwar city became arenas where inequality was shaped and contested.[8]

In the following pages, I hope to complicate the conventional narratives of post–World War II American history. The United States at midcentury was a far more complicated and troubled place than emerges from most histories and popular accounts. The nation was at a peak of economic and global strength in the 1940s and 1950s. America's aggregate rate of economic growth was nothing short of stunning. Observers marvelled—accurately—at an "affluent society" whose members could purchase a plethora of consumer goods, from cars to refrigerators to television sets. But the cele'-bration of affluence masked significant regional variations and persistent inequality. The remarkable growth of the postwar American economy was profoundly uneven; capitalism left behind huge sections of the United States, mainly older industrial cities in the North and East and rural areas in the South and Midwest.

The cities of America's industrial heartland were the bellwethers of economic change. The rusting of the Rust Belt began neither with the much-touted stagflation and oil crisis of the 1970s, nor with the rise of global economic competition and the influx of car or steel imports. It began, unheralded, in the 1950s. As pundits celebrated America's economic growth and unprecedented prosperity, America's midwestern and northeastern cities lost hundreds of thousands of entry-level manufacturing jobs. In the industrial belt that extended from New England across New York, Pennsylvania, and West Virginia, through the Midwest to the banks of the Mississippi, major companies reduced work forces, speeded up production, and required more overtime work. The manufacturing industries that formed the bedrock of the American economy, including textiles, electrical appliances, motor vehicles, and military hardware, automated production and relocated plants in suburban and rural areas, and increasingly in the low-wage labor markets of underdeveloped regions like the American South and the Caribbean. The restructuring of the economy proceeded with the full support and encouragement of the American government. Federal highway construction and military spending facilitated and fueled industrial growth in nonurban areas.[9]

In the midst of these wrenching changes, economic inequality remained largely off the agenda of politicians and scholars. A few astute policymakers, like Senators Paul Douglas of Illinois and Joseph Clark of Pennsylvania, recognized the corrosion beneath the facade of postwar prosperity. In the 1950s, they proposed legislation to shore up "depressed areas" of the nation. But their agenda remained on the fringes of postwar economic policy. Critics on the left, like Harvey Swados and C. L. R. James, recorded the travails of industrial workers for the few who cared to listen. The invisibility of economic hardship in the affluent age became visible in the shock that greeted the depictions of skid rows, black inner cities, and poverty-ridden Appalachian hollows in Michael Harrington's 1962 book, *The Other America*. Harrington and others identified a world that countless Americans already knew, but whose harsh realities barely penetrated the postwar veneer of consensus and civility.[10]

Setting the boundaries of debates over the economic changes that beset Detroit and the Rust Belt were several currents in national politics. First, and most important, was antiradicalism. Anticommunists silenced some of the most powerful critics of the postwar economic and social order. Red-baiting discredited and weakened progressive reform efforts. By the 1950s, unions had purged their leftist members and marginalized a powerful critique of postwar capitalism. McCarthyism also put constraints on liberal critics of capitalism. In the enforced consensus of the postwar era, it became "un-American" to criticize business decisions or to interfere with managerial prerogative or to focus on lingering class inequalities in the United States.[11]

Further limiting the political vision of policymakers and reformers in the postwar era were the conceptual tools that they used to grapple with questions of political economy. Three interrelated assumptions shaped economic and labor policy after World War II. First was the orthodoxy of neoclassical economics that interpreted the structural changes of the postwar era as temporary dislocations, and looked to national aggregate indicators of economic prosperity rather than to regional variations. Second was the emerging labor relations "manpower" theory that explained unemployment as the result of individual educational or behavioral deficiencies, and deemphasized the structural causes of joblessness. Third was a fundamental optimism about the capacity of the private sector to absorb surplus labor. The reality of rusting cities in the Northeast and Midwest challenged these orthodoxies, but those who bucked mainstream economic and labor market theory, or spoke pessimistically about the economy, remained on the political margins. The result is that urban economic decline in the postwar years has remained largely absent from historical accounts of the 1940s and 1950s.[12]

The problems that beset Detroit were not solely economic. The fate of Northern industrial cities was fundamentally entangled with the troubled history of race in twentieth-century America. By 1960, a majority of America's African American population lived in cities, most of them north of the Mason-Dixon line. The steady loss of manufacturing jobs in northeastern and midwestern cities occurred at the same time that millions of African Americans migrated to the urban North, driven from the rural South by disruptions in the agricultural economy and lured by the promise of freedom and opportunity denied to them in Jim Crow's last, desperate days. The complex and pervasive racial discrimination that greeted black laborers in the "land of hope" ensured that they would suffer disproportionately the effects of deindustrialization and urban decline. For a large number of African Americans, the promise of steady, secure, and relatively well-paid employment in the North proved illusory.[13]

The most visible and intractable manifestation of racial inequality in the postwar city was residential segregation. Blacks in Detroit and other northern metropolises found themselves entrapped in rapidly expanding, yet persistently isolated urban ghettos. Despite the supposedly liberal mores of the North, despite successful court challenges to housing market discrimination, despite open housing advocacy and legislation, northern cities experienced rates of segregation that barely changed between the 1940s and the present. Segregated housing compounded the urban crisis. The combination of deindustrialization, white flight, and hardening ghettoization proved devastating. Residence in the inner city became a self-perpetuating stigma. Increasing joblessness, and the decaying infrastructure of inner-city neighborhoods, reinforced white stereotypes of black people, families, and communities.[14]

Racial conflict and tension surfaced as a persistent refrain in the lives of urban Americans in the postwar era. Discrimination by race was a central fact of life in the postwar city. But the dimensions, significance, and very meaning of race differed depending on its cultural, political, and economic context. Relationships across racial lines took myriad forms and had differing consequences. Many scholars have painted the history of racial discrimination with broad brush strokes. Race, in many accounts, is a transhistorical constant rather than a historical variable. Racism is portrayed as a pathological condition, an unchanging part of white culture. But the word "racism" oversimplifies what was a complicated and multifaceted reality. Race relations in the postwar city were the product of a variety of racial beliefs and practices that changed greatly in the postwar period.[15]

Racial ideology, a shifting and fluid popular vernacular of race, served as the backdrop to the relationship between blacks and whites in the postwar city. Discriminatory attitudes and actions were constructed and justified in part by the images of African Americans to which white city-dwellers were exposed. In mid-twentieth-century Detroit, as in the rest of the nation, racial identities rested on widely held assumptions about the inferior intelligence of blacks, notions that blacks were physiologically better suited for certain types of work, and stereotypes about black licentiousness, sexual promiscuity, laziness, and dependence. But Detroiters were a part of a national culture that began to project contradictory images of African Americans for mass consumption. Perceptions of racial difference and inferiority were informed by music, radio, and movies, in countless ways from the smiling face of Aunt Jemima to the shuffling of Amos 'n Andy, to the crooning voice of Chubby Checker, to the brawny arms of boxer Joe Louis, to the celluloid images of Sidney Poitier and Bessie Smith. On the other side was the persistent association of whiteness with Americanism, hard work, sexual restraint, and independence. These assumptions about racial difference were nourished by a newly assertive whiteness, born of the ardent desire of the "not-yet-white ethnics" (many of them Roman Catholic, second- and third-generation southern and eastern European immigrants) to move into the American mainstream. To be fully American was to be white. Popular images of whiteness and blackness—and the ways in which they changed—influenced the day-to-day encounters between whites and blacks at work and on city streets.[16]

Perceptions of racial differences were not, I argue, wholly, or even primarily, the consequences of popular culture. If they were, they would not have had such extraordinary staying power. In the postwar city, blackness and whiteness assumed a spatial definition. The physical state of African American neighborhoods and white neighborhoods in Detroit reinforced perceptions of race. The completeness of racial segregation made ghettoization seem an inevitable, natural consequence of profound racial differences. The barriers that kept blacks confined to racially isolated, deteriorating, inner-city neighborhoods were largely invisible to white Detroiters. To the majority of untutored white observers, visible poverty, overcrowding, and deteriorating houses were signs of individual moral deficiencies, not manifestations of structural inequalities. White perceptions of black neighborhoods provided seemingly irrefutable confirmation of African American inferiority and set the terms of debates over the inclusion of African Americans in the city's housing and labor markets.[17]

Perhaps most important in shaping the concept of race in the postwar period, I argue, were local and national politics. Race was as much a political as a social construction. The place of race both in party politics and in government policies was in flux in the postwar era. In the aftermath of the struggle against fascism, racialist ideologies lost their official credibility. Beginning in World War II, the federal government promoted a pluralist vision of nationhood that emphasized integration rather than inherent difference. At the same time, the balance of power in national and local politics began to shift as the black population moved northward and became an important part of the Democratic constituency for the first time. Wielding the growing clout of the African American vote, newly empowered civil rights groups demanded the attention of Democratic politicians. Black activists gained new access to government and pursued an aggressive judicial and legislative strategy to eliminate racial inequality. Yet government policies, including Social Security, welfare, and jobs programs, also reinforced and reconstructed racial stereotypes and inequalities. Most importantly, government housing programs perpetuated racial divisions by placing public housing in already poor urban areas and bankrolling white suburbanization through discriminatory housing subsidies. The liberal state communicated an ambivalent message on matters of race that had a powerful impact on individual and group interactions at the local level.[18]

Overall, political activity affected a gradual, if unsteady, shift in the boundaries of what was acceptable racial practice in the postwar years. But the changes were hard fought and bitterly contested. For most of the period between the 1930s and the mid-1960s, nominal liberals dominated the governing coalition in Washington, in northern industrial states, and in major cities. The New Deal coalition was forged in working-class cities like Detroit, and urban elected officials and voters played a crucial role in implementing New Deal policies. Liberal politicians won loyalty by promising their constituents that the government would actively protect their economic and social security. White and black Americans took the promise of liberalism seriously and mobilized in the 1940s and 1950s to assert their rights as citizens.

But the New Deal state was riddled with ambiguities and contradictions that left room for opposing interpretations of what constituted proper government action. Most threatening to the seeming unity of the New Deal order were unresolved questions of racial identity and racial politics, dilemmas that would become inseparable from the mission of liberalism itself. Part the story of the African American challenge to liberalism is well known: civil rights groups in the 1950s launched a fierce attack on Jim Crow in the South. But at the same time, the combination of deindustrialization and black population growth upended the racial order of Detroit and other northern cities. The disruption of old patterns of work, residence, and race coincided with a massive political challenge to the structures of racial inequality nationwide. The history of race relations and civil rights in the North remains, however, largely unexamined by historians. Racial tensions, prejudices, and debates over civil rights played out on the shop floors and in the streets of the urban north, with consequences as far-reaching as those of the southern civil rights movement. Two visions of the polity came into collision in Detroit, both rooted in a newfound rights consciousness at the center of postwar liberalism. African Americans forcefully asserted their rights to equal opportunity in employment and housing. But they faced opposition from working- and middle-class whites who also claimed the mantle of the authentic New Deal state. White Detroiters expected the state to protect the privileges associated with property ownership and race. Debates over housing and race had profound ramifications for the fate of federal policy in the city for the next half-century. The rhetoric, the battles, and the compromises of the 1940s and 1950s, in Detroit and all over the nation, set the terms for the debate over social policy into the Great Society years and beyond.[19]

The convergence of the disparate forces of deindustrialization, racial transformation, and political and ideological conformity laid the groundwork for the urban crisis in Detroit and its northern counterparts. But the emphasis in this study on structural forces shaping the city should not obscure the role of human agency and contingency in the city's development. In many social-scientific studies of American cities, urban problems seem almost inevitable. The shape of the postwar city, I contend, is the result of political and economic decisions, of choices made and not made by various institutions, groups, and individuals. Industrial location policy is not solely the result of technological imperatives; it is the result of corporate policies to minimize union strength, to avoid taxes, and to exploit new markets. Racially segregated neighborhoods are not alone the foreordained consequence of centuries of American racial prejudice; rather, they are the result of the actions of the federal and local governments, real estate agents, individual home buyers and sellers, and community organizations. Economic and social structures act as parameters that limit the range of individual and collective decisions. The consequences of hundreds of individual acts or of collective activity, however, gradually strengthen, redefine, or weaken economic and social structures. The relationship between structure and agency is dialectical and history is the synthesis.[20]

The ideologies and actions of myriad groups shaped the evolution of postwar Detroit. Corporate executives and managers who controlled the city's industry determined the range of employment opportunities through their labor policies and their long-term corporate planning strategies. They had a disproportionate influence on the city's development because of their economic power: a single corporate decision could affect thousands of workers. Company hiring and upgrading policies established and reinforced discriminatory patterns in the workplace. The introduction of new technology and decisions about plant size, expansion, and relocation affected the city's labor market and reshaped the economic geography of the Detroit region.

Though less powerful than their bosses, labor unions and their rank-and-file members also had a hand in Detroit's development. By the 1940s, Detroit was a bastion of industrial unionism, home to the mighty United Automobile Workers, one of the nation's most powerful and influential labor organizations. Over half of Detroit's workers belonged to unions in 1950. Union victories on such issues as work rules, wages, and seniority advanced the economic security and employment stability of the city's unionized workers. At the same time, however, unions often reinforced or quietly acquiesced in employers' discriminatory hiring and upgrading policies, and only seldom challenged management decisions on plant location and expansion that had significant long-term ramifications for Detroit's workers.

In the public sector, federal, state, and local governments buttressed corporate policies through the allocation of resources. Decisions about spending for defense production and transportation profoundly altered the shape of Detroit in the boom years during and after the Second World War. State and local taxation policies influenced corporate decisions on plant location and movement. Most importantly, because most federal urban programs were administered locally and relied on the support of local constituencies, urban politicians, bankers, developers, real estate brokers, and citizens groups all used federal and local housing policies to reconfigure urban geography by class and race in the postwar era.

Individual white Detroiters challenged and reformulated local and federal policies both in the workplace and in their neighborhoods, and contributed to the racial and socioeconomic division of metropolitan Detroit. Workers who benefited from the systematic exclusion of blacks from white jobs often promoted discriminatory policies in the workplace. White working-class and middle-class homeowners played a crucial role in the racial division of the city. Detroit's neighborhoods became a fiercely contested terrain as the city's black population expanded. Through collective organization to resist black mobility, white homeowners redrew the city's racial boundaries and reinforced patterns of racial inequality.

Black Detroiters were far less powerful than employers, white workers and homeowners, and the federal government as actors shaping the social and economic geography of Detroit. They were not, however, powerless. In the postwar years, black homeowners and black renters, the working class and middle class, sometimes collaborated with white organizations, sometimes unwittingly abetted racial divisions, and often challenged patterns of segregation and discrimination. Black organizations such as the Urban League and the NAACP confronted employers, unions, and government agencies over the issue of equal opportunity in the labor and housing markets, and succeeded in expanding the horizons of opportunity for black Detroiters. But growing class divisions within the city's black population inhibited the efforts of black reform groups to address the plight of poor and unemployed Detroit residents. Well-to-do black homeowners, like their white counterparts, fled to outlying sections of the city, and contributed to the residential segregation of the black poor. Black homeowners and white homeowners also joined forces to oppose publicly funded housing for the poor.

The intricate dynamics of personal and group interaction—and their interplay with structural forces—are most visible only at the local level. I have chosen a case study precisely because it allows for a rich description and analysis of the processes that are all too often left in the realm of generalizations such as discrimination, deindustrialization, and racism.[21] Detroit is a logical site for such a close analysis. Its mid-twentieth-century history was shaped by the interplay of the mighty forces of racial conflict and economic change. A magnet for black migrants from the South, Detroit became a test-

ing ground for race relations, a place wracked with racial tensions and conflicts. In Detroit, as in every other Northern city with a sizeable black population, conflicts over race and housing moved to the center of local political
debates. Detroit's whites, like their counterparts in Chicago, Cincinnati,
Philadelphia, and Trenton, resisted the African American migration regardless of the size of the influx of black newcomers. Elected officials in almost
every major northern city grappled with public policies, from housing to
antidiscrimination laws, intended to address the problems generated by
racial conflict.[22]

As a major manufacturing center, the headquarters of the automobile industry, and a hub of union activism, Detroit offers a lens into the dynamics
of American industrial capitalism. The economic fate of the automobile industry in Detroit was not simply a matter of local peculiarity or local interest.
Automobile and related industries led the American industrial economy
after World War II, accounting for about one-sixth of the country's employment at midcentury. In the 1940s and 1950s, the American auto industry
was at its peak of profitability and power, still unchallenged by foreign imports and the management crises that would plague it in the 1970s and
1980s. Because of its dominance in auto production, Detroit was the center
of a regional web of industries vital to the nation's economy. What befell
Detroit directly affected other major manufacturing sectors—steel in Chicago, Pittsburgh, Youngstown, and Gary; rubber and tires in Akron; machine
tools in Cincinnati; glass and electronics in Toledo and Dayton; and more
autos in Cleveland, Milwaukee, and South Bend. When Detroit sneezed,
the adage went, other cities caught pneumonia. In addition, Detroit was
home to a wide range of other industries, including chemicals, steel, phar-
maceuticals, construction, and brewing, in which the dynamics of economic
restructuring and race played out in ways that allow for comparisons with
other cities.[23]

To view Detroit (or any place) as typical would be erroneous. Much about
the city's economy, most notably its dependence on manufacturing employment, distinguished it from other cities with more diverse economic bases.
Detroit was not a global city like New York or Los Angeles, where in the
1970s and 1980s, a large, internationally linked information and service
sector emerged to replace manufacturing jobs. And in some cities, most notably New York, Los Angeles, and Chicago, the presence of other minority
groups, particularly Hispanics and Asians, complicated racial politics in
ways that diverge from the experience of Detroit, which had a small Mexi-
can-American population, a tiny Asian enclave, and hardly any Puerto Ri-
cans, Dominicans, or Cubans. The presence of new immigrants, particularly
in the last twenty years, has undoubtedly complicated the histories of some
other cities. But because the color line between black and white has remained America's most salient social division, the experiences of Detroit

and other cities with sizeable African American populations share much in common. In the end, I contend that the differences between Detroit and other Rust Belt cities are largely a matter of degree, not a matter of kind.

As with any case study, it is important to be attentive to differences and commonalities. At appropriate points, primarily in the notes, I offer readers the opportunity to read further and consider comparisons between Detroit and other cities. Since the history of postwar America, and its cities, remains largely unwritten, many of the larger arguments in this book await the arrival of future books and articles. It is only with many more detailed studies that we will be able to make thorough comparisons and test the arguments that I advance here.

One finding pervades the thousands of letters, pamphlets, newspaper stories, census statistics, government documents, maps, workplace studies, investigative reports, survey data, organizational records, and memoirs that provide the basis for my chronicle of postwar Detroit. The fate of the city is the consequence of the unequal distribution of power and resources. Inequality is by no means a new feature in history—but its manifestations differ widely in different places and different times. What follows is a social and political history of inequality in a twentieth-century city. How those residents of the city who have little access to political power survive, resist, adapt, and gain access to power is a story that I also touch upon. For the actions of the poor can be fully understood only in the context of the larger structures that limit their choices and constrain their options. This book by no means offers a complete history of postwar Detroit; rather, it offers a starting point for an examination of the causes of the vexing problems of urban poverty, inequality, and urban decline, and a tale of the struggles for equality and survival in the postindustrial American city.

Part One

ARSENAL

1.1. The enormous Ford River Rouge plant, one of the largest industrial complexes in the world, was a symbol of Detroit's industrial might. In 1927, photographer Charles Sheeler captured the might of the Rouge in his view of "Criss-Crossed Conveyors." At the end of world War II, over eighty-five thousand workers were employed in the sprawling complex. The River Rouge plant was also Detroit's major employer of African Americans in the wartime era.

1

"Arsenal of Democracy"

IN 1927, Charles Sheeler photographed the Ford Motor Company's enormous River Rouge plant. His most famous print depicts two starkly angular conveyor belts that transported coal into the power plant. In the background piercing the sky are eight tall, narrow smokestacks. Sheeler's striking image revealed the might of Detroit's industry, and did so by portraying only one small section of an industrial complex that consisted of nineteen separate buildings covering more than two square miles. The Rouge included a man-made harbor for Great Lakes coal and iron barges, the largest foundry in the world, and ninety-two miles of railroad track. In 1933, Mexican muralist Diego Rivera captured the monumentality of automobile production at the Rouge. His frescoes at the Detroit Institute of Arts depict workers dwarfed by furnaces belching fire, engaged in seemingly mortal combat with machinery so overwhelming that it called forth herculean labors.[1] These powerful images of Detroit conveyed the sense that the city was the very essence of American industry.

Mid-twentieth-century Detroit embodied the melding of human labor and technology that together had made the United States the apotheosis of world capitalism. Visitors flocked to the Motor City to marvel at its industrial sites. Crowded into the observation areas at auto plants, they stood rapt as the twentieth century's premier consumer object, the automobile, rolled off the assembly lines by the dozens an hour. The scene was a drama of might and violence, of human ingenuity and sheer physical labor, punctuated by the noise of pounding machinery, the sight of hundreds of workers moving rhythmically to the pulse of the line, the quiet but never unnoticed hovering of foremen and inspectors, the interplay of mechanical power and the brawn of human arms and backs, the seemingly endless rush of workers through the gates at shift change time. Detroit's brooding horizon of factories and its masses of industrial laborers became icons of modernity.

Sheeler's photographs and Rivera's murals depicted one part of Detroit: its role as a center of mass production. Ford, Chrysler, and General Motors had their headquarters in the Detroit area. The outlines of dozens of major automobile plants punctuated the low skyline of Detroit. Some, like Dodge Main in Hamtramck, nearly as large as the Rouge, loomed on the horizon; others, like the Packard plant on East Grand Boulevard, spread out over several long city blocks. But throughout the city were many less imposing but still significant enterprises. Also prominent on the city's landscape were a score of large plants where car parts were built: several stamping plants that produced car bumpers and chassis frames, a number of engine plants, one of the largest tire manufactories in the country, and four independent car body manufacturers.[2]

Thousands of relatively inconspicuous factories lined Detroit's major thoroughfares, most employing a few hundred workers, too ordinary in their design and function to attract the attention of artists like Sheeler and Rivera, but no less essential to the city's economy. "Around the work-stained skirts of the town," noted a reporter in 1955, sprawl "miles of one-cylinder tool-and-die shops." The production of a car involved the assembly of thousands of small parts, the building of hundreds of machine tools, the stamping of dies, the forging of metal, the casting of tubes and coils and springs, the molding of plastics, and the manufacture of paints, glass, fabrics, bearings, electronics, and wire. To supply machinery and parts to the automobile industry, a myriad of small manufacturing operations thrived around the city.[3]

To focus merely on the automobile-related factories would miss whole sectors of Detroit's industrial economy. Over 40 percent of the city's industrial jobs were in nonautomotive plants. Some were descended from nineteenth-century enterprises: stove making, brewing, furniture building. Also in Detroit were chemical companies, aircraft part fabricators, oil refineries, salt mines, steel mills, garment manufacturers, food processing plants, the largest pharmaceutical manufacturer in the world, and a major producer of adding machines and typewriters.

Early twentieth-century Detroit was, in the words of historian Olivier Zunz, a "total industrial landscape." Factories, shops, and neighborhoods blurred together indistinguishably, enmeshed in a relentless grid of streets and a complex web of train lines. To the casual observer, the design of Detroit seemed anarchic. The city's sprawling form and its vast array of manufactories made little sense. But Detroit's industrial geography had a logic that defied common observation. Rail lines formed the threads that tied the city's industries together. Automobile manufacturing and railroad transportation were inseparably bound in a symbiotic relationship. Every major automobile factory had its own rail yard. Plants were, in the eyes of one observer, "ringed round with . . . snarls and tangles of railroad tracks." Trains brought raw materials and parts to the auto plants and carried the finished products to distributors throughout the country.[4]

The Detroit River was another essential element in the city's industrial geography. The fast-flowing channel that marked the southern and eastern boundaries of the city passed by Detroit's steel mills and chemical plants. Its waters provided egress to the Great Lakes and easy access to coal and ore, which were prohibitively expensive to transport by land. Chemical and steel manufacturers also depended on water for their cooling systems, and on the river as a ready place to discharge industrial wastes.

In the age of the truck and automobile, roads were a vital conduit linking Detroit's numerous industries to each other. Five wide arterial avenues—Michigan, Jefferson, Gratiot, Woodward, and Grand River—the remnants of Pierre L'Enfant's neoclassical, early national plan for the city—allowed for speedy transit in and out of the city center. A network of surface streets, laid out by nineteenth-century planners in an enormous checkerboard, proved tremendously convenient for the speedy transport of car parts, machine tools, and casts and dies from the small plants where they were built to the larger plants that put them to use in car production. Suppliers and machine tool companies, and other smaller operations, fanned out throughout the city, generally within short range of auto plants, but not confined to the riverside or to railroad rights-of-way.[5]

In the early 1940s, Detroit was at its industrial zenith, leading the nation in economic escape from the Great Depression. Between 1940 and 1947, manufacturing employment in Detroit increased by 40 percent, a rate surpassed only by Los Angeles, San Francisco, and Chicago. Demand for heavy industrial goods skyrocketed during World War II, and Detroit's industrialists positioned themselves to take advantage of the defense boom. Detroit's automobile manufacturers, led by Ford, quickly converted their assembly lines to the mass production of military hardware, airplanes, tanks, and other vehicles, making metropolitan Detroit one of the birthplaces of the military-industrial complex. Observers christened the city "Detroit the Dynamic," the "arsenal of democracy" for a war-torn world. Almost overnight, Detroit had gone from one of the most depressed urban areas in the country to a boomtown, a magnet that attracted workers from all over the United States. The demand for manufacturing labor seemed boundless. Thousands of newcomers flooded the city, coming from places as diverse as rural Appalachia, depressed farm counties in central Michigan, Ohio, and Indiana, and the declining Black Belt regions of the Deep South. The rapid expansion of wartime production drastically reduced unemployment in the city. Between 1940 and 1943, the number of unemployed workers in Detroit fell from 135,000 to a mere 4,000.[6]

The workers who toiled in Detroit's factories forged some of the nation's most powerful trade unions. The end of the Great Depression and the onset of World War II marked the triumph of industrial unionism in Detroit. In the late 1930s, the United Automobile Workers battled the major automobile manufacturers in a series of sitdown strikes, pickets, and protests. The UAW brought together industrial workers from a wide range of ethnic and cultural backgrounds—Lithuanians, Hungarians, Poles, Jews, Scottish, Irish, Mexicans, Canadians, Lebanese, Palestinians, Italians, Germans, and many more. It overcame initial resistance from African Americans whose

1.2. In the 1940s, Detroit's booming defense and automobile industries made the city a blue-collar mecca, magnet to tens of thousands of migrants who found relatively secure, well-paying jobs. At shift change time, shown here, workers rushed out of their plants, heading to their homes in Detroit's innumerable working-class neighborhoods.

church and community leaders were suspicious of trade union activity and from southern white migrants who often worshipped in staunchly antiunion storefront churches and belonged to organizations like the Black Legion and the Ku Klux Klan. The UAW and other industrial unions succeeded in obtaining relatively high wages and benefits, and some job security, for a sizable fraction of Detroit's manufacturing workers. Still, especially in the 1940s, the shop floor was a battleground of contesting visions of unionism. White rank-and-file members protested the upgrading of black workers, unions split into left-led and centrist factions, and union leaders alternated between militance and accommodation with employers.[7]

At the end of the workday, Detroit's laborers rushed to their cars and to the trolleys and buses of the Detroit Street Railway, clogging the streets that led to the innumerable blue-collar neighborhoods of the city. Surrounding

1.3. Detroit's West Side was home to tens of thousands of blue-collar workers whose single-family detached homes made Detroit a low-rise city.

the smoky factories of Detroit and spreading out for miles and miles on the horizon in every direction was a sea of frame and brick houses. "The proto-plasmic cells of Detroit," observed traveler Edmund Wilson, "are . . . drab yellow or redbrick houses, sometimes with black rock-candy columns or a dash of crass Romanesque." Lining the streets of the city's "Polak and Negro sections" were "little dull one-story frame houses." However "small, square, [and] ugly" they might appear to an outsider, two-thirds of all residential structures in the city were single-family homes and another one-fifth were two-family homes. The city's skyline was unassuming, for outside of down-town with its Art Deco skyscrapers and the industrial areas with their multistory factories and belching smokestacks, Detroit had virtually no tall buildings. Unlike its east coast counterparts, Detroit lacked both tenements and high-rise apartments. Only 1.3 percent of the city's residential struc-tures were apartment buildings. A quintessential twentieth-century city in its amorphous sprawl, Detroit lacked the density of older cities in large part because of the vast amount of open land available within the city's boundaries as late as mid-twentieth century. In most parts of the city, the highest visible buildings were church steeples, most of them monuments to the religious fervor and diligence of Catholic immigrants.[8]

Detroit in the 1940s was also a city rife with social tensions. By the outbreak of World War II, the geography of Detroit had come to be defined in terms of white and black. This racial division of the metropolis came in the wake of the dissolution of ethnic communities. By the 1920s, the city's tightly knit ethnic clusters had begun to disperse, and fewer and fewer white neighborhoods were ethnically homogeneous. Important and highly visible immigrant enclaves like Polish Hamtramck and Hungarian Delray continued to exist throughout the twentieth century, but a dwindling number of Detroit residents found themselves living in communities defined by ethnicity. Beginning in the 1920s—and certainly by the 1940s—class and race became more important than ethnicity as a guide to the city's residential geography. Residents of Detroit's white neighborhoods abandoned their ethnic affiliations and found a new identity in their whiteness.[9]

There were many white Detroits. The Detroit of automobile company executives, bankers, lawyers, and doctors could be found in neighborhoods like Boston-Edison, where cathedral-like stands of elm trees towered over staid boulevards lined with ten- to twenty-room mansions, and Palmer Woods and Rosedale Park, whose curvilinear streets passed through a romantic landscape of mock-French châteaux, Tudor-style mansions, formal Georgian estates, and stately New England–style colonials. The Detroit of clerks, engineers, accountants, and midlevel white-collar workers consisted of more modest neighborhoods in the northwest and far northeast sections of the city, like West Outer Drive, Russell Woods, and Chalmers Park, where many lived in substantial three- and four-bedroom brick homes, small-scale versions of the architecture of Palmer Woods.[10]

The majority of white Detroiters lived in the lesser homes of the city's innumerable blue-collar neighborhoods. Small bungalows, most of frame construction, some of brick, crowded together on twenty-five-by-one-hundred-foot lots that allowed just enough room for small vegetable gardens or flower patches. Many, like Oakwood in southwest Detroit, were huddled in the shadow of Detroit's plants, offering their residents easy access to jobs. Increasingly, in the age of the automobile, blue-collar workers built neighborhoods far from the soot of older industrial sections of the city. Areas like Brightmoor on the far West Side, Courville on the Northeast Side, or De Witt–Clinton on the Northwest Side attracted workers who wanted a little green space and did not mind commuting to their jobs. Typical was Brightmoor, an area of one-story "white frame houses, built largely on wooden piles," cheaply built "without adornment of any kind, and strictly utilitarian."[11] Whatever the condition of their houses, many working-class Detroiters had deep attachments to their neighborhoods and the houses they

TABLE 1.1
Detroit's Population, 1910–1970

Year	Total Population	Black Population	Percent Black
1910	465,766	5,741	1.2
1920	993,675	40,838	4.1
1930	1,568,662	120,066	7.7
1940	1,623,452	149,119	9.2
1950	1,849,568	300,506	16.2
1960	1,670,144	482,229	28.9
1970	1,511,482	660,428	44.5

Source: U.S. Department of Commerce, Bureau of the Census, *United States Census of Population*, 1910–1970 (Washington, D.C.: U.S. Government Printing Office, various years).

had built there. "It's a pretty city," recalled auto worker Mike Kerwin, comparing Detroit favorably to his hometown of Chicago. "Almost every street had trees all up and down." Detroit was, above all, a city of homes.[12]

Black Detroit in 1940 was large and rapidly growing. Like other major northern urban centers in the twentieth century, Detroit had a sizable black ghetto that had emerged in the midst of the World War I–era Great Migration of blacks from the South to the urban North. Detroit's reputation as a city of unsurpassed economic opportunity, combined with wrenching changes in the southern economy, attracted thousands of new migrants northward to the Motor City. Migrants came with the hope that the booming northern city would be free of the harsh segregation that had perpetuated Jim Crow on the docks, in the mines, and in the warehouses of the South. Some observers called Detroit "the northernmost southern city" or "the largest southern city in the United States," but it was, after all, a place where blacks could vote, ride side by side with whites on streetcars and buses, and share the same drinking fountains and bathrooms.[13] In the wake of waves of migration, Detroit's black population expanded dramatically over the course of the twentieth century (Table 1.1). Fewer than 10 percent of Detroit's population at the outbreak of World War II, African Americans comprised more than a quarter of the city's residents by 1960.

Detroit's racial boundaries had their origins in the Great Migration of blacks to the city between 1916 and 1929. As early as the mid-nineteenth century, blacks had settled primarily on Detroit's East Side, many in the small "Black Bottom" neighborhood just east of downtown. But blacks and recent immigrants in the nineteenth and early twentieth centuries shared the same streets; seldom did blacks find themselves concentrated in predominantly black neighborhoods. The Great Migration changed the racial geography of Detroit markedly. From the 1920s through the 1940s, the majority of Detroit's black population was confined to a densely populated, sixty-square-block section of the city's Lower East Side which migrants named, perhaps with more than a tinge of irony, Paradise Valley. Black churches, clubs, and stores concentrated in areas where the new migrants settled. Small pockets of several hundred to several thousand blacks lay scattered throughout the city, on Grand River and Tireman on Detroit's West Side, on the northern boundary of heavily Polish Hamtramck, and in the Eight Mile–Wyoming area in northwest Detroit.[14] These areas, especially Paradise Valley, received the enormous number of black workers who came to the city during the Second World War. In the 1940s, the black sections of the city that were already crowded in the 1920s and 1930s burst over with new migrants.

White neighborhoods, especially enclaves of working-class homeowners, interpreted the influx of blacks as a threat and began to defend themselves against the newcomers, first by refusing to sell to blacks, then by using force and threats of violence against those who attempted to escape the black sections of the city, and finally by establishing restrictive covenants to assure the homogeneity of neighborhoods. In the 1920s, white Detroiters began to define their communities in terms of racial homogeneity, and to make apparent to blacks the high cost of penetrating those communities. In 1925, Ossian Sweet, a prominent African American doctor, was tried for murder after shooting into a crowd of several hundred angry whites who surrounded his newly purchased house in a white neighborhood. Even though Sweet was acquitted, the incident demonstrated the risk of violating the sanctity of racial boundaries. Other whites, especially those with the means to relocate, simply fled what they considered to be the inevitable black invasion.[15]

A visitor to Detroit in 1940 could have walked or driven for miles in large sections of the city and seen only white faces. At the outbreak of World War II, nearly 90 percent of Detroit's white population would have had to move from one census tract to another for there to have been an equal distribution of blacks and whites over the city's nearly 140-square-mile area.[16] But if a large number of white Detroiters lived nowhere near blacks, a growing number of blacks and whites met in the workplace. The war was a remarkable moment of opportunity for black workers. Through the first four decades of the twentieth century, the overwhelming majority of Detroit's blacks—like blacks throughout the United States—were employed in the service sector, women in domestic work, men in hotel, restaurant, and maintenance work. In the 1940s, industrial work began to eclipse service employment. The niche that blacks held in hotel and restaurant work declined steadily throughout the early twentieth century. Changes in the organization of department stores in the 1940s eliminated many stock handling and maintenance jobs held by black men. Most importantly, the number of blacks working in domestic service waned during the Great Depression. The introduction of labor-saving appliances resulted in a reduction in jobs for

household servants. The shrinking number of white households that continued to seek domestics, grounds and maintenance workers, and chauffeurs
were less likely to hire blacks. A survey of orders for domestic workers with
the Michigan State Employment Service during the 1940s found a growing
number of households requested white help, perhaps in reaction to the
negative perceptions of African American migrants and the hostile climate
of race relations in the city.[17]

Few blacks lamented the decline of personal service jobs. They were,
after all, remnants of black employment patterns that dated back to the era
of slavery. They paid little, seldom offered fringe benefits, and were ex-
empted from the Social Security program. The decline in demand for domestics corresponded to a rebellion against domestic work by younger black
women in Detroit (and in other parts of the country as well). As social worker
Geraldine Bledsoe pointed out, younger black women in Detroit in the
1930s and 1940s shared "a deep resentment against household employment." Fewer and fewer looked for domestic work, and those employed as
domestics were "constantly trying to escape to other fields" where they
would have more control over their time. Moreover, the rapid growth in
factory and clerical work opened up new opportunities for former personal
service workers. The gains were perhaps greatest for those who were attracted to relatively high-paying manufacturing jobs that lured them away
from the service sector.[18]

Before World War II, only a handful of Detroit's major manufacturers
had employed African Americans. Ford, Briggs, and Dodge—major auto
manufacturers—opened their doors to a small number of African American
workers beginning in the World War I era. Detroit's most welcoming employer was Ford, which recruited an elite corps of black male workers
through carefully cultivated contacts with leading black ministers. By 1940,
nearly 12 percent of Ford workers were African American. Henry Ford's
idiosyncratic paternalism toward black migrants, combined with the company's interest in finding workers willing to accept the dirtiest and most
grueling jobs, led the Ford Motor Company to turn toward black migrants.
Half of all blacks in the automobile industry nationwide were Ford employees; nearly all of these workers were concentrated in the Ford River Rouge
plant.[19] Wherever they were employed, most blacks worked in service jobs,
especially on plant janitorial and maintenance crews, or in hot, dangerous
jobs in foundries or furnace rooms.

Black auto workers before the 1940s were a blue-collar elite. Most found
jobs with the recommendation of their churches or, in some cases, the Urban
League. In the 1930s, Ford hired two respected black leaders, Donald
Marshall and Willis Ward, to serve as liaisons to black Detroit, exploiting
their networks in the black community to recruit for Ford. Black churches
were an especially fruitful recruiting ground. Ford officials donated money

to several major black churches in Detroit, occasionally attended their services, and fostered close relationships with leading clergy. One of Ford's most important contacts was Saint Matthew's Protestant Episcopal Church. On the brink of World War II, the Reverend F. Ricksford Meyers, pastor of Saint Matthew's, corresponded regularly with Ford Motor Company officials and met with Timken-Detroit Axle Company officials to request work for his parishioners, continuing a long relationship with the automobile industry that began in 1923. By recruiting in the churches, Ford reaped the benefits of positive public relations, but more importantly, church recruitment allowed the company to draw from a black labor aristocracy. By using ministers to prescreen potential employees, Ford ensured that it brought in mature, reliable, long-term workers.[20]

World War II represented a turning point in black employment prospects. In 1941 and 1942, firms with predominantly white work forces gradually opened their doors to blacks. Three factors contributed to the opening of industrial jobs to black men and women during the 1940s. First, and most important, was the tight labor market. Detroit firms could barely meet the high demand for labor during the massive wartime defense buildup and the postwar economic boom. A chronic shortage of labor forced manufacturers to hire blacks and women for jobs that had been restricted to white men, although "the vast majority of these jobs," as a 1945 study noted, "were in labor and service classifications." Still, blacks who migrated to Detroit in this period could expect to find jobs that had been closed to them in the South, and wages that far surpassed those in the even the best-paid southern industries.[21]

Second, unions and civil rights organizations played a central role in changing the terms on which blacks were hired. Beginning in the last years of the Great Depression, industrial unions, led by the UAW, opened many locals to black membership, lobbied for civil rights protection, and supported the hiring of black workers. The leadership of the UAW also made a tremendous push for inclusion of blacks in the workplace during World War II, despite opposition from rank-and-file workers and corporate managers.[22] Auto employers had most frequently used black labor as part of a classic divide-and-conquer strategy in the workplace: in times of industrial tumult, the auto companies hired blacks as strikebreakers. The pattern broke in the early 1940s, when the UAW forged an alliance with black churches and reform organizations, especially the NAACP.[23] The success of interracial unionism in the automobile industry hindered employers' strategies of fragmenting the work force by race to curb union militancy.

During the war, moreover, the NAACP, and other, shorter-lived civil rights and labor organizations, like the National Negro Congress and the Civil Rights Congress, played an important role in highlighting the issue of employment discrimination. Agitation for workplace equality in Detroit was part of a national wartime campaign for racial justice. Civil rights organizations used newspaper articles and advertisements, employer outreach programs, and workplace education campaigns, to pressure employers to hire black workers and to persuade a skeptical white public that hiring blacks was a wartime necessity and a moral duty. Double victory meant the vanquishing of Nazism abroad and racism at home. With great effectiveness, black activists used pickets and boycotts to bring discriminatory practices to the public eye. Protestors preyed on companies' fears of negative publicity, by suggesting that discrimination was unpatriotic and hindered the war effort. And they put pressure on government officials to use the strong arm of the law to combat discrimination in defense industries.[24]

The most powerful weapon in the wartime battle for racial equality in the workplace was President Franklin D. Roosevelt's Executive Order 8802, mandating nondiscrimination in war industries and creating the President's Fair Employment Practices Commission (FEPC). Roosevelt hoped that the FEPC would diffuse the growing black protest movement, with little cost to the federal government.[25] The FEPC had few enforcement powers, but used its investigations to challenge recalcitrant employers and racist workers. Not uniformly activist in its support for black workers, the FEPC responded to pressure from Detroit's NAACP and UAW, and conducted investigations at Detroit plants. The FEPC forced reluctant employers to hire and upgrade blacks, and wary white employees to accept new black coworkers. It curbed some of employers' discriminatory excesses, although some employers disregarded federal directives, and the government enforced them selectively at best. Perhaps most importantly, the alliance between blacks and government—despite its fragility—raised expectations and spurred thousands more blacks and whites to civil rights activism.[26]

The cumulative effect of economic forces, activism, and government assistance was that blacks made significant gains in Detroit's industrial economy during the war. The biggest gains came in former auto plants: most had black workers. The smallest came in tool and die, machine, and metal fabricating firms. Only 11 of 44 firms surveyed by the UAW in late 1942 had black workers, and only one had more than eight black workers. As late as 1942, 119 of 197 Detroit manufacturers surveyed had no black employees. But the shortage of labor in Detroit was so great by 1943 that companies by necessity opened doors for blacks that had previously been shut. A 1944 report found that "a 44% advance in wartime employment brought with it an advance of 103% in the total number of Negroes employed." As Chrysler worker James Boggs recalled, "You could get a job anywhere you went." Even if Boggs exaggerated somewhat, his comment reflected the enormous optimism that wartime employment gains generated among Detroit's blacks. During the period of critical labor shortage, black workers no longer had to rely on the recommendations of ministers and influential community members to find work. The proportion of black men working as factory operatives rose from 29 percent in 1940 to 45 percent in 1950.[27]

Wartime opportunities diverged greatly by sex as well as race. The war effort drew women into defense industries to replace men who had joined the military. A growing number of women became their households' primary breadwinners during the war, and relied on defense employment to support their families. Employers channeled women into jobs like riveting and wiring, where their presumed "nimbleness" would be an asset. Women were almost entirely closed out of employment in industries whose jobs could not be easily redefined as traditionally female, such as steel, machine tool making, chemicals, and construction. The result was that the war employment experience for women in Detroit was decidedly mixed. Women got jobs that had been denied them before the war, but still found themselves in sex-typed work, almost always paid less than their male counterparts. Because of unresolved conflicts between child care, housework, and paid labor, women's work tended to be less stable than men's. Female war workers had higher rates of absenteeism and quit their jobs more frequently than men.[28]

Black women gained the least from war employment. Many firms hired white women first, and black women only in response to protest and pressure. Detroit civil rights activists angrily protested companies' failure to hire black women. In 1942, bus loads of black picketers targeted Ford for its unwillingness to hire black women at its Willow Run aircraft plant. But even after they were hired in defense industries, black women faced an uphill battle. White male workers often harassed their women co-workers and reacted even more vehemently to the double affront to their racial and gender privileges when firms hired black women to work beside them. At Packard, whites walked out on a hate strike in 1943 when three black women were placed as drill operators. As a result of resistance to black women at all levels from the boardroom to the assembly line, their entrance into war work was hard fought. In January 1943, fifty leading war production plants in Detroit had women workers, but only nineteen hired black women. Wartime necessity eventually opened new opportunities for black women in Detroit's factories. Although a majority remained "employed in such capacities as janitresses and matrons," the number of black women operatives doubled in the 1940s. Nearly one-fifth of black women had factory jobs by 1950.[29]

In the crucible of war, resentment between blacks and whites simmered. Detroit's public spaces, from city parks to schools, became the scenes of countless minor skirmishes. In 1943, a British traveler to the city wrote that "obnoxious to everyone is the crowding, in public places, on the street, in transport, in parks, lifts, shops, and places of amusement." Blacks and whites, often in close proximity for the first time, jostled and brawled. Mundane interracial encounters were laden with uncertainty. Anxious whites accused blacks of forming a "bump club," whose members, they believed, deliberately pushed and shoved white pedestrians and bus riders.[30]

Such incidents were symptoms of far greater racial animosities that played out in the two most hotly contested arenas of Detroit life: workplaces and neighborhoods. In the midst of a severe wartime housing shortage, the city's rapidly growing black population sought decent homes beyond the borders of the black ghetto. Violence flared on the streets of areas like the near Northeast Side, where whites fought to prevent black occupancy in the Sojourner Truth housing project and blacks gathered to protest and to fight back. Between 1941 and 1944, workers at dozens of Detroit-area plants engaged in wildcat strikes over the hiring and upgrading of black workers to jobs formerly restricted to whites.[31]

Wartime racial tensions came to a violent climax in June 1943. Detroit was one among many booming cities across the United States that were seething with racial conflict. During the war, race riots broke out in Harlem, Mobile, and Brownsville, Texas; whites attacked Mexican and African American zoot-suiters in Los Angeles and Chicago; hate strikes shut down workplaces in Chicago, Baltimore, and Philadelphia; and countless minor clashes between blacks and whites occurred on the overcrowded streets, parks, streetcars, and buses of virtually every major city in the country. The situation in Detroit was especially tense. "Detroit is Dynamite," read a banner headline in *Life* magazine in 1942. "It can either blow up Hitler or blow up the U.S."[32]

It was in this context of wartime strife that Detroit experienced one of the worst riots in twentieth-century America. The trouble began when nearly one hundred thousand Detroiters gathered on Belle Isle, Detroit's largest park, on a hot summer Sunday. Brawls between young blacks and whites broke out throughout the afternoon, and fights erupted on the bridge connecting Belle Isle to southeast Detroit in the evening. In the climate of racial animosity and mistrust bred by the disruptions of World War II, the brawls were but a symptom of deeper tensions. Rumors of race war galvanized whites and blacks alike, who took to the streets near Belle Isle and in the downtown area, and launched fierce attacks against passersby, streetcars, and property. Blacks in Paradise Valley looted white-owned stores. The following day more than ten thousand angry whites swept through Paradise Valley, and rampaged along nearby thoroughfares. Many Detroit police openly sympathized with the white rioters, and were especially brutal with blacks; 17 blacks were shot to death by the police, no whites were. Over the course of three days, 34 people were killed, 25 of them blacks. 675 suffered serious injuries, and 1,893 were arrested before federal troops subdued the disorder.[33]

Yet however serious were Detroit's problems, black newcomers continued to arrive in the wartime and postwar eras with high expectations. During World War II and the immediate postwar years, African Americans continued to flood into the city, lured by the prospect of stable, secure employment and by the high wages and seemingly endless supply of jobs in Detroit's preeminent industry, automobile production. In the 1940s and 1950s, the rapidly growing metropolitan area offered significant opportunities for work in its burgeoning manufacturing, construction, and retail sectors. The migration continued unabated in the 1950s, as a new generation of blacks, displaced by the mechanization of southern agriculture, moved to the city that many of their relatives and friends called home. Black migrants fled poverty rates that soared as high as 80 percent in the rural black belt. They also sought freedom from a political climate that grew harsher as Jim Crow desperately fought for survival. Whether attracted to the opportunities of the Motor City, or pushed from the tiny farm plots where they had toiled for generations, southern blacks looked to Detroit as a land of hope, a "New Caanan."[34]

Like sojourners in an unknown land, they did not know exactly what fate would befall them in the postwar city. They remained hopeful because they lived in a political and social world that was in tremendous flux. The 1940s were an optimistic time for Detroiters, both black and white. The city's tremendous economic growth seemed a portent of still better things to come. That the period of "reconversion" from military to civilian production was so mild and short-lived quelled many lingering uncertainties about the city's future. "Detroit's adjustment to peacetime production," boasted state officials, "was accomplished with the same efficiency that brought it fame as an arsenal of democracy." In the immediate aftermath of the war, "Detroit's production machine really rolled into high gear"; and by 1948 auto production rates were higher than in any year except for 1929. The postwar boom in civilian production ensured that unemployment in the city remained at wartime lows. Employers complained that jobs were going begging and economists lamented the city's "critical labor shortage." If Detroit had an economic golden age, the decade of the 1940s seems as likely a candidate as any.[35]

The immediate postwar years also brought a period of guarded optimism about race relations in the city and nationwide. In the wake of the 1943 riot, city officials created the Mayor's Interracial Committee to address the grievances of black city residents and to cool racial tensions. Its apparent successes inspired other cities around the country to form similar organizations.[36] Detroit's chapter of the NAACP grew to be the largest in the nation, and allied itself closely with the powerful United Automobile Workers to combat discrimination in the workplace. The wartime rhetoric of racial equality, pluralism, and rights added to the hope that significant change was possible—that a combination of civil rights legislation, education and dialogue between whites and blacks, and an overall climate of prosperity would calm racial tensions and eventually eliminate racial divisions. But the raw memories of the hate strikes and the riot gave Detroiters pause. Throughout the 1940s, the underlying causes of racial inequality in Detroit—housing and employment—remained unaddressed. The city's neighborhoods and shop floors continued to be contested terrain. Detroit's blue-collar workers, blacks and whites, politicians, unions, corporate managers, real estate brokers, and homeowners joined in a struggle over their competing agendas, often in conflict with each other. The city's future was up for grabs.[37]

2.1. This streetscape of frame houses built in the late nineteenth century was described by an Office of War Information photographer as a "typical Negro neighborhood." During the housing shortage of World War II and afterward, these already old and crowded dwellings were often subdivided into temporary apartments to accommodate additional families and boarders.

2

"Detroit's Time Bomb": Race and Housing in the 1940s

Housing is Detroit's time bomb.
—Lester Vellie (1946)

[We] have talked about taking an area and moving
the whites the hell out—and moving the Negroes
in. You won't have peace and quiet until you have
such an area. I'd like to see the Negro get a city
of his own, with his own school. We need a
Harlem for them.
—Common Councilman William Rogell (1946)

IN 1949, an unknown African American woman named Ethel Johnson wrote a short letter to Michigan Governor G. Mennen Williams. She recounted the difficulty of finding rental housing for her family, and described the substandard house she lived in. "My husband, baby and I sleep in the living room. When it rain or snow it leap through the roof. Because of the dampnes of the house my baby have a bad cold. We have try very hard to fine a place, and every where we go we have been turn down because of my baby." The same year, Donald Stallings, a black city sanitation worker, and his wife Irma, found themselves in similar straits. The Stallings lived with their five children in a "partitioned basement utility room" in the Black Bottom, the oldest and poorest section of Detroit. Their dreary one-room apartment was often covered with coal soot from a poorly functioning furnace.[1] The housing situations of these two African American families were not atypical in the 1940s. Detroit blacks were entrapped in the city's worst housing stock, half of it substandard, most of it overcrowded. They lived in overwhelmingly black neighborhoods, a reflection of the almost total segregation in the city's housing market. Detroit's black population had doubled between 1940 and 1950, but the pool of available housing had grown painfully slowly.

An enormous gap separated the reality of overcrowded, substandard housing and the aspirations of black migrants to the city. Black migrants to the urban North brought with them expectations of independence, economic security, and property ownership, all of which had been systematically thwarted in the postemancipation South. Since emancipation, most southern blacks aspired to own their own property, build their own homes, and work for themselves. Black landownership was not unheard of in the postbellum South, but it was not common. Sharecropping, debt-peonage, and systematic violence bound many southern blacks to the enforced dependence of landlessness and labor for landowning whites. Many whites simply refused to sell land to blacks, even to the few who had the means to purchase property. Migration to the North held out the promise of steady, well-paid employment and the prospect of saving to purchase property. As Charles Butler, an Arkansas-born Detroit minister, recalled, "One of the things that was inbred in us in the south is that land is extremely important—a home and some land. My parents used to say to me . . . 'get you a piece of land because that's the only thing nobody can move you off.' It was that kind of mentality that formed the background for small parcel acquisitions of housing in the city of Detroit." But if black migrants had great expectations about the possibility of independence through home-ownership, at the same time the reality of housing became a source of tremendous frustration.[2]

African Americans in Detroit faced formidable barriers in the city's housing market, a combination of forces that proved almost insurmountable. Finances were a major obstacle to equal housing. Because blacks were confined to the poorest-paying, most insecure jobs, they had less disposable income than their white counterparts, and could not afford the city's better housing. The rental market was small and expensive, controlled by landlords who profited handsomely from the huge black demand for housing and the inadequate supply of apartments. Overpriced rental housing added to blacks' economic woes, forcing them to spend a higher percentage of their income on housing than whites, and to double or triple up with other black families if they wanted to save any money. Homeownership was also an unrealistic expectation for a majority of black Detroiters in the 1940s. Although Detroit had a stock of well-built if modest homes that blue-collar workers could afford, blacks were systematically shut out of the private real estate market. White real estate brokers shunned black clients and encouraged restrictive covenants and other discriminatory practices that kept blacks out of most of the city's single-family houses. Bankers seldom lent to black home buyers, abetted by federal housing appraisal practices that ruled black neighborhoods to be dangerous risks for mortgage subsidies and home loans. The result was that blacks were trapped in the city's worst housing, in strictly segregated sections of the city.

The process of housing segregation set into motion a chain reaction that reinforced patterns of racial inequality. Blacks were poorer than whites and they had to pay more for housing, thus deepening their relative impoverishment. In addition, they were confined to the city's oldest housing stock, in most need of ongoing maintenance, repair, and rehabilitation. But they

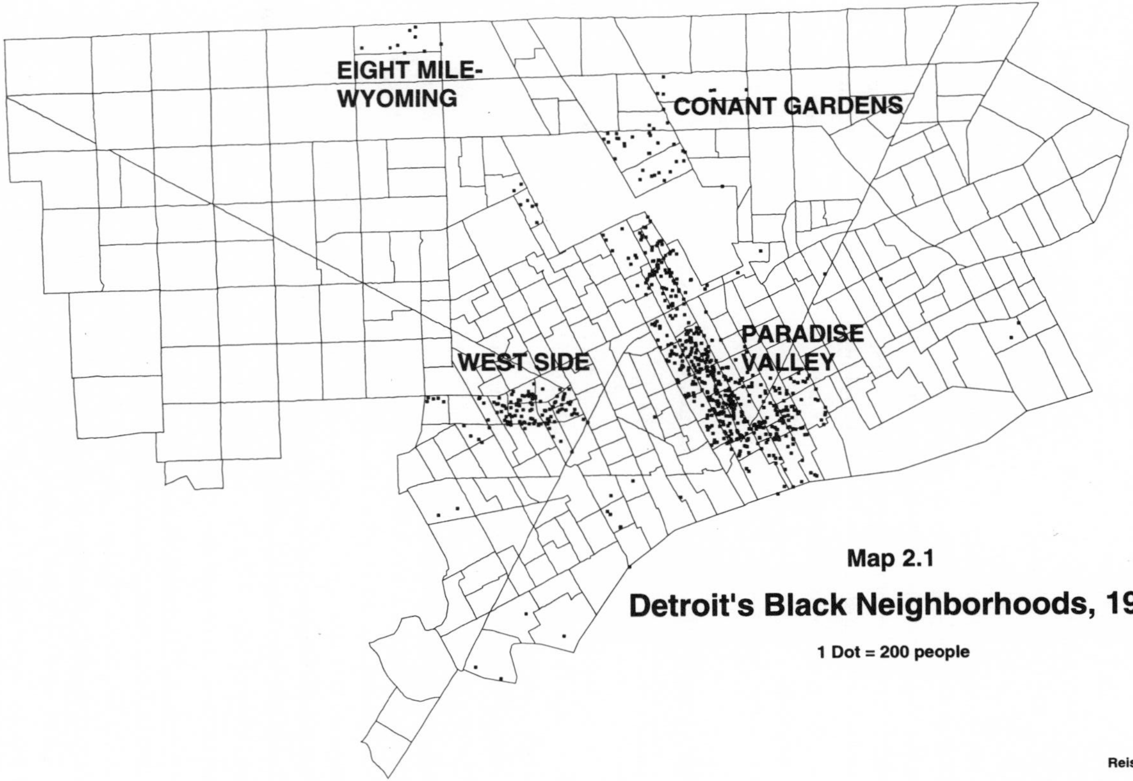

Map 2.1

Detroit's Black Neighborhoods, 1940

1 Dot = 200 people

CONANT GARDENS

PARADISE VALLEY

WEST SIDE

EIGHT MILE-WYOMING

Reiser/Sugrue

could not get loans to improve their properties. As a result, their houses deteriorated. City officials, looking at the poor housing stock in black neighborhoods, condemned many areas as blighted, and destroyed much extant housing to build highways, hospitals, housing projects, and a civic center complex, further limiting the housing options of blacks. Moreover, the decaying neighborhoods offered seemingly convincing evidence to white homeowners that blacks were feckless and irresponsible and fueled white fears that blacks would ruin any white neighborhood that they moved into. Finally, neighborhood deterioration seemed definitive proof to bankers that blacks were indeed a poor credit risk, and justified disinvestment in predominantly minority neighborhoods. To understand the processes of black occupancy, impoverishment, disinvestment, and decline, this chapter will look at the housing patterns in segregated Detroit and the role that homeowners and institutions played in maintaining racial barriers and perpetuating the social, economic, and political marginalization of African Americans.

The Traditional "Ghetto": Paradise Valley and the East Side

During and after World War II, black migrants flooded into Detroit's Lower East Side, a section of the city that extended from the Detroit River on the south to Grand Boulevard, about three miles to the north. The poorest section, nicknamed the Black Bottom, was between the river and Gratiot Avenue, on the site of Detroit's earliest settlements. On its narrow streets stood tiny, densely packed frame homes jerry-built by poor European immigrants in the mid and late nineteenth century. Just to the north, between Gratiot and Grand Boulevard, nearly a third of Detroit's black population lived on the streets clustered around St. Antoine and Hastings. Known as Paradise Valley, the area had been the commercial center of Detroit's black population since the World War I era. Paradise Valley was the destination of tens of thousands of migrants, and the point of departure for a future of opportunity and promise. "Paradise Valley is a misnomer," wrote Detroit NAACP president Gloster Current in 1946. The name was a reflection of the hope of black newcomers to the city, and an ironic comment on hopes still unmet. Current described the area as "a mixture of everything imaginable— including overcrowding, delinquency, and disease. It has glamor, action, religion, pathos. It has brains and organization and business. Not only does it house social uplift organizations, but it supports the militant protest groups." In 1940, Paradise Valley was home to most of black Detroit's most venerable institutions, including churches, social organizations, and business associations. Among the busy storefronts along Hastings and St.

Antoine Streets were Detroit's famous jazz and blues clubs, barber shops, groceries, and clothing stores catering to black Detroiters. Yet Paradise Valley was hardly a promised land, for it was also an area with densely packed tenements and visible poverty, plagued by disease and crime.[3]

Living conditions in the area were bleak. Paradise Valley dwellings were among the oldest in the city, many dating to the 1860s and 1870s. Most of the buildings were owned by absentee landlords, and most were poorly maintained. During the Great Migration, the owners of old hotels and once-grand nineteenth-century row houses chopped up large rooms and converted them into small apartments and boarding houses, over a quarter of them without modern amenities like plumbing and full kitchen facilities.[4] As the district's population expanded during the 1940s, living conditions worsened. Federal housing officials classified over two-thirds of Paradise Valley residences as substandard (a category that included dwelling units without a toilet or bath, running water, heating, and lighting; buildings that needed major repairs; and low-rent apartments that were overcrowded). Rents were among the lowest in the city, but they were disproportionately high given the quality of housing in the area.[5]

Nearly a third of Detroit residential fires occurred within three miles of downtown, most in predominantly black neighborhoods that contained only 12 percent of the city's housing. Fire was an ever-present hazard, especially in older wood-frame buildings that held too many people and had outdated electrical and heating systems. Poor inner-city residents often had family or friends deprived of their homes or killed by fire.[6] In inner-city areas, sanitary conditions also left much to be desired. Because the city picked up garbage only once a week in most residential neighborhoods, enormous piles of trash accumulated in the alleys of densely packed sections of the city. Residents of rundown houses facing rubbish-strewn alleys battled infestations of rats and mice. In the cold months, foraging vermin found easy food and shelter in the old wooden buildings that predominated in the inner city. Residents of the predominantly black Lower East Side, known disparagingly as the "rat belt," reported 206 rat bites to city officials in 1951 and 1952.[7]

Beyond the Ghetto: Black Enclaves

About a quarter of Detroit's blacks lived outside of the Lower East Side in the early 1940s. Most settled in black enclaves or "colonies," as federal bank appraisers called them, where they sought refuge from the overcrowded and rundown housing of the inner city. The history of these smaller black neighborhoods, where black migrants cobbled together the resources to buy or build single-family homes, is little studied in Detroit or elsewhere.[8] The largest enclave outside Paradise Valley, home to about a third of Detroit's African American population, was the black West Side, a neighborhood centered around the intersection of Tireman and West Grand Boulevard. The black West Side was "an attractive neighborhood" settled in the 1920s by upwardly mobile Detroit blacks fleeing Paradise Valley as it attracted growing numbers of southern-born migrants. West Side residents, in the words of a black observer, "took pride in their achievement." They founded a community organization, the Entre Nous Club, to "keep their homes on a high level" by sponsoring community home improvement and gardening activities. The neighborhood contained some substantial turn-of-the-century homes, especially on its western periphery, that attracted many of Detroit's Great Migration–era business leaders, ministers, and professionals. Their motto, "The West Side is the Best Side," aptly summed up their sense of distinction from other sections of black Detroit.[9]

Government officials responsible for rating Detroit communities for the Federal Home Loan Bank System noticed a difference between the status of residents of the black West Side and other sections of the city. Like every other black section of Detroit, the West Side was marked "D" or "red" on the Home Owners Loan Corporation appraisal maps of Detroit, flagging the area as unsuitable for federal loans and subsidies. Despite its low rating, HOLC officials noted that the residents of the area consisted of the "better class" of "Negro," and pointed out that several streets in the area had expensive homes.[10] The West Side differed considerably from Paradise Valley in its housing and social characteristics. At the beginning of World War II, 37 percent of West Side residents were homeowners, compared to only 10 percent in Paradise Valley. And only 17 percent of West Side dwellings were substandard, compared to over 60 percent of Paradise Valley homes. The western section of the West Side had rates of homeownership between 40 and 49 percent, greatly exceeding the rate of the city as a whole.[11]

The influx of migrants during World War II put real burdens on the West Side neighborhood. Its population expanded dramatically during the 1940s, but newcomers were confined to the extant housing stock. Families doubled and tripled up in single-family homes. Many landlords divided the area's modest homes into apartments and boarding houses to accommodate the influx of defense workers and their families. Strained by overpopulation and poor maintenance, the West Side's housing deteriorated, and the community lost some of its luster as a center of Detroit's black bourgeoisie. Although certain blocks retained African American businessmen and professionals, the area began to suffer some of the same problems as Paradise Valley. Overcrowding brought sanitation, safety, and fire hazards. Elizabeth Jenkins and her six children were among the poor residents who crowded into illegally converted apartments in the West Side during and after the war. Forced to move from place to place because of the size of her family,

Jenkins ended up in a tiny attic apartment in a crowded Twenty-fourth Street house. In December 1948, Elizabeth Jenkins and her six children died when a fire gutted the building.[12]

Other blacks lived in racially segregated neighborhoods distant from the inner city. The Eight Mile–Wyoming area, nearly ten miles from Paradise Valley on the northern boundary of the city, barely resembled the inner-city neighborhoods where most Detroit blacks lived. About a thousand migrants settled on former farmland in the area in the 1920s with the encouragement of the Detroit Urban League and the assistance of an enterprising white land speculator. On the open fields of the Eight Mile area, they hoped to build their own houses on their own land. According to Horace White, a leading Detroit minister and the first African American member of the Detroit Housing Commission, blacks had settled in the Eight Mile area "because it was their one opportunity, as they saw it, to own their own homes and rear their families."[13]

Burneice Avery, a southern migrant who arrived in Detroit in 1919 with her parents, described the "dream homes" that the residents of the Eight Mile–Wyoming community hoped to build after they had paid off their land contracts and saved enough money to purchase building supplies. Construction in the neighborhood was piecemeal, as residents scraped together their meager resources, gathered building materials from junkyards and demolition sites, and purchased the occasional fitted window or door. "Building material," Avery recalled, "was purchased on the pay-day plan—$10.00 worth now, and $15.00 worth again. . . ." She continued, "Tar paper siding was the fashion, rooms were added as the family grew." Of the tumble down houses in the neighborhood, Avery stated that "we all knew that these were our temporary homes—someday we would build a beautiful permanent home with running water instead of the old pump, and modern sanitation to take place of the outside toilets and the tin tub to bathe in." Unable to obtain loans and mortgages, residents of the Eight Mile Road community pooled their resources and built what they could afford.[14]

Eight Mile residents spoke proudly of their houses and land, even if their living quarters were little more than "a neat little house undoubtedly once intended to be a garage," a four-room shack, or an old city bus converted into a small dwelling.[15] One elderly woman spoke of the independence and security of her three-room house:[*] "This little place is mine—ah got a place to live in till ah die an' ah'm happy knowin' ah'm safe . . . ah sleeps bettah nights knowin' nobody can put me outa mah own little house." Another homeowner stated that "Day ain't no place like dis place. We has a gahden—

---

[*] Sociologist Marvel Daines, who interviewed Eight Mile–Wyoming residents in 1938, transcribed her interviews in dialect, a standard convention of white writers in the 1930s. The use of dialect simultaneously conveyed to a white readership the authenticity of black voices, and a message of black inferiority. I have left Daines's quotations unedited.

2.2. The Eight Mile–Wyoming neighborhood, with ample open land, attracted black migrants from the South who sought the independence and security of homeownership. The simple frame structure, photographed in 1942, was typical of the self-constructed houses in the area. Residents often converted undeveloped lots, like the one on the right, into cornfields and vegetable gardens.

flowahs—trees—sunshine—nice neighbahs." Most residents found the abundant land for gardening the most appealing feature of the neighborhood. Vacant lots became cornfields and vegetable gardens in the summer, assisting families' subsistence.[16]

By the time the Works Progress Administration and the Detroit Housing Commission conducted the 1938 Real Property Survey of Detroit, residents of the Eight Mile area were among the city's poorest residents. They lived in dire housing conditions. Still, in stark contrast to the majority of Detroit's African American population, 91.7 percent of Eight Mile residents lived in single-family, detached homes. Two-thirds of the homes were owner-occupied, in contrast to only 37.8 percent of homes in the city. Nearly 43 percent of Eight Mile area homeowners had fully paid off their land contracts or mortgages. The high rates of homeownership belied poor living conditions. The Real Property Survey found that more than two-thirds of the buildings in the area were in substandard condition, and only 45.5 percent of the homes had at least one toilet and bath.[17]

On the Northeast Side, nearly eight miles from Paradise Valley, lay Detroit's most exclusive African American enclave, Conant Gardens. Settled by black ministers, teachers, lawyers, and businesspeople fleeing the inner city, the area was more suburban than urban, surrounded by open fields and remote from the city's business and industrial districts. The quiet tree-lined streets of the neighborhood passed modern single-family detached homes, often with large, well-manicured lawns. Conant Gardens was the wealthiest area of black Detroit. In 1950, the median income of black families and unrelated individuals in tracts 603 and 604 ranked first and second of all tracts in the city with more than five hundred blacks. Over 60 percent of area residents owned their own homes. Conant Gardens residents also had the highest levels of education of blacks in any section of the city.[18]

Protective of their homes and investments, Conant Gardens residents, like their counterparts in white, middle-class neighborhoods throughout the city, used restrictive covenants to bar multiple housing and other "undesirable uses." In defense of their exclusive status, Conant Gardens residents staunchly (but unsuccessfully) opposed the construction of federally subsidized public housing at the nearby Sojourner Truth site in the early 1940s, forming an unlikely alliance with conservative white homeowners' groups in the area. Conant Gardens residents established a pattern that the black middle class would repeat throughout the postwar years: whenever new housing opportunity was available they would be the first to take advantage of it.[19]

The Housing Shortage

Apart from the lucky few who lived in Conant Gardens, few black Detroiters had access to high quality housing. The main force confining blacks to the overcrowded inner city and a few scattered outlying enclaves in the 1940s was the city's construction industry and real estate market. Between 1929 and 1960, Detroit's building industry went through two distinct stages. From the onset of the Great Depression through 1946, construction of new housing was sluggish. The Depression hit the homebuilding industry especially hard, and in Detroit, as in most parts of the country, few residents could afford to build new homes. The onset of World War II ossified the private housing industry, depriving contractors of both labor and building materials. The effects of the Depression and war were most apparent in the shortage of skilled construction labor. Two years after the war ended, the median age of bricklayers in metropolitan Detroit was an astonishing fifty-seven years. Since the Crash, few young men had apprenticed in the building trades, thus virtually depriving the construction industry of experienced craftsmen.[20]

At the end of the war Detroit's housing industry began a gradual renaissance, as labor and materials became less scarce and contractors rushed to take advantage of federal subsidies for new developments. It was not until the late 1940s and early 1950s that new residential construction surpassed its pre-Depression peak. Thousands of new houses filled the vacant lots of far northeast and northwest Detroit and its booming suburbs. Still, the supply of housing lagged well behind unmet demand. From the early 1940s to the mid-1950s, Detroit and other major metropolitan centers throughout the United States faced housing shortages of unprecedented magnitude. Popular magazines like *Fortune* lamented the nation's "housing mess." Detroit's population increased by over 220,000 between 1940 and 1950, but new housing starts failed to keep pace. Families shared houses and crowded into tiny apartments and Quonset huts hastily erected to provide shelter for defense workers. Compounding the crisis was the return of thousands of war veterans, many of whom started families as soon as they could. Rapidly growing industrial centers like Detroit simply did not have enough houses and apartments to shelter new migrants and returning GIs and their baby-boom families.[21]

Both blacks and whites suffered from the shortage of housing, but blacks bore a disproportionate share of the burden. Detroit's black population expanded much more rapidly than the available housing stock in the small neighborhoods to which they had been confined. About 150,000 new Detroiters in the 1940s were black, accounting for more than two-thirds of the city's population growth. During the war, "housing for Negroes was . . . the Number One problem of the area," noted the Citizens Housing and Planning Council in 1944, but the city gained virtually no new housing for blacks. Despite a demand for ten thousand units of housing for blacks who migrated to the city during the war, only 1,895 units of public housing and 200 units of private housing were built for black occupancy between 1941 and 1944.[22]

Resourceful black workers converted stables, storefronts, garages, attics, and cellars into makeshift housing. In 1943, eighteen black families lived in a former church that had been converted to a crowded apartment building.[23] Living conditions were often miserable. A black Packard worker who lived with his family in a rundown former saloon proclaimed that "It's hell living here"—undoubtedly a sentiment that many war workers shared.[24] Another family lived in a jerry-built illegal apartment on the city's East Side. A journalist reported that the apartment's walls were "stuffed with rags and papers to keep out the weather and rodents," and "tin cans are suspended from the ceiling to catch the water that is always coming through."[25]

When war veterans returned, the housing shortage became even more acute. Between July 1946 and March 1947, 43 percent of married black veterans shared quarters with another family, or lived in rented rooms, trailers, or tourist cabins.[26] Frequently whole families had to share apartments that would have been small for even one or two people. Typical was Lena Williams, who lived for over five years in a single room with her family of four.[27] Despite the housing shortage, more than half of black veterans surveyed hoped to move and buy or build their own homes. But the demand far exceeded the supply. Of 545,000 housing units available in the Detroit area in 1947, only 47,000 were available to blacks.[28]

There were many reasons for the low supply of housing for workers in the city. First, a relatively small portion of Detroiters could afford newly constructed homes. Throughout the city, builders preferred to construct homes for well-to-do buyers. Common Council member George Edwards testified in 1947 that "the houses we are building are either for sale at prices the vast majority of us cannot afford or are offered at monthly rents twice what most of us can afford."[29] Edward Connor, director of the Citizens Housing and Planning Council, concurred, noting that most new housing in 1947 cost $7,500 to $8,000, while the greatest unanswered demand was for housing under $6,000.[30]

Not only were new homes out of the price range of working Detroiters, but they were almost always unavailable to African Americans. A mere 1,500 of the 186,000 single-family houses constructed in the metropolitan Detroit area in the 1940s were open to blacks. As late as 1951, only 1.15 percent of the new homes constructed in the metropolitan Detroit area were available to blacks.[31] "Vast amounts of new housing on the periphery of the city are being marketed to white buyers," reported Mayor's Interracial Committee chair George Schermer in 1950. "These conditions result in a situation where properties in older neighborhoods tend to command a higher price from Negro buyers than from white."[32] Black buyers faced large down payments, difficulties in financing, and high-interest land contracts, as well as the expensive maintenance costs of old houses, all of which added to their housing expenditures.[33]

Private-sector discrimination was neither the reflection of the invisible hand of the free market, nor the consequence of blacks acting in accordance with a preference to live in segregated neighborhoods. Rather, it was a direct consequence of a partnership between the federal government and local bankers and real estate brokers. In fact the boundaries between the public and private sectors in housing were blurry in the postwar period. Leading developers, bankers, and real estate executives frequently traveled the road between private practice and government service.

Federal housing policy gave official sanction to discriminatory real estate sales and bank lending practices. The primary sources used by brokers and lenders to determine eligibility for mortgages and home loans were the Residential Security Maps and Surveys, developed by Federal Home Loan Bank Board officials in collaboration with local real estate brokers and lenders. The maps carefully subdivided the entire Detroit metropolitan area into sections ranked from A (green) through D (red), based on a survey of the age of buildings, their condition, and the amenities and infrastructure in the neighborhood. Most important in determining a neighborhood's classification was the level of racial, ethnic, and economic homogeneity, the absence or presence of "a lower grade population." Residents of areas rated "C" and "D" were unlikely to qualify for mortgages and home loans. Builders and developers, likewise, could expect little or no financial backing if they chose to build in such risky neighborhoods. The appraisal practices of the Home Owners' Loan Corporation thus perpetuated a vicious cycle of neighborhood decline.[34]

Every Detroit neighborhood with even a tiny African American population was rated "D," or "hazardous" by federal appraisers, and colored red on the HOLC Security Maps. Areas where there was "shifting" or "infiltration" of "an undesirable population" likewise warranted "D" ratings. The FHA perpetuated private industry's opposition to funding black residential development in or near white neighborhoods. The FHA regularly refused loans to black homebuilders while underwriting the construction of homes by whites of a similar economic status a few blocks away. Race relations official John Feild captured the tragedy of federal home ownership programs in his statement that "most discrimination was a consequence of public policy." Federal housing policy legitimated systematic discrimination against African Americans in housing.[35]

HOLC appraisers awarded higher ratings to white neighborhoods whose properties were covered by restrictive covenants. An innovation of the early twentieth century, covenants were clauses incorporated into deeds which had as their intention the maintenance of "desirable residential characteristics" of a neighborhood. They sought to preserve both architectural and social homogeneity. Restrictive covenants included prohibitions against commercial activity, the division of buildings into rental units, the placement of signs on property, the construction of multiple-residence homes in predominantly single-family areas, and the purchase and occupancy of homes by racial and ethnic minorities.[36]

Covenants barring purchase or occupancy by certain racial, religious, or ethnic groups were the most conspicuous type of restriction. In a survey of deeds for ten thousand subdivisions in Detroit, sociologist Harold Black found that racial restrictions were ubiquitous by the 1940s. More than 80 percent of property in Detroit outside of the inner city (bounded by Grand Boulevard) fell under the scope of racial restrictions. Whereas no land developed before 1910 was restricted, deeds in every subdivision developed between 1940 and 1947 specified the exclusion of blacks. A typical racial covenant stipulated that property along Seebaldt Avenue between Firwood and Beechwood Avenues on Detroit's near Northwest Side "shall not be used or occupied by any person or persons except those of the Caucasian race."[37]

To enforce restrictive covenants, real estate brokers and developers encouraged the formation of neighborhood improvement associations. In 1940, Phillip Kale, president of the Eastern Detroit Realty Association, offered an address to fellow realtors on the "Benefits of an Improvement Association to a Community." Kale suggested the use of restrictive covenants to preserve the homogeneity of a neighborhood, and encouraged the organization of areas "by streets, or subdivisions, or square miles." Realtors should carefully choose a "community most likely to have trouble, or better yet, one in which a Negro family is already resident. The people of that section will be in a most receptive mood." Many real estate agents and builders also founded neighborhood associations or played an active role in already existing groups. The Northwest Detroit Realty Association and the Northwest Civic Association, to take one example, worked together to create and enforce restrictive covenants in one section of the city. Miller Homes, a major developer of FHA-subsidized housing, proudly announced the construction of a "highly restricted and carefully controlled community" of affordable homes, "where as a member of an association of residents you can pass judgment upon who shall be your neighbor and the type and value of the home he builds."[38]

Above all, the success of racial covenants depended on neighborhood cohesiveness. In neighborhoods on the margins of the expanding black ghetto, white residents frequently disregarded covenants when "racial transition" seemed inevitable. Neighbors had to be willing to go through the costly procedure of suing property owners suspected of breaching covenants. And as civil rights groups, particularly the NAACP, began to challenge restrictive covenants, court battles went on for years. By the early 1940s, the outcome in courts was by no means certain. During the wartime emergency, judges sometimes allowed for temporary exceptions to covenants forbidding multiple-family occupancy.[39] And local judges began to overturn racial restrictions—albeit sporadically, and usually on narrow grounds—in the years preceding the Supreme Court's *Shelley v. Kraemer* decision (1948) which found the enforcement of race-specific covenants illegal. Even if they could not be enforced in a court of law, however, deed restrictions remained an effective signal to builders, real estate agents, and developers. When the land in a subdivision was restricted to "Caucasians only," contractors found it impossible to get financial backing to construct homes for nonwhites. Covenants also retained moral force. Real estate agents who refused to honor deed restrictions risked the wrath of white homeowners and jeopardized their businesses.[40]

Racial restrictions were a blunt tool for maintaining the exclusivity of neighborhoods. Other types of covenants were more effective, and immune to court challenges. Restrictions that determined architectural standards, regulated lot size, and prohibited multiple-family occupancy subtly preserved social homogeneity. Covenants that banned the taking of boarders or the division of homes into apartments effectively kept away the majority of blacks who could not afford to rent or buy a whole house, or who needed to supplement family income by renting out rooms. Lot size and architectural restrictions preserved large sections of the metropolitan area for wealthy landowners. In effect, middle-class and wealthy homeowners could stem much racial change without the legal cost or stigma of racial restrictions.

More effective than restrictive covenants in maintaining Detroit's racial boundaries were the practices of the real estate industry. Whether a neighborhood was covered by a restrictive covenant or not, if it was all white, realtors kept it that way. HOLC appraisals of Detroit neighborhoods became self-fulfilling prophecies in the hands of real estate brokers. A web of interlocking real estate interests—brokers, speculators, developers, and banks—built on the base of racial animosity to perpetuate racial divisions in the housing market. Even after racially restrictive covenants were ruled unenforceable in 1948, the Detroit Mayor's Interracial Committee reported that "credit controls and the restrictive practices of the real estate brotherhood are holding the line in all areas where restrictive covenants previously existed."[41]

The Detroit Real Estate Board (DREB) followed the Code of Ethics of the National Association of Real Estate Boards, and pledged that real estate agents would "never be instrumental in introducing into a neighborhood a character of property or occupancy, members of any race or nationality, or any industry whose presence will be clearly detrimental to real estate values." A realtor who violated the guidelines faced penalties or expulsion from the Real Estate Board, and was denied access to the board's cross-listing service. Gerald Lawson, president of the Detroit Real Estate Board, warned members of the Eastern Detroit Realty Association "not to sell to Negroes in a 100 percent white area." An agent who violated the admonition "is not given access to circulating listings and is shunned by other real estate companies who comprise the membership of the Detroit Real Estate Board." Brokers were especially sensitive to the impact of accusations of "blockbusting" on their business. Offended white customers often harassed and boycotted real estate companies that breached racial barriers.[42]

Lending institutions were also unwilling to challenge residential segregation. Sometimes they justified their policy in actuarial terms: they were risk-averse and did not want to make loans in poor neighborhoods where they expected a high default rate. But white-owned banks were also largely unwilling to make safe loans in areas that attracted well-to-do blacks. And they systematically refused to lend to blacks who were among the first to move to all-white neighborhoods or to developers building new homes for blacks near white neighborhoods. As an Urban League study found, investors believed "that to make such mortgages . . . would incur the hostility and wrath of their white depositors" and "court the great disfavor of other investors, realtors, and builders." Because of bankers' racial conservatism, blacks found it almost impossible to get conventional home financing. There were African American–run savings and loan associations that financed black homebuyers, but because they were undercapitalized, they made little impact. Blacks looking for their own homes were left to turn to loan sharks or to buy homes using land contracts at high interest rates.[43]

Urban Redevelopment

Postwar highway and urban redevelopment projects further exacerbated Detroit's housing crisis, especially for blacks. Detroit's city planners promised that the proposed system of cross-city expressways would dramatically improve the city's residential areas, as well as bolster the city's economy. For the thousands of blacks who lived in the path of Detroit's first expressways, both promises were false. Detroit's highway planners were careful to ensure that construction of the new high-speed expressways would only minimally disrupt middle-class residential areas, but they had little such concern for black neighborhoods, especially those closest to downtown. Instead, they viewed inner-city highway construction, in Detroit as in other major American cities, North and South, as "a handy device for razing slums."[44]

Beginning in the late 1940s, the most densely populated sections of black Detroit were devastated by highway construction. The Oakland-Hastings (later Chrysler) Freeway blasted through the black Lower East Side, Paradise Valley, and the Hastings Street business district, wiping out many of the city's most prominent African American institutions, from jazz clubs to the Saint Antoine branch of the YMCA. The John C. Lodge Freeway cut through the Lower West Side, the increasingly black area bordering Twelfth Street, and the heavily black neighborhoods bordering Highland Park. The Edsel Ford Freeway, an extension of "Bomber Road" which connected Detroit to the Willow Run defense complex west of the city, bisected the black West Side, and cut through the northernmost fringe of Paradise Valley.[45]

Left behind was what one black businessman called a "no man's land" of deterioration and abandonment. The announcement of highway projects came years before actual construction. Homeowners and shopkeepers were trapped, unable to sell property that would soon be condemned, unable to move without the money from a property sale. Building owners had no incentive to invest in improvements. An enormous number of buildings were condemned and leveled to make way for the new expressways. By 1950, 423 residences, 109 businesses, 22 manufacturing plants, and 93 vacant lots had been condemned for the first three-mile stretch of the Lodge Freeway from Jefferson to Pallister; by 1958, the Lodge Freeway from its terminus in downtown Detroit to Wyoming Avenue (about 7 miles) displaced 2,222 buildings. Similar destruction cleared the path for the Edsel Ford Expressway: in the 1950s about 2,800 buildings were removed for its construction. Homeowners did not suffer the effects of highway construction to the same extent as renters; of the 900 structures cleared in a largely white area between Wyoming and Warren Avenues, about 700 were moved intact to other sites. Renters, in contrast, suffered disproportionately, and the leveled black areas had few homeowners and few buildings that could be physically relocated elsewhere.[46]

Black residents of the expressway construction areas often pointed to the folly of highway plans, but few government officials took their complaints seriously. They had little political power in a majority white city. Poor residents of center-city neighborhoods, mainly renters, had to fend for themselves when relocated by highway construction because the state highway commission had no legal obligation to assist households that had been forced to move because of highway clearance.[47] Blacks who lived along proposed freeway routes worried about the difficulty of finding rental housing in other parts of the city. Harvey Royal, who lived along the route of the future Edsel Ford Freeway, wrote, "I think it would have been so much nicer to have built places for people to live in than a highway & just put people in the street."[48] Maud W. Cain, a widow who lived in a one-room apartment behind a storefront on Hastings Street, expressed her desperation about finding an affordable apartment when she was relocated for highway construction. "I do not have money to rent a $75.00 house [with] no heat."[49] Mayor Albert Cobo, the city's most ardent supporter of the new expressway system (and a Republican who was elected with virtually no black support), discounted the hardship wrought by construction: "Sure there have been some inconveniences in building our expressways and in our slum clearance programs, but in the long run more people benefit. That's the price of progress."[50] The problem of expressway displacement persisted through the 1950s. Public officials did little to assist families forced to move and, like Cobo, downplayed the high human costs of highway projects. In 1958, the Wayne County road commissioner predicted "that little difficulty will be experienced by families facing displacement because of highway construction," even though the families on highway sites received only a thirty-day notice to vacate and the commission made no efforts to assist families in relocation.[51]

Compounding the housing woes of inner-city blacks was the city's extensive urban renewal program. The centerpiece of Detroit's postwar master plan was the clearance of "blighted areas" in the inner city for the construction of middle-class housing that it was believed would revitalize the urban economy. Like most postwar cities, Detroit had high hopes for slum removal. City officials expected that the eradication of "blight" would increase

2.3. The clearance of land for urban renewal displaced tens of thousands of Detroit blacks, putting great pressure on the city's already saturated housing market. Shown here is the area around Gratiot and Orleans Streets in the heart of Detroit's Black Bottom. The most densely populated section of the city in the 1940s, it was a target of "slum clearance." City officials began condemning properties and evicting residents here in 1950 to make way for a proposed middle-income apartment complex.

city tax revenue, revitalize the decaying urban core, and improve the living conditions of the poorest slum dwellers. Overcrowded, unsanitary, and dilapidated districts like Paradise Valley and the Lower East Side would be replaced by clean, modern, high-rise housing projects, civic institutions, and hospitals.[52] Four of the city's most important redevelopment projects—the Gratiot Redevelopment Site, the Brewster and Douglass public housing projects, and the Medical Center Area—were premised on the destruction of some of the most densely populated black neighborhoods in the city. Plans to relocate blacks displaced by the projects utterly failed.

The Gratiot Redevelopment site on over one hundred acres of Detroit's Lower East Side was the centerpiece of the "Detroit Plan," a comprehensive proposal for a partnership between the city and private developers to clear the Lower East Side slum and rebuild the area as a private housing project. Proposed by Detroit Mayor Edward Jeffries and the Detroit City Plan Commission in 1946, it offered an alternative to public housing, thus appealing to conservative real estate and business interests in the city. With funding from the federal government under the 1949 Housing Act, and with the enthusiastic support of private developers allied with the Cobo adminis- tration, the city began the comprehensive renewal of the Gratiot area and evicted the first area residents in 1950.[53]

The other major thrust of redevelopment was the construction of high-rise public housing to replace cleared slums in the center city. Less than a mile north of the Gratiot site stood a tract of land condemned for the Douglass Homes, to be constructed between 1950 and 1954; a mile to the west stood the area to be cleared for the new, high-rise Jeffries Homes. Both sites, like Gratiot, stood in the center of densely populated, poor neighborhoods. Few disagreed with redevelopers that the nineteenth- and early twentieth-cen- tury tenements that lined the streets of the redevelopment sites comprised some of the city's worst housing stock. More than 90 percent of the buildings on the Gratiot site were occupied by renters who paid an average of $19 per month in 1946, by far the lowest rents in the city. Landlords compensated for low rents by subdividing buildings and packing families into small, cramped apartments. More than half of the buildings in the neighborhood had substandard facilities and no indoor plumbing, or were classified as fire and safety hazards. But redevelopment did not ameliorate the living condi- tions of the impoverished residents of sites slated for slum clearance.

The most obvious problem with slum clearance was that it forced the households with the least resources to move at a time when the city's tight housing market could not accommodate them. Hugo C. Schwartz, local di- rector of the Federal Public Housing Authority, noted the irony that "from the standpoint of income and race," residents of the redevelopment areas "are the families who will find it most difficult to find a place to live if they are pushed out of their present dwellings." The Detroit Council on Better Housing, a liberal housing reform group, argued that the leveling of down- town slums would worsen the city's housing shortage. "By not building a supply of low rent homes on vacant land sites . . . the city is ignoring the plight of thousands of Detroit families living in sub-standard housing, dou- bled or tripled up with relatives, or otherwise in need of a decent place to live." And city planner Astrid Monson noted the result of inner-city redevel- opment would be "to increase congestion in the already over-populated areas of the city." Their dire predictions came true.[54]

The city's redevelopment projects soon demonstrated the commonplace wisdom of the streets that "slum removal equals Negro removal." The city had no adequate relocation plans for residents uprooted by urban renewal. Common Council member Edward Connor was most critical of "the admin- istration's rosy picture" of relocation programs. City housing officials, in fact, expected most households to find new dwellings without any government assistance. In a letter to families about to be evicted from buildings on the Gratiot site, Detroit Housing Commission Secretary Harry Durbin offered aid in finding adequate housing, but advised them to "make every possible effort to find housing in the private market." At a 1951 Common Council hearing on relocation, Durbin was blunt: "We can't clear slums without hardship."[55]

Relocation did involve great hardship. Because of the housing shortage, many evicted families were "temporarily relocated in blocks adjacent to the one they have moved from," to buildings at least as dilapidated as those that they had left.[56] Families who moved off-site often found "the same over-crowding and sharing pattern that existed in the project area."[57] The Detroit Housing Commission could not find enough housing for renewal-area residents. City housing officials held out hope that private organizations would be able to offer additional assistance to slum removal families, but social service agencies were even more poorly equipped than the city to house evicted families. The Urban League's housing advocate, William Price, asked city officials, "If you who are skilled in finding vacancies can't find them—how can we?"[58] Ultimately, the relocation assistance offered by the Detroit Housing Commission was inadequate. The city's relocation office was understaffed and often unsympathetic to the plight of evicted families.[59] About one-third of the Gratiot area's families eventually moved to public housing, but 35 percent of the families in the area could not be traced. The best-informed city officials believed that a majority of families moved to neighborhoods within a mile of the Gratiot site, crowding into an already decaying part of the city, and finding housing scarcely better and often more overcrowded than that which they had left.[60]

Low-Rent Housing

Complicating the situation for families relocated from highway and urban renewal projects was a dearth of low-rent apartments and public housing in the city. Non–property owners, a large portion of those relocated from inner-city redevelopment areas, faced an impossibly difficult rental market. A 1951 report stated that "the amount of rental housing being built in Detroit has dropped to a trickle." White single-family neighborhoods staunchly resisted the construction of "multiple housing," and fought zoning changes that allowed for the construction of apartment buildings, even on marginal land that bordered commercial or industrial areas.[61]

Detroit had few apartment buildings compared to cities like New York and Chicago, and Detroit homeowners viewed "multiple housing" as an unwanted intrusion in their neighborhoods. Their opposition was rooted in fears that apartments would attract disorderly lower-class residents to their neighborhoods. Apartments, contended the *Brightmoor Journal*, would "open the way for 'ill fame' houses," including "professional rooming houses and professional boarding houses." Residents of outlying single-family residential areas also feared that "multiple homes in single residence areas threaten . . . additional blight." White homeowners intertwined racial prejudices with their class-based opposition to multiple housing. Apartment complexes would become "tenements" that would attract low-income residents, especially blacks. Lamented one housing reform group, "people seem to have the idea that multiple rental housing brings in minority groups."[62]

Detroit's Northwest Side, one section of the city that had a considerable amount of vacant land in the 1940s, became the site of dozens of local battles over multiple-family residential zoning. In 1947, residents of the Southfield Woods and College Woods–Southfield Court subdivisions in far northwest Detroit joined with the Miller Construction Company, a large single-family subdivision developer, to file a lawsuit against the developers of an apartment complex in the area. The Evergreen Village Civic Association, another group of Northwest Side homeowners, lobbied against a zoning variance that would have allowed the construction of a five-hundred-unit apartment complex on Evergreen Road. In 1949 and 1950, when Detroit's housing shortage was at its worst, the City Plan Commission bowed to the demands of community groups and rejected several multiple-dwelling sites in northwest Detroit.[63]

With a virtual freeze on the construction of low-rent housing in the city, Detroit's poor fought over the scraps that remained. New migrants to the city, rapidly growing postwar families, returning veterans, and people displaced by urban redevelopment and highway projects all competed for the same scarce private housing. Finding affordable housing in the 1940s and early 1950s was nearly impossible. In a typical September week in 1950, the Office of the Housing Expediter of the Housing and Home Finance Agency found only thirty-seven rental units available in the entire city. Eighteen were too expensive for "the average industrial worker," twenty-five did not allow children, and ten "were one or two room units unsuitable for family occupancy."[64] A 1950 survey found that a quarter of the city's residents ranked housing as "the most urgent single problem" in Detroit, and over half of the respondents placed housing on their list of the top three problems of the city. "Negroes and people in the low socio-economic stratum" gave "particularly bad ratings" to Detroit's housing situation. Seventy-two percent of Detroit blacks rated the "handling of housing needs" in the city as "not good" or "definitely bad."[65]

Even when the housing market slowly opened up in the mid-1950s, lower-income families had few grounds for optimism in the housing search. A survey of ads for rental housing in the Sunday, January 31, 1954 edition of the *Detroit News* found that of 816 listings, only forty-seven were "suitable

for family occupancy," and available for under $100 per month. Only three
of the forty-seven rented for under $70. Eleven of the forty-seven ads speci-
fied white only, and 40 percent of the ads specified adults only. The apartments advertised were by no means luxurious. Almost half were in the
center-city area, which had the oldest and most rundown housing stock.[66]

Migrants and relocated families scrambled to find a place to live. One
woman reported standing in line with sixty people for an hour and a half for
an interview with a landlord for a single rental unit. "Besides the porch and
sidewalk being packed, there was a constant flow of cars," she stated. They
"came, paused, and drove on, realizing how little chance they stood of renting."[67] Many newcomers attracted to the city's booming industry left after a
vain search for adequate housing: in a fluid job market white workers were
especially prone to pick up and move if they could not find adequate housing. Three employees a day resigned from their jobs at Great Lakes Steel
because of lack of housing for their families. Other companies also lost workers who could not cope with the housing shortage. E. A. Cheetham, a Fisher
Body supervisor, reported that two hundred workers quit their jobs and
returned to out-of-state homes between April and October 1950 "because of
their inability to find housing."[68]

In the tight postwar housing market, landlords took advantage of their
power to screen out any tenants who might be risky. Blacks, especially those
with large families, suffered the greatest hardships. Landlords regularly
turned away prospective tenants with children, and the birth of a child was
often cause for an eviction.[69] In the early 1950s, the *Detroit Free Press* reported that ten thousand families were homeless each year, because "When
places to rent are hard to find, prices go up, and landlords get extra fussy
about children."[70] One of dozens of poorly housed blacks who wrote of her
plight to Michigan Governor G. Mennen Williams, Essie Mae Jordan lived
with her seven children in one room, and was consistently turned away by
landlords who did not allow families. Another correspondent, Mary Felder,
also recounted her difficulty in finding rental housing: "They don't want
children, even though children will have to have living facilities to survive."
She continued: "I am tired of the struggle to survive. I wonder if life is worth
the struggle negroes have made."[71]

High demand for scarce housing inflated the values of some of the city's
most decrepit and overcrowded buildings. In 1949, property in the largely
black section ringed by Grand Boulevard cost between $35,000 and $60,000
an acre, in part because of "the speculative value of the land" close to downtown, and in part because "with the housing shortage, these properties are
extremely valuable as money-makers and have a high market value."[72] Even
if their buildings were run down, scarcity permitted landlords regularly to
overcharge housing-starved Detroiters. "Bootleg landlords" illegally divided
single-family homes into apartments, and charged high rents. "Out around

Chrysler," recalled a black wartime worker, "they used to rent the houses by shift, rent the rooms by shift." By breaking up buildings into several small "housekeeping rooms," landlords met the rising demand for space, evaded rent control laws, and doubled or tripled their rental income. Others converted formerly all-white apartment buildings into housing for blacks, often dividing rooms, cutting services, and increasing rents.[73]

The economic boom of the 1940s and early 1950s lost its luster for families who were forced to spend a large portion of their income on inadequate housing. It was not unusual for blacks to pay 20 to 40 percent more for rent than whites in equivalent apartments. One inner-city landlord increased rents during the war from $25 per month to $15 to $18 per week in an apartment building "converted" from white to black occupancy.[74] As long as the rental housing shortage for blacks persisted, black apartment dwellers suffered from rent gouging. When a landlord on West Hancock Street decided to open a formerly all-white building to black occupancy in 1957, he raised the rent 30 percent, and cut back on building maintenance. Residents of a Rochester Street building a few years later reported that the landlord charged blacks one-third higher rent than whites.[75] Landlords often demanded weekly or biweekly rent payments, summarily evicted tenants who could not meet high rents, and quickly found other housing-starved tenants to take over at the same price. As late as 1960, the median monthly rent for blacks in Detroit was $76 per month, but only $64 for whites. Over 40 percent of black-occupied dwellings cost renters more than 35 percent of their income.[76]

The desperate housing situation in the inner city provided great opportunities for unscrupulous landlords. William Burton, the owner of dozens of rundown inner-city apartments and houses, charged unusually high rents. Families in his buildings often took in boarders to make ends meet, often with his encouragement. After four people were killed in a fire in one of Burton's buildings, city officials fined him for overcrowding and rat infestation (he had rented one three-bedroom apartment to twelve people). Burton was undeterred by city regulators. He continued to pack desperate renters into his buildings and mercilessly threw out tenants who were the least bit late with payments. Between January and August 1953, Burton evicted sixty-four families from his buildings. One family in a Burton-owned "ugly, weatherbeaten frame building" could not meet the $100 per month rent he charged (average rents in Detroit were less than $50 per month); another family in a "depressed area" of the city was driven out because of inability to pay Burton the $75 due for three weeks' rent.[77]

Landlords who charged high rents often had little stake in their buildings: to maximize profit they minimized repairs. Likewise, tenants who could barely afford to make rent payments had few resources to maintain their apartments in decent condition. The high turnover of tenants meant that few had any long-term commitment to the quality of life in their buildings. The result was detrimental to all concerned. Members of a group representing apartment dwellers in a West Side neighborhood described the self-perpetuating cycle of ghettoization: "When apartment buildings are poorly maintained, the whole neighborhood is downgraded. When rents are exorbitant, people cannot long afford to pay; this leads to a constantly changing community rather than to stable neighborhood relations."[78]

Detroit's housing shortage and its racial boundaries held firm for most of the 1940s. The result was the confinement of blacks to densely packed, run-down, and overpriced housing in the same neighborhoods that had entrapped blacks since the Great Migration. The decrepit housing stock that had already held several generations of poor Detroiters burst with new residents in the 1940s. Living conditions in the center city, never good, deteriorated rapidly. Civil rights and welfare advocates lamented the disruptions wrought by ghettoization. The housing shortage, wrote NAACP officials, led to "serious congestion and overcrowding" and "ill health, delinquency, unrest, distrust, and disunity within the community."[79]

Black Detroiters' dire living conditions in the 1940s were not inevitable, and the patterns of racial segregation in housing established by the World War II era were not immutable. Observers in the early 1940s were hopeful that Detroit's pattern of housing segregation would be disrupted by the wartime migration and by the rise of racial liberalism in the 1940s. Even after Detroit's violent riot of 1943, many held out hope for peaceful integration in the city. Optimists made reference to the fact that the race riot did not affect neighborhoods where blacks and whites lived together. And as some blacks began to move into formerly all-white neighborhoods in the late 1940s, many sociologists and social workers pointed to statistics that showed a growing number of mixed-race areas as evidence of trends toward integration. The 1940s and 1950s seemed to many a moment of hope, a time of opportunity to reverse the trends toward racial segregation and discrimination of the previous quarter-century. The result was that housing became a major arena for organized political activity in the 1940s, where Detroiters, black and white, fought a battle that would define Detroit politics for decades to follow.

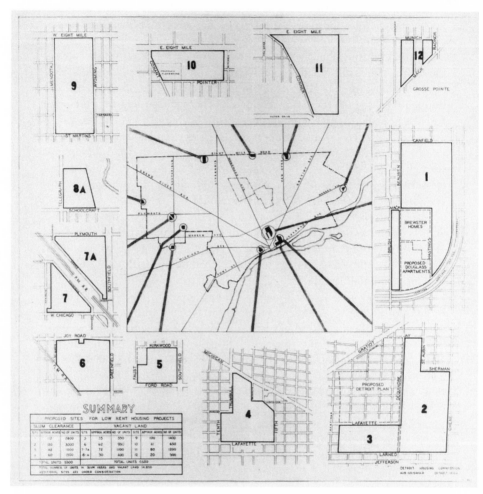

3.1. Of twelve proposed public housing sites in Detroit in the 1940s, only three were built. The outlying sites met with stiff opposition from neighborhood groups and were tabled by Mayor Albert Cobo and the Detroit Common Council in 1950.

3

"The Coffin of Peace": The Containment of Public Housing

> We have won the war and are striving to win a com-
> plete peace. Each time Negroes are discriminated
> against, veterans or otherwise, a nail is driven into
> the coffin of peace.
> —Charles Johnson, an African American veteran
> (1945)

> Our boys are fighting in Europe, Asia, and Africa to
> keep those people off our soil. If when these boys
> return they should become refugees who have to
> give up their homes because their own neighbor-
> hood with the help of our city fathers had been in-
> vade[d] and occupied by the Africans, it would be a
> shame which our city fathers could not outlive.
> —Michael J. Harbulak, a white resident of the
> Oakwood section (1945)

IN SEPTEMBER 1945, veteran Charles Johnson returned to Detroit from service in the Pacific, hoping to make a life for himself and his family in the
booming city. Johnson arrived at a particularly difficult time, especially for
African Americans like himself. Tens of thousands of returning veterans put
pressure on a housing market that could not even absorb the thousands of
defense workers who had migrated to the city during the war. The small
apartment buildings and houses in Detroit's black neighborhoods were
bursting with tenants. Johnson found a temporary apartment on the West
Side. He hoped that, like other veterans, he would be able to move into
public housing. He spoke to another veteran, a white, who "had been given
a list of several places to investigate." Even if it was just one of the hundreds
of Quonset huts that housed homeless veterans and their families, it would
be better than a dreary, overcrowded, vermin-infested inner-city apartment.
On September 21, 1945, Johnson applied for public housing.[1]

Johnson's hopes were quickly dashed. A Detroit Housing Commission
staff member informed him that "the Negro housing situation is extremely
acute," and "we have many more applications than dwelling units." He was

put on a waiting list. But "while waiting for his interview," Johnson heard
white veterans "receive assurances that they would be placed in housing
developments in the very near future." He heard correctly. During World
War II, blacks flooded the city with applications for public housing, but only
1,731 of 14,446 black applicants were placed.[2]

Johnson was infuriated. He told the Housing Commission interviewer
that "he had not fought for this country to uphold racial discrimination."
When she tried to explain the commission's policy to him, he "was extremely
angered and hardly appeared to be listening." Johnson left the office determined to get an answer. He moved up the chain of command, "determined
to make an issue of the matter." He headed straight for the office of the
director of the Detroit Housing Commission, then to the mayor's office, and
finally ended up meeting for an hour with George Schermer, the director of
the Mayor's Interracial Committee. Schermer reported that "Johnson displayed very strong feeling." The veteran boldly stated he "would refuse to
accept placement in a segregated Negro project" and "would insist on
his right to be placed in any housing development of his own choosing."
Schermer was sympathetic to Johnson and suggested that he testify to the
Common Council about his situation. Johnson left frustrated, "thoroughly
convinced that the Mayor, the Common Council, the Housing Commission
and the Interracial Committee are unanimously committed to an anti-Negro
policy." He followed up with a letter to the Detroit Common Council. "We
have won the war," he wrote, "and are striving to win a complete peace.
Each time Negroes are discriminated against, veterans or otherwise, a nail
is driven into the coffin of peace."[3]

Johnson's fate is unknown. But the situation for blacks like him improved
little in the postwar decade. From January 1947 through July 1952, 37,382
black families and 56,758 white families applied for public housing. 41
percent of white applicants and only 24 percent of black applicants made it
onto the waiting list. Whites also moved off the waiting list more quickly
than their black counterparts. The result was a striking discrepancy in the
fortunes of black and white applicants: 9,908 whites, but only 1,226 blacks
obtained public housing in the city. Because of the city's discriminatory
policy, most black demand for public housing went unmet through the
mid-1950s. Blacks remained confined to a few inner-city projects, and despite tremendous efforts to alleviate the housing shortage by constructing
subsidized low-income developments on the city's periphery, virtually nothing was built.[4]

Johnson's frustrations highlighted a fundamental dilemma in postwar
public policy. A nation committed (at least rhetorically) to assist its neediest
citizens found it difficult to translate rhetoric into reality. Underlying federal
social policy in the New Deal era were two competing ideals: one calling for
the provision of assistance to the disadvantaged, the other supporting an

expansion of opportunities for those who already had significant resources. The New Deal created a newly empowered citizenry, one that looked to the government to provide economic and social security. World War II further contributed to ordinary Americans' new sense of citizenship. Like Charles Johnson, they drew a direct connection between their service to their country and the rights and entitlements that would be their reward.

The new rights-based liberalism that emerged from the crucible of the Great Depression and World War II shaped responses to government initiatives in general, but the tension between the two ideals was clearest in the case of housing policy. In cities like Detroit, social reformers and federal officials fought to erect public housing sufficient to meet the needs of those whom the market failed to serve. But public housing advocates were repeatedly stymied by homeowners who asserted their own interpretation of New Deal social policy. They demanded that the government privilage the stability of their homeownership, over and above its support for public housing.

The fate of most New Deal social programs was decided in cities like Detroit, where local governments bore the responsibility of implementing federal policy. In Detroit, battles over public housing were shaped by the actions of new community organizations, both black and white, which emerged to represent the interests of the various constituents of the New Deal state. The local political activism of the 1940s turned on domestic issues, like family, housing, and homeownership. Whatever their differences, newly empowered blacks and whites in Detroit attempted to define and challenge—really to appropriate on their own terms—the New Deal state. In the case of homeownership, their activism—drawing from the Democratic party's promise of entitlement—was often conservative and individualistic, even when it involved collective action. The debates over housing in the 1940s were to have profound ramifications for the fate of federal policy in the city for the next twenty years and would set the terms for debate on—and limit—the next generation of social policy, the Great Society.[5]

A New Deal in Housing

From the 1930s through the early 1950s, the federal government, city officials, and housing reformers looked to an alternative to Detroit's private market to solve the city's housing crisis. In place of inferior accommodation for the poor, government-subsidized developments would be built throughout the city. The construction of public housing, argued its advocates, would eliminate the city's overcrowded, dangerous slums. Not only would public housing offer workers and the poor clean, new, affordable shelter, it would serve as a tool of social engineering. Public housing, in the words of urban historian Robert Fairbanks, would "make better citizens." Some of the most optimistic reformers of the 1930s and 1940s hoped that the construction of public housing would also overcome the hostility that arose as blacks and whites competed for scarce private-sector housing.[6]

New Deal liberalism set the context for debates in Detroit that persisted through the 1950s. In 1937, Congress held President Franklin D. Roosevelt to a pledge made in his second inaugural address to mitigate the hardships of the "one-third of a nation ill-housed" by passing the Wagner-Steagall Housing Act, which provided for the construction of public housing under the auspices of the United States Housing Authority.[7] In 1949, Congress and the Truman administration reaffirmed the New Deal's goal of providing for the housing needs of America's poor in the Taft-Ellender-Wagner Act, which provided millions of dollars for the construction of new public housing throughout the country.[8] New Deal and Fair Deal legislation allocated over a billion dollars to provide shelter for the poorest Americans.

The New Deal commitment to the construction of public housing coexisted uneasily with a second promise: government subsidies for the purchase of private homes and loans for new single-family home construction. In 1933, when Roosevelt proposed legislation to create the Home Owners' Loan Corporation (HOLC), he declared the government's commitment to protect homeownership from foreclosure. The HOLC would subsidize home purchases and improvements with low-interest loans.[9] The Federal Housing Administration (FHA), founded in 1934, with its policy of guaranteeing long-term residential mortgages, became the most prominent government agency to embody FDR's notion of an empowered, self-sufficient, homeowning public. Roosevelt viewed the stability of private homeownership as central to the nation's security and self-preservation.[10] The extension of homeowners' benefits to returning veterans in the Servicemen's Readjustment Act of 1944 (the GI Bill of Rights) solidified the government's new responsibility to finance private housing for millions of Americans.

The policy goals of the Roosevelt and Truman administrations were reshaped in the crucible of state and local politics. The deference to localism built into most liberal social programs preserved a concentration of power in city and state governments, particularly concerning issues of housing, social welfare, and land use. As a result, in Detroit, as elsewhere, local elected officials controlled the implementation of federal policies.[11] On the matter of public housing, officials of the United States Housing Authority (responsible for planning), the Federal Works Agency (responsible for construction), and the National Housing Agency (which took over planning and construction activities in 1942) worked closely with local officials, but local governments had the final say over the expenditure of federal funds, the location of projects, and the type constructed. In Detroit, the city's Housing Commission drafted plans for the implementation of federal policy. The City Plan

Commission, headed by Harvard graduate and planner George Emery, administered city zoning regulations and approved zoning changes necessary for the construction of public housing. The Detroit Housing Commission (DHC) and City Plan Commission directors served at the pleasure of the Mayor.[12] And all of their decisions regarding the selection of sites had to meet the approval of the nine-member Detroit Common Council, elected at large in citywide elections. FHA and HOLC funds, in contrast, were unencumbered by local politics. Both were administered by federal officials, assigned to regional, state, and local offices, and responsible to their Washington headquarters.

City officials were especially sensitive to the demands of the local electorate. Crucial to the outcome of New Deal housing policy was the reaction of local organizations, of the New Deal's grassroots constituents.[13] The fate of public housing in Detroit was shaped by a contest between liberal pro-housing advocates and homeowners, both of whom lobbied and attempted to influence local and federal officials. Both groups battled for what they considered to be the heart of New Deal housing policy, struggling to attain one or the other New Deal goal: public housing or private homeownership.

City planners, labor organizations, and many inner-city residents, especially blacks, coalesced around the New Deal's public housing agenda. They viewed the provision of decent low-income housing as a fundamental responsibility of the government. The problem of housing the poor, in their view, was too intransigent to be left to the market. On the other side were real estate brokers, housing developers, and above all, homeowners—both black and white—all of whom hoped to benefit from New Deal subsidies for private housing. These competing interest groups attempted to direct federal policy to their own ends, and, working within the confines of localism, shaped the implementation of federal programs in ways that no legislators or policymakers could have anticipated.[14]

The single most important pro–public housing organization in Detroit was the Citizens' Housing and Planning Council (CHPC), one of dozens of similar organizations formed in cities all over the United States in the New Deal era. Founded in 1937 by a group of social workers, business leaders, planners, and architects, the CHPC shared with many early twentieth-century reform organizations a commitment to the reconstruction of urban slums. It saw itself as a sort of brain trust of professionals who could "bridge the real gap between the bewildered layman and the technical, official city planner."[15] The CHPC had as its primary mission the improvement of the environmental conditions of Detroit's slums through the elimination of crowded, dirty, and substandard housing, and the construction of sanitary, well-lit, and well-ventilated public housing in its place. The CHPC explained its goals for housing and neighborhood development in terms familiar to early twentieth-century reformers. Improved housing would have ameliorative effects on living conditions and would modify the behavior and character of urban residents. A clean, hygienic environment, the CHPC argued, would dramatically improve public health, especially of infants and children. Public housing would also uplift the "morale" of urban dwellers, and increase the likelihood of their gainful employment, political participation, and self-help.[16] CHPC literature put forth its message of social and individual improvement through orderly planning and urban redevelopment with a near religious fervor that combined altruism with paternalism. According to the council's statement of purpose, "we are the VOICE OF THE INARTICULATE. If we do not speak, the THOUSANDS IN OUR DETROIT SLUMS will not be heard."[17]

On the other side of the divide on the public housing issue were working-class and middle-class homeowners. The political language of New Deal reforms, and the creation of public programs that offered employment, social security, and individual housing subsidies raised the expectations of American workers in the 1930s and 1940s. Their newfound sense of entitlement led them to expect the government to provide, at least in part, for their security as workers, retirees, and homeowners. President Roosevelt frequently alluded to the ideal of a nation of free homeowners in his speeches, and included the right to a decent home in his 1944 "Second Bill of Rights." Workers responded with tremendous loyalty. Ninety percent of blue-collar Detroiters surveyed in 1957 and 1958 considered FDR America's greatest President because, as one put it: "He was the best for the working man. He brought in social security, ended Prohibition, and brought in FHA." Another recalled: "He put people up. In my neighborhood a $15,000 house can be bought for $800 down because of Roosevelt. Nobody else like him, nor will there ever be."[18]

The working-class and middle-class Americans who benefited from HOLC, FHA, and VA housing policies took the New Deal's promise of stable homeownership very seriously. New Deal rhetoric touched a deep nerve among Detroiters who had struggled, usually without the benefit of loans or mortgages, to build their own homes in the city. It reinforced the deeply rooted values of homeownership and family stability held by striving immigrants in the early twentieth century (especially Italians and Poles), and appealed to the seldom-met aspirations for landownership and independence held by blacks since emancipation.[19] With government-backed mortgages and loans, they were able to attain the dream of property ownership with relative ease.

Homeowners welcomed government assistance; in fact by World War II, they began to view homeownership as a perquisite of citizenship. Subsidized loans and mortgage guarantees, promised by New Deal legislation, became a fundamental right. The FHA and HOLC's insistence that mortgages and loans be restricted to racially homogeneous neighborhoods also resonated strongly with Detroit's white homeowners. They came to expect a vigilant government to protect their segregated neighborhoods. These constituents of the New Deal state reinterpreted the government's rhetoric of homeownership to their own ends.[20] As working-class Detroiters exercised their newfound sense of political empowerment, they played a crucial role in the implementation of federal housing policy in the city. The success of Detroit property owners in availing themselves of government assistance for private homeownership ensured that Detroit would construct little public housing, and that the projects that were built would be racially segregated.[21]

Public housing in Detroit met with staunch opposition from community groups, real estate interests, developers, and elected officials. Neighborhood groups were most adamant in their opposition to public housing, and elected officials were generally sensitive to the enormous anti–public housing backlash. Business groups chafed at the threat that federally funded housing developments posed to the sanctity of private enterprise. They viewed the availability of affordable public housing as an unwarranted interference in the workings of the real estate market. Above all, homeowners and business leaders alike came to see New Deal public housing projects as a taxpayer-subsidized handout for the feckless.

Support for public housing in Detroit was confined to liberal activists, whereas in cities like New York and Chicago business groups, contractors, and construction workers played a major role in backing public housing proposals.[22] Lacking a well-oiled urban machine, the Detroit city government felt little pressure to reward political supporters with lucrative public housing contracts. Detroit's large construction firms and building trades unions were busy enough with private construction after the war to remain relatively uninterested in contracts and jobs offered by public housing development.[23] The relative indifference of developers and unions dampened support for public housing, but opposition from the grass roots, especially homeowners, played the most important role in constraining Detroit's housing reform agenda.

Black Homeownership and the FHA: The Eight Mile–Wyoming Area

The battle between two visions of New Deal housing policy occurred in Detroit's unassuming working-class neighborhoods, both black and white. In the late 1930s and 1940s, the modest black settlement in the Eight Mile–Wyoming area became a battleground for one of the city's fiercest debates over government housing policy. The Eight Mile–Wyoming area was a black island in a section of the city that was nearly all white—one, moreover, that was ripe for development. Over 72 percent of the property in the half-square mile black community was vacant. Many plots were owned by African Americans who held them in hopes of eventually building their own homes. Many more were possessed by banks or real estate firms because impoverished residents had defaulted on high-interest land contracts. And a large number of lots had reverted to the city or state government in lieu of unpaid back taxes.[24] The United States Housing Authority eyed the Eight Mile area as a site for slum clearance and the construction of public housing. The FHA viewed the neighborhood as an obstacle to subsidies and insurance for the construction of single-family residential areas in northwest Detroit. The city of Detroit hoped to clear and redevelop the "blighted area" as a means of increasing its tax base. Liberal reform groups, city planners, and members of the community reacted differently to the potential of government intervention in the neighborhood.

Although the site of the Eight Mile community was marginal in 1920, by the early 1940s it lay squarely in the path of new housing and commercial development. West of the Eight Mile neighborhood lay scattered houses among a landscape of truck farms and woodlands, an area slated for new construction as the city expanded outward. A quarter-mile south of the three-by-fourteen-block black community was West Outer Drive, lined with newly built, spacious middle-class homes, separated from the Eight Mile neighborhood by a barrier of undeveloped land and a sand quarry. Less than a mile to the east, enormous two- and three-story homes, many with pools and tennis courts, graced the winding, picturesque streets of Palmer Woods and Sherwood Forest, two of Detroit's newest and most exclusive neighborhoods. The black enclave, an anomaly on Detroit's Northwest Side, appeared to many as an impediment to the continued development of middle-class neighborhoods on the city's periphery. The developer of a proposed all-white subdivision immediately to the west of the black neighborhood could not get FHA funding for home construction because of its proximity to a slum, considered a high-risk area by government appraisers. The developer worked out a compromise with the FHA, garnering loans and mortgage guarantees in exchange for the construction of a foot-thick, six-foot-high wall, running for a half-mile on the property line separating the black and white neighborhoods.[25]

Eight Mile residents viewed the wall as a setback, but most hoped to find a solution in the Roosevelt administration and its housing policy. As recipients of New Deal job assistance, Aid to Dependent Children, and Social Security (over half of the area's residents got some federal benefits in the 1930s), many came to expect government entitlements. Eight Mile–Wyoming residents used their clout as New Deal voters to lobby the Roosevelt administration to extend its housing benefits to their neighborhood. In the late 1930s and early 1940s, residents of the area persistently—and unsuc-

3.2. The foot-thick, six-foot-high cement wall shown here separated the African American community in the Eight Mile–Wyoming area from the adjoining white neighborhood. Known by area residents as the "wailing wall," the barrier was erected by a white developer to meet the actuarial standards of the Federal Home Loan Bank Board.

cessfully—tried to get HOLC and FHA assistance for home improvement and construction. One woman sent a letter to Roosevelt with the poignant but unanswerable inquiry: "Why, when ones credit is good, is he still denied F.H.A.? Why are banks allowed to be evaisive [*sic*] and filled with excuses while turning down application after application for help?" The Eight Mile residents were "desperate-DESPERATE," and "wept bitter tears at our failure to get FHA assistance."[26]

Because their individual efforts to get federal subsidies had failed, the Eight Mile settlers resorted to collective action. In the late 1930s, area residents founded two community groups, the Carver Progressive Association and the Eight Mile Road Civic Association, to agitate for the development of their area with single-family detached homes funded by the FHA, and to protest plans for the redevelopment of the neighborhood with private housing for whites or public housing. Burneice Avery, a thirty-five-year-old schoolteacher who had been among the first blacks to settle in the Eight Mile community, organized the Eight Mile Road Civic Association, and served as its most outspoken representative. Avery spoke eloquently of Eight Mile residents' desire to own their own homes.[27]

Avery felt that the "disreputable shacks owned by some black people who had the audacity to dream of building a home on these lots someday" were worthy of FHA guarantees. If the government were to fulfill its promise to encourage single-family homeownership, why should black landowners be disqualified? Another community spokesperson stated "we want to be allowed to develop our property—to build homes with government insured financing." The black residents of the area found the federal housing policy especially unfair, given that in Detroit's factories, they were "working side by side with homeowners who are paying off their mortgage through F.H.A." To Avery, the government's plans to relocate the landowners of the Eight Mile area to make way for public housing was analogous to the arbitrary evictions of sharecroppers in the South. "Now in Detroit, even though we own the land," she wrote, "we are being told to 'Get Off' because we are not able to develope [*sic*] it in the way some people think it should be developed."[28]

In the early 1940s, the strenuous efforts of the Eight Mile Civic Association and local developers gained the attention of Raymond Foley, the Michigan director of the FHA. Foley, a New Deal Democrat who became the national director of the FHA in the Truman administration, found the efforts of black neighborhood residents and developers to construct their own homes a compelling cause. Foley, like Roosevelt, envisioned federal housing policy as a means of encouraging residential stability through the promotion of homeownership. The black residents of the Eight Mile community, who strove for self-sufficiency and homeownership, and who had attempted to build their own homes against the odds of an unfavorable real estate market and the Depression-era economy, were no less worthy of federal subsidy than their white counterparts. Yet Foley's interest in the small black community by no means signaled a new federal commitment to integrated housing. Foley had no intention of departing from the FHA policy which mandated racial homogeneity in housing developments; like many social reformers of the New Deal era, he believed in a separate-but-equal philosophy of housing finance.[29]

Avery and the members of the Eight Mile Civic Association rearticulated the Roosevelt administration's philosophy of independent homeownership to persuade Foley and the FHA of their neighborhood's worthiness for government subsidies. After the Detroit Common Council sponsored a hearing in August 1943 on development plans for the Eight Mile community, Foley decided to visit the area and examine its housing conditions for himself. On the eve of Foley's visit, community organizers led an enormous clean-up drive. "Late that night," Avery recounted, "windows were being washed, curtains were being hung, bon fires blazed consuming rubbish, trees were whitewashed—everything was in order—then we waited and prayed." The community effort impressed Foley. At the City Plan Commission hearing, he praised "the efforts being made toward the reclamation of the Wyoming–Eight Mile area." Burneice Avery and the Civic Association "felt we had found an understanding friend in Mr. Foley."[30]

As Avery and the Eight Mile community groups sought the independence of single-family homeownership, they faced the staunch opposition of other reform organizations. The most prominent organization to envision a different future for the Eight Mile community was the Citizens Housing and Planning Council. In 1938, as one of its first major investigative and reform efforts, the CHPC targeted the Eight Mile Road community for a detailed study of housing conditions, and a major redevelopment proposal. In 1939, sociologist Marvel Daines, a white University of Michigan graduate, surveyed the community for the CHPC and photographed some of the community's bleakest residences. In her report, entitled "Be It Ever So Tumbled: The Story of a Suburban Slum," Daines described the neighborhood in great detail. The pamphlet, published by the CHPC and distributed widely to government officials, planners, and corporate leaders, included interviews with Eight Mile residents about housing, employment opportunity, and living conditions. Daines's report combined indignation at the economic conditions that led to the impoverishment of the area's residents, shock at the dilapidated housing conditions in the neighborhood, admiration of the persistence and "decency" of the residents, and paternalism toward them for their poverty and lack of education. "An economic hurricane," Daines wrote, "had swept them relentlessly before it—bringing poverty and destruction.

Their homes deteriorated gradually into shacks, unpainted and dilapidated." Daines was also concerned with the effects of the slum on future development in the adjacent white communities. The section to the west of the development, she feared, "possibly may be retarded in its development by the fact that a slum area lies in close proximity. What is to keep this deteriorated area from spreading?"[31]

Daines considered several proposals for the neighborhood, including the construction of public housing, which seemed unlikely because of the government's desire "to limit its future building program to clearing the slums within the congested part of the city." A private-public project, she concluded, would be no better, for it would drive out poor residents who could not afford the rents demanded by private developers. And the wholesale conversion of the area to a white community would leave the present residents with no low-cost alternative to their housing. "Would we force them back into the already congested downtown slums from which they came twenty years ago in quest of air and sunshine and a garden spot?" Daines's CHPC report concluded with a proposal "which seems feasible from both the point of view of the Negro, and his more fortunate white neighbor in the adjacent areas." The CHPC recommended that land in the existing black neighborhood be sold to white buyers, who could maintain the quality and character of their neighborhoods adjacent to the Eight Mile community by redeveloping the area for white middle-class homeowners. To meet the needs of the existing black residents, a new community would be built "in a comparable area . . . close to an industrial center of employment . . . where Negroes have already settled, and garden space is available." The CHPC proposal, in effect, called for a government-subsidized expansion of the black ghetto, preserving the choice land of the Eight Mile area for white settlement.[32]

The city of Detroit also had its eye on the Eight Mile area. In 1941, as the rapidly expanding city sought land for a new airport accessible to the city center, the Mayor's Airport Committee found the Eight Mile–Wyoming community the "most desirable location" for a major airport. Because much of the land in the area was still vacant, and because the developed sections were largely inhabited by poor blacks, the city expected little objection to the airport proposal. Moreover, commercial development around the airport would bring more tax money into the city's coffers. By 1942, however, the city turned to cheaper or more convenient alternative sites, closer to the industrial belt on Detroit's East Side, or in virtually undeveloped suburban areas, where land costs were low. Although the city reconsidered the Eight Mile area for an airport in 1945, vociferous objection of community groups and developers who planned middle-class development in the vicinity persuaded the government officials of the impracticality of the Eight Mile site.[33]

Detroit's City Plan Commission (CPC) proposed an alternative suburban airport site, and called for the "orderly" redevelopment of the Eight Mile Community. The CPC's proposals were part of an emerging program to create a totally planned metropolis, combining public housing with strictly regulated private development. To that end, the CPC administered Detroit's first zoning law, enacted in 1940, and began composing a master plan to guide city and regional growth. Crucial to the success of the CPC's vision was the reconstruction of Detroit's "blighted" neighborhoods as modern planned communities.[34] CPC officials believed that if the Eight Mile area were left in the hands of private developers or its black residents, it would simply remain a disorderly slum. Thus, the CPC supported the construction of temporary housing to house war workers, while giving the commission time to devise a plan for the redevelopment of the community as a whole. Here the CHPC agreed with the CPC: temporary housing was acceptable "providing that planning be carried out with a view to post-war growth."[35]

Perhaps influenced by the CHPC report, the CPC suggested a plan "for the redeeming of the area, perhaps by moving the people to some slum clearance project." In early 1942, the City Plan Commission sent its "Blight Committee" to study public housing and private, FHA-subsidized redevelopment projects in the Eight Mile area that they now called "Blight Area D." The City Plan Commission envisioned public-private partnerships as the vehicle for the "rehabilitation" of blighted areas. In 1941, city lawyers had approved a Blight Committee suggestion that the city could condemn property in slum areas and sell "land unneeded for municipal purposes to private parties for housing development." The City Plan Commission's support for public-private housing ventures may have stemmed from the widespread suspicion that public housing would stunt the growth of the private housing market. Many city officials, among them Detroit's Mayor Jeffries, were skeptical of all public housing projects, even those required for the accommodation of wartime defense workers. Expressing his favor of private alternatives to government-funded construction, Jeffries worried that "there might remain a great surplus of housing after the emergency which will substantially interfere with the new private construction program we already have."[36]

The wartime emergency, the sluggishness of the construction industry because of wartime manpower and material shortages, and the influx of thousands of new workers to the city in the early 1940s, rendered Jeffries's desires moot. Because of the growing housing shortage in the city during the war, federal and city planning officials sought open land throughout the city for the construction of temporary wartime housing. During the Second World War, the Federal Public Housing Authority (FPHA) and the Detroit Housing Commission (DHC) built hundreds of permanent public housing units and thousands of temporary units in barracks-like wooden structures and Quonset hut–type buildings throughout the city. In 1942, the FPHA and the DHC proposed the erection of one thousand five hundred units of temporary wartime housing for black workers on the vacant land in the Eight Mile community. The Eight Mile area was one of the few solidly black sections of the city with land available for development. Housing officials knew that with few white residents in the area, the project would not disrupt existing racial patterns and thus would be immune from protest.

At the same time housing reformers and city officials discussed the eradication of the Eight Mile Road "slum," individual contractors saw potential for profitable development in the area through the acquisition of "scavenger lots" held by the city or state for nonpayment of taxes. In 1943, black developers M. M. Robinson and Nash Russ petitioned the City Plan Commission for the release of property that had fallen under state control. Both promised to repair existing homes and to construct new houses for black residents with newly approved FHA subsidies.[37] In addition, the Eight Mile Civic Association attempted to create its own private development group. In June 1943, the secretary of the City Plan Commission reported "that there is a colored group who claim they have funds for the reclamation of the blighted area on Eight Mile and Wyoming." The black group incorporated under the Urban Redevelopment Corporation law in an attempt to garner federal funds and city approval for its redevelopment plan.[38] Other contractors also expressed interest in developing the area. Wayne County Better Homes, a new corporation spearheaded by black businessman and politician Charles Diggs, which became the leading builder of new homes for black Detroiters, couched its proposal for redevelopment in the language of the City Plan Commission that the neighborhood should be "developed as a community," rather than piecemeal.[39] The struggle for the future of the Eight Mile Road community became public at a September 1943 hearing over the Russ petition for the release of land, and at a March 1944 hearing over the sale of 850 tax-delinquent parcels in the Eight Mile area. Those offering testimony included a representative of Wayne County Better Homes, three members of the Eight Mile Road Civic Association, State Senator Charles Diggs, two representatives from United Automobile Workers (UAW) Local 600 (which drew a large black membership from Ford's River Rouge plant and had a leftist leadership), and Raymond Foley, the director of the Michigan office of the FHA. Having returned from a personal visit to the neighborhood, Foley praised the residents of the Eight Mile-Wyoming area for their redevelopment initiatives and lauded "the improvement of individual properties by tenants and occupants in the past few years."[40]

Black Detroit was by no means unanimous in support of the efforts of Eight Mile community organizations, the FHA, and private developers to build single-family homes in the area. Prominent members of the black community joined the CPC and CHPC in support for planned public housing in the Eight Mile community. Numerous advocacy and reform groups, most notably the UAW and especially its locals with sizable black memberships, like Local 600, put pressure on city and federal officials to alleviate the acute shortage of housing for the thousands of southern blacks who had flooded the city in search of work since the outbreak of the war. William Nicholas, the director of the Congress of Industrial Organizations' International Housing Department, called for the construction of two thousand five hundred public housing units in the Eight Mile community. Horace Sheffield, a leading black UAW official, likewise supported the construction of temporary public housing until the area could be comprehensively redeveloped as a "model Negro community." Detroit's most prominent black housing advocates also sided with the proposals to build public housing in the Eight Mile neighborhood. Horace White, a leading Detroit minister who had played a crucial role in mediating the Sojourner Truth controversy, used his influential column in Detroit's major black newspaper to argue for planned development in the area. He feared that Eight Mile residents were being manipulated by private developers seeking quick profits from FHA loans, and warned that they "ought not to allow themselves to be used as pawns in the fight between private builders and public housing people."[41]

The result of the contentious meetings was a compromise, backed by the FHA and city planning officials, to construct six hundred units of temporary war housing—the Robert Brooks Homes—and to allow FHA subsidy of the construction of single-family homes in the neighborhood. It was a partial victory for black community groups, a showpiece for the FHA, which could claim that it worked for the benefit of black Detroiters, and an acceptable result for public housing officials, who hastily constructed temporary structures in the Eight Mile Road area. The CHPC made the best of its defeat, calling the neighborhood "a laboratory in city planning" where "all interested agencies, public and private, have joined together in planning."[42] City Plan Commission officials held out for a more comprehensive strategy, and hoped that the one thousand five hundred acres set aside for temporary war housing would come under its control for the construction of a park and recreation center.[43]

In the end, the Eight Mile community groups—acting out of aspirations for homeownership and a sense of entitlement from the federal government—changed the course of FHA policy. Their neighborhood became a bastion of black homeownership, "one of the very few areas in Detroit where Negroes can buy land, build, and own their own home." More than one thousand five hundred new single-family homes were built in the area between 1940 and 1950, the year that the expanding black population jumped the infamous "dividing wall" and moved into the formerly white neighborhood to the west. By 1960, a remarkable 88 percent of the area's homes were owner-occupied.[44] But the unprecedented triumph of the black community groups was tinged with irony. The discriminatory lending policies of the FHA remained intact, although the boundaries of federal action had expanded slightly. Above all, the events in the Eight Mile–Wyoming area revealed the tension at the heart of New Deal housing policy which remained unresolved throughout the 1940s and 1950s. The government's encouragement of single-family homeownership unleashed the aspirations of many urban blacks, and led them to demand funds for private housing. Efforts by community groups to obtain HOLC and FHA funds undermined support for the New Deal's program to provide public housing. When working-class whites, the most powerful voting bloc in the city, fought against public housing to preserve their New Deal right to homeownership and the "integrity" and security of their neighborhoods, they ultimately undermined the entire enterprise of public housing in Detroit.

Public Housing on the Periphery: "Biracial" Housing in the 1940s

In the 1940s, city planners, community groups, and housing reformers engaged in intense debates over the location of public housing. An especially vexing question was where to construct public housing for blacks. It was clear to many planners that there simply was not enough adequate housing in the concentrated ghetto of inner-city Detroit for the city's rapidly growing black population. Any attempt to eliminate the shortage and to overcome the overcrowding of center-city areas would fail, barring a comprehensive plan to disperse the inner-city population to undeveloped land on the city's periphery. Proposals to construct public housing in or near largely white areas were the most contentious political issue of the 1940s and early 1950s in Detroit. Federal agencies responsible for providing wartime housing, and the city agencies responsible for implementing urban policy, the City Plan Commission and the Detroit Housing Commission, faced a political conundrum regarding public housing. The fate of public housing construction in white areas rested in the hands of a range of well-funded, well-connected, and well-organized opponents. Opponents of racial integration challenged public housing on the grounds that it would foster the indiscriminate mixing of races. Suburban governments, concerned with homogeneity, refused to allow the construction of public housing within their jurisdictions. Real estate developers and business groups opposed government-built projects as creeping socialism that threatened to erode the values of private enterprise. And Detroit's elected officials were increasingly reluctant to support projects that met with vociferous opposition from their white working- and middle-class constituents.

Sojourner Truth

The controversy over the construction of the Sojourner Truth housing project in northeast Detroit, in the midst of World War II, set a precedent that would shape Detroit public housing policy for another decade. In 1941, the Detroit Housing Commission and the USHA announced plans for the construction of a two-hundred-unit housing project to alleviate the wartime housing shortage. The site they chose in northeast Detroit sat in the heart of the Seven Mile–Fenelon neighborhood, an area that government officials believed would be uncontroversial, because of its proximity to an already existing concentration of blacks. The firestorm that exploded around Sojourner Truth caught government officials off guard. Between June 1941 and February 1942, white residents in the area formed the Seven Mile–Fenelon Improvement Association to coordinate opposition to the project; they were joined in a brief alliance by middle-class black residents in nearby Conant Gardens.[45]

White neighborhood pressure grew, as members of the Seven Mile–Fenelon association held regular meetings and protests, set up picket lines at city offices, deluged government officials with thousands of angry letters, met with city officials, attended Common Council meetings, and lobbied their congressman against the project. White homeowners were especially infuriated with the seeming indecision of the federal government, which switched its official position on the racial occupancy of the project at least three times. Even more galling to white area residents was the FHA's "refusal to insure any more mortgage loans" in the Seven Mile–Fenelon area in the aftermath of the decision to build public housing there. Public housing for blacks, residents believed (with some justification) jeopardized their ability to improve their homes and finance new construction on the many vacant lots in the area.[46] While Seven Mile–Fenelon neighbors rallied against the project, civil rights groups, left-leaning unionists, and pro–public housing groups pressured the federal government to maintain its commitment to house blacks at Sojourner Truth. In 1941, only one other project in the city housed blacks, despite the growing inner-city housing shortage.

Federal officials and the Detroit Housing Commission seemed to bow to white pressure when, in January 1941, they officially designated Sojourner Truth a project for white occupancy. But less than two weeks later, after an outburst of protest, city and federal officials, in a remarkable volte-face, promised the project to black war workers. White Seven Mile–Fenelon members responded with massive protest, picketing the site throughout February, and demanding their "Rights to Protect, Restrict, and Improve Our Neighborhood."[47] When the first black families moved into the project on February 28, 1942, crowds of black supporters and white opponents

3.3. White residents of the Seven Mile–Fenelon area fiercely resisted the designation of the Sojourner Truth Homes as a "Negro" housing project. This billboard was erected in February 1942, just before the first black families arrived. Notice both the American flags and the sign's bold assertion of whiteness.

gathered near the project, and by the end of the day, more than a thousand blacks and whites filled the streets. Fighting erupted. At least 40 people were injured, 220 were arrested, and 109 were held for trial—all but three black—before police restored order in the area.

In the wake of the Sojourner Truth riot, the Detroit Housing Commission established a policy mandating the continuation of racial segregation in public housing projects. Echoing the language of the National Association of Real Estate Boards, city officials promised that public housing projects would "not change the racial pattern of a neighborhood."[48] The policy was, in large part, an admission that the success of public housing depended on the support of the communities in which it was to be built. In fact, the Detroit Housing Commission, the City Plan Commission, and the Common Council were especially sensitive to the demands of white community groups that opposed public housing. Community groups flooded city offi-

3.4. Public housing for African Americans was scarce and the waiting lists to get in were enormous. Shown is one of the first black families to move into the Sojourner Truth Homes in 1942. The low-rise Northeast Side project was spartan, but it provided a modern, clean alternative to the overcrowded inner city.

cials with letters when they perceived the threat of public housing construction in their neighborhoods, packed public hearings with vocal crowds, and spoke forcefully for the "protection" of their neighborhoods and property from projects. After the Sojourner Truth incident and the Detroit Riot of 1943, white community groups learned to use the threat of imminent violence as a political tool to gain leverage in housing debates. City officials, desperately hoping to avoid racial bloodshed, had no choice but to take seriously the specter of civil disorder.

Suburban Resistance to Public Housing

During the war, the opposition of suburban communities to public housing greatly limited the options available to reformers. FPHA projects proposed for Ecorse and Dearborn, which allowed easy access to the Ford Rouge complex and other factories in the Dearborn and Downriver industrial areas, met with stiff resistance from suburban mayors. In September 1944, the FPHA announced plans to construct four hundred to one thousand units of temporary wartime housing in Dearborn.[49] Although twelve thousand blacks worked in war production in Dearborn, only a few dozen—all of them live-in servants—resided in the community. White war workers, in contrast, lived throughout Dearborn, often in neighborhoods convenient to their workplaces. UAW Local 600 and NAACP officials joined the lobbying effort for defense workers' housing. But FPHA officials recognized the difficulties of the Dearborn site, noting "that Dearborn will undoubtedly attempt to make things as miserable as possible for the people who live in the houses which are built."[50] Victory against Dearborn's skeptics was, to the FPHA, necessary for the success of integration and government-provided housing. Officials recognized the "social, political, and psychological significance of overcoming Dearborn's resistance to the Negro and toward the whole idea of public housing."[51]

Immediately Dearborn officials pledged to fight the construction of public housing in their city. Mayor Orville Hubbard, first elected in 1941 and reelected thirteen consecutive times through 1973, had built his reputation on his promise to keep Dearborn "lily white."[52] Hubbard combined anti-communist rhetoric, thinly veiled racial references, and stalwart localism in his opposition to the construction of public housing in Dearborn. Because Dearborn had few black residents, he contended that it bore no responsibility for the wartime housing shortage: "Housing the Negroes is Detroit's problem."[53] At a public forum on housing, Hubbard played to his white supporters and stated his position even more bluntly: "When you remove garbage from your backyard, you don't dump it in your neighbor's."[54] His fierce resistance to public housing, noted a black critic, "makes one wonder if Dearborn is a city in Michigan or Mississippi."[55]

Hubbard was joined in his opposition to war housing by officials and workers from Dearborn's largest employer, the Ford Motor Company. Ford management sanctioned the circulation of petitions among its work force opposing federal housing in Dearborn.[56] In November 1944, the Dearborn City Council passed an anti–public housing resolution.[57] When the FPHA, responding to political pressure, decided to reject the Dearborn site for one in neighboring Ecorse Township, Dearborn officials were just as indignant. Again Hubbard led the reaction with his statement that "We don't want any projects on Dearborn's outskirts, Negro or white. They couldn't get in Dearborn, so they stuck it on the city's veranda." The proposal, argued Hubbard, was a "sneak move" of "federal housing agents with their stratosphere social ideas" to built "a shack town under the guise of aiding national defense." Recalling the controversy, Hubbard referred to federal officials as "goddamn nigger-lover guys"; FPHA spokesman George Schermer, he said, had a "warped mind."[58] Ford Motor Company, which owned part of the hundred-acre parcel on which the project was to be constructed, joined with the Dearborn City Council and the board of Ecorse Township to sue the FPHA to prevent construction on the Ecorse site.[59]

Detroit officials hoped to avoid the suburban housing impasse by constructing public housing within the city's borders, on marginal land in neighborhoods considered to be racially transitional. Constrained by the proscription against changing the residential character of a neighborhood, and by fears of "race trouble," the DHC had problems finding uncontroversial sites for housing for blacks. In September 1944, the DHC rejected a proposal for a three-hundred-unit expansion of the Sojourner Truth Homes, on the grounds that they "would be inviting a major controversy while gaining only a very small percentage of the houses needed to solve the immediate housing problem."[60] Despite the protests of housing advocates that the decision was "a go-ahead for those pro-fascist groups to increase and project their anti-Negro activities," the DHC felt that the project "could . . . lead to another Sojourner Truth incident."[61]

The Defeat of Public Housing in Oakwood

In early 1945, the DHC offered another proposal for housing on a site it expected to be less controversial in the Oakwood neighborhood on Detroit's far Southwest Side, only two miles from the proposed Ecorse project. The working-class neighborhood, close to the Ford River Rouge Plant, the steel mills of the Downriver area, and Detroit's salt mines, was predominantly white, but had already attracted a few hundred black workers. Oakwood had few apartments or duplexes, and 83.2 percent of Oakwood residents lived in detached one-family houses. Oakwood was also a community of homeowners. 64.5 percent of Oakwood's houses were owner-occupied, a percentage almost identical to that of the Eight Mile–Wyoming neighborhood. Oakwood was a modest and affordable neighborhood, home to many recent immigrants or children of immigrants from Poland, Hungary, and Italy. Its small one- and two-story houses, mainly built in the boom years of the 1920s, had an average value of $3,621, substantially less than the $4,684 average for the entire city. In general, Oakwood's homes were well maintained, and fewer than 15 percent were classified as substandard in a 1938 survey of the neighborhood.[62] For Oakwood's residents, the small houses represented a substantial investment of their meager resources, and a permanent stake on American soil.

Because Oakwood was a relatively poor and marginal working-class neighborhood, federal authorities eyed it for redevelopment. Unlike older parts of the city, Oakwood had open land, and it was home to an already existing public housing project for white defense workers, the Fisher Houses. Property in Oakwood was unencumbered by racial covenants, and thus posed no legal barriers to the construction of a black housing project. In 1944 the FHA had approved the construction of three hundred single-family homes for blacks in a new subdivision on the western border of Oakwood. The neighborhood's distance from middle-class residential areas, its relatively low level of racial violence, and its proximity to many of Detroit's largest factories, made it particularly desirable for a low-income housing development.[63]

The Oakwood project, however, encountered enormous grassroots resistance from whites adamant that the government should preserve the racial and architectural homogeneity of their neighborhood. In the two-week period before a March 1945 Common Council hearing on the Oakwood proposal, 446 white residents of the eleven-hundred-family surrounding neighborhood sent letters of protest to city hall. Common to the letters, despite their diverse themes, was the belief that the city government would abdicate its responsibility to its loyal working-class constituents if it allowed the project to be built. The letters occasionally duplicated the style of a form letter circulated by a community association, but most were personal and rich with anecdote. The letter writers stressed security and stability, echoing Roosevelt's pro-homeownership rhetoric. They often demonstrated a humble "bootstraps" mentality derived from the acquisition of property through hard work. They expressed fear, laden with racist resentments, that their status as homeowners and their life investments were profoundly threatened by the influx of blacks. The letters combined the personal and the political, combining family sentiment with the themes of patriotism, rights, and equality. Above all, the letters were a resounding defense of the promise of homeownership at the core of New Deal housing policy, a promise that their writers hoped would be kept in the insecure postwar era.[64]

Many writers recounted in poignant detail their struggles to build a home in the area, their financial insecurity, and their concern for the future. "I do not want negroes living in my neighborhood," wrote Frank Berge, "as we take pride in our homes and streets." Like many of his neighbors, Berge feared that "our property would depreciate in value" if a public housing project were constructed nearby.[65] Others expressed concern over racial mixing, that proximity to blacks threatened the identity of Oakwood residents. As one resident stated: "We firmly believe in the God-given equality of man. He did not give us the right to choose our brothers ... but he did give us the right to choose the people we sleep with."[66] Father Henry P. Fadanelli, pastor of Our Lady of Mount Carmel Catholic Church, expressed the sentiments of many of his parishioners with a colorful fable: that "one can love both dogs and cats, but no sane person would throw a number of both into the same cage and pretend that they will get along—Anyway the SPCA would take up the case."[67] Another common theme was crime and civil disorder: the Oakwood project "will deprive us of the peace and equanimity we have enjoyed and turn the whole area into an armed camp."[68] Dozens of residents warned that the construction of a project for blacks would catalyze a race riot. In the wake of the violence surrounding black admission to the Sojourner Truth Homes, and Detroit's bloody 1943 riot, public officials were particularly sensitive to the threat of civil disorder.

Several letters highlighted the theme of wartime patriotism and its implications for citizenship. They appealed to the sentiments that undergirded federal entitlements for returning veterans. As Michael J. Harbulak wrote, "Our boys are fighting in Europe, Asia, and Africa to keep those people off our soil. If when these boys return they should become refugees who have to give up their homes because their own neighborhood with the help of our city fathers had been invade [sic] and occupied by the Africans, it would be a shame which our city fathers could not outlive."[69] Many of the sentiments were couched in the language of Americanism, a language that included allusions to the Constitution and grudging acknowledgments of racial equality. A large number included the formula "I have nothing against the colored" or "I believe in the God-given equality of man," and qualified these shibboleths with statements like "But I wouldn't want them for a neighbor nor growing up with my children."[70] Others believed that the proposed project was a violation of white "rights" to "peace and happiness." John Watson stated succinctly, "It looks as if, we the white people are being discriminated against. Let the colored people make their own district, as we had to."[71] Oakwood residents, like many working-class, white Detroiters, turned to a language of entitlement to justify their call for racial exclusion. As one observer noted, "the white population has come to believe that it has a vested, exclusive, and permanent 'right' to certain districts." The government, they believed, had an obligation to protect that "right."[72]

At a March 9, 1945, Common Council hearing on public housing in Oakwood, thirty-five hundred people crowded into City Hall, the majority white. Of the six hundred people who actually made it into the auditorium where the hearing was held, only twenty were black. The UAW Housing Department endorsed the plan, although many local union officials were reluctant to support Oakwood for fear of alienating white rank-and-file workers. Members of liberal pro–housing reform groups, including the

CHPC, addressed the council, but Oakwood residents set the tone of the meeting. Their representatives presented the Common Council with a petition signed by over three thousand area residents. Louis J. Borolo, president of the Oakwood Blue Jackets Athletic Club, appealed to the Common Council using the same patriotic language and rights rhetoric that many of the letter writers had used. "There are 1,500 blue stars in the windows of homes of that neighborhood," he testified. "Those stars represent soldiers waiting to come back to the same neighborhood they left." Acknowledging the "moral and legal right" of blacks to adequate housing, he contended that "we have established a prior right to a neighborhood which we have built up through the years—a neighborhood which is entirely white and which we want kept white."[73]

The massive outpouring of opposition to the Oakwood project was successful: on March 20, 1945, the Detroit Common Council rejected the proposal to build public housing in Oakwood.[74] The victory of the Oakwood residents was not solely their own. Behind Oakwood were thousands of other white working-class and middle-class Detroiters, who exerted formidable electoral clout as a majority of the city's electorate. The political cost of supporting the construction of the Oakwood project was potentially great. Several Detroit politicians used the housing issue to their advantage in reelection bids later that year; incumbent Mayor Edward Jeffries, in a campaign laden with racial innuendo, attacked UAW-backed mayoral candidate Richard Frankensteen, flooding Northwest and Northeast Side neighborhoods with literature warning of his opponent's support for public housing and ties to black organizations.[75]

Jeffries and his supporters combined antiblack and anticommunist sentiments into a potent political brew. Frankensteen, warned Jeffries and his supporters, was a "red" who would encourage "racial invasions" of white neighborhoods. Unlike Frankensteen, Jeffries would uphold community interests. "Mayor Jeffries is Against Mixed Housing" proclaimed a boldly printed campaign poster. It quoted Jeffries: "I have tried to safeguard your neighborhoods in the character in which you, their residents, have developed them."[76] The *Home Gazette*, a Northwest Side neighborhood newspaper, editorialized that "There is no question where Edward J. Jeffries' administration stands on mixed housing." It praised the Detroit Housing Commission for "declaring that a majority of the people of the city of Detroit do not want the racial character of their neighborhoods changed," and for reiterating "its previous stand against attempts of Communist-inspired Negroes to penetrate white residential sections."[77]

Black observers of the election and union supporters of Frankensteen were appalled by the blatant racial claims of Jeffries's campaign, and attempted to use economic populist and anti-Nazi rhetoric to deflate Jeffries's charges. Black journalist Henry Lee Moon, writing in the NAACP's monthly, *Crisis*, accused Jeffries of appealing "to our more refined fascists, the big money interests, and the precarious middle class whose sole inalienable possession is a white skin."[78] Jeffries's racial appeals were remarkably successful. They bolstered his flagging campaign, and gave him a comfortable margin in November against the UAW-backed candidate in a solidly union city. On the local level, the link between black and red was a clever strategy for attracting white Democrats, suspicious of liberalism and its capacity for egalitarian political and social rhetoric.

The result of wartime housing battles in Sojourner Truth, Dearborn, and Oakwood was that whites began to view public housing as "Negro housing," and grew increasingly skeptical of the federal agenda that called for the housing of America's poor. Erosion of support for public housing on grounds of race also eroded support more generally for New Deal programs. One astute observer noted in 1946 that

> In the field of housing, there has tended to develop a tie-up in our thinking between Negroes and government. Public housing and housing for Negroes is synonymous or nearly so in the minds of many people. This is bad for public housing and bad for Negroes. Many people are concerned about government interference of all kinds. This tends to create a separation in their minds between themselves and "the government." . . .[79]

Peripheral Public Housing after Oakwood

Oakwood was but the first skirmish in an ongoing battle over public housing in Detroit that continued throughout the 1940s and early 1950s. In 1946, the CPC issued its Master Plan for Detroit, and called for the construction of public housing in outlying areas as part of a comprehensive slum removal and reconstruction project. City planning officials began investigating potential outlying sites, to fulfill the goals of the Master Plan. Finally in 1949, in anticipation of funding available under the recently passed Taft-Ellender-Wagner Housing Reform Act, the Detroit Housing Commission proposed twelve sites for the construction of new public housing. Four large tracts in the center city were to be "slum clearance" projects, three in largely black neighborhoods. The housing commission slated the remaining eight projects for vacant land sites on the Northeast and Northwest sides of the city, all but one in predominantly white neighborhoods.[80]

The vacant land sites were by no means Detroit's choicest residential real estate. All fronted major thoroughfares, two were bounded by railroad tracks, and three sat in largely industrial areas, on sites zoned for manufacturing. Despite their location on marginal land, each proposal generated enormous resistance from the residents of the surrounding communities. Community groups around the city mobilized to fight the construction of public housing in their neighborhoods, local newspapers lambasted housing reform proponents, and white neighborhood resistance to public housing remained at the top of the city's political agenda.

The most intense conflicts involved sites on Detroit's far Northwest Side, an area of neat, tree-lined streets with 1920s-style bungalows and modest three-bedroom homes constructed with FHA and HOLC financing in the 1930s and 1940s. A large part of the remaining vacant land within the city limits lay in this area, although rapid government-subsidized single-family housing development left less and less land available for public housing. The white residents of the Northwest Side lived more than ten miles from the crowded tenements of Paradise Valley, but the spread of slums to their areas nevertheless seemed to them an imminent threat to their precarious hold on middle-class status and to their fiercely guarded "homeowners' rights." In the words of one community resident, public housing would "ruin Northwest Detroit."[81]

Leading the community resistance to public housing was Floyd McGriff, editor and publisher of a chain of neighborhood newspapers on the Northwest Side. McGriff used his papers as a vehicle for his conservative views on such matters as communism, fluoridation of the water supply, unions, race relations, and public housing. For McGriff, and for many of his Northwest Detroit readers, the issues of race, left-wing politics, and government action were inextricably linked. Public housing projects were part of the conspiratorial effort of well-placed communists and communist sympathizers in the government to destroy traditional American values through a carefully calculated policy of racial and class struggle. McGriff warned that multiple-family homes would "threaten local areas with additional blight," and blamed "fringe disruptionists, the political crack-pots, and the socialist double-domes" who "injected racial issues" into housing debates. The city planned to "move the slum-area residents into city-built housing projects in Northwest Detroit," and "to force pioneering families to move out."[82]

The political tensions of race and public housing came to a head in the mayoral election of 1949. Liberal Common Council member George Edwards faced conservative City Treasurer Albert Cobo. Edwards, a one-time UAW activist, former public housing administrator, and New Deal Democrat, was the political antithesis of Cobo, a corporate executive, real estate investor, and Republican.[83] Cobo focused his campaign on the issues of race and public housing. Armed with the endorsement of most white neighborhood improvement associations, Cobo swept the largely white precincts on the Northeast and Northwest sides, where voters were especially concerned about the threat of public housing. The distinction between Cobo and Edwards was crystal clear. Cobo adamantly opposed "Negro invasions" and public housing, whereas Councilman Edwards had consistently

3.5. George Edwards, the Democratic candidate for Mayor of Detroit in 1949, was a former UAW activist and an advocate of public housing. He was defeated overwhelmingly by Albert Cobo, a conservative Republican and ally of white homeowners' groups.

championed the right of blacks to decent housing anywhere in the city, and regularly voted in favor of proposals to locate public housing in outlying areas.[84]

Liberal leaders were baffled when conservative Cobo beat prolabor councilman Edwards in a heavily Democratic city, and that Cobo did particularly well among union voters. The Edwards campaign was coordinated by the UAW and other CIO unions, which provided him with nearly thirty thousand dollars in funding, printed and distributed over 1.3 million pro-Edwards pamphlets, and sent union members canvassing door-to-door throughout the city. Pamphlets in English, Polish, and Hungarian lambasted Cobo for his connections with bankers and slumlords who "live in Grosse Pointe, Birmingham, and Bloomfield Hills"; radio spots featured a "snotty woman's voice" urging voters to "vote Republican in the Detroit election for mayor"; and UAW sound trucks blasted pro-Edwards messages at local un-

employment offices. Yet despite the massive and well-organized union effort, Edwards lost to Cobo even in predominantly blue-collar precincts.[85]

Stunned in the aftermath of the overwhelming Edwards defeat, UAW
political activists met to discuss the election. On the East Side, one organizer reported, many union members refused to place Edwards placards in
their windows. In one heavily Democratic ward on the West Side, blue-
collar voters told a UAW canvasser that they supported Edwards, yet on
election day, they turned out for Cobo two-to-one. A West Side coordinator
explained the seeming paradox of union members' support for Cobo: "I
think in these municipal elections we are dealing with people who have a
middle class mentality. Even in our own UAW, the member is either buying
a home, owns a home, or is going to buy one. I don't know whether we can
ever make up this difficulty." The problem was that "George was beaten by
the housing program."[86]

The 1949 election revealed the conflict between the politics of home and
the politics of workplace, a conflict exacerbated by racial tensions in rapidly
changing neighborhoods. Blue-collar workers, one activist lamented, failed
to "see the relationship between their life in the plant and their life in the
community." Racial fears and neighborhood defensiveness made the political unity of home and workplace impossible. And many UAW local officials
were unwilling to support their union's position in favor of integrated public
housing. East Side UAW shop stewards, many of whom were open Cobo
supporters, told one UAW Political Action Committee organizer that "the
Union is okay in the shop but when they buy a home they forget about it.
You can tell them anything they want to but as long as they think their
property is going down, it is different."[87] The Edwards defeat marked the
beginning of a retreat of the UAW from labor politics in the city; the disillusioned UAW Political Action Committee continued to endorse liberal candidates, but offered only half-hearted support to Cobo's opponents in Detroit's
biennial mayoral races in the 1950s. The combination of racial resentment
and homeowners' politics that defeated Edwards dimmed future hopes for
the triumph of labor liberalism on the local level in Detroit.[88]

Cobo's term as mayor, beginning in 1949, put to rest many of the fears of
community groups. A fiscal conservative who had entered politics after a
career as a utility company executive, Cobo carried to the mayoralty a strong
distrust of government economic intervention, and a faith in the unhindered
operation of the free market. Cobo owed much of his support to well-organized neighborhood improvement associations throughout the city, and immediately pledged that "It will not be the purpose of the administration to
scatter public housing projects throughout the city, just because funds may
be forthcoming from the Federal Government. I WILL NOT APPROVE
Federal Housing Projects in the outlying single homes areas."[89] He justified
his policies as necessary protection of the investment of single-family home-

owners, for "when people move and invest in a single-family area, they are entitled to consideration and protection."[90]

Cobo wasted no time fulfilling his anti–public housing promises. In his first weeks of office, he vetoed eight of the twelve proposed public housing sites, all but one in outlying, predominantly white sections of the city. By putting brakes on all public housing development outside of heavily black inner-city neighborhoods, Cobo finally killed public housing as a controversial political issue.[91] Real estate agents and community groups immediately applauded Cobo's stance. Roman Ceglowski, president of the Detroit Civic League, who opposed "attempts to change the racial character of any Detroit neighborhood," praised Cobo's public housing policy as "healthy . . . and truly American."[92] Orville Tenaglia, president of the Southwest Detroit Improvement League, stated that "we who have come to look upon this community as 'our home,' living with people of our 'own kind,' do most humbly . . . thank you for the courageous stand you have taken" on the housing issue. Ralph Smith, president of the Michigan Council of Civic Associations, was confident that "minority pressure groups" would "collapse" because of the mayor's uncompromising position.[93] Suburban civic leaders also took sustenance from Cobo's stance on public housing.[94]

Armed with endorsements from white community groups, Cobo quickly dismantled Detroit's public housing program. James Inglis, the head of the Detroit Housing Commission under Mayors Jeffries and Van Antwerp, resigned in outrage because he was "in almost complete disagreement" with Cobo on the issue of housing. Cobo's program, he contended, "falls far short of meeting the real needs of the community" and "completely disregards the seriousness of the housing shortage." Cobo immediately replaced Inglis with Harry J. Durbin, a prominent developer and former president of the National Association of Home Builders. The roster of housing officials in Detroit in the Cobo years reads like a Who's Who of the city's real estate and construction industries. Other Cobo appointees included real estate magnate Walter Gessell and property manager George Isabell.[95] Two other members of the Housing Commission, Ed Thal and Finlay C. Allan, were officers of the Detroit Building Trades Council of the American Federation of Labor.[96] These officials represented the interests of private industry and the building trades in their government positions. It is not surprising that city housing policy, like federal housing policy, reinforced the practices of private industry. Like their counterparts in Chicago and Boston, they turned their energies toward urban renewal projects, including the proposed Civic Center, Medical Center, and a middle-income apartment project, all in the predominantly black inner city.[97]

The staffs of the City Plan Commission and the Federal Public Housing Authority continued to fight in vain for the dispersal of public housing in outlying sites in the city. CPC officials argued that "locating small projects in various areas rather than large ones in one general area" would offer "better means of integration with neighborhoods, better overall relationship to sources of employment, less evidence and feeling of institutionalism."[98] The housing commission, however, succumbed to political pressure and placed its whole emphasis on the redevelopment of slums and the construction of large projects in heavily black inner-city areas.[99] The Mayor's Interracial Committee was scathing in its rebuke of Cobo, noting that "the present program is to be concentrated in the Negro area for the sole purpose of rebuilding and perpetuating the Negro ghetto."[100] The Cobo administration policy, another critic contended, was "determined to preserve a monopoly by the building industry and bigoted racial prejudice."[101] A report in 1951 complained that because of opposition to the construction of multiple housing in outlying areas, "the amount of rental housing being built in Detroit has dropped to a trickle."[102]

Cobo's staunch refusal to consider outlying sites and his close alliance with the opponents of public housing marked a final blow to Detroit's troubled public housing efforts. As a result of the events of the 1940s, Detroit, unlike New York and Chicago, had relatively little permanent public housing. Only 8,155 units of public housing were constructed in Detroit between 1937 and 1955, substantially fewer than in a city like Chicago where nearly 5 percent of the city's population lived in public housing. The three largest projects, the Jeffries, Brewster, and Douglass Homes, were all high-density complexes located in the inner city.[103] From 1950 through 1956, when cities throughout the country took advantage of federal funds made available in the 1949 Housing Act, Detroit ranked eighteenth among the twenty-five largest cities in the ratio of low-rent starts to all housing starts. Smaller cities like Boston, Newark, Norfolk, St. Louis, and New Orleans all built more public housing during the early 1950s than Detroit.[104]

The Strange Death of Public Housing in Detroit, 1950–1960

Public housing in Detroit, like its troubled counterparts in cities like Chicago, Philadelphia, and New York, played a decisive role in deepening racial inequality in the city. Detroit's public housing was racially segregated. And the small amount of public housing built in Detroit was concentrated in largely black inner-city neighborhoods. The gap between blacks and whites in public housing grew even wider in the 1950s, as thousands of blacks were relocated for urban renewal and highway construction projects, while the admissions policy of the Housing Commission remained unchanged. Detroit was slow to desegregate its public housing projects, and offer equal housing facilities to blacks and whites. Officially sanctioned segregation in public housing legitimated private-sector housing discrimination. Cyril Lawrence, a critic of the Housing Commission's approval of segregation, noted that the "public has interpreted the policy as applicable to all housing, including private housing."[105] George Schermer of the Mayor's Interracial Committee was even more critical of the policy. Official approval of segregation, he argued, "has a detrimental effect," fostering "distrust and disbelief in government on the part of minority and liberal" groups, and giving "official sanction to the prejudices of others."[106] During the Cobo administration, DHC policy remained unrelentingly segregationist, as officials defended "the right of the landlord to operate his property as he wishes or take the tenants he wants to take in."[107] In response to pressure from civil rights orgnaizations, city officials began the token integration of public housing projects in 1953 and 1954, but not until 1956, after the Detroit Branch of the NAACP won a lawsuit that challenged the city's racial policy, did the city open all public housing to blacks, and even then desegregation was haltingly slow. As late as the early 1960s, four public housing projects were virtually all-white, with token black residents, and two projects were all-black.[108]

The dilemma of the housing crisis for Detroit's poor was still unresolved in the late 1950s. The city directed blacks needing homes to its already crowded center-city projects, and defended the concentration of blacks as the necessary consequence of slum removal. James Inglis, director of the City Housing Commission in 1949, stated that black housing projects were by necessity high-density because of the high land prices in the center-city areas where slum housing had been cleared. In a critical response to Inglis, Edward Turner, a member of the board of the Detroit Branch of the NAACP and the Mayor's Interracial Committee, pointed to the ironic consequence of the city's public housing policy that forced black Detroiters to live in developments that, like the slum areas they replaced, were crowded. In effect, argued Turner, construction of high-rise public housing would "provide approval of the congested pattern they have been forced to live in."[109] Turner suggested that the only solution to the city's housing dilemma would be the construction of new public housing on open land outside of the black ghetto: "I think the outlying areas should be given to Negroes if you are to do anything." By the early 1950s, Turner's views were quixotic. The pro–public housing Citizens' Housing and Planning Council was defunct, the NAACP was putting its energies into the desegregation of existing projects, and the UAW and other unions had abandoned their efforts in favor of integrated public housing. What had seemed feasible in 1940 was now politically impossible.

After a decade of struggle over government-provided housing, its opponents had won a clear victory. One observer, looking back at the efforts of Detroit's public housing advocates from the vantage point of the 1960s, commented bitterly that "elephantine labors have brought forth a mouse." Public housing in Detroit was "only a token force in the total housing picture."[110] Support for the construction of housing for black Detroiters in segregated white neighborhoods was thwarted by community groups and elected officials at every turn, and the result was a further solidification of the spatial barriers of race in the city. It ushered in an era that civil rights advocates, including Joseph Coles, a prominent black Democratic party activist, considered "the dark ages of Detroit."[111]

Part Two

RUST

4.1. Black workers, like this janitor in the Allison Motors plant in 1942, were disproportionately represented in unskilled factory jobs and in the service sector. Janitorial work was almost always a dead end. Separate seniority lines prevented maintenance workers from moving into semiskilled and skilled jobs.

4

"The Meanest and Dirtiest Jobs": The Structures of Employment Discrimination

If they don't stop this discrimination, there's going
to be a civil war.
—Unemployed black worker, Detroit (late 1950s)

In following his aspirations, the Negro has crossed
over his Jordan in multitudes to a land of Canaan in
America—a city named Detroit.
—*Detroit Free Press* (1957)

IN MARCH 1948, Joseph Mays, an unemployed African American, joined the
line in front of the employment office at Dodge Main, Chrysler Corporation's flagship plant. Laid off from a welding job when the Fruehauf Trailer
Company downsized its Detroit plant, Mays saw an ad that Chrysler had
put in all three Detroit daily newspapers: "Wanted: Die Makers, Template
Makers, Machine Operators, Assemblers, Production Workers, Dodge Main
Plant, 7900 Jos. Campau." Mays was confident that he would be hired
right away. Production at Dodge Main was booming and the plant was
hiring hundreds of workers a day. And Mays came with impeccable credentials. He had extensive experience as a welder, both at Fruehauf and in
shipyards as a defense worker during World War II. But when he showed
up at the Dodge Main employment office, Mays's hopes were quickly
dashed. When he asked about the machine operator openings, the personnel representative told him that all the positions had been filled. Mays
then inquired about the production worker openings and listed his qualifications. The employer's representative turned Mays away without a job
application.

Undaunted, Mays returned to the Dodge Main hiring office the following
day and tried to apply for a job as a welder. The company agent responded
brusquely that they were not hiring welders. Mays did not give up. Later in
the day, he joined the line of prospective workers at the Dodge Truck Plant.
There he was treated even more rudely. Although several white workers in
the employment office were filling out application forms when Mays came
in, the hiring agent told him that no jobs were available and refused to give
him a form. Adding indignity to injury, the agent interviewed the next man

in line, who was white, as Mays walked away still unemployed. Mays was not alone; several other black workers were rebuffed by the Dodge Main employment office that week, and later that summer several black women complained that they had also been refused applications at the Dodge Main hiring gate.[1]

Joseph Mays understood that he had been denied a job because of the color of his skin. He and countless other black workers, who watched white men and women move easily into jobs that were closed to them, readily recognized discrimination. Even if it was not a part of their own personal experience, most African Americans in industrial cities like Detroit could relate a story of a relative, friend, or neighbor who had been denied or lost a job "because he was black." More than just a collection of impressions, employment discrimination was manifest in the underrepresentation of African Americans in most of the city's better paid, safer, and higher-status jobs (see Appendix B). Employment discrimination in postwar Detroit appeared endemic, but it also seemed inconsistent and capricious. The plight of black workers had improved as a result of the Second World War. Defense mobilization created unprecedented economic opportunities. In addition, industries varied in their openness to African American employees. An individual worker might not be able to predict when and where he would encounter a seemingly arbitrary rebuff. Nonetheless, by all objective measures, white Detroiters citywide enjoyed preferential treatment at hiring gates, in personnel offices, in union halls, and in promotions to better positions.

Viewed either from the perspective of an individual worker, or from citywide labor statistics, racial discrimination in employment was an undeniable outcome of hiring processes in postwar Detroit. The causes of inequitable hiring decisions, however, are more difficult to determine. Racism and discrimination alone are not satisfactory explanations for the myriad individual decisions that determined the makeup of the labor force. Racial practices in the workplace took shape in the changing ideological and political context of the mid-twentieth century.

The structure of the labor market also shaped discriminatory practices. The industrial labor market in the mid-twentieth century was divided into heavily capitalized "primary sector" firms, and poorly capitalized, small-scale "secondary sector" ones. Within large firms, the division of labor was intricate, as skilled, semiskilled, and unskilled laborers often worked under the same roof. Black workers were disproportionately concentrated in poor-paying secondary sector jobs (in service work, for example) or in the worst "subordinate jobs" in the primary sector (unskilled, janitorial, and assembly work). In World War II–era Detroit, primary sector employers, especially the auto and steel industries, discovered a readily available surplus of African American labor, particularly among new migrants from the South. Employers were more than willing to take advantage of that surplus, offering inferior jobs to black migrants, many of whom were desperate and grateful for employment in industries from which they had been systematically excluded before World War II.[2]

Also structuring race in the workplace were internal firm considerations. Employers were concerned about the costs of hiring, training, and placing new groups of workers. In the short run, personnel managers sometimes found it easier to exclude whole classes of workers to simplify hiring procedures or to minimize the costs of training. Race became a proxy for a number of characteristics that they believed would affect the efficiency of a work force and the profitability of a firm. Many employers, basing their decisions on racial stereotypes, assumed that black workers would be unproductive, prone to high absenteeism, and unreliable. Finally, managers often based their decision whether or not to hire an African American on their assumptions about the impact of racial mixing on the camaraderie of the shop floor. For example, if managers feared that white workers would strike or lose morale if the color line were breached, they might be reluctant to hire blacks. Such considerations were especially important in small, paternalistically organized companies that valued homogeneity and often tapped kinship or friendship networks to find workers.[3]

Employers were not alone in shaping firms' racial policy. Labor markets were also structured by workers' culture, attitudes, customs, and work rules. When workers formed a sense of "brotherhood" on the shop floor, they often defined it through the practice of racial and gender exclusion. But how effective exclusion was—and what forms it took—depended on whether or not workers were unionized, and what racial politics their unions practiced. Racially progressive unions could—and sometimes did—challenge corporate hiring and internal labor market policies. But the effectiveness of union antidiscrimination efforts depended on the willingness of union leadership to support civil rights initiatives and the cooperation or resistance of workers. Union-negotiated rules on matters like seniority and apprenticeship often fostered racial and gender segmentation and exclusion.

Racial ideology and culture, politics, labor market structures, and internal firm dynamics all interacted in shaping patterns of black employment. Managers, union members, and individual employees all brought racial perceptions and racial politics with them to the job. Each of these actors brought to the table a particular set of ideological and political views, which were, to one degree or another, structured by macro- and microeconomic forces. Workplace discrimination was widespread but not universal, either during the war or afterward. Its causes and manifestations varied enormously from workplace to workplace. A close examination of race in a number of Detroit's crucial industries—automobile manufacturing, steel making, machine tool production, retail work, city employment, and construction labor—adds several layers of complexity to theoretical discussions of discrimination, revealing a dense and tangled web of forces that kept blacks, in the aggregate, entrapped in Detroit's worst, most insecure jobs.

Screening by Race: Employment Agencies and Ads

A small number of workers—black and white—found jobs through listings at unemployment offices, through private employment agencies, and through want ads. Until the state of Michigan passed a Fair Employment Practices Law in 1955, employers regularly specified racial preferences in job listings. Racial classifications were ubiquitous in job orders placed with state agencies. The Michigan State Employment Service (MSES) reported that in December 1946, 35.1 percent of all job orders placed in its offices contained discriminatory clauses, rising to 44.7 percent in April 1947, and 65 percent in June 1948. The trend toward discriminatory hiring continued through the early 1950s. In 1951, 55.5 percent of job orders placed with the Michigan Employment Security Commission (the successor to the MSES) "were closed to non-whites by written specifications."[4] Even employers seeking unskilled labor, the types of jobs historically most open to blacks, consistently refused to consider hiring black workers. In May 1948, the MSES reported that three-fourths of listings for unskilled jobs were closed to blacks. At the same time, 67.5 percent of all unemployed unskilled workers registered with the MSES were nonwhite. An inquiry into employment practices in 1948 reported that "Discrimination in hiring is on the increase. . . . Despite a serious labor shortage in Detroit, employers refuse to employ qualified non-white workers."[5]

One Detroit company which sought four thousand workers during the labor shortage in early 1949 requested only white workers, despite the large number of available black workers in the city. State employment officials were unable to fill the company's demand for 250 referrals per day with white workers alone, yet the company refused to consider hiring blacks. The unwillingness of employers to hire nonwhite workers, despite a readily available surplus of black workers, was again clear in 1951: in one month of acute labor shortage, 508 unskilled jobs, 423 semiskilled jobs, and 719 skilled jobs listed in Detroit MSES offices went unfilled, although 874 unskilled, 532 semiskilled, and 148 skilled black applicants were available for immediate employment. In many cases employers recruited out-of-state workers before considering hiring local blacks.[6]

Blacks who sought work through the city's numerous private employment agencies faced equally daunting obstacles. Through the mid-1950s, employment agencies listed in Detroit's yellow pages carried the designations "Colored" and "White." Most "Colored" agencies catered to employers seeking domestic and other service workers. Many job listings in Detroit's major newspapers also specified "white" or "colored"; and occasionally "American" and "Protestant." Small employers were most likely to include race preferences in their want ads. All in all, however, employment agencies and newspaper advertisements played a relatively small role in postwar Detroit's divided labor market. And in 1955, racial preferences in advertising became illegal under state law. More important were the actions of firms, unions, and workers at the employment office, in the hiring hall, and on the shop floor.[7]

The Automobile Industry

The motor vehicle industry was the single largest employer in mid-twentieth-century Detroit, providing a quarter to a third of all jobs in the city. It was also the city's largest employer of blacks. At the outbreak of World War II, blacks made up only 4 percent of the auto work force; by 1945, they comprised 15 percent; by 1960, they made up about 16 percent of the work force. By any measure, auto work paid well. The average earnings of workers in the automobile industry were significantly greater than those of employees of other manufacturing concerns, and of nonmanufacturing workers. By the late 1940s, the fruits of collective bargaining between the UAW and the major automobile companies offered workers a pay package and benefits that were almost unsurpassed in American industry. And union-negotiated seniority rules meant that auto work was more stable and secure than many other jobs.[8]

But if auto work offered blacks their greatest opportunities in the postwar era, it was also the source of some of their greatest frustrations. Black auto workers faced formidable discriminatory barriers at some plants and relatively few at others. Many black workers found the automobile industry's hiring practices bewildering and unpredictable. The location and rigidity of the color line varied widely. At times, employers discriminated and unions resisted discrimination. Some plants had large numbers of blacks; others had very few. Sometimes UAW locals were in the vanguard of civil rights, sometimes they blatantly disregarded the rights of African American workers. The experience of blacks in the auto industry revealed in microcosm the complexity of race relations in this era of flux.

The uneven opportunities for blacks in Detroit auto plants are most evident in a comparison of plant-level employment statistics. Even as the proportion of blacks in auto manufacturing remained high, black workers were well represented in certain plants, and underrepresented in others. Statis-

tics on black employment in major plants in 1960 make clear the capriciousness of decentralized hiring practices (Table 4.1). The number of blacks employed at Chrysler plants ranged from a handful to nearly 50 percent. Two
General Motors plants had a mere six black workers while at another over
60 percent of employees were black. Blacks found employment in large
numbers at Chevrolet plants, whereas Fisher Body plants tended to be
heavily white. General Motors generally hired more blacks in its center-city
plants, whereas Chrysler was as likely to employ blacks in its suburban as in
its city plants.

What is most striking about these statistics is the arbitrary distribution of
blacks. It might be expected, for example, that plants with a high number of
skilled workers would have a smaller percentage of blacks. That is in part
true: Fisher Body Plants 23 and 37, for example, had large numbers of
skilled workers and virtually no black employees. But the occupational composition of plants with few blacks and those with a large number of black
workers was generally similar.[9] The difficulty of the tasks demanded of semiskilled operatives and laborers differed little at the Fisher Body Livonia
Plant which employed few blacks and the Chevrolet plants which employed
many. In only two cases can the high proportion of white employees be
explained by educational differences between blacks and whites. The General Motors Tech Center and Chrysler Engineering Centers, both centers of
research and development, employed highly educated white-collar workers,
especially engineers and design specialists, with college and postgraduate
degrees in business, science, and engineering.

Plant location mattered surprisingly little in auto industry hiring. Livonia,
an all-white suburb west of Detroit, had two General Motors plants, one
with a work force over two-fifths black, the other with virtually no blacks at
all. Likewise, black employment at plants in Warren, an all-white suburb
north of Detroit, ranged from one-tenth to one-quarter. The only plant
whose location can explain the lack of black workers was Chrysler's Chelsea
facility, which was in a heavily white rural area more than forty-five miles
west of Detroit. Within the limits of Detroit, black employment in auto
plants also ranged from one in fifty at the Fisher Body Plant 53 to three out
of five at Chevrolet Forge.

Why the variations? The answer can be found in large part in the discretion that company officials exercised at the hiring gate. Within the automobile companies, hiring practices were decentralized, leading to wide variations in black employment from plant to plant. Often the whim of a single
plant manager or entrenched practice in a particular factory limited black
opportunities in certain plants. Louis Seaton, a General Motors vice president, stated that his company left hiring to the discretion of "the individual
divisions, and other employing units of the corporation."[10] The lack of over-
sight in hiring practices meant that personnel managers in individual plants

TABLE 4.1
Black Workers in Detroit-Area Automobile Plants, 1960

	Total	Total Black	Percent Black
GENERAL MOTORS (total)	39,723	9,185	23
Cadillac, Detroit	8,400	2,100	25
Detroit Transmission, Warren	4,700	658	14
Detroit Diesel, Romulus	1,549	451	29
Fisher Body, Livonia	2,384	20	1
Fisher Body 23, Detroit	915	15	2
Fisher Body 37, Detroit	185	6	3
Fisher Body Fleetwood, Detroit	3,900	650	17
Ternstedt Division, Detroit	4,000	502	13
Chevrolet Forge, Detroit	1,407	845	60
Chevrolet Gear and Axle, Detroit	6,500	3,270	50
Chevrolet Spring and Bumper, Livonia	1,630	662	41
General Motors Tech Center, Warren	4,153	6	0
CHRYSLER (total)	41,892	10,759	26
Dodge Main, Hamtramck	7,500	3,375	45
Chrysler Jefferson, Detroit	3,000	669	22
Dodge Forge, Detroit	1,000	300	30
Plymouth Assembly, Detroit	2,300	506	22
Plymouth Engine, Detroit	1,000	150	15
Dodge Truck, Detroit	1,800	360	20
Amplex, Detroit	297	32	11
Automotive Body Division, Detroit	9,700	1,649	17
Imperial (export and glass), Detroit	1,410	465	33
Trenton Engine, Trenton	3,077	923	30
Engineering (hourly), Highland Park	3,100	124	4
Highland Park	2,200	814	37
Nine Mile Press, Warren	1,560	343	22
Lynch Road, Detroit	1,529	739	48
Detroit Tank, Warren	536	145	27
Michigan Missile, Warren	1,148	115	10
MoPar	470	56	12
Chelsea	265	3	1
FORD (total)	n.a.[a]	n.a.[a]	n.a.[a]
River Rouge	30,000	12,500	40
Steel Division (part of Rouge)	5,550	1,650	30
Mound Road, Sterling Township	5,600	n.a.[a]	38

Source: United States Commission on Civil Rights, *Hearings Held in Detroit, Michigan, December 14–15, 1960* (Washington, D.C.: U.S. Government Printing Office, 1961), 63–65, data submitted by UAW. Ford Steel Division figures are from Job Development Quarterly Report, DUL, Box 56, Folder A20–10.

[a] Employment totals for all Detroit-area Ford plants were not submitted to the commission. Likewise, incomplete data were submitted for the Ford Mound Road plant.

could establish arbitrary criteria for the hiring and upgrading of minorities. In 1954, several blacks complained to the Detroit NAACP that they had been turned away from the gates of Detroit-area Chrysler plants. The complaint gained legitimacy because of the statement of a Chrysler official that "We are not employing Negroes; we may employ a few when the situation becomes desperate enough."[11] The Michigan Employment Security Commission also reported in December 1954 that it was still receiving job orders from some Chrysler plants that specified white only, despite the Chrysler headquarters' promise to avoid discriminatory language in job orders. Even plants with large numbers of black workers sometimes turned away black applicants arbitrarily. At the Ford River Rouge plant, for example, a UAW official complained in 1950 that the company was only hiring new white employees.[12]

Plant personnel managers had a number of rationalizations for refusing to hire black workers. At predominantly white plants, management was reluctant to risk disrupting the workplace by hiring blacks. There is also evidence that plant managers followed custom in their hiring practices. Racial patterns at certain plants were institutionalized during World War II and changed little thereafter. In 1940, for example, General Motors' Fisher Body plants were "well known for their 'lily-white' policy," and in 1960, Fisher Body plants were still largely white. Plants with large black work forces in the 1940s, like Chevrolet Spring and Bumper, Dodge Main, and Chevrolet Forge, remained heavily black in 1960.[13] At other plants, management refused to consider blacks for positions in white-dominated departments. And they refused to challenge male-dominated job classifications by hiring women, particularly African American women. Many managers apparently believed that racial homogeneity on the shop floor was essential to worker morale. The rash of wartime hate strikes in Detroit automobile factories, precipitated by the upgrading of black workers, made employers fearful of disrupting the status quo. Although the UAW swiftly suppressed each hate strike in the postwar era by supporting the expulsion of leaders and participants, the possibility of racial unrest, slowdowns, and strikes remained real in the minds of employers.[14]

Employers were also often chary about the dedication of black workers to their jobs. Given the rising demand for labor in Detroit during and after World War II, large companies experienced frequent turnover in their work forces, when workers who were not satisfied with their jobs or work conditions simply quit and sought work elsewhere. Yet, for reasons that are not clear, employers exaggerated the danger of high black turnover. The best available evidence, the Ford Motor Company employment records surveyed by Thomas Maloney and Warren Whatley, show that black workers were actually more stable than their white counterparts.[15] It is quite possible that employers like Ford simply held black workers to a higher standard than whites, knowing that they could easily replace unproductive black workers.

Given the fears of high black turnover, black job applicants, more so than whites, had to take extra steps to demonstrate to prospective employers their willingness to work. Jordon Sims, a recent high-school graduate seeking auto work in the late 1940s, discovered that blacks were more likely to be hired if they made repeat visits to company employment offices. When Sims sought work with Chrysler, plant hiring officials told him that they were not hiring, although the company offered jobs to many of his white acquaintances. The key to success was "to come back the following week, and the week after that if it's necessary, to let the man know that you sincerely want to work."[16]

Once hired, blacks found themselves placed in the least desirable jobs, disproportionately in unskilled and semiskilled sectors, usually in the dirtiest and most dangerous parts of the plant. Some employers based hiring decisions on straightforward racial antipathy. One auto company official hired blacks to work in the dangerous paint room. He explained his rationale: "Yes, some jobs white folks will not do; so they have to take niggers in, particularly in duce work, spraying paint on car bodies. This soon kills a white man." Asked if it killed blacks, he responded, "It shortens their lives, it cuts them down but they're just niggers."[17] Employers held contradictory views about the ability and discipline of black workers. Implicit in the decision of large manufacturers who often placed black employees in the most demanding and dangerous jobs was the assumption that blacks were singularly capable of the most physically demanding work. But most importantly, employers took advantage of the insecure position of blacks in the labor market to place black workers in undesirable jobs. Black workers who had experienced discrimination in the past were more likely to accept jobs that white workers, with a wider range of employment options, would summarily reject. And for many black migrants from the South, the worst factory jobs were better than the immiseration they had left behind.[18]

Not all black workers, however, accepted the dangerous, inferior jobs offered them in Detroit's factories. Some workers, either unaccustomed to the rigorous demands of the highly mechanized automobile industry or resentful of their inferior jobs, chafed at the routine of the assembly line. Others resisted domineering and racially biased foremen and managers. H. Matheny, a Chrysler vice president during World War II, noted that many foundry workers "are shirking on the job"; E. T. Weiniger, personnel director at Dodge Main, noted that many black workers "have some trouble getting adjusted and they ruin many tools."[19] Yet employers made similar complaints about southern white workers, many of whom had even less industrial labor experience than black migrants who often had worked as seasonal laborers in the lumber or tar industries, or who had come to Detroit with experience in the steel or shipbuilding industries in the South. But discrimination against white southerners was sporadic; most benefited from their whiteness and were able to vanish into an increasingly undifferentiated white working class. In contrast, black shirking and soldiering on the job often reinforced racial stereotypes, and firms continued to recruit and hire whites in preference to blacks. Many black migrants shared the experience of black worker Charles Denby who, despite his background in the Mobile shipyards, was summarily rejected for a riveting job in Detroit in favor of a white migrant from Tennessee who, bemused at his fortune, told Denby that he "just come in from the fields.".[20]

As a result of discrimination at the hiring gate, blacks remained overrepresented in unskilled occupations, were most susceptible to layoffs, and most vulnerable to replacement when plants automated. Unfortunately, no data exist on the departmental breakdown of blacks working within each plant for the late 1940s and 1950s—data that could help explain plant-by-plant differences. That blacks were disproportionately represented at plants with forges (Chevrolet Forge, Dodge Main, and Ford River Rouge) supports the hypothesis that they remained concentrated in certain unpleasant and high-risk jobs. Companies seldom hired blacks in certain job classifications, and auto company work orders regularly requested black or white workers for particular jobs. Not until 1952 did Chevrolet, Chrysler, and Ford agree to stop sending discriminatory job orders to MESC, a gain achieved only "after exhaustive discussion of the issue" with MESC and Urban League officials.[21] Although they refrained from publishing race-specific job listings, companies continued to practice discrimination without fanfare. At the Ford Wayne assembly plant in 1953, for example, blacks were confined to difficult jobs in the body shop and on the final assembly line, and entirely excluded from the "nice, easy, soft jobs" in the trim and cushion department.[22]

Management jealously protected its absolute prerogative over hiring and promotion decisions. Although contracts allowed unions some control over work rules, grievance procedures, and seniority, employers' hiring decisions were sacrosanct well into the 1960s. Former black UAW official George Robinson recounted the difficulty of eradicating discrimination in the plants in the 1950s: "management, especially in Chevrolet, had taken a hard-nosed position, and there was nothing too much the union could do at the time."[23]

As a unionist, Robinson went too far in excusing the UAW for its reluctance to press recalcitrant employers to adopt antidiscrimination clauses and to hire and upgrade workers without regard to race. The UAW's record on race relations was mixed. On the national level, the UAW was on the cutting edge of civil rights activism throughout the 1940s, 1950s, and early 1960s. The UAW supported the creation of a permanent federal Fair Employment Practices Committee after World War II to extend the pioneering role of the wartime FEPC. Beginning in the early 1940s, the UAW funded black organizations, including the NAACP and CORE, sponsored conferences on civil rights, and offered support to civil rights protests. The UAW also backed open housing campaigns, and advocated integrated housing projects in white neighborhoods, despite the unpopularity of such efforts among white Detroiters, and many rank-and-file union members.[24]

Notwithstanding its progressive stand on national civil rights issues, the UAW's record in achieving racial equality in the workplace and in union offices was inconsistent. Officially, the union had no tolerance for blatant opposition within its ranks to black hiring and upgrading. During World War II, union leaders adamantly opposed the explosive outbreak of wildcat hate strikes over the promotion of black workers, ordered hate strikers back to work on pain of expulsion, and expelled strike leaders. And in the aftermath of World War II, the UAW established a Fair Practices Department, which handled discrimination grievances and served as a clearing house for civil rights education in the union.[25]

On the other hand, UAW locals varied widely in their commitment to African American equality. Hate strikes continued to erupt sporadically in auto plants well into the 1950s, and white rank-and-file union members, often abetted by local leaders, worked to protect the color line in many plants. The organizational structure of the UAW—especially its localism—permitted discriminatory practices to flourish on the shop floor. As a matter of principle and electoral expediency, UAW International officials were reluctant to interfere in the internal affairs of union locals. Reuther and other officials were especially loath to challenge the powerful skilled trades workers in the UAW, who often threatened to rebel against union leadership. The result was that separate seniority lists for blacks and whites—reflecting local custom and negotiated individually from plant to plant—limited the job advancement of black workers at a number of plants. In addition, white local officials often ignored charges of racial discrimination filed by black workers.[26]

While the UAW had a mixed record in supporting integration on the shop floor, it moved at an even slower pace to integrate the ranks of union leadership. In plants with sizable black work forces, disproportionately few blacks held union posts. In some locals, like UAW Local 3, which represented workers at Dodge Main, white officials gerrymandered elections to dilute black votes and influence. Local practices shadowed what occurred at UAW headquarters. Blacks were underrepresented in high-level union positions through the 1960s, and it took the extraordinary efforts of the Trade Union Leadership Council, a black-led union reform movement, to persuade the UAW to appoint a black to the union's executive board.[27]

Most significantly, the UAW, despite its oft-stated support for fair employment practices, failed to make nondiscrimination a major issue in contract negotiations, and directed its energies to seniority clauses, higher wages, and comprehensive benefits packages. As early as 1946, George Crockett, head of the UAW's Fair Practices Department, criticized union leadership for its failure to press General Motors for an antidiscrimination clause in contract negotiations.[28] Walter Reuther, in his testimony to the United States Commission on Civil Rights fifteen years later, claimed that the union "spent some of the most precious hours of our collective bargaining time" pushing for a fair employment clause. Ultimately, faced with strike deadlines, the UAW did not press hard on the issue, probably because union leaders knew that antidiscrimination policies did not have widespread support among the white rank and file.[29] As a matter of principle, the UAW also placed economic issues that affected the bulk of the rank and file ahead of race-specific measures. Writing of the 1940s, militant unionist Charles Denby recalled that "Reuther says Negroes shouldn't raise any problems about Negroes as Negroes in the union. He says they should raise the questions about workers in general."[30] Ultimately, it was this rationale that prevented the UAW in the postwar decades from using its organizational clout to force employers to hire and upgrade black workers without discrimination.

The one area in auto employment where racial discrimination was almost complete was the skilled trades, such as tool and die makers and electricians. The skilled trades included about 15 percent of auto workers. Both unions and management bore responsibility in varying degrees for the almost complete exclusion of African Americans from the crafts. Among the demands that the UAW successfully negotiated into its contracts was the establishment of some union control over the hiring of skilled apprentices. The first UAW-Ford contract in 1941 established a Joint Apprenticeship Committee, consisting of union and management representatives, which had the power to accept or reject applicants. Ford did, however, protect its managerial prerogative for a time. Applicants went before the Joint Committee only after "preliminary examination and approval by the Personnel Director of the Company." The program also gave preference to graduates of the Henry Ford Trade School.[31] Ford prided itself on its apprenticeship program, one of the largest and oldest in the industry. The Henry Ford Trade School, a centerpiece of Ford's social reform efforts, had trained young men for the crafts since 1916; the Apprentice School at the Rouge plant, created in 1923, provided the company with another source of skilled workers.[32] By offering the union some control over admission to its apprenticeship programs, Ford preserved the pride of craft among its skilled workers, while simultaneously maintaining its corporate power over hiring.

Auto industry apprenticeship requirements varied from company to company and changed over time. Throughout the 1940s and early 1950s, international union guidelines recommended a hiring system similar to that established at Ford. Corporation personnel staff screened applications and the Joint Apprenticeship Committee gave "final approval."[33] At Chrysler, applications went to the company's Department of Industrial Education or its Personnel Department. There the contract specified preferential treatment to "sons and close relatives of employees and to individuals of the local community." General Motors also gave preference to sons of employees, and required that applicants provide the names of relatives who worked at the company.[34] By 1955, however, it appears that Ford relinquished its prerogative over the hiring of apprentices and gave full responsibility to the Joint Committee.[35] In each case, the hiring of apprentices was a cooperative union-management effort, in which both parties achieved a delicate balance between maintaining management's hiring prerogatives and allowing skilled trades a degree of autonomy and exclusivity. Both left blacks and women out.

Apart from apprenticeship, however, the power to hire remained firmly in the hands of corporation officials. Firms staunchly opposed antidiscrimination clauses in contracts, state fair employment legislation, and federal antidiscrimination legislation on the grounds that it interfered with management's rights to employ whomever it wanted. Thus, before the passage of civil rights laws, neither unions nor the government oversaw hiring practices. Personnel decisions were discretionary, based solely on the judgment of hiring officials. The Big Three auto companies rejected the union-proposed antidiscrimination contract clause on the grounds that the union "cannot bargain for persons not yet employed."[36]

Once blacks were hired, the contract provision that affected their employment patterns most was seniority. Seniority rationalized corporate hiring and firing practices by making length of service the primary criterion for layoff and rehiring. Seniority also served as a basis for promotion to better-paying jobs. Above all, seniority provided job security for a segment of the work force that had once been vulnerable to employers' arbitrary layoff policies. The privileges of seniority also made possible promotion from unskilled to semiskilled or supervisory jobs. In the aftermath of the Great Depression, seniority became a linchpin of labor contracts. In the automobile industry, seniority was, for the most part, divided by department or company division (for example, assembly work, engine production, foundry work, inspection, tool and die), and often within divisions to workers with specific responsibilities, what contracts called "non-interchangeable occupational groups."[37]

Seniority had tremendous potential to eliminate discriminatory practices, yet it could also work to reinforce the barriers of race and sex. To blacks' advantage, it curbed employers' tendency to indulge their racial prejudice by selectively firing blacks. The first blacks to be hired by the automobile companies benefited enormously from seniority. Black workers themselves recognized the importance of seniority for their opportunity: during World War II, black workers were less likely to lead wildcat strikes for fear of losing their hard-won seniority.[38] Seniority safeguarded their niche in industry, since workers were laid off on the basis of length of employment, rather than on arbitrary grounds like race. In the case of women workers, however, the seniority system failed altogether. Union and company officials viewed women's work as temporary, and refused to defend women's seniority rights during the wartime reconversion. Women were invariably assigned to separate seniority lines, with separate pay schedules, reflecting and hardening the gendered division of labor that prevailed in auto work. The result was that the tentative gains that women—black and white—made during the war were rolled back when male veterans returned to reclaim their old jobs.[39]

For the vast majority of blacks who were hired in the postwar period, seniority had mixed results. Seniority tended to reinforce the traditional hiring pattern of black workers—last hired and first fired. The flurry of layoffs at the end of World War II affected black workers disproportionately, for most had been hired since 1942 and had not accumulated much seniority. That a greater percentage of black workers suffered from the postwar reconversion layoffs demonstrated the double-edged consequences of seniority in an industry that had long excluded blacks but was beginning to change. Because the automobile industry continued to grow in the late 1940s and early 1950s, however, seniority protected a growing number of black workers from the insecurity of layoffs. But the generation of workers who entered the automobile factories in the early 1950s found seniority less beneficial to them, as they were most vulnerable to the waves of layoffs that hit Detroit between 1953 and 1961. Seniority created an elite stratum of securely employed blacks, but hurt the career prospects of those workers who entered the auto industry as it began to restructure and reduce the size of its work force.

Seniority had its most pronounced effects on promotions. Because the auto industry confined black workers to disproportionately black sections of the plants, with separate, dead-end job classifications, upward mobility was nearly impossible. White workers got the lion's share of seniority-based promotions. Departmental and occupational seniority rules entrapped black workers in the departments in which they had been hired, and afforded them no opportunity to move from one department to another or from one occupation to another. Efforts to replace departmental seniority with plant-wide seniority gained support from neither management nor unions. And left-labor calls for "flexible" or "preferential" seniority to protect recently hired blacks and maintain racial balance in the workplace (an interesting precursor of affirmative action) never gained adherents outside of Communist circles.[40]

Blacks found it difficult to move out of unskilled and semiskilled positions in automotive plants, and were virtually absent from ranks of craftsmen,

skilled operatives, and supervisors. In 1954, a mere 43 blacks held management positions in the automobile industry. Only 24 of 7,425 skilled Chrysler
workers and only 67 out of 11,125 skilled General Motors workers in 1960
were black. Even after civil rights groups put pressure on the automobile
companies to upgrade black workers, companies frequently promoted a
token black or two to offer evidence of their openness. Among Ford's
"white-collar" positions open to blacks in 1963 were valets, porters, security
guards, messengers, barbers, mail clerks, and telephone operators.[41]

Throughout the postwar period discrimination in the auto industry remained a Gordian knot. Intricately interwoven were the prejudices of company managers and union members. Decentralized hiring policies led to a
haphazard pattern of black opportunity. And discrimination was institutionalized in union practices and in customary divisions of the shop floor. The
inroads that African Americans made in the auto industry were undeniable:
blacks gained a permanent niche in auto work during and after World War
II. Black assembly-line workers, like their white counterparts, obtained a
relatively high standard of living because of high union-negotiated wages
and excellent fringe benefits. They became an aristocracy of labor among
the city's African American population, able to buy houses and move out of
the inner city. "Blacks working in the automobile industry," recalled black
Detroiter Clyde Cleveland, "were able to live a middle-class life." But a
patchwork of discriminatory practices persisted in the auto industry, limiting the opportunities of blacks in countless ways.[42]

Hiring Practices in Other Detroit Industries

The best opportunities for blacks outside of the automotive industry in Detroit came in the steel industry, where the 1940s marked an era of major
gain. The fifth largest steel-producing state in the country, Michigan's steel
production and employment patterns followed those of other major northeastern and midwestern steel producing cities. In 1940, only 4.2 percent of
the state's steelworkers (mainly concentrated in the Detroit area) were
black, a figure that rose to 17.9 percent in 1950. Most of the black gains came
during World War II; but once blacks made inroads into certain jobs, their
gains slowed. The percentage of black steelworkers stagnated in the 1950s,
rising to only 18.5 percent in 1960. As in the automobile industry, blacks
were disproportionately concentrated in unskilled and semiskilled jobs; virtually no blacks found employment as skilled craftsmen, the most lucrative
jobs in steel plants.[43]

Steel mill shop floors were intricately divided by race and ethnicity.
Charles Younglove, employed at Great Lakes Steel, the Detroit area's largest steel manufacturer, described the deeply entrenched ethnic niches in his

plant. Some department managers preferred members of the same fraternal organization or Catholic parish, others hired predominantly from a single ethnic group. As he recalled, "if you weren't Italian you couldn't get in the millwright gang in the open hearths; and if you *were* Italian you couldn't get in the soaking pits." At the bottom of the rung were blacks, a small part of the work force, largely confined to the dangerous, scalding hot blast furnaces or to unskilled maintenance jobs.[44]

The United Steelworkers of America (USWA), like the UAW, vocally supported civil rights legislation, funded national civil rights organizations, and sponsored civil rights conferences for its members. But as with the UAW, the gap between official union policy and local practice was often large. In a 1950 USWA civil rights survey, one Detroit local reported that there was only "slight variation" in the range of jobs open to blacks since unionization. Most locals denied practicing discrimination, but provided little evidence of race-blind policies. And one local unwittingly betrayed the actual state of affairs, reporting that "We haven't any jobs for the minority groups," and that somehow, at the same time, "We don't have any racial discrimination at our shops." Blacks in steel, like their counterparts elsewhere in the country, remained confined in the most strenuous and dangerous jobs.[45]

By 1965, blacks had established beachheads in steel industry employment in Detroit; 18 percent of the metropolitan area's nonautomotive steelworkers were black. But as in the case of the automobile industry, the number of blacks employed in different plants ranged widely (Table 4.2). Although the black population was large, only two firms had greater than 20 percent black work forces: Great Lakes Steel and Detroit Steel. Salaried positions were largely unavailable to blacks: of the 159 blacks who held salaried jobs in the industry, 150 were employed by Great Lakes Steel.

Detroit's chemical industry likewise employed few blacks. Most of the metropolitan area's chemical plants were in the downriver area, in the all-white industrial suburbs of Southgate, Wyandotte, Trenton, Riverview, and Grosse Ile. Although most chemical workers were classified as semiskilled, chemical work required more technical training and skill than assembly-line work. In many respects, chemical work was organized like a skilled craft. Barriers to employment were greater than in the automobile industry: job applicants had to pass a preemployment test. But it was not test scores that prevented blacks from being hired by chemical firms. Instead it was hiring practices. Wyandotte Chemical Company was typical. Joseph Kanthack, President of Oil, Chemical, and Atomic Workers Local 11–627, which represented Wyandotte Chemical Company employees, reported that "very few Negroes make application for employment in this chemical industry." The company hired primarily local residents, but did not recruit in black communities in nearby Ecorse, River Rouge, and southwest Detroit. Above all, hiring officials relied on personal references. Kanthack noted that "it is not

TABLE 4.2
Black Workers in Selected Detroit-Area Steel Plants, 1965

	Total	Total Black	Percent Black
Great Lakes Steel	10,500	2,400	22.9
McLouth Steel	4,600	453	9.8
Jones and Laughlin	1,610	260	16.0
Kasle Steel and Aluminum	350	25	7.1
Detroit Steel	290	76	26.2
Ryerson Steel	250	30	12.0
Bliss and Laughlin	155	0	0
Plymouth Steel	60	0	0
Total	17,815	3,244	18.2

Source: Job Development Quarterly Report, DUL, Box 56, Folder A20–10. I have excluded Ford Motor Company's Steel Division from the total; it is included in Table 4.1 above.

unusual to find a grandfather, father, and son employed in the plant." Segregated housing patterns reinforced discriminatory hiring practices. As a result, blacks made up only 3.2 percent of chemical workers in Detroit in 1950, and only 3.9 percent in 1960.[46]

Blacks were far less likely to be found in Detroit's secondary sector industries, notably small automotive parts plants, machine and tool companies, and local nonautomotive industries like brewing. In five breweries surveyed by the Detroit Urban League in 1950, only 39 out of 3,300 employees were black. Pfeiffer Brewing Company employed only three blacks out of a workforce of more than a thousand. Underrepresented in beer production and bottling, blacks were entirely absent from the ranks of shipping and delivery workers. Like Pfeiffers, E and B Brewery and even the National Brewing Company, which aggressively marketed its beers to Detroit blacks, had no black delivery truck drivers in the 1950s. Even in the wake of a boycott of National Bohemian in 1955, brewing industry practices changed little.[47]

The main cause of discrimination in the brewing industry was the importance of personal connections in hiring decisions. The Brewery Workers' Union, the primary hiring agent for beer manufacturers, was responsible for excluding blacks from production and driver-sales jobs. According to the union's 1955 contract with local breweries, employers had to report all job vacancies to the union, which supplied new workers from its own employment office. Prospective workers found their way to the union through references from friends and relatives. Here, housing segregation reinforced hiring discrimination. Because few blacks lived near whites, they had few opportunities to develop the relationships that would provide them access to jobs.

The brewing industry's hiring arrangements allowed employers to pass responsibility for nondiscriminatory hiring to the union, and the union to avoid charges of discrimination by reiterating its policy of relying on the references of union members. Urban League officials reported a "strong bottleneck" in its negotiations with the brewery union and brewers, and lamented the "buck-passing by all concerned." In 1955, the union did not place any of twenty-three black men, carefully selected by the Urban League's Vocational Services Department, in brewing jobs. Until 1957, Brewery Workers' Union officials refused to meet with officials of the Urban League to discuss hiring practices, and failed to respond to entreaties to admit blacks to union membership. Union recalcitrance ensured that blacks remained grossly underrepresented in brewing jobs. As late as 1962, a Detroit civil rights group complained that fewer than 120 blacks were among the brewing industry's 12,000 workers. Stroh's, Detroit's largest brewer, had 15 black employees out of a workforce of 1,435; Pfeiffer had tripled its number of black employees to a total of 9 out of about 700.[48]

Small manufacturers in Detroit tended to be more paternalistic in organization than large manufacturers. Often owned by a family or a partnership, small companies emphasized face-to-face contact with workers and placed much more emphasis on workplace amenities. Small manufacturers relied on word of mouth and employee recommendations to fill open positions in their plants. A 1961 survey of hiring practices found that 73 percent of companies with fewer than one hundred employees rated recommendations "important or very important" in job applications, compared to only 34 percent of larger companies.[49] These companies may not have consciously discriminated against blacks, but the consequence of referrals, given the segregation of blacks and whites throughout the metropolitan area, was the virtual exclusion of blacks from employment by small companies.

To take one example, few blacks could be found working in the machine and fabricated metals industries, Detroit's second and third largest sources of manufacturing employment. Only 1.7 percent of metropolitan Detroit's more than 44,000 workers in the machinery industry in 1950 were black; only 2.4 percent of the nearly 68,000 machinery workers in 1960 were black.[50] Most tool and die companies were small, run by families or partners who often participated in hiring decisions. These firms were often paternalistically organized, in many respects similar to nineteenth-century enterprises in which owners and managers played an important role in workplace relations, unmediated by layers of hierarchical management. It was to ensure a homogeneous work force that tool and die firms relied on employee recommendations, and on networks of friends and relatives. Despite their qualifications, as one tool and die course instructor reported, "colored men are not wanted in the field." The introduction of black workers would be an infringement on the "family" of the workplace.[51]

The obstinacy of machine tool employers was clear when Detroit Urban League official Francis Kornegay wrote to the secretary of the Automotive Tool and Die Manufacturers Association, arguing that the shortage of labor in the early 1950s compelled the hiring of black workers. Although Kornegay hoped that "some employers would be liberal because of a manpower need to accept Negro youth in the tool and die industry," his entreaties went unheeded.[52] Unions in the machine tool industry proved equally intransigent on the hiring of blacks. In UAW Local 155, for example, skilled white workers jealously protected their monopoly on well-paying crafts jobs by systematically denying blacks entry into apprenticeship programs. Although this violated international union regulations, neither the local nor the international enforced nondiscriminatory practices in tool and die apprenticeship programs throughout the postwar years.[53]

Blacks fared little better in larger auto parts and machine companies. The reluctance of these firms to hire blacks was reinforced by local union indifference to civil rights issues or rank-and-file hostility to blacks. At Champion Spark Plug's Ceramic Division in Detroit, the only black employees had been hired under the federal FEPC law during World War II. In a period of expansion between 1945 and 1951, the firm hired only two black workers. Champion officials were responsible for turning away black job-seekers at the hiring gate, but UAW Local 272 officials who represented workers at the spark plug plant did nothing to investigate or respond to allegations of discrimination there.[54]

Black workers faced even more inhospitable conditions at Ex-Cell-O, a major machinery manufacturer. The firm had a long-standing history of what NAACP officials called "flagrant job discrimination." Leaders of UAW Local 49, representing Ex-Cell-O workers, supported the principle of nondiscriminatory hiring and upgrading. In 1950, Local 49 officers complained when the firm failed to promote a black worker. Under pressure, Ex-Cell-O management promoted him "to a better job," but did little more. Complicating the picture, Ex-Cell-O's white rank and file fiercely resisted racial integration. When a skilled black worker was offered a job in an all-white department in 1951, 146 of the 149 white workers walked out in a hate strike and planned a work stoppage when they returned. Local 49 officials refused to support the strikers and the black worker kept his job, but race relations remained tense. The combination of company hiring policy and rank-and-file racism kept the doors at Ex-Cell-O virtually shut to blacks. More than a decade after the hate strike, the firm had barely improved its hiring practices, despite promises to eliminate discrimination. In 1962 black Ex-Cell-O workers complained that the company's managers "either overly place Negroes in certain classifications or pick one or two to place in different classes to say they don't discriminate." Ex-Cell-O's tokenism riled black workers. One complained that Ex-Cell-O promoted "the average white worker," but only upgraded blacks who were "exceptionally outstanding, above the white workers." He continued: "I deserve to be rated as any 'average' man, working with and being compared to 'average' men." Even in the civil rights era, white racial privileges remained firmly in place.[55]

Municipal Employment

Perhaps the most promising arena of opportunity for blacks in postwar Detroit was government employment. Here political calculations broke down long-standing racial barriers. In 1935, only 202 of Detroit's 23,684 municipal employees were black, and in 1940, only 396 of 30,324. The breakthrough for black workers came during the Second World War. By 1946, blacks comprised a remarkable 36 percent of city employees. Why the dramatic expansion? In part, the reason for the movement of blacks into city work resulted from the efforts of civil rights activist Snow Grigsby and his Civic Rights Committee, who put pressure on the city government to hire African Americans throughout the 1930s and early 1940s. But Grigsby's efforts amounted to little until Mayor Edward Jeffries came to office.

Jeffries, elected in 1939, was sympathetic to black demands for municipal employment, at least until the riot of 1943, when he shifted to the right on racial matters. In his first three years in office, Jeffries broke the barriers against black employment in dozens of city departments. His reasons were threefold. First, Jeffries made extraordinary efforts to distinguish himself from his predecessor Richard Reading, who had resigned in a corruption scandal after taking bribes from job-seekers. Second, and more important, Jeffries was an astute political operative who realized that he could cement the loyalty of Detroit's rapidly expanding black population by bringing them into city offices. Detroit's blacks had, after all, just joined the New Deal coalition, and Jeffries, like his Democratic counterparts in other major cities, rewarded them for their votes. Further contributing to black gains, the city lost white employees during World War II. Military service called away many city workers, and more importantly, city jobs became less attractive because they paid relatively poorly compared to defense industry jobs. As whites left for well-paying private-sector jobs, blacks filled the gap.[56]

If the city government showed remarkable flexibility in opening positions to blacks during the war, it did not entirely buck conventional racial wisdom. Four tracks of employment in city government were open to blacks. The first, and largest, was unskilled work. The vast majority of black city workers toiled as janitors, heavy laborers, groundskeepers, and sanitation men. Most of these jobs were unpleasant; many were part-time. In 1946, 4,450 of 8,037 black city employees were seasonal workers, primarily in the Departments of Public Works and Parks and Recreation. Blacks were offered such jobs, in

4.2. City employment was an important niche for African Americans beginning in the 1940s, although black municipal workers, like their counterparts in private industry, were largely restricted to the most unpleasant and poorly paying jobs like sanitation work.

part, because they bore the stigma of Depression-era relief programs. Several hundred more blacks worked as janitors, cleaners, building attendants, and boiler operators, all service jobs to which they had traditionally been confined. The second area was one in which blacks made a genuine breakthrough—city transportation jobs. At the end of World War II, 2,310 blacks were employed on the Detroit Street Railway (DSR), mainly as conductors and motormen, the result of a serious shortage of white workers and the liberal hiring policy of DSR head Fred Nolan. The third area was low-level clerical work, for which the city hired a tiny minority of blacks, primarily highly educated women. City clerical jobs for blacks, numbering under a hundred, were concentrated in departments like Public Health, Housing, and Welfare that served large numbers of black clients. The final area was primary education. About 187 blacks, most of them women, found employment as teachers in Detroit's several predominantly black elementary schools. Intermediate and secondary education, on the other hand, remained almost entirely white: only 29 blacks taught at these schools. The numbers increased gradually through the early 1950s, but blacks remained

grossly underrepresented in education-related positions. The police department also remained a white domain throughout the postwar era. In 1953,
Detroit had only 117 blacks in its police force all assigned to a few predominantly black precincts.[57]

The situation for black city workers had changed little by 1963, when 35.4
percent of city workers were black. Most were still concentrated in jobs at
the lower end of the occupational ladder. Two-thirds of black city employees
were still in unskilled work. Some had moved up to managerial positions,
but they were confined largely to the service departments where blacks had
been concentrated since 1946—sanitation, public works, parks and recreation, and welfare. The biggest gains came in education, a reflection of the
growing number of black-majority schools in Detroit. By the late 1960s,
nearly half of Detroit's public school teachers were African American, and a
large proportion of them were women. Particularly impressive were gains in
intermediate and high-school teaching, both of which attracted thousands of
blacks in the 1950s and 1960s as a new generation of liberal school adminis-
trators opened doors to them for the first time. And Detroit's Police and Fire
departments were slowly integrating, but remained overwhelmingly white.
Even if blacks remained concentrated in the least desirable municipal jobs,
however, unlike other service-sector jobs, these offered a high degree of
security and good benefits. Just as government had provided an employment niche for Irish immigrants at the turn of the century, so in the mid-
twentieth century it became a beachhead for blacks. The great irony for
blacks, however, was that city government by the 1960s would not be a
growth industry for much longer, as it had been in the late nineteenth and
early twentieth centuries. A declining municipal tax base and growing anti-
government sentiment diminished public-sector job opportunities as the
black working-age population continued to grow.[58]

Retail Sales

Blacks found very little employment in the postwar era in high-visibility jobs
that involved public contact, and remained grossly underrepresented in
sales jobs, compared to whites (see Appendix B). Their exclusion from retail
trade was not inconsequential. In 1950 and 1960, the retail sector provided
jobs for about one-seventh of all male Detroit workers, and more than one-
fifth of all female workers. Salespeople and counter clerks were the public
face of a firm, and store owners were especially sensitive about the interactions between their staff and customers. They believed that black sales
clerks would alienate white shoppers. By employing blacks, store owners
would have had to buck the pattern of segregation in the postwar city, where

whites had no regular contact with blacks. The barriers were even greater in opulent department stores and in shopping malls. A 1963 survey found that only 326 of 7,436 jobs in Detroit-area shopping malls were held by blacks. Only twenty blacks were salespeople; the remainder worked as porters, janitors, cleaners, shoe shiners, stockroom laborers. The employment of black salespeople from blue-collar or poor families would undermine the thoroughly bourgeois atmosphere of high-end retail shopping. In addition, most stores catered to a primarily female clientele, and were especially careful to avoid offending female customers. The presence of a black man in a sales position would affront the sexual conventions so intimately interwoven with race. Finally, store owners sometimes acted on their fears that black employees would steal from the cash register or pilfer store merchandise.[59]

The result was that retail firms that catered to whites either hired no blacks or placed them in behind-the-scenes jobs in the stockroom, or in jobs traditionally reserved for blacks that would not offend the sensibilities of white shoppers, like shoe shiners, janitors, and elevator operators. In the case of Kilgore and Hurd, a downtown retailer, the Urban League found the store's owners were reluctant to hire blacks because they had few black customers and because the store's owners believed that most blacks routinely pilfered. In fact Kilgore, a partner in the company, was so concerned about the potential damage to business if a black were seen on the premises that he refused to meet with an Urban League investigator inside the store. Kilgore answered his questions outdoors. A few stores with a large black clientele, notably Sam's Cut Rate, hired black salespeople by the early 1950s, but most other retailers refused to hire blacks for jobs that required interaction with white customers. Only 86 of 1,200 employees in Detroit's major men's clothing stores in Detroit in 1959 were black; no blacks held professional, managerial, or sales jobs. About 40 worked in stockhandling, shoe shining, or maintenance jobs.[60]

Blacks also found very little employment in chain grocery stores in the 1940s and 1950s, although certain stores that relied on black customers had some black cashiers and stockboys. When the Detroit Urban League surveyed Detroit grocery stores in 1954 and 1955, it found pervasive discrimination. The most integrated chain, King Cole Stores, which primarily served inner-city shoppers, employed about 110 blacks in a work force of eight hundred. Two other chains with stores in black sections of the city employed black workers, but these were largely token hirings. Nineteen of the twenty-six blacks employed in Detroit's seventeen A&P stores worked in three locations, all within three miles of downtown. All ten Big Bear supermarkets in the city had at least one black worker, although none had more than seven. Other large chains had few or no black workers. Kroger, one of Detroit's largest supermarket chains, with twelve stores, employed only five blacks citywide, and Wrigley, with fourteen stores, employed none. Smaller chains, LaRose, National, Food Fair, and Foodtown, employed only two blacks in their sixteen locations throughout Detroit.[61]

Small neighborhood grocery and convenience stores also hired few blacks. Stores and markets provided an especially important base of jobs for teenagers, often their first entry-level jobs. But the vast majority of those jobs went to whites. Many markets and small shops were family-run; employers turned to family members, relatives, and acquaintances for help. As in the machine tool industry, many small shopowners had personal contacts with each employee, and also relied on employee recommendations to find staff. A 1955 Urban League survey of markets in a heavily black section of the city, however, found virtually no black employees. Of the twenty-seven stores surveyed that hired teenage workers, all but seven ranked "recommendations from individuals you know personally" as the first or second most important factors in hiring decisions; sixteen rated it first. Without family connections or friends and neighbors already employed in supermarkets, young blacks found even entry-level checkout, stockroom, and bagging jobs entirely closed to them. Few blacks worked where they shopped. Fewer felt any loyalty to neighborhood stores. Only a decade after the survey, inner-city grocery stores were among the most prominent targets of young looters. White-owned and -operated stores were the most prominent businesses in Detroit's African American neighborhoods and the most convenient symbol of the systematic exclusion of blacks from whole sectors of the city's economy.[62]

The Building Trades

The sector of Detroit's labor market where discrimination was most entrenched was the building trades. Postwar Detroit was a veritable promised land for construction workers. In the late 1940s, the city had an enormous unmet demand for construction labor. Postwar housing construction boomed, as thousands of new houses, many of them underwritten by the Federal Housing Administration, the Home Owners' Loan Corporation, and the Veterans Administration, rose daily on vacant land in northeast and northwest Detroit and its booming suburbs. The erection of new automobile and defense plants in Warren, Livonia, and Willow Run demanded thousands of carpenters, electricians, plumbers, roofers, pipe fitters, painters, glaziers, brickmasons, plasterers, sheet metal workers, and common laborers. Postwar Detroit had a desperate shortage of building tradesmen, as a whole generation of workers was lost by the unemployment of the Great Depression and the demands of the defense industry and military during World War II. Yet few blacks found work in the skilled crafts.[63]

On the official record, at least, the construction industry was remarkably free of discriminatory hiring. In October 1947, Senator Joseph McCarthy called two leading Detroit contractors to testify before the Joint Committee on Housing about the city's housing shortage. Concerned with the dearth of building trades workers, McCarthy asked them to respond to allegations that blacks faced discrimination in the construction industry. The executive secretary of the Detroit Builders' Association stated: "I know of no restriction against a Negro." Rodney Lockwood, president of the Builders' Association, concurred that "There is no restriction either as a matter of policy or practice." Senator McCarthy, displaying none of his famous combativeness, took both men at their word and asked no follow up questions.[64]

Had John Crews testified, McCarthy's committee would have heard a different story. A black migrant to Detroit, Crews was rebuffed again and again in his search for construction work. His daughter Burneice Avery recalled:

> About eight o'clock he would try construction. They always had as many common laborers as they needed. . . . "Could he handle the machines? Any training as a brick mason?" These questions always made John angry because he knew this was their way of saying, "We can't use you." Everybody knew black men were not permitted to train on the machines or lay bricks. The union did not allow black apprenticeship.[65]

Even full training did not guarantee admission to the building trades. The Brick Masons and Plasterers were most open to hiring "the cream of the crop" of skilled black masons who had been trained in the South. Other unions were less open. Alan Morton, a successful electrical apprentice who was black, found that his credentials were not enough for admission to the electrical workers' union. Black electricians, reported the Urban League, faced the "critical and aggravating problem" that despite their skills, they could not get jobs because they were denied union cards.[66]

Like John Crews and Alan Morton, a large number of black Detroiters had come to the city seeking work in the crafts. Black migrants seemed an ideal source for construction labor. Many had extensive experience in construction in the South, especially in carpentry and masonry. And they did get construction employment—by 1960, the construction industry in Detroit was the third largest employer of black men, after the vehicle industry and retail trade. But the vast majority of blacks employed in construction worked as unskilled laborers and haulers, without union wages and benefits. They were especially vulnerable to layoffs and temporary unemployment. Despite the high demand for construction labor, blacks could not gain entry to permanent, unionized construction labor jobs. In 1951, the Detroit Mayor's Interracial Committee noted that "Negroes are conspicuous in their absence from the building trades."[67] The Urban League found in 1961 that blacks remained locked out of virtually every building trade union. Only "a few" blacks belonged to the International Brotherhood of Electrical Workers, one of the largest building trades unions in the city. No black plumbers had gained admission to the Plumbers and Steam Fitters Union. The only building trade union with a substantial number of black members was the Laborers Union, and most of them belonged to a local that was 90 percent black. In lieu of union membership, many blacks formed craft associations, such as the Electrical Association, but without union affiliation they lacked access to Detroit's most lucrative jobs. Detroit's patterns were by no means peculiar. In fact, levels of black apprenticeship and union membership were nearly identical in Detroit and other major American cities.[68]

The barriers that black construction workers faced began with apprenticeship. Admission to building trades apprenticeship programs in the late 1940s required a high-school diploma or its equivalent, a qualification that excluded most black migrants from the south. Crafts unions, however, regularly bent the rules for whites. According to Louis Goodenow of the Bricklayers Union, apprenticeship programs regularly accepted men (neither he nor anyone else interviewed mentioned women) with a seventh-grade education or greater. Admission under the relaxed standards, however, seems to have been discretionary. In many trades, apprentices had to be sponsored by a contractor. As a rule, apprentices could not be older than their early twenties, unless they were veterans or had "exceptional qualifications." Defense workers, regardless of the importance of their work to the war effort, and regardless of their prewar experience, could not shift to the trades at the end of the war if they were past the age of majority.[69] Few black men, however ready, could surmount these obstacles.

By the early 1950s, employers made apprenticeship requirements somewhat more flexible, in response to the shortage of young skilled workers. Most trades still required a high-school education, but many extended the age limit to the midtwenties, or in a few cases as high as thirty. Potential apprentices still had to run a gauntlet of applications, interviews, and tests, most of which deterred or excluded blacks. Young men applied for training through the Joint Apprenticeship Committee, composed of both union and management representatives. Over two-thirds of the crafts required a written promise of employment as a prerequisite for admission to apprentice training.[70] As an Urban League official stated in 1960, unions and management were "both culprits" in the pattern of discrimination in the workplace. "[G]entleman's agreements" between unions and management "perpetuate this kind of vicious circle" which prevented young blacks from entering apprenticeship programs.[71]

Statistics on apprenticeship enrollment make clear the magnitude of the exclusion of blacks from the construction industry (Table 4.3). Ten years

TABLE 4.3
Black Enrollment in Apprenticeship Programs in Detroit, 1957–1966

	Total Apprentices	Black Apprentices	Percent Black
1957	3,009	59	2.0
1960	2,000	36	1.8
February 1962	1,314	10	0.8
June 1963	1,341	12	0.9
October 1963	1,623	22	1.4
June 1964	1,585	28	1.8
October 1964	1,902	34	1.8
June 1965	2,056	34	1.7
October 1965	2,321	44	1.9
February 1966	2,363	41	1.7

Sources: 1957 and 1960: "Apprenticeship Data (Detroit Area)," DUL, Box 47, Folder A11–27; all other dates from Ray Marshall and Vernon M. Briggs, Jr., *The Negro and Apprenticeship* (Baltimore: Johns Hopkins University Press, 1967), 139.

after the onset of the national civil rights movement, and eight years after Michigan passed a statewide Fair Employment Practices act, blacks remained effectively shut out of well-paying, skilled, and unionized jobs in the construction trades. Whether in union or public-school apprenticeship programs, black enrollments were, in the words of a labor activist, "quite dismal."[72]

The building trades have served as the classic example of a segment of the American working class steeped in prejudice. The dark side of the working-class community that thrived in the skilled trades was xenophobia and exclusivity. The "barons of labor" in the building trades were a self-styled aristocracy of workers who protected their whiteness at the expense of blacks and Asians. American Federation of Labor (AFL) craft unions had a long history of exclusion, and union leadership was generally unsupportive of attempts to admit minorities as members with full privileges. Craft union leaders reinforced the attitudes of their members in their refusal to combat discrimination in union ranks.[73]

Members of the Detroit's building trades in part followed a path that had been established well before the 1940s. In the postwar period they perpetuated their unions' long-held policy of discrimination. But historical racism alone did not determine the shape of Detroit's construction industry labor market. In other industries, employers and unions shared some degree of racial prejudice, but incorporated blacks into their work forces with less resistance than did the building trades. The story is more complicated. Explanations that ascribe workplace discrimination to individual racism or to the AFL's history of racial exclusion overlook the subtle combination of cultural and economic forces at work in the postwar era that reinforced the trades' discriminatory history.

The culture of construction workers helps to explain the exclusion of blacks from skilled labor. Perhaps most important in shaping the construction labor market was the powerful sense of brotherhood among construction workers, a masculine identity reinforced by close relationships with fellow workers both in and outside the workplace. Working relatively unsupervised, on jobs that were often physically demanding and hazardous, construction workers bonded in a solidarity of the trenches, one that valued risk taking and machismo. The fraternal atmosphere of the trades was, in large part, the result of the wholesale exclusion of women. But construction workers' bonds were even stronger because they were forged outside of the workplace as well as at the job site. Union recruiting practices strengthened workers' sense of brotherhood. More so than most other occupations, contractors and unions relied on personal references to hire apprentices. Sons of construction laborers, relatives, and neighbors received the highest priority on hiring. Employers often did not publicize job openings; they did not use ads or employment agencies to recruit. Instead, they simply passed the word of openings along to their families, friends, and staff. Systematic nepotism guaranteed that members of particular ethnic groups and extended families enjoyed unusual access to crafts jobs. The importance of friendship and kin networks in the building trades also served as a nearly insurmountable barrier for black workers because virtually no blacks and whites lived in the same neighborhoods or belonged to the same churches and clubs and even fewer intermarried.[74]

Blacks were not excluded from the building trades simply for cultural reasons, however. Perhaps the most significant reason for the exclusion of blacks after the war was the artificial monopoly that ready-trained tradesmen had on the construction market. Contractors and union construction workers, after suffering the vicissitudes of the Depression and war, found themselves profiting handsomely from the postwar boom. Housing prices in postwar Detroit rose phenomenally in the years following World War II, in part because of overcrowding, but also in part because of the lack of material and labor. In the tight market, skilled workers commanded high wages. Building tradesmen had it in their interest to restrict entry into their craft. Restriction also guaranteed that in lean times, union members would have a corner on the labor market. Either way, by restricting the number of skilled workers, white craftsmen eliminated much potential competition for jobs. The Detroit Branch of the NAACP argued that the trades had constructed a "vocational iron curtain" which protected a "self-contained monopoly for white labor."[75]

The Casual Labor Market

The form that building trades discrimination took was a direct consequence of the structure of Detroit's labor market. Because black men suffered high unemployment rates and were especially vulnerable to layoffs in other Detroit industries, they formed an easily exploitable labor surplus, desperate for work. Taking advantage of the ready supply of black men, many white construction workers subcontracted black workers for a fraction of the regular hourly wage. The black workers who assisted white workers did not threaten their monopoly over high wages and, because of their clearly inferior status, did not challenge the rough culture of masculinity that prevailed on job sites. It is likely that having a black hand on the job buttressed white construction workers' sense of independence and masculinity; by supervising black day laborers, white workers became temporary bosses.[76]

Casual labor reinforced patterns of racial discrimination, and entrapped many blacks in a cycle of deprivation. Because blacks were hired temporarily, they were more vulnerable to the cyclical fluctuations of the construction industry than the workers who hired them; their jobs were day-to-day rather than week-to-week. Black construction workers in Detroit followed a pattern of adaptation to the labor market familiar to them from the South. As Jacqueline Jones argues, they "scuffled," holding a series of temporary jobs, none of them well-paying, but together enough to allow them to patch together a subsistence-level income.[77] The fact that black construction workers were trapped in a casual labor market explains the extraordinary $2,228 gap in median earnings between black and white construction laborers in metropolitan Detroit in 1960. The per capita annual income of blacks in the building trades was a mere $3,530, just above the poverty line for a family of three; whites made an average of $5,758, enough to place them in the top half of Detroit's income range.[78]

Detroit's black day laborers gathered at an informal outdoor labor market on the city's periphery, known to local whites as the "slave market." The large "open air labor mart" thrived between the 1940s and 1960s on Eight Mile Road near Wyoming Avenue and Livernois Avenues, major intersections in northwest Detroit in the heart of the black enclave that was the site of housing battles in the 1940s, and convenient to construction sites in the booming northern suburbs. "Many of the men" who waited for work at the intersection, observed reporter Charles Wartman in 1946, "have the badges of their trade with them, bags of tools, trowels, and the like." Throughout the day contractors and construction workers drove past the clusters of workers hanging out on the Eight Mile Road sidewalks and chose one or two to join them on the job site.[79]

The sight of a casual labor market would have been familiar to anyone from the South, but was frowned upon by middle-class black residents of the area and by disapproving suburban whites who drove by. Local residents complained that traffic along Eight Mile backed up for blocks as employers checked out and selected day laborers. On slow days, jobless men loitered on the streets, leading one black community group to complain of "women, young and old being molested on the sidewalks, the usage of vile language," and "gambling and drinking." Despite community complaints, the police only sporadically arrested men for loitering, and courts were usually sympathetic to the claim that the men were looking for work. Police interference in the market would deprive Detroit employers of a ready supply of cheap labor. Even the Urban League, which called for increased police patrols and arrests in the area, supported a police presence only in the late afternoon and evening to curb vice but avoid disrupting the labor market.[80]

The atmosphere of "hanging out" in the Eight Mile–Wyoming area, however disturbing to local observers, was in the nature of casual construction work. Except in the most flush of times, the supply of potential workers far exceeded the number of jobs available, and construction work was especially vulnerable to unpredictable stoppages. A rainy day, muddy ground, a sudden change in temperature, or lack of material could shut down a building site for hours or even days. Most construction projects were also short-term, offering no guarantee of steady employment. Day laborers also generally got the most grueling and exhausting tasks, from lugging support beams, to pushing wheelbarrows of bricks, to lifting enormous bags of cement mix. Day construction labor was both physically taxing and relatively low-paying, and many men fortified themselves for a day of grueling work with a drink, or steeled themselves against another day or week of joblessness with the camaraderie of the northwest Detroit sidewalks.

Casual Labor and the Construction of an "Underclass"

The sight of underemployed African American men hanging out on street corners on the city's northern boundary had an important and unintended effect that reinforced patterns of racial discrimination and ensured the persistence of a racially segmented labor market. The existence of the "slave market" in Detroit (and similar casual labor markets in many other cities) helped to crystallize an image of black male shiftlessness that came to represent the African American urban "underclass." In the 1960s, the "street-corner society" of African American men became one of the most potent symbols of the "culture of poverty" and the subject of several important sociological investigations into African-American urban life in the North. Street corner life, shaped by informal labor markets, according to social-scientific observers in the 1960s, fostered a "pathological" sense of present-orientation, self-defeat, personal failure, and hopelessness.[81] Conservative politicians and the police saw the informal labor markets in less sympathetic terms. They saw on street corners dangerous "gangs" of men who threatened law and order by "loitering." It is perhaps not surprising that in the wake of growing fears of black urban crime in the 1960s, and as the economies of cities turned more sour, police began to crack down on the young men who hung out on street corners.[82]

No less significantly, the creation of a large and growing class of underemployed or jobless African American men reinforced the ideology of race held by northern whites in the era of the Second Great Migration. The "slave market" was not simply a place on the city's map; it was also became the basis of an ideological construct. Every time suburban whites drove past the "slave market" (tens of thousands of commuters passed through the Eight Mile–Wyoming intersection every day) they saw an embodiment of the stereotypes that they held about black men. The "slave market" thus became a metaphor for perceived racial difference. Whites created a cognitive map of the city shaped by these perceptions.[83] Their racial geography of the city became, in part, the basis of their decisions about where to live, what areas to avoid, and what federal social policies to support and to contest. Above all, the perception of black male shiftlessness and undependability became rationalizations for discriminatory hiring practices.[84]

The existence of the "slave market" thus allowed whites to redefine and reinforce the color line. The sight of a seemingly feckless, rough crowd of black men who drank and hung out on street corners reinforced images of white respectability and black indolence—images that became central to debates over poverty. Able-bodied, unemployed black men became in 1960s political debates the epitome of the undeserving poor, unworthy of public assistance, and a threat to urban law and order.[85] The picture of chronic black joblessness became a tool that reinforced the politics of racial domination.

The Continuing Significance of Discrimination

Writing in 1953, Charles Wartman, editor of Detroit's largest black weekly, stated that "with a few outstanding exceptions, practically nothing happened with regard to employment for Negroes outside the accepted pattern."[86] Wartman was largely right. In the late 1940s and early 1950s, during a prolonged period of what observers called a "critical labor shortage," Detroit's auto manufacturers, its tool and die companies, its construction industry, and its stores and restaurants could not find enough workers for all of their unfilled positions. In the decade after Wartman wrote, the situation for black workers in most industries remained the same or changed for the worse. To be sure, many blacks obtained jobs that provided security and offered opportunities for upward mobility. But they continued to struggle with myriad forms of discrimination in Detroit's workplaces. Even as union activity and fair employment legislation began to undermine patterns of workplace discrimination, blacks remained concentrated in what civil rights activist William Seabron called "the meanest and dirtiest jobs," disproportionately in the ranks of unskilled workers, in low-paid, insecure jobs, most susceptible to layoffs and long-term unemployment.[87]

Regardless of industry or sector of the labor market, discrimination in Detroit must be understood as historically specific. It occurred for a variety of complex reasons and had a wide variety of manifestations, none of which can be reduced to a single theory. Pure racial prejudice undoubtedly motivated some employers and unions, but discriminatory hiring and promotion practices varied widely from workplace to workplace. The experience of black workers was shaped by a variety of discriminations. When discrimination made economic sense, in terms of white workers' competitive advantage (building trades), or internal labor market decisions (auto industry), or pandering to customers' racism (retail), it was practiced widely. It often provided what David Roediger has called a "psychological wage," that reinforced white identity (building trades, skilled work, auto work). It was often reinforced by patterns of residential segregation (chemicals, machinery, and brewing). Patterns of discrimination fluctuated depending on the relative supply of black and white labor, in response to pressures from union members, and in response to labor contract provisions. The choices of employers and unions—like seniority—also had unintended consequences, improving the employment opportunities of one segment of the black population (those with longevity in a firm) at the expense of another (those recently hired).

In the end, the fact that black workers in Detroit did not enjoy unlimited access to a free labor market had important consequences for the history of the postwar city. Employers, hiring offices, and unions discriminated in so many seemingly unpredictable ways that even the most seasoned veterans of the labor market had difficulty figuring out the situation. The bewildering array of discriminatory practices and the range of motivations from the blunt to the subtle ensured that discrimination would remain an intransigent problem in the postwar city. Those who sought to better the situation of black workers in Detroit's labor market often reduced their diagnosis to a single cause—racial prejudice. In so doing, they overlooked the variety of causes and manifestations of workplace discrimination. It would take far more than the eradication of individual racism to transform the urban labor market, for racial discrimination was the result of far more than the sum of individual preferences and prejudices. Thus remedies—many of which had their origins in the 1950s—such as Fair Employment Practices legislation, nondiscrimination clauses in contracts, and pressure on employers to expand the hiring of minorities—met with only partial success (see Chapter 6). To be sure, they gradually expanded the opportunities of black workers in certain sectors of the economy. But the final irony was that just as attempts to provide blacks with a greater slice of the labor market pie began in earnest, the pie shrank. Blacks made gains in occupations that became increasingly scarce in the postwar decades. The combination of discrimination and profound changes in the city's industrial base left a sizable segment of the black population bereft of hope in the land of Caanan.

5.1. The transformation of Detroit's industrial economy in the 1950s left a growing number of African Americans underemployed or jobless. Robert Frank's stark photograph, "Factory—Detroit" (1955–56) captured the impact of deindustrialization and discrimination on the city's African American population.

5

"The Damning Mark of False Prosperities": The Deindustrialization of Detroit

Obsolescence is the very hallmark of progress.
—Henry Ford II (1955)

Unemployment is not a crime. It is a social ill full of
hardships, set-backs, anxieties, needs and sacrifices
which would be lauded under any other circumstances. It is truly the weakest spot in Democracy's
armor, the likely erosion point in the social structure, and the damning mark of false, unstable or lopsided prosperities.
—William Wakeham (1951)

THE INTERSECTION OF Grand Boulevard, John R Street, and the Milwaukee and Junction Railroad, just four miles north of downtown Detroit, seemed the heartbeat of the industrial metropolis in the 1940s. Within a two-square-mile area extending along the Grand Trunk and Michigan Central railroads was one of the most remarkable concentrations of industry in the United States. To the north was Detroit's second largest automobile factory, Dodge Main, which employed over thirty-five thousand workers in a five-story factory building with over 4.5 million square feet of floor space. Studebaker had a plant at the corner of Piquette Avenue and Brush where it produced its luxury sedans. Just to the north, on Russell Street, was a cavernous red-brick building that housed Murray Auto Body, a major independent pro-ducer of automobile chassis. Packard Motors produced cars in a sprawling ninety-five-building complex that extended for nearly a mile along East Grand Boulevard. At shift change time, the area came to a virtual standstill, as cars, buses, and pedestrians clogged the streets. The whole area was often covered in a grayish haze, a murky combination of pollutants from the factories and car exhaust. Even at night the area bustled, as the factory win-dows emitted an eerie "blue-green glow," and echoed with the "screams and clank of the machinery."[1]

By the late 1950s, this industrial landscape had become almost unrecog-nizable. The Milwaukee-Junction area was hard hit by layoffs and plant clos-ings. Murray Auto Body, Packard, and Studebaker shut down between 1953 and 1957. Dodge Main cut its work force by several thousand in the late 1950s. The shells of several empty multistory factories stood as cavernous hulks on the horizon, unobscured by smoke and haze on all but the foggiest days. Dozens of taverns and restaurants that had catered to workers were boarded up. And the neighborhoods surrounding the plants, which had housed thousands of industrial workers, had quickly become run-down. Property values fell, because plant closings deprived the small frame houses on the East Side of their only real advantage, their proximity to the workplace. Their largely white residents followed the flight of jobs to suburban and exurban areas. Traffic on the new Chrysler and Ford Freeways whisked past the former plants, the drivers oblivious to the blighted landscape around them. Similar rotting industrial areas could be found throughout the city, most notably on the city's far East Side, near Connor Road between Gratiot and Jefferson, where Mack, Briggs, Hudson, and Motor Products plants had closed. Even the area around the enormous Ford River Rouge plant lost some of its luster, as whole sections of the plant were modernized and thousands of workers who had patronized local stores, bars, and restaurants were laid off or transferred.

The 1950s marked a decisive turning point in the development of the city—a systematic restructuring of the local economy from which the city never fully recovered. Detroit's economy experienced enormous fluctuations in the 1950s. Between 1949 and 1960, the city suffered four major recessions. Because the auto industry was tremendously sensitive to shifts in consumer demand it weathered recessions badly. The unpredictability of demand for automobiles, especially in times of economic uncertainty, had serious ramifications for Detroit's working class. A slight shift in interest rates or a small drop in car sales resulted in immediate layoffs.[2] That the auto industry was especially vulnerable to economic vagaries was, however, nothing new. What was new in the 1950s was that auto manufacturers and suppliers permanently reduced their Detroit-area work forces, closed plants, and relocated to other parts of the country.

Looking out onto the city in 1952, social welfare worker Mary Jorgensen observed that "Detroit is in the doldrums." But what she observed, unknowingly, were the first signs of long-term economic problems that beset Detroit, not just a momentary economic lull. More important than the periodic downswings that plagued the city's economy was the beginning of a long-term and steady decline in manufacturing employment that affected Detroit and almost all other major northeastern and midwestern industrial cities. Between 1947 and 1963, Detroit lost 134,000 manufacturing jobs, while its population of working-aged men and women actually increased. Workers who had enjoyed a modicum of stability in the boom years of the 1940s suffered repeated bouts of unemployment in the 1950s. Laid-off workers were also consumers whose loss of buying power rippled through-out the city's economy, affecting local businesses from department stores and groceries to restaurants and bowling alleys. The growing gap between job seekers and job opportunities would have profound ramifications in subsequent decades.[3]

Capital Mobility

The transformation of Detroit's economy in the 1950s is best understood from a long-term perspective. Throughout the nineteenth and early twenti-eth centuries, American industry followed a pattern of centralization. Con-siderations of topography, access to transportation routes (either water or railroad), and the availability of raw materials determined plant location. The process of deindustrialization—the closing, downsizing, and relocation of plants and sometimes whole industries—accelerated throughout the twentieth century. Advances in communication and transportation, the transformation of industrial technology, the acceleration of regional and in-ternational economic competition, and the expansion of industry in low-wage regions, especially the South, reshaped the geography of American industrial cities. Beginning with the New Deal, the federal government channeled a disproportionate amount of resources to the South, culminating in the Sunbelt-dominated military-industrial complex of the Cold War era. Postwar highway construction, spurred by state and local expressway initia-tives in the 1940s, and federally funded highway construction after 1956, made central industrial location less necessary by facilitating the distribu-tion of goods over longer distances. Companies also moved to gain access to markets in other sections of the country, especially rapidly growing areas like California and the urban West.[4]

The forces of capital mobility reshaped the landscape of industrial Amer-ica. New factories appeared on rural hillsides, in former cornfields, and in cleared forests, and the shells of old manufacturing buildings loomed over towns and cities that were depopulated when businesses relocated produc-tion in more profitable places. In the 1920s, New England textile towns were ravaged by the flight of mills to the Piedmont South, presaging similar shifts of capital that would transform much of the industrial North later in the century. By midcentury, what had been a trickle of manufacturing jobs out of the industrial heartland became a flood. In the 1950s, the flight of industry and the loss of jobs reconfigured the landscape of the most prominent industrial cities across the region that came to be known as the Rust Belt. Detroit, Chicago, New York, Pittsburgh, Philadelphia, Baltimore, Trenton, Boston, Buffalo, and St. Louis all lost hundreds of thousands of manufacturing jobs beginning in the 1950s, as firms reduced employment in center-city plants, replaced workers with new automated technology, and constructed new facilities in suburban and semirural areas, in medium-sized cities, often in less industrialized states or regions, and even in other countries.[5]

Automobile manufacturers were in the vanguard of corporate decentralization. The growth of a national and international market for automobiles led firms like Ford and General Motors to construct plants throughout the country. Technological advances, especially in transportation, made industrial decentralization possible. Yet decentralization was not simply a response to the inexorable demands of the market; it was an outgrowth of the social relations of production itself. Decentralization was an effective means for employers to control increasing labor costs and weaken powerful trade unions. The deconcentration of plants gave employers the upper hand during periods of labor unrest. General Motors, the first firm to deconcentrate production on a wide scale, built new plants in the 1930s in rural parts of the country, as a means of reducing wages and inhibiting union militancy in manufacturing cities like Detroit, Pontiac, and Flint, where most of its facilities had been located. The early decentralization experiments had little impact on Detroit. The city's share of national automobile production remained large throughout the first half of the twentieth century. But the pre–World War II decentralization efforts foreshadowed the auto industry's aggressive efforts to deconcentrate production and reduce its Detroit workforce after World War II.[6]

In the late 1940s and 1950s, Detroit's economy began to feel the effects of the mobility of the Big Three automobile manufacturers—Ford, General Motors, and, to a lesser extent, Chrysler. Between 1946 and 1956, General Motors spent $3.4 billion on new plants and facilities. Equally ambitious in its restructuring plans was Ford, which made aggressive decentralization the central part of its postwar corporate policy. From the end of World War II through 1957, Ford alone spent over $2.5 billion nationwide on a program of plant expansion. Chrysler, whose finances for capital expansion were small compared to its rivals, still spent $700 million on plant expansion in the same period.[7] Between 1947 and 1958, the Big Three built twenty-five new plants in the metropolitan Detroit area, all of them in suburban communities, most more than fifteen miles from the center city.[8] The lion's share of new plants, or "runaway shops," as Detroiters called them, however, went to small- and medium-sized cities in the Midwest, like Lima, Lorain, and Walton Hills, Ohio; Kokomo and Indianapolis, Indiana; and to the South and West, especially California.[9] In 1950, 56 percent of all automobile employment in the United States was in Michigan; by 1960, that figure had fallen to 40 percent.[10] As they expanded in other regions of the country, the major automotive producers reduced employment in their older Detroit-area plants.

A major reason that employers cited for the construction of new plants outside Detroit was the lack of available land for expansion. With new assembly-line technology, auto companies found the multistory plants of the 1910s and 1920s outdated. A few plants in the 1930s, and all new postwar auto plants, were built on one level. As more workers commuted to their jobs by car (71 percent of manufacturing employees in 1955 went to work by private car), firms also looked for large sites to accommodate massive parking lots. In addition, after World War II, Detroit lacked large sites with railroad frontage. A 1951 survey found only 367.5 acres of undeveloped land adjacent to railroad lines. The land was scattered about in 36 parcels, the largest site covering only 54 acres. The entire stretch of land abutting the Detroit Terminal railroad between Highland Park and Dearborn was fully developed; the Wabash Railroad line had only 48.5 acres of undeveloped frontage on the East Side and only 2.1 acres on the West Side. These small sites were simply insufficient for any large-scale factory construction. As a 1956 report noted, expanding firms could find "elbow room" only in the "outlying fringe areas."[11]

First to follow the auto industry out of the city were auto-related industries, in particular machine tool manufacturers, metalworking firms, and parts manufacturers. Between 1950 and 1956, 124 manufacturing firms located on the green fields of Detroit's suburbs; 55 of them had moved out of Detroit. Leading the flight were metals-related firms—manufacturers of metalworking tools, wire, stampings, and dies. These small plants (most with between eight and fifty workers) employed about 20 percent of Detroit-area workers in 1950, forming the second largest category of employment in the city after automobile production. It is impossible to calculate the number of metal and auto parts firms that moved outside the Detroit metropolitan area altogether, but undoubtedly many followed auto plants to their new locations in other parts of the country. The mobility of large auto producers and small firms alike reconfigured Detroit's industrial landscape, leaving empty factories and vacant lots behind, and bringing runaway shops to areas that just a few years earlier had been farms.[12]

Yet it was not foreordained that the auto companies would construct single-story automobile plants and downsize or abandon their older multistory factory complexes, nor was it inevitable that smaller machine tool and parts firms would prefer plants in outlying areas. The assumption that companies in the postwar period had no choice but to move to sprawling suburban and rural sites, surrounded by acres of parking lots and manicured lawns, is wrongly based in an ahistorical argument about the inevitability and neutrality of technological decisions. Industrial location policy was not a neutral response to market forces or an inexorable consequence of economic progress. Corporations made decisions about plant location and employment policy in a specific political, cultural, and institutional context, in the case of postwar Detroit in the aftermath of the rise of a powerful union movement and in the midst of a shop-floor struggle over work rules and worker control.[13]

Automation

The most important force that restructured Detroit's economy after World War II was the advent of new automated processes in the automobile, auto parts, and machine tool industries. In the late 1940s and 1950s, many Detroit industries, ranging from major automobile manufacturers to small tool and die firms, embraced automation. Automation had roots in earlier technological innovations in the automobile industry: it was the most refined application of the Fordist system of production.[14] In the wake of the long General Motors strike of 1946, GM began to experiment with labor-reducing machinery in its Flint Buick plant. Ford, however, led the automotive industry in experimentation with automation. In 1947, Ford set up an "Automation Department" to direct the reorganization of its manufacturing operations; its competitors and many other industries followed suit over the next fifteen years.

Automation offered two major benefits to manufacturers: it promised both to increase output and to reduce labor costs. Chrysler executive Harry R. Bentley described the purpose of automation as the "optimum use of machines to produce high-volume, high-quality products at the lowest possible cost." Although automation's advocates exaggerated its utility and underestimated its costs, automation sometimes did have dramatic effects. Before the introduction of automated engine production at Ford's Cleveland plant, it took 117 workers to produce 154 engine blocks per hour; after automation the same output required a mere 41 workers.[15]

Industrialists touted automation as a way to improve working conditions and workers' standard of living. Del S. Harder, a Ford vice president and Detroit's most energetic proponent of automation, argued that "the era of automation is nothing more than a continuation of the industrial revolution which greatly increased our national wealth . . . and helped bring about the highest standard of living in the world." In Harder's view, automation would improve working conditions, reduce hours, and improve workplace safety. It was simply "a better way to do the job."[16]

Certainly automated production replaced some of the more dangerous and onerous factory jobs. At Ford, automation eliminated "mankilling," a task that demanded high speed and involved tremendous risk. "Mankilling"

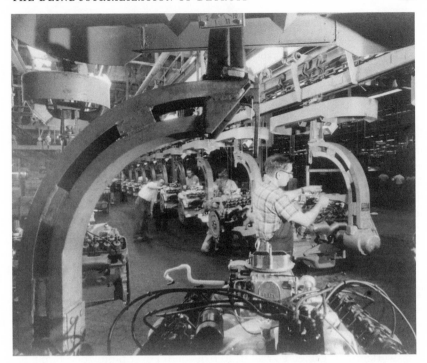

5.2. When Ford introduced automated assembly lines in its newly opened Lima, Ohio plant in 1954, it relocated production from the River Rouge plant, displacing hundreds of Detroit workers. Lima was typical of towns that attracted relocating industry in the 1950s. It was small and overwhelmingly white.

required a worker to remove hot coil springs from a coiling machine, lift them to chest height, turn around, and lower them into a quench tank, all within several seconds. In Ford's stamping plants, new machines loaded and unloaded presses, another relatively slow, unsafe, and physically demanding job before automation. Here automation offered real benefits to workers.[17]

Despite these occasional benefits, automation was primarily a weapon in the employers' antilabor arsenal. Through automation, employers attempted to reassert control over the industrial process, chipping away at the control over production that workers had gained through intricately negotiated work rules. Manufacturers hoped that self-regulating, computerized machinery would eliminate worker-led slowdowns, soldiering, and sabotage on the line. Contended one of automation's advocates: "Changing times have raised the idea around Detroit" that in the future, industrialists would look to "how to get the most out of machines rather than how to get the most out of people. Personnel men of the future, they say, may be automation experts." Automation would lower the risk "of considerable damage to parts through worker carelessness." Automation also provided engineers and plant managers a seemingly foolproof way to reduce industry's dependence on labor and reduce labor costs. Above all, automation counteracted the "increasing cost of labor . . . given a sharp hike by recent Reuther assistance."[18]

Corporate leaders bluntly stated that automation would ensure that they retained the upper hand in labor-management relations. Only a little more than a decade after the emergence of the UAW, in a period of tremendous labor strength, automation was a formidable tool for management. A manager in the newly automated Ford engine plant in Cleveland reminded UAW President Walter Reuther that "you are going to have trouble collecting union dues from all of these machines."[19] The reduction of the work force in certain plants after the introduction of automation eviscerated some of the most powerful bastions of labor activism.

Automation had a devastating impact on the work force at the Ford River Rouge plant. Rouge workers were represented by UAW Local 600, one of the most militant in the industry. The plant was also the largest employer of blacks in the Detroit area, and throughout the 1940s, a majority of black workers there consistently supported the left-wing caucus of the UAW. Slowdowns or wildcat strikes at the Rouge could paralyze Ford production nationwide. In key sections of the plant, like the Motor and Plastics buildings, workers had gained a great degree of control over production through a mix of custom and work rules. Ford officials, hoping to weaken union strength on the shop floor, targeted the Rouge for automation. In 1950, Rouge workers assembled all Ford and Mercury engines; by 1954, Ford had shifted all engine production to the new automated Cleveland plant. Rouge workers with seniority were transferred to Cleveland or to the new Dearborn Engine Plant that built engines for Lincolns. Stamping, machine casting, forging, steel production, glassmaking, and dozens of other operations were shifted from the Rouge to new Ford plants throughout the 1950s.[20] As a result, employment at the Rouge fell from 85,000 in 1945, to 54,000 in 1954, to only 30,000 in 1960.[21]

In the early, experimental stages of automation, the Big Three auto companies set up sections of new plants whose processes paralleled those at already existing plants. They compared productivity at old and new plants, and either modernized or closed older plants to increase productive capacity, or used the threat of a plant closing to prod workers to speed up production. New automated plants often replaced part or all of the production at existing facilities and eliminated whole job classifications. In Ford's first heavily automated plant, the Buffalo Stamping Plant, "workers were chiefly inspectors." Ford officials found that productivity at the older Dearborn stamping plant lagged behind Buffalo, and proceeded to automate Dearborn and reduce its work force. Ford further automated and decentralized stamping, opening a new Chicago plant in 1956, where company officials cut the number of job classifications by more than two hundred. The decentralization and automation of Ford stamping eliminated thousands of jobs, and weakened union shop floor control.[22]

Automation had its most far-reaching consequences in engine production, one of the most labor-intensive jobs in the auto industry before the 1950s. In 1951, Ford shifted a large part of its engine production from the Motor Building in the Rouge Complex to its new highly mechanized Cleveland plant and its new Dearborn plant. In the process, Ford eliminated close to three thousand jobs at the Rouge. By 1953, the Cleveland and Dearborn plants were running parallel production. Where 950 workers made piston connecting rods at the Rouge, they were replaced by two units of 146 workers each at Cleveland and Dearborn, resulting in a net loss of 804 jobs in the Detroit area. In addition, Ford paid its new Cleveland workers an average of eleven cents less per hour than at Dearborn. A similar pattern followed in every engine-related job. The hemorrhage of jobs continued in 1953 and 1955, when Ford announced the construction of new engine production facilities at Brookpark Village, Ohio, and in Lima, Ohio.[23]

The effects of automation on job opportunities in communities like Detroit were a well-guarded corporate secret. Responding to labor union criticism of automation, employers downplayed the possibility of significant job loss. When Ford began automating and decentralizing the Rouge plant, John Bugas, Ford's vice president for industrial relations, told workers that they had nothing to fear. "I do not believe," wrote Bugas in 1950, "that the over-all reduction in employees in the Rouge operations resulting from the building of new facilities will be substantial." Ford labor relations official Manton Cummins dismissed claims that automation led to job loss as a union-led "scare campaign." Yet the only detailed statistics on automation and its effects on employment, a UAW-sponsored study of Ford from 1950 to 1953, indicated a net loss of 4,185 jobs in the first years of industrial restructuring (Table 5.1).[24]

In the first flush of automation campaigns, industry publications like *Automation* magazine argued that automation reduced labor costs, but by the mid-1950s, they seldom raised labor as a rationale, because automation's effect on jobs had become a sensitive political issue. Instead, the magazine's editors went on the defensive against charges that automation led to job loss. In February 1960, for example, the magazine noted that "lest anyone be deluded into thinking of [the Plymouth Detroit assembly plant] as a workerless automaton, it should be reported that this place employs in excess of 5,000 people."[25]

Corporate leaders expressed unbounded optimism about automation. "Obsolescence is the very hallmark of progress," argued Henry Ford II, in a 1955 address. Technological change brought with it short term hardship,

TABLE 5.1

Automation-Related Job Loss at Detroit-Area Ford
Plants, 1951–1953

	Job Loss
Engine Division (Rouge)	1,727
Gear and Axle (Rouge)	231
Crankshaft (Motor Building, Rouge)	18
Piston (Motor Building, Rouge)	575
Frame and Cold Header Unit (Rouge)	531
Plastic Unit (Rouge)	30
Dearborn Stamping	940
Highland Park	85
Mound Road Plant	48
TOTAL	4,185

Source: J. O'Rourke, Memo on Automation in Ford Plants,
January 31, 1957, UAW-RD, Box 65.

but long term gain. "The faster we obsolete products, machines, and anti-
quated, costly means of working, the faster we raise our living standards and
our national wealth." Ford recognized that "In some areas where industries
have been partly obsoleted whole communities may suffer real hardship." In
his view, such suffering was inevitable, for there would be "no direct way I
can imagine to avoid by private means the dislocations that come from technological obsolescence."[26]

General Motors Vice President Louis Seaton was even more sanguine
than Ford, but more disingenuous. He railed against the belief that automation "is a grim reaper of jobs" and noted that General Motors employment
had gone up since the introduction of automation. He was quick to cite
national-level statistics, but made no reference to the local consequences of
GM modernization. Interestingly, he advocated early retirement as "one
means of cushioning the effect of reduced employment," and noted that
thousands of workers had retired under the "flexible retirement age provision" of the GM pension plan.[27]

The UAW, for the most part, worried about automation only insofar as it
affected employment levels nationwide. National-level data gave little reason for concern. In the 1950s, there was little evidence to show that the
number of auto industry jobs nationwide would fall because of automation.
Some economists argued that over the long run, the introduction of automated processes would increase jobs nationwide. Aggregate employment
statistics, however, masked profound local variation. Local economies in
places like Detroit reeled from the consequences of automation-caused
plant closings or work force reductions. Walter Reuther and other UAW
officials initially expressed some concern about the effects of automation on

employment and union strength in industrial cities, but for the most part they poured their energy into cushioning the effects of layoffs through extended unemployment benefits, improved pension plans, and preferential hiring plans for displaced workers. Labor leaders also became staunch advocates of government funding for education and retraining programs to prepare workers for new automated jobs. Contract provisions guaranteed that workers who lost their jobs because of automation would be protected by seniority and transferred to other jobs. Their programs offered remedies for the symptoms of automation, rather than grappling with the root causes of unemployment.[28] While transfer guarantees mitigated the effects of displacement in the auto industry for workers with seniority, the introduction of automated processes led to "silent firing," a term that referred to the unheralded reduction of entry-level auto industry jobs in Detroit. Silent firing aroused little controversy, but it cut into the pool of available unskilled and semiskilled jobs in the city, and, over the long run, weakened union strength in what had been a union stronghold.[29]

Detroit's workers bore the burden of technological changes in the 1950s. Automation had two other important consequences for the Detroit-area labor market. First, it gave a competitive advantage to General Motors and Ford, which hurt Chrysler and destroyed the independent automobile manufacturers in the city. Second, it led auto companies to take on productive capacities formerly left to independent manufacturers, driving many parts suppliers out of business and further reducing Detroit's employment base. Automation affected virtually every sector of the city's economy, reshaping Detroit's industrial labor market, and unleashing forces whose destructive powers no one—industrialists and workers alike—could fully anticipate.

Chrysler, the Independent Auto Producers, and Suppliers

Advances in productive technology brought disproportionate benefits to two of the Big Three manufacturers. The third, Chrysler, attempted to follow its competitors' lead in automating and decentralizing its production facilities. At the flagship Dodge Main plant, new technologies reduced employment in the paint shop by nearly twenty-five hundred; in body assembly by twenty-one hundred; and on the motor line by eleven hundred. Before automation in the late 1950s, the Plymouth Detroit assembly plant on Lynch Road produced 180 cars per hour on two assembly lines. With the introduction of labor-saving technology, one newly automated line at the old Plymouth plant turned out 60 cars per hour, while "Other assembly plants in dispersed geographical locations make up the difference in schedule and produce closer to the marketplace." Engine production, which had occupied

25 percent of the floor space at the Plymouth Detroit plant, was shifted to the new Trenton Engine Plant, in a suburb south of Detroit.[30]

Despite its efforts, Chrysler Corporation spent far less on automation and decentralization than its competitors in the 1950s. Because of poor management, the company lacked the funds to invest in new development. The result was two-edged. Chrysler jobs stayed in Detroit to a much greater extent than Ford and General Motors jobs; in fact by 1960, Chrysler was Detroit's largest employer. But the company struggled to remain economically viable. It speeded up production dramatically in the late 1950s, laid off thousands of workers, and relentlessly used overtime to increase output without dramatically increasing labor costs. As a result, Chrysler employment plummeted. During the recession of 1958, the number of Chrysler production workers bottomed out at 59,440, nearly half of the number employed in the peak year of 1950.[31]

The scramble to automate production crushed independent auto manufacturers. Automated machinery was very costly, requiring massive capital investments. As Ford and General Motors engaged in an intense battle for market share in the early 1950s, their technological innovations, productivity, and profits far surpassed those of smaller firms like Nash, Hudson, Willys, Kaiser-Frazer, Studebaker, and Packard. Big Three sales bit into the independents' already small niche in the automotive market—their combined market share fell from 18 percent in 1948 to 4 percent in 1955.[32] In the 1950s, in their drive to remain competitive with the Big Three, independent producers began to invest heavily in automation. Unlike General Motors or Ford, however, they were poorly capitalized and struggled to remain profitable while retooling their plants. Typical was Packard, which cut employment in its Detroit plant from 16,000 to 4,000 between 1952 and 1956 to remain competitive. Packard merged with Studebaker in 1954, and its Detroit plant closed in 1956, leaving the 4,000 remaining workers, most of whom were over forty years old, unemployed.[33] Hudson Motors followed a similar route. At its peak in 1950, Hudson employed 25,330 workers in its two outdated Detroit plants. Those jobs soon disappeared. The new conglomerate American Motors, which absorbed Hudson, removed all production from Detroit between 1954 and 1957. As a fitting coda to its troubled history, the Hudson plant on Jefferson and Connor was torn down and replaced by a parking lot in July 1959.[34]

Corporate restructuring had its most dramatic consequences in smaller manufacturing concerns around Detroit. In the mid-1950s, Ford, Chrysler, and General Motors began to produce auto bodies and other parts in integrated, automated facilities, rather than relying on independent suppliers. Three independent car body and parts manufacturers, all based in Detroit, closed in the mid-1950s. In 1953, Briggs Auto Body was absorbed by Chrysler Corporation. In 1954, another major independent, Murray Auto Body,

5.3. Two of the several plants that closed on Detroit's East Side in the 1950s were the Motor Products and Briggs plants. Altogether, the East Side lost more than seventy-thousand jobs between 1954 and 1960.

closed its doors permanently. And in 1956, Motor Products shut its Mack Avenue plant after Chrysler took over its stamping business. In three years, over ten thousand workers were displaced in these three closings alone.[35]

The case of Murray Auto Body starkly revealed the combined impact of automation, decentralization, and plant closings. In 1947, Ford employed 13,000 workers in its stamping division and contracted parts from Murray, a nearby supplier which employed 5,000 workers. In the early 1950s, Ford took over all stamping production. Murray lost its contract and closed its plant in 1954; its 5,000 workers lost their jobs. Ford, following the policy of decentralization, reduced employment in its Dearborn stamping operation to 6,000 workers, and shifted most of its production to two new stamping plants which employed 7,000 workers elsewhere in the midwest. In the process of reorganization, Detroit lost 11,000 jobs and one manufacturer.[36]

Equally striking was the decline in peripheral manufacturing jobs in Detroit. Detroit's nonautomotive manufacturers averaged only 140 employees per plant at the end of World War II.[37] These plants, manufacturers of machine tools, wire, castings, stampings, and other metal products, were subject to violent cyclical fluctuations related to automotive production. As larger, better-capitalized machine tool plants were automated, many small companies failed. And although the automobile companies continued to rely on an extensive network of independent suppliers, automation and the integration of parts production also decimated many of Detroit's "one-cylinder" manufacturing companies. Ford, for example, took over production of forgings, axles, wheels, stampings, and other parts formerly provided by outside suppliers, crippling many independent firms.[38] General Motors also shifted parts production from independent suppliers, largely based in the Detroit area, to its own new parts plants in Ohio and Illinois.[39] Firms such as Bohn Aluminum, Falls Spring and Wire, F. L. Jacobs, Thompson Products, Richard Brothers, and Federal Mogul shut down their Detroit operations in the mid-1950s. Several thousand employees of these smaller firms, unlike workers with seniority in the Big Three who had the option to be transferred when displaced by automation, entered the ranks of the unemployed.[40]

Costs: Labor and Taxes

Automation was not the only force contributing to job loss in Detroit. Smaller firms that did not automate production or suffer automation-related job losses still fled the city in increasing numbers in the 1950s. Labor relations were especially important in motivating firms to relocate outside of Detroit, or to expand facilities outside of the city. Employers left industrial centers with high labor costs for regions where they could exploit cheap, nonunion labor. One such firm, Ex-Cell-O, a major machine tool manufacturer, built six new plants in rural Indiana and Ohio in the 1950s, and none in metropolitan Detroit. Ex-Cell-O's president, H. G. Bixby, argued in 1960 that the reason for the failure of firms like his to expand in metropolitan Detroit was that "there was something seriously wrong with our business climate." Bixby blamed union activity for the flight of industry from Detroit. The "militant and venomous attitude toward industry has and will continue to limit job opportunity. . . . Industries, like people, will not go where they are insulted and vilified daily. If Michigan labor union leadership is seriously interested in job opportunity for their members, they must change their attitude from one of conflict to one of cooperation with industry."[41] Forty-nine percent of Michigan industrialists interviewed in 1961 felt that "the labor situation" was worse in 1960 than it had been ten years earlier.[42]

Wage costs were also an important consideration in plant location, especially for small firms. From the 1950s through the 1970s, high wage costs ranked first in small manufacturers' complaints about the Detroit business climate. One small industrialist lamented that "the unions are so strong that they have more influence than they should have. Make unreasonable de-

mands and get them." In his words, "Unions have killed a lot of small industries. They raise union rates. This means costs go up and then prices have to
go up. Then a small firm cannot compete. And that is the end." One small
Michigan firm opened a new plant in Alabama, citing "labor demands" and
the "wage rate" as reasons for leaving Detroit.[43] Fruehauf Trailer also moved
out of Detroit to cut labor costs. In 1950, it laid off its thirty-five hundred
Detroit workers, and opened a new plant in Avon Lakes, Ohio, where it
reduced the workforce to twenty-five hundred, imposed higher production
quotas, and cut wages by 25 cents an hour.[44]

Tax rates also ranked as a major factor in plant location policy, although
corporate leaders exaggerated the effect of the tax burden on their operations. In 1954, *The Detroiter*, the organ of the Detroit Chamber of Commerce, stated that the "excessive burden of taxation on inventories is an
important factor in causing the location of new plants outside the Detroit
city limits."[45] Ex-Cell-O's Bixby also complained of the high taxes in metropolitan Detroit. In 1957, General Motors cited tax increases as a rationale
for halting expansion in Michigan. And in 1959, Chrysler Vice-President
W. C. Newberg warned that taxes "dictate some decisions about plant location" and hinted that in the absence of a "fair and even distribution of property taxes," Chrysler might leave Detroit.[46] One industrialist worried that his
firm paid "three and four times the amount of taxes per net worth that our
competitors are paying in Ohio, Pennsylvania, Illinois, California." Detroit's
real and personal property taxes were particularly galling to members of the
city's business community.[47]

Detroit officials were responsive to fears of high property taxes: Detroit
did not increase its property tax levy between 1948 and 1958. But business
leaders, tempted by lower tax rates in nonmetropolitan areas, frequently
used the threat of mobility to push for changes in tax laws favorable to industry. In the meantime, the flight of industry diminished Detroit's tax base.
Runaway shops took with them tax revenue essential to the provision of city
services, and the city was forced to rely on state and federal aid, running up
a growing deficit. City officials, discouraged by threatened business flight,
attempted to maintain a tax structure favorable to businesses by keeping
property taxes low and shifting the burden to income earners, who faced a
1 percent levy beginning in 1962. With an aging infrastructure, an enormous
school district, an expensive city-funded social welfare program, and a growing population of poor people, Detroit could not reduce its taxes to the level
of its small-town and rural competitors.[48]

Neighboring states took advantage of the plight of Detroit and other large
cities and encouraged panic over urban tax rates; many held out the promise
of low business taxes as a lure to Michigan firms who wanted to cut overhead
costs. Some state chambers of commerce and economic development officials placed advertisements in trade publications trumpeting their favorable

tax climates. According to Bixby, Detroit taxes "were 2⅓ times as high as the state and local taxes per plant in Ohio, and 1¾ high as in Indiana."[49] The combination of low taxes and low-wage labor markets lured firms away from Detroit to small towns throughout the Midwest and South.

Federal Policy and Decentralization

The federal government also actively encouraged industrial deconcentration. Beginning during World War II, it fostered military-industrial development in suburban areas at the expense of center cities, in part as a precaution in case of air attack. Firms also frequently took advantage of federal largesse to subsidize new plant construction on green-field sites. The Chrysler Warren Tank Plant, built in 1941 in an undeveloped suburban area fifteen miles north of downtown Detroit, and the enormous Willow Run aircraft complex, constructed in 1942 on over fifteen hundred acres of rural land twenty-five miles west of the city, stood as models to postwar industrial planners.[50]

Government support for industrial decentralization went even further during the Korean War and afterward. During the Korean War buildup, for example, only 7.5 percent of $353 million allocated for the purchase of equipment and new plant construction in metropolitan Detroit went to firms located within the city of Detroit; 92.5 percent of the funding went to "outlying parts of the region."[51] In addition, the Department of Defense also pioneered a "parallel plant" policy, building new defense plants outside of traditional industrial centers that duplicated existing production.[52] Chrysler shifted tank engine production to New Orleans and tank production to Newark, Delaware. Ford, which had constructed aircraft engines in Detroit during World War II, shifted production to sites in Chicago and Missouri. And Cadillac began the manufacture of light tanks in Cleveland.[53]

The growing power of Sun Belt politicians in Congress further diminished Detroit's share of the massive federal defense budget. By the end of the Korean War, the northeastern and midwestern share of the Cold War defense budget had shrunk greatly. Southern members of Congress, many heading influential committees, steered federal military spending toward their home states. Between 1951 and 1960, the South's share of the national defense budget doubled. Even more impressive was the impact of defense dollars on the West. California was the major beneficiary of defense spending. In 1951, it was awarded 13.2 percent of national defense contract dollars; by 1958, its share was 21.4 percent. Detroit and other industrial centers in the Northeast and Midwest, all of which had benefited from the flow of defense dollars during the 1940s, suffered the effects of the Pentagon-financed development of the Sun Belt.[54]

The major automobile manufacturers also contributed to the loss of defense contracts in the immediate postwar years. They quickly reconverted plants from defense to civilian production, in anticipation of high demand for cars after the war, while manufacturers in other regions positioned themselves for continued military research and development and defense production. The result was the Detroit area did not attract new high-technology aircraft and electronics manufacturers that benefited from government largesse during the Cold War.[55]

Detroit, the World War II "arsenal of democracy," had become, in the words of a critic of defense policy, a "ghost arsenal."[56] In 1954 alone, the Detroit area lost nearly 56,000 defense jobs; it lost another 26,000 between 1955 and 1957. By 1957, only 33,000 workers in all of metropolitan Detroit worked in defense industries. At a time when the national military-industrial complex was growing by leaps and bounds, Detroit's share of Defense Department contracts shrunk rapidly. The loss of defense jobs in the city occurred simultaneously with the decline in employment in other industries. Detroit's loss of defense jobs only added to its already deep economic troubles.[57]

The movement of firms out of the city, whether spurred by government subsidies or by market considerations, created a spatial mismatch between urban African Americans and jobs. Persistent housing discrimination combined with job flight to worsen the plight of urban blacks. The mismatch was not as perfect as many theorists have contended; some large suburban plants, as we have seen, did hire blacks. But most smaller firms did not. Tool and die companies that located in the all-white suburbs north of Detroit, for example, tended to rely on local contacts to find new employees. The gap between black workers and job opportunity grew the further firms moved from the metropolitan area. And increasingly firms, from automobile manufacturers to parts suppliers, relocated in small towns and rural areas with minuscule black populations. Firms that moved to the South seldom broke Jim Crow customs, offering the lion's share of their jobs to white workers. Discrimination combined with nonmetropolitan industrialization to limit black economic opportunity.[58]

Overtime

Automation and decentralization combined with a third industrial change that reduced the size of Detroit's work force: the increasing use of overtime. Beginning in the mid-1950s, employers began to favor the use of overtime in lieu of hiring additional workers. In January 1954, Ford's decision to put all workers in its Lincoln-Mercury plants on fifty-four-hour weeks made the daily papers. The use of overtime was not unprecedented, but it had generally been restricted to model changeover season, at the end of the summer when plants needed to be retooled quickly for the production of a new year of cars. Ford's overtime announcement attracted attention because it came in the middle of a production year, and was controversial because at that time more than 107,000 Detroit workers were unemployed.[59]

The use of overtime became even more common as the decade went on. Between 1958 and 1962, UAW workers put in between 2.3 and 4 hours of overtime per week over the course of the year. UAW economists estimated that 37,600 additional workers could have been employed over that period if overtime were abolished. By 1965, overtime was fully entrenched as a labor policy, in the auto industry and in most other American manufacturing enterprises. That year, the average manufacturing worker put in 3.5 hours of overtime per week and the average auto worker put in 5.9 hours of overtime.[60] In the late 1950s and early 1960s, managers in the auto industry increased output by putting whole plants on periods of sustained overtime. Some plants went on fifty-eight-hour-per-week schedules for three-month periods. In one plant, managers scheduled at least forty-eight hours of work for the entire work force for fifty-six of eighty consecutive weeks.[61]

Overtime was one of few management strategies that appealed both to many workers and to corporate accountants. Overtime allowed managers to reduce the costs of hiring and training new workers, as well as benefits packages, while maintaining high production levels. It also diluted union strength by reducing membership. Union leaders argued, quite plausibly, that overtime reduced the size of the labor force and added to the ranks of the unemployed. Corporate leaders, however, rejoined that because "the unemployed are, *on the average* less qualified than those who are employed," the abolition of overtime "will not necessarily shift the margin of employability for those out of work."[62]

If union leadership saw the dangers of overtime, not all rank and file members did. Many workers supported overtime, for the reason described by John Kenneth Galbraith, that overtime ended "the barbarous uniformity of the weekly wage" premised on the belief that "all families have the same tastes, needs."[63] Overtime was appealing because it offered workers the rare opportunity to increase their wages substantially, given the barriers within plants that prevented workers from moving to higher-paying jobs. Moreover, overtime provided workers with extra pay which offered a hedge against the frequent layoffs that plagued the automobile industry, especially in the 1950s. Workers occasionally went on wildcat strikes to protest what they considered to be the unequal assignment of overtime. In 1955, when the Ford Livonia Transmission Plant gave eight hours of overtime to its Saturday afternoon shift workers, 150 final assembly workers who were not assigned overtime walked out in protest.[64] Employers also used the prospect of overtime pay as a lure to prospective workers. Advertisements for tool and die jobs in Detroit papers frequently mentioned the availability of overtime work. On the other hand, because it was usually mandatory, overtime was often unpopular, especially among younger workers. Those who had no desire to work nine- to twelve-hour days were involuntarily subject to grueling hours and pressure to keep productivity high.[65]

Industrial Job Loss and Economic Distress

Detroit seemed to embody American confidence and affluence in the aftermath of the triumph of World War II, but just when the city's boosters proclaimed an industrial rebirth, the destructive forces of industrial capitalism began the process of economic corrosion that made Detroit the epitome of the Rust Belt. Between 1948 and 1967, Detroit lost nearly 130,000 manufacturing jobs. The number of manufacturing jobs fell by almost half in the 1950s (Table 5.2). The trend of job loss continued through the next four decades, mitigated only slightly by the temporary boom in the local economy and in automobile production from 1964 through 1969. Bolstered by the views of postwar social scientists who emphasized American affluence, the perception of Detroit's decline lagged far behind reality. While social scientists were writing of Detroit as the home of the "embourgeoised" auto worker, the face of industrial Detroit was being transformed by enormous economic upheavals. A growing number of Detroit residents joined the ranks of "displaced workers," dislocated by industrial changes and trapped in the declining metropolis.

The restructuring of Detroit's industrial economy diminished opportunity for several segments of the Detroit work force. First, the loss of manufacturing jobs removed a rung of the ladder of economic opportunity for the poorest workers, especially those with little education and few skills. The testimony of workers who lost their jobs when Detroit's Packard plant shut its doors in 1956 revealed the high costs of industrial decline. "I felt like some one had hit me with a sledge hammer," stated one worker. Recalled a stockhandler with twelve years seniority: "It was such a shock . . . I had been there so long. . . . They just threw us out and didn't say nothing . . . they just threw us out on the street." A worker with thirty years of seniority perhaps best summed up the effects of plant closings in the 1950s: "It hit and hit hard, hit the man who was a common assembler the hardest."[66]

In the aftermath of the wartime and postwar boom, the bust of the 1950s was devastating. The city's economy had seemed dynamic and unstoppable, insatiable in its demand for labor. Making the process all the more traumatic, layoffs and plant closings were unpredictable. Seemingly secure jobs could be eliminated without notice when a plant automated. Events in the 1950s reminded workers that even the factory buildings that seemed like perma-

TABLE 5.2
Decline in Manufacturing Employment in Detroit, 1947–1977

	1947	1954	1958	1963	1967	1972	1977
Manufacturing Firms	3,272	3,453	3,363	3,370	2,947	2,398	1,954
Total Manufacturing Employment[a]	338.4	296.5	204.4	200.6	209.7	180.4	153.3
Total Production Employment[a]	281.5	232.3	145.1	141.4	149.6	125.8	107.5

Source: U.S. Department of Commerce, Bureau of the Census, *City and County Data Books* (Washington, D.C.: U.S. Government Printing Office, 1949, 1956, 1962, 1967, 1972, 1977, 1983).
[a] In thousands.

nent landmarks on Detroit's skyline were mortal. Bustling plants were abandoned and boarded up as companies moved production outside the city or went out of business. In the midst of celebratory descriptions of national prosperity, as pundits spoke of embourgeoisement, the gap between rhetoric and reality grew.

If many workers were affected in some way by changes in the city's economy, blacks bore the brunt of restructuring. Persistent racial discrimination magnified the effects of deindustrialization on blacks. Data from the 1960 census make clear the disparate impact of automation and labor market constriction on African American workers. Across the city, 15.9 percent of blacks, but only 5.8 percent of whites were out of work. In the motor vehicle industry, the black-white gap was even greater. 19.7 percent of black auto workers were unemployed, compared to only 5.8 percent of whites. Discrimination and deindustrialization proved to be a lethal combination for blacks. Seniority protected some black workers from permanent layoffs, but it disproportionately benefited white workers. Blacks had not gained footholds in most plants until after 1943—most were hired in the late 1940s and early 1950s, well after large numbers of white workers had established themselves in Detroit's industries. Thus they were less likely to have accumulated enough seniority to protect their jobs. And because blacks were concentrated in unskilled, dangerous jobs—precisely those affected by automation—they often found that their job classifications had been eliminated altogether.[67]

By the early 1960s, observers noted that a seemingly permanent class of underemployed and jobless blacks had emerged, a group that came to be called the "long-term unemployed." In 1962, the editors of the *Michigan Labor Market Letter* looked back at the troubled 1950s. The last decade, they noted, had been marked by "significant and sometimes violent changes in our economy." They looked with chagrin on the "creation of a very large and alarmingly consistent list of long-term unemployed." Each year from

5.4. The enormous Packard plant on East Grand Boulevard closed in 1956. By the early 1960s, the Packard complex had become a white elephant, and its machinery, furniture, and equipment were offered for auction.

1956 to 1962, state officials ranked Detroit as an area of "substantial labor surplus." While black and white workers alike suffered from economic dislocations, black workers faced a particularly gloomy future. Overrepresented in Detroit's labor surplus were two groups of African American workers: older, unskilled workers and youth.[68]

The most poignant stories of unemployment and dislocation involved older workers, those who had seniority at plants that had closed down altogether, or those who did not have enough seniority to qualify for a transfer to new jobs. They often had years of experience working in heavy industry, but few skills easily transferable to other jobs. The experience of older black workers was somewhat worse than that of older whites. A survey of workers unemployed when Detroit's Packard plant closed in 1956 found that black workers suffered longer bouts of unemployment (thirteen months compared to ten for whites; 38 percent unemployed for more than nineteen months compared to 26 percent for whites). Blacks also took more substantial pay cuts than whites when reemployed.[69] When Murray Auto Body closed in 1954, 76 percent of black employees surveyed exhausted their unemployment benefits, compared to only 27 percent of whites. Those blacks who found new employment went "to an average of twice as many places to find work as the sample as a whole," and suffered a wage drop twice that of reemployed white workers.[70]

Less visible, but even more momentous than the emergence of a pool of unemployed older, disproportionately black workers, was the dramatic reduction of entry-level jobs. As a committee investigating the city's labor market in the late 1950s noted, "the real loss comes not so much in lay-offs as in a falling off in the number of new hires." As manufacturing industries restructured, decentralized, and cut back plant work forces, experienced workers protected by seniority moved into jobs that would have earlier been filled by recent migrants to the city and young workers entering the work force for the first time.[71] Firms that were decentralizing and automating saved costs by relying on trained, experienced workers. Whenever possible, employers tried to minimize the union backlash against automation and decentralization by reducing employment through attrition and curbs on new hiring, instead of layoffs. Responding to workers' fears of job loss at the River Rouge plant, Ford managers noted that a reduction of the labor force "can be handled by the simple expedient of not hiring new employees rather than laying off older ones."[72]

The decline in the number of entry-level manufacturing jobs disproportionately affected black migrants and black youth. Black migrants were less likely in the 1950s to find entry-level jobs in manufacturing that had provided security and relatively good pay to their predecessors in the 1940s. Detroit's pool of manufacturing jobs decreased at the same time that the population of working-age black adults continued to rise. In 1959, the *Detroit News* noted that "Too many Negro families who have moved here to work in the automobile plants are now unemployed. For most there are no prospects of jobs. Many are unemployable and either illiterate or nearly so." They had followed the path of migration to the North, with expectations of entry-level industrial work that required few skills—the sort of work that had attracted blacks to the North since the beginning of the Great Migration. But all too often, upon arrival in Detroit, they found that factories simply were not hiring new workers. "There is little hope for them to regain employment," Urban League vocational counselors reported. "There will be very few employment opportunities open to these people."[73]

TABLE 5.3

Percentage of Men between Ages 15 and
29 Not in Labor Force, Detroit, 1960

Age	White	Nonwhite
15	76.3	76.2
16	56.6	77.7
17	42.3	61.6
18	15.0	41.0
19	8.9	35.3
20	7.8	24.9
21–22	4.9	20.5
23–24	3.4	12.5
25–29	2.3	10.1

Source: Detroit Metropolitan Area Employment by Age, Sex, Color, and Residence, copy
in DNAACP, Part II, Box 10, Folder 10–5,
ALUA. Those in school are not included in
the figures.

The combination of discrimination and deindustrialization weighed most
heavily on the job opportunities of young African American men. Young
workers, especially those who had no postsecondary education, found that
the entry-level operative jobs that had been open to their fathers or older
siblings in the 1940s and early 1950s were gone. The most dramatic evidence of the impact of industrial changes on young black workers was the
enormous gap between black and white youth who had no attachment to the
labor market (Table 5.3). The exclusion of a generation of young men from
the work force, at a vital time in their emergence as adults, prevented them
from gaining the experience, connections, and skills that would open opportunities in later years. It also confirmed their suspicions that they were entrapped in an economic and political system that confined them to the very
bottom. By the end of the 1950s, more and more black job seekers, reported
the Urban League, were demoralized, "developing patterns of boredom and
hopelessness with the present state of affairs." The anger and despair that
prevailed among the young, at a time of national promise and prosperity,
would explode on Detroit's streets in the 1960s.[74]

Only fifteen years after World War II, Detroit's landscape was dominated
by rotting hulks of factory buildings, closed and abandoned, surrounded by
blocks of boarded up-stores and restaurants. Older neighborhoods, whose
streets were lined with the proud homes that middle-class and working-class
Detroiters had constructed in the late nineteenth and early twentieth centuries, were now pockmarked with the shells of burned-out and empty build-

5.5. The flight of industry, the loss of population, and the decline of
Detroit's economy in the postwar period devastated the city's numerous
commerical strips. Unrented stores were often abandoned and vandalized, scarring the city's landscape.

ings, lying among rubbish-strewn vacant lots. Deteriorating housing and
abandoned storefronts were but signs of the profound social and economic
changes that were reshaping the metropolis.

The effects of the loss of industry and of jobs rippled throughout the local
economy. Over a million square feet of space in seven inner-city factories
were vacant in 1956; over 9.9 million square feet of factory space were idle
in the entire city in 1957.[75] The area worst hit by the industrial changes of
the 1950s was Detroit's East Side. The Michigan Employment Security
Commission reported that its Connor Road office (which served all of Detroit's East Side south of the Ford Freeway) had been the state's busiest.

Serving an area with twenty-three plants and 102,967 workers in March of 1953, the MESC office had processed thousands of orders for firms seeking employees. The situation had changed drastically by 1960. Between 1953 and 1960, the area had lost ten plants and 71,137 jobs. Seven plants had closed altogether, two had moved to the suburbs, and one had moved out of Michigan altogether. The MESC office reported that in the depressed economic climate of the late 1950s "an order for 25 [job placements] creates excitement." The East Side, once the epicenter of the auto industry, had become "an economic slum" in the course of a decade.[76]

Detroit's East Side was devastated by the sudden loss of its manufacturing base. Local stores that had relied on the business of regularly employed factory workers suffered. In 1957, the mile-long strip of East Jefferson between Connor and Alter Roads on the city's far East Side had forty-six vacant stores. Similar decline beset other former industrial sections of the city. By 1961, a survey of twenty-five miles of commercial streets in Detroit showed a vacancy rate of over 11 percent. The inner core of the city (within a three-mile radius of downtown) had a vacancy rate of 22 percent. Business districts adjoining former industrial areas were especially hard hit. Detroit's suburbs, by contrast, had only a 4 percent commercial vacancy rate.[77] Most indicative of the city's deteriorating economic health, the number of shops and factories constructed or modified in Detroit fell tenfold between 1951 and 1963 (Table 5.4).

Not only commercial construction was hurt by the devastation of the city's industrial economy. The stunted labor market made homeownership in the city all the more insecure. Workers who managed to hold onto their well-paying, unionized, industrial-sector jobs were able to achieve a level of comfort that few of their blue-collar counterparts in the American past had been able to achieve. They became homeowners. But a growing number of workers found that the status that they had achieved as propertyholders was extremely tenuous. Again African Americans suffered disproportionately. As more blacks found well-paying work in the city's primary industrial sector in the 1940s and 1950s, they bought homes in unprecedented numbers. But because they were at great risk of layoffs and unemployment, their hold on property was all the more precarious.

The process of industrial decline had other far-reaching consequences. It imperiled Detroit's fiscal base. As jobs left the city, so too did white workers with the means to move to suburbs or small towns where factories relocated. Wealthier whites also followed investments outward. As a result, Detroit's population began an unbroken downward fall in the 1950s. As Detroit's population shrank, it also grew poorer and blacker. Increasingly, the city became the home for the dispossessed, those marginalized in the housing market, in greater peril of unemployment, most subject to the vagaries of a troubled economy.

TABLE 5.4

Building Permits Issued for Factories and
Shops, Detroit, 1951–1963

1951	148	1958	31
1952	106	1959	35
1953	124	1960	29
1954	72	1961	24
1955	91	1962	16
1956	86	1963	14
1957	49		

Source: Comprehensive Division, Detroit
City Plan Commission, March 10, 1964, City
Plan Commission Papers, Box 3, Folder: Inter-
Office Memos, February 1961–December
1964.

The 1940s had been a rare window of opportunity for blue-collar workers
in Detroit, especially for African Americans. During World War II, the
number of entry-level jobs in manufacturing grew so fast in Detroit that
discriminatory barriers lost some of their salience. Even if large segments of
the Detroit labor market remained largely closed to black workers, they still
found operative jobs in the automobile industry and in other related industries during the wartime and postwar boom. The decline of manufacturing in
Detroit in the 1950s, however, hit black workers with real force. Rates of
unemployment and joblessness in Detroit rose steadily beginning in the
1950s especially among African Americans (Table 5.5).

One of the tens of thousands of Detroiters who entered the ranks of the
jobless was Tecumseh Haines. A metal polisher, Haines had survived temporary layoffs and managed to hold onto his job until 1959, when he was laid
off indefinitely. Like most black workers, Haines held one of the auto industry's less desirable jobs, one that paid him only eighty-nine dollars a week.
However difficult, the job had seemed secure. At age thirty-four, married,
with one child, one of the nearly 20 percent of blacks who was unemployed
in 1960, Haines looked for another job. His persistence and resourcefulness
paid off. He eventually found employment as a bottle washer at a fruit products factory, although at sixty-three dollars per week he took a substantial
pay cut. After he had been employed in his new job for ten months, the fruit
company cut its work force, and Haines, a new employee with no seniority,
found himself unemployed again.[78]

Haines shared the experience of employment and unemployment in Detroit in the late 1950s and early 1960s with a lot of other workers, both black
and white. But the differences between Haines and his white coworkers
outweighed the similarities. In the heady days of the early 1950s, when

TABLE 5.5
Joblessness in Detroit, 1950–1980 (percent)

	1950	1960	1970	1980
All Workers Unemployed[a]	7.5	7.6	6.9	11.7
Not in Labor Force[b]	16.5	19.5	26.7	37.9
Not Working[c]	22.8	25.7	32.6	45.1
Blacks Unemployed[a]	11.8	18.2	9.8	22.5
Blacks not in Labor Force[b]	18.7	23.3	25.4	43.9
Blacks Not Working[c]	28.3	37.2	32.7	56.4

Sources: Author's calculations from U.S. Department of Commerce, Bureau of the Census, *Census of Population, 1950* (Washington, D.C.: U.S. Government Printing Office, 1952), vol. 2, part 22, Tables 35, 36; *1960*, PC1-24C, Tables 73, 77; *1970*, PC1-C24, Tables 85, 92; *1980*, PC80-1-C24, Tables 120, 134.

[a] Includes all males over fourteen who were in the civilian labor force and seeking work for 1950 and 1960; sixteen years and older in the civilian labor force seeking work for 1970 and 1980.

[b] Has as its denominator all males aged fourteen or older for 1950 and 1960; sixteen years and older for 1970 and 1980.

[c] Includes total unemployed plus total not in labor force divided by total working-age male population.

Haines was in his early twenties and planned to start a family, a job at an auto plant was his ticket to upward mobility. Thrown out of work in the late 1950s, he had few options. The best opportunities for semiskilled workers were in the small midwestern towns and suburbs where many automobile plants and suppliers had relocated. But such places were generally inhospitable to blacks. Following the migration of jobs to the South was even less appealing an option. And based on his experiences in Detroit, he probably felt that he could expect little more in another major city. Whatever became of Tecumseh Haines, his choices were few.[79]

In the eyes of many at the time, and of most commentators since, the 1950s was a decade of prosperity. The decade was the era of the embourgeoised auto worker, the "golden age of capitalism," the era of affluence. In the corporate boom of the decade, some workers did indeed attain the dream of economic security and employment stability. But the forces unleashed by automation, decentralization, and relocation wrecked many workers' lives. Another displaced worker, William Wakeham, worked in one of the most unpleasant jobs in the Ford River Rouge complex, the core room of the iron foundry. Foundry work, relegated largely to blacks, was unbearably hot and dangerous, but it provided a steady wage and secure employment for Wakeham and his coworkers. In 1951, however, Ford eliminated its foundry, laying off thousands of workers. To add insult to injury, when Ford opened a new "specialized foundry," it replaced former foundry workers with "special workers," mostly whites, who had been transferred from other plants. Wakeham lashed out against the inequities of the economic changes that left him unemployed and would provide fewer and fewer opportunities for his children and grandchildren. "Unemployment is not a crime," he wrote. "It is a social ill full of hardships, set-backs, anxieties, needs and sacrifices which would be lauded under any other circumstances. It is truly the weakest spot in Democracy's armor, the likely erosion point in the social structure, and the damning mark of false, unstable or lopsided prosperities." No words could better describe the failed promise of postwar Detroit.[80]

6

"Forget about Your Inalienable Right to Work": Responses to Industrial Decline and Discrimination

> Detroit is known the world over as the "Motor
> City." Are you trying to change it? Where is your
> gratitude to your men, your city? We ask what will
> happen to the thousands who will be let out? What
> is going to happen to the thousands who are buying
> homes?
> —Bill Collett, open letter to Henry Ford II (1951)
>
> Forget about your inalienable right to work.
> —John Szluk (1950)

ON LABOR DAY 1951, the national economy was running at a feverish pitch. The atmosphere at Detroit's annual Labor Day parade was celebratory. Auto workers, machinists, chemical workers, building tradesmen, bus drivers, and a myriad of other laborers thronged Woodward Avenue waving American flags, singing union songs, cheering lustily at Miss CIO, and roaring to applaud Michigan's popular Democratic governor G. Mennen Williams. Capturing the mood of optimism was the parade's prize-winning float, a glistening metallic horn of plenty built by members of two Sheet Metal Workers locals. Not everyone was in a festive mood, however. The parade's largest contingent, workers from the sixty-thousand-strong United Automobile Workers (UAW) Local 600, employed in Ford's River Rouge Plant, struck a dissonant chord. The Rouge contingent was notably interracial— about a third of the union's members were black. In a festival of consensus, they were strikingly militant. Local 600 was one of a few embattled left-led unions remaining in Detroit during the McCarthy era. Their defiance and anger could be heard in their chants and read in their placards. "SPEED UP AND DIE SOONER," read one banner. "SUPPORT OUR FIGHT AGAINST JOB RUNAWAY," proclaimed dozens of boldly scripted signs. Local 600 workers were in a struggle against automation and decentralization, against the profound transformation of the city's economy in the early 1950s. In their battle against "runaway shops," they were the first to recog-

6.1. When the Ford River Rouge plant began eliminating jobs and firing workers in the early 1950s, workers campaigned for the reduction of the work week to thirty hours. In the fall of 1951, UAW Local 600 members filled the lobby of the UAW headquarters with petitions asking the international union to join their call for a shorter work week.

nize that the city's employment base was being ravaged by the forces that economists would later call deindustrialization.[1]

The Local 600 picketers recognized that deindustrialization was not simply an economic issue. The flight of manufacturing jobs in the 1950s raised fundamental political questions about rights, responsibilities, power, and inequality that were unresolved in mid-twentieth-century America. What obligations, if any, did corporations have toward the communities in which they were located? Should workers have a say in corporate decisions that affected their livelihood? How should government respond to job flight? What about the troubling fact that African American workers, because of entrenched workplace discrimination, bore the brunt of economic restructuring? How unions and corporations, judges and local elected officials, civil rights groups and reformers responded to these questions would have profound implications for the American political economy for the remainder of the twentieth century.

The economic changes that affected the workers at the Rouge and other plants in Detroit at midcentury perplexed most observers. While sociologists argued that America was home to a uniquely embourgeoised working class and was witnessing the end of class struggle, and popular writers were lauding the age of affluence in the United States, places like Detroit were left behind. African American workers bore the brunt of economic change, their options limited by discrimination, and their tenuous hold on factory jobs threatened by deindustrialization. Yet urban economic troubles were marginalized in a national debate that was framed by the discourses of growth, affluence, and consensus. Mainstream economists focused on national-level statistics that showed phenomenal growth in the gross national product, in consumer buying power, and in industrial output. Even those who acknowledged that some workers suffered the effects of economic restructuring nonetheless remained confident that it was just a matter of time before market forces pulled the labor market back to equilibrium. Growth economists were optimistic that a "rising tide would lift all boats," and hoped that tinkering with the federal budget would solve the country's lingering employment problems. There were, of course, prominent dissenters. Paul Douglas, Democratic U.S. Senator from Illinois and a former economics professor, distrusted the easy optimism of growth economics. As early as 1953, Douglas predicted that "Detroit is going to have rough times." When Douglas, Pennsylvania Senator Joe Clark, Minnesota Senator Hubert Humphrey, and other labor Democrats proposed legislation in 1955 to deal with the special problems of "depressed areas," they bucked conventional economic wisdom. Eisenhower twice vetoed proposed Area Redevelopment Acts intended to deal with the problems of islands of poverty in the midst of an affluent society.[2]

The trend against a structural understanding of poverty and unemployment was reinforced by the work of industrial psychologists and "manpower" experts who stressed the importance of individual skills in the workplace. The reason that large numbers of workers had been displaced was their lack of "human capital." African American migrants, these experts argued, came with backward values and few marketable skills; African American youth were sullen and hardened. Their troubles in the labor market were compounded by family dysfunctionality. To solve the problem of unemployment meant behavior modification. Job training, the improvement of interpersonal skills, and the inculcation of a work ethic would solve the problem of urban joblessness.[3] The pro-business sentiment of the 1950s bolstered arguments that individual deficiencies rather than structural economic and racial barriers were at the root of urban joblessness and poverty. To highlight the problems of industrial workers, to emphasize workplace inequity, was fundamentally un-American. After World War II, as Elizabeth Fones-Wolf has argued, major corporations orchestrated an extraordinarily successful propaganda campaign that associated big business with "true" American values, and tainted its critics with charges of communism. To challenge corporate policy was to risk political marginalization and disdain, and radical voices in the 1950s were muffled in the free enterprise crusade.[4]

McCarthyism also silenced the most vocal critics of racial inequality. Civil rights organizations in the North expended tremendous political energy deflecting accusations of communism. Afraid to be labeled un-American, civil rights groups in Detroit in the 1950s fashioned a centrist gradualism in response to racial inequalities. Democrats and moderate Republicans also shared a belief in gradualism, and their civil rights proposals were more symbolic than transformative. Even the most liberal Democrats were reluctant to upset their party's precarious racial balance, and Republicans were generally unwilling to accept the large-scale governmental intervention that was necessary to overturn the racial status quo.[5]

In this context, Detroiters who recognized the fundamental economic and racial conflicts that plagued the city at midcentury were left to improvise. Labor activists, city officials, and civil rights groups had few models for coping with the plight of displaced workers, especially African Americans. They groped toward political solutions, but were stymied at all levels. In a political climate that stressed consensus, where both parties downplayed racial conflict and censored any serious discussion of class structure, inequality, and income maldistribution, they fashioned compromise solutions that did little to address the underlying causes of the city's economic woes. They were forced to strike compromises with big business. They butted heads with unsympathetic government officials. And they drew from the conventional wisdom of industrial relations specialists and race relations experts in ways that hindered their efforts to challenge racial discrimination. The result was that the flight of industry and jobs continued unchecked, as persistent urban unemployment, especially among black workers, became an increasingly intransigent problem.

The UAW's Lost Opportunity: The Battle Against "Runaway" Jobs

The workers at the Ford River Rouge plant who broke the atmosphere of consensus at the 1951 Labor Day parade were the first to see Detroit's industrial economy dramatically changing for the worse. The Rouge was the target of Ford's aggressive automation and decentralization plans, and Rouge workers felt the pinch. In May 1949, in response to Ford's attempts to speed up production on its assembly lines, Rouge workers walked out in a twenty-five-day strike.[6] As Rouge workers began to see the link between speedups, automation, and plant decentralization, Local 600 extended its battle against Ford's industrial policy from the shop floor to local city halls and to federal courtrooms.

In February 1950, James Simmons, a worker in the Plastics Department at the Rouge, warned that the introduction of automated machinery would put jobs at risk. Simmons saw changes in the Rouge as "part of a pattern that calls for taking these jobs to new unorganized sections of the country to be manned by green workers at higher speeds and less pay."[7] Simmons was not off base. Beginning in 1949, Ford accelerated plastics production from 650 to 740 pieces a day, then to 870. Workers who failed to keep up the grueling pace lost their jobs. In the fall of 1949 one of Simmons's coworkers, Earl Filban, had been laid off by Ford for failing to meet the new, higher quota of hourly parts production in plastics. Plastics building workers feared for their jobs. "We want everybody to know we want our jobs," wrote Filban and three coworkers. "Each of us have families to support. We have many years of seniority. We need your help."[8] Throughout 1950 and 1951, workers in plastics, the foundry, and the motor building faced continuous speedups.[9]

Ford officials kept workers in the dark about decentralization plans, while suddenly laying off hundreds of workers and surreptitiously moving machinery from River Rouge to new plants. In August 1951, Ford went so far as to haul machines out of the Rouge under the cover of darkness because they feared "action by Ford workers to protect their jobs." "It's thievery in the night," wrote one anonymous Rouge worker angrily.[10]

Throughout 1950 and 1951, Ford and Local 600 engaged in regular skirmishes over automation and decentralization at the Rouge. Local 600 established a Committee on Decentralization both to examine the impact of Ford's industrial location policy on Rouge workers and to shape a campaign to respond to it. In the summer of 1950, the committee predicted that thirty thousand Rouge workers would be affected by decentralization, a figure that turned out to be remarkably accurate.[11] They feared that decentralization would irreparably weaken their local's financial and bargaining power. Union officers concerned themselves with the rights of transferred workers, but worked even more assiduously to prevent "runaway shops" altogether.[12] In response to automation-related speedups, Rouge workers went on dozens of wildcat strikes and engaged in countless individual acts of shop-floor resistance. To protect workers' rapidly eroding control over the production process, Local 600 officials encouraged workers to avoid the company's "suggestion box," fearing that the company would translate worker suggestions into further automation, speedups, and layoffs.[13]

In the crucible of rapid economic change, Rouge workers fashioned a critique of corporate policy using the potent political language of rights, just as in the context of housing, Detroiters had pushed for recognition of their entitlement to a home. Again and again union officials and workers referred to "the inalienable right to a job," a right rooted in the New Deal notion of economic security. This notion of rights took on special resonance with African American workers. Local 600's ally in the battle against runaway shops was the National Negro Labor Council (NNLC), a Detroit-based organization that allied itself with the CIO's left-led unions. The NNLC, in fact, drew heavily from Local 600 for both its rank-and-file membership and its leadership.[14] "THE RIGHT TO WORK," argued a NNLC pamphlet, "is the most burning issue of our time." The NNLC offered a wide-ranging critique of decentralization, especially of the construction of new plants in the Jim Crow South. The movement of industry to the South, argued the NNLC, hurt northern workers, especially blacks, who lost their jobs, hurt southern workers who were paid less than their northern counterparts, and especially hurt blacks who were closed out of most of the well-paying jobs below the Mason-Dixon line.[15] Runaway shops threatened the rights of workers north and south.

Workers' rights would be unattainable without corporate responsibility. Local 600 members and their allies offered a communitarian critique of Ford policy. Ford, they contended, had an obligation to the greater Detroit community. Tommy Thompson, Local 600 president in 1950, denounced the "forced migration of workers." What about the "worker who has lived most of his life in the Detroit area, who has 'roots' buried deep in this community"? he asked. Should a worker be "forced to pull out those 'roots,' sell his home, leave friends and relatives and start all over again in some new city, not of his or his family's choosing"?[16] In an open letter to published in the Local 600 newspaper, Rouge worker Bill Collett chastised Henry Ford II: "Detroit is known the world over as the 'Motor City.' Are you trying to change it? Where is your gratitude to your men, your city?"[17]

Local 600 officials turned to the shop floor and began an uphill battle to reduce the number of work hours to save jobs. In late 1951, angry Rouge workers, frustrated by the UAW International's refusal to negotiate a reduction in work hours, descended on Solidarity House, the UAW International headquarters. The Rouge delegation filled the Solidarity House lobby with thirty thousand petitions calling for a thirty-hour week, which they argued would stem job loss in the decentralizing auto industry. UAW International officials dismissed their demands, convinced that the militant unionists were trying to subvert the recent five-year contract with the Big Three and sabotage the Korean War effort. Employers also adamantly opposed the shortened work week. The call for a thirty-hour week came as firms were turning to overtime to increase production and reduce the costs of hiring new workers, training them, and providing them with benefits. Despite stiff resistance from both employers and UAW International officials, Local 600 continued its demands for a thirty-hour week throughout the 1950s.[18]

Rouge workers also took their battle against decentralization to local city halls. In January 1950, Tommy Thompson, president of Local 600, entreated Detroit Mayor Albert Cobo to establish a committee to examine the "migration of industrial operations and jobs from this area and to seek ways and means of ending such migration."[19] Cobo, a former businessman and conservative Republican, ignored the request, but political leaders in a few nearby communities responded to Local 600's calls for support. In the wake of the Labor Day 1951 protests, Local 600 persuaded the Dearborn city council to pass an anti–runaway job resolution. City councils in the heavily blue-collar suburbs of Ecorse, Garden City, River Rouge, and Melvindale joined Dearborn in passing antidecentralization resolutions.[20] Such gestures were largely symbolic. Local officials were too timid or too powerless to stand up to the giant Ford Motor Company; alone they could not hope to affect the industrial policy of the automotive multinational.

Protests and symbolic political gestures did little to stem the flow of Ford jobs away from the Rouge. In a creative and desperate move, Local 600 shifted the battleground to the courtroom. In late 1951, the local filed a suit seeking an injunction against Ford's decentralization policy or a nullification of their five-year contract with Ford signed in 1950. The basis of the suit was breach of contract.[21] "No member of our union or any union would consciously sign a five-year contract which would leave him helpless while his employer moved his job from under him," argued Local 600 President Carl Stellato (who replaced Thompson in the post in 1951).[22]

The suit was also based on what Stellato had called "moral and economic issues." Ford's decentralization policy went "beyond the realm of pure industrial relations" to issues of economic equality and justice. "We owe it to ourselves, to our members, and to the surrounding communities to prevent this disastrous result for the Ford Rouge workers," argued Stellato.[23]

The suit offered a fundamental challenge to the prevailing assumption that companies owed nothing to the towns and cities whose viability depended on them or to the workers who lived there. The complaint reminded the court that "The economic life, the growth and the development of this Greater Detroit area has been and is dependent in substantial measure upon the continuation of the high level of production activities of the Rouge Plant and the affording of continued and substantial employment to the plaintiffs."[24] Decentralization brought "increased relief rolls, increased un-employment compensation claims, decreased retail sales and a lowering of public morale in the Greater Detroit area." Ford's policy, in other words, did not only affect Rouge workers, it affected other Detroit-area workers, especially in auto-related industries, as well as shopowners, taxpayers, and homeowners. Ford's decentralization policy was detrimental to the public good.[25]

Local 600's brief built a case around an expansive definition of workers' rights. The plaintiffs argued that the right to work was embedded in the five-year contract negotiated by Ford and the UAW in 1950. Under the terms of the contract, workers "became entitled to and received certain valu-able rights, including . . . security of tenure in their employment classifi-cation at said Rouge Plant, [and] the right to employment in accordance with seniority at said plant." The contract's guarantees of paid holidays, benefits, seniority, and retirement "have value for the plaintiffs only in the continued employment of the plaintiffs" at the Rouge Plant. By laying off workers at the Rouge plant, Ford had "substantially reduce[d] the employment rights and opportunities" of its employees.[26]

Perhaps the boldest aspect of the lawsuit was its attempt to narrow the license that labor law gave employers to lay off or fire workers at will. Under the law, workers had little legal protection against firings and layoffs. The National Labor Relations Act of 1935 prohibited employers from firing workers for engaging in union activity, but otherwise, discharged workers had little recourse. As UAW International staff lawyer Harold Cranefield argued, the Local 600 suit, if successful, would limit the freedom of employ-ers "to withdraw employment for any reason whatsoever (except one which would violate the National Labor Relations Act)" and would represent "a great gain for labor."[27]

The Local 600 suit also challenged a basic assumption of labor law, that the mobility of capital was an inalienable property right, not subject to worker input or negotiation. Embedded in labor law was the tenet that cer-tain spheres of business activity were protected as "managerial prerogative," not subject to collective bargaining. Workers and unions had long struggled for control over the work process, and often gained tenuous control over promotion and work rules on the shopfloor, but companies seldom allowed

workers even a small voice in firms' long-term planning and economic decision making. Most significantly, the courts and the National Labor Relations
Board tenaciously protected companies from labor interference in "enterprise affairs." In the key 1945 *Mahoning Mining Company* case, the National
Labor Relations Board had ruled that an employer could "change his [*sic*]
business structure, sell or contract out a portion of his operations, or make
any like change" without consulting "the bargaining representatives of the
employees affected by the proposed business change." There was little precedent in labor law that challenged Ford's right to move at will, regardless
of its effects on workers or the surrounding community.[28]

Local 600's suit also had the potential to expand the notion of corporate
responsibility beyond the narrow bounds of corporate law. Business law, as
legal historian Lawrence Friedman has argued, "is less concerned with the
economic power of corporations than with their everyday behavior." Its
primary concern is to assure fair and honest dealings between corporations
and their officials and investors and stockholders, "in a way that would not
interfere with business efficiency." Implicit in the suit against Ford was
a call for the extension of the realm of corporate responsibility from everyday behavior to economic power. The suit challenged the assumption
that the company's obligation to shareholders was greater than that to its
employees.[29]

Local 600's legal battle against Ford's decentralization policy faced serious resistance within the UAW itself. On November 12, 1951, Rouge workers held a mass meeting to persuade the UAW International office to support the suit.[30] Behind the scenes, UAW Legal Department officials were
intrigued by Local 600's legal gambit. Staff lawyer Cranefield noted that the
suit was "novel in its conception," but added that "almost all lawyers would
probably agree instantly that such a suit is wholly untenable." Yet Cranefield
warned against treating the legal action "cavalierly." The suit's theory, he
wrote, "has been very carefully thought out," and he pointed out that its
premise of "fraud in the inducement" was "an ancient ground upon which
courts of equity have relieved parties from their contracts."[31]

Whatever the merits of the case, UAW International officials, embroiled
in a dispute with the oppositional local, refused to join the lawsuit and took
no public position on the issues that it raised, either pro or con. In February
1952, the UAW International office took Local 600 into trusteeship, in part
because of the local's staunch oppositional politics, in part because five local
officers were suspected Communist party members. It removed the leftist
officers, took over the local's newspaper, and assumed control of the daily
operations of the union until new elections could be held in September.[32]
Local 600's militant stand against runaway jobs was a casualty of the takeover. The International took a moderate position on decentralization, calcu-

lated to maximize union power without challenging management's traditional prerogative to move capital and labor at will. Its strategy was twofold. The UAW would organize every runaway plant so that "Ford, no matter where it sprang up, was forced to pay Detroit Area Rates, to establish Detroit Area Conditions (or better), and to set up Seniority Systems similar to those in Detroit." Second, the union worked out an arrangement with Ford that Rouge workers' seniority would be honored in all Ford plants in Michigan.[33] As long as the UAW could build a base in new plants and protect the seniority of existing workers, the International office had few worries about decentralization. In the case of Local 600, International officials probably welcomed the reduction in the size and power of the largest oppositional local in the union.[34]

Even if Local 600 had somehow managed to gain the support of the UAW leadership, its legal battle against Ford would have faced formidable odds at a federal bench dominated by a cautious, pro-business jurisprudence. *Local 600 v. Ford Motor Company* met with a predictable fate in the United States District Court. In a short, acerbic opinion, Judge Thomas P. Thornton dismissed the suit. Nothing in the contract, Thornton argued, prohibited the company from decentralizing Rouge operations. The judge found no evidence to support Local 600's charge that Ford had engaged in "concealment, misrepresentations and false denials." If indeed the contract between Ford and its workers had been obtained fraudulently, the judge contended (without mentioning the bitter factional battle within the UAW) then the UAW International officials who had signed the contract would certainly have joined Local 600 in its suit. That the UAW International refused to be party to the complaint was proof to Thornton that the disputed contract was valid. Most importantly, Thornton refused to challenge Ford's plant relocation decisions. Above all, the contract "vests in the company, and only in the company, the right" to manage its business as it sees fit.[35] In Thornton's chambers, Rouge workers lost their last possible redress against the runaway shop.

During the profound transformation of the city's economy, Local 600 stood almost alone against the runaway shops. What explains the militancy of the Rouge workers and the complacency of most other Detroiters? Part of the story lies in the radical vision of union activists at the Rouge. They offered a more systematic critique of management prerogative and indeed of capital mobility itself than did more mainstream unionists who focused increasingly on collective bargaining and directed their energies toward incremental gains in wages and benefits. Local 600's leadership was far more willing to confront Ford when cooperation was the norm. By the 1950s, under the leadership of Walter Reuther, the UAW was increasingly unwilling to challenge corporate leadership openly on controversial issues such as plant location policy and discriminatory hiring policy. The reluctance of the

UAW International (and most other unions) to challenge sacrosanct business practices limited the possibilities of resistance to deindustrialization.[36]

By the mid-1950s, the UAW leadership began to address the impact of automation, but with much greater caution than the dissenters at Local 600. International union leaders took a middle-ground position, expressing optimism about new technologies, but concerned with mitigating their effects on UAW members. Automation could be a blessing, but if misused, it could endanger the well-being of industrial workers. Automation, as Michigan CIO leaders noted, could lead to the "virtual end of back-breaking toil for our people, a total end to want." But if it were unregulated, it could be abused. Automation could "serve man, or enslave man," as the *Michigan CIO News* reminded its readers. Careful planning was necessary to protect workers from the abuses of new technologies.[37]

Mainstream unionists took a multipronged approach to solving the crisis of automation. According to UAW officials, government, unions, and management should work together to prepare for the changes that would inevitably result from the introduction of automated machinery. Walter P. Reuther argued for such proposals as early retirement programs, a guaranteed annual wage, and the extension of unemployment benefits and welfare. Central to the union's call for reform was vocational counseling and worker retraining. Schooled in the burgeoning field of "manpower" studies, unionists emphasized the problem of mismatch between individual abilities and employers' demands. Unemployment would remain high unless the skills gap was closed. Employers and schools needed to retrain workers. In the meantime, union leaders called for an extension of unemployment benefits to assist "displaced workers." Finally, Reuther, AFL-CIO President George Meany and other mainstream unionists offered a tepid endorsement of a shorter work week that they had withheld in the early 1950s.[38]

Democratic party leaders, including Michigan Governor G. Mennen Williams, were more than happy to cooperate with the UAW. By the late 1950s, calls for "manpower development" and job training had become a staple of liberal politics. Williams created a state commission that would research the effects of automation, and work with employers, unions, and schools to retrain workers in the high technology skills they would need to cope in the automated workplace. Michigan Democrats joined with other northern liberals to push for another union demand—federally subsidized job training programs—that would become an important element of the Kennedy adminstration's domestic agenda and eventually part of Lyndon Johnson's Great Society.[39]

Industrialists, in contrast, resisted even the most tepid union proposals to soften automation's effects. In the midst of the recession of 1957, officials from General Motors and American Motors rejected Reuther's invitation to discuss the thirty-hour week. At a time when Michigan had a "chronic labor surplus," and when employers were increasing the use of overtime, employers had no incentive to accept shorter work week proposals. The only proposal that had any significant support among auto company officials were early retirement programs, which would contribute to worker loyalty and, simultaneously, give less productive workers with seniority the incentive to retire. As a result, organized labor's agenda remained largely unachieved. Instead, labor leaders, corporate leaders, and city government officials turned to a second strategy: the attempted reindustrialization of Detroit.[40]

Industrial Renewal

While deindustrialization went largely unchecked in the courts and on the picket lines, Detroit's city government embarked on a policy of trying to work within the constraints of the "free market." Rather than intervening to regulate corporate decentralization policies, city officials attempted to lure manufacturers to Detroit, with the carrots of cleared land and tax breaks. Planners based the city's reindustrialization proposals on two premises. First, they believed that the major cause of industrial flight was the lack of new land for industrial development within the city. Second, they believed that most of Detroit's existing factories were superannuated or unusable in the age of automation. Their understanding of the industrial change of the 1950s rested on the fallacy of technological determinism. Automation, in their estimate, was the inevitable consequence of the march of industrial progress. If only city planners could figure out how to accommodate the demands of new automated plants, they could maintain the city's industrial base and prevent the further hemorrhage of manufacturing jobs.[41]

The centerpiece of Detroit's reindustrialization policy was "industrial renewal," a complement to the downtown commercial and housing redevelopment plans that the Detroit City Plan Commission had begun proposing in the early 1940s. As early as 1950, the City Plan Commission called for "an aggressive redevelopment program" to revitalize Detroit's industrial base. To attract industry to Detroit, the city established "industrial corridors" and proposed the condemnation and "demolition of substandard residential structures which have a blighting effect on industrial districts." Planners hoped that the cleared land would attract the new single-story, largely automated plants that employers favored. Detroit was by no means alone in placing hope in industrial renewal. Trenton, Philadelphia, St. Louis, Cleveland, Buffalo, and Cincinnati all cleared run-down residential and business areas with great fanfare and optimism. Industrial renewal plans in Detroit and elsewhere, however, faced serious problems, in part because they were premised on the destruction of existing neighborhoods and housing. Residents of the areas that were to be condemned mounted fierce resistance to industrial clearance. And the city had no guarantee that after it cleared sections of land it would find companies willing to construct new plants there.[42]

Detroit officials developed industrial renewal plans piecemeal. Beginning in the early 1950s, the Detroit City Plan Commission proposed to clear a seventy-five-acre site in the ethnically heterogeneous and declining Corktown neighborhood on the city's West Side for the development of a district of warehouses and small businesses, something analogous to a suburban industrial park. The West Side Industrial Project, as it was tagged, would provide land for small plants and warehouses, especially those dislocated from the sites of urban renewal areas near downtown. Clearance plans, however, met with the staunch opposition of neighborhood church leaders, civic associations, and ethnic clubs. The city ultimately dismissed the opposition of community groups, cleared acres of houses and other buildings, and redeveloped the land as an industrial park.[43]

The fate of the West Side Industrial Project foreshadowed the fate of later industrial revitalization plans. The development of the area was painfully slow. More than ten years passed between the announcement of plans to redevelop the area and the construction of the first warehouses and small plants. The costs of displacement were great, and the benefits of reindustrialization were few. The result was that the positive impact of the West Side Industrial Project on Detroit's economy was minimal. The gain from the construction of a few small plants and warehouses required a tremendous expenditure of political and economic resources, and in the end, failed to stem Detroit's economic decline. Finally, the West Side Industrial Project proved difficult to replicate. It was a piecemeal attempt to solve an economic problem with far deeper roots.[44]

The Urban League's Two-Tiered Employment Policy

The City Plan Commission's attempt to draw industry to the city, for all of its flaws, nonetheless started with the recognition that the primary problem facing Detroit's economy was industrial flight. Few other public officials or reform groups saw industrial flight as the major cause of unemployment in Detroit. Social service and employment agencies in the city turned their energies toward what they perceived as a growing gap between automated jobs and workers who were so inadequately trained or educated that they could not qualify for those jobs. Black agencies were especially concerned about the effect of automation on black job prospects.

The Detroit Urban League (DUL) ran the most important black employment agency in the city. From its founding in 1916 through the 1940s, the

DUL had offered counseling to recent migrants, served as a social service agency, and operated as an employment agency for recent arrivals. The DUL had long served as a conduit for black workers into unskilled and semiskilled service and industrial jobs. In the 1920s and 1930s, John Dancy, DUL secretary, made close contacts with Dodge and Ford Motor Company and placed some young men with these firms, optimistic that business leaders could be gently persuaded to abandon racial discrimination.[45] The DUL steered even more workers—men and women alike—into maintenance and household service positions. DUL officials were, for the most part, reluctant participants in the city's service-sector labor market. By the 1940s, the DUL began to direct more resources toward "breakthrough" jobs for well-educated and highly skilled blacks.[46]

The DUL's new policy emerged from the optimism of the late 1940s and early 1950s. DUL officials assumed that a rapidly growing economy would absorb most unskilled and semiskilled black workers. In response to its perception of new opportunities for blue-collar black workers, the DUL gradually reduced its role throughout the 1940s as an employment agency for new migrants. In 1952, the DUL eliminated its job placement program for recent migrants and unemployed blacks altogether, and referred jobless workers to the Michigan Employment Security Commission. In its place, the DUL Vocational Services Department made its major mission "job development"—opening formerly all-white jobs in skilled and white-collar work to black "pioneers."[47]

DUL officials, most of whom had professional degrees and enjoyed middle-class status, were especially sympathetic to the plight of underemployed blacks with college and graduate degrees. Urban League officials received hundreds of depressing letters, often with résumés, from blacks with MBAs who worked in factory jobs because they could not find white-collar employment, black accountants who were rejected again and again when they applied for jobs with white-owned banks, and black doctors rejected for internships at major city hospitals. "I have 600 young Negroes," recalled DUL Vocational Services Secretary Francis Kornegay, "men and women with degrees . . . and there isn't any place to send them." Particularly galling to DUL officials was the absence of black faces on the floors of major department stores, at the ticket counters and in the aisles of major airlines, in the tellers' booths in local banks, and at receptionists' desks in law firms, ad agencies, and auto companies. Opening "pioneer" jobs for blacks served two purposes. It provided a semblance of dignity and status to blacks who had been denied access to the white-collar world. But, more importantly, for the Urban League, it would be a major step toward civil rights by encouraging "public acceptance of the Negro both as a citizen and as a worker."[48]

DUL officials noted with pride the accomplishments of their placement service. Of 356 placements in 1951, 26 were in professional careers, 208 in clerical and sales jobs, 8 in skilled, 1 in semiskilled, 22 in unskilled, and 91 in service jobs. The DUL placed 386 workers in 1953: 11 in professional occupations, 330 in clerical and sales work, and only 7 in skilled and 11 in semiskilled jobs. The mission of the DUL was clear: to find positions for the budding black middle class. The search for middle-class jobs, however, took a tremendous amount of energy. The DUL, like its counterparts in other cities like Cincinnati, eschewed the tactics of protest and direct confrontation, preferring quiet, behind-the-scenes negotiations with employers. Throughout the 1950s, DUL Vocational Services staff members spent hours in exhausting meetings with corporate officials over the hiring of blacks in high-visibility jobs. In a typical month in 1956, DUL officials met or spoke with 108 industrial managers, corporate executives, and business owners.[49]

The process of convincing businesses to hire a token black or two often took years. To meet with employers who were skeptical of blacks' native intelligence and ability or outright hostile to equal employment demanded a tremendous amount of patience. In 1953 and 1954, as part of a National Urban League campaign to open the transportation industry to blacks, DUL officials met with executives from every major airline to persuade them to hire black stewardesses, and black employees in sales, management, and supervisory positions. In October 1956, they met with airline officials again, to no avail. Finally, in 1957 the DUL arranged a conference for airline executives. DUL officials followed a similar pattern with the major bus companies. By early 1957, DUL had met or spoken to major airline officials sixty-eight times and major bus company officials fifty-nine times.[50] DUL Vocational Services reports noted with pride their successes in placing black pioneers with formerly segregated firms: in 1957, they placed one driver with Greyhound, an airline reservation clerk with American Airlines, and another with Capital Airlines.[51] The same year, the DUL placed a grand total of 116 workers in breakthrough jobs, 16 in firms that had never had a black employee before.

Through its job placement and pioneering program, the DUL assisted well-educated and highly skilled blacks. The League also directed resources toward the employment problems of unskilled workers and the poor, but these efforts had a markedly different focus. They began with the assumption that lower-class blacks were unemployable, and thus emphasized the development of personal skills and the modification of individual behavior, rather than job creation. On the matter of employment for the poorest blacks, the DUL contended that discrimination was only one part of the problem: "Many people are not prepared to hold the jobs that are available," regardless of discriminatory patterns in employment.[52]

DUL officials were especially concerned that unemployed black workers were unprepared to meet the demands of automated industry. The DUL took little notice of the deindustrialization of the city, but it did note the dangers of automation. Ernest L. Brown, Jr., a Vocational Services Department staff member, warned: "Education will be a necessity for everyone in the coming generation. There will be no place for unskilled labor."[53] By 1959 DUL staff worried that "the continuing installation of automation in most manufacturing processes produced a drastic shift from past manpower skills to new ones with high technical content." With few skills, young blacks faced the prospect of permanent unemployment.[54]

The solution to the dilemma of automation, according to the DUL, was emphasis on "the factors of family structure, community influences, and basic schooling, as they relate to training and preparation for jobs at all levels."[55] Beginning in the late 1950s, the DUL directed an increasing amount of its resources toward the preparation of black youth for work in automated industries. DUL officials spoke to high-school students around the city, prepared conferences on vocational guidance, and worked with city churches to inform ministers about job advice. Its projects included a Stay-in-School and a Back-to-School campaign "directed at potential school drop-outs and adults who lack saleable skills," a church guidance council which arranged monthly meetings between vocational counselors and church leaders citywide, and a "Vocational Opportunities Campaign" which emphasized "the relationship between school and future work experiences."[56]

Most important to the strategy of the DUL was the counseling of displaced workers and youth. DUL guidance programs started with the premise that self-improvement was the first step toward gainful employment. In 1958, the Urban League ran a series of "Job Tips" columns in the weekly black *Michigan Chronicle*, including columns on job applications, employment agencies, and interviews. "Underlying [the advice]," wrote the DUL columnist, "is the fundamental requirement that an individual must develop strength of character if he is to succeed in a career."[57]

The Urban League also continued its efforts to help blacks, especially migrants, to assimilate to the urban workplace. Job counselors and social workers with the Urban League paid especially close attention to the appearance and demeanor of black youths, and offered them tips on job application procedures, interviews, and dress at work. Typical was a series of short plays prepared by an Urban League staff member which admonished black youth to present themselves well when applying for jobs. In one, "Jenny Notready" appears at her interview chewing gum and "wearing high heels, slacks and a midriff." She answers her interviewers with curt "uh, huhs" and with flippant comments. And despite her slovenly dress, she insists on a job that pays eighty-five dollars a week rather than the advertised sixty-five dollars. Predictably, she is not hired. In another, "Mo Humphrey," a young man "sloppily dressed," goes to a department store with a friend to apply for a job.

Personnel Director: Have you filled out your application?

       Mo: Uh huh. (*Slouches down in seat, one foot on desk*).

      P.D.:   May I see it please?

       Mo: Uh huh. (*Slides application onto desk, it falls off side, P.D. has to bend over to pick it up*).

      P.D.:   Well, I see your name is MO THOMPSON. Is that your full name, Mr. Thompson?

       Mo: Naw, my full name's Moses Aloysius Contrusious Federaoutious Thompson. . . .

      P.D.:   Now, let me see, the application is so smudged I can't make out what it says. Is this a new school? Sathewestun or Soteweten?

       Mo: Naw, man that's Southwest'n.

      P.D.:   Oh, that's S-O-U-T-H-W-E-S-T-E-R-N. (*Shakes head as he writes*). Now one other thing I do not see written here is your social security number.

       Mo: Yeah, uh, ta tell yuh the truth, I forget what it is and I didn't bring the card.

Not only is Mo sullen and illiterate, he is also a high-school dropout and "the toughest thing on wheels," with ten points on his driving record. Mo, like the feckless Jenny Notready, fails to get a job. In a follow-up play, a reformed Mo, dressed impeccably, presents an immaculate job application, speaks in impeccable standard English, and gets hired immediately at a job that pays ten dollars a day more than he had expected.[58]

The Urban League vocational services programs—whether negotiations for "breakthrough" jobs or guidance and education programs—met with limited success. Most impressively, the DUL contributed to employers' growing acceptance of African-American women as clerical workers. The number of black female clerical workers nearly doubled between 1950 and 1960 and doubled again between 1960 and 1970. But the percentage of blacks employed as managers and sales workers fell in the 1950s and rose only slightly in the 1960s. The DUL's hope that opening clerical, management, and executive positions would lead to a "dispersion of Negro workers throughout the workforce" remained unfulfilled. With the exception of clerical work, the DUL's program created token positions for the most elite job seekers. Moreover, the emphasis on jobs for the elite took away resources from programs to create jobs and improve working conditions for the poor. The second prong of the DUL approach to employment also met with mixed success at best. DUL training and guidance programs may have succeeded in improving the "human capital" of some unskilled workers and youth. The DUL was right in pointing to the declining number of unskilled jobs in the city. Still, the best interview skills and personal manners were of limited value in stiff competition for a shrinking pool of jobs in a market still plagued by discrimination. DUL employment policy was a limited solution to a growing structural problem.[59]

The NAACP, the UAW, and Fair Employment Practices

The NAACP had the reputation of being far more militant than the Urban League in its response to the problems of blacks in Detroit's labor force. The reality was more complicated. The largest local branch in the country during World War II, Detroit's NAACP grew in power and influence because of its alliance with the UAW. The NAACP joined with the UAW to battle wartime hate strikes, enforce the wartime Fair Employment Practices regulations, and work for the passage of antidiscriminatory legislation. The wartime alliance between the UAW and the NAACP brought civil rights politics to the workplace, where the combination of protest and union clout helped to expand job opportunities for black workers. The NAACP-UAW alliance endured after World War II, but it changed shape as the wartime insurgency was institutionalized and bureaucratized. The NAACP turned its energies away from the shop floor and toward courtrooms and the halls of the state legislature and Congress. And the UAW took a middle-ground position on civil rights, adamantly supporting national and state efforts for racial equality, propagandizing among its workers for civil rights, but largely leaving shop-floor and hiring-gate discrimination unaddressed.[60]

By the late 1940s, Detroit's NAACP had lost members and political clout, a trend that would continue through the 1950s. From its wartime peak of 25,000, Detroit Branch membership plummeted to a nadir of 5,162 in 1952. In the late 1940s, the NAACP purged many of its more militant members, among them former Branch President Reverend Charles Hill, who left under a cloud of suspicion for his activism and his refusal to sever ties with Communist-front civil rights organizations. The specter of McCarthyism shaped the Detroit NAACP's new nonconfrontational strategy. As a result, many of its grassroots and labor activist members grew disillusioned with the moderation of its leaders and quit the organization.[61] By the early 1950s, the major role of the Detroit Branch was fund-raising for national litigation efforts. NAACP officials also expended a tremendous amount of energy battling such left-led organizations as the Civil Rights Congress and the Detroit-based National Negro Labor Council, even when they worked toward common goals.[62]

On a national level, the NAACP Labor Department, led by the indefatigable Herbert Hill beginning in 1948, attempted to open employment opportunities for blacks in unions and industries all over the country. The

NAACP's strategy was to investigate, negotiate, legislate, and, if necessary, litigate. Under Hill, the NAACP challenged Jim Crow union locals in textiles, steel, and the auto industry, worked to improve the conditions of migrant farm laborers, battled discrimination in government contracts, and investigated racial barriers in apprenticeship programs. Most striking was how seldom any of these efforts involved industries in Detroit. In part, the situation of Detroit workers was not as urgent as that of their counterparts in the border states and the South, where the NAACP targeted Jim Crow locals. Herbert Hill frequently visited Detroit for three reasons: to promote trade union membership in the NAACP, to fundraise, and to meet with UAW officials to coordinate national efforts to pass and enforce antidiscrimination laws.[63]

Overshadowed by the battles against racial inequality, hobbled by anticommunism, directed by cautious, gradualist leaders, and with a dwindling base of grassroots support, the Detroit Branch NAACP turned its energies toward the legislative arena. The Detroit Branch NAACP's most active antidiscrimination efforts in the 1950s centered around the statewide campaign for a Fair Employment Practices (FEP) law. Efforts to pass a state Fair Employment Practices law began in the immediate aftermath of World War II. Civil rights and labor activists, inspired by Franklin Roosevelt's wartime Executive Order 8809 prohibiting discrimination in the defense industry, pushed for permanent legislation to protect the civil rights of black workers in all industries. The drive brought together a wide range of labor and civil rights groups including the UAW Fair Practices and Anti-Discrimination Department, the Mayor's Interracial Committee, liberal organizations like the Lawyers' Guild and the American Civil Liberties Union, religious groups like the Association of Catholic Trade Unionists and the Detroit Council of Churches, and Communist-front organizations like the Civil Rights Congress and the National Negro Labor Council.[64]

The passage of FEP legislation was hindered by political inertia at the state level and by intense infighting among civil rights organizations. The major issue splitting FEP advocates was communism. Many of Detroit's most vocal proponents of workplace civil rights measures were Communists or fellow travelers. Militant and fired by a intense ideological commitment to racial equality, Detroit leftists who pushed for an FEP law included lawyer George Crockett (who went on to become one of the McCarthy era's most outspoken defenders of accused Communists), the Reverend Charles Hill (who had led black protesters during the Sojourner Truth public housing debate), left-wing labor activists Coleman Young and William Hood (under suspicion by anticommunist union leaders), and civil libertarians Jack Raskin and Art McPhaul (who faced Smith Act prosecutions for subversion). By the late 1940s, these activists were outcasts in Detroit's labor and civil rights movements. Just as Reverend Hill had been ousted from the

NAACP, Crockett lost his job as head of the UAW Fair Practices Committee, Young was fired from his CIO staff position, Hood and dissident auto workers were ostracized by the Reutherite caucus of the UAW, and Raskin and McPhaul and their colleagues in the Civil Rights Congress faced relentless harassment by local anticommunists and the House Un-American Activities Committee.[65]

The factional struggle between Communist and anticommunist civil rights advocates came to a head in 1951. A coalition of left-wing organizations, led by the Civil Rights Congress, the National Negro Labor Council, and Communist-led unions organized a drive in Detroit for a city Fair Employment Practices Ordinance. They hoped to gather thirty thousand signatures in support of a city ordinance, which would force the Common Council to vote on the initiative or put it on the November 1951 municipal ballot. Communist party officials argued that the Common Council must be "pressured into [passing an FEP law] by labor and the people."[66] Labor and the people, however, split deeply over the proposal.

Every mainstream liberal civil rights and labor group opposed the left-wing FEP initiative. Their critique was twofold: that the local FEP referendum was a "fiendish little plot," which if placed on the ballot would "be defeated by hate groups who would run an anti-black and anti-minority campaign," and provide Communists with "propaganda against democracy throughout the world."[67] To "take the ball from the Communists and deny them this issue for their propaganda," the United Automobile Workers, the NAACP, the Mayor's Interracial Committee, the Catholic Interracial Council, the Michigan Council of Churches, and other liberal organizations founded the Detroit Citizens Committee for Equal Employment Opportunities to lobby Detroit's Common Council to pass an FEP ordinance. (Urban League officials supported the ordinance, but less vocally than other groups, for fear of jeopardizing their negotiations with local employers.) Liberal civil rights advocates viewed their counterinitiative as an inconvenience: most wanted to direct their energies toward a statewide FEP law rather than toward a largely symbolic local law.[68]

The leftist and liberal FEP campaigns ran on parallel tracks in the summer and fall of 1951. While NNLC activists and their radical allies continued to solicit signatures for an initiative petition, Citizens Committee officials lobbied, took to the airwaves, and continued their battle against left-wing civil rights activists.[69] Both measures failed. In September, city officials invalidated eleven thousand signatures on the leftists' initiative petition, keeping the referendum off the ballot. And in late October, six out of nine Detroit Common Council members tabled the Citizens Committee's FEP proposal, caving in to fear that they would jeopardize their reelection bids if they supported the measure.[70]

Left-wing civil rights activists reeled from their loss in 1951. Battered by growing anticommunist sentiment and under scrutiny by the House Un-American Activities Committee, the Detroit Negro Labor Council and the Civil Rights Congress faded to insignificance. Liberal groups again directed their energies toward the Michigan State legislature. UAW and NAACP activists lobbied behind the scenes and built a coalition of Democrats and moderate Republicans in favor of civil rights legislation. NAACP and labor groups held pro-FEP rallies in Detroit in fall 1952 and at the State Capitol in spring 1953.[71]

Despite the best orchestrated efforts of civil rights groups, the FEP proposals ran up against a solid wall of opposition, especially among Michigan Republicans, who controlled both the State Senate and House of Representatives. Many GOP legislators were persuaded by the anti-FEP arguments of corporate leaders. Ford Motor Company Vice President Benson Ford, an opponent of the FEP, proclaimed that "you cannot legislate good human relations." Adding his voice to the chorus of opposition, National Time and Signal Corporation President George Fulton argued that "If I apply for a job and any prospective employer does not want to hire me . . . that is his business. And thank God for this." State FEP bills went down to defeat on the floor of the Michigan Senate in 1952. In 1953 and 1954, organized GOP opposition kept the FEP bill trapped in committee.[72] The breakthrough came in 1954, when Democrats picked up enough seats in the midterm election to pass a statewide FEP law in coalition with some liberal Republicans. Governor G. Mennen Williams signed Michigan's FEP law in June 1955.[73]

The Michigan FEP Act was the product of compromise, emblematic of the gradualism and caution that prevailed among most civil rights supporters in both parties. The law represented an important symbolic blow to workplace racism. It outlawed discrimination on the basis of race, creed, and color, prohibited advertisements that specified race, and forbade employers to keep lists of employees by color and race. But, like many 1950s-era civil rights laws, its power and reach were sharply limited. Enforcing the law was a six-member, bipartisan Fair Employment Practices Commission (FEPC). The FEPC could only respond to formal complaints brought by aggrieved workers. It was empowered to investigate claims that came to its attention, and to issue cease-and-desist orders against offending parties.[74]

Michigan's FEPC offered a scattershot approach to the systematic problem of workplace discrimination. The commission was so small that it could not devote sufficient time and resources to investigations. Adjudication was time-consuming and difficult. In addition, the standards of proof were often too high for individual complainants to meet. In its first four years, the FEPC settled 829 cases, and dismissed nearly 60 percent for insufficient

6.2. In 1955, Michigan Governor G. Mennen Williams signed the Fair Employment Practices Act. This was Michigan's first statewide law that forbade workplace discrimination by race, creed, or color. Civil rights and labor leaders had lobbied for the law since the end of World War II, but their victory was largely symbolic.

evidence. Most importantly, under the FEP law it was extremely difficult to attack the systematic exclusion of blacks from certain jobs. The results were, at best, token placements of blacks who successfully filed charges against employers. Eager for visible triumphs, FEPC officials tended to direct their attention toward the exclusion of blacks from white-collar employment. A small number of black workers benefited from the FEPC, but structural flaws in the law and in the commission itself guaranteed that the law made a tiny dent in a major problem.[75]

An unintended consequence of the FEPC was a rekindling of radical civil rights activism. Many black labor activists grew impatient at the glacial pace of integration in the city's workplaces. In the summer of 1955, just after the FEPC law was passed, the Cotillion Club, an organization of black business and community leaders, launched a boycott against National Bohemian Beer for failing to hire black delivery truck drivers. Cotillion leaders also lobbied for the integration of Detroit's virtually all-white police force.[76] The Trade Union Leadership Conference (TULC) a black-led reform group within the UAW, founded in 1957, took the quest for workplace civil rights a step further. TULC members worked hard for the upgrading of black workers to skilled jobs in the auto industry, for the opening of apprenticeship programs for black youth, and for the expansion of the executive leadership of the UAW to include blacks. The TULC succeeded in winning concessions from the UAW leadership and in negotiating antidiscrimination contracts with the major auto producers. But TULC efforts to open apprenticeship programs met with little success. Ultimately, the TULC program primarily benefited a handful of aspiring union leaders and insurgent politicians in Detroit, but did little to change the job prospects of unemployed and underemployed African Americans.[77]

By the late 1950s and early 1960s, the Detroit Branch of the NAACP began to pursue a more militant strategy, but directed its efforts, much like the Urban League, to improving the status of skilled and white-collar workers. Prodded to action by the increasing militancy of the TULC, and motivated by the strategies and successes of the ongoing southern civil rights movement, the NAACP began targeting employers who failed to hire blacks for white collar positions. Like DUL officials, NAACP officials conducted negotiations with Detroit-area firms to convince them to hire blacks, but unlike the DUL, the NAACP also resorted to more confrontational tactics to oppose workplace discrimination. In the early 1960s, the Detroit Branch of the NAACP succeeded in persuading five Detroit-area department stores to hire black sales workers.[78] They were joined by local black ministers who directed a "selective patronage" campaign "aimed at opening doors of employment for our people that were formerly closed." Boycotts of Tip Top Bread and Borden Dairies led to the hiring of blacks in white-collar positions at both companies.[79] Spurred to further radicalism, the NAACP began a series of highly publicized pickets against First Federal Bank and General Motors in 1963 and 1964, protesting the firms' failure to hire blacks in management positions.[80] The NAACP met with some success in challenging discriminatory employment practices, but also failed to address the issue of the effects of industrial flight on the most disadvantaged workers.

The NAACP and the TULC, although their boycott and picketing tactics were more confrontational than those of the DUL, responded to the demands of their largely middle-class and stable working-class constituencies. In the early 1960s, the NAACP emphasized the opening of highly skilled and clerical and management jobs to black workers, at the expense of efforts to get jobs for the unemployed and improve working conditions for the unskilled. Meanwhile, the TULC focused on the grievances of skilled workers and union leaders. Although each organization successfully highlighted the problems of discrimination, they failed to respond to the changing structure of the city's economy. As Detroit's major black organizations directed most of their energy toward antidiscrimination cases that affected white-collar and employed blue-collar workers, the city's manufacturing base continued to atrophy.

The efforts of the Urban League, the NAACP, and the TULC were simultaneously buttressed and limited by what Evelyn Brooks Higginbotham calls the "metalanguage of race."[81] On the one hand, reformers' emphasis on racial discrimination provided a powerful rallying cry for working- and middle-class African Americans in Detroit, most of whom had experienced the effects of racial prejudice in the workplace. On the other hand, it left unchallenged growing class divisions among black Detroiters. As Higginbotham argues, "The totalizing tendency of race precludes recognition and acknowledgment of intragroup social relations as relations of power."[82] The DUL, NAACP, and TULC claimed to speak for all Detroit blacks, but, in effect, represented only one segment. Detroit's African American reform organizations assumed that by improving the job opportunities for professionals and skilled workers, they would uplift the entire race. Their programs for black youth emphasized "skills development," the development of interview skills and work habits that would demonstrate the worthiness of the poor for employment by white employers. The reform organizations' racialized vision obscured the structural forces that profoundly limited the opportunities of the poor.

The battles over discrimination and deindustrialization in Detroit played out in microcosm the political debates of the 1950s and anticipated the dilemmas of many 1960s-era social programs. Kennedy and Johnson administration officials put into action on the national level many of the programs that had played out on an experimental level in Detroit. The Manpower Development Training Act built on the prescriptions of mainstream unionists, many of whom served as advisers and consultants to the Kennedy administration. Great Society programs like the Job Corps started with the assumption that the problem of joblessness was primarily one of individual skills, not the fundamental restructuring of industry. Government officials eschewed a comprehensive industrial planning program, and adopted place-based urban redevelopment programs that used soft incentives to lure industry back to inner cities, with few successes. And federal civil rights laws, while they were far more successful than state FEP laws, were most effective in bolstering the fortunes of highly educated and skilled African Americans rather than those who remained chronically unemployed. The results were eerily foreshadowed in 1950s Detroit—a persistent gap between the haves and the have nots, and the continued, vexing phenomenon of "hard core unemployment."[83]

Despite the best efforts of Detroit's civil rights and labor organizations, the deindustrialization of Detroit continued apace throughout the 1950s and 1960s. The flight of jobs from the center city was even more damaging, however, because as jobs left, the city's black population remained behind.

Black workers remained to a great extent confined to decaying center-city neighborhoods, trapped by invisible barriers of race. As industry fled the city, a large number of white workers were willing and able to follow. Those working-class whites who lacked the resources to move, however, grew angrier and more defensive. As the city's economy soured in the 1950s, and as its black population continued to grow, Detroit's unassuming tree-lined neighborhoods and their modest single-family homes became the major battlegrounds where blacks and whites struggled over the future of the city.

Part Three

FIRE

7.1. In the postwar era, class and status divisions became increasingly pronounced in Detroit. Well-to-do blacks fled the inner city for enclaves like Conant Gardens, shown above, where they moved into spacious suburban-style ranch houses. Detroit's poorest blacks, however, were increasingly concentrated in the city's oldest neighborhoods, trapped in decrepit houses. The scene of children playing in a trash-filled alley, shown below, was taken in 1963, but could have been photographed twenty years earlier.

7

Class, Status, and Residence: The Changing Geography of Black Detroit

> The family who moves in next door to you or down
> the block, whether white or colored, is not the ad-
> vance guard of an invasion. They are just folks fol-
> lowing the old American custom of bettering their
> living conditions by seeking a finer place to live.
> —Maceo Crutcher, president of the Detroit Realtist
> Association, and Walker E. Smith, Chairman of the
> Committee on Race Relations, the Detroit Realtist
> Association (1948)

THE SCENE was tense with drama. The place was the Wayne County Circuit Court in May 1945. The case was a civil suit against a middle-class black couple who had bought a house in an all-white West Side neighborhood. The defendants, Minnie and Orsel McGhee, were upwardly mobile, better off than most Detroit blacks at the end of World War II. She was one of Detroit's two hundred black school teachers, he was a relatively well-paid automobile worker. The plaintiffs were Benjamin and Anna Sipes and other members of the Northwest Civic Association. With the assistance of the NAACP and two leading black lawyers, Willis Graves and Francis Dent, Minnie and Orsel McGhee used the defense to challenge racially restrictive covenants, agreements that covered virtually all Detroit neighborhoods outside the center city. Their immodest goal was "to wipe out Detroit's ghetto walls."[1]

When the McGhees bought a house on Seebaldt Street, in a white neighborhood just beyond the black enclave near Grand Boulevard and Tireman Avenue, Benjamin Sipes, their next-door neighbor, along with a delegation from the all-white Northwest Civic Association, sent the McGhees a letter asking them "to kindly vacate the property." When the McGhees refused, Sipes and the Northwest Civic Association filed suit to prevent them from moving in, on the grounds that the entire neighborhood was covered by a covenant that specified that houses could not be "sold nor leased to, nor occupied by any person other than one of the Caucasian race." Sipes testified that Orsel McGhee "appears to have colored features," and that Minnie

McGhee "appears to be the mulatto type." Attorneys Dent and Graves tried to challenge Sipes's testimony, to no avail, on the grounds that "there is no simple way to determine whether a man is a member of the Mongoloid, Caucasoid, or Negroid race." The Wayne County Circuit Court held that the McGhees were indeed "colored" and that the covenant was valid.

That was only the beginning of the McGhees' legal assault on Detroit's ghetto walls. With the assistance of the NAACP Legal Department, they appealed to the Michigan State Supreme Court, this time deploying a more powerful legal weapon. They argued that the covenants violated state antidiscrimination laws and were unconstitutional under the Fourteenth Amendment. Again, their arguments fell on deaf ears. Michigan's conservative senior jurists denied their appeal and wrote an opinion reaffirming the validity of restrictive covenants. Still confident of the merits of their case, the McGhees' lawyers appealed to the United States Supreme Court.

Sipes was one of dozens of restrictive covenant cases that the NAACP and other civil rights groups argued before the courts in the 1940s (including several others in Detroit), with the hopes of undermining residential Jim Crow throughout the United States. Judges around the country had regularly upheld such covenants as necessary and proper to protect the rights of property owners. In addition, the Home Owners' Loan Corporation and Federal Housing Administration used racial restrictions to determine the actuarial soundness of a neighborhood. FHA underwriting manuals, in fact, encouraged developers to put racial restrictions on their properties to protect the "character" of a neighborhood and to maintain high housing values.[2]

In 1948, the U.S. Supreme Court heard arguments on *Sipes* along with three other covenant cases, including *Shelley v. Kraemer*, a similar case from Saint Louis after which the court's decision would be named. A team of lawyers, led by the NAACP's talented Thurgood Marshall, argued against racially restrictive covenants using both sociological evidence about the impact of covenants on black housing opportunities, and constitutional arguments about the illegality of state action that sanctioned racial discrimination. Persuaded by the NAACP's effective combination of constitutional and sociological arguments, the Vinson court unanimously ruled that restrictive covenants, including that at issue in *Sipes*, could not be enforced by the state. Detroit blacks were elated at the decision. "We Can Live Anywhere!" ran a banner headline in the *Courier*. "This far reaching decision means that a mortal blow has been struck at racial restrictions in homes, artificially created ghettoes, . . . and countless other jim-crow manifestations made possible because of heretofore enforced segregation in home ownership." The attack on restrictive covenants raised blacks' hopes that their housing woes would soon be over. And it inspired blacks in Detroit to move forth more boldly, looking for housing in the predominantly white neighborhoods beyond the city's racial frontier.[3]

In the era of *Sipes v. McGhee*, civil rights activists were optimistic that Detroit would soon be a racially integrated city. The wartime rhetoric of pluralism, tolerance, and antiracism, forged in response to Nazi atrocities, promised a future free of racial conflict. Even though the failure of public housing was a portent of resistance to racial change, the creation of a "second ghetto" in Detroit hardly seemed inevitable to observers of the postwar city. Liberals pointed to statistics showing mixed racial composition in certain neighborhoods as the herald of an era of equality. And civil rights groups clung to the hope that a combination of litigation, legislation, and moral suasion would break down the barriers of race that had kept blacks confined to the inner city. Just five years after the *Shelley* decision, Charles Wartman, editor of the *Michigan Chronicle*, Detroit's most important black weekly, believed that "private housing has become the means of bringing the Negro housing problem nearer solution, with every indication that ultimately it will solve the whole problem of the ghetto."[4]

Motivated by a hopeful vision of an interracial metropolis, civil rights organizations and city officials took an active role in challenging Detroit's racial boundaries. At the same time that African Americans battled to gain access to equal opportunities in the workplace, civil rights organizations directed their energies toward the private housing market. Their beneficiaries were growing numbers of black "pioneers" like the McGhees. Many were members of the city's African American elite.

Beginning in the late 1940s, black Detroit began to expand outward from the prewar concentrations on Detroit's East Side and the outlying enclaves (Map 7.1). Detroit blacks moved beyond the inner city to the east, and especially to the northwest. Between 1940 and 1950, the number of census tracts in Detroit with more than five hundred blacks increased from 56 to 73; between 1950 and 1960, the number increased to 166. The impact of the movement out of the traditional ghetto was mixed. Between 1948 and 1960, black housing conditions in Detroit improved significantly. The number of blacks in substandard buildings (dilapidated buildings or those that lacked running water or indoor toilets) plummeted between 1950 and 1960 from 29.3 percent to only 10.3 percent, and the number of overcrowded residences fell from 25.3 percent to 17.5 percent. The reason for the decline was simple: blacks moved out of the oldest, most run-down sections of the city into newer neighborhoods, including some that contained some of Detroit's finest housing stock, that had been all-white through World War II.[5]

Even though black housing conditions improved, patterns of residential segregation remained intact. Virtually all of Detroit's blacks—regardless of class and education, occupation, age, or place of birth—shared the experience of discrimination in the city's housing market. Only a handful of blacks ever lived for any significant period of time within predominantly white sections of the city, unless they were living-in servants. But to describe the

Map 7.1 (a). Black Population in Detroit, 1940. 1 Dot = 200.

Map 7.1 (b). Black Population in Detroit, 1950. 1 Dot = 200.

Map 7.1 (c). Black Population in Detroit, 1960. 1 Dot = 200.

Map 7.1 (d). Black Population in Detroit, 1970. 1 Dot = 200.

experience of blacks after World War II as a single process of "ghettoization" is to simplify a complex reality. Within the constraints of the limited housing market, Detroit's blacks created distinct subcommunities. The universality of the experience of segregation should not obscure other aspects of the residential life of black Detroiters. An unintended consequence of the opening of Detroit's housing market was a hardening of class divisions within black Detroit. As white movement increased the housing options available to black city dwellers, blacks began the process of sifting and subdividing, replicating within Detroit's center city the divisions of class that characterized the twentieth-century metropolis as a whole.[6]

In the rapidly changing economic climate of postwar Detroit, blacks had two increasingly divergent residential patterns. Those who were able to obtain relatively secure, high-paying jobs were able to purchase their own homes. Increasingly, they put pressure on the racial boundaries that confined them to the center city. But those who were trapped in poor-paying jobs and thrown out of work by deindustrialization remained confined in the decaying inner city neighborhoods that had long housed the bulk of Detroit's black population.

Pushing at the Boundaries: Black Pioneers

As one observer noted in 1946, "it is physically impossible to keep the Negro population imprisoned in its present warren."[7] Families with resources found the housing shortage especially frustrating, because their expectations far exceeded the reality of housing in the city. As sociologists Alfred McClung Lee and Norman D. Humphrey observed: "Take an already crowded situation, add half again as many people, give them a great purchasing power, and still attempt to confine them within . . . the old area, and the pressures developed within the increasingly inadequate 'container' will burst the walls."[8] Adequate housing for African Americans remained one of the great unfulfilled promises of postwar Detroit.

First to push at the city's racial boundaries was the rapidly growing black bourgeoisie. Since the early twentieth century, black entrepreneurs in Detroit had carved out an important niche in the city's economy by providing services to a clientele that white businessmen largely ignored. Because of systematic discrimination in public facilities, blacks created a separate system of "race" businesses—black-owned private hospitals, hotels, restaurants, and funeral homes. Hotelier A. G. Wright made his fortune through his ownership of Detroit's Hotel Gotham, known for providing luxurious accommodations to black travelers who were closed out of Detroit's white-owned hotels. Democratic political leader and U.S. Representative Charles Diggs had followed the typical trajectory of Detroit's black bourgeoisie, starting his career in his family's enormous "House of Diggs" Funeral Home. In addition, many African Americans in the city moved into the black elite through the traditional route of the ministry or education, and a growing number of women joined the ranks of the professions, primarily teaching and social work, after World War II.[9]

As the city's black population grew in the 1940s and 1950s, Detroit's black bourgeoisie kept pace. In 1953, Detroit boasted the largest number of independently owned black businesses of any city in the United States. Most black business leaders continued to find opportunities in traditional "race" businesses, which grew to meet the needs of the city's expanding African American population. As blacks joined the postwar consumer culture with the same fervor, if not the same resources, as whites, a number of black entrepreneurs began to cross over into sectors of the economy that had been white-dominated. Like white Americans, if they could afford it, blacks purchased radios, televisions, cars, and new electric appliances. Some of Detroit's wealthiest African Americans made their fortunes by bringing the fruits of postwar prosperity to well-paid black auto workers and their families. One, Edward Davis, opened the nation's first black-owned car dealership in Detroit on the brink of World War II and profited handsomely from the postwar boom. Another, Sidney Barthwell, followed the trend of franchising and consolidation that reshaped the postwar retail industry. He owned a ten-store chain of pharmacies in black neighborhoods, catering to a rapidly growing base of customers that white-owned firms ignored. Black-owned savings and loan associations and insurance companies filled the niche left by bankers and actuaries who relentlessly redlined African American neighborhoods. Real estate brokers and developers like Pete W. Cassey, Jr., James Del Rio, and Samuel Gibbons profited from the growing demand of Detroit blacks for single-family homes. Detroit was also home to two of the nation's largest black-owned financial institutions: the Great Lakes Mutual Life Insurance Company and the Home Federal Savings and Loan Association. And cultural entrepreneurs also fueled a creative expansion of the consumer market in radio and music, starting the city's first black radio station, and marketing (to an increasingly interracial audience) the Detroit sounds of blues, jazz, and Motown.[10]

Detroit's black elite sought the status and security of residence in districts outside of the traditional inner-city neighborhoods that had confined blacks through World War II. They looked for houses of the size and grandeur appropriate to their economic and social status. Paradise Valley, reported the elite, boosterish *Color* magazine, "can no longer hold the ambitious Negro. He wants to get out of this mecca for card sharks, numbers players, cult leaders, 'prophets,' and shady entertainment." By the late 1940s, Detroit's well-to-do blacks had the desire and the means to flee the overcrowded and decrepit inner city.[11]

Detroit's high-status blacks were not alone in their aspirations to escape the inner city. Also seeking to escape Detroit's "rat belt" were black city employees and automobile and defense workers, especially those who were able to obtain seniority in relatively high-paying factory jobs. Chrysler worker James Boggs recalled that "everybody saved some money during the war. That's how they bought all those houses when the war was over, because people had four years there when they just worked and there wasn't nothing to buy." For the first time, as a city race relations official reported in 1946, black workers had "sufficient funds . . . to free themselves from the tragic overcrowding" in inner-city Detroit.[12] Working-class blacks looked in white neighborhoods on the periphery of black enclaves, whose streets, lined with modest frame and brick houses, had fulfilled the aspirations of a generation of blue-collar homeowners. In addition, by the early 1950s, they hoped to benefit from the new housing opportunities in outlying Detroit neighborhoods and suburbs. Thousands of new houses were constructed on vacant land in northeast and northwest Detroit, and in the booming suburbs to the north and west of the city. Once the Detroit housing market became fluid, the pent-up black demand for housing spilled over racial boundaries. As the housing market opened, black "pioneers" with more modest incomes began moving into neighborhoods on the periphery of black Detroit. By the late 1940s, several neighborhoods, most on the city's near Northwest Side, attracted upwardly mobile blacks fleeing the inner city. Many who moved into the older neighborhoods being abandoned by whites did not view their new homes as permanent residences, but instead treated their purchases or rentals as "a temporary route to the 'best' neighborhoods." Movement to older, formerly white areas gave black strivers a boost in status, while allowing them to build up equity or savings to fund the purchase of a better home in the future.[13] They hoped that eventually they would have the opportunity to live anywhere in the city, and that, like whites, they would enjoy unrestricted residential mobility.

The Open Housing Movement

The aspirations of Detroit's black elite and steadily employed working-class blacks coincided with the rapidly growing integrationist movement. Civil rights activists believed that blacks should have equal access to the housing market, but more than that, they should live side by side with whites to create a racially harmonious city. Only daily contact between the races would solve the nation's pressing dilemma of racial prejudice and inequality. Beginning modestly in the late 1940s, and expanding dramatically in the 1950s, a coalition of civil rights groups, religious organizations, and African American leaders directed their energies toward desegregating the city's

housing market. They found a powerful ally in the Detroit Mayor's Interracial Committee (MIC), which had been founded after the race riot of 1943
to monitor racial tension in the city and advocate civil rights reform. Dominated by liberal whites and blacks who had close ties with civil rights organizations, the MIC consistently opposed segregation in public housing and
other facilities, worked to abolish restrictive covenants, and investigated incidents of racial conflict in the city. The MIC, despite its name, was a largely
independent city agency whose members were protected by civil service
laws. Under Jeffries and Cobo, it became a refuge for a small, dedicated
band of integrationists, who maintained close ties with civil rights groups
throughout the country. In the late 1940s, the MIC spearheaded a joint
campaign with civil rights and religious groups around the city to open the
housing market to blacks.[14]

Inspired by the victory in *Shelley v. Kraemer*, open housing advocates
hoped that with concerted action, they could abolish residential segregation
once and for all. At first their attempts were primarily educational. The
Coordinating Council on Human Relations (CCHR), founded in 1948,
brought together the MIC and dozens of religious and civil rights organizations to persuade whites that they should support racial integration for
moral and economically rational reasons. Throughout the 1950s, the CCHR
held meetings with white church groups, parent-teacher associations, and
community organizations. The primary goal was to convince whites to
"act with intelligence and courage" when blacks moved in. Open housing
activists attempted to persuade skeptical white homeowners that "racial
change was inevitable," and that it was in their self-interest to "work for a
sound, stable, liveable community." The CCHR's primary task was to challenge the conventional wisdom that "the movement of Negroes into your
community will inevitably cause depreciation of value." If whites acted
rationally rather than panicking and fleeing, their property values would
remain stable or rise.[15]

To further their goal, civil rights organizations published pamphlets, brochures, and booklets extolling the virtues of integrated housing. They wrote
articles and letters for local newspapers on the dangers of racial division and
the benefits of racial integration, and published materials attempting to as-
suage homeowners' fears of property depreciation and crime following black
movement into their neighborhoods. They looked to other cities for models
of successful racial change. Open housing groups in Philadelphia, Cleveland, and Chicago shared materials with their Detroit counterparts. Detroit
open housing advocates also assiduously cultivated contacts with national
newspapers and magazines and worked with authors to develop stories
on successful racial integration. A typical story, authored by NAACP head
Walter White in *Saturday Evening Post* in the summer of 1953 and reprinted by civil rights groups around the country, added an interracial twist

to typical 1950s depictions of family life. Included as an example of how "Detroit is now setting an example" of integration were photographs of black and white children playing together, and black and white housewives amiably chatting on their lawns.[16]

Religious leaders also joined together in an ecumenical call for racial harmony, even if many of their rank-and-file clergy members and coreligionists did not support them. In 1957, Edward Cardinal Mooney, the Roman Catholic Archbishop of Detroit, Reverend G. Merrill Lenox of the Detroit Council of Churches, and Rabbi Morris Adler of the Jewish Community Council issued a joint call for integration. To "deny the right of homeownership" to blacks, they argued, "is contrary to our American Constitution and an affront to the righteousness of God." In a typical exchange with a correspondent who denounced racial integration as "the hysterical championing of the primitive black minority," the Reverend Lenox challenged her to avoid the "course that is comfortable and in line with our accustomed thinking," and to act "in agreement with the will of God." But because most Protestant churches were congregationally controlled, many of their members paid little heed to the exhortations of the Detroit Council of Churches, particularly those that challenged conventional racial wisdom. As a result, Presbyterian, Congregationalist, Baptist, and Reformed churches tended to move quickly from racially changing neighborhoods.[17]

The Catholic response was somewhat different. Unlike Protestants, the vast majority of Catholics lived in territorial parishes, whose boundaries were strictly defined and whose churches were permanent fixtures on the cityscape. Local priests and their parishioners had long resisted black encroachment onto parish turf. Yet in the 1950s, a growing number of Catholic bishops and clergy, and a vocal minority of laypeople, began to speak out on civil rights issues. In 1957, Cardinal Mooney met with the pastors of St. Brigid and St. Cecilia parishes to work out a strategy to dampen white parishioners' resistance to blacks moving into their area. Liberal Catholic clerics like University of Detroit Professor John Coogan, S.J. joined in calls for racial equality. Taking a stand alongside Coogan were members of the small but vocal Catholic Interracial Council, and in the late 1950s, the Archdiocesan Council for Catholic Women. And in 1960, then-conservative Archbishop John Dearden (Mooney's successor) heeded the voices of racial liberalism in the Church and established a Commission on Human Relations. The hierarchy's growing racial tolerance brought it into conflict with parishioners who lived in racially changing neighborhoods and with pastors who often shared racial prejudices and looked with chagrin on white flight from their parishes. Angry Catholics barraged Father Coogan, a long-standing member of the Commission on Community Relations, with hate mail. And parishioners often greeted Catholic interracial activists with suspicion and hostility.[18]

Motivated by the burgeoning national civil rights movement, open housing groups moved beyond moral suasion to political action. In the mid-1950s, DUL officials lobbied the Federal Housing Administration and Home Owners' Loan Corporation to allow blacks to purchase foreclosed houses in white neighborhoods. United Automobile Workers officials also supported behind-the-scenes efforts to open the housing market to blacks (although they worked quietly, so as to avoid rankling the white rank and file who had so vocally repudiated the union on public housing issues in the 1940s). And by the late 1950s, civil rights groups began targeting the racially exclusionary practices of real estate brokers. Civil rights groups allied with liberal Democrats in the state legislature to extend the principles of the FEPC to the real estate market. In 1958 and 1959, Michigan's Senate and House of Representatives debated bills that would have fined real estate brokers who failed to sell or rent to anyone because of race. The bills did not pass, but increasing pressure from civil rights groups kept the issue on the table for the next decade.[19]

The challenge to real estate discrimination in Detroit burst onto the national scene in 1960, in the wake of revelations that realtors in suburban Grosse Pointe used a "point system" that ranked perspective home buyers by race, nationality, occupation, and "degree of swarthiness." Blacks and Asians were excluded from Grosse Pointe altogether, and Poles, Southern Europeans, and Jews needed higher rankings than families of northwestern European descent to be approved to move into the community. Private detectives, paid with money from assessments on property owners and real estate brokers, investigated the backgrounds of potential residents, excluding them for such offensive practices as using outdoor clotheslines or painting their houses in gaudy colors. Even though the "point system" affected a relatively small segment of the metropolitan area's housing market, it brought the issue of discriminatory real estate practices to the center of political debate. In the wake of public hearings on Grosse Pointe, the state corporation and securities commissioner issued a regulation that would prevent the issuance of licenses to real estate brokers who discriminated on the basis of race, religion, or national origin.[20]

More importantly, the Grosse Pointe revelations led to a dramatic expansion of open housing activity in Detroit. In 1962, Catholic, Protestant, and Jewish leaders formed the Open Occupancy Conference (later renamed the Religion and Race Conference) to promote housing integration, particularly in suburban communities. The Conference had as its primary goal "to assist middle-class blacks to move into the larger community." As Leonard Gordon, one of the Conference's organizers, noted, "the inner city areas per se were not a programmatic focus." Like earlier open occupancy efforts, the Conference targeted the "small part of the Negro community that could afford outer-city and suburban housing." To that end, conference organizers

7.2. In the late 1950s and early 1960s, civil rights activists made neighborhood integration a central political issue in Detroit. In 1963, Detroit NAACP members and church leaders picketed at the Detroit Civic Center in favor of open housing.

embarked on a "challenge to conscience" campaign "to teach whites their moral duty" to support integration. A related open housing group, the Greater Detroit Committee for Fair Housing Practices, also appealed to religious sentiments. Greater Detroit Committee organizers handed out fair housing "Covenant Cards" in white churches, that churchgoers could sign and carry as proof of their commitment to housing integration. Committee members also assisted blacks trying to move to white areas and escorted blacks to real estate offices in Detroit's suburbs. Beginning in 1964 and 1965, open housing advocates began using testers—paired black and white home buyers who met separately with real estate brokers—to document discriminatory sales practices. Their efforts ensured that open housing remained a central issue in discussions of race, politics, and civil rights in Detroit throughout the 1960s.[21]

"Blockbusting" Real Estate Agents

Open housing groups fostered an intense public debate about the merits of integrated housing. But it was not the discourse of integration that propelled black movement into Detroit's formerly all-white neighborhoods. Real estate brokers played the most important role in helping blacks challenge the city's racial boundaries. Their motivations were complicated. Some, like African American James Del Rio, head of Associate Brokers, one of the city's most successful black-run businesses, genuinely believed in open housing and racial integration. And members of the all-black Detroit Realtist Association championed the right of blacks to live where they pleased. But many other less scrupulous real estate agents took advantage of the tremendous economic opportunities to be found in racially changing neighborhoods. They exploited the frustrated expectations of blacks who desperately wanted to own their own homes, and fueled the deep-seated fears of white homeowners who dreaded black encroachment on their turf. "Blockbusting" real estate brokers, as they came to be called, offered real opportunities to blacks, while sowing panic among whites. Working both sides of the embattled racial frontier made a lot of real estate brokers rich.[22]

Blockbusting brokers and speculators worked on the margins of Detroit's official real estate industry. Members of the Detroit Real Estate Board (the only group allowed to use the trademark name "realtor," hence the black use of the term "realtist") were forbidden under their Code of Ethics to change the racial character of neighborhoods. Into the gap left open by the realtors were agents and brokers who had no affiliation to the Real Estate Board and who operated on the frontier of changing black and white communities. Many were blacks and Jews who had been excluded from membership in the DREB on racial or ethnic grounds. These unaffiliated real estate agents took advantage of their marginal status and profited enormously from speculation in property in neighborhoods considered to be on the brink of black "invasion."

The tactics of blockbusting brokers and speculators were simple. They began by selling a house in an all-white block or neighborhood to a black family, or using devious techniques like paying a black woman to walk her baby through a white neighborhood to fuel suspicion of black residential "takeover." Most susceptible to the manipulation of real estate brokers were whites who lived near the borders of predominantly black neighborhoods. "The uneasy, tenuous and emotional climate under which many of these white families live," reported William L. Price of the Urban League, "renders them easy prey for avaricious speculators in real property."[23] Some brokers brazenly displayed a house for sale in a white neighborhood to a black family, waited a day for rumors to spread, and then inundated residents with leaflets and phone calls, informing them that "Negroes are 'taking over' this block or area" and that they "had best sell now while there is still a chance of obtaining a good price . . ." One clever agent sent black children door to door in a white Northeast Side neighborhood to deliver handbills reading: "Now is the best time to sell your house—you know that."[24] Real estate agents also widely publicized early home sales to nonwhites to offer proof that white fears were justified. One broker went as far as lying about the sale of several homes to blacks on Spokane Street on the West Side to drum up business.[25]

Mary Czechowski, a resident of a largely white working-class neighborhood adjacent to the black West Side, described the events of the first year after a black family moved onto her block in 1950. She lamented that real estate agents "took opportunity to make the most out of this [c]haos, sending their agent to urge people to sell, many times using unfair tactics, and constantly bombarding with postcards, advertising, and proding [sic] to sell."[26] Countless white Detroiters like Czechowski complained about the aggressive tactics of real estate brokers. In one West Side neighborhood of fifty-five hundred homes undergoing racial transition, more than sixty real estate companies vied for white customers.[27] A working-class white homeowner stated his exasperation at persistent real estate solicitation. "It gets so tiresome being asked all the time to sell your house. I bet they don't call out in Grosse Pointe or Bloomfield Hills or Palmer Park all the time asking those people if they want to sell."[28]

Real estate brokers were so persistent because there were huge profits to be made in racially transitional neighborhoods. They bought houses from panicked white sellers at below-market prices. Often, to sweeten the deal, they offered sellers full cash payment for their houses. Then they placed ads in African American newspapers, offering residents of overcrowded and substandard inner-city housing the chance to escape. They quickly sold the houses at substantial markups to blacks willing to pay a premium for good-quality housing in an ostensibly racially mixed neighborhood. As a result, only families with "the financial means to make large initial and monthly payments" could afford to purchase the homes abandoned by panicked whites.[29]

Blockbusting speculators also often served as lenders, filling the gap left by banks and savings and loan associations. It was difficult enough for blacks to qualify for conventional mortgages because of redlining practices. But banks also seldom offered loans to blacks who were the first purchasers in a neighborhood, for fear of alienating their white clients and investors, and because they considered racially transitional neighborhoods to be risky investments.[30] As an alternative to conventional financing, speculators offered land contracts to black home buyers who paid a premium through high down payments and often exorbitant interest rates. Land contracts were far less secure than mortgages. Speculators held onto the title of the property until the contract was fully paid off, thus preventing contract holders from building up equity. The combination of high housing prices and above-market interest rates meant that contract holders had to make large monthly payments to meet their debt obligations. If they defaulted, speculators simply evicted them and quickly offered the house to another desperate black buyer. The arrangement brought speculators a handsome profit with relatively little risk.[31]

In the early 1960s, city officials attempted, unsuccessfully, to curb blockbusting. Open housing groups called for a tough law that would ban all housing discrimination. If blacks had equal access to the housing market, they argued, blockbusting would fade as a practice. They proposed a Fair Neighborhoods Practices Ordinance (FNPO), modeled on the Fair Employment campaign. Led by William Patrick, Detroit's first black Common Council member, FNPO advocates wanted a law that would prohibit racial discrimination by real estate brokers and private sellers, and called for substantial fines to be levied against those who violated civil rights. But the FNPO was hijacked by white opponents of blockbusting, led by white councilman James Brickley, whose racially changing northwest Detroit neighborhood was barraged by aggressive real estate brokers. NAACP officials denounced the Brickley proposal because it "does not touch the basic and wide-ranging practices of racial discrimination in the housing market. . . . Indeed it has no interest at all in the goal of achieving housing integration." The compromise version of the FNPO passed in October 1962 did little to respond to civil rights groups' charges. The ordinance forbade brokers from using racial appeals in their sales pitches and limited the display of "For Sale" and "Sold" signs, in an attempt to stem panic about neighborhood change. As a palliative to civil rights groups, it also authorized the Commission on Community Relations to conduct "appropriate educational and community organizational programs." The law was disregarded by real estate brokers, loosely enforced, and interpreted by whites as authorization to file complaints against the actions of any black real estate broker who sold houses in racially transitional neighborhoods.[32]

Separation by Class

Speculation and lending practices had unintended consequences for the social geography of black Detroit, particularly in the economically troubled 1950s and 1960s. The scarcity of housing options and the high prices that speculators charged meant that well-to-do blacks were the first to move into transitional neighborhoods. Those who followed, usually working-class blacks, often had a tenuous grasp on homeownership. As a result of the widespread use of land contracts, they found themselves pushed to the brink of solvency when they purchased a house in a racially changing neighborhood. To meet monthly payments, they often took in boarders or doubled up with other families. In addition, they often deferred property maintenance, which posed serious problems because so many new black neighborhoods

contained relatively old houses. And because of layoffs and economic vulnerability, particularly during the economic restructuring that began in the
1950s, blacks often defaulted on their monthly payments. During economic
slumps, houses in predominantly black neighborhoods changed hands with
alarming frequency. As a result, housing values fell and all but the most
exclusive black neighborhoods were unstable. The instability of newly black
neighborhoods and the rapid deterioration of older housing stock drove
many middle-class black homeowners out in search of better housing opportunities on the city's ever-changing racial frontier.[33]

The consequence of the process of neighborhood change was twofold. As
one city official charged, the "ghetto crept outward block by block." But
even more importantly, it fueled a pattern of growing spatial segregation of
African Americans by class. Most recent literature on urban poverty has
assumed that the 1970s marked a turning point in the fortunes of the American black middle class. William Julius Wilson argues that the gains of affirmative action and the opening of the suburban housing market to blacks
in the 1970s allowed middle-class blacks the opportunity to leave the inner
city, thus contributing to the isolation and concentration of the urban poor.
Before 1970, he claims, the "institutional ghetto," created by persistent
housing segregation, had the unintended benefit of bringing the "regularly
employed" middle- and working-class black population and the urban poor
together in a shared environment. Jobless and poor blacks, living in close
proximity to those better off than themselves, thus gained from the "social
buffer" of an example of steady, gainful employment and independence, and
had access to job networks that allowed them to escape from joblessness.
The contrast between the ghetto's "golden age" and the present is a common
theme in recent social-scientific literature on the urban underclass, but one
that historical research is beginning to challenge.[34]

An examination of city maps and census data for tracts undergoing racial
transition offers a clear picture of the process of differential residential mobility and class segregation that took place in postwar black Detroit. It is
important to remember that class segregation took place within the confines
of systematic discrimination in housing, and that all black Detroiters experienced the effects of isolation by race. But data show that within the confines
of the divided metropolis, subcommunities within the black population separated by class. The isolation of the urban black poor in deteriorating center-
city areas is a phenomenon with origins in the aspirations of black residents
of the prewar black enclaves of Conant Gardens and the West Side, and
became even more deeply rooted in the postwar decades as steadily employed blacks fled to the boundaries of segregated Detroit.

The gradual sifting of the black population of Detroit by income can be
seen very clearly in black income data in the 1950 and 1960 censuses.
In 1950 black residents of the West Side and Conant Gardens had the high-

TABLE 7.1

Black Household Income in Census Tracts with More than 500 Blacks, Detroit, 1950 and 1960

Percent black in 1940	1950 Income	Number of Tracts
0–10 (transitional)	$2,779	15
11–49 (infill)	$2,513	24
50+ (ghetto)	$2,197	26
Enclaves	$2,897	8

Percent black in 1950	1960 Income	Number of Tracts
0–10 (transitional)	$4,082	65
11–49 (infill)	$3,767	46
50+ (ghetto)	$2,995	55

Sources: Calculated from U.S. Department of Commerce, Bureau of the Census, *1950 Census of the Population, Census Tract Statistics for Detroit, Michigan and Adjacent Area* (Washington, D.C.: U.S. Government Printing Office, 1952), Table 2; *1960 Census of Population and Housing, 1960, Census Tracts, Detroit, Michigan Statistical Area*, Final Report PHC (1)–40 (Washington, D.C.: U.S. Government Printing Office, 1962), Table P.4. The categories "transitional," "infill," and "ghetto" come from Karl and Alma Taeuber, *Negroes in Cities* (Chicago: Aldine, 1965).

est incomes of black residents in the city—$2,897. Outside the enclaves, the most prosperous sections of black Detroit were transitional tracts—those with a black population of less than 10 percent in the previous decennial census—that attracted black "pioneers." The income of blacks in infill tracts—those with a black population of greater than 10 percent but fewer than 50 percent in the previous census year—was lower than that of blacks in transitional tracts. Infill tracts were those that no longer attracted black pioneers, where the process of racial transition from white to black occurred rapidly. Majority-black (ghetto) tracts that remained stable or increased their African American populations remained the poorest in both years (Table 7.1). The gap between transitional and ghetto areas was especially pronounced in 1960: blacks who lived in former all-white neighborhoods had average incomes 73 percent greater than residents of majority-black tracts.[35]

An examination of the geographic distribution of the black population by income offers a graphic representation of the growing geographic isolation of the poorest black Detroiters (Map 7.2). From 1950 through 1970, the census tracts with the highest median income were on the periphery of black Detroit. The poorest tracts were all well removed from the higher-income

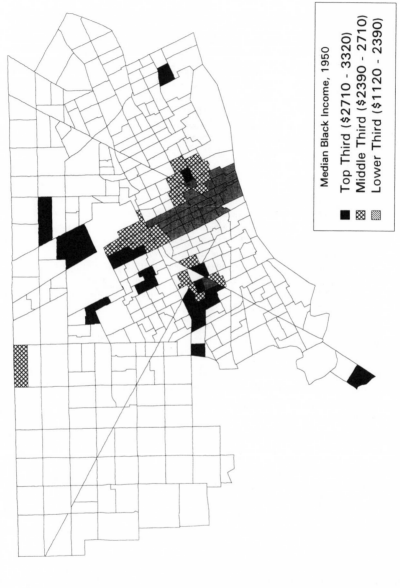

Map 7.2 (b). Detroit's Black Population by Median Income, 1960.

Median Black Income, 1970

Top Third ($7800 - 22600)
Middle Third ($6000 - 7800)
Lower Third ($1800 - 6000)

Map 7.2 (c). Detroit's Black Population by Median Income, 1970.

areas, clustered in the oldest section of the city, close to downtown. As one moved outward from the downtown area, black median income by tract rose. The process of the outward movement of Detroit's black population seems in many respects to resemble in microcosm the solar model of urban population succession developed by the Chicago School. Detroit's black population was distributed in concentric circles by economic status, the center containing the poorest and most immobile population, and each succeeding ring containing a progressively wealthier population.[36]

Status and Conflict

The growing division of black Detroit by class was not simply the result of the dynamics of the housing market. It was also, in part, a manifestation of a status and class consciousness that had long divided urban black communities in the United States. Already in 1940, some well-to-do black Detroiters like Edward Gibbons, real estate broker and head of Detroit's NAACP in the 1950s, lived in elite enclaves like Conant Gardens. In the postwar period, these islands of prosperity expanded. Grixdale Park, a westerly extension of Conant Gardens, attracted black professionals, entrepreneurs, teachers, municipal employees, and an aristocracy of black auto workers, all of whom had the means to pay for its newly built "attractive red brick" ranch-style houses. Grixdale Park residents were not only better off than the majority of blacks in the city, they were also richer than many of the white residents of the surrounding area, who lived in "small two bedroom asbestos shingled homes."[37] Likewise, the substantial homes of the West Grand Boulevard area, just beyond the black West Side, attracted well-to-do black home buyers like Austin W. Curtis, Jr., head of the A. W. Curtis Laboratories and a protégé of George Washington Carver. But increasingly Detroit's leading African Americans were attracted to the substantial homes, many of them mansions, that lined the streets of turn-of-the-century neighborhoods near downtown that had been left behind as well-to-do whites moved to fashionable suburbs.[38]

In the aftermath of *Shelley*, Detroit's black professional elite found a haven in the stately homes in Detroit's Arden Park and Boston-Edison neighborhoods. Only a few miles from downtown, the area's substantial homes, ranging in size from eight rooms to "palatial mansions" of twenty rooms, had been home to wealthy white executives, bankers, and brokers since their construction in the 1910s and 1920s. After the war, the two areas lost some of their appeal as housing values fell and wealthy whites headed for spacious homes in racially exclusive suburbs like Grosse Pointe, Birmingham, and Bloomfield Hills. Remaining white residents had held back the black "invasion" with restrictive covenants, and many left when the *Shelley* decision came down. Well-heeled blacks quickly replaced the fleeing whites. By the early 1950s, Boston-Edison had become a "high status Negro community," known colloquially as "Millionaires' Row."[39] The area's wealthy African American residents included car dealer Ed Davis, Motown magnate Berry Gordy, Urban League head John Dancy, pharmaceutical giant Sidney Barthwell, U.S. Representative Charles Diggs, and leading black lawyers, ministers, and doctors.[40]

Detroit's black elite found status and distance from the majority of the city's black population in Boston-Edison and Arden Park. Many black residents of the Boston-Edison area viewed Detroit's Lower East Side contemptuously. A 1954 survey found that Boston-Edison's blacks had a "firmly fixed idea" that the Lower East Side was an irremediable "slum," and that "any move to the East Side, or even toward the center of the city, would be a backward step." Above all, "their concepts of social prestige and residential desirability" propelled them outward from the center city.[41]

Divisions of class and status were no less evident in more modest African American neighborhoods. Most of Detroit's better-off African Americans moved to neighborhoods like Twelfth Street, Russell Woods, and the Bagley area, all in northwest Detroit. These neighborhoods, as native Detroiter Wilson Moses recalled, were home to the city's "Elites" or "E-Lights," as they were known to the predominantly working-class and poor East Side "Hoods."[42] At the heart of African American northwest Detroit was Twelfth Street, a formerly Jewish neighborhood that began attracting blacks in the immediate aftermath of World War II. Its homes, unrestricted by racial covenants, cost $8,000 to $12,000 in 1947, substantially higher than the citywide average of $5,500. As a result, the neighborhood attracted what one resident called "a kind of middle class," including "doctors, factory workers, postal employees, bus drivers, salesmen, and the like." They shared "the desire to fix up their homes and keep the neighborhood nice," and viewed Twelfth Street as an area of "high status, one to which a hard working family climbs, and one it is an opportunity to live in." Most of the new black residents saw residence in the area as a chance to escape the poverty of the Lower East Side, and took pains to dissociate themselves from the poorer blacks they had left behind.[43]

Exacerbating class divisions was the growing gulf between the regularly employed and the "chronically unemployed." Jobless African Americans, whether they were rebuffed at the hiring gate, unprotected from layoffs by seniority, or fired when plants closed or relocated, could not afford to own their own homes or even to rent in desirable neighborhoods outside the inner city. They continued to crowd together in inner-city neighborhoods like Paradise Valley, suffering disproportionately from evictions and defaults. Joblessness rates were highest in the oldest neighborhoods where blacks had been concentrated before World War II. It was in those same neighborhoods that black social workers found alarmingly high rates of juvenile delinquency, and where crime rates rose precipitously in the late 1950s.[44]

Better-off blacks, like their white counterparts, often sought to regulate the behavior of their neighbors and ensure the exclusiveness of their neighborhoods. African American Boston-Edison residents, for example, strictly enforced restrictive covenants and zoning codes that regulated building type, enforced single-family occupancy, and prohibited boarding houses. As late as 1976, when a Capuchin monastery purchased a house in the area for its novices, Boston-Edison residents battled against the "incompatible use." Grixdale Park residents established a property owners' association in 1953 to "protect their investments, to control their community, to raise maintenance standards, and . . . to prevent the spread of blight." The Grixdale Park Property Owners Association battled "rowdyism" at a local theater in the 1950s, out of fear that the "situation could easily put us in the category of theaters on Hastings or Russell [in Paradise Valley], which we in this neighborhood should not tolerate." And they fought the construction of houses marketed to lower-income African Americans. When a low-cost "asbestos shingled, basementless" home was built at the corner of Wexford and Nevada in 1961, Amos Wilder, president of the Grixdale Park Property Owners Association, argued that small frame houses did not "compliment the area." Association members picketed in front of the model home and negotiated with the builder to "modify the house to meet neighborhood standards."[45]

Other black newcomers to formerly all-white neighborhoods had views shaped by the "politics of respectability." In a climate of intense racial antagonism, they sought to disprove negative racial stereotypes, and did so by distancing themselves physically and symbolically from the African American poor. Black pioneers moving in the mid-1950s to the Russell Woods area on Detroit's near Northwest Side aspired to middle-class status. The blacks who were the first to move onto the streets of this section of stately homes had a history of movement into predominantly white or "mixed" neighborhoods, and moving out of those neighborhoods when they became predominantly black. "H," a restaurant owner, and his family had lived for fifteen years in an increasingly black center-city area. The "H"s sought better housing in Russell Woods because their old neighborhood had become "run down and rough." A young couple, the "J"s, moved to the area with hopes that it would "stabilize as a mixed racial neighborhood." "J," a law student, and her husband, a lawyer, had lived in five different neighborhoods in the city, two of which had become predominantly black. Another black family, the "L"s, had moved several times from neighborhoods that had started "to go down hill." They left their old neighborhood when "loud, vulgar people . . . who had wild parties and used vulgar language" moved into the area.

The "L"s hoped that Russell Woods would remain predominantly white, or at least not attract any "poor class" people.[46]

African Americans who moved to the Bagley neighborhood in northwest Detroit had similar attitudes. The square-mile area between McNichols, Seven Mile Road, Livernois, and Wyoming was an area of fairly substantial middle-class homes, many of them four-bedroom Colonial- and Tudor-style houses, with large lawns and well-manicured gardens, built in the 1930s and 1940s for white families with means. Sociologists Eleanor Paperno Wolf and Charles Lebeaux interviewed twenty-one black families who moved into the area between 1962 and 1964 and found that the new black residents had a higher average income and higher education levels than the departing white residents. Wolf and Lebeaux found that most of the black newcomers expressed dissatisfaction with their old neighborhoods (fifteen of the respondents had come from near Northwest Side neighborhoods). Their responses revealed a deep concern with changes in the economic and social composition of their former neighborhoods—many referred to the growing number of poorer people as their reason for moving. Some referred to "congestion," others spoke frankly about their concerns about crime, "rowdy people," "hoodlums," "transients," gang activity, and "ADC people [welfare recipients] and their boyfriends." Their desire for respectability underlay their worries about problems with the "upkeep of property" and the depreciation of real estate values in their old neighborhoods, and their desire to live in an area with houses that boasted "all the comforts that I was seeking," plus good schools.[47]

These black Detroiters shared a common set of aspirations with white middle-class Detroiters. They sought peaceful neighborhoods where they could live without the fear of disorder and crime. They sought single-family homes, with yards and space, antidotes to the overcrowding they had experienced in the inner city. They sought the status of "high-class" neighbors, and the beneficial influence of good schools and good role models for their children. Patterns of segregation limited their options, but most moved to the city's racial frontier. In so doing, they fulfilled their middle-class aspirations, at least for a time.[48]

Not all middle-class blacks expressed their distaste for the poor as vocally as did residents of Russell Woods and Bagley. Many stayed in the homes that they had struggled to purchase, even as the surrounding neighborhoods became increasingly poor. And those who moved from the inner city often retained close contacts with their old neighborhoods, through social organizations, businesses, and churches. Black business leaders may have escaped to their quiet homes in Boston-Edison or Russell Woods, but most still relied on the patronage of inner-city customers. In addition, many of the most important African American institutions, like the prestigious Second Baptist Church, the Urban League, and the Young Men's Christian Association, remained in the oldest and poorest inner-city neighborhoods, even if their leadership and a growing number of their members resided elsewhere. On the near Northwest Side, churches like the Reverend C. L. Franklin's New Bethel Baptist Church and the Reverend Albert Cleage's Shrine of the Black Madonna served the area's increasingly poor population.[49]

Still, the movement of better-off blacks into Detroit's outlying enclaves and formerly all-white neighborhoods contributed to the transformation of the social geography of Detroit after World War II. Many historians have described the process of "community formation" that occurred during the First Great Migration. But in the increasingly heterogeneous postwar black metropolis, the process might better be described as the formation of several distinct communities. Differences in income, occupation, and status within black Detroit manifested themselves in a growing residential segregation of the black population by class. Blacks fortunate enough to marshal the resources to flee the crowded center city left behind a segment of the population that would continue to bear the brunt of segregation, by both class and race, trapped in the city's worst housing. They set into motion a process that over the long run would leave inner-city neighborhoods increasingly bereft of institutions, businesses, and diversity.

As a growing number of African American Detroiters attempted to lift their status, assisted by an increasingly well-organized open housing movement, they faced one of the most powerful, well-organized political movements in Detroit's history, a grassroots movement that had as its primary purpose the maintenance of Detroit's racial boundaries. Their desire for better homes along the city's racial frontier came into collision with the wishes of insecure whites, motivated by racial, economic, and political considerations, who wanted to maintain all-white neighborhoods. Detroit's shifting racial borderlands became battlegrounds for the future of the city.

8.1. With Federal Housing Administration, Home Owners' Loan Corporation, and Veterans' Administration mortgage guarantees and loans, more than 60 percent of white Detroiters owned their own homes by the 1960s. These modest homes on the city's West Side, probably brand new when they were photographed in 1953, were a source of pride for many first-time blue-collar homeowners.

"Homeowners' Rights": White Resistance and the Rise of Antiliberalism

> Men and women who own homes, which they have
> purchased in order to raise their children in conge-
> nial neighborhoods, have invested their stake in the
> future of Detroit. . . . They are ambitious to make
> Detroit a better place in which to live and to work,
> for themselves, their families and their neighbors. It
> has been well said, "A Liberal is one who is liberal
> with the other fellow's money, and a Conservative is
> a man who has saved a little money and has a home
> of his own."
> —Allen B. Crow, president of the Economic Club of
> Detroit (1945)

> The white population . . . has come to believe that it
> has a vested, exclusive, and permanent "right" to
> certain districts.
> —Henry Lee Moon, black journalist (1946)

TENS OF THOUSANDS of white Detroiters rebelled against the open housing movement in the 1950s and 1960s. One of their leaders was a local lawyer and Democratic party activist, Thomas Poindexter. A tall, heavy-set man with flaming red hair and a deep, booming voice, Poindexter made a first try for political office in 1954, running for an open congressional seat against popular party regular Martha Griffiths. An economic populist, Poindexter argued "that the government has the power and responsibility to see that there is a job for every man who wants to work." He was one of the few politicians to respond immediately to the wave of plant closings and automation-related layoffs ravaging the city. Poindexter's fiery rhetoric won him the endorsement of the United Automobile Workers Political Action Committee, but his first foray into electoral politics failed miserably nonetheless. His economic message fell flat among his district's largely white-collar constituents. In addition, he had little campaign experience, virtually no name recognition, and a minuscule campaign war chest. Despite his drubbing in the 1954 Democratic primary, Poindexter continued his populist crusade.

In 1955, he "accused General Motors of monopolizing the Republican Party," and filed a lawsuit against the automobile giant, seeking to bar it from political activity.[1]

Sometime in the late 1950s, Thomas Poindexter discovered the issues that would lift him from obscurity and make him one of Detroit's most popular elected officials in the 1960s. He jettisoned his critique of big business and directed his animus against integration, crime, and taxation. Blacks and the government officials who pandered to them, he argued, were responsible for the insecurity that plagued hardworking white Detroiters. In 1960, he ran as an unsuccessful "law and order" candidate for the Detroit Court of Common Pleas, and in 1962, he campaigned against Detroit's new income tax. He began working closely with the John Birch Society, although he never joined the radical rightist organization. And in 1963, he expressed sympathy with Alabama's segregationist Governor George Corley Wallace, who was just beginning to extend his political reach to the North.[2]

Poindexter's populism propelled him toward the hot-button issues of race and homeownership. Disturbed by the growing prominence of civil rights politics, he founded the Greater Detroit Homeowners' Council in 1962, for the sole purpose of battling racial integration and preserving white home-owners' insecure investments. In the contentious debates over blockbusting and open housing, Poindexter's voice was the loudest and clearest. He became the official voice of angry white Detroiters who fought vigorously to maintain neighborhood homogeneity.[3] Poindexter's crusade launched him to national prominence. In August 1963, Dixiecrat Senator Strom Thurmond invited Poindexter to Washington, where he testified before the Senate Committee on Commerce on behalf of "99 percent of Detroit white residents" against the Kennedy administration's proposed civil rights legislation. Poindexter warned that "when integration strikes a previously all-white neighborhood . . . there will be an immediate rise in crime and violence . . . of vice, of prostitution, of gambling and dope." With a "general lowering of the moral standards," racially mixed neighborhoods "will succumb to blight and decay, and the residents will suffer the loss of their homes and savings."[4] Poindexter capped his political efforts by winning a seat on the Common Council in 1964 as the "Home Owners' Champion," the top vote-getter in a thirty-six-candidate field. Although he still called himself a "moderate liberal," Poindexter built a base of support among working-class Democrats and middle-class Republicans alike.[5]

Poindexter was one of tens of thousands of white Detroiters who forged a new antiliberal political vision in the postwar years. In reaction to the economic and racial transformation of the city, Detroit's whites began fashioning a politics of defensive localism that focused on threats to property and neighborhood. They directed their political energy toward the two groups they believed were the agents of change: blacks and their liberal allies. Acting on their perception of the threat of the black newcomers to their stability, economic status, and political power, many of Detroit's working- and middle-class whites banded together in exclusive neighborhood organizations, in what became one of the largest grassroots movements in the city's history. By moving the politics of race, homeownership, and neighborhood to center stage, they reshaped urban politics in the postwar era, and set into motion the forces that would eventually reconfigure national politics.[6]

The Rise of the Homeowners' Movement

Between 1943 and 1965, Detroit whites founded at least 192 neighborhood organizations throughout the city, variously called "civic associations," "protective associations," "improvement associations," and "homeowners' associations."[7] Few scholars have fully appreciated the enormous contribution of this kind of grassroots organization to the racial and political climate of twentieth-century American cities.[8] Their titles revealed their place in the ideology of white Detroiters. As civic associations, they saw their purpose as upholding the values of self-government and participatory democracy. They offered members a unified voice in city politics. As protective associations, they fiercely guarded the investments their members had made in their homes. They also paternalistically defended neighborhood, home, family, women, and children against the forces of social disorder that they saw arrayed against them in the city. As improvement associations, they emphasized the ideology of self-help and individual achievement that lay at the very heart of the American notion of homeownership. Above all, as home and property owners' associations, these groups represented the interests of those who perceived themselves as independent and rooted rather than dependent and transient.

The surviving records of homeowners associations do not, unfortunately, permit a close analysis of their membership. From the hundreds of letters that groups sent to city officials and civil rights groups, from neighborhood newsletters, and from improvement association letterheads, it is clear that no single ethnic group dominated most neighborhood associations. Names as diverse as Fadanelli, Csanyi, Berge, and Watson appeared on the same petitions. Officers of the Greater Detroit Homeowners' Association, Unit No. 2, in a blue-collar northwest Detroit neighborhood, included a veritable United Nations of ethnic names, among them Benzing, Bonaventura, Francisco, Kopicko, Sloan, Clanahan, Klebba, Beardsley, Twomey, and Barr. Groups met in public-school buildings, Catholic and Protestant churches, union halls, Veterans of Foreign Wars clubhouses, and parks. Letters, even from residents with discernibly "ethnic" names, seldom referred to national heritage or religious background. Organizational newsletters and neighborhood newspapers never used ethnic modifiers or monikers to describe neighborhood association members—they reserved ethnic nomenclature for "the colored" and Asians (and occasionally Jews). The diversity of ethnic membership in neighborhood groups is not surprising, given that Detroit had few ethnically homogeneous neighborhoods by midcentury. But the heterogeneity of Detroit's neighborhoods only partially explains the absence of ethnic affiliation in remaining records. Homeowners' and neighborhood groups shared a common bond of whiteness and Americanness—a bond that they asserted forcefully at public meetings and in correspondence with public officials. They referred to the "white race," and spoke of "we the white people." Some called for the creation of a "National Association for the Advancement of White People," and others drew from the "unqualified support of every white family, loyal to white ideas."[9]

Detroit was a magnet for southern white migrants, but there is no evidence of a distinctive southern white presence in neighborhood organizations. "Hillbillies," as they were labeled, were frequently blamed for racial tension in the city, but their role was greatly exaggerated. Most of them dispersed throughout the metropolitan area, and quickly disappeared into the larger white population. There were a few concentrations of poor white southerners in the city, like the Briggs neighborhood near Tiger Stadium. Even in these neighborhoods, however, they tended not to form civic or political organizations. Scattered evidence from voter surveys suggests that they tended to vote solidly Democratic; indeed, in 1949 and 1951 they were more likely to support liberal candidates than were Italians and Poles. In addition, as historical anthropologist John Hartigan has shown, southern whites often lived in close proximity to blacks with little long-term resistance. Most importantly, a 1951 public opinion survey found that "Southerners who now live in Detroit express no more negative attitudes about Negroes and are no more in favor of segregation than are people from other parts of the country." The racial politics of Detroit's neighborhood associations were thoroughly homegrown.[10]

Racial exclusion had not always been the primary purpose of neighborhood associations. Real estate developers had originally created them to enforce building restrictions, restrictive covenants and, later, zoning laws. Their members served as watchdogs, gathering complaints from neighbors and informing the City Plan Commission of zoning violations. Frequently, they lobbied city officials for the provision of better public services such as street lighting, stop signs, traffic lights, and garbage pickup. Improvement associations were also social clubs that welcomed new neighbors and brought together residents of adjacent streets for events such as block parties, dinner dances, and excursions to local amusement parks or baseball games. They sponsored community cleanup and home improvement competitions. Their newsletters included admonitions to association members to drive safely, announcements of local dinner dances, neighborhood gossip, and home improvement and homemaking tips.[11]

During and after World War II, these organizations grew rapidly in number and influence, as hundreds of thousands of working-class whites became homeowners for the first time. Detroit's industrial workers had used their relatively high wages, along with federal mortgage subsidies, to purchase or build modest single-family houses on the sprawling Northeast and Northwest sides. The proportion of owner-occupied homes in the city rose from 39.2 percent in 1940 to 54.1 percent in 1960.[12] Yet the working-class hold on affluence was tenuous. Many city residents had spent a large part of their life savings to buy a home, and they usually had little else to show for their work. Most Detroiters viewed homeownership as a precarious state, always under siege by external forces beyond their control. Even those who held steady employment found that mortgage or land contract payments stretched family budgets to the breaking point. In a comprehensive survey of Detroit residents conducted in 1951, Wayne University sociologist Arthur Kornhauser found that white Detroiters ranked housing needs as the most pressing problem in the city. Homeownership required a significant financial sacrifice for Detroit residents: the most frequent complaint (voiced by 32 percent of respondents) was that the cost of housing was too high.[13] To a generation that had struggled through the Great Depression, the specter of foreclosure and eviction was very real. For working Detroiters, the vagaries of layoffs, plant closings, and automation jeopardized their most significant asset, usually their only substantial investment—their homes.

Homeownership was as much an identity as a financial investment. Many of Detroit's homeowners were descendants of immigrants from eastern and southern Europe, for whom a house and property provided the very definition of a family. They placed enormous value on the household as the repository of family values and the center of community life. In addition, for many immigrants and their children, homeownership was proof of success, evidence that they had truly become Americans. A well-kept property became tangible evidence of hard work, savings, and prudent investment, the sign of upward mobility and middle-class status.[14]

To white ethnics, homeownership was more than the product of individual enterprise. Detroiters, by and large, lived in intensely communal neighborhoods. In Detroit's working-class districts, houses were close together on small lots. Day-to-day life was structured by countless small interactions among neighbors; little was private. Property maintenance, behavior, and attitudes seldom escaped the close scrutiny of neighbors. Reinforcing the ties of proximity were the common bonds of religion. In the mid-1950s, about 65 percent of Detroit's population was Roman Catholic; the white population was probably closer to 75 or 80 percent Catholic. Catholic familial and institutional bonds ordered urban life in ways that cannot be underestimated. Paul Wrobel, a third-generation Polish American, recalled that life in the heavily Catholic East Side neighborhood of his youth "centered around three separate but related spheres: Family, Parish, and Neighborhood." In largely Catholic neighborhoods, improvement associations grew out of parish social organizations, frequently held meetings in church halls, and often got material and spiritual support from pastors. Improvement associations in largely Polish neighborhoods on Detroit's East Side, reported the Mayor's Interracial Committee (MIC), "conform to the bounds of Catholic Church parish lines rather than subdivisions." Although many Catholic clergy supported civil rights, priests at some Detroit-area churches encouraged their parishioners to support homeowners' associations, for fear that black "invasions" would hurt parish life. Parishioners at Saint Andrew and Saint Benedict, a large Catholic church in a racially changing southwest Detroit neighborhood, were active in the Southwest Civic Improvement League. MIC officials reported a "prevailing sentiment of antagonism and fear" and a "feeling that this investment [in a new parish school building] and the social life of the church will be affected by the movement out . . . of large numbers of church members."[15] Catholic parishes were not the only bases for homeowners' groups, however. White civic associations also found religious and political support among evangelical Protestants. Many white fundamentalist churches, such as the Temple Baptist Church and the Metropolitan Tabernacle, fostered racial prejudices and often sponsored neighborhood association meetings.[16]

The homeowners' movement, then, emerged as the public voice of proud homeowners who defined themselves in terms of their tightly knit, exclusive communities. But the simultaneous occurrence of economic dislocation and black migration in postwar Detroit created a sense of crisis among homeowners. Both their economic interests and their communal identities were threatened. They turned to civic associations to defend a world that they feared was slipping away. Increasingly, they blamed blacks for their insecurity. In the era of open housing, responding to the threat of black movement into their neighborhoods became the raison d'être of white community groups. One new group, the Northwest Civic Association, called its founding meeting "So YOU will have first hand information on the colored situation in this area," and invited "ALL interested in maintaining Property Values in the NORTHWEST section of Detroit." The Courville District association gathered together residents of a northeast Detroit neighborhood to combat the "influx of colored people" to the area, and rallied supporters with its provocatively entitled newsletter, *Action!* When a black family moved onto Cherrylawn Street on the city's West Side, between six hundred and a thousand white neighbors attended an emergency meeting to form a neighborhood association. The founders of the Connor-East Homeowners' Association promised to "protect the Area from undesirable elements." Members of the San Benardo Improvement Association pledged to keep their neighborhood free of "undesirables"—or "Niggers"—as several who eschewed euphemism shouted at the group's first meeting. Existing organizations took on a new emphasis with the threat of black "invasion." In 1950, Orville Tenaglia, president of the Southwest Detroit Improvement League, recounted his group's history: "Originally we organized in 1941 to promote better civic affairs, but now we are banded together just to protect our homes." The league was engaged in a "war of nerves" over the movement of blacks into the community.[17]

The issues of race and housing were inseparable in the minds of many white Detroiters. Economically vulnerable homeowners feared, above all, that an influx of blacks would imperil their precarious investments. "Stop selling houses to the colored," advocated one white Detroiter. "Where would we move? No place—poor people have no place to move," he added. "What is the poor people to do?" Speaking for homeowners who felt threatened by the black migration, a self-described "average American housewife" wrote: "What about us, who cannot afford to move to a better location and are surrounded by colored? . . . Most of us invested our life's savings in property and now we are in constant fear that the neighbor will sell its property to people of different race."[18] Kornhauser found that race relations followed a close second to housing in Detroiters' ranking of the city's most pressing problems. Only 18 percent of white respondents from all over the city expressed "favorable" views toward the "full acceptance of Negroes" and 54 percent expressed "unfavorable" attitudes toward integration. When asked to discuss ways in which race relations "were not as good as they should be," 27 percent of white respondents mentioned "Negroes moving into white neighborhoods." 22 percent answered that the "Negro has too many rights and privileges; too much power; too much intermingling." Another 14 percent mentioned "Negroes' undesirable characteristics." Only 14 percent mentioned the existence of discrimination as a problem in race relations.[19]

Whites in Detroit regularly spoke of the "colored problem" or the "Negro problem."[20] In their responses to open-ended questions, Kornhauser's informants made clear what they meant by the "colored problem." Of blacks: "Eighty percent of them are animals," stated one white respondent. "If they keep them all in the right place there wouldn't be any trouble," responded another. "Colored treat the whites in an insolent way," added a third white, "They think they own the city." A majority of whites looked to increased segregation as the solution to Detroit's "colored problem."[21] When asked, "What do you feel ought to be done about relations between Negroes and whites in Detroit?" a remarkable 68 percent of white respondents called for some form of racial segregation—56 percent of whites surveyed advocated residential segregation. Many cited the Jim Crow South as a model for successful race relations.[22]

Class, union membership, and religion all affected whites' attitudes toward blacks. Working-class and poor whites expressed negative views toward blacks more frequently than other respondents to Kornhauser's survey. 85 percent of poor and working-class whites supported racial segregation, in contrast to 56 percent of middle-income and 42 percent of upper-income whites. Union members were slightly "less favorable than others towards accepting Negroes." CIO members were even more likely than other white Detroiters to express negative views of African Americans—65 percent—although more CIO members were also likely to support full racial equality (18 percent) than ordinary white Detroiters. And finally, Catholics were significantly more likely than Protestants to express unfavorable feelings toward blacks.[23]

Neighborhood groups responded to the threat of "invasion" with such urgency because of the extraordinary speed of racial change. Most blocks in changing neighborhoods went from being all-white to predominantly black in a period of three or four years. They also reacted viscerally against the tactics of blockbusting real estate brokers, whose activities fueled their sense of desperation. Whites living just beyond "racially transitional" areas witnessed the rapid black movement into those areas. They feared that without concerted action, their neighborhoods would turn over just as quickly.

White Detroiters also looked beyond transitional neighborhoods to the "slum," a place that confirmed all of their greatest fears. Whites saw in the neighborhoods to which blacks had been confined in the center city area, such as Paradise Valley, a grim prophecy of their own neighborhoods' futures. The rundown, shabby appearance of inner-city housing, the piles of uncollected garbage, and the streets crowded with children and families escaping tightly packed apartments seemed confirmation of whites' worst fears of social disorder. To them, the ghetto was the antithesis of their tightly-knit, orderly communities. They also noticed the striking class difference between blacks and whites. The median family income of blacks in Detroit was at best two-thirds of that of whites between the 1940s and the 1960s. Although the poorest blacks were seldom the first to move into formerly white neighborhoods (in fact black "pioneers" were often better off than many of their white neighbors), whites feared the incursion of a "lower-class element" into their neighborhoods.[24]

To white Detroiters, the wretched conditions in Paradise Valley and other poor African American neighborhoods were the fault of irresponsible blacks, not greedy landlords or neglectful city officials. Because housing was such a powerful symbol of "making it" for immigrant and working-class families, many Detroit whites interpreted poor housing conditions as a sign of personal failure and family breakdown. Wherever blacks lived, whites believed, neighborhoods inevitably deteriorated. "Let us keep out the slums," admonished one East Side homeowners' group. If blacks moved into white neighborhoods, they would bring with them "noisy roomers, loud parties, auto horns, and in general riotous living," thus depreciating real estate values and destroying the moral fiber of the community. A middle-aged Catholic woman living in a racially changing Detroit neighborhood offered a similar view. Blacks "just destroy the whole neighborhood," she told an interviewer. "They neglect everything. Their way of life is so different from ours."[25] A Northwest Side neighborhood association poster played on the fears of white residents afraid of the crime that they believed would accompany racial change: "Home Owners Can You Afford to . . . Have your children exposed to gangster operated skid row saloons? Phorno-graphic [sic] pictures and literature? Gamblers and prostitution? You Face These Issues Now!"[26]

As black joblessness rates rose in the 1950s, such fears were not totally without basis. As more and more young African American men faced under-employment or unemployment, many spent time hanging out on street-corners, a scene that whites found threatening. And as the city's economy began its downward spiral in the mid-1950s, rates of burglary, robbery, and murder began to rise. In the city's poorest black neighborhoods, an alternative economy of gambling, drugs, and prostitution flourished. Even though whites were seldom the victims of black-initiated crimes, Detroit's white-owned daily newspapers paid special attention to black-on-white crimes, giving prominent billing to murders and rapes. Often sensationalistic accounts mentioned the race of a black perpetrator, but seldom, if ever, mentioned that of whites.[27]

Whites also commonly expressed fears of racial intermingling. Black "penetration" of white neighborhoods posed a fundamental challenge to white racial identity. Again and again, neighborhood groups and letter writers referred to the perils of rapacious black sexuality and race mixing. The politics of family, home, and neighborhood were inseparable from the containment of uncontrolled sexuality and the imminent danger of interracial liaisons. Neighborhood newsletters ominously warned of the threat of miscegenation. One Northwest Side newspaper praised a Common Council candidate with a banner headline: "Kronk Bucks Mixing Races." Members of the Courville District association discussed "interracial housing," "interracial marriage," and "interracial dancing in our schools and elsewhere." Proximity to blacks risked intimacy. "Do you want your children to marry colored?" asked one woman at an improvement association rally in 1957. At a meeting at Saint Scholastica Catholic Church in northwest Detroit nine years later, fears of racial intermarriage remained the most pressing concern. Parishioners expressed concerns about the supposed sexual potency of black men.[28]

The undistilled sentiments of youth offer a revealing glimpse into the racial attitudes that undergirded Detroit's battles over housing. In the mid-1940s, a teacher at the all-white Van Dyke School in northeast Detroit asked students in a sixth-grade class to write essays on "Why I like or don't like Negroes." The students frequently mentioned cleanliness, violence, and housing conditions as grounds for disliking blacks, and often offered pejorative comments about blacks' living habits. Several students expressed concerns about black neighbors. "They are durty fighters and they do not keep their yardes clean," wrote one sixth-grader. In the words of another student, "they try to mix in with white people when they don't want them." A classmate stated that "they wanted to live out on Van Dyke and we didn't want them to." Another argued (in words that must have come right from his parents), that "if you give them a inch they take a mile and they are sneaky." Mary Conk drew up a list which encapsulated most of her class-mates' sentiments:

1. Because they are mean
2. And they are not very clean.
3. Some of them don't like white people
4. They leave garbage in the yard and it smells
5. And in the dark the skare you
6. And they pick you up in a car and kill you. at nite
7. And they start riots

Most of the students at the Van Dyke School had never lived near a black person. Few spoke from experience. But the children, fearful of the prospect of blacks as neighbors, expressed attitudes that they had heard again and again from their parents and friends. As white Detroiters continued to fight against black movement throughout the city, they ensured that subsequent generations of children and adults would share Mary Conk's fears about blacks.[29]

Homeowners' Rights versus Civil Rights

In the battles over open housing, neighborhood groups refined and ex-tended the potent political language of rights that they developed during the public housing debates. As black journalist Henry Lee Moon noted, "the white population . . . has come to believe that it has a vested, exclusive, and permanent 'right' to certain districts." Civic associations cast their demands for racially segregated neighborhoods in terms of entitlement and victimiza-tion. Homeowners' groups were by no means alone in couching their politi-cal demands in the language of rights. They were part of the post–World War II rights revolution that empowered other groups, including African

Americans, trade union members, and military veterans, to use rights talk to express their political discontent and their political vision.[30]

The rhetoric linking homeownership and citizenship echoed throughout the newsletters and petitions of neighborhood associations. The National Association of Community Associations met "to keep the colored race from encroaching on the rights of the property owners by buying into the neighborhood." The Federated Property Owners of Detroit was founded in 1948 "To promote, uphold and defend the rights of home and property ownership and small business as the cornerstone of American opportunity and prosperity." The promise of government-sanctioned racial homogeneity also resounded in neighborhood association rhetoric. In 1949, the Greater Detroit Neighbors Association, Unit No. 2, rallied its members around "the right to live in the type of neighborhood that you choose." Homeowners' rights were precarious and needed to be defended vigorously from grasping blacks and acquiescent federal officials who threatened to usurp them. "Help Stamp Out Oppression—Fight for Our Rights," exhorted organizers of a "Vigilantes Organizational Meeting" in 1945 which appealed to "the oppressed Homeowners" of Detroit.[31]

"Homeowners' rights" was a malleable concept, one that derived its power from its imprecision. Some whites argued that they had acquired property and earned their rights through hard work and responsible citizenship. Homeowners' rights were, in this view, a reward for sacrifice and duty. Echoing the patriotic language of the anti–public housing groups, the Courville District Improvement Association reminded its members of wartime sacrifice. "Our boys fought to uphold freedom and safeguard our present rights. Are you willing to pick up the torch and carry on? There is no freedom without responsibility." Others drew from an idiosyncratic reading of the Declaration of Independence and Bill of Rights to justify their neighborhood defensiveness. Some defined homeowners' rights as an extension of their constitutional right to freedom of assembly. They had a right to choose their associates. That right would be infringed if their neighborhoods were racially mixed. "We believe in equal opportunity for all in employment, housing, and all phases of life," wrote officers of the Ruritan Park Civic Association, but nothing that "necessitates our having to give up our homes and go in search of another place to live, or suffer the depreciation . . . that occurs as soon as the area becomes a mixed neighborhood and to suffer the deterioration that follows." Rights for blacks were acceptable in the abstract, as long as blacks remained in their own neighborhoods and kept to themselves. But many whites believed that civil rights for blacks were won only at the expense of white rights. Many expressed a majoritarian conception of rights. "Let us not get so concerned with minority group welfare," wrote one white Detroiter in 1949, "that we forget all about the rights of the majority."[32]

In the battle against open housing, neighborhood associations forged a close alliance with real estate firms. Improvement associations unwittingly served the interests of landowners in heavily black areas, who took advantage of the enforced overcrowding of blacks to raise rents, and made exorbitant profits on decrepit buildings in the center city. Improvement associations also fit into the real estate industry's ideal of the planned community. Builders and real estate agents relied on grassroots enforcement of covenants prohibiting inharmonious uses, and depended on improvement associations to preserve the exclusionary character of neighborhoods. The interests of community builders dovetailed well with the status consciousness of single-family homeowners, their desire to see property values increase, and their obsession with homogeneity. Developers used the language of democracy and Americanism to give a patina of respectability to their community organization efforts. Karl H. Smith, a partner in the Smith-Bischop, Inc., one of the city's largest real estate agencies, praised improvement associations as "examples of true Americanism." These groups did "splendid work in upholding property values and property restrictions, and in fighting unjust tax levies for the benefit of shiftless drifters who have not guts enough to want to own a home of their own."[33]

Self-interested real estate agents and panicky white homeowners fearful of black encroachment collaborated closely to fight integration. Real estate agents were regular guests at improvement association meetings throughout the postwar period, and served as board members and advisers to white community groups. The Lower West Side Property Owners' Association included a local real estate agent, John Hamilton, among its officers. The Southwest Detroit Homeowners Association, to take another example, had as its chair Staunton Elsea, one of the city's most prominent realtors. Perhaps the most visible and influential neighborhood association was the Seven Mile–Fenelon Improvement Association, closely associated with Joseph P. Buffa and John Dalzell, both real estate brokers and developers with substantial property interests on Detroit's Northeast Side. The Seven Mile–Fenelon association furthered both Buffa's goal of protecting his substantial land investments from losses he anticipated if blacks moved into the area, and the interests of individual homeowners in the vicinity of the expanding black enclave of Conant Gardens. White homeowners and realtors had different but equally strong stakes in the future of their communities.[34]

In response to the judicial attack on restrictive covenents, homeowners' groups, often with the assistance of real estate agents, began to organize collectively to increase their political clout. As realtor Karl Smith argued, "There are so many of these little improvement associations along with a dozen or more big ones, that they get all tangled up and in each others' way; and they overlap, especially on important issues."[35] Groups heeded Smith's advice and began to form citywide organizations. In 1946, twenty-five homeowners' associations acted in concert to file an amicus curiae brief support-ing racially restrictive covenants in the *Sipes v. McGhee* case. In 1950, George Schermer, the director of the Mayor's Interracial Committee, noted "mounting organized resistance" from organizations "now being federated and acting together."[36] New umbrella organizations represented their nu-merous constituent groups throughout the city at public hearings. Efforts to consolidate met with mixed success; like-minded groups from different sec-tions of the city banded together in a number of citywide associations. The most prominent were the Michigan Council of Civic Associations, Inc., which included eleven organizations; the North East Council of Home Owners Associations, which had twelve member groups; and the enormous Federated Civic Associations of Northwest Detroit, which had at least fifty members and claimed to be "the largest known association of home owner groups in the country."[37]

Neighborhood associations began their battle against open housing in the aftermath of *Shelley v. Kraemer*. In 1948, the Federated Property Owners of Detroit, an umbrella organization of homeowners' groups, lashed out against those who breached restrictive covenants. "Property owners violating these principles have larceny in their hearts. They are worse than outlaw hood-lums who hold you up to steal your money. They have blood on their hands for having cut deep into [our] hearts and homelife." To mitigate the effects of *Shelley*, Federated Property Owners called for a citywide network to monitor the selling of homes to blacks, to harass real estate brokers who sold homes to blacks, and to keep house prices high to deter black buyers. "Watch for ad sections specifying colored—call them, pretend their prices sound very reasonable—that will make them keep their prices up."[38]

Neighborhoods reacted to the *Shelley v. Kraemer* decision differently. Wealthy whites in Boston-Edison pledged the "continuation of vigilant ac-tion to preserve the high character" of the area. The association would con-tinue to fight against "non-conforming uses," for "the best protected neigh-borhoods will be those such as ours where multiple family occupancy and business uses are prohibited."[39] Boston-Edison homeowners continued to express concern about black residents in the neighborhood. In 1949, the secretary of the association remarked with chagrin that "the colored care-taker" of a house in the neighborhood left his garage residence and "now lives in the house and uses the front door any time."[40] The transition to integration was tense. John P. Heavenreich, a longtime white resident of the community, stated that "the first years were tough for everybody. The origi-nal residents were afraid of what was going to happen." Eventually their "deep dark fears" about the area's future abated, mainly because the neigh-borhood association fiercely upheld its restrictions against mixed use.[41]

Other white neighborhoods attempted to subvert the Supreme Court decision through extralegal means. The Eastside Civic Council, serving a middle-class neighborhood on the far Northeast Side, attributed the victory of anticovenant forces to NAACP funding and "the organization and cooperation of the Colored groups." Success in maintaining the neighborhood would depend on similar community organization among whites: "Let us organize and cooperate and victory will be ours."[42] The Palmyra Home Owners' Association, on the Northwest Side, called for the discussion of "mutual reciprocal agreements" that replaced the racially specific language of racial covenants with vague references to "undesirable peoples." Several neighborhood associations circulated such dubiously legal voluntary agreements to "take place of the outlawed use restrictions and safeguard us against a mixed neighborhood."[43] And, in an ingenious scheme to revitalize racial restrictions in a legal guise, the Plymouth Manor association made its members sign a contract promising to sell their houses only through approved real estate brokers and to offer the association the right to match the offer of any prospective buyer. The first bastion of defense against black "invasion" came from the concerted efforts of such community groups throughout the city.[44]

Race and housing had been potent political issues since the early 1940s, but the election of Albert Cobo as mayor in 1949 represented the coming of age of the civic association movement. When Cobo came to office, he rewarded the improvement associations with close attention. Most significantly, he bent to the wishes of the neighborhood federations and gave them a prominent role on city commissions that handled matters of urban development, race relations, and housing. In 1951, Cobo appointed Alan E. Mac-Nichol, president of the Federated Civic Associations of Northwest Detroit, to the City Plan Commission. Cobo also created a citizens' advisory committee to consult on matters of zoning and city planning, comprised primarily of improvement association officers, including Ross Christie of the Gratiot-Chalmers Property Owners' Association and Alden C. Laird of the Park Drive–Ravendale Improvement Association.[45]

Homeowners' groups began an attack on "pressure groups, be they labor, government, or other impractical idealists," who supported the civil rights agenda. The most prolonged battle of the first years of the Cobo administration was over the construction of the union-supported and privately funded Schoolcraft Gardens Cooperative on Detroit's far Northwest Side. This project, a well-publicized venture, was scarcely a public housing project: it was designed as model "workers'" housing. The proposed spacious, modern townhouses overlooking beautifully landscaped terraces more closely resembled a suburban development than the sterile towers and featureless low-rises of public housing projects. It received financial and administrative backing from the powerful United Automobile Workers, which hoped that it would inspire similar developments throughout the city. The UAW and the other proponents of Schoolcraft Gardens refused to bow to pressure

8.2. Republican Mayor Albert Cobo (1950–1957) was sworn in for his third term in 1954. Cobo built a solid base of support among white working- and middle-class homeowners, and forged close alliances with white civic associations and anti–civil rights activists. Although he was a Republican in an overwhelmingly Democratic city, Cobo was handily reelected three times before his death in office in 1957.

from community groups to ensure that the development would remain all-white. Many of the project's advocates, in fact, hoped that Schoolcraft Gardens would serve as "an ideal testing ground to see whether whites and Negroes could live side by side without difficulties."[46]

Opponents of Schoolcraft Gardens found vice where its proponents found virtue. William Louks, speaking on behalf of the Detroit Real Estate Board, argued that proponents of Schoolcraft Gardens sought "to inject the century-worn strategy of pitting class against class or race against class or race and to promote the socialistic theory of a cooperative society."[47] Newspaper editor Floyd McGriff led a year-long campaign against the project in his Northwest Side neighborhood newspapers with articles attacking the "Bi-Racial Co-op" and warning his readers of the "socialistic" challenge to the "vested rights" of homeowners.[48] Northwest Detroit homeowners' associations, led by the Tel-Craft Association, barraged city officials with over ten thousand postcards protesting the project. Twelve fundamentalist Christian ministers in the area signed a resolution denouncing the project.[49] Cobo agreed with DREB, McGriff, and the neighborhood groups, and vetoed the City Council's authorization of a zoning change to allow the construction of Schoolcraft Gardens. The defeat of the Schoolcraft Gardens proposal was the opening battle in a two-decade-long struggle against liberal advocates of open housing. Just as the Cobo administration had torpedoed attempts to construct public housing on outlying sites, it now preserved "homeowners' rights" by blocking a significant private attempt to integrate the city.[50]

The Cobo administration's pro-homeowner stance emboldened civic associations to demand city intervention in changing neighborhoods. In May 1950, Roy E. LaVigne, a director of the Courville District Improvement Association, asked city officials to assist the association in its attempt to buy back the first house on a block sold to a black family. LaVigne warned city officials that if the association did not prevent the family from settling into their new house, "property values would be adversely affected," and "the people of the neighborhood would move out in droves to Dearborn, Royal Oak and other suburbs, leaving Detroit 'holding the bag.'" The city refused to intervene in the situation on the grounds that blacks had the right to live where they pleased.[51] In June 1952, Marx Street residents sent a petition to Detroit Common Council requesting that the city "exclude Negroes" from the area. However sympathetic Cobo administration officials may have been to the apartheid scheme, it was blatantly illegal, and the petition remained unanswered. Despite these rebuffs, white Detroit residents continued to send letters of protest to Cobo administration officials when blacks moved into their neighborhoods.[52]

Neighborhood groups were more effective in marshaling their newfound political influence to agitate for changes in the city government. Their most conspicuous victory came with the evisceration of the Mayor's Interracial Committee. Vilified by many white Detroiters for its increasingly vocal pro-civil rights stance, the MIC consistently opposed restrictive covenants, segregation in public housing, and discrimination in public places. In 1951, a neighborhood association–backed group, which called itself the Legislative Research Committee, issued a report calling for the abolition of the MIC. It accused director George Schermer of bias because he was a member of the liberal Americans for Democratic Action, and argued that under his guidance the MIC fostered racial animosity in the city. "Instead of lessening and assuaging interracial tensions, Schermer's outfit, by devious means, has accentuated them, stirring up racial strife."[53]

The anti-MIC campaign combined an anti–civil rights stance with anti-bureaucratic and antitax sentiments. Neighborhood group respresentatives charged that the MIC wrongfully used public funds to assist civil rights

organizations. C. Katherine Rentschler, a member of the Warrendale Improvement Association and chair of Home-Owner Civic and Improvement
Associations, proposed the elimination of the MIC. She accused the "watch-
dog commission" of "using our TAX MONEY to create agitation." According
to Rentschler, "A review of the work of the Mayor's Interracial Committee
indicates that it has continually functioned solely for the Negro race."[54] As
an alternative to the MIC, she called for a "Home Owner Participation Ordinance" that would give neighborhood associations "a voice in planning and
regulating the activities" of city agencies.[55]

Cobo took such proposals seriously. After the Detroit Common Council
authorized the restructuring of the MIC as the Commission on Community
Relations (CCR), Cobo used his appointment power to weaken the new
body. In perhaps the most controversial move of his administration, Cobo
appointed neighborhood association advocate John Laub to head the commission. Laub, a high-school coach and counselor, had no qualifications for
the job apart from his presidency of the staunchly pro-Cobo Northwest Civic
Federation.[56] The mayor passed over two inside favorites. He rejected
Beulah Whitby, a member of the MIC since its founding, because of her
opposition to segregated public housing, and race relations expert John
Feild, a highly regarded MIC staff member who had become director of
the Toledo Human Relations Board. Members of integrationist groups in
Detroit bitterly attacked Laub, who had no experience in race relations
issues, and compared him unfavorably with his predecessor George
Schermer, a national advocate of urban racial integration. Joining Laub was
Isabel Wieterson, another improvement association veteran and staunch
anti–civil rights activist.[57]

Civil rights groups in the city were especially concerned about the chill-
ing effect of the commission's rightward turn. According to the Wayne
County Council of the CIO, the restructured CCR failed "to show real leadership or activity in the fields of education and positive action in areas of
tension."[58] Horace White, a leading black minister in the city, charged that
under Laub's leadership, the CCR had "gracefully sidetracked every fundamental issue that rightfully belonged to them in the last two years." Even
black businessman Ed Davis (who, as a Republican, generally supported
Cobo) agreed that Laub was an "ineffectual novice," who was "not qualified
to carry out the mandate of the commission." The Detroit Branch of the
NAACP lamented that "what was a model human relations agency" had "de-
generate[d] into a mockery."[59] Four longtime members, including two of the
CCR's three black members, resigned in 1955 before Laub, under considerable community pressure, resigned in 1956.[60]

At the same time, neighborhood groups launched into open warfare
against open housing advocates. As domestic anticommunism reached its
peak of political prominence, neighborhood groups began to articulate their

concerns in McCarthyite terms. A growing number of white Detroiters believed that open housing advocates were part of a conspiracy that linked together government bureaucrats, civil rights organizations, and liberal religious groups, many influenced by Communism or socialism (terms used interchangeably), who sacrificed white homeowners to their experiments in social engineering for the benefit of "pressure groups"—repudiating, in the process, property rights and democratic principles.

Homeowners' groups and sympathetic politicians used McCarthyite rhetoric against public housing and open housing advocates and their liberal supporters. Red-baiting was, to be sure, a crass smear tactic, but in the perfervid atmosphere of the anticommunist crusade, many whites believed that a sinister conspiracy was at hand. Open housing, according to conservative editor Floyd McGriff, was the product of a "leftist political brigade" that had as its mission "political activity to provide colored persons with homes they cannot afford to live in." Calls for racial integration were part of an effort of communists and their sympathizers to weaken the American family, the nation's best defense against the Soviet threat.[61]

Detroit's realtors reinforced the rights rhetoric that animated white neighborhood groups. In their campaign against proposed open housing legislation, state regulation of real estate brokers, and the Fair Neighborhood Practices Ordinance, realtors flooded the city with anti–open occupancy propaganda. According to the Michigan Real Estate Association, a proposed state law to ban discrimination in real estate sales would "ROB the individual of his 'property rights' which are truly inseparable from 'human rights.'" Detroit Real Estate Board flyers reminded homeowners of the risk that open housing posed to the very tenets of democracy. "THIS IS YOUR PERSONAL WAR TO SAVE YOUR PROPERTY RIGHTS" read one real estate industry political sheet. Another called on homeowners to "HELP CRUSH DICTATOR RULE" by liberal government officials who were motivated by the "Communist creed."[62]

In the early 1960s, the struggle between civil rights and homeowners' rights culminated at the ballot box. In 1963, open housing groups, upset at the weak Fair Neighborhood Practices Ordinance, pushed for a stronger city law that would outlaw all racial discrimination in real estate transactions. The open housing law was backed by the Commission on Community Relations, religious groups, and Detroit's new liberal Mayor Jerome Cavanagh.[63] But only two of nine Common Council members supported the open housing law, and it did not stand a chance of passing. Neighborhood groups counterattacked. In 1963, they proposed a "Homeowners' Rights Ordinance" that would preserve their "right" to segregated neighborhoods and their "right" to discriminate in real estate sales. The competing ordinances pitted blacks, white racial liberals, and civil rights groups against a solidly white, bipartisan, antiliberal coalition.

Advocates of the Homeowners' Rights Ordinance linked class resentments with an indictment of civil rights groups and government. Organizers of the Butzel-Guest Property Owners Association railed against "the 'Civil Wrongs' that are being forced on us more and more every day," and pledged to "put out of office those who are working just for the minority and put in someone who will work for all the people."[64] Many whites combined a populist rage against both civil rights organizations and their allegedly well-off white supporters. "The hypocrites who scream about the homeowners' refusal to be dictated to by pressure groups and who advocate open housing," wrote one angry woman, "are the very ones who live in ultraexclusive neighborhoods."[65] Another chastised the hypocrisy of "Bishops, ministers, and union leaders [who] lecture about brotherhood ... confident that their means of income will never force them to live among their black brothers." The open housing movement, in their view, elevated minority rights over the rights of the majority. "You can't ram people down people's throats," argued another angry white Detroiter who opposed open housing.[66]

Building on the rights rhetoric of the neighborhood movement, the Homeowners' Rights Ordinance pledged to protect the individual's "right to privacy," the "right to choose his own friends and associates," "the right to freedom from interference with his property by public authorities attempting to give special privileges to any group," the "right to maintain what in his opinion are congenial surroundings for himself, his family, and his tenants," and the "right" to choose a real estate broker and tenants and home buyers "for his own reasons."[67] More was at stake than the preservation of rights, for as Greater Detroit Homeowners' Association spokesman Thomas Poindexter contended, the ordinance would stop "the spread of crime, disease, and neighborhood blight," and the takeover of the city by "persons living on public assistance."[68]

Supporters of the Homeowners' Rights Ordinance quickly collected over forty-four thousand signatures to put it on the 1964 primary ballot, more than twice the number required for ballot initiatives. On Detroit's Northeast Side, more than two thousand volunteers went door-to-door, rallying supporters. The campaign was remarkably successful. Voter turnout, over 50 percent, was especially high for a local primary election. The ordinance passed by a 55-to-45 margin. In the city's two largest, predominantly white wards, the margin was two to one; the ordinance lost by nearly four to one in predominantly African American wards in the inner city. The Homeowners' Rights Ordinance was declared unconstitutional by the Wayne County District Court in 1965 and never implemented.[69]

Detroit's Homeowners' Rights Ordinance was but one salvo in nationwide battle against the open housing movement. In 1964, California voters approved a homeowners' rights amendment to the state constitution, and voters in Akron, Ohio, amended the municipal charter to prohibit its city

8.3. A reactionary populist who rose to fame as an opponent of housing integration, Thomas Poindexter (second from right) was known as the "Home Owners' Champion." Here Poindexter and the officers of the Greater Detroit Home Owners' Association present Homeowners' Rights Ordinance petitions to the city clerk in July 1963. Advocates of the anti–open housing ordinance gathered forty-four thousand signatures, more than double the number necessary to get a place on the city ballot.

council from passing an open housing ordinance without a citywide referendum. In Milwaukee, Gary, and Baltimore, whites in urban neighborhoods threatened by open housing supported George Corley Wallace in the Democratic presidential primary. Two years later, white homeowners in Chicago attacked the Reverend Martin Luther King, Jr., when he led open housing marches through white working-class neighborhoods.[70]

The consequences of the creation of the divided metropolis were profound. The physical separation of blacks and whites in the city perpetuated inequality in housing and access to jobs, but, no less significantly, it reinforced the ideology of race held by northern whites. The "ghetto" was not simply a physical construct; it was also an ideological construct. Urban space became a metaphor for perceived racial difference. Whites created a cognitive map of the city based on racial classifications and made their decisions about residence and their community action in accordance with their vision of the racial geography of the city. They established "invisible stone walls of prejudice," and through defensive activity ensured that despite their invisibility those walls were well known to black and white Detroiters.[71] In the very act of defining the boundaries of the "ghetto," whites also continually defined and reinforced the boundaries of race. Throughout the postwar period, Detroit's racial barrier shifted again and again, as blacks moved into formerly all-white neighborhoods. Even as it shifted, the racial wall remained intact. With remarkable alacrity, whites fled changing neighborhoods, and mounted their defenses elsewhere.[72]

Neighborhood improvement associations saw their agenda implemented in the Cobo administration, but ultimately, their political clout was not enough to address the issue that most concerned them, black mobility. As the city's black population began to spread beyond the confines of the prewar ghetto, improvement associations adopted increasingly sophisticated strategies to preserve neighborhood homogeneity. Their alliances with elected officials, businessmen, realtors, and other Detroiters like themselves were, in their view, insufficient to stem the tide of disorder overtaking their neighborhoods and threatening their way of life. These organizations turned to a variety of legal and extralegal activities from picketing to harassment to vandalism and violence to fight against the threat of black movement. Detroit's crabgrassroots organizations combined mainstream political activism with organized resistance. The struggle against the "colored threat" would move fluidly between the political arena and the battleground of the streets.

Je. 1/6.00

EMERGENCY MEETING

SAT., MARCH 11, 1950 - 7 P.M.

All Residents on Streets - Dequindre
Marx, Orleans, Riopelle, Greeley and
all streets up to Oakland
6 Mile to 7 Mile Roads

NEIGHORHOOD INVADED BY COLORED PURCHASE ON ORLEANS & MINNESOTA

EVERY RESIDENT ASKED TO BE PRESENT TO VOTE ON MEASURES TO BE TAKEN, SIGN PETITIONS, AND ELECT BLOCK CAPTAINS

PLACE - LAZAR HALL
Dequindre and Minnesota

9.1. Courville area residents called an emergency meeting when a black family violated the invisible racial boundary of Dequindre Avenue. Like many homeowners' associations, they rallied neighbors with militaristic language, referring to an "invasion" and calling for the election of block "captains."

9

"United Communities Are Impregnable": Violence and the Color Line

Pitch for your civic rights and the protection of your women.
—*Action!*, the newsletter of the Courville District Association (1948)

We hate Niggers
—Painted on the front of a house purchased by a black family on San Juan Street (1963)

LIFE WAS GOOD for Easby Wilson in the spring of 1955. The city was in a recession, but Wilson was still steadily employed on the day shift at the Dodge Main plant. At a time when many of his fellow black workers were being laid off, Wilson was lucky. He had saved enough money so that he, his wife, and their five-year-old son could move from the crowded and run-down Paradise Valley area to the quiet, leafy neighborhood around the Courville School on Detroit's Northeast Side. The Courville area was popular with Dodge Main workers because it was affordable, attractive, and only three miles from the plant. Wilson could drive from his house to the factory gate in about ten minutes, or take a fifteen-minute bus ride down Dequindre Avenue.[1]

After looking at a few houses in March 1955, the Wilsons chose a modest frame house on Riopelle Street. They knew that the neighborhood was predominantly white and had heard rumors of racially motivated violence in changing Detroit neighborhoods. But their real estate agent reassured him that "the situation" (a euphemism for race relations) "was fine." What the broker failed to tell them was that they were breaching an invisible racial boundary by buying a house west of Dequindre Avenue. The neighborhood to the east of Dequindre had a rapidly growing black population, but only one other black family lived on the blocks to the west. The Wilsons also did not know that over the preceding decade, white residents of the surrounding neighborhood had formed a powerful homeowners' association to resist the black "invasion" of their area, had harassed whites who offered their houses to blacks, and had driven out several black newcomers. Less than two years before the Wilsons bought their house, neighbors in the same block had threatened a white family who put their house on the market with a black broker.[2]

Shortly after the Wilsons closed on the real estate deal, their new house became a racial battleground. Indignant white neighbors launched a five-month siege on 18199 Riopelle. In late April, just before the Wilsons moved in, someone broke into the house, turned on all the faucets, blocked the kitchen sink, flooded the basement, and spattered black paint on the walls and floors. Later that day, after the Wilsons cleaned up the mess and left, vandals broke all the front windows in the house. Despite the noise, no neighbors reported the attack to the police. On Tuesday, April 26, the Wilsons moved in. The onslaught escalated. White members of the Cadillac Improvement Association approached the Wilsons and demanded that they sell the house. That evening, someone threw a stone through the bathroom window. For two straight nights, the phone rang with angry, anonymous calls.

On Friday, after dinner, a small crowd gathered on Riopelle Street in front of the Wilsons' house. They were soon joined by more than four hundred picketing and chanting whites, summoned by young boys who rode their bikes up and down the street, blowing whistles. The crowd drew together a cross-section of neighborhood residents: as Mrs. Wilson reported, "it was children; it was old people; it was teen-agers; in fact all ages were there." Demonstrators screamed epithets. "You'd better go back where you belong!" shouted an angry neighbor. A rock shattered the dining room window. Trapped inside, Easby Wilson could barely contain his rage. "He lost his head" before he was calmed by his wife and a police officer. The following evening, more protesters filled the street in front of the Wilson house; despite police surveillance, someone threw a large rock toward the house so hard that it stuck in the asbestos siding.

In the aftermath of the demonstrations, some of Wilson's friends from UAW Local 3 stood guard occasionally on the Wilsons' porch. The police stationed a patrol car near the house twenty-four hours a day. Gradually the pickets subsided, but over the next two months, hit-and-run vandals launched eggs, rocks, and bricks at the Wilsons' windows, splashed red, black, and yellow paint on the facade of the house, and put several snakes in the basement. An older white woman who lived next door threatened the family and was caught one evening pouring salt on the Wilsons' lawn. "At night," reported Mrs. Wilson, "when the lights are out, you can expect anything." Despite the police protection, the attacks went unabated; in fact many of the attacks occurred while police officers sat in their car nearby. At the end of the second month of the siege, Mrs. Wilson was exasperated. "I don't know whether it's worthwhile. I believe in Democracy; I believe in what my husband fought for [in World War II]. . . . They fought for the peace and I wonder if it's worthwhile. I have a question in my mind: where is the peace they fought for—where is it?"

The beleaguered Wilsons reported a "terrific strain" because of the incidents. Easby Wilson suffered from a mild heart condition that was aggravated by the stress of constant harassment. Their son Raymond, a five-year-old, began having "nervous attacks," waking up in the middle of the night complaining that he felt like "something was crawling over him, maybe ants." Raymond's affliction proved to be the last indignity the Wilsons would suffer. They moved out of their Riopelle Street house when a psychologist warned the Wilsons that Raymond risked "becoming afflicted with a permanent mental injury" because of the relentless attacks. The siege on the Wilsons, and other attacks on black newcomers to the area, served as an effective deterrent to black movement onto the streets west of Dequindre Avenue, between McNichols and Seven Mile Roads. In 1960, almost five years after the Wilsons were driven out, only 2.9 percent of the area's residents were black.[3]

Violent incidents like the attacks on the Wilsons' home were commonplace in Detroit between the Second World War and the 1960s. The postwar era, as a city race relations official recalled, was marked by many "small disturbances, near-riots, and riots." The city "did a lot of firefighting in those days." White Detroiters instigated over two hundred incidents against blacks moving into formerly all-white neighborhoods, including harassment, mass demonstrations, picketing, effigy burning, window breaking, arson, vandalism, and physical attacks. Most incidents followed improvement association meetings. The number of attacks peaked between 1954 and 1957, when the city's economy was buffeted by plant closings, recession, and unemployment, limiting the housing options of many white, working-class Detroiters. Incidents accelerated again in the early 1960s, reaching a violent crescendo in 1963, when the Commission on Community Relations reported sixty-five incidents. A potent mixture of fear, anger, and desperation animated whites who violently defended their neighborhoods. All but the most liberal whites who lived along the city's racial frontier believed that they had only two options. They could flee, as vast numbers of white urbanites did, or they could hold their ground and fight.[4]

The violence that whites unleashed against blacks was not simply a manifestation of lawlessness and disorder. It was not random, nor was it irrational. In the arena of housing, violence in Detroit was organized and widespread, the outgrowth of one of the largest grassroots movements in the city's history. It involved thousands of whites, directly affected hundreds of blacks, mainly those who were among the first families to break the residential barriers of race, and indirectly constrained the housing choices of tens of thousands of blacks fearful of harassment and physical injury if they broke through Detroit's residential color line. The violent clashes between whites and blacks that marred the city were political acts, the consequence of perceptions of homeownership, community, gender, and race deeply held by white Detroiters. The result of profound economic insecurities among working- and middle-class whites, they were, above all, desperate acts of neighborhood self-determination, by well-organized community groups, in response to an array of social and economic changes over which they had little control.

Racial incidents encoded possession and difference in urban space. Residents of postwar Detroit carried with them a cognitive map that helped them negotiate the complex urban landscape. In a large, amorphous twentieth-century city like Detroit, there were few visible landmarks to distinguish one neighborhood from another. But residents imposed onto the city's featureless topography all sorts of invisible boundaries—boundaries shaped by intimate association, by institutions (like public-school catchment areas or Catholic parish boundaries), by class, and, most importantly, by race. As the city's racial demography changed in the postwar years and as blacks began to move out of the center city, white neighborhood organizations acted to define and defend the invisible boundaries that divided the city. Their actions were, in large part, an attempt to mark their territory symbolically and visibly, to stake out turf and remind outsiders that to violate those borders was to risk grave danger.[5]

The sustained violence in Detroit's neighborhoods was the consummate act in a process of identity formation. White Detroiters invented communities of race in the city that they defined spatially. Race in the postwar city was not just a cultural construction. Instead, whiteness, and by implication blackness, assumed a material dimension, imposed onto the geography of the city. Through the drawing of racial boundaries and through the use of systematic violence to maintain those boundaries, whites reinforced their own fragile racial identity. Ultimately, they were unsuccessful in preventing the movement of blacks into many Detroit neighborhoods, but their defensive measures succeeded in deepening the divide between two Detroits, one black and one white. On one side of the ever-shifting, contested color line were insecure white workers who expressed their racial sentiments politically and depended on the most extreme among them to patrol racial borders. On the other side of the line were blacks, initially optimistic about the prospects of residential integration, but increasingly unwilling to venture into territory they justifiably considered hostile.

Fight or Flight: The Social Ecology of White Resistance

Despite the frequency of racial conflict in the city's streets, postwar Detroit's violent past remains hidden from history.[6] Although "racial incidents popped up in almost monstrous frequency," city race relations officials and white-owned newspapers downplayed the city's race-motivated violence. The Detroit Mayor's Interracial Committee (MIC) feared that widespread publicity about racial incidents would provoke a race riot. The MIC did not censor news reports, but commission staff met regularly with reporters and editors to discuss coverage of housing incidents.[7] In public statements, city officials engaged in a conspiracy of silence about racial violence in the city. In 1955, when the Easby Wilson disturbances and twenty other major housing incidents shook the city, Common Council President and future Mayor Louis Miriani told the black Pioneers Club that "the Common Council knew nothing of racial incidents in the community." Not until 1956, when a Detroit daily carried an article about a two-week long siege against blacks who bought a house on Robson Street in northwest Detroit, did race-motivated violence become visible to whites in the city, although plenty of large, angry, rock-wielding crowds as aggressive as those on Robson Street had terrorized blacks in the 1940s and 1950s. Whites who lived beyond racially transitional neighborhoods remained, by and large, blissfully unaware of the racially motivated violence directed at Detroit's blacks.[8]

Black Detroiters were, however, painfully aware of the racial strife that ravaged Detroit's neighborhoods in the postwar years. Detroit's black weeklies carried detailed reports of the numerous attacks on black homeowners in Detroit in the postwar period. The coverage of racial violence in the black papers gave the lie to optimistic reports about improving race relations in the city. Well informed about the skirmishes on Detroit's racial frontier, many blacks grew increasingly pessimistic about the possibility of harmonious race relations in Detroit, and skeptical toward the public authorities who seemed to do little or nothing to curb the fury of angry white homeowners.[9]

Defended Neighborhoods

Violent attacks against blacks occurred in just about every racially changing neighborhood in the city in the postwar years. But the fiercest resistance to black movement occurred in three predominantly working-class sections of the city (Map 9.1) whose residents were members of the city's most powerful homeowners' organizations: the Northeast Side (represented by the Courville District and Seven Mile–Fenelon Improvement Associations), the Wyoming Corridor (represented by the Ruritan Park, De Witt–Clinton, and States-Lawn Neighborhood Associations), and the Lower West Side (represented by the Property Owners' Association).

These defended neighborhoods had several important characteristics in common. All of them had predominantly blue-collar populations with median incomes slightly above the city average (Table 9.1). Skilled workers were overrepresented in each neighborhood: all had above-average percentages of craftsmen. Defended neighborhoods also had lower rates of female

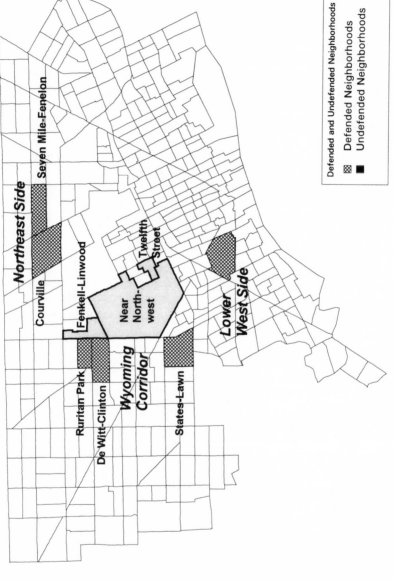

Map 9.1. Defended and Undefended Neighborhoods

TABLE 9.1

Housing and Employment Characteristics, Defended and Undefended Neighborhoods, Detroit, 1940 and 1950[a]

	Home Price (as percent of city average)	Percent of Homes Owner-Occupied	Percent Blue-Collar, of males in work force	Percent Craft, of males in work force	Percent Female in work force
	DEFENDED NEIGHBORHOODS				
Northeast Side					
Courville	83.0	72.5	77.8	28.3	25.4
Seven Mile–					
Fenelon	76.3	63.0	85.8	25.3	26.7
Wyoming Corridor					
De Witt–Clinton	90.2	72.4	67.0	29.8	26.1
Ruritan Park	97.3	61.6	61.5	28.5	26.4
States-Lawn	93.8	71.7	60.5	26.7	27.4
Lower West Side	64.7	24.3	80.0	25.2	22.5
	UNDEFENDED NEIGHBORHOODS				
Fenkell-Linwood	85.5	63.2	55.8	24.6	29.0
Twelfth Street	99.7	10.8	51.3	19.8	32.2
Near Northwest	110.3	35.0	43.4	17.6	31.6
Detroit (1950)	100.0	52.9	66.7	21.7	27.3
Detroit (1940)	100.0	39.2	68.1	22.5	28.3

Sources: U.S. Department of Commerce, Bureau of the Census, *Census of Population and Housing, 1940, Census Tract Statistics for Detroit, Michigan and Adjacent Area* (Washington: U.S. Government Printing Office, 1943), tract 603 (Seven Mile–Fenelon); tracts 187–88 (Twelfth Street); tracts 9–10, 36–39, 41 (Lower West Side). *Census of Population, 1950, Census Tract Statistics for Detroit, Michigan and Adjacent Area* (Washington: U.S. Government Printing Office, 1953), tract 606 (Courville); tract 261 (De Witt–Clinton); tract 263 (Ruritan Park); tracts 201–3 (States-Lawn); tracts 153–56, 159–69, 175–84, 190–91 (Near Northwest); tracts 170–71 (Fenkell-Linwood). [a] The data have been selected for the nearest census year before black movement into a neighborhood.

labor force participation than the city as a whole. The neighborhoods were bastions of single-family homeownership. With the exception of the Lower West Side, the percentage of owner occupancy far exceeded the citywide average. The residential architecture in these communities was undistinguished. Most homes were modest two- or three-bedroom bungalows of frame construction, built in the 1920s and 1940s, crowded together on forty-foot lots. However, they sat neatly on tree-lined streets, which gave them a quasi-suburban atmosphere. And none of the defended neighborhoods was located in the midst of a major industrial area, but all were within a few miles of large auto plants, and most were even closer to Detroit's innumerable small machine and tool shops. Finally, all but one were ethnically heterogeneous, with sizable Roman Catholic populations.

The Northeast Side was a hotbed of racial unrest beginning with the controversy over the Sojourner Truth Homes in 1942 and continuing through the mid-1960s. A green refuge from more crowded and older sections of the city, northeast Detroit was settled in the 1920s, largely by blue-collar workers of Italian and Polish descent. Its tiny houses attracted both auto and crafts workers, many of whom worked in the nearby Chrysler plants or in the dozens of small tool and die shops that lined Nevada Street and McNichols Road.[10] Northeast Side residents took special pride in their neighborhood's several impressive Catholic parishes—Saint Rita's, Saint Bartholomew's, and the Polish national Corpus Christi (all in the Courville district) and the enormous Saint Louis the King (home base of the powerful Seven Mile–Fenelon Improvement Association). The sight of Catholic schoolchildren in uniform on weekdays, and the crowds on the sidewalks in front of the churches on Sundays, were visible reminders of the importance of Catholic identity in the area.[11]

In the midst of the Northeast Side were two sizable black enclaves, the Conant Gardens area and the Sojourner Truth Homes. The surrounding streets, some still undeveloped in the early 1950s, became magnets for black homeowners and builders. As blacks began to move into houses on the formerly all-white blocks of the Courville and Seven Mile–Fenelon neighborhoods, violence exploded. The first battles occurred between 1948 and 1952, as demonstrators vandalized new, substantial single-family homes being built in the area for middle-class blacks. That many of the new houses "were above the standards of existing structures" in the area enraged white neighbors all the more.[12] Failing to deter the black newcomers, white Northeast Side residents tried to confine the black population, by drawing invisible racial lines along three major arteries that passed through the area—Dequindre on the west, Seven Mile on the north, and Mound on the east. (Dequindre and Seven Mile also served as parish boundaries, an example of the mutual reinforcement of religious and racial territories). Through violence, whites made clear to blacks the high cost of transgressing the color line. When the first black families tried to cross the invisible line along Dequindre, white neighbors set their houses afire and broke their windows. Throughout the 1950s, every black family that tried to move across Dequindre, including the unfortunate Wilsons, was rebuffed by angry white crowds and vandals.[13]

The violence that beset black pioneers on the Northeast Side was matched on the streets of the Wyoming Corridor, a band of West Side neighborhoods between Livernois and Meyers avenues, centered along Wyoming Avenue. The Wyoming Corridor was distant from Detroit's smoky riverfront, but centrally located for blue-collar commuters, easily accessible to the Rouge and Downriver areas via car or bus, and a short ride to the Chrysler plants on the East Side. The Wyoming Corridor was also dotted with

9.2. This 1920s-era bungalow on Tuller Street was typical of homes in the defended Wyoming Corridor. Blue-collar homeowners in the area fiercely resisted black movement into their neighborhood, protecting their investments and their status through organized protest and violent demonstrations.

small factories that employed many area craftsmen. It was more ethnically diverse than the Northeast Side: the residents were a mixture of first- and second-generation Irish, Germans, Italians, native-born whites, Anglo-Canadian immigrants, and a few Poles and other Slavs. Its small bungalows, most built in the 1920s, were home to a largely Roman Catholic population. The imposing stone facades of Saint Gregory's, Saint Francis de Sales, Saint Luke's, and Saint Brigid's parish churches all loomed on the horizon, monuments to the piety of the area's faithful.[14]

Whites in the Wyoming Corridor, fearful that their neighborhoods would be engulfed in the black migration from inner-city Detroit, began organizing against "undesirables" in 1949, a full seven years before the first black family tried to move into the area. Resistance was spearheaded by the well-organized De Witt–Clinton association, whose leaders helped residents in nearby Ruritan Park and States-Lawn form their own homeowners' organizations.[15] From 1956 through 1965, Wyoming Corridor residents fiercely attacked black pioneers and real estate agents who dared enter their neighborhood. Typical was the case of black auto worker Henry Love and his family, who moved into a house on Chalfonte in 1955. A thousand angry white neighbors filled the street, pelting the house with stones and "a burning fuse," and injuring two policemen who were standing guard. Henry Love told Urban League investigators that he "was not interested in being a pioneer," and stated that "he could not stomach this hostility."[16] Ruritan Park Association members, inspired by the victory against the Love family, pledged "to keep Negroes out of the area" by "using any methods available which are not specifically illegal."[17] States-Lawn area residents also attacked black home buyers, but directed special animus against the hundreds of real estate agents who fanned through the community in the late 1950s and early 1960s sowing the seeds of panic in hopes of reaping handsome profits from white flight.[18]

The one defended neighborhood that was significantly different from the others was the Lower West Side. It was the epicenter of white protest in the immediate postwar years. Wedged between the downtown business district, the industrial corridors of Jefferson and Michigan Avenues, and the black West Side, the Lower West Side was not one of Detroit's more attractive neighborhoods. Its housing stock was old and rather run-down, and its residents were poorer whites, fewer than a quarter of them homeowners. And in contrast to the other defended neighborhoods, few of the residents were Roman Catholics. Appalachian whites, mainly Protestant, were the neighborhood's most visible group.[19]

On the fringe of an expanding black section of the city, the Lower West Side was rocked by eighteen racial incidents between the fall of 1945 and early 1950.[20] Lower West Side residents torched a black veteran's newly purchased house on Seventeenth Street, pulled off the porch of a black-owned Vermont Street house, drove two blacks from their Sycamore Street apartments, harassed landlords and real estate agents, cut the power lines to a house on Brooklyn Street, broke thirty-five windows on two houses on Harrison Street, and regularly filled the streets with crowds of fifty to one thousand demonstrators.[21]

Violence on the West Side stopped as abruptly as it had started, and sizable black and white populations coexisted in the area for decades after the explosions of the 1940s. There are two explanations for the different trajectories of the Lower West Side and other defended neighborhoods. First, the violence in this neighborhood was a direct response to the desperate shortage of housing after World War II, a shortage that poor whites in the area felt especially acutely. Residents of the West Side—white and black—had to compete for scarce space in the 1940s, unlike their homeowner counterparts in the Wyoming Corridor and the Northeast Side. Second, the area—because of its cheap housing stock—continued to attract southern white migrants, who—unlike Roman Catholics—had few institutional roots. It is speculative, but quite possible, that migrants from the South, where the degree of residential segregation never equaled that of the North, were less concerned with the prospect of having African American neighbors. What is certain is that southern white migrants on the Lower West Side reached an accommodation with their black neighbors and did not defend their racial identity with the desperation of the "not-yet-white" ethnics who lived in the Wyoming Corridor and the Northeast Side.[22]

Residents of Detroit's defended neighborhoods shared much in common with their counterparts in other cities. Like antiblack protesters in Chicago, Detroit's resisters were primarily "an 'ethnic' amalgam of working-class Catholics." They tended, like their counterparts in Boston, to live in neighborhoods whose identities were strongly shaped by the presence of large, vital Catholic parishes. As in Cleveland and Cincinnati, Detroit's white resistance was spearheaded by homeowners with a precarious hold on their middle-class identity, fearful of association with "any group bearing the stigma of low status." And white neighborhood defenders in Detroit had less mobility and fewer resources than their middle- and upper-class neighbors, who could flee rather than resort to violence. There were differences. Detroit's flat, featureless topography prevented the formation of isolated white enclaves, like Charlestown and South Boston, cut off from the rest of the city and intensely protective of their turf. And unlike whites who lived in Philadelphia and Trenton, who were more likely to react violently to black movement into neighborhoods within walking distance of major factories, working-class white Detroiters tried to protect their quasi-suburban turf.[23]

Undefended Neighborhoods

The distinctive characteristics of Detroit's defended neighborhoods can be seen most clearly in contrast with formerly all-white neighborhoods where blacks settled with little resistance. One blue-collar area with a housing stock and population almost identical to the six defended neighborhoods was the Fenkell-Linwood area on Detroit's West Side. Located just west of an established black neighborhood, Fenkell-Linwood was the site of a few serious racial disturbances in the late 1940s and early 1950s as blacks began to move into the area. The first rumblings of unrest came in 1948, when whites protested against black residents moving into homes at 15010 Quincy and 15532 Baylis. In February 1950, when black Chrysler worker James Waterman moved onto Princeton Street, enraged protesters stoned his house, slashed his car tires, and burned a cross on his front lawn. Nine days after Waterman moved in, Unit 5 of the Greater Detroit Neighbors Association attracted about 150 area residents to discuss ways of preventing other "Samboes" and "niggers" from moving into the area.[24]

Despite the initial outburst of violence, resistance to black movement into

Fenkell-Linwood was short-lived. The eastern half of the neighborhood was simply too close to established black neighborhoods to prevent realtors from speculating in the area and encouraging panic selling. Even more importantly, however, the city announced plans to construct the Lodge Freeway through the area in the late 1940s. Running for nearly two miles along Keeler Street, the new highway cut a swath through the area and devalued homes on nearby streets. Because of the highway construction, homeowners began to sell or rent houses along the expressway route to blacks—the Baylis, Princeton, and Quincy Street houses were all close to the proposed path of the Lodge. The disruptive effects of highway construction dampened any incipient resistance to black movement into the area. The depreciation of property values in blocks adjacent to the expressway, along with the flight of hundreds of white families, opened formerly closed streets to black newcomers. Whites who had patrolled the borders to prevent black movement quickly abandoned their defenses and left the racial boundary unguarded. As a result, large sections of the Fenkell-Linwood area seemed to lose their white population and gain a black population virtually overnight. The racial transformation of the census tracts along the expressway took place with shocking speed: two census tracts in the area that were virtually all-white in 1950 saw their black populations increase four-thousand- and six-thousand-fold by 1960.[25]

Neighborhoods with large Jewish populations, in contrast to their Catholic counterparts, also experienced rapid racial transition. The Twelfth Street area, north of Grand Boulevard between Linwood and Hamilton Avenues, was the center of Detroit's Jewish population in 1940. Its business district bustled with shoppers going to its kosher butchers, bakeries, and delicatessens, and its haberdasheries. Twenty synagogues met the religious needs of the community's residents. Economically and demographically, the Twelfth Street area differed considerably from the other areas considered. Buildings in the neighborhood had been constructed during the first two decades of the twentieth century, but a majority were apartment buildings or two-family homes. Unlike the defended neighborhoods, Twelfth Street had few homeowners. Only 11 percent of the dwellings in the Twelfth Street area were owner-occupied.[26]

As the first black families moved into the area in 1947 and 1948, city officials and religious leaders in the area expected an onslaught of interracial violence. During the summer of 1947, the first three black residents of the area suffered several window breakings and small fires. But the perpetrators of each incident turned out to be two fourteen-year-old boys and one sixteen-year-old, caught by police during a botched arson attempt. The boys, who had experimented with crude explosives in their garage, directed their arson against their black neighbors, but unlike vandals in other parts of the city, they had no apparent attachment to an improvement association.[27]

Apart from these isolated incidents, however, blacks moved peacefully into the Twelfth Street area. City officials were unaware of any "organized movement in the neighborhood to oppose Negro occupancy."[28] The responses of white area residents questioned by the police investigating the arson cases revealed a profound antipathy to black newcomers to their community, but also resignation to the inevitability of racial transition. Most white residents announced plans to move rather than to stay and fight. Mrs. W. J. Snyderman, for example, stated that "she will have to move because of expected colored occupancy." Three other residents interviewed had recently sold their homes to blacks or planned to move.[29]

Twelfth Street area residents interviewed in a 1947 survey of the neighborhood expressed feelings of sadness, anger, and resignation over the movement of blacks into the area. Twelfth Streeters shared the same racial prejudices as whites in other parts of the city. One woman who lived in the area for thirty-two years stated: "It makes me sick, I would have stayed here the rest of my days, except there is colored next door." Another opined: "Colored and white can't mix . . . they think its theirs and begin shoving around." But despite their antipathy to black newcomers, Twelfth Street residents did not violently resist racial change. Most residents stated that they planned to move; as one resident grumbled: "what can we do [with] 6 or 7 families coming everyday[?]" Even those with few resources seemed ready to move out as soon as possible: "We'll move out and let them have it . . . when we can."[30]

That the Twelfth Street area was predominantly Jewish minimized overt racial tension there. The pattern of little resistance to black movement had ample precedent in Detroit's older Jewish neighborhoods. The Hastings Street area on the East Side, a Jewish enclave before World War I, became a largely black area during the 1920s, as Jewish residents fled to the Twelfth Street area. In other parts of the country, Jewish center-city areas also generally turned over rapidly when black families moved in. Blacks moving to Harlem, Chicago's Lawndale area, Boston's Roxbury and Mattapan, and parts of Cleveland's East Side, all former Jewish settlements, faced little resistance.[31] Sociologists examining the Twelfth Street area in the mid-1940s found that Jewish residents were least likely to organize against black newcomers; instead, racial tensions "reach their most overt and hostile form in those areas where the proportion of non-Jewish to Jewish residents is the greatest."[32]

Black-Jewish relations in Detroit had been marked by moments of tension, to be sure. Some members of the Jewish community encouraged Twelfth Street Jews to hold their ground; others circulated petitions and called for racially restrictive covenants. But such activity was marginal. Detroit's Jews had little use for covenants; they were concerned that techniques to bar blacks from white neighborhoods could be used with equal effectiveness against themselves. But there were three more important reasons for the rapid turnover and the lack of interracial violence in the Twelfth Street area. Most importantly, Jews had a lower rate of homeownership than Catholics and Protestants in the city, making it easier for them to pick up and flee. They did not have the financial or personal stake in their own homes that motivated homeowners to defend their neighborhoods against black newcomers in other parts of the city.[33] Secondly, Jewish institutions were more mobile than Catholic parishes, which were bound geographically; an institutional move did not result in residents' deracination from their community. In the 1920s, several important Jewish institutions had fled the Hastings Street area on Detroit's East Side, and beginning in the late 1940s, they moved out with equal speed from the Twelfth Street area.[34] Third, Jewish leaders were generally sympathetic to the civil rights of blacks, and many spoke of a common history of oppression shared by both groups. Whereas Catholic priests and Protestant ministers often preached resistance, Jewish leaders advocated racial accommodation. The Jewish Community Council of Detroit warned of the pernicious consequences of discrimination: "We recognize that prejudice exercised against any one group is harmful to all groups and to the entire community." Even if residents of Twelfth Street did not always share the racial progressivism of their leaders, they avoided out-and-out resistance and fled rather than fought.[35]

The consequences of flight were clear in the racial composition of the Twelfth Street area. Whereas virtually no blacks lived there in 1940 (the area was 98.7 percent white), the area was over one-third (37.2 percent) nonwhite in 1950. By 1960, the proportion of blacks to whites had nearly reversed: only 3.8 percent of the area's residents were white. Given that the first blacks did not move to the area until 1947 and 1948, the area underwent a complete racial transition in a little more than a decade. Fleeing Twelfth Street whites left a vacuum that was quickly filled by blacks.[36]

Neighborhoods with predominantly middle- and upper-class white populations also offered little violent resistance to black pioneers. One such section of the city was the near Northwest Side. Its streets were lined with solidly built, often substantial, twentieth-century houses. But rates of homeownership were lower in this area than in the city as a whole, and many well-appointed, 1920s-era apartment buildings dotted the area. More near Northwest Side residents worked in white-collar jobs than in the defended neighborhoods, and more women worked outside the home. Houses in the area were considerably more expensive than in other areas of the city: indeed, the area's homes cost an average of $6,386 in 1940, nearly $2,000 more than the citywide average.[37]

Black newcomers faced little violence, little taunting, and little opposition from whites when they moved into near Northwest Side neighborhoods.

Only about a dozen racial incidents accompanied black movement into this sizable section of Detroit. Most of the incidents were minor, and they followed no discernible pattern. Racial transition in this area was rapid. In 1950, only 2.5 percent of the area's population of over 145,000 was black; in 1960, 73.5 percent of the area's population of almost 140,000 was black. Because white residents were less attached to their neighborhood and many had the means to move when their blocks were threatened by black "invasion," few stayed and fought.

Residents of the undefended neighborhoods were attracted to Detroit's booming suburbs. Suburban life offered many advantages to fleeing whites. They could move into new ranch, split-level, and Colonial-style homes, with standard amenities like two-car garages, aluminum siding, spacious kitchens, and large lawns. But the attractions of suburbia were not merely architectural. Suburban communities were themselves defended communities, whose invisible walls against "invasions" were far more difficult to breach than the constantly shifting, insecure lines that divided the city. Suburban developers touted the "exclusive" nature of their communities and contrasted them with the undesirable city. "Plan now to move out of the smoke-zone into the ozone in beautiful Beverly Hills," read a brochure for one suburban development. Real estate agents and developers targeted their markets carefully, quickly giving suburbs reputations based on the class and ethnicity of their residents. Downriver Taylor, Lincoln Park, Ecorse and northeastern Warren, Roseville, and Madison Heights became blue-collar suburbs with small FHA- and VA-subsidized houses that were new versions of the working-class bungalows of the center city. Southfield and Oak Park became magnets for Jews, who followed their institutions out of the city. Grosse Pointe, Birmingham, Franklin, and Bloomfield Hills remained the metropolitan area's most prestigious addresses, attracting automobile company executives, lawyers, developers, and other corporate elites. Livonia, Dearborn Heights, and Royal Oak were solidly middle-class areas, bedroom communities for middle-level managers, salesmen, and clerks. Like their urban counterparts, suburban developers often used restrictive covenants and, after *Shelley v. Kraemer*, resorted to barely legal subterfuges to preserve neighborhood homogeneity.[38]

Suburban exclusiveness and homogeneity were not just the sum of individual choices about housing. Without the support of governments, both federal and local, suburbs would not have been able to maintain their character. Most important were the actuarial policies of the Federal Housing Administration and Home Owners' Loan Corporation, which systematically excluded African Americans. Solidifying the invisible walls that separated city and suburb (and suburbs from one another) were the hard-and-fast lines of municipal boundaries. Each suburb had its own school district, recreation programs, libraries, and public services, paid for by local taxes. Suburban governments guarded their autonomy jealously, regularly refusing to join in metropolitan government schemes. Outlying towns also strictly enforced zoning, prohibiting the division of single-family houses into apartments, strictly limiting multiple-family housing, and stipulating lot size. Residents of suburbs lived in communities whose boundaries were firmly established and governmentally protected, unlike their urban counterparts who had to define and defend their own fragile borders.[39]

Territoriality

For those white Detroiters unwilling or unable to flee, black movement into their neighborhoods was the moral equivalent of war. As the racial demography of Detroit changed, neighborhood groups demarcated racial boundaries with great precision, and, abetted by federal agencies and private real estate agents, divided cities into strictly enforced racial territories. In the postwar years, white urban dwellers fiercely defended their turf. They referred to the black migration in military terms: they spoke of "invasions" and "penetration," and plotted strategies of "resistance." White neighborhoods became "battlegrounds" where residents struggled to preserve segregated housing. Homeowners' associations helped whites to "defend" their homes and "protect" their property.[40]

In defended neighborhoods, white organizations served as gatekeepers by diplomacy and by force. Their goal was nothing short of the containment of Detroit's black population, a domestic Cold War to keep the forces of social disorder, represented by blacks, at bay.[41] White community organizations served the double function of social club and neighborhood militia. On the Lower West Side, homeowners formed the "Property Owners Association" in 1945 to combat the expansion of the black West Side into their neighborhood with "every means at our command."[42] "United Communities are Impregnable," noted founders of the National Association of Community Councils, a grandiosely named "protective, vigilant, American organization" on the West Side.[43]

Most neighborhood improvement associations that battled black newcomers assumed a paramilitary model of organization. The Courville District Association divided the neighborhood into "danger spots," that were "in the process of disintegration by an influx of colored families in the past year." Each section had "captains" and "supervisors" who would lead residents to "retard and diminish this influx, and prevent our white families from exodus."[44] Residents of the De Witt–Clinton area adapted the civil defense system from World War II to their new racial battleground. They formed as "Unit Number 2" of the Greater Detroit Neighbors Association (later renamed the De Witt–Clinton Civic Association) in 1949, a full seven years before the first black family attempted to move into the area. "Block wardens" were responsible for the defense of every street in the area. Residents of other Wyoming Corridor neighborhoods invited De Witt–Clinton officials to help them organize in 1955, 1956, and 1957. They formed a tightly knit network of neighborhood groups that covered every subdivision along the West Side's racial frontier and that shared leadership and passed on information about black movements in the area.[45]

One of the most important roles of improvement associations was to mark the city's racial borders. Frequently, groups used signs to make visible the invisible boundaries of race. In November 1945, for example, white residents of a neighborhood that was beginning to attract blacks to its low-rent apartments posted a sign on a building: "Negroes moving here will be burned, Signed Neighbors."[46] Residents of a West Side street posted "Whites Only" and "KKK" on a house sold to a black family.[47] Blacks seeking homes on American Street in Saint Luke's parish could not miss two large signs at each end of the block that boldly proclaimed "ALL WHITE."[48] Protesters in front of a new house built for an African American in the "white section" of the Seven Mile–Fenelon area carried signs reading, "If you're black, you'd better go back to Africa where you belong."[49] Signs often greeted the first black families who crossed invisible racial lines, warning them of their proper place in the city. The first black family to cross into the Northeast Side neighborhood surrounding Saint Bartholomew's parish in 1963, for example, was greeted with a sign that read "Get back on the other side of 7 Mile."[50] And countless variations on the theme "No Niggers Wanted" (posted on a West Side house in 1957) appeared throughout the city. Signs sometimes conveyed a more subtle message. Some whites in neighborhoods threatened by racial change attempted to stake their turf and deter "blockbusting" real estate agents by posting signs declaring "This House is Not for Sale."[51]

Often protesters chose boundaries as the site of demonstrations. In the Seven Mile–Fenelon area, in November 1948, two men burned an effigy at the corner of Nevada and Conley, only a block from the Sojourner Truth site, on the edge of their threatened white neighborhood. Their ominously simple symbolic act made clear to blacks the risks of crossing racial barriers. When private developers announced plans to construct homes in a formerly all-white section of the area to be sold "on a non-restricted basis," Seven Mile–Fenelon residents tore down signs advertising the new homes and vandalized the houses that breached the racial divide.[52] In the Courville area, residents of Nevada and Marx Streets joined a "car parade," for the purpose of "keeping undesirables out." Led by a sound truck, the paraders ritualistically marked the line that they did not want breached.[53]

In the crucible of racial change, white protesters targeted and stigmatized outsiders whom they believed threatened their communities. The consummate outsiders were blockbusting real estate agents, who violated community boundaries and acted as the catalyst of racial "invasions." In 1948, a coalition of homeowners' organizations published a list of brokers who sold homes to blacks and encouraged members to "Get busy on the phone." Even though the pamphlet asked members to "Never threaten or argue," whites in defended neighborhoods regularly called and harassed offending brokers. Especially galling to white groups was the prominence of blacks and Jews in real estate firms conducting business in changing neighborhoods. Both suffered relentless abuse from members of community groups. When Nathan Slobin, a Jewish real estate agent working in the Lower West Side, sold a home on Poplar Street to a black family, unnamed women barraged him with over a hundred phone calls, many with "obscene and menacing language." Area residents carrying anti-Semitic signs picketed his office and his home. Members of the Seven Mile-Fenelon Association threatened Charles Taylor, a black real estate broker who worked with contractors in the area, and warned him that any new homes for blacks constructed north of Stockton Street "will be burned down as fast as you can build them."[54] In the Courville area, white residents made death threats to a real estate agent who sold a house to a black family. On Woodingham, a crowd catcalled James Morris, a black real estate agent showing a house to a black family. In another incident on Woodingham, the police demonstrated their solidarity with protesting whites when they arrested Morris, after he had requested police intervention to quell the hostile mob that had gathered. On nearby Tuller and Cherrylawn Streets, gangs of youths harassed black real estate agents and their clients.[55]

Equally galling to residents of defended communities were white neighbors who listed their homes with known blockbusting real estate agents. Protesters reserved special venom for white "race traitors" who sold their homes to African Americans. Frequently, threats were ominous. Whites hid behind the cloak of anonymity "to intimidate and terrify white people who might sell to Negroes." In one case, Mrs. Florence Gifford, a Lower West Side white woman who offered her house with a black real estate agent, received a hundred phone calls over a ten-day period in early 1948. All the calls came from women, but only three were willing to identify themselves, all members of the neighborhood improvement association. Callers threatened property damage and offered more vague warnings like "It will be too bad if you sell to Negroes." Protesters also followed blockbusting white sellers to their new neighborhoods and tried to poison their relations with their new neighbors. Lower West Side picketers tracked Edward Brock to his new house on Detroit's far West Side, and circulated copies of his business card to his new neighbors along with a handbill that read: "WATCH ED BROCK . . . IS ATTEMPTING TO PUT *COLORED* IN OUR *WHITE* NEIGHBORHOOD 3420 HARRISON. HE WOULD DO THE SAME TO YOU!!" In 1956, white residents of Ruritan Park followed Mr. and Mrs. Peter Hays to their new suburban Livonia home after they sold their Detroit house to a family suspected to be black. They warned the Hays' Livonia neighbors that the couple was "just the type who would sell a home to Negroes."[56]

Occasionally, community groups sought reprisals in the workplace. In 1955, the president of one neighborhood association gleefully reported that his group "had taken care of the white seller on his job." The owner of the chain store where the seller worked "asked us not to boycott [his] business because of this man." In 1957, protesters on Cherrylawn Street tried a similar tactic, threatening officials at Federals Department Store with a boycott if they did not fire Stella Nowak, a white woman who had sold her house to an African American family. Such threats deterred many whites from being the first on a block to sell to blacks.[57]

Threats were most effective when combined with diplomacy. In well-organized neighborhoods, delegations from improvement associations approached parties involved in the sale of a house to offer them alternatives. Often, community groups offered to purchase the house, usually for a sum greater than the asking price. If they lacked the financial resources, delegations often simply approached buyers and sellers and warned them of the dire consequences of breaching the residential color line. By approaching the offending seller or customer, whites presented a united community front, making clear their determination to preserve the neighborhood's racial homogeneity.[58]

Family Affairs: Containing the "Negro Invasion"

When diplomacy and threats failed, neighborhood defenders escalated confrontations, protesting, picketing, and attacking those who tried to cross racial boundaries. Protesters reserved their strongest opprobrium for African Americans who had the temerity to "invade" their neighborhoods. In the anxious days preceding and following a black "invasion," community groups held "emergency meetings," to plot their strategies. Most common were large demonstrations in the streets in front of blacks' newly purchased homes and surreptitious attacks on property. The nature of the white resistance to the black movement deserves closer examination. The attacks on property were not irrational outbursts of an angry mob. They were political acts, carefully calculated to intimidate individual black families, but even more importantly they were hortatory acts, intended to announce racial boundaries and serve as a warning to blacks of the high costs of breaching Detroit's racial frontiers.

The battles in defended neighborhoods were thoroughly communal affairs, like the siege of the Wilsons' Riopelle Street home. They did not involve a mere violent fringe of the community. Protests attracted a wide cross-section of neighbors. Young parents, teenagers, pre-adolescent boys and girls, and elderly people all rallied to the defense of their neighborhoods. Embattled whites deployed their entire families, in roles appropriate to their age and gender, to defend their turf when a black family bought a house or moved in. The motivation and tactics of protesters drew from and reinforced the prevailing ideologies of race, family, and gender in the postwar era.

Women played a crucial role in threatening those who transgressed racial boundaries. Standing on a picket line or distributing leaflets, or speaking up at community meetings, working-class women formed the vanguard of a neighborhood's defense. From the safety of their kitchens and bedrooms, they launched anonymous threats at offending real estate agents, sellers, and new black neighbors. When a black molder purchased a three-family frame house on the Lower West Side, "countless" women callers harassed the white former owner, while others warned the real estate agent who handled the sale that "there would be a repetition of the June 1943 race riots." Angry women in the Courville area also used the telephone to harass Easby Wilson and his family, until the Wilsons got an unlisted phone number.[59]

As the first line of family defense, women policed the boundaries of race and sex. The overlapping concerns of neighborhood integrity, racial purity, and domestic tranquillity gave particular urgency to protests led by women. When Edward Brock, the white owner of two houses on the Lower West Side, sold them to black families in 1948, women led the resistance. Groups of ten to twenty-five women, many pushing strollers, gathered every day for a week, carrying hand-painted signs that read: "My home is my castle, I will die defending it"; "The Lord separated the races, why should Constable Brock mix them"; "We don't want to mix"; and "Ed Brock sold to colored in white neighborhood." Protests composed of women and their preschool children attracted a lot of attention. Passersby were taken aback by picket lines of white mothers and babies, an uncommon sight at a time when most demonstrations in Detroit were labor-oriented and male-led. Replete with the symbols of motherhood and family, these protests often touched a deep, sympathetic nerve among onlookers, many of whom saw black movement into a neighborhood as a threat to virtuous womanhood, innocent childhood, and the sanctity of the home.[60]

The role that Detroit women played in neighborhood improvement associations and in communal protest grew directly out of the postwar domestic ideology. They sought a secure home and healthy and safe neighborhood life for the benefit of their children. Even as norms about women working outside the home were changing, and a growing number of mothers supplemented the family income, several major institutions attempted to circumscribe women's role as homemaker and caregiver. One was the Catholic Church, whose theology of maternal sacrifice played an important role in shaping the beliefs and practices of men and women in the heavily Catholic city. In addition, trade union rhetoric and policies reinforced women's domestic role. In Detroit, auto workers and their families had long been exposed to the gendered promise of a "family wage" offered by the United Automobile Workers and the Congress of Industrial Organizations. Under union-negotiated contracts, men would earn sufficient pay to support their families. Women could thus avoid paid labor and direct their energies toward child rearing and homemaking. Neighborhood association newsletters promoted the ideology of domesticity. *Action!*, the belligerent newsletter of the Courville Association, included "recipes of interest to the ladies," and *The Civic Voice*, the organ of a Wyoming Corridor association, included advice on "how to help the busy hostess become the successful hostess," along with an article about the innate racial inferiority of blacks. The role of motherhood was inseparable from the postwar domestic ideology, which elevated the nuclear family to an almost sacrosanct status and associated the health and survival of the family with a defensive attitude toward extramural threats.[61]

Women, far more than men, depended on the neighborhood networks for both economic and emotional subsistence. In the defended neighborhoods, where large numbers of women left the work force to raise their baby-boom families, the affective ties of neighborhood grew even stronger. Even relatively transient women, newcomers to urban neighborhoods, quickly became part of female networks of support, borrowing and lending food and kitchen supplies and relying on each other for assistance with child care and babysitting. Moreover, the sidewalks of city neighborhoods became gathering places where women forged friendships and found emotional support. The neighborhood provided an outlet, a place to escape the monotonous routine of housekeeping and to relieve the loneliness and isolation of urban life.[62]

Concerns about family, domesticity, and community all undergirded white women's role in neighborhood resistance in the postwar city. A 1951 survey of Detroit residents showed that women, to a far greater degree than men, ranked housing and race relations as the city's top two problems. The survey found that when asked to name "undesirable" groups, women were also twice as likely as men to mention blacks. These sentiments were undoubtedly even stronger in defended neighborhoods where more women remained at home than in undefended neighborhoods (see Table 9.1). Women in these areas had even more at stake than men in the preservation of a neighborhood. They viewed neighborhood transition as a profound threat to the sense of community that they had constructed. And they feared the introduction of outsiders—in the case of Detroit, blacks—as a threat to the domestic unit. If, as they had heard, blacks brought with them family disruption, profligate lifestyles, and crime, then neighborhood integration seriously jeopardized the health and safety of children. Thus the National Association of Community Councils, a West Side neighborhood group, offered a "full share of feminine program activities" that would "afford each woman member opportunities to participate in molding the character of the community and enable them to build stronger defenses against child delinquency."[63]

Gender offered a strategic advantage to protesters as well. Police were usually reluctant to arrest women and their children, even when their protests broke the law. They feared that hauling off mothers and their children would exacerbate already tense situations. When a crowd of one to two hundred protesters, most of them women and children, gathered on Maine Street near the Courville area in 1947, the police inspector called to the scene let them obstruct the street because he feared that a mass arrest "would have created a much worse incident." The woman caught vandalizing Easby Wilson's house in 1955 was released by the police on a technicality. Few women, however, participated in acts of vandalism. It was men who took resistance a step further, from protest to violence.[64]

The gender dynamics of protest changed at night, when most demonstrations took place, with crowds far larger and more menacing than the banner-wielding mothers who filled the streets during the day. Despite its seeming anarchy, crowd activity under the cover of darkness was no less organized than daytime pickets. Demonstrations followed a predictable pattern. Early in the evening, community members would drive slowly in the vicinity of a newly purchased black home, beckoning neighbors to join the protest. Crowds gathered after the dinner hour, drawing men who had just returned home from work, and school-age children, especially teenagers, who played in the streets in the evening. Often outdoor protests followed emergency improvement association meetings. Mob activity ranged from milling about in front of targeted houses, to shouting racial epithets, to throwing stones and bricks. The intensity of violence in the early stages depended on the presence of the police. Frequently, officers were slow to respond to housing incidents, and residents had ample time to hurl objects at the offending houses. After police arrived they often passively watched crowds gather, without dispersing them for parading without a permit, disorderly conduct, or riot. When the police broke up crowds for obstructing traffic or for crowding the sidewalk, smaller groups usually reconstituted themselves on neighbors' lawns and porches, safe havens from the police who did not venture onto private property to control crowds. From the sanctuary of nearby yards, enraged neighbors continued to taunt their new black neighbors, to shout their disapproval at the police, and to throw cans, stones, or bottles toward the targeted house.

Neighbors of all ages, male and female alike, joined the nighttime demonstrations, but men dominated these events. Their involvement was an extension of their role as protectors of home and property. Whereas women held signs and issued anonymous threats, men put their bodies on the line in defense of their families. In the context of fears of black sexuality, neighborhood defense became more than a struggle for turf. It was a battle for the preservation of white womanhood and innocent childhood. Men had a duty, as the Courville District Improvement Association admonished, to "pitch for your civic rights and the protection of your women." That a disproportionate number of men in defended neighborhoods were craftsmen probably added an additional urgency to their protests. It is impossible to determine fully the role that artisans played in neighborhood protests. But the tightly knit masculine world of the skilled trades flowed so naturally from the close networks of neighborhood and parish that it is likely that craftsmen found the threat of neighborhood change especially acute. Tradesmen recruited fellow workers from their relatives, neighbors, and fellow churchgoers, a process that reinforced communal ties at work and at home. Just as a black hire would threaten the exclusive identity that bound together craftsmen on the shopfloor, so too would black neighbors challenge the security of the craftsmen's homes and neighborhoods.[65]

Late in the evening and in the dark hours of the morning, violence accelerated. After the crowds and police had dispersed, neighborhood defenders attacked their unwanted neighbors' property, throwing garbage on the lawns, shattering windows with bottles, bricks, stones, and other convenient projectiles, ranging from pumpkins to tree stumps. Window breaking was by far the most common sort of vandalism: it required relatively little effort and it could be done from a safe distance providing vandals with time to flee before police could catch them. Demonstrators also marred properties with paint, tore down fences, pulled off cornices, trampled gardens, poured salt and gasoline on lawns, slashed car tires, broke car windshields, and in one case, used a truck and cables to tear down a porch.[66] Arson, also carried out under the cover of darkness, was common too, because it was both surreptitious and dramatic. Enraged neighbors set the offending houses afire (usually rear porches or garages which offered easy, undetectable access). Arsonists severely damaged three homes on the Lower West Side. Seven Mile–Fenelon residents threatened black home builders with a "burning party," destroyed three newly built houses for black occupancy, and used the threat of arson to persuade developers to restrict new home sales to whites. Other arsonists burned down several garages in Courville and torched three houses in the Wyoming Corridor, one with a firebomb. They also built bonfires, lit trash cans on fire, and burned crosses, a practice that became increasingly common in the 1960s.[67]

In virtually every case, protesters directed their violence against property. In postwar Detroit, housing was the most visible symbol of status, and, for the vast majority of homeowners, it was their most substantial investment. Houses were symbolic extensions of the self, of the family. To break windows, mar houses with paint, destroy woodwork, or burn down buildings was a direct challenge to a family's privacy and security, the very essence of homeownership. Interestingly, protesters seldom did more than attack property. Despite their taunts and threats, in only a few cases did white adults physically attack their black neighbors during housing protests. Interracial physical assaults almost always involved teenagers and youths.[68]

Juveniles played an essential role in the defense of their neighborhoods against black encroachment. Their actions mirrored the animosities of adults. In the Courville area, for example, gangs of teenage boys told investigators that they hung out on street corners "to protect people against Negroes," actions they justified on the basis of "their parents' fear and resentment that Negroes were buying houses in the area." Across town in the De Witt–Clinton area, teens defended their own symbolic turf, the Clinton School, which many of them had attended. In the schoolyard, they staged attacks on black schoolchildren after school hours and engaged in pitched battles with groups of black teens at night.[69]

Often youths served as community sentinels, warning neighbors of black move-ins and gathering together angry crowds. Carloads of teenagers drove through the neighborhood around Maine Street in 1947, shouting "There is going to be a riot tonight at nine o'clock." Youths blowing whistles as they rode up and down Riopelle Street summoned the crowd that protested in front of Easby Wilson's house.[70] Fearless teenagers often threatened black homeowners and frequently vandalized black homes. At 3414 Harrison Street, on the Lower West Side, a group of white teens, including one who lived across the street, stoned a house occupied by blacks. In the DeWitt–Clinton area in the early 1960s, teens led mobs of stone throwers. And on Greenlawn Street in the Wyoming Corridor, teens threw firecrackers at a black woman and hurled mud and stones at her newly purchased house.[71] Teens also brought their indefatigable spirit to demonstrations, rousing crowds with songs and chants. When Leroy Dudley and his fiancée Bessie Young purchased a house on Birwood Street on Detroit's West Side, a group of teenagers rallied adult protesters with two hours of spirited chanting.[72] Younger children also joined protests. On the West Side, several pre-adolescents dragged a "stuffed dummy" behind their bikes to harass their new black neighbors. In Ruritan Park, "little Sunday School, parochial school girls" jeered when a black family moved onto their all-white block. And on Ohio Street, several young children, goaded on by their mother, dumped rotting garbage on the porch of their new next-door black neighbors.[73]

All too often, the acts of teen vandals and the visibility of teens in angry crowds were dismissed by the authorities as the acts of unruly, undisciplined youth. The boys who threw signs reading "Beat It Nigger" onto the porch of a black family that moved into a house on Tuller Street, or who broke windows on Greenlawn Street, might be viewed as delinquents alienated from the community. And occasionally defensive white residents blamed neighborhood protests on outside agitators or "hoodlums." What was most evident about teen participation in housing protests was not, however, its deviance. Instead, it was closely linked to adult activities. Acts of violence committed by youths almost always followed emergency community meetings or street demonstrations. And adults often harbored youthful protestors from the authorities. When police dispersed large crowds of teenagers protesting on Tuller Street, several adult residents let the chanting and stone-throwing youths gather on their lawns across the street from a home sold to a black family. In many neighborhoods, parents and neighbors protected their children with a code of silence. When police discovered that five boys had hung an effigy on the house of the first black family that moved across Seven Mile Road on the Northeast Side, their parents refused to identify the clothes the boys had used.[74] Such tolerance is especially striking given pervasive fears about juvenile delinquency in the postwar years. Parents clearly did not view the violent acts of youth committed during battles over housing as deviant, lawless behavior. Instead, they tolerated it, indeed sanctioned it. Vandalism that occurred in a climate of intense community organization was an approved expression of communal sentiment.[75]

The effect of systematic attacks and harassment on black pioneers cannot be fully measured. The families whose anonymity and privacy were challenged by white racial violence all too quickly vanished from the historical record. Many, like Easby Wilson and Henry Love, moved out of defended neighborhoods because of concern for their families' safety. Others remained in their houses despite the harassment, and waited for the violence to abate. But scattered material not lost to the historical record makes clear that some black pioneers resisted white neighborhood defenders, often through acts of what historian Robin D. G. Kelley calls "infrapolitics." Jennie Overton, one of the first black residents on Harrison Street on the Lower West Side, refused white neighbors' entreaties to buy back her house. Overton recalled how she and her husband confronted window breakers from their front porch, and then, emboldened by the presence of a police escort, took every occasion to come and go conspicuously from their new house, flaunting their hard-won freedom. Jennie Overton turned the indignity of white harassment into a badge of honor, and by demonstrating her fearlessness, reminded her white neighbors of her class and her pride.[76] Other black pioneers sometimes mocked white homeowners' organizations. An African American who moved into the Courville area demanded that the civic association pay him four thousand dollars more than his house was worth, a demand he knew they could not meet. The Reverend David Mitcham, a new black resident of Roselawn Street in Ruritan Park, craftily rebuffed homeowners' association attempts to force him to sell his house, "playing cat and mouse with us," as a neighborhood association representative bitterly reported. Mitcham also scorned the fear-mongering real estate agents who went door to door in the neighborhood.[77] On occasion, black pioneers resisted more aggressively. A family that moved into the embattled States-Lawn area in the early 1960s brandished a gun to fend off angry white protesters and protected their yard with a large, mean dog.[78]

Black resisters were the exception rather than the norm. White-initiated violence or the threat of it was a powerful deterrent to black pioneers. The effect of white resistance was to create a sieve through which a relatively small number of black Detroiters passed. The Seven Mile–Fenelon Association's activity did not fully preserve the racial status quo in the area, but it severely limited the residential options open to black home buyers, and slowed black residential movement. 26 percent of the population in the area was black in 1940, and only 35 percent was black in 1950. Considering that 250 black families had moved into the Sojourner Truth project, black movement to other parts of the neighborhood was at best incremental. 1960 census data make more clear the dynamics of racial transition in the area. Blacks were confined to the section of the neighborhood sandwiched between Conant Gardens and Sojourner Truth and to certain blocks immediately to the east.[79] Whites maintained the invisible boundary of race along Dequindre Avenue and slowed black movement further west. In 1960, the section of Courville west of Dequindre was only 2.7 percent black.[80] The De Witt–Clinton area also preserved its racial homogeneity for nearly fifteen years. Although the neighborhoods to the east steadily gained black population, from 1949, when they formed an association, to 1963, not a single black family successfully moved into the neighborhood.[81] The one exception to the norm was the Lower West Side. The number of blacks living in the area increased between 1940 and 1950, but relatively slowly. Of the entire area, only 11.2 percent of the population was black in 1950; and over one-third of the black population was concentrated in the one census tract closest to the Tireman–Grand Boulevard area. By 1960, however, all but one of the tracts in the former turf covered by the Property Owners Association had a black population of at least 30 percent, but the western part of the district attracted more blacks and fewer whites.[82]

By preoccupying blacks in block-by-block skirmishes, and hastily retreating when blacks finally "broke a block," residents of defended neighborhoods offered a small safety valve to residents of the overcrowded inner city. The rearguard actions of the defended neighborhoods essentially preserved—indeed strengthened—the principle of racial segregation in housing. They protected the homogeneity of all-white neighborhoods beyond the contested blocks. Over the long run, most of the defended neighborhoods became majority black communities. Whites, as one observer noted, "hold 'til the dam bursts, then run like hell." Those whites who remained were, with a few exceptions, older people who could not afford to move.[83]

Detroit was not alone in its pattern of racial violence. Urban whites responded to the influx of millions of black migrants to their cities in the 1940s, 1950s, and 1960s by redefining urban geography and urban politics in starkly racial terms. In Chicago and Cicero, Illinois, working-class whites rioted in the 1940s and 1950s to oppose the construction of public housing in their neighborhoods. White Chicagoans fashioned a brand of Democratic party politics, especially under mayors Martin Kennelly and Richard Daley, that had a sharp racial edge. In Newark, New Jersey, in the 1950s, blue-collar Italian and Polish Americans harassed African American newcomers to their neighborhoods. And in the postwar period, white Philadelphians and Cincinnatians attacked blacks who moved into previously all-white enclaves, and resisted efforts to integrate the housing market.[84] Countless whites retreated to suburbs or neighborhoods on the periphery of cities where they prevented black movement into their communities with federally sanctioned redlining practices, real estate steering, and restrictive zoning laws.[85]

Racial violence had far-reaching effects in the city. It hardened definitions of white and black identities, objectifying them by plotting them on the map of the city. The combination of neighborhood violence, real estate practices, covenants, and the operations of the housing market sharply circumscribed the housing opportunities available to Detroit's African American population. Persistent housing segregation stigmatized blacks, reinforced unequal race relations, and perpetuated racial divisions.

A visitor walking or driving through Detroit in the 1960s—like his or her counterpart in the 1940s—would have passed through two Detroits, one black and one white. Writing in 1963, sociologists Albert J. Mayer and Thomas Hoult noted that blacks in Detroit "live in essentially the same places that their predecessors lived during the 1930s—the only difference is that due to increasing numbers, they occupy more space centered around their traditional quarters."[86] Segregation in housing constrained black housing choices enormously. Whole sections of the city and the vast majority of the suburbs were entirely off limits to blacks. Racial discrimination and the housing market confined blacks to some of Detroit's oldest and worst housing stock, mainly that of the center-city area, and several enclaves on the periphery of the city.[87] Through sustained violence, Detroit whites engaged in battle over turf, a battle that had economic and social as well as political and ideological consequences.

But more than that, it added to Detroit blacks' already deep distrust of whites and white institutions. Speaking to an open housing conference in 1963, the Reverend Charles W. Butler, a prominent African American minister and civil rights advocate, reminded his audience of the anger that seethed among Detroit's blacks. "The desire and ability to move without the right to move," he argued, "is refined slavery." Butler summed up his remarks with a warning that racial segregation "spawned and cultivated the spirit of rebellion. . . . This rebellion is evident in many forms, from nonviolent resistance to vandalism. This rebellion is proof positive that the Negro has grown weary of being the eternal afterthought of America." Racial violence left blacks in neighborhoods increasingly bereft of capital, distant from workplaces, and marginalized politically. In a city deeply divided by racial violence, it was only a matter of time before blacks retaliated. The results of housing segregation, in combination with persistent workplace discrimination and deindustrialization, were explosive.[88]

Conclusion _____

Crisis: Detroit and the Fate of Postindustrial America

We Shall Rise Again from the Ashes
We Hope for Better Things
—Mottos on the official seal of the City of Detroit
(1826)

By the time of the civil disturbance in 1967, the
seeds of destruction were already sown.
—Roger Robinson, union activist (1994)

IN LATE JULY 1967, one of the most brutal riots in American history swept through Detroit. On July 23, 1967, in the middle of a summer heat wave, the police decided to bust a "blind pig," an illegal after-hours saloon on Twelfth Street in the center of one of Detroit's largest black neighborhoods. Arrests for illegal drinking were common in Detroit, but usually the police dispersed the crowd and arrested a handful of owners and patrons, taking the names of the remainder. On the steamy July night, they decided to arrest all eighty-five people present and detained them—hot, drunk, and angry—outside the saloon until reinforcements could arrive.[1]

By four in the morning, an hour after the bust, nearly two hundred people, attracted by the commotion behind the blind pig, had gathered to watch the proceedings. As the arrestees shouted allegations of police brutality, tempers rose. The crowd began to jeer and to throw bottles, beer cans, and rocks at the police. William Scott II, a son of one of the bar's owners, threw a bottle at a police officer and shouted "Get your god damn sticks and bottles and start hurtin' baby." By 8:00 A.M., a crowd of over three thousand had gathered on Twelfth Street. The riot raged out of control until it was suppressed by a combined force of nearly seventeen thousand law enforcement officers, National Guardsmen, and federal troops. After five days of violence, forty-three people were dead, thirty of them killed by law enforcement personnel. Altogether 7,231 men and women were arrested on riot-related charges. The property damage, still visible in vacant lots and abandoned buildings in Detroit, was extensive. Rioters looted and burned 2,509 buildings. $36 million in insured property was lost and undoubtedly millions more were lost by those without insurance, not to mention wages, income, and government costs.

10.1. Hundreds of stores on Twelfth Street were looted and burned during Detroit's 1967 racial uprising. The rioters, largely young black men, bore a disproportionate share of the burden of economic restructuring in postwar Detroit.

Detroit was twice torn by cataclysmic violence in a period of less than twenty-five years. The extent of social and economic changes in the postwar period, however, made the context of Detroit's long hot summer of 1967 profoundly different from the violent summer of 1943. The vast majority of participants in the 1967 Detroit uprising were black (with the exception of armed officials who were overwhelmingly white); 1943 had involved black and white participants in roughly equal proportions. The changed racial demography of 1967 was hardly surprising, for over a third of Detroit residents were black in 1967, and few whites lived anywhere near the riot's epicenters on Linwood and Twelfth Street on the West Side and on Mack and Kercheval on the East Side. The riot of 1943 came at a time of increasing black and white competition for jobs and housing; by 1967, discrimination and deindustrialization had ensured that blacks had lost the competition. White resistance and white flight left a bitter legacy that galvanized black protest in the 1960s. Detroit's attempts to take advantage of the largesse of the Great Society offered too little, too late for Detroit's poor, but raised expectations nonetheless. Growing resentment, fueled by increasing militancy in the black community, especially among youth, who had suffered the brunt of economic displacement, fueled the fires of 1967.

For those who cared to listen, there were rumblings of discontent in the late 1950s and the early 1960s. The problems of limited housing, racial animosity, and reduced economic opportunity for a segment of the black population in Detroit had led to embitterment. When sociologist John Leggett and his colleagues interviewed black Detroiters in 1957 and 1958, they found that many were seething with anger about their living and working conditions. When Leggett asked unemployed blacks to predict what would happen if there were another Great Depression, their answers were grimly prophetic. "There'd be widespread riots," answered one. "The young people won't take it," stated another. "They will steal. A lot of them steal now because they aren't working." A third also raised the issue of a youthful rebellion. "The younger generation won't take it; a lot of bad things would happen." "Oh Hot!" remarked another. "Everybody would get a ball bat and start swinging."[2] Black youths, as Leggett's respondents knew, were increasingly alienated. They were most severely affected by the city's shrinking job market. Young people coming of age in Detroit in the mid- and late 1950s and 1960s faced a very different economic world from that of the previous generation. A black male in Detroit in 1945 or 1950 could realistically expect factory employment, even if his opportunities were seriously limited by discrimination. Blacks continued to suffer levels of unemployment disproportionate to those of Detroit residents in general, although labor force participation rates fluctuated with economic cycles. Still, even in the most flush of times, somewhere close to 10 percent of Detroit's black population was unemployed. Over the next three decades, with the exception of a cyclical boom in automobile employment in the mid- and late 1960s, few could rely on steady employment.

A survey of over three hundred young people in one of Detroit's most depressed inner-city neighborhoods in the early 1960s revealed the extent to which limited opportunities in Detroit's job market had narrowed the horizon of Detroit's young African Americans. Not a single respondent mentioned a career in "the broad middle range of occupations such as skilled trades, office, clerical or technical occupations." The report noted that "replacing the whole middle range of occupations" in the "perceptual worlds" of the youth were a "whole range of deviant occupations—prostitution, numbers, malicing, corn whiskey, theft, etc." A growing number of young people turned to criminal activity, for "Under conditions where a gap in legitimate opportunity exists in the world, such deviant occupations grow up to fill the void. The motif is one of survival; it is not based on thrill seeking. What we call deviant occupations are in fact perceived to be common and in fact legitimate within the context of the culture in which these youths live." The situation changed little in the mid-1960s, even though the overall economy of Detroit improved. At the time of the 1967 riot, somewhere between 25 and 30 percent of young blacks (between ages eighteen and twenty-four) were out of work.[3]

The combination of persistent discrimination in hiring, technological change, decentralized manufacturing, and urban economic decline had dra-

matic effects on the employment prospects of blacks in metropolitan Detroit. What was even more striking was the steady increase of adults who
were wholly unattached to the urban labor market. Nearly one in five of all
Detroit adults did not work at all or worked in the informal economy in
1950. The number grew steadily in the 1960s. The economic transformation
of the city launched a process of deproletarianization, as growing numbers
of African Americans, especially young men, joined the ranks of those who
gave up on work. By 1980, nearly half of the adult male population had only
tenuous connections to the city's formal labor market. The deproletarianization of the city's black population had far-reaching consequences: it shaped
a pattern of poverty in the postwar city that was disturbingly new. Whereas
in the past, most poor people had had some connection to the mainstream
labor market, in the latter part of the twentieth century, the urban poor
found themselves on the economic margins.[4]

The deproletarianization of a growing number of Detroit's black workers
was exacerbated by the persistent racial divide between blacks and whites in
the metropolitan area. Detroit's blacks lacked the geographic mobility—
common to other groups in other periods of American history—to adapt to
the changing labor market. A visitor to Detroit in the 1960s would have
found that despite the tremendous growth of Detroit's black population, the
pattern of segregation in the metropolitan area remained intact. Throughout
the postwar period whole neighborhoods lost their white populations as
hundreds of thousands of white Detroiters fled to the burgeoning ring of
suburbs that surrounded the city. Detroit's black population was mobile, but
its movement was contained within sharply defined racial barriers.

Plant relocations, especially to rural areas and the South, severely limited
the economic opportunities of Detroit's blacks. Detroit's waning industrial
economy had less and less to offer them. But few black Detroiters in the
1960s had the option of following the exodus of employment; residential
segregation and lack of resources kept most trapped in the city. In addition,
the alternatives were hardly more appealing. Few considered moving to
other major Rust Belt cities, whose economies, like Detroit's, were rapidly
declining. And fewer had any desire to move to the small, overwhelmingly
white Midwestern towns that attracted much of the nonmetropolitan industrialization of the postwar era. Small numbers headed west, and beginning in the 1970s, some began to return to the South. But opportunities in
Detroit were, for many, still better than in Alabama's Black Belt, the Mississippi Delta, or the coal mines of West Virginia. Many remembered the
promise of the 1940s and early 1950s and clung to the reasonable expectation that Detroit's economy would pick up again. Hope about the city's
future was one option available to the unemployed and jobless. But more
and more black Detroiters responded with anger to the city's economic and
racial crisis.[5]

Beginning in the late 1950s, African American civil rights activists in the city, after a period of retrenchment, engaged in a renewed militancy. As part of the nationwide civil rights movement, black Detroiters founded new, insurgent organizations like the Trade Union Leadership Council and began to refashion the agenda of established groups like the National Association for the Advancement of Colored People. In the early and mid-1960s, organized African American resistance to discrimination in work and housing accelerated. In 1963, nearly 250,000 blacks and whites, led by the Reverend Martin Luther King, Jr., marched through Detroit. Inspired by the successes of the civil rights movement in the South, African American activists in Detroit led boycotts against local stores and businesses that discriminated against blacks. And interracial liberals took the struggle for open housing in a new direction, turning their sights on Detroit's middle- and upper-class suburbs, including Birmingham and Livonia, and lobbying hard for state and federal legislation that would prohibit discriminatory real estate practices.[6] In all these ways, 1960s-era Detroit witnessed the emergence of a revitalized civil rights movement.

But many civil rights activists grew impatient with the glacial pace of change in Detroit. Black power organizations burgeoned in Detroit in the 1960s, offering an alternative to the mainstream civil rights activism of the postwar years. Detroit was home to the Reverend Albert Cleage, founder of the nationalist Shrine of the Black Madonna and an early and outspoken advocate of black power. At the same time, a younger generation of African Americans, who watched entry-level jobs vanish and who chafed at ongoing discrimination in Detroit's factories, grew more militant on the shop floor, eschewing the consensus politics and integrationism of the UAW for a new "revolutionary unionism." The black-led Revolutionary Union Movement (RUM) established footholds in Dodge and Chrysler plants, where whole departments remained devoid of African Americans, and where blacks remained underrepresented in local union offices.[7]

The 1960s was a paradoxical time in Detroit. From the perspective of national politics, it seemed hopeful. The federal government enacted the most sweeping civil rights legislation since Reconstruction. At the same time, Detroit benefited tremendously from the expansion of federal urban spending during the Kennedy and Johnson administrations. In local politics, the balance of power also began to shift to the left, as Detroit's rapidly growing black population gained electoral power. City politics remained stiffly polarized by the issues of race and housing, but as more blacks voted and were elected to office, they (and a small but vocal segment of white liberals) broke the stranglehold of the white neighborhood associations on local politics. Mayor Albert Cobo's successor, Louis Miriani, was initially sympathetic to the homeowners' movement when the took office in 1957, but he recognized the power of blacks as a swing vote and tried, unsuccessfully, to accommodate both white neighborhood groups and blacks. His successor, Jerome Cavanagh, a little-known insurgent, won an upset victory in 1961 over Miriani. Cavanagh's election was almost accidental: he was supported by an unlikely alliance of African Americans and white neighborhood groups, both alienated (for different reasons) by Miriani's equivocal, middle-of-the-road position on race and housing.[8]

Under Cavanagh, who astutely lobbied government officials for assistance, War on Poverty dollars flooded into Detroit. Detroit was second only to New York in the amount of federal dollars that it received in the 1960s. But officials channeled government assistance down familiar routes and established programs that did not fundamentally deviate from the limited agenda that social welfare, labor, and civil rights groups had set in the 1950s. By and large, War on Poverty programs embodied the conventional wisdom of mainstream economists and social welfare advocates, and focused on behavioral modification as the solution to poverty. The most far-reaching antipoverty programs targeted jobless youth. In 1962, Cavanagh established the Mayor's Committee on Community Action for Detroit Youth, and in 1963, the Michigan Employment Security Commission established a special Detroit Metropolitan Youth Center. Both directed their energies largely toward black youth "deprived because of social, economic, cultural, or . . . personal conditions." Government, it was argued, should play a role in the transformation of youth culture. The problem with such initiatives as Thomas F. Jackson has argued in his seminal article on antipoverty policy in the 1960s, was that they "failed to eliminate income poverty or reduce income inequality [or] to increase the aggregate supply of jobs in urban and other labor markets." The education, job training, and youth programs that were at the heart of the War on Poverty in Detroit were built on the same premises and suffered many of the same limitations as the previous generation of ad hoc programs. None responded adequately to deindustrialization and discrimination.[9]

Simultaneous with the organized protest of civil rights groups were spontaneous outbursts of violent resistance on the streets of Detroit. A growing segment of the black population, especially young people who had little attachment to civil rights and reform organizations, began to vent their discontent at shopkeepers and police officers, the only two groups of whites who regularly appeared in largely black neighborhoods. Protests surrounding the shooting of a black youth by an East Side shopkeeper in 1964, a "mini-riot" on the Lower East Side in 1966, and the massive 1967 riot were the symptoms of growing discontent among Detroit's black poor in the 1960s. Detroit's rioters were disproportionately young black men, the group most affected by racial and economic dislocations, and the most impatient with the slow pace of civil rights reforms.[10]

Further complicating the situation in the postwar era were hardening white racial prejudices. Whites grew increasingly bitter at the failure of their efforts to contain the city's expanding black population. The city was racked with housing protests throughout the mid-1960s, as mobile blacks continued to trangress the city's precarious racial boundaries. White neighborhood groups grew even more militant in their opposition to civil rights and open housing. In 1965, fresh off the Homeowners' Rights Ordinance campaign, white civic association advocate Thomas Poindexter revived the effort to abolish the Detroit Commission on Community Relations. The same year, twenty-five crosses burned throughout Detroit, including some in the Courville area, Lower West Side, and Wyoming Corridor, whose residents were involved in a last-ditch effort to stem racial transition. White Detroit groups pressured local politicians to oppose civil rights legislation. Their votes played a crucial role in the defeat of Michigan's Democratic governor, G. Mennen Williams, in 1966, and in the defeat of local referenda to raise taxes to pay for Detroit's increasingly African American public schools.[11]

Most importantly, working- and lower middle-class whites continued to rally around racially conservative candidates. In 1968 and 1972, Detroit whites provided an impressive base of support for Alabama segregationist George C. Wallace as he forayed northward. The politician whose most famous declaration was "segregation now, segregation forever" found a receptive audience in one of the supposed bastions of liberal northern urban voters. Wallace's outspoken opposition to open housing, school integration, and the expansion of civil rights in the workplace resonated deeply with alienated white Detroiters. Wallace voters, to a far greater extent than supporters of other candidates, denounced racial integration and believed that the civil rights movement was moving too fast. Cheering crowds of thousands greeted Wallace when he appeared at Cobo Hall, the riverfront convention center. Like Wallace supporters elsewhere in the North, stalwart Democratic voters roared in applause when their candidate derided civil rights, "forced housing," welfare spending, urban crime, and big government. Wallace also tapped into the economic vulnerability of his blue-collar supporters. Pollsters found that Wallace voters were more pessimistic about the economy than the electorate at large. A UAW local in Flint, Michigan, endorsed Wallace, and Ford workers at the company's shrinking River Rouge plant supported him in a straw poll. Wallace's troubled campaign faltered in Detroit in 1968. But emboldened by the depth of grassroots support that he found in the Rust Belt, Wallace returned stronger than ever in 1972. He won the 1972 Michigan Democratic primary, sweeping every predominantly white ward in Detroit. Wallace found some of his most fervent support on Detroit's Northwest and Northeast sides, the final remaining bastion of homeowners' association activity in a city that was now over 45 percent African American. Following the lead of Wallace, Richard Nixon and Spiro Agnew repudiated their party's moderate position on civil rights, wooed disaffected urban and southern white Democrats, and swept predominantly white precincts in Detroit in 1968 and 1972.[12]

Racial cleavages also persisted in local politics. Whites provided the crucial margin of support to conservative Polish American mayoral candidate Roman Gribbs in 1969, who edged out his African American opponent Richard Austin. They rallied in support of Detroit's overwhelmingly white police force, including its paramilitary STRESS (Stop Robberies, Enjoy Safe Streets) squad that was regularly accused of brutality toward black suspects. Anti-integration sentiment came to a head when white Detroiters rebelled against the *Milliken v. Bradley* court decision that called for interdistrict busing to eliminate metropolitan-wide educational segregation. The combination of the riot and growing black political power gave urgency to white resistance, but opposition to school integration and support of white conservative candidates for public office was the logical extension of the white racial politics that had divided Detroit in the 1940s and 1950s.[13]

As the invisible boundaries within Detroit frayed, whites continued to flee from the city. Within the secure confines of suburban municipalities, working-class whites created a world that looked remarkably like the city they had left behind. The grid-like streets of Warren, a community of nearly 180,000 on Detroit's northern perimeter, were lined with the 1950s and 1960s ranch-style equivalents of the little bungalows that housed the residents of Courville, Seven Mile–Fenelon, and other parts of the East Side. Likewise, the tract houses of Southgate, Taylor, Wayne, Westland, and Garden City bore a striking resemblance to their counterparts on Detroit's West Side. Fleeing whites brought the politics of local defensiveness with them to the suburbs, and found protection behind the visible and governmentally defended municipal boundaries of suburbia. By 1980, metropolitan Detroit had eighty-six municipalities, forty-five townships, and eighty-nine school districts. It was far more difficult for African Americans to cross suburban lines than it was for them to move into white urban neighborhoods. But when a few intrepid blacks tried to move into communities like Redford, Wayne, and Warren, they faced attacks and hostility like those that had plagued them in the city. Window breakings, arson, and threats largely prevented blacks from joining the ranks of working-class suburbanites. Whites also fiercely battled the Department of Housing and Urban Development's attempt to mandate the construction of integrated low-income housing in all-white suburbs.[14]

More importantly, the grassroots racial politics that had dominated Detroit since the 1940s took deep root in suburbia. As the auto industry continued to reduce its Detroit labor force and shut down Detroit-area plants in the 1970s and 1980s, blue-collar suburbanites turned their anger against government-sponsored programs for African Americans, particularly affirmative action. Macomb County, the refuge for so many white East Side residents who fled black movement into their neighborhoods, became a bellwether for the troubled Democratic party in the 1970s and 1980s. Like whites still living in the city of Detroit, Macomb residents overwhelmingly supported Wallace in 1972. And in the 1980s, Macomb County became a bastion of "Reagan Democrats," angry antiliberal white voters who repudiated the party of Franklin D. Roosevelt for the Republican Party. Macomb was combed by pollsters and pundits alike who sought to explain why its Catholic, blue-collar workers had abandoned the New Deal for the New Right.[15]

The virulence of the white backlash of the 1970s and 1980s seems to lend support to the thesis of many recent commentators that the Democratic party made a grievous political error in the 1960s by ignoring the needs of white, working-class and middle-class voters in favor of the demands of the civil rights movement, black militants, the counterculture, and the "undeserving" poor. "The close identification of the Democratic party with the cause of racial justice," argues Allen Matusow, "did it special injury."[16] Jonathan Rieder contends that the 1960s rebellion of the "silent majority" was in part a response to "certain structural limitations of liberal reform," especially "black demands" that "ran up against the limits of liberalism."[17] Wallace's meteoric rise seems to sustain Thomas and Mary Edsall's argument that the Alabama independent "captured the central political dilemma of racial liberalism and the Democratic party: the inability of Democrats to provide a political home for those whites who felt they were paying—unwillingly—the largest 'costs' in the struggle to achieve an integrated society."[18]

The Edsalls, Rieder, and Matusow, although they correctly emphasize the importance of white discontent as a national political force, err in their overemphasis on the role of the Great Society and the sixties rebellions in the rise of the "silent majority." To view the defection of whites from Democratic ranks simply as a reaction to the War on Poverty, civil rights, and black power movements ignores racial cleavages that shaped local politics in the north well before the tumult of the 1960s. Urban antiliberalism had deep roots in a simmering politics of race and neighborhood defensiveness that divided northern cities well before George Wallace began his first speaking tours in the Snowbelt, well before Lyndon Johnson signed the Civil Rights Act, well before the long, hot summers of Watts, Harlem, Chicago, Newark, and Detroit, and well before affirmative action and busing began to dominate the civil rights agenda. From the 1940s through the 1960s, Detroit whites fashioned a language of discontent directed against public officials, blacks, and liberal reformers who supported public housing and open housing. The rhetoric of George Wallace, Richard Nixon, Spiro Agnew, and Ronald Reagan was familiar to the whites who supported candidates such as

Edward Jeffries, Albert Cobo, and Thomas Poindexter.[19] The "silent majority" did not emerge de novo from the alleged failures of liberalism in the 1960s; it was not the unique product of the white rejection of the Great Society. Instead it was the culmination of more than two decades of simmering white discontent and extensive antiliberal political organization.

The most enduring legacy of the postwar racial struggles in Detroit has been the growing marginalization of the city in local, state, and national politics. Elected officials in Lansing and Washington, beholden to a vocal, well-organized, and defensive white suburban constituency, have reduced funding for urban education, antipoverty, and development programs. At the same time, Detroit—like its counterparts around the country—grapples with a declining tax base and increasingly expensive social, economic, and infrastructural problems.[20]

Urban Transformation

The legacy of postwar Detroit's economic and social history has weighed heavily on the city in the last three decades of the twentieth century. Manufacturers have continued their flight from the city, entirely unchecked by government. Stable and secure blue-collar jobs have grown scarce. In response to industrial decline, city officials have attempted to attract new industries to the city to stem the flow of manufacturing-sector jobs, but their efforts have met with little success. Building on the precedent of the industrial renewal proposals of the 1950s, city officials used the law of eminent domain to help firms acquire land for plant construction and offered tax abatements to firms that located in the city. The city condemned and cleared nearly half a square mile of land on the East Side for the General Motors Poletown plant, and several hundred acres for a new Chrysler industrial complex in the late 1980s, but both operations, surrounded by acres of beautifully landscaped parking lots, employed only a few thousand workers, most transferred from other area plants. Blue-collar jobs have continued to disappear, to be replaced by service-sector jobs, attached to corporate headquarters, the hotel and restaurant business, the health care industry, and burgeoning suburban shopping malls. The largest area of job growth since the early 1980s has been part-time, contingent work.[21]

Discrimination has also persisted in Detroit's labor market, despite civil rights legislation. Employers, as a 1993 survey pointed out, continue to use race to screen prospective employees. Remedies for systematic discrimination have met with limited success, primarily in the governmental sector (a part of the economy that was already opening to blacks after World War II) and in clerical employment. In other sectors, affirmative action has had little impact. Government-enforced affirmative action programs continued the trajectory of the antidiscrimination efforts of the Urban League and the NAACP in the 1950s. They played an important role in opening employment to middle-class blacks, and in breaking the deeply rooted barriers of discrimination in the city's police and fire departments. They resulted in the token hiring of blacks in the building trades, where their numbers still remain small. Racial preferences in government contracts also created a lucrative niche for African American–owned businesses. Detroit's first African American mayor, Coleman Young, much like his white predecessors, used city employment and city contracts to reward loyal supporters over the course of his twenty-year mayoralty (1974–1994). But in the private sector, companies and workers continued to resist affirmative action programs, and blacks have remained underrepresented in skilled and white collar work throughout the post-riot years. By and large untouched by affirmative action programs have been the displaced working-class and poor black Detroiters most in need of assistance.[22]

Detroit has also remained intensely segregated by race and by class. Open housing and antidiscrimination efforts had little effect on metropolitan Detroit's housing market. Patterns of segregation actually worsened in the 1970s and 1980s. Real estate steering and discrimination against blacks have persisted, as audits of brokers' racial practices have demonstrated. Whites remained reluctant to live in racially mixed neighborhoods, and even when middle-class African Americans moved into prosperous suburbs like Southfield, just north of Detroit, the white population has fled, creating new segregated enclaves. Within the confines of persistent housing segregation, well-to-do African Americans, following the trend of the residents of Conant Gardens, Grixdale Park, and Boston-Edison in the postwar years, have continued to segregate by class.[23]

The confluence of residential segregation by race and by class with lack of employment opportunity and poverty is conveyed most vividly in an analysis of poor neighborhoods in the center city. Poverty statistics by census tract for 1970 and 1980 reveal a growing concentration of poverty in certain sections. The black neighborhoods that had housed the poorest third of the city's black population in 1950 and 1960 were even poorer in 1970 and 1980. An increasing number of Detroiters lived in high-poverty areas—those with 40 percent or more of their population living below the official poverty line.[24] Between 1970 and 1980, the number of high-poverty tracts in Detroit doubled, and the population of the city living in these areas nearly doubled as well. In 1970, only about one-tenth of the city's poor lived in high-poverty areas, a figure rising to nearly one-fifth by 1980. Table 10.1 indicates the increasing number of high-poverty areas in the city.

Residents of high-poverty areas were twice as likely as the average Detroiter to be unemployed, and were substantially less likely to be in the labor force. Table 10.2 summarizes the economic status of residents in high-pov-

TABLE 10.1
High-Poverty Tracts in Detroit, 1970 and 1980

	Number	Population	Population Poor	Percent of Detroit Poor
1970	22	55,547	24,039	10.8
1980	44	110,111	50,670	19.6

Source: Author's calculation from U.S. Department of Commerce, Bureau of the Census, *Census of Population and Housing: Census Tracts, Detroit, Michigan Standard Metropolitan Statistical Area* PHC(1)–58 (Washington, D.C.: U.S. Government Printing Office, 1970), Tables P3 and P4; and 1980, Tables P10 and P11.

TABLE 10.2
Joblessness in Detroit's High-Poverty
Areas, 1970 and 1980 (percent)

	1970	1980
Unemployed	14.0	28.4
Not in Labor Force	45.9	59.1
Not Working	53.5	70.7

Sources: See Table 10.1.
Notes: For citywide statistics on joblessness and explanation of denominators of percentages, see Table 5.5.

erty tracts in both 1970 and 1980. Detroit's poor were increasingly likely to live in neighborhoods with other poor people, and in neighborhoods where a growing majority of their associates were likely to be wholly unattached to the labor market.

It is a commonplace observation that Detroit's urban crisis began with the riot of 1967 and worsened with the inauguration of Coleman Young as Detroit's first black mayor in 1974. Detroit, argued journalist Ze'ev Chafets in an influential *New York Times* article and subsequent book, became America's "first major Third World city" in the wake of the 1967 riot. The image of a largely black and very poor city surrounded by a ring of affluent white suburbs gives resonance to images of Detroit as a center of American apartheid. What has become of Detroit, however, is not the product of post-riot panic or the alleged misrule of Coleman Young. By the time Young was inaugurated, the forces of economic decay and racial animosity were far too powerful for a single elected official to stem. Efforts to revitalize the city over the last two decades have foundered on the shoals of inadequate finances: industrial and population flight have drained the city of resources necessary to maintain infrastructure, and the federal government, especially since the Reagan administration, has drastically cut urban spending. Celebrated public-private partnerships, including the Ford-financed Renaissance Center hotel and office project, and the General Motors Poletown plant, have done little to enlarge the city's employment base, and have drained city coffers of more tax money. The bleak landscapes and unremitting poverty of Detroit in the 1970s and 1980s are the legacies of the transformation of the city's economy in the wake of World War II, and of the politics and culture of race that have their origins in the persistent housing and workplace discrimination of the postwar decades. What hope remains in the city comes from the continued efforts of city residents to resist the debilitating effects of poverty, racial tension, and industrial decline. But the rehabilitation of Detroit and other major American cities will require a more vigorous attempt to grapple with the enduring effects of the postwar transformation of the city, and creative responses, piece by piece, to the interconnected forces of race, residence, discrimination, and industrial decline, the consequences of a troubled and still unresolved past.[25]

Appendix A

Index of Dissimilarity, Blacks and Whites in Major American Cities, 1940–1990

	1940	1950	1960	1970	1980	1990
Boston	86.3	86.5	83.9	81.2	77.6	68.2
Buffalo	87.9	89.5	86.5	87.0	79.4	81.8
Chicago	95.0	92.1	92.6	91.9	87.8	85.8
Cincinnati	90.6	91.2	89.0	76.8	72.3	75.8
Cleveland	92.0	91.5	91.3	90.8	87.5	85.1
Columbus	87.1	88.9	85.3	81.8	71.4	67.3
Detroit	**89.9**	**88.8**	**84.5**	**88.4**	**86.7**	**87.6**
Gary	88.3	93.8	92.8	91.4	90.6	89.9
Indianapolis	90.4	91.4	91.6	81.7	76.2	74.3
Kansas City	88.0	91.3	90.8	87.4	78.9	72.6
Milwaukee	92.9	91.6	88.1	83.9	83.9	82.8
Newark	77.4	76.9	71.6	81.4	81.6	82.5
New York	86.8	87.3	79.3	81.0	82.0	82.2
Philadelphia	88.0	89.0	87.1	79.5	78.7	77.2
Pittsburgh	82.0	84.0	84.6	75.0	72.7	71.0
St. Louis	92.6	92.9	90.5	84.7	81.3	77.0

Sources: Annemette Sorensen, Karl E. Taeuber, and Leslie J. Hollingsworth, Jr., "Indices of Racial Residential Segregation for 109 Cities in the United States, 1940 to 1970," *Sociological Focus* 8 (1975): 128–30; Douglas S. Massey and Nancy A. Denton, *American Apartheid: Segregation and the Making of the Underclass* (Cambridge, Mass.: Harvard University Press, 1993), 222. The 1940–70 figures are for cities; the 1980–90 figures are for Standard Metropolitan Statistical Areas.

Appendix B

African American Occupational Structure in Detroit, 1940–1970

Detroit's black men (Table B.1) made their most significant gains as operatives (semiskilled workers in industrial jobs). The most pronounced gain in semiskilled work came in the 1940s. Fewer than one in three black men worked as operatives in 1940, compared to nearly half in 1950. Black gains in better manufacturing jobs came as the percentage employed in the most menial of jobs declined appreciably. At the outbreak of World War II, a quarter of all black men held positions as unskilled laborers; three decades later, a mere one in twelve held unskilled jobs. This decline was primarily a consequence of automation: manufacturers eliminated unskilled jobs throughout the period (see Chapter 5). The fraction of blacks employed in the service sector also fell significantly in the postwar period. More than one-fifth of black men held service jobs in 1940, compared to only one-eighth in 1970. The proportion of black men in white-collar positions remained small throughout the period, and the proportion in the professions and in clerical positions did not rise until the 1960s. The proportion of black men employed as managers and proprietors also remained low and changed little between 1940 and 1970.

The situation of black women workers in Detroit's labor market also changed considerably in the period from 1940 to 1970 (Table B.2). The percentage of black women in service jobs dropped sharply in the 1940s and the 1960s. In 1940, four-fifths of black women worked in service jobs; by 1970, only a third did so. The decline in service work was overcome by a wartime increase in operative work (although the percentage of black women employed in semiskilled factory positions actually fell during the 1950s and 1960s). Black women also made gains in the professional and management sectors. Their most striking gains were in the clerical sector, where their representation nearly doubled each decade.

In other occupations, black representation changed little. Until the 1960s, the percentage of blacks (male and female) in the skilled crafts remained almost constant (see Chapter 4), and black gains in skilled employment in the 1960s were minimal. In other occupations, the percentage of black male workers remained ossified throughout the postwar period. The proportion of black managers, proprietors, officials, and sales workers remained constant or increased only slightly through the postwar period. Black female workers

TABLE B.1

Black Male Occupational Distribution in Detroit, 1940–1970 (percent)

	1940	1950	1960	1970
Professional	2	2	3	6
Manager, proprietor, or official	3	3	2	3
Clerical worker	3	4	6	8
Sales worker	2	2	2	3
Crafts	14	12	13	17
Operative	29	45	44	39
Service worker	22	12	12	13
Laborer	25	20	17	11

Sources: Calculated from U.S. Department of Commerce, Bureau of the Census, *Census of Population, 1940*, vol. 3, part 3 (Washington, D.C.: U.S. Government Printing Office, 1943), Table 19; *Census of Population, 1950*, vol. 2, part 22 (Washington, D.C.: U.S. Government Printing Office, 1952), Table 76; *Census of Population, 1960*, vol. 1, part 24 (Washington, D.C.: U.S. Government Printing Office, 1963), Table 122; *Census of Population, 1970*, PC(1)–C24 (Washington, D.C.: U.S. Government Printing Office, 1972), Tables 86 and 93. Data for 1940 are for Detroit; data for 1950–1970 are for the Detroit Standard Metropolitan Statistical Area. Figures are rounded.

TABLE B.2

Black Female Occupational Distribution in Detroit, 1940–1970 (percent)

	1940	1950	1960	1970
Professional	4	6	8	11
Manager, proprietor, or official	1	2	1	4
Clerical worker	4	9	16	30
Sales worker	2	3	3	4
Crafts	0	1	1	1
Operative	9	20	15	14
Service worker	79	57	54	35
Laborer	1	2	2	2

Sources: See Table B.1.

made their most pronounced gain in the professions, largely because of the opening of teaching positions as the number of black students in Detroit's public schools increased dramatically (See Chapter 4).

A comparison of the occupational concentration of black workers with that of white workers (Tables B.3 and B.4) makes clear a gradual convergence of black and white work experiences in postwar Detroit. An index of 100 indicates that the occupational structure of blacks and whites was identical. An index of less than 100 signals the underrepresentation of blacks in certain occupations; an index of greater than 100 indicates that blacks were concen-

TABLE B.3

Index of Relative Concentration of Black Males in Detroit by
Occupation, 1940–1970

	1940	1950	1960	1970
Professional	38	24	29	37
Manager, proprietor, or official	32	26	23	32
Clerical worker	35	59	82	104
Sales worker	29	25	31	44
Craftsman	62	56	61	102
Operative	104	171	194	180
Service worker	355	236	251	194
Laborer	400	435	409	287

Sources: See Table B.1.

Methodological note: On the construction of the index, see Stephan Thernstrom, *The Other Bostonians: Poverty and Progress in the American Metropolis,
1880–1970* (Cambridge, Mass.: Harvard University Press, 1974), 190–91, 200
(Table 8.11) for comparable Boston data. In his index, Thernstrom calculates the
distribution of blacks compared to the distribution of all workers in the economy.
Because his denominator includes both black and white workers, it does not offer
an accurate measure of the effects of discrimination, particularly in the lower
ranks of employment (operative and laborer) where blacks were concentrated. I
have reworked the index to offer a direct comparison of the occupational distribution of blacks and whites.

trated in certain professions disproportionate to whites. Had the occupational structure for black and white men been identical in 1940, three to four
times as many blacks would have to be represented in the professions, in
management, and in sales. Black and white men, however, were almost
equally represented in semiskilled operative positions in 1940. As more
blacks entered manufacturing jobs in 1950 and 1960, they held two to three
times as many semiskilled positions as would be expected if the black and
white occupational structures were identical.

The one area in which black male representation in the work force con-
verged with whites was clerical work. Whereas in 1940, three times more
blacks needed to be employed in clerical positions to reach parity with
whites, by 1970, representation of black and white men in clerical positions
was nearly equal. Between 1960 and 1970, the gap between black and white
men in the skilled trades also began to narrow, although through the 1960s,
blacks still remained primarily confined to nonunionized crafts. The proportion of blacks in semiskilled occupations increased, as black males maintained their large foothold in manufacturing. The most striking improvement for black men was the significant decrease in their representation on
the lowest rungs of the city's occupational ladder, especially in unskilled
laboring positions.

TABLE B.4

Index of Relative Concentration of Black Females in Detroit by
Occupation, 1940–1970

	1940	1950	1960	1970
Professional	32	52	69	81
Manager, proprietor, or official	41	47	45	126
Clerical worker	13	28	49	80
Sales worker	20	33	36	47
Craftsman	31	67	83	90
Operative	54	129	128	141
Service worker	383	416	356	230
Laborer	103	283	314	202

Sources: See Table B.1.
Methodological Note: See Table B.3.

The gap between black and white women in Detroit's labor market also narrowed considerably in most occupations between 1940 and 1970. In 1940, black women were underrepresented in every occupational category except service work, where they were disproportionately concentrated, and in unskilled labor, where their representation was comparable to that of white women. In the 1940s, black women made significant gains relative to white women in virtually every occupation in the 1940s; yet they remained overrepresented in the manual occupations, and underrepresented in sales, clerical, management, and professional positions. From 1950 through 1970, black women remained concentrated in operative positions relative to whites; but the 1960s marked a narrowing of the gap between black and white women employed as service workers and laborers. Still, despite gains, black women were two times as likely to be found in service and labor positions than white women. The period from 1940 to 1970 saw some significant advances for black women relative to white women. The representation of black women in white- and pink-collar jobs moved toward convergence with that of whites, especially in the professions, managerial, clerical and crafts.

To overemphasize gains, however, would be to misrepresent trends. The index of occupational representation makes clear the enormous chasm which separated the occupational structure of whites and blacks in Detroit, even as late as 1970. All blacks in Detroit remained disproportionately represented in service jobs and as unskilled laborers, areas in which they had traditionally found employment. The occupational structure of blacks and whites began to converge in the postwar decades, but a distinctive pattern of occupational inequality persisted in most sectors of the city's labor market through 1970.

Abbreviations in the Notes

Archives and Libraries

AAD	Archives of the Archdiocese of Detroit, Detroit, Michigan
ALUA	Archives of Labor and Urban Affairs, Walter P. Reuther Library, Wayne State University, Detroit, Michigan
DPL	Burton Historical Collection, Detroit Public Library
LC	Manuscript Division, Library of Congress, Washington, D.C.
MHC	Michigan Historical Collections, Bentley Library, University of Michigan, Ann Arbor
MSRC	Moorland-Spingarn Research Center, Howard University, Washington, D.C.
NA	National Archives and Records Service, College Park, Maryland
PL	Labor History Collection, Pattee Library, Pennsylvania State University, University Park, Pennsylvania
WSU-UA	University Archives, Wayne State University, Walter P. Reuther Library, Detroit, Michigan

Manuscript Collections

BA	Burneice Avery Papers, DPL
BEP	Boston-Edison Protective Association Papers, DPL
CAH	Charles A. Hill Papers, ALUA
CCR	Detroit Commission on Community Relations Collection, ALUA
CHPC	Detroit Citizens Housing and Planning Council Papers, DPL
CPC	Detroit Archives—City Plan Commission Papers, DPL
CRC	Civil Rights Congress of Michigan Collection, ALUA
DMP	Donald Marsh Papers, WSU-UA
DNAACP	Detroit Branch National Association for the Advancement of Colored People Papers, ALUA
DSL	Donald S. Leonard Papers, MHC
DUL	Detroit Urban League Papers, MHC
ECP	Edward Connor Papers, ALUA
FHLBS	Federal Home Loan Bank System, Record Group 195, NA
FK	Francis Kornegay Papers, MHC
FM	Floyd McGriff Papers, MHC
GMW	G. Mennen Williams Papers, MHC
HOLC	Home Owners' Loan Corporation, Record Group 39, NA
Mayor's Papers	Detroit Archives—Mayor's Papers, DPL
MDCC	Metropolitan Detroit Council of Churches Collection, ALUA
MJ	Mildred Jeffrey Papers, ALUA
NAACP	National Association for the Advancement of Colored People Papers, LC

NUL	National Urban League Papers, LC
RH	Robert Halbeisen Collection, ALUA
RK	Rose Kleinman Papers, ALUA
SEMCOG	Southeastern Michigan Council of Governments Collection, ALUA
SLAA	South Lakeview Area Association Papers, DPL
SMSJ	St. Matthew and St. Joseph Church Papers, MHC
SP-AME	St. Paul AME Zion Church Papers, MHC
UAW-CAP	United Automobile Workers Community Action Program Collection, ALUA
UAW-FP	United Automobile Workers Fair Practices Department Collection, ALUA
UAW-PAC	United Automobile Workers Political Action Committee—Roy Reuther Collection, ALUA
UAW-RD	United Automobile Workers Research Department Collection, ALUA
UAW-WPR	United Automobile Workers President—Walter P. Reuther Collection, ALUA
UAW-49	United Automobile Workers Local 49 Collection, ALUA
UAW-600	United Automobile Workers Local 600 Collection, ALUA
USWA-CRD	United Steel Workers of America Civil Rights Department Collection, PL
VF	Vertical Files, ALUA
WS	William Seabron Papers, ALUA

Notes

Introduction

1. See the arresting images of Detroit in Camillo José Vergara, *The New American Ghetto* (New Brunswick, N.J.: Rutgers University Press, 1995) and Camillo José Vergara, Richard Plunz, Dan Hoffman, and Kyong Park, "Detroit is Everywhere," Exhibit Program, Store Front for Art and Architecture, N.Y., May 20–July 1, 1995.

2. Douglas S. Massey and Nancy A. Denton, *American Apartheid: Segregation and the Making of the Underclass* (Cambridge, Mass.: Harvard University Press, 1993), 57. For a comparison of levels of segregation in Detroit and other major American cities in 1940, 1950, and 1960, see Karl E. Taeuber and Alma F. Taeuber, *Negroes in Cities: Residential Segregation and Neighborhood Change* (Chicago: Aldine Publishing Company, 1965), 39–41. On economic restructuring and job loss, see John D. Kasarda, "Urban Change and Minority Opportunities," in *The New Urban Reality*, ed. Paul E. Peterson (Washington, D.C.: The Brookings Institution, 1985), 43–47, esp. Tables 1 and 2. According to Kasarda, the most marked difference between Detroit's labor market and that of other major cities was the decline in employment in Detroit's service sector, mainly after 1967 (45). In 1970, 1980, and 1987–88, the percentage of blacks in metropolitan Detroit living below the poverty line has remained lower than in Chicago and Cleveland. In 1970 and 1980 the Detroit-area black poverty rate was lower than in Baltimore, Philadelphia, and New York; in 1987–88, it was higher than in all three. See Reynolds Farley, "Residential Segregation of Social and Economic Groups Among Blacks, 1970–1980," in *The Urban Underclass*, ed. Christopher Jencks and Paul E. Peterson (Washington, D.C.: The Brookings Institution, 1991), 295.

3. I have developed this point at length in Thomas J. Sugrue, "The Structures of Urban Poverty: The Reorganization of Space and Work in Three Periods of American History," in *The "Underclass" Debate: Views from History*, ed. Michael B. Katz (Princeton, N.J.: Princeton University Press, 1993), 85–117.

4. Edward C. Banfield, *The Unheavenly City: The Nature and Future of Our Urban Crisis* (Boston: Little, Brown, 1968); E. Franklin Frazier, *The Negro Family in the United States* (Chicago: University of Chicago Press, 1939); Lee Rainwater and William L. Yancey, eds., *The Moynihan Report and the Politics of Controversy* (Cambridge, Mass.: MIT Press, 1967). More recent works include George Gilder, *Wealth and Poverty* (New York: Basic Books, 1981); Charles Murray, *Losing Ground: American Social Policy, 1950–1980* (New York: Basic Books, 1984); Myron Magnet, *The Nightmare and the Dream: The Sixties Legacy to the Underclass* (New York: William Morrow, 1993); Lawrence Mead, *The New Politics of Poverty* (New York: Basic Books, 1992). Many liberal authors have picked up these themes as well. See, especially, Ken Auletta, *The Underclass* (New York: Random House, 1982); Nicholas Lemann, "The Origins of the Underclass," *Atlantic*, June 1986, 31–55, July 1986, 54–68; Christopher Jencks, *Rethinking Social Policy* (Cambridge, Mass.: Harvard University Press, 1993); Isabel Sawhill, "The Underclass: An Over-

view," *Public Interest* 96 (Summer 1989): 3–15. Overviews of this literature are Michael B. Katz, *The Undeserving Poor: From the War on Poverty to the War on Welfare* (New York: Pantheon, 1989); James T. Patterson, *America's Struggle Against Poverty, 1900–1994* (Cambridge: Harvard University Press, 1995); Thomas J. Sugrue, "The Impoverished Politics of Poverty," *Yale Journal of Law and the Humanities* 6 (1994), 163–79; Herbert Gans, *The War Against the Poor* (New York: Basic Books, 1995).

5. William Julius Wilson, *The Truly Disadvantaged: The Inner City, the Underclass, and Public Policy* (Chicago: University of Chicago Press, 1987); Kasarda, "Urban Change and Minority Opportunities," and "Urban Industrial Transition and the Underclass," *Annals of the American Academy of Political and Social Science* 501 (1989): 26–47, and other articles by Kasarda. For authors who emphasize race, see Massey and Denton, *American Apartheid*; Gary Orfield, "Ghettoization and Its Alternatives," in Peterson, *The New Urban Reality*, 161–96, and "Separate Societies: Have the Kerner Warnings Come True?" in *Quiet Riots: Race and Poverty in the United States*, ed. Fred R. Harris and Roger Wilkins (New York: Pantheon Books, 1988); Susan Fainstein and Norman Fainstein, "The Underclass/Mismatch Hypothesis as an Explanation for Black Economic Deprivation," *Politics and Society* 15 (1986–87): 403–51.

6. Thomas Byrne Edsall and Mary D. Edsall, *Chain Reaction: The Impact of Race, Rights, and Taxes on American Politics* (New York: Norton, 1991); Jim Sleeper, *The Closest of Strangers: Liberalism and the Politics of Race in New York City* (New York: Norton, 1990); Jonathan Rieder, *Canarsie: The Jews and Italians of Brooklyn Against Liberalism* (Cambridge, Mass.: Harvard University Press, 1985); Edward G. Carmines and James A. Stimson, *Issue Evolution: Race and the Transformation of American Politics* (Princeton, N.J.: Princeton University Press, 1989). On Detroit, see Ze'ev Chafets, *Devil's Night and Other True Tales of Detroit* (New York: Random House, 1990). Important critical reviews of this literature include James R. Grossman, "Traditional Politics or the Politics of Tradition?" *Reviews in American History* 21 (September 1993): 533–38; Adolph Reed and Julian Bond, "Equality: Why We Can't Wait," *The Nation*, December 9, 1991, 723–37; and Adolph Reed, "Review: Race and the Disruption of the New Deal Coalition," *Urban Affairs Quarterly* 27 (December 1991): 326–33. Important alternatives to this scholarship include Margaret Weir, "Cities and the Politics of Social Policy in the United States," in *Prospects for a Social Europe*, ed. Stephan Leibfried and Paul Pierson (forthcoming); Weir, "Urban Poverty and Defensive Localism," *Dissent*, Summer 1994, 337–42: and John H. Mollenkopf, *The Contested City* (Princeton, N.J.: Princeton University Press, 1983).

7. An important first foray into the topic are the essays in Michael B. Katz, ed., *The "Underclass" Debate: Views from History* (Princeton, N.J.: Princeton University Press, 1993); a useful overview of the small historical and larger social-scientific literature on recent American cities is Kenneth L. Kusmer, "African Americans in the City Since World War II: From the Industrial to the Post-Industrial Era," *Journal of Urban History* 21 (1995): 458–504. Also extremely important is Loïc J. D. Wacquant, "Urban Outcasts: Stigma and Division in the Black American Ghetto and the French Urban Periphery," *International Journal of Urban and Regional Research* 17 (1993): 366–83.

8. Joseph Schumpeter, *Capitalism, Socialism, and Democracy* (New York: Harper, 1942).

9. Every major Northern and Midwestern city lost jobs in the 1950s. For a concise summary, see Kasarda, "Urban Change and Minority Opportunities," 43–47, esp. Tables 1 and 2. On industrial decline, see Sugrue, "Structures of Urban Poverty," 100–117; John Cumbler, *A Social History of Economic Decline* (New Brunswick, N.J.: Rutgers University Press, 1989); Gary Gerstle, *Working-Class Americanism: A History of Labor in a Textile City, 1920–1960* (Cambridge: Cambridge University Press, 1989), 318–30; on the electrical industry, see Ronald W. Schatz, *The Electrical Workers: A History of Labor at General Electric and Westinghouse* (Urbana: University of Illinois Press, 1983), 232–37. On the government-subsidized rise of the sunbelt, see Bruce Schulman, *From Cotton Belt to Sunbelt: Federal Policy, Economic Development and the Transformation of the South, 1938–1980* (New York: Oxford University Press, 1990); Roger Lotchin, *Fortress California, 1910–1961: From Warfare to Welfare* (New York: Oxford University Press, 1992).

10. On Douglas, Clark, and the fate of depressed areas legislation, see James L. Sundquist, *Politics and Policy: The Eisenhower, Kennedy, and Johnson Years* (Washington, D.C.: The Brookings Institution, 1968), 57–83; Irving Bernstein, *Promises Kept: John F. Kennedy's New Frontier* (New York: Oxford University Press, 1991), 160–91. Harvey Swados, *On the Line* (1957; reprint, with an introduction by Nelson Lichtenstein, Urbana: University of Illinois Press, 1990); Charles Denby, *Indignant Heart: A Black Worker's Journal* (1956; reprint Detroit: Wayne State University Press, 1989); Michael Harrington, *The Other America: Poverty in the United States* (New York: Macmillan, 1962).

11. Elizabeth Fones-Wolf, *Selling Free Enterprise: The Business Assault on Labor and Liberalism, 1945–1960* (Urbana: University of Illinois Press, 1994); William Chafe, "Postwar American Society: Dissent and Social Reform," in *The Truman Presidency*, ed. Michael J. Lacey (New York: Cambridge University Press, 1989), 156–73; Robert Griffith, "Forging America's Postwar Order: Domestic Politics and Political Economy in the Age of Truman," ibid., 57–88; Thomas J. Sugrue, "Reappraising the History of Postwar America," *Prospects: The Annual of American Culture Studies* 20 (1995) 493–509; Steve Rosswurm, ed., *The CIO's Left-Led Unions* (New Brunswick, N.J.: Rutgers University Press, 1992).

12. Margaret Weir, "The Federal Government and Unemployment: The Frustration of Policy Innovation from the New Deal to the Great Society," in *The Politics of Social Policy in the United States*, ed. Margaret Weir, Ann Shola Orloff, and Theda Skocpol (Princeton, N.J.: Princeton University Press, 1988), 149–90; Ira Katznelson, "Was the Great Society a Lost Opportunity?" in *The Rise and Fall of the New Deal Order*, ed. Steve Fraser and Gary Gerstle (Princeton, N.J.: Princeton University Press, 1989), 185–211; Gary Mucciaroni, *The Political Failure of Employment Policy, 1945–1982* (Pittsburgh: University of Pittsburgh Press, 1990), 17–53.

13. The literature on the post–World War II black migration is slim. See Nicholas Lemann, *The Promised Land: The Great Black Migration and How It Changed America* (New York: Random House, 1991); Jacqueline Jones, *The Dispossessed: America's Underclasses from the Civil War to the Present* (New York: Basic Books, 1992), 205–65.

14. Arnold R. Hirsch, "With or Without Jim Crow: Black Residential Segregation in the United States," in *Urban Policy in Twentieth-Century America*, ed. Arnold R. Hirsch and Raymond A. Mohl (New Brunswick, N.J.: Rutgers University Press, 1993), 65–99; Massey and Denton, *American Apartheid*; Loïc J. D. Wacquant, "The New Urban Color Line: The State of the Ghetto in Postfordist America," in *Social Theory and the Politics of Identity*, ed. Craig Calhoun (Oxford: Basil Blackwell, 1994).

15. Economists and sociologists have long offered influential monocausal explanations of racial discrimination. See, for example, Gary Becker, *The Economics of Discrimination*, 2d ed. (Chicago: University of Chicago Press, 1971); Richard Edwards, *Contested Terrain: The Transformation of the Workplace in the Twentieth Century* (New York: Basic Books, 1979), 184–99; Lester C. Thurow, *Poverty and Discrimination* (Washington, D.C.: The Brookings Institution, 1969), 111–38. More sensitive to historical complexity, but still reductionist, are Michael Reich, *Racial Inequality: A Political-Economic Analysis* (Princeton, N.J.: Princeton University Press, 1981) and Stanley Lieberson, *A Piece of the Pie: Blacks and White Immigrants Since 1880* (Berkeley: University of California Press, 1980), esp. 363–83. For a searching critique of scholarship that takes an ahistorical view of race, which has strongly influenced my analysis, see Barbara Jeanne Fields, "Ideology and Race in American History," in *Region, Race, and Reconstruction: Essays in Honor of C. Vann Woodward*, ed. J. Morgan Kousser and James M. McPherson (New York: Oxford University Press, 1982), 143–77.

16. David R. Roediger, *Toward the Abolition of Whiteness: Essays on Race, Politics, and Working-Class History* (London: Verso, 1994); the term "not-yet-white ethnics" is from an unpublished essay by John Bukowczyk, quoted ibid., 194; see also David Roediger, "Race and the Working-Class Past in the United States: Multiple Identities and the Future of Labor History," *International Review of Social History* 38 (1993): suppl., 127–43.

17. See Chapter 2.

18. I borrow the term "political construction" from Robert Lieberman, "Social Construction (Continued)," *American Political Science Review* 89 (1995): 437–41. On the importance of World War II in the history of civil rights and race relations, see Harvard Sitkoff, "Racial Militancy and Interracial Violence in the Second World War," *Journal of American History* 58 (1971): 661–81; Richard M. Dalfiume, "The 'Forgotten' Years of the Negro Revolution," *Journal of American History* 55 (1968): 90–106. On federal policy and race, see Jill Quadagno, *The Color of Welfare* (New York: Oxford University Press, 1995); on urban policy, see Kenneth T. Jackson, "Race, Ethnicity, and Real Estate Appraisal: The Home Owners Loan Corporation and the Federal Housing Administration," *Journal of Urban History* 6 (1980): 419–52; John Bauman, *Public Housing, Race, and Renewal: Urban Planning in Philadelphia, 1920–1974* (Philadelphia: Temple University Press, 1987); Arnold R. Hirsch, *Making the Second Ghetto: Race and Housing in Chicago, 1940–1960* (New York: Cambridge University Press, 1983), 212–75; for an overview, see Raymond A. Mohl, "Shifting Patterns of American Urban Policy Since 1900," in Hirsch and Mohl, *Urban Policy in Twentieth-Century America*, 1–45.

19. On the centrality of the 1940s for the coalescence of the New Deal order, and on the future of American social policy, see Fraser and Gerstle, *The Rise and*

Fall of the New Deal Order. In their introduction, Fraser and Gerstle note that the "1940s transformations decisively shaped and limited the social programs of the 1960s" (xix).

20. My thinking on these matters has been influenced by Pierre Bourdieu and Loïc J. D. Wacquant, *An Introduction to Reflexive Sociology* (Chicago: University of Chicago Press, 1992); Pierre Bourdieu, "The Uses of the 'People,'" in *In Other Words: Essays toward a Reflexive Sociology*, trans. Matthew Adamson (Cambridge, Mass.: Polity Press, 1990), 150–55.

21. See Joe R. Feagin, Anthony M. Orum, and Gideon Sjoberg, *The Case for the Case Study* (Chapel Hill: University of North Carolina Press, 1991).

22. Hirsch, *Making the Second Ghetto*, and "Massive Resistance in the Urban North: Chicago's Trumbull Park, 1953–1966," *Journal of American History* 82 (1995): 522–50; Cumbler, *A Social History of Economic Decline*, 153; John F. Bauman, *Public Housing, Race, and Renewal: Urban Planning in Philadelphia, 1920–1974* (Philadelphia: Temple University Press, 1987); Charles F. Casey-Leininger, "Making the Second Ghetto in Cincinnati: Avondale, 1925–1970," in *Race and the City: Work, Community, and Protest in Cincinnati, 1820–1970*, ed. Henry Louis Taylor, Jr. (Urbana: University of Illinois Press, 1993), 239–40, 247–48.

23. Nelson Lichtenstein, "Introduction: The American Automobile Industry and Its Workers," in *On the Line: Essays in the History of Auto Work*, ed. Nelson Lichtenstein and Stephen Meyer (Urbana: University of Illinois Press, 1989), 1–16; Jon Teaford, *Cities of the Heartland: The Rise and Fall of the Industrial Midwest* (Bloomington: Indiana University Press, 1993), 176–78.

Chapter 1
"Arsenal of Democracy"

1. Charles Sheeler, *Crisscrossed Conveyors, River Rouge Plant, Ford Motor Company*, 1927, gelatin silver print, Ford Motor Company Collection, The Metropolitan Museum of Art, New York; Diego Rivera, *Detroit Industry*, frescoes, Detroit Institute of Arts, Detroit. For descriptions of the Rouge Plant, see Allan Nevins and Frank Ernest Hill, *Ford: Decline and Rebirth: 1933–1962* (New York: Scribner, 1963), 8; Nelson Lichtenstein, "Life at the Rouge: A Cycle of Workers' Control," in *Life and Labor: Dimensions of American Working Class History*, ed. Charles Stephenson and Robert Asher (Albany: State University of New York Press, 1986), 237–38.

2. On Dodge Main, see Charles Hyde, "Dodge Main and the Detroit Automobile Industry, 1910–1980," *Detroit in Perspective* 6, no. 1 (1982): 1–21; Writers' Program of the Work Projects Administration, *Michigan: A Guide to the Wolverine State*, American Guide Series, Illustrated (New York: Oxford University Press, 1941), 267.

3. George Tripp, "Detroit: The Fashion is R.P.M.," *Esquire*, June 1955, p. 73. Thanks to Mary Panzer for this citation.

4. Gloria Whelan, "The First City," *Michigan Quarterly Review* 25 (1986): 184. Whelan refers here to the Packard plant on East Grand Boulevard.

5. Olivier Zunz, *The Changing Face of Inequality: Urbanization, Industrial Development, and Immigrants in Detroit, 1880–1920* (Chicago: University of Chicago Press, 1982), 292–309; and Robert Sinclair, *The Face of Detroit: A Spatial Synthesis* (Detroit: Department of Geography, Wayne State University, 1972), 36–41.

6. On Detroit's rapid recovery from the Great Depression, see Detroit Metropolitan Area Regional Planning Commission, *The Manufacturing Economy of the Detroit Region, Part I (Revised)* (1950), 3–4, copy in the United States Department of Labor Library, Washington, D.C. For a discussion of Detroit boosters, see Laurence Goldstein, "Images of Detroit in Twentieth Century Literature," *Michigan Quarterly* 25 (1986): 269–91; the image of Dynamic Detroit comes from Julian Street, "Detroit the Dynamic," *Colliers*, July 4, 1914, 9–10, and from Arthur Pound, *Detroit: Dynamic City* (New York: Appleton-Century, 1940).

7. There is a voluminous literature on the rise of the UAW and industrial unionism in Detroit. For a readable overview, see Steve Babson, *Working Detroit: The Making of a Union Town* (Detroit: Wayne State University Press, 1986). More specialized studies include Peter Friedlander, *The Emergence of a UAW Local, 1936–1939* (Pittsburgh: University of Pittsburgh Press, 1975) and Steve Babson, *Building the Union: Skilled Workers and Anglo-Gaelic Immigrants in the Rise of the UAW* (New Brunswick, N.J.: Rutgers University Press, 1991), both of which focus on ethnicity in the workplace. For a list of twenty-four ethnic groups represented at Ford during the World War I era, see Jonathan Schwartz, "Henry Ford's Melting Pot," in *Ethnic Groups in the City*, ed. Otto Feinstein (Lexington, Mass.: D.C. Heath, 1971), 195; on Mexicans, see Zaragosa Vargas, *Proletarians of the North: A History of Mexican Industrial Workers in Detroit and the Midwest, 1917–1933* (Berkeley: University of California Press, 1993). As Vargas notes (189), repatriation during the Great Depression reduced Detroit's Mexican population by 90 percent; only twelve hundred Mexicans remained in the city in 1936. The population increased slowly beginning in the 1940s, but Detroit's Mexican population remained small. On union battles, see Sidney Fine, *Sit-Down: The General Motors Strike of 1936–37* (Ann Arbor: University of Michigan Press, 1969); August Meier and Elliot Rudwick, *Black Detroit and the Rise of the UAW* (New York: Oxford University Press, 1979); Nelson Lichtenstein, *Labor's War at Home: The CIO in World War II* (Cambridge: Cambridge University Press, 1982); Martin Halpern, *UAW Politics in the Cold War Era* (Albany: State University of New York Press, 1988); Martin Glaberman, *Wartime Strikes: The Struggle Against the No-Strike Pledge in the UAW During World War II* (Detroit: Bewick Editions, 1980). On southern whites and their storefront churches, see "Survey of Racial and Religious Conflict Forces in Detroit," CRC, Box 71.

8. Edmund Wilson, *American Earthquake: A Documentary of the Twenties and Thirties* (New York: Doubleday, 1958), 230; Edmund Wilson, *The Thirties From Notebooks and Diaries of the Period*, ed. Leon Edel (New York: Farrar, Straus and Giroux, 1980), 53. Wilson visited Detroit in 1931. Detroit Housing Commission and Work Projects Administration, *Real Property Survey of Detroit, Michigan*, vol. 1 (Detroit: Detroit Bureau of Governmental Research, 1939), 38–39.

9. On the decline of ethnicity, see Zunz, *The Changing Face of Inequality*, esp. 320–71. Hamtramck is a separately incorporated municipality within the boundaries of Detroit.

10. Federal Home Loan Bank Board, "Summary of Economic, Real Estate, and Mortgage Survey and Security Area Descriptions of Greater Detroit, Michigan," hereafter referred to as "Security Area Descriptions," HOLC, Box 18, Area A-1 (Palmer Woods), Area A-6 (Chalmers Park), Area B-6 (Rosedale Park).

11. On Brightmoor, see *Brightmoor: A Community in Action* (Detroit: Brightmoor Community Center, 1940), 1–8.

12. Interview with Mike Kerwin, in *Detroit Lives*, ed. Robert H. Mast (Philadelphia: Temple University Press, 1994), 224.

13. Bruce Nelson, "Organized Labor and the Struggle for Black Equality in Mobile During World War II," *Journal of American History* 80 (1993): 952–88; "largest Southern city": *Pittsburgh Courier* (Detroit edition), April 5, 1947.

14. National Urban League Department of Research, "Observations of Conditions Among Negroes in the Fields of Education, Recreation and Employment in Selected Areas of the City of Detroit, Michigan," June 1941, 6–7, in DUL, Box 74, Folder: History. On the naming of Paradise Valley, see Gloster Current, "Paradise Valley: A Famous and Colorful Part of Detroit as Seen Through the Eyes of an Insider," *Detroit*, June 1946, 32–34. Overviews of black Detroit before and after the Great Migration include David M. Katzman, *Before the Ghetto: Black Detroit in the Nineteenth Century* (Urbana: University of Illinois Press, 1973), especially 53–80, on residential patterns; Richard W. Thomas, "From Peasant to Proletarian: The Formation and Organization of the Black Industrial Working Class in Detroit, 1915–1945" (Ph.D. diss., University of Michigan, 1976); Richard W. Thomas, *Life for Us is What We Make It: Building Black Community in Detroit, 1915–1945* (Bloomington: Indiana University Press, 1992); David Allen Levine, *Internal Combustion: The Races in Detroit, 1915–1926* (Westport, Conn.: Greenwood Press, 1976); Zunz, *The Changing Face of Inequality*, 372–98; Dominic J. Capeci, Jr., *Race Relations in Wartime Detroit: The Sojourner Truth Housing Controversy of 1942* (Philadelphia: Temple University Press, 1984), 3–8.

15. For examples of housing tensions in the 1920s, see Robert W. Bagnall, "Michigan—The Land of Many Waters," *The Messenger*, April 1926, 101–2, 123; the best discussion of the Sweet case is Levine, *Internal Combustion*, 158–98.

16. For a comparison of Detroit and other cities, see Appendix B.

17. M. Geraldine Bledsoe, "Service Occupations: Domestic and Personal—Hotel and Restaurant—Building and Custodial," in "Report for Michigan State Conference on Employment Problems," 44–49, VF—Pre 1960s, Box 4, Folder: Fair Employment Practices 1940s; Sixth Civilian Defense Region, "Report of Survey of Race Relations in Detroit," September 11, 1943, 2–3, copy in NAACP, Group II, Box A505, Folder: Racial Tension, Detroit, MI, 1943.

18. Bledsoe, "Service Occupations," 47. For similar patterns in Washington, D.C., see Elizabeth Clark-Lewis, *Living in, Living Out: African American Domestics in Washington, D.C., 1910–1940* (Washington, D.C.: Smithsonian Institution Press, 1994). The number of black women in service employment in Detroit fell from 79 percent in 1940 to 57 percent in 1950; the number in factory work rose from 9 percent to 20 percent in the same period. See Appendix B, Table B.2.

19. Lloyd H. Bailer, "The Negro Automobile Worker," *Journal of Political Economy* 51 (1943): 416–17.

20. For a series of letters regarding employment of blacks, see F. Ricksford Meyers to D. J. Marshall, Ford Motor Company, February 5, 1940, April 2, 1940, April 8, 1940, June 3, 1940 (2 letters), June 17, 1940 (2 letters), June 18, 1940, June 24, 1940; Meyers to Frederick Searle, Ford Motor Company, September 9, 1940;

Meyers to Mr. Judson, Timken-Detroit Axle Company, October 25, 1940, all in SMSJ. For an example of a black recruited to Ford, see interview with Walter Rosser, in *Untold Tales, Unsung Heroes: An Oral History of Detroit's African American Community, 1918–1967*, ed. Elaine Latzman Moon (Detroit: Wayne State University Press, 1994), 139–40. On the history of the relationship of black churches to the automobile industry, see Thomas, *Life for Us Is What We Make It*, 272–77; Meier and Rudwick, *Black Detroit*, 9–11. A detailed economic study of black workers at Ford is Thomas N. Maloney and Warren C. Whatley, "Making the Effort: The Contours of Racial Discrimination in Detroit's Labor Markets, 1920–1940," *Journal of Economic History* 55 (1995): 465–93. Ford's public relations with blacks remained positive well into the 1950s because of its early efforts to hire blacks. See for example, A.L. Foster, "This is Detroit," *Color*, July 1948; "The Negro and Henry Ford," *Our World*, December 1953, 44–55.

21. Field Report to Robert C. Weaver from William E. Hill, June 1, 1945, p. 4, in NAACP, Group II, Box A505, Folder: Racial Tension, Detroit, Mich., 1944–46.

22. Meier and Rudwick, *Black Detroit*, 34–222. There is no comprehensive overview of CIO racial practices, but a starting point is Michael Goldfield, "Race and the CIO: Possibilities for Racial Egalitarianism during the 1930s and 1940s," *International Labor and Working-Class History* 44 (1993): 1–32. The piece should be read in conjunction with the critical responses to it by Gary Gerstle, Robert Korstad, Marshall Stevenson, and Judith Stein, ibid., 33–63.

23. Meier and Rudwick, *Black Detroit*, 3–33.

24. For an overview of wartime antidiscrimination efforts, see Metropolitan Detroit Fair Employment Practice Council, "In Support of Fair Employment Practice, January 1942–December 1945," DUL, Box 21, Folder 21–5. On the role of unions, see Meier and Rudwick, *Black Detroit*; Alan Clive, *State of War: Michigan in World War II* (Ann Arbor: University of Michigan Press, 1979), 131–32, 137, 141–42; and Robert Korstad and Nelson Lichtenstein, "Opportunities Found and Lost: Labor Radicals and the Early Civil Rights Movement," *Journal of American History* 75 (1988): 786–811. On similar campaigns in other cities, see Merl Reed, "Black Workers, Defense Industries, and Federal Agencies in Pennsylvania," *Labor History* 27 (1986): 356–84; Cheryl Lynn Greenberg, *Or Does It Explode: Black Harlem in the Great Depression* (New York: Oxford University Press, 1991), 198–210; Earl Lewis, *In Their Own Interests: Race, Class, and Power in Twentieth-Century Norfolk, Virginia* (Berkeley: University of California Press, 1991), 173–87.

25. On the history of the wartime FEPC, see Louis Ruchames, *Race, Jobs, and Politics: The Story of FEPC* (New York: Columbia University Press, 1951); and Herbert Garfinkle, *When Negroes March: The March on Washington Movement in the Organizational Politics for FEPC* (Glencoe, Ill.: Free Press, 1959).

26. *Pittsburgh Courier* (Detroit edition), January 16, 1943; Robert C. Weaver, "Detroit and Negro Skill," *Phylon* 4 (1943): 131. Meier and Rudwick, *Black Detroit*, 108–74, trace the history of the wartime struggle against discrimination in Detroit, and offer dozens of examples of the reluctance of FEPC officials to intervene aggressively in discrimination cases in Detroit plants. Still, they note that by 1943 "striking improvement" in fair employment practices came about "through the determined and sustained efforts of the reorganized and rejuvenated FEPC" (172). See also Clive, *State of War*, 134–36, 144.

27. Lists of "Total Number of Negroes Employed," November 1942, April 21, 1943, October 1941–November 1944; "Employment of Negroes in Detroit," January 1943; "Negro Employment in Detroit Area," December 12, 1944 all in UAW-RD, Box 9, Folder 9–24; interview with James Boggs, in Moon, *Untold Tales, Unsung Heroes*, 152.

28. The best discussions of women's work during the war are Ruth Milkman, *Gender at Work: The Dynamics of Job Segregation by Sex during World War II* (Urbana: University of Illinois Press, 1987); Nancy F. Gabin, *Feminism in the Labor Movement: Women and the United Autoworkers, 1935–1975* (Ithaca, N.Y.: Cornell University Press, 1990), 47–110; Clive, *State of War*, 185–213; Alice Kessler-Harris, *Out to Work: A History of Wage-Earning Women in the United States* (New York: Oxford University Press, 1982), 273–99; Susan M. Hartmann, *The Home Front and Beyond: American Women in the 1940s* (Boston: Twayne Publishers, 1982); and Karen Anderson, *Wartime Women: Sex Roles, Family Relations, and the Status of Women During World War II* (Westport, Conn.: Greenwood Press, 1981).

29. "Employment of Negroes in Detroit," January 1943; *Michigan Chronicle*, November 7, 1942, November 14, 1942, January 16, 1943, September 12, 1943; *Pittsburgh Courier* (Detroit edition), August 29, 1942, December 12, 1942, April 10, 1943, Bailer, "The Negro Automobile Worker," 426–27; conversation with Ray Hatcher, September 25, 1943, in "Survey of Racial and Religious Conflicts in Detroit," CRC, Box 71; Robert C. Weaver, *Negro Labor: A National Problem* (New York: Harcourt, Brace, and World, 1946), 81, 285–86; Meier and Rudwick, *Black Detroit*, 136–38, 147–54, 166; Gabin, *Feminism in the Labor Movement*, 78–79; Milkman, *Gender at Work*, 55–56. On the number of black women operatives, see below, Appendix B, Table B.2; on the proportion of black to white women in operative jobs, see Appendix B, Table B.4.

30. Arthur Bray, "The Tempo of Detroit Life," July 1943, reprinted in *Michigan Voices: Our State's History in the Words of the People Who Lived It*, ed. Joe Grimm (Detroit: Detroit Free Press and Wayne State University Press, 1987), 168; Clive, *State of War*, 156.

31. On Sojourner Truth and other wartime housing disputes see Chapter 3; see also Capeci, *Race Relations*. On hate strikes, see Weaver, "Detroit and Negro Skill," 36–43; Lloyd Bailer, "Automobile Unions and Negro Labor," *Political Science Quarterly* 59 (1944): 568–75; Meier and Rudwick, *Black Detroit*, 125–36, 162–74.

32. "Detroit is Dynamite," *Life*, August 17, 1942, 15. See, for example, Richard Polenberg, *War and Society: The United States, 1941–1945* (New York: J. D. Lippincott, 1972), 120–22, 126–30; Harvard Sitkoff, "Racial Militancy and Interracial Violence in the Second World War," *Journal of American History* 58 (1971): 661–81; Robin D. G. Kelley, "We are Not What We Seem: Black Working-Class Opposition in the Jim Crow South," ibid., 80 (1993): 102–10; Bruce Nelson, "Organized Labor and the Struggle for Black Equality in Mobile During World War II," ibid., 952–88; Dominic Capeci, Jr., *The Harlem Riot of 1943* (Philadelphia: Temple University Press, 1977).

33. Alfred McClung Lee and Norman Daymond Humphrey, *Race Riot* (New York: Dryden Press, 1943); Meier and Rudwick, *Black Detroit*, 192–97; Robert Shogan and Tom Craig, *The Detroit Riot: A Study in Violence* (Philadelphia: Chilton Books, 1964); Harvard Sitkoff, "Detroit Race Riot of 1943," *Michigan History* 53

(Fall 1969): 183–206; B. J. Widick, *Detroit: City of Race and Class Violence* (Chicago: Quadrangle, 1972), 99–112; Clive, *State of War*, 157–62; Dominic Capeci and Martha Wilkerson, *Layered Violence: The Detroit Rioters of 1943* (Jackson: University Press of Mississippi, 1991), esp. 3–31.

34. Weaver, "Detroit and Negro Skill," 31–43; Jacqueline Jones, *The Dispossessed: America's Underclasses from the Civil War to the Present* (New York: Basic Books, 1992), esp. 205–65; on the poverty rate among blacks in the South, see Mark Stern, "Poverty and Family Composition Since 1940," in *The "Underclass" Debate: Views from History*, ed. Michael B. Katz (Princeton, N.J.: Princeton University Press, 1993), 236.

35. "Postwar Trends in Detroit's Labor Force," *Michigan's Labor Market* (February 1949), 3; see also Clive, *State of War*, 227.

36. On the formation of the Mayor's Interracial Committee, see material in CCR, Part I, Series 1, Box 1; see also Alfred McClung Lee and Norman Daymond Humphrey, "The Interracial Committee of the City of Detroit: A Case History," *Journal of Educational Sociology* 19 (1946): 278–88; Tyrone Tillery, *The Conscience of a City: A Commemorative History of the Detroit Human Rights Commission and Department, 1943–1983* (Detroit: Detroit Human Rights Department, 1983); Robert A. Burnham, "The Mayor's Friendly Relations Committee: Cultural Pluralism and the Struggle for Black Advancement," in *Race and the City: Work, Community, and Protest in Cincinnati, 1820–1970*, ed. Henry Louis Taylor, Jr. (Urbana: University of Illinois Press, 1993), 258–79.

37. Meier and Rudwick, *Black Detroit*; Korstad and Lichtenstein, "Opportunities Found and Lost," 786–811.

Chapter 2
"Detroit's Time Bomb": Race and Housing in the 1940s

1. Mrs. Ethel L. Johnson to Governor G. Mennen Williams, GMW, Box 4, Folder: Housing 1949 (1); Robert Conot, *American Odyssey* (New York: Bantam, 1975), 522–25.

2. On the desire of Detroit blacks for homeownership, see National Urban League, Department of Research, "Observations of Conditions Among Negroes in the Fields of Education, Recreation and Employment in Selected Areas of the City of Detroit," June 1941, 6–8, in DUL, Box 74, Folder: History. Quote from interview with Charles Butler, in *Detroit Lives*, ed. Robert H. Mast (Philadelphia: Temple University Press, 1994), 191. On black aspirations to home and landownership, see Leon Litwack, *Been in the Storm So Long: The Aftermath of Slavery* (New York: Pantheon, 1979), 401; James Grossman, *Land of Hope: Chicago, Black Southerners, and the Great Migration* (Chicago: University of Chicago Press, 1989), 21–26, 33–34; John Bodnar, Roger Simon, and Michael Weber, *Lives of Their Own: Blacks, Italians, and Poles in Pittsburgh, 1900–1960* (Urbana: University of Illinois Press, 1982), 154–83, 255–59. Bodnar et al. downplay black aspirations to homeownership (154, 256), but they draw their evidence from only one interview.

3. Gloster Current, "Paradise Valley: A Famous and Colorful Part of Detroit as Seen Through the Eyes of An Insider," *Detroit*, June 1946, 32, 34; Walter White

noted the irony of the name Paradise Valley in "How Detroit Fights Race Hatred," *Saturday Evening Post*, July 18, 1953, 26.

4. David Katzman, *Before the Ghetto: Black Detroit in the Nineteenth Century* (Urbana: University of Illinois Press, 1973), 80. U.S. Department of Commerce, Bureau of the Census, *Census of Population, 1950, Census Tract Statistics for Detroit, Michigan and Adjacent Area*, vol. 2, part 24 (Washington, D.C.: U.S. Government Printing Office, 1952), Table 1, data for tracts 508, 528, 529, 534, 535, 536, 537, 543, 544, 547. (Hereafter referred to as *1950 Census*.)

5. Detroit Housing Commission and Works Progress Administration, *Real Property Survey of Detroit, Michigan*, vol. 2 (Detroit: Bureau of Governmental Research, 1939), data for tracts 508, 528, 529, 534, 535, 536, 537, 543, 544, 547; for definitions of "substandard," see vol. 1, pp. 33–34. (Hereafter referred to as *Real Property Survey*.) See also Alfred McClung Lee and Norman D. Humphrey, *Race Riot: Detroit 1943* (New York: Octagon Books, 1968), 93; *Detroit Tribune*, July 3, 1943.

6. *Detroit Free Press*, April 9, 1950.

7. "Report of the Executive Secretary, Detroit Branch, NAACP," May 9, 1944–August 1, 1944, 3–4, in NAACP, Group II, Box 87, Folder: Detroit, Aug.–Sept. 1944. Unidentified clipping, February 16, 1945, in CHPC, Box 50, Folder: Clippings, 1944–45. The article "City's 'Rat Belt' Residents Fight Losing Battle," describes the belt as the area bounded by Warren on the north, Monroe on the south, Dequindre on the east, and Beaubien on the west. *Detroit Free Press*, August 23, 1953. The rat problem did not abate: see "The Rat Bit a City's Conscience," ibid., April 29, 1956.

8. The most thorough discussion of enclaves of black homeowners is Henry Louis Taylor, Jr., "City Building, Public Policy, the Rise of the Industrial City, and Black Ghetto-Slum Formation in Cincinnati," in *Race and the City: Work, Community, and Protest in Cincinnati, 1820–1970* (Urbana: University of Illinois Press, 1993), 175–76. A glimpse at maps of black residence in several northern cities reveals the existence of small black concentrations, most of which have not been examined historically. See Arnold Hirsch, *Making the Second Ghetto: Race and Housing in Chicago, 1940–1960* (Cambridge: Cambridge University Press, 1983), 6; Bodnar, Simon, and Weber, *Lives of Their Own*, 275; and Laurence Glasco, "Internally Divided: Class and Neighborhood in Black Pittsburgh." *Amerikastudien* 34 (1989): 223–30; Kenneth L. Kusmer, *A Ghetto Takes Shape: Black Cleveland, 1870–1930* (Urbana: University of Illinois Press, 1976), insert between 146 and 147. Thomas L. Philpott, *The Slum and the Ghetto: Neighborhood Deterioration and Neighborhood Reform, Chicago 1880–1930* (New York: Oxford University Press, 1978), 181–83 offers a brief discussion of Chicago's "pocket ghettoes." James Grossman, *Land of Hope: Chicago, Black Southerners, and the Great Migration* (Chicago: University of Chicago Press, 1989), 139, offers a brief discussion of "old settlers" who fled the incursion of black migrants in Chicago by moving to Morgan Park on Chicago's far South Side, and other middle-class blacks who fled to the periphery of the black South Side.

9. Forrester B. Washington, "The Negro in Detroit: A Survey of the Conditions of a Negro Group in a Northern Industrial Center during the War Prosperity Period" (Detroit, 1920), DPL; John C. Dancy, *Sand Against the Wind: The Memoirs of John C. Dancy* (Detroit: Wayne State University Press, 1966), 58–59. Olivier Zunz is

skeptical of the existence of a black middle class in Detroit in the 1920s, and finds Washington's account of black homeownership in the Tireman–Grand Boulevard area exaggerated: *The Changing Face of Inequality: Urbanization, Industrial Development, and Immigrants in Detroit, 1880–1920* (Chicago: University of Chicago Press, 1982), 393–98, esp. 397.

10. Area Description, Security Map of Detroit, Michigan, Area No. D-28, March 1, 1939, Division of Research and Statistics, Federal Home Loan Bank Board, City Survey, Metropolitan Detroit, HOLC, Box 17.

11. *Real Property Survey*, vol. 2, data for tracts 13–15, 118–121.

12. Bette Smith Jenkins, "The Racial Policies of the Detroit Housing Commission and Their Administration" (M.A. thesis, Wayne State University, 1951), 33–35; *Pittsburgh Courier* (Detroit edition), December 11, 1948.

13. On the founding of the Eight Mile area, see "A Short History of the Community," in NAACP, Group II, Box A505, Folder: Racial Tension, Detroit, Michigan, 1945–46; "Housing Survey, 1952," 2, DUL, Box 43, Folder A7–12; Dancy, *Sand Against the Wind*, 57–58; *Michigan Chronicle*, April 22, 1944.

14. Burneice Avery, "The Eight Mile Road . . . Its Growth . . . 1920–1952," BA, Box 1, Folder 1: "A Short History of the Community," 1. On the dual housing market, see Zunz, *The Changing Face of Inequality*, 161–76.

15. Marvel Daines, "Be It Ever So Tumbled—The Story of a Suburban Slum," (1940), 23, 29, 40, CHPC, Box 48.

16. Ibid., 23, 28, 38–39.

17. *Real Property Survey*, data for tract 305.

18. *1950 Census*, vol. 2, part 22. The Bureau of the Census did not publish tract-level income data in 1940.

19. Dominic J. Capeci, Jr., *Race Relations in Wartime Detroit: The Sojourner Truth Housing Controversy of 1942* (Philadelphia: Temple University Press, 1984), 76–77; Joseph Coles, oral history, interviewed by Roberta McBride and Jim Keeney, 12, Blacks in the Labor Movement Collection, ALUA; Gloster Current, oral history, interviewed by John Britton, 8, Civil Rights Documentation Project, MSRC. Interview with Robert Bynum, Jr., in *Untold Tales, Unsung Heroes: An Oral History of Detroit's African American Community, 1918–1967*, ed. Elaine Latzman Moon (Detroit: Wayne State University Press, 1994), 199.

20. U.S. Congress, Joint Committee on Housing, *Study and Investigation of Housing, Hearings, Proceedings at Detroit, Michigan, October 22, 1947*, 80th Congress, 1st sess., 1948, 413–16, 419, 479.

21. On the national dimensions of the housing crisis, see "The Great Housing Shortage," *Life*, December 17, 1945, 27–36; "Housing," *Fortune*, April 1946, esp. 101–32; "The Housing Mess," ibid., January 1947, 81–93.

22. Citizens Housing and Planning Council of Detroit, Annual Report, 1944, in CHPC, Box 1. See also "The Current Racial Situation in Detroit," August 6, 1945, NAACP, Group II, Box A505, Folder: Racial Tension, Detroit, 1944–46.

23. Field Report to Robert C. Weaver from William E. Hill, June 1, 1945, p. 6, ibid.; Lee and Humphrey, *Race Riot*, 93.

24. James Sweinhart, "What Detroit's Slums Cost Its Taxpayers" (Detroit: Detroit News Reprints, 1946), in CHPC, Box 73, Folder: Racial Relations.

25. *Michigan Chronicle*, March 25, 1944, May 6, 1944.

26. Housing and Home Finance Agency, "The Housing of Negro Veterans: Their Housing Plans and Living Arrangements in 32 Areas," January 1948, Table 11, in CHPC, Box 60, Folder: Negro Housing.

27. Lena Williams to Governor G. Mennen Williams, March 1, 1949, in GMW, Box 4, Folder: Housing 1949 (3).

28. "The Housing of Negro Veterans," Table 8B.

29. Testimony of George Edwards to Joint Committee on Housing, *Study and Investigation*, 396.

30. Ibid., 426–27.

31. "Analysis of Certain Racial Aspects of the Present Detroit Slum Clearance, Redevelopment and Public Housing Program," April 5, 1951, 1, CHPC, Box 41.

32. Resume—Group Meeting, September 14, 1950, attached to letter of George Schermer to Mayor Albert Cobo, March 27, 1951, in Mayor's Papers, Box 4 (1951), Folder: Interracial Committee (2).

33. Memorandum on Negro Veterans' Housing in the Detroit Area, February 18, 1948, HOLC, Box 9, Folder: Economists' Reports on Housing, March 1948–September 1950; see also "Analysis of Certain Racial Aspects," 2.

34. Summary of Economic, Real Estate and Mortgage Survey and Security Area Descriptions of Greater Detroit, Michigan, 2–4, in FHLBS, Box 18. Other studies that have used these records include Kenneth T. Jackson, "Race, Ethnicity, and Real Estate Appraisal: The Home Owners Loan Corporation and the Federal Housing Administration," *Journal of Urban History* 6 (1980): 419–52; and Raymond A. Mohl, "Trouble in Paradise: Race and Housing in Miami during the New Deal Era," *Prologue* 19 (1987): 7–21.

35. "City Survey, Metropolitan Detroit, Michigan," June 30, 1939, Division of Research and Statistics, Federal Home Loan Bank Board, City Survey, Metropolitan Detroit, FHLBS, Box 17. John C. Feild, oral history (interviewed by Katherine Shannon, December 28, 1967), 36, in Civil Rights Documentation Project, MSRC. Feild is incorrectly identified as Fields in the typescript. For a discussion of the long-term impact of FHA and HOLC practices in Philadelphia, see David W. Bartelt, "Housing the 'Underclass,'" in *The "Underclass" Debate: Views from History*, ed. Michael B. Katz (Princeton, N.J.: Princeton University Press, 1993), 118–57.

36. On covenants generally, see Marc Weiss, *The Rise of the Community Builders: The American Real Estate Industry and Urban Land Planning* (New York: Columbia University Press, 1987), 68–72; Patricia Burgess Stach, "Deed Restrictions and Subdivision Development in Columbus, Ohio, 1900–1970," *Journal of Urban History* 15 (1988): 42–68.

37. Harold Black, "Restrictive Covenants in Relation to Segregated Negro Housing in Detroit" (M.A. thesis, Wayne University, 1947), 6, 42; Clement Vose, *Caucasians Only: The Supreme Court, the NAACP, and the Restrictive Covenant Cases* (Berkeley: University of California Press, 1959), 125–26.

38. *Detroit Tribune*, August 10, 1940. For an example of residents of an unrestricted subdivision signing restrictive covenants, see "Statement by Allen V. Brett Relative to Proposed Restrictions Against Negroes in the Eason Palmer Park Subdivision," December 6, 1945, CCR, Part III, Box 25, Folder 25–36. "Stop Paying Rent: Sign a Lifetime Lease on Happiness," n.d. [1945] in CHPC, Box 16, Folder: Statements of Availability. On the role of real estate agents in the creation of neighborhood

improvement associations, see Herman H. Long and Charles S. Johnson, *People vs. Property: Race Restrictive Covenants in Housing* (Nashville: Fisk University Press, 1947), 67–69, Charles Abrams, *Forbidden Neighbors: A Study of Prejudice in Housing* (New York: Harper, 1955), 182–85.

39. A copy of the restriction agreement for the Boston-Edison neighborhood can be found in BEP, Box 1, Folder 1–1. The case discussed is *Boston Edison Protective Association v. Home Owners' Loan Corporation and Maurice Trimble*, State of Michigan in the Circuit Court for the County of Wayne in Chancery, No. 354,469, October 25, 1944, ibid., Box 8, Folder 4.

40. Before 1948, courts often struck down restrictive covenants on narrow grounds, for example the precedent of a black family inhabiting an allegedly re-stricted area, or the lack of signatures of a majority of area residents on covenants. See Capeci, *Race Relations*, 34–35. For an example of a case where a racially restric-tive covenant was upheld, see *Northwest Civic Association v. Sheldon*, State of Mich-igan in the Circuit Court for the County of Wayne in Chancery, No. 377,790, April 5, 1946; copy in CRC, Box 65, Folder: Negro Discrimination 1945–46. An overview of court opinions on restrictive covenants in Detroit can be found in Gloster Current to Shirley Adelson, July 12, 1946, NAACP, Group II, Box B135, Folder: Sipes v. McGhee, 1946; Memorandum to Mr [Thurgood] Marshall from Marian Wynn Perry, May 1, 1946, NAACP, Group II, Box B74, Folder: Legal, Detroit, Mich., General 1946, 1947.

41. Report on Meeting, Detroit Mayor's Interracial Committee, 5, CCR, Part I, Series 1, Box 5, Folder: 48–124 H.

42. William V. Louks to Edward Connor, March 14, 1950, CHPC, Box 60, Folder: Detroit Real Estate Board; Quotes from *East Sider* newspaper, July 1956, in "Detroit Area Study Paper," n.d., DUL, Box 70, Folder: Housing General (2). For a vivid description of DREB practices, see B. J. Widick, *Detroit: City of Race and Class Violence* (Chicago: Quadrangle, 1972), 144–48. The Neighborhood Property Stabili-zation Committee of the Federated Property Owners of Detroit called for intimida-tion of white real estate brokers who sold homes to blacks, see *Michigan Chronicle*, December 4, 1948; for an example of harassment of a real estate broker who sold to blacks, see "Protest of Negro Occupancy at 18087 Shields (September 1949)," CCR, Part I, Series 1, Box 6, File 49–33.

43. "Report on Meeting," ibid., Box 5, Folder: 48–124H; Detroit Urban League Speech, n.d. [c. 1959], DUL, Box 44, Folder A8–1, MHC; Testimony of Mel J. Ravitz, *Hearings Before the United States Commission on Civil Rights Held in Detroit, Mich-igan, December 14–15, 1960* (Washington, D.C.: U.S. Government Printing Office, 1961), 212, 222. On land contracts, see Chapter 7.

44. Robert J. Mowitz and Deil S. Wright, *Profile of a Metropolis: A Case Book* (Detroit: Wayne State University Press, 1962), 405, 412. Detroit planners were care-ful to note that expressway construction would only minimally interfere with the operation of the central business district. Another principle in the choice of highway sites was "maintaining compact neighborhoods and communities unbroken by major traffic channels." Yet in the case of black neighborhoods, such principles were disre-garded. See Detroit City Plan Commission, *The Planner*, March 1945, 1–2, ibid. September 1945, 4–5, in possession of the author. For a discussion of similar issues

in other cities, see Ronald Bayor, "Roads to Racial Segregation: Atlanta in the Twentieth Century," *Journal of Urban History* 15 (1988): 3–21; and Raymond A. Mohl, "Race and Space in the Modern City: Interstate-95 and the Black Community in Miami," in *Urban Policy in Twentieth-Century America* (New Brunswick, N.J.: Rutgers University Press, 1993), 100–158.

45. The Master Plan of Detroit stated: "Wherever possible, the expressways will be routed along belts of industry. Thus they will avoid carrying heavy traffic through residential neighborhoods, and at the same time serve as buffer strips, separating industrial installations from residential areas." City of Detroit, *Proposed System of Trafficways, Master Plan Report No. 4* (Detroit: Detroit City Plan Commission, December 1946), 10, in GMW, Box 2, Folder: Detroit 1949. The earliest expressway plans for the city were considered by the Detroit City Plan Commission in 1943: see City Plan Commission Minutes, September 23, 1943, vol. 11, 131, DPL; Committee of Management Meeting, St. Antoine Branch, April 1, 1959, YMCA of Metropolitan Detroit Collection, Box 5, MHC; *Detroit News*, April 26, 1960.

46. Ed Davis, *One Man's Way* (Detroit: Edward Davis Associates, 1979), 96–97; *Michigan Chronicle*, November 26, 1955; *Detroit Free Press*, July 25, 1950; Minutes, Relocation Advisory Council, February 26, 1958, DUL, Box 42, Folder A6–6; Report on Expressway Displacement, June 7, 1950, ibid., Box 41, Folder A4–18; "Profile of Critical Problems Facing Negro People in the Detroit Community," April 18, 1959, ibid., Box 39, Folder A3-14.

47. William Price, "The Magnitude of the Relocation Problem," November 21, 1950, 4, DUL, Box 38, Folder A2–1; Summary Report of Community Services Department, July 1952, ibid., Folder A2–7; Maceo Crutcher to Harry Durbin, May 12, 1950, UAW-PAC, Box 64, Folder 64–12.

48. Petition to Governor G. Mennen Williams from several Detroit residents, May 4, 1950, GMW, Box 27, Folder: Detroit 1950; Harvey Royal to G. Mennen Williams, May 4, 1950, ibid.

49. Maud W. Cain to G. Mennen Williams, September 13, 1951, ibid., Box 49, Folder: Housing A-I.

50. *Detroit Free Press*, March 16, 1954.

51. V. S. Stryjak, paraphrased in Relocation Advisory Council Minutes, February 26, 1958, DUL, Box 42, Folder A6–6.

52. For a national perspective on urban redevelopment projects, see Jon C. Teaford, *Rough Road to Renaissance: Urban Revitalization in America* (Baltimore: Johns Hopkins University Press, 1990), esp. 10–167. On urban redevelopment in Detroit, see Conot, *American Odyssey*, 514–21, 536–38, 573–75; Mowitz and Wright, *Profile of a Metropolis*, 11–139; Joe T. Darden et al., *Detroit: Race and Uneven Development* (Philadelphia: Temple University Press, 1987), 155–74; June Manning Thomas, "Detroit: The Centrifugal City," in *Unequal Partnerships: The Political Economy of Urban Development in Postwar America*, ed. Gregory D. Squires (New Brunswick, N.J.: Rutgers University Press, 1989), 142–60; June Manning Thomas, "Neighborhood Response to Redevelopment in Detroit," *Community Development Journal* 20 (1985): 89–98.

53. Mowitz and Wright, *Profile of a Metropolis*, 13–27; see Detroit Housing Commission, "The Detroit Plan: A Program for Blight Elimination," February 18, 1947,

and Detroit Housing Commission, "The Detroit Plan: A Private Enterprise Redevelopment Project," 1949, both in CHPC, Box 73, File: Racial Relations.

54. *Detroit Free Press*, April 13, 1950; *East Side Shopper*, July 6, 1950; Astrid Monson, "Slum Clearance, Public Housing, and a Municipal Land Policy," September 1949, mimeograph in CHPC, Box 81.

55. Hearing before the Common Council, April 6, 1951, 6, DUL, Box 38, File A2–2; Mowitz and Wright, *Profile of a Metropolis*, 36.

56. William Price, "The Magnitude of the Relocation Problem," November 21, 1950, DUL, Box 38, Folder A2–1; see also Mowitz and Wright, *Profile of a Metropolis*, 34–35, 38.

57. Community Organization Advisory Committee Minutes, January 25, 1951, DUL, Box 38, Folder A2–2.

58. William Price, "Supplementary Information Presented Before the City of Detroit Common Council," April 6, 1951, ibid.; Minutes of Meeting Held in Store Front Baptist Church at 648 Adelaide, April 13, 1950, ibid.

59. Detroit Housing Commission officials were loath to be assigned to the Relocation Office, because it was it was a division of the Tenant Selection Office, which atrophied in significance during the anti–public housing Cobo administration. See Mowitz and Wright, *Profile of a Metropolis*, 35. For an example of a tenant who faced the apathy of the Relocation Office, see Willie Mae Johnson to William Price, October 31, 1951 in DUL, Box 38, Folder A2–4.

60. Mowitz and Wright, *Profile of a Metropolis*, 40–46; at the 1951 Common Council hearing on relocation, William Price of the DUL charged that one-third of the families relocated from the Gratiot area "have bought beyond their purchasing ability" (Price, "Supplementary Information," 4).

61. Joint Committee on Housing, *Study and Investigation*, 396; Detroit Chapter, Americans for Democratic Action, "Does Detroit Have a Housing Problem?" (1951), CHPC, Box 41.

62. "Request for Action to Board of Directors, Future Detroit, Inc., from the Housing Committee," n.d. [c. 1940s], ibid., Box 73, File: Special Committee on Housing, Metropolitan Detroit; "ill fame," *Brightmoor Journal*, March 30, 1950; "blight," ibid., February 3, 1949 (this article "Multiple Homes Here Blocked By Court: 22 Month Legal Fight Won By Northwest Residents," also reminded readers of the implications of the Supreme Court's *Shelley v. Kraemer* decision which rendered racially restrictive covenants unenforceable in court). *Shelley v. Kraemer* is discussed in greater detail in Chapter 7. Quote about "tenements" is from *Brightmoor Journal*, March 9, 1950.

63. Ibid., February 27, 1949, March 10, 1949, March 9, 1950. On April 6, 1950, the Evergreen Village Civic Association, Joy Road Community Association, and Grandale Civic Association petitioned the City Plan Commission against the rezoning of a site on Chicago and Staehlin for multiple housing, on grounds that they had bought homes in the area with the understanding that it was zoned for single-family rather than multiple-family residence: City Plan Commission, Minutes, vol. 15 (1949–50), 342–44, DPL.

64. Office of the Housing Expediter, "Housing Survey for Detroit, Michigan,"

Washington, D.C., September 1950, in CHPC, Box 41; *Detroit News*, October 29, 1950.

65. Arthur Kornhauser, *Detroit as the People See It: A Survey of Attitudes in an Industrial City* (Detroit: Wayne University Press, 1952), 75, 77–82, Table 26B, 213. For other accounts, see *East Side Shopper*, June 15, 22, 29, 1950; *Detroit News*, October 29, 1950; *Detroit Free Press*, August 20, 1953; *Detroit Free Press*, October 10, 1953.

66. Detroit Housing Commission, Monthly Report, February–March 1954, 4–5, in Mayor's Papers (1954), Box 4, Folder: Housing Commission (2).

67. Mrs. N. W. Chase to Governor G. Mennen Williams, September 27, 1950, GMW, Box 28, Folder: Housing 1950 (1).

68. Office of the Housing Expediter, Housing and Home Finance Administration, "Housing Survey for Detroit, Michigan, September 1950," 6–7, CHPC, Box 41; *Detroit News*, October 29, 1950.

69. Detroit Housing Commission, "Children Not Wanted," May 1948, CHPC, Box 81.

70. *Detroit Free Press*, August 20, 1953.

71. Essie Mae Jordon to Governor G. Mennen Williams, October 4, 1950, GMW, Box 28, Folder: Housing 1950 (1), MHC; Mary E. Felder to Williams, April 28, 1950, ibid.

72. Astrid Monson, "Slum Clearance, Public Housing, and a Municipal Land Policy," 3, September 1949, CHPC, Box 81.

73. "Arsenal of Democracy," in *Detroit Perspectives: Crossroads and Turning Points*, ed. Wilma Wood Henrickson (Detroit: Wayne State University Press, 1991), 398; interview with James Boggs, in Moon, *Untold Tales, Unsung Heroes*, 152; *Detroit Free Press*, March 13, 1952.

74. Lee and Humphrey, *Race Riot*, 116.

75. "To All My Friends from Blanche Rinehart, Re: Change of Address," August 25, 1957, NAACP, Group III, Box C64, Folder: Michigan: Detroit: Aug.–Dec. 1957; *Michigan Chronicle*, December 16, 1961; *Detroit Free Press*, February 26, 1962. For other examples, see Sylvia W. Lee to Jerome Cavanagh, August 14, 1962, in DNAACP, Part I, Box 18, Folder: Miscellaneous Material, 1962, and "Detroit Urban League Annual Report," March 1962, 3, ibid., Box 20, Folder: Urban League 1962.

76. *Report of the National Advisory Commission on Civil Disorders* (New York: Bantam Books, 1968), 471; Paul R. Dimond, *Beyond Busing: Inside the Challenge to Urban Segregation* (Ann Arbor: University of Michigan Press, 1985), 46–47.

77. *Detroit News*, May 4, 1951; *Detroit Free Press*, May 9, 1951; *Detroit Times*, May 10, 1951; *Detroit Free Press*, August 22, 1953. The article described three other landlords with abnormally high eviction rates: Sam Barak evicted twenty-six tenants in the eight-month period; David Rott evicted thirty-three; and Nathan Tarabelo evicted twenty-eight. The average rent figure in 1950 was $43.23. Figure from *1950 Census*, Table 3.

78. Community Tenants League, flyer, n.d. [c. 1961–62] in DUL, Box 44, Folder A8–18.

79. Detroit Branch NAACP, Proceedings of Housing Conference, August 29–30, 1945, 5, CHPC, Box 60.

Chapter 3
"The Coffin of Peace": The Containment
of Public Housing

1. The information about Johnson comes from Memorandum "Re Charles B. Johnson," September 25, 1945; George Schermer to Charles B. Johnson, October 1, 1945; City of Detroit Housing Commission, interoffice correspondence to George Schermer from C. J. Laurence, October 2, 1945; all in CCR, Part III, Box 27, Folder 27–1.

2. Citizens Housing and Planning Council, "Housing the Negroes is a War Measure: A Few Facts on the Present Situation," n.d. [c. 1945], copy in CRC, Box 66, Folder: Housing Conference 1945.

3. Quoted in Bette Smith Jenkins, "The Racial Policies of the Detroit Housing Commission and Their Administration" (M.A. thesis, Wayne University, 1951), 28.

4. William Price, "Housing Situation in Detroit as it Effects Minorities," June 5, 1951, DUL, Box 38, Folder A2–4, 3–4. Memorandum to Mayor's Interracial Committee from George Schermer, Re: Public Housing—Racial Occupancy Policy, September 24, 1952, 2, ibid., Box 6, Folder 6–18; Letter from William Price, Detroit Urban League, to William Hill, Federal Public Housing Administration, January 27, 1954, ibid., Box 38, Folder A2–11.

5. On the centrality of the 1940s for the coalescence of the New Deal order and for the future of American social policy, see Steve Fraser and Gary Gerstle, eds., *The Rise and Fall of the New Deal Order, 1930–1980* (Princeton, N.J.: Princeton University Press, 1989), xix.

6. Robert B. Fairbanks, *Making Better Citizens: Housing Reform and Strategy in Cincinnati, 1890–1960* (Urbana: University of Illinois Press, 1988).

7. On the background and passage of the 1937 act, see Robert Moore Fisher, *Twenty Years of Public Housing: Economic Aspects of the Federal Program* (New York: Harper, 1959), 8–12, 92–125. A superb overview of federal housing policy in the 1930s is Gail Radford, *Modern Housing for America: Policy Struggles in the New Deal Era* (Chicago: University of Chicago Press, forthcoming).

8. Richard O. Davies, *Housing Reform During the Truman Administration* (Columbia: University of Missouri Press, 1966).

9. C. Lowell Harriss, *History and Policies of the Home Owners' Loan Corporation* (New York: National Bureau of Economic Research, 1951), 9.

10. Ronald Tobey, Charles Wetherell, and Jay Brigham, "Moving Out and Settling In: Residential Mobility, Home Owning, and the Public Enframing of Citizenship, 1921–1950," *American Historical Review* 95 (1990): 1415–20.

11. There is a vast literature on the implementation of the New Deal on the state and local levels. The classic introductions are James T. Patterson, *The New Deal and the States: Federalism in Transition* (Princeton, N.J.: Princeton University Press, 1969); John A. Braeman, Robert H. Bremner, and David Brody, eds., *The New Deal*, vol 2: *The State and Local Levels* (Columbus: Ohio State University Press, 1975); on urban policy, in particular, see Philip J. Funigiello, *The Challenge to Urban Liberalism: Federal-City Relations during World War II* (Knoxville: University of Tennessee Press, 1978), and Mark Gelfand, *A Nation of Cities: The Federal Government and*

Urban America, 1933–1965 (New York: Oxford University Press, 1975), 23–156; Margaret Weir, "Urban Poverty and Defensive Localism," *Dissent,* Summer 1994, 337–42.

12. Robert J. Mowitz and Deil S. Wright, *Profile of a Metropolis: A Case Book* (Detroit: Wayne State University Press, 1962), 82, 86, 93–94.

13. My view of the role of the New Deal's constituents is informed by two important books: Lizabeth Cohen, *Making a New Deal: Industrial Workers in Chicago, 1919–1939* (New York: Cambridge University Press, 1990); and Jo Ann E. Argersinger, *Toward a New Deal in Baltimore: People and Government in the Great Depression* (Chapel Hill: University of North Carolina Press, 1988).

14. Many of the "new institutionalists," in their emphasis on the "autonomous" role of the state, have little to say about the reaction of the state's constituents in shaping the development or implementation of policy. An important revision is Theda Skocpol's "polity-centered" approach, developed in *Protecting Soldiers and Mothers: The Political Origins of Social Policy in the United States* (Cambridge, Mass.: Harvard University Press, 1992), esp. 41–57.

15. Detroit Citizens Housing and Planning Council, *Annual Report 1947,* CHPC, Box 1. On the CHPC's membership, see 1945 Statistical Report, ibid. On similar organizations elsewhere, see Jon C. Teaford, *The Rough Road to Renaissance: Urban Revitalization in America* (Baltimore: Johns Hopkins University Press, 1990), 45–54.

16. CHPC *Newsletter,* May 1939, 1, CHPC, Box 70. For a study of the ideological bases of liberal housing reform in Cincinnati (which paralleled those in Detroit), see Fairbanks, *Making Better Citizens.*

17. CHPC *Newsletter,* April 1939, 1, CHPC, Box 70.

18. Franklin Delano Roosevelt, "Message to Congress on the State of the Union," January 11, 1944, in *The Public Papers and Addresses of Franklin D. Roosevelt,* vol. 13 (New York: Harper, 1950), 41. For examples of the impact of New Deal rhetoric on working-class Detroiters in the late 1950s, see John C. Leggett, *Class, Race, and Labor: Working-Class Consciousness in Detroit* (New York: Oxford University Press, 1968), 88, 167–69; quotes from 168 and 169. On the New Deal and homeownership, see Tobey, Wetherell, and Brigham, "Moving Out and Settling In," 1395–1422, esp. 1415–20; Cohen, *Making a New Deal,* 272–77. For more elaboration on this point, see Thomas J. Sugrue, "Crabgrass-Roots Politics: Race, Rights, and the Reaction against Liberalism in the Urban North, 1940–1964," *Journal of American History* 82 (1995), 551–78.

19. On immigrants and homeownership, see for example, Olivier Zunz, *The Changing Face of Inequality: Urbanization, Industrial Development, and Immigrants in Detroit, 1880–1920* (Chicago: University of Chicago Press, 1982), 129–76; Humbert Nelli, *The Italians in Chicago, 1880–1930: A Study in Ethnic Mobility* (New York: Oxford University Press, 1970), 33–40.

20. Henry Lee Moon, "Danger in Detroit," *Crisis* 53 (January 1946): 28; Seven Mile–Fenelon Improvement Association, poster, "WE DEMAND OUR RIGHTS," CRC, Box 66, Folder: Property Owners Association. On immigrants and home-ownership in Detroit, see Zunz, *The Changing Face of Inequality,* 129–76; on the discriminatory nature of FHA and HOLC programs, see Kenneth T. Jackson, "Race, Ethnicity, and Real Estate Appraisal: The Home Owners Loan Corporation and the Federal Housing Administration," *Journal of Urban History* 6 (1980): 419–52.

21. In his pathbreaking study of race and housing in Chicago, Arnold Hirsch moves beyond the notion of the state as an all-powerful force, to examine how the actions of inner-city whites and the real estate market combined with the discriminatory policies of local reformers and the needs of local politicians to create the second ghetto. As he writes, "a perspective based in Washington, D.C. is fragmentary at best and misleading at worst." But for a book that focuses on the rise of the ghetto, Hirsch surprisingly downplays the role of urban blacks, and views them as powerless in the political battles over postwar housing. See Arnold R. Hirsch, *Making the Second Ghetto: Race and Housing in Chicago* (New York: Cambridge University Press, 1983), 269. On Hirsch's view of the black role in Chicago's public housing controversies, see ibid., xii.

22. See, for example, Allen B. Crow, president of the Economic Club of Detroit, "How Detroit Should Rehabilitate Its 'Blighted Areas,'" CRC, Box 66, Folder: Housing 1945. On New York, see Joel Schwartz, *The New York Approach: Robert Moses, Urban Liberals, and the Redevelopment of New York City* (Columbus: Ohio State University Press, 1993).

23. On the reform tradition in Detroit politics, see especially Melvin G. Holli, *Reform in Detroit: Hazen S. Pingree and Urban Politics* (New York: Oxford University Press, 1969); and Sidney Fine, *Frank Murphy: The Detroit Years* (Ann Arbor: University of Michigan Press, 1975). Detroit officials were not wholly immune to corruption, despite their the city's lack of machine politics. Richard Reading, who served as mayor from 1938 to 1940, was involved in illegal pay schemes and gambling. Reading did not, however, last in office, nor did his malfeasance have a lasting effect on Detroit's politics. See Robert Conot, *American Odyssey* (New York: William Morrow, 1974), 368–69. On the relationship of public housing to machine politics in Chicago, see Arnold R. Hirsch, "The Cook County Democratic Organization and the Dilemmas of Race," in *Snowbelt Cities: Metropolitan Politics in the Northeast and Midwest Since World War II*, ed. Richard M. Bernard (Bloomington: Indiana University Press, 1990), 77; in Pittsburgh, see Michael Weber, *Don't Call Me Boss: David L. Lawrence, Pittsburgh's Renaissance Mayor* (Pittsburgh: University of Pittsburgh Press, 1988).

24. *Real Property Survey of Detroit, Michigan*, vol. 2 (Sponsored by the Detroit Housing Commission as a Report on Official Project No. 665–51–3–124, Conducted under the Auspices of the Work Projects Administration), (Detroit: Bureau of Governmental Research, 1939), 186; Marvel Daines, "Be It Ever So Tumbled—The Story of a Suburban Slum" (1940), 6–16, CHPC, Box 48.

25. The Home Owners' Loan Corporation appraiser rated the Eight Mile area as "D" or "hazardous." See "Security Area Map, Detroit, Michigan," and "Area Description," Area No. D-7," FHLBS Box 18; See also Burneice Avery, "The Eight Mile Road . . . Its Growth . . . 1920–1952," 3, BA, Box 1, Folder 1. The wall is also depicted on a map in NAACP, Group II, Box A 505, Folder: Racial Tension, Detroit, Michigan, 1945–1946. For a photograph of the wall, see Burneice Avery, *Walk Quietly Through the Night and Cry Softly* (Detroit: Balamp Publishers, 1977), 190. The wall still stands today, although by the early 1950s, blacks had crossed it into the previously all-white neighborhood on the other side.

26. Avery, "The Eight Mile Road," 5–6; Nancy J. Weiss, *Farewell to the Party of Lincoln: Black Politics in the Age of FDR* (Princeton, N.J.: Princeton University Press, 1983), 205–6.

27. On Avery's background, see *Detroit Tribune*, June 7, 1952; *Pittsburgh Courier* (Detroit edition), October 10, 1953; *Detroit Free Press*, November 30, 1987.

28. Burneice Avery, "Never All (Detroit) 1941–1953," 2, 4–5, in BA, Box 1, File: Literary Works—2.

29. On Foley, see *Michigan Chronicle*, January 13, 1940, January 27, 1940; see also Dominic J. Capeci, Jr., *Race Relations in Wartime Detroit: The Sojourner Truth Housing Controversy of 1942* (Philadelphia: Temple University Press, 1984), 35.

30. Avery, "The Eight Mile Road," 8, 10; Detroit City Plan Commission Minutes, vol. 11 (1942–43), 118, DPL.

31. Daines, "Be It Ever So Tumbled," 2.

32. Ibid., 48–51.

33. Detroit City Plan Commission Minutes, vol. 10 (1941–42), 103, 232–33, 242, 300, 313, 328, 358, DPL. On the 1945 proposal, see Mowitz and Wright, *Profile of a Metropolis*, 299–311.

34. The City Plan Commmission considered the future of the Eight Mile area as early as 1940; City Plan Commission Minutes, vol. 9 (1940), 200, DPL. For an early proposal of a master plan, see ibid., 308.

35. Minutes of the Subcommittee on Housing for Negro Occupancy, October 27, 1943, CHPC, Box 41.

36. City Plan Commission Minutes, vol. 9 (1940), 200, DPL; ibid., vol. 10 (1941–42), 38, 97, 387.

37. Ibid., vol. 11 (1943–44), 57, 93, 110.

38. Ibid., 84.

39. Ibid., 116–19; *Michigan Chronicle*, October 23, 1943.

40. City Plan Commission Minutes, vol. 11 (1943–44), 116–19, DPL; Avery, "The Eight Mile Road," 9–11; *Michigan Chronicle*, April 22, 1944.

41. On union support for public housing, see telegram to CHPC from William Nicholson, October 26, 1943, CHPC, Box 41. In September 1943, the representatives of UAW Local 600 testified to the City Plan Commission in favor of the construction of temporary public war housing: City Plan Commission Minutes, vol. 11 (1943–44), 117, DPL. Memo Concerning Eight Mile–Wyoming Area, March 10, 1944, CHPC, Box 58; *Detroit News*, March 14, 1944; *Michigan Chronicle*, April 22, 1944.

42. *Detroit News*, May 3, 1944; "Experience in City Planning," n.d., 1, 3, CHPC, Box 58.

43. The "deprogramming" of the Robert Brooks Homes in 1953 renewed debate in the Eight Mile community over its future development, this time pitting the City Plan Commission and advocates of a community recreation project against community activists who called for further redevelopment of the area with single-family homes. See "Housing Survey, 1953–1954," DUL, Box 38, Folder A2–11.

44. City Plan Commission Minutes, vol. 14 (1948), 342d, DPL; Mayor's Interracial Committee Minutes, January 16, 1950, CCR, Part I, Series 1, Box 11; Minutes, April 27, 1950, p. 7, ibid., Part III, Box 25, Folder 25–114. John Bublevsky, Tom Gates,

Lola Gibson, Victor Harbay, and Sally Stretch, "A Spatial Study of Racial Tension or 'The Walls Come Tumbling Down,'" typescript, ibid., Box 13, Folder 13–20; U.S. Bureau of the Census, *U.S. Census of Population and Housing: 1960, Census Tracts, Detroit, Michigan Standard Metropolitan Statistical Area*, Final Report PHC (1)-40 (Washington, D.C.: United States Government Printing Office, 1962), Table H-3, data for tracts 305A and 305B; *Michigan Chronicle*, July 30, 1955.

45. Capeci, *Race Relations in Wartime Detroit*, 75–99, offers the most thorough discussion of the event; a brief description of the riot can be found in Alan Clive, *State of War: Michigan in World War II* (Ann Arbor: University of Michigan Press, 1979), 145–50. The following paragraphs draw from Capeci's account unless otherwise cited.

46. Seven Mile–Fenelon Improvement Association, poster, "WE DEMAND OUR RIGHTS," CRC, Box 66, Folder: Property Owners Association; Capeci, *Race Relations in Wartime Detroit*, 80; Charles Abrams, *Forbidden Neighbors: A Study of Prejudice in Housing* (New York: Harper, 1955), 95.

47. Capeci, *Race Relations in Wartime Detroit*, 88.

48. Mayor's Interracial Committee, "Analysis and Recommendations Regarding the Racial Occupancy Policy and Practice of the Detroit Housing Commission," March 24, 1952, 6, CCR, Part I, Series 1, Box 12, Binder 3/7/52–12/52. For the background to this policy, see Jenkins, "The Racial Policies of the Detroit Housing Commission," 21.

49. Detroit Area Office, NHA, to Edward Connor, September 27, 1944, CHPC, Box 42.

50. "Analysis of Social and Political Factors Pertaining to the Selection of a Site for an Unrestricted Public Housing Project in the Detroit Area," n.d., 2, CHPC, Box 41; "Housing Crisis in the Detroit Area," p. 27, ibid., Box 68; *Daily Worker*, December 3, 1944; Gloster B. Current to Thurgood Marshall, January 15, 1945, NAACP, Group II, Box B74, Folder: Housing, Dearborn, Mich., 1944–45.

51. "Summary of Meeting in Mr. Klutznick's Office on the Detroit Situation," February 28, 1945, CHPC, Box 41.

52. David L. Good, *Orvie: The Dictator of Dearborn: The Rise and Reign of Orville L. Hubbard* (Detroit: Wayne State University Press, 1989).

53. "Dearborn Meeting, 12/18/44," CHPC, Box 42, DPL.

54. Gloster Current, "What's Wrong With Detroit," n.d. [1944?], 7, DNAACP, Part I, Box 1, Folder: "Miscellaneous Material."

55. "Where is Dearborn?" *Chicago Defender*, December 30, 1944. Thanks to Eric Arnesen for a copy of this article.

56. Report on conversation with Ford Motor Company Engineer, December 4, 1944, CCR, Part I, Series 1, Box 3, Folder: Incidents—Housing 1944. See also Resolution on the Immediate War Housing Need for Metropolitan Detroit, 1945 Housing Conference, CRC, Box 66, Folder: Housing Conference 1945.

57. *Dearborn Press*, November 22, 1944; Resolution Passed By Dearborn City Council, November 17, 1944, in NAACP, Group II, Box B74, Folder: Housing, Dearborn, Mich., 1944–45.

58. *Detroit Times*, May 24, 1945; for Hubbard's recollections, see Good, *Orvie*, 142.

59. *Detroit News*, May 15, 1945.

60. Ibid., Sept. 22, 1944.

61. Ibid., Sept. 26, 1944. Dearborn continued to oppose low-income housing. When John Hancock Life Insurance proposed to build private rental housing in Dearborn in 1948, the project was defeated because Hubbard raised the spectre of black occupancy. See Abrams, *Forbidden Neighbors*, 99–101.

62. "Southwest Area Under Consideration," Detroit Housing Commission, Monthly Report to the Commissioners, vol. 3, no. 2 (February 1945), 7, Mayor's Papers (1945) Box 3, Folder: Housing Commission. Statistics on Oakwood calculated by the author from data in *Real Property Survey of Detroit*, vol. 2, 5, 90–91.

63. *Detroit News*, January 18, 1945, February 16, 1945. On the black residential development see also *Michigan Chronicle*, October 7, 1944; and Gloster Current, "The Detroit Elections: Problem in Reconversion," *Crisis* 52 (November 1945): 325. The black development did meet with some resistance: the Southeast Detroit Improvement Association filed a suit against the development's occupancy by blacks, and one house suffered some fire damage in an attack by two disgruntled white neighbors. See *Michigan Chronicle*, October 14, 1944.

64. On the values of home and family in the postwar era and their relationship to New Deal rhetoric, see Elaine Tyler May "Cold War—Warm Hearth: Politics and the Family in Postwar America," in Fraser and Gerstle, *The Rise and Fall of the New Deal Order*, 156–58.

65. Frank Berge to Mayor Jeffries, February 23, 1945, in Mayor's Papers (1945), Box 3, Folder: Housing Commission 1945.

66. Alex Csanyi and family to Mayor Jeffries, February 20, 1945, ibid.

67. Fadanelli to Mayor Jeffries, March 6, 1945, ibid., Box 2, Folder: Interracial.

68. *Detroit News*, February 28, 1945.

69. Michael J. Harbulak to Mayor Jeffries, February 21, 1945, Mayor's Papers (1945), Box 3, Folder: Housing Commission 1945.

70. Mr. and Mrs. Fred Pressato to Mayor Jeffries, March 6, 1945, ibid.

71. Harbulak to Jeffries; John Watson to Mayor Jeffries, March 6, 1945, ibid.

72. Henry Lee Moon, "Danger in Detroit," *Crisis* 53 (January 1946): 28.

73. *Detroit News*, March 9, 1945, March 10, 1945; *Detroit Free Press*, March 10, 1945; Current, "The Detroit Elections," 325; Report of the Executive Secretary, Detroit Branch NAACP, February 6–March 12, 1945, in NAACP, Group II, Box C87, Folder: January–April 1945. On the reluctance of UAW locals to support the controversial housing project, see Field Report to Robert C. Weaver from William E. Hill, June 1, 1945, p. 8, in NAACP, Group II, Box A505, Folder: Racial Tension, Detroit, Mich., 1944–46.

74. *Detroit News*, March 20, 1945.

75. Copies of handbills in DMP, Box 3, Folder 3–8. See also "The 1945 Mayoral Campaign—National Lawyers Guild," January 10, 1946, attached to Memorandum to Thurgood Marshall from Gloster Current, NAACP, Group II, Box A505, Folder: Racial Tension Detroit, Mich., 1944–46.

76. "Mayor Jeffries is Against Mixed Housing," in NAACP, Group II, Box A475, Folder: Politics/Michigan 1945–53.

77. "White Neighborhoods Again in Peril: Frankensteen Policy Up On Housing Negroes Here," ibid., October 11, 1945; "Kronk Bucks Mixing Races," *Home Gazette*, October 25, 1945: copies in CAH, File: Clippings; see also Current, "The

Detroit Elections," 319–21. Jeffries's housing commissioner, Charles Edgecomb, a UAW member and former union activist, staunchly supported segregation. See *Twin Cities Observer*, November 1, 1945. Thanks to Eric Arnesen for this clipping.

78. Moon, "Danger in Detroit," 12.

79. Fourth Meeting of the Speaker's Study Group of Intercultural Affairs, February 4, 1946, 2, CHPC, Box 74, Folder: Interracial Resolutions/Intercultural Council.

80. *Master Plan for the City of Detroit* (Detroit: City of Detroit, 1946); for a comprehensive list of sites and map, see Mayor's Interracial Committee Minutes, April 4, 1949, CCR, Part I, Series 1, Box 11.

81. Allan MacNichol, quoted in *Brightmoor Journal*, December 22, 1949.

82. For a sketch of McGriff's background and for a few examples of his anticommunist activity in the 1940s, see FM. Quotes from McGriff editorials in *Brightmoor Journal*, February 3, 1949, May 12, 1949, January 12, 1950. I wish to express my gratitude to the staff of the Michigan Historical Collections, Bentley Historical Library, University of Michigan, who allowed me to consult the as yet uncatalogued and unprocessed collection of Northwest Side neighborhood newspapers edited by McGriff.

83. For Cobo's background, see Melvin G. Holli and Peter d'A. Jones, *Biographical Dictionary of American Mayors, 1820–1980: Big City Mayors* (Westport, Conn.: Greenwood Press, 1981), 69–70; on Edwards, see *Detroit News*, October 31, 1947, copy in UAW-RD, Box 10, Folder 10–4; see also "Biographical Data, George Edwards," VF—Biography.

84. *Brightmoor Journal*, September 22, 1949; *"HI" NEIGHBOR* (newsletter of the Outer–Van Dyke Home Owners Association), vol 1., no. 5 (November 1949), copy in UAW-CAP, Box 5, Folder 5–5; *Detroit News*, November 8, 1949; interview with Joseph Coles (Jim Keeney and Roberta McBride, interviewers) July 8, 1970, 17, Blacks in the Labor Movement Collection, ALUA.

85. Labor's Municipal Campaign Committee, Schedule 1: Liabilities, UAW-PAC, Box 62, Folder 62–10. Labor spent $28,455.51 on Edwards's campaign, as noted in Al Barbour to Roy Reuther, November 17, 1949, ibid., Folder 62–19. Notes, "East Side Meeting, Thursday November 17, 9:00 a.m.," ibid., Folder 62–13; "Material for Sound Trucks and Leaflets at MUCC Offices," ibid., Folder 62–7; "Suggested Slot Announcements," ibid., Folder 62–16; poster: "Housewives—Don't Stay Home Nov. 8th," ibid., folder 62–10; and flyer: "750,000 Detroiters *Did Not Vote* in the Primary Election," ibid. Edwards also targeted women voters. See Mildred Jeffrey to Ralph Showalter, October 24, 1949, UAW Community Relations Department—Mildred Jeffrey Collection, Box 9, Folder 9–5, ALUA. According to UAW analysis of returns from selected precincts, Edwards did better in blue-collar areas than in "middle-class" white districts, although he lost in both. Edwards won only among black voters (82 percent) and white public housing project residents (59 percent). The only other group that came close to majority support (49 percent) for Edwards were "hillbillies," presumably recent Southern white migrants to the city. Untitled tables, UAW-PAC, Folder Box 63, 63–2.

86. Notes, "West Side Coordinators Meeting, Wednesday, November 16, 1949," ibid., Box 62, Folder 62–11.

87. Notes, "East Side Meeting, Thursday November 17, 9:00 a.m.," p. 6, ibid., Folder 62–13.

88. A clear overview of Detroit politics in the 1950s can be found in J. David Greenstone, "A Report on the Politics of Detroit," unpublished paper, Harvard University, 1961 (in possession of Kresge-Purdy Library, Wayne State University Library, Detroit, Michigan). For an excellent analysis of the 1949 election and its legacy, see Kevin G. Boyle, "Politics and Principle: The United Automobile Workers and American Labor-Liberalism, 1948–1968," (Ph.D. diss., University of Michigan, 1991), 94–100. My analysis of the Detroit election of 1949 bears out Ira Katznelson's hypothesis about the importance of the separation of home and work as a constraint on American radical politics. See Ira Katznelson, *City Trenches: Urban Politics and the Patterning of Class in the United States* (New York: Pantheon, 1981). It is important not to overstate the contrast between neighborhood and union politics, because ongoing research on CIO unions in the North has shown that shop-floor conflicts over racial issues such as upgrading and seniority lists continued well into the 1950s. See below, Chapter 4, and Kevin Boyle, "'There Are No Union Sorrows That the Union Can't Heal': The Struggle for Racial Equality in the United Automobile Workers, 1940–1960," *Labor History* 36 (1995): 5–23; Bruce Nelson, "Race Relations in the Mill: Steelworkers and Civil Rights, 1950–1965," paper delivered at the conference, "Toward a History of the 1960s," Madison, Wis., April 1993 (in author's possession).

89. Detroit Housing Commission Monthly Report (December 1949), 1–2, Mayor's Papers (1950), Box 5, Folder: Housing Commission. On Cobo's support among white homeowners groups, see interview with Joseph Coles, 17.

90. City Plan Commission Minutes, vol. 16 (1950–51), 44, DPL.

91. Detroit Housing Commission Monthly Report (December 1949), 1–2, in Mayor's Papers (1950), Box 2, Folder: Detroit Housing Commission; City Plan Commission Minutes, vol. 16 (1950–51), 44, DPL; *Detroit Free Press*, March 14, 1950.

92. Roman Ceglowski to Cobo, June 27, 1951; Bertha Joslin to Cobo, September 18, 1951 both in Mayor's Papers (1951), Box 2, Folder: Civic Associations; see also Louis Eppolito to Cobo, April 19, 1950, ibid. (1950), Box 2, Folder: Civic Associations.

93. Orville Tenaglia to Cobo, March 28, 1950; and Ralph Smith to Cobo, March 23, 1950, both ibid.

94. Lucille McCollough to Cobo, December 27, 1949, ibid.

95. Detroit Housing Commission, Monthly Report (November–December 1949), 1, in ibid., Box 5, Folder: Housing Commission; *Detroit News*, December 15, 1949; *Detroit Free Press*, December 30, 1949; *Detroit Free Press*, March 8, 1950.

96. Detroit Housing Commission, "Public Housing in Detroit, 1946–1948," 9–10, CHPC, Box 71, Folder: Housing Shortage. Until his death in October 1947, Thal, executive secretary of the Building Trades Council, also served as president of the Detroit Housing Commission. Allan, president of the Building Trades Council, was appointed president of the Housing Commission in February 1948.

97. Detroit Housing Commission, Monthly Report (November-December 1949), 2, Mayor's Papers (1950), Box 5, Folder: Housing Commission; *Detroit Free Press*, March 14, 1950. On connections between housing reformers and business interests elsewhere, see Hirsch, *Making the Second Ghetto*, 100–134; Schwartz, *The New York Approach*, 108–43; Thomas H. O'Connor, *Building a New Boston: Politics and Urban Renewal, 1950–1970* (Boston: Northeastern University Press, 1993).

98. City Plan Commission Minutes, vol. 16 (1950), 241, DPL; Speech by Hugo Schwartz to the Eastern Detroit Exchange Club, April 12, 1950, in UAW-PAC, Box 64, Folder 64–12; *Detroit Times*, April 12, 1950.

99. City Plan Commission Minutes, vol. 16 (1950), 241, DPL.

100. "The City Administration's Housing Program: An Analysis," attachment to Mayor's Interracial Committee Minutes, May 1, 1950, CCR, Part I, Series 1, Box 11.

101. Robert Roberge to Cobo, March 4, 1950, Mayor's Papers (1950), Box 5, Folder: Housing Schoolcraft Gardens.

102. Detroit Chapter, Americans for Democratic Action, "Does Detroit Have a Housing Problem?" (1951), CHPC, Box 51.

103. Detroit Housing Commission Material Describing Low Rent Housing Program of the City, August 1966, DNAACP, Part I, Box 11, Folder 11–11; Chicago figure from Hirsch, *Making the Second Ghetto*, 13.

104. Fisher, *Twenty Years of Public Housing*, Table 2, 18.

105. Draft transcript of WJBK radio interview with Cyril Lawrence, Supervisor of Tenant Relations, Detroit Housing Commission, August 7, 1946, CHPC, Box 74, Folder: Interracial Res., 1945–1948.

106. Memo to Members of the Mayor's Interracial Committee from George Schermer, re: Housing Policy, May 16, 1949, 3–4, ibid., Folder: Interracial Committee.

107. MIC Minutes April 4, 1949, CCR, Part I, Series 1, Box 11.

108. Petition of George Isabell to Detroit Common Council, n.d. [1954], DUL, Box 38, Folder A2–11; *Michigan Chronicle*, September 28, 1957; *Saturday Evening Post*, October 19, 1957; *Detroit News*, August 18, 1959; "Racial Factors in Admission to Detroit Public Housing," n.d. [1959], CCR, Part I, Series 4, Box 3, Folder: Minutes, August 1959. Detroit Commission on Community Relations, *1960 Annual Report*, Appendix A, includes figures of integration in Detroit's public housing projects. In August of 1960, Brewster, Douglass, and Sojourner Truth Homes were all black; Jeffries was 86 percent black. Parkside and Charles Homes were more than 94 percent white; Smith Homes were 96 percent white; and Herman Gardens was 98 percent white.

109. Mayor's Interracial Committee, Minutes, April 4, 1949, CCR, Part I, Series 1, Box 11.

110. Albert J. Mayer, "Public Housing, Urban Renewal, and Racial Segregation in Detroit," Department of Sociology, Wayne State University, 3 (June 1962), DNAACP, Part I, Box 30, Folder 30–9.

111. Interview with Joseph Coles, 17.

Chapter 4
"The Meanest and Dirtiest Jobs": The Structures of
Employment Discrimination

1. Memo to Nat Weinberg from Ralph Showalter, Subject: Discrimination at the Hiring Office of Chrysler Corporation, March 30, 1948; William Oliver to Mike Novak, April 22, 1948; William Oliver to Mildred Jeffrey, July 16, 1948; all in UAW-FP, Box 14, Folder 14–8.

2. David M. Gordon, Richard Edwards, and Michael Reich, *Segmented Work,*

Divided Workers: The Historical Transformation of Labor in the United States (New York: Cambridge University Press, 1982).

3. Peter Doeringer and Michael Piore, *Internal Labor Markets and Manpower Analysis* (Lexington, Mass.: D. C. Heath, 1971); on signaling, Michael Spence, "Job Market Signalling," *Quarterly Journal of Economics* 87 (1973), 355–74. For a particularly sophisticated application and revision of theories of discrimination, see Joleen Kirschenman and Kathryn M. Neckerman, "'We'd Love to Hire Them, But . . .': The Meaning of Race for Employers," in *The Urban Underclass*, ed. Christopher Jencks and Paul E. Peterson (Washington, D.C.: The Brookings Institution, 1991), 203–232. On the use of racial division to curtail worker solidarity, see Michael Reich, *Racial Inequality: A Political-Economic Analysis* (Princeton, N.J.: Princeton University Press, 1981); Gordon, Edwards, and Reich, *Segmented Work, Divided Workers*.

4. "Michigan State Employment Service Experiences in the Placement of Minority Group Workers"; see also *Detroit Focus*, December 1951, in DUL, Box 21, Folder 21–14.

5. Memorandum from the Michigan Committee on Civil Rights to the Governor's Committee on Civil Rights, December 29, 1948, in VF, Box 4, Folder: Fair Employment Practices, Michigan, 1940s; *Michigan's Labor Market* 3, no. 6 (June 1948): 3–4.

6. "Michigan State Employment Services Experiences in the Placement of Minority Group Workers," 6. The company is unnamed in the report.

7. City of Detroit, Mayor's Interracial Committee, "Racial Discrimination in Employment and Proposed Fair Employment Measures, A Report to the Common Council," December 7, 1951, 6, in CCR, Part I, Series 1, Box 11. For similar patterns in Philadelphia, see Walter Licht, *Getting Work: Philadelphia 1840–1950* (Cambridge, Mass.: Harvard University Press, 1993), 125–26, 136–39.

8. In 1950, 33.4 percent of metropolitan Detroit workers were employed in the motor vehicle industry; in 1960, 23.4 percent of Detroit area workers were employed in the motor vehicle industry. Figures from U.S. Bureau of the Census, *1950 Census of Population* (Washington, D.C.: United States Government Printing Office, 1953); and U.S. Bureau of the Census, *1960 Census of Population* (Washington, D.C.: United States Government Printing Office, 1962). The increase in black motor vehicle industry employment during World War II is well documented in reports on "Employment of Negroes in Detroit," UAW-RD, Box 9, Folder 9–24. See also August Meier and Elliot Rudwick, *Black Detroit and the Rise of the UAW* (New York: Oxford University Press, 1979), 213–14; Robert C. Weaver, *Negro Labor: A National Problem* (New York: Harcourt, Brace, and World, 1946), 285. For a snapshot of auto industry employment in 1960, see figures from UAW data submitted to *Hearings Before the United States Commission on Civil Rights Held in Detroit, Michigan, December 14–15, 1960* (Washington, D.C.: United States Government Printing Office, 1961), 63–65. Data for Ford plants was, unfortunately, incomplete. For a comparison of wages in the auto industry with wages in other sectors of the economy, see Nelson Lichtenstein, "From Corporatism to Collective Bargaining: Organized Labor and the Eclipse of Social Democracy in the Postwar Era," in *The Rise and Fall of the New Deal Order, 1930–1980*, ed. Steve Fraser and Gary Gerstle (Princeton, N.J.: Princeton University Press, 1989), Table 5.1, 145.

9. My generalization is based on a breakdown of workers in General Motors plants in 1955, 1958, 1961, and 1964 by production, skilled trades, maintenance, and tool and die positions (unfortunately, not by race or gender), in "Survey of Population in General Motors Plants," UAW-RD, Box 69, Folder: GM Productivity, 1946–63.

10. Louis Seaton to Francis Kornegay, DUL, Box 78, Folder: Gp 2, Kornegay, Exec. Dir., General Motors; Herbert R. Northrup, *The Negro in the Automobile Industry*, Report No. 1, The Racial Policies of American Industry (Philadelphia: Industrial Research Unit, The Wharton School of Finance and Commerce, University of Pennsylvania, 1968), 11, 20, argues that General Motors hiring policies were decentralized prior to the Second World War, but "adopted a much stronger corporate-wide stance on integration rather than leaving the problem totally to decentralized management" during World War II. The Seaton quote and data for General Motors plants in Detroit for 1960 seem to point to some capriciousness in hiring practices by plant, indicating more decentralization than Northrup concedes.

11. Edward M. Turner to John C. Dancy, December 2, 1954, in FK, Box 4, Folder 124; for earlier instances of discrimination at Chrysler, see above, note 1.

12. "Discriminatory Job Orders Placed With State Employment Offices by Chrysler Corporation," December 6, 1954, in FK, Box 4, Folder 124; UAW Local 600, Executive Board Minutes, February 14, 1950, in UAW-600, Box 2.

13. Lloyd Bailer, "The Negro Automobile Worker," *Journal of Political Economy* 51 (1943): 416–19, has excellent data on black employment distribution in the 1940s.

14. *Pittsburgh Courier*, April 10, 1943; for examples of hiring-gate discrimination directed toward black women, see William Oliver to Mildred Jeffrey, July 16, 1948, all in UAW-FD, Box 14, Folder 14–8; Detroit Urban League Vocational Services Department, Monthly Report, December 1952, FK, Box 6, Folder 184; on postwar discrimination against women generally, see Ruth Milkman, *Gender at Work: The Dynamics of Job Segregation by Sex during World War II* (Urbana: University of Illinois Press, 1987), 118–27; "NAACP Study Concerning Trade Union Apprenticeship" (prepared by Herbert Hill), 1960, 48–49, NAACP, Group III, Box A180, Folder: Labor: Apprenticeship Training.

15. Thomas N. Maloney and Warren C. Whatley, "Making the Effort: The Contours of Racial Discrimination in Detroit's Labor Markets, 1920–1940," *Journal of Economic History* 55 (1995). For more detail, see also Warren Whatley and Gavin Wright, "Getting Started in the Automobile Industry" (unpublished paper, 1990), 483–86. Unfortunately other major automobile companies do not have, or have not released, comparable employment data. The Ford data that Maloney and Whatley use is only available through 1947.

16. Jordon Sims, interviewed by James A. Geschwender, January 1974, quoted in James A. Geschwender, *Class, Race, and Worker Insurgency: The League of Revolutionary Black Workers* (New York: Cambridge University Press, 1977), 39. For another example of a worker being told to return to the hiring gate, see Memo to Nat Weinberg from Ralph Showalter, Subject: Discrimination at the Hiring Office of Chrysler Corporation, March 30, 1948, UAW-FD, Box 14, Folder 14–8.

17. Quoted in B. J. Widick, "Black Workers: Double Discontents," in *Auto Work and Its Discontents* (Baltimore: Johns Hopkins University Press, 1976), 54.

18. National Urban League Department of Research, "Observations of Conditions Among Negroes in the Fields of Education, Recreation and Employment in

Selected Areas of the City of Detroit, Michigan," June 1941, 35–36, in DUL, Box 74, Folder: History.

19. See Conversations with "BIG THREE" (Motor Industry) Vice Presidents in Charge of Personnel, Detroit, September 29, 1943, in "Survey of Racial and Religious Conflicts in Detroit," CRC, Box 71; Charles Denby, *Indignant Heart: A Black Worker's Journal* (Detroit: Wayne State University Press, 1989), 124–34, 138–41.

20. Ibid., 87–88; on black shipyard workers, see Bruce Nelson, "Organized Labor and the Struggle for Black Equality in Mobile During World War II," *Journal of American History* 80 (1993): 952–88. See also Erdman Doane Beynon, "The Southern White Laborer Migrates to Detroit," *American Sociological Review* 3 (1938): 333–43; Elmer Akers, "Southern Whites in Detroit," typescript, Ann Arbor, 1936 (University Microfilms, OP 70, 108); Alan Clive, *State of War: Michigan in World War II* (Ann Arbor: University of Michigan Press, 1979), 175, 179–84. For a systematic comparison of the experiences of Appalachian white and black migrants to the North, see Jacqueline Jones, *The Dispossessed: America's Underclasses from the Civil War to the Present* (New York: Basic Books, 1992), esp. 205–65. See also the rich statistical survey by James N. Gregory, "The Southern Diaspora and the Urban Dispossessed: Demonstrating the Census Public Use Microdata Samples," *Journal of American History* 82 (1995): 111–34. Apart from findings in a 1951 survey of intergroup relations in Detroit that showed that 21 percent of respondents made negative comments about "Poor southern whites, hill-billies, etc.," I was able to find little mention of southern whites, and nothing on discrimination against them, in newspapers and social agency records in the postwar period. See Arthur Kornhauser, *Detroit as the People See It: A Survey of Attitudes in an Industrial City* (Detroit: Wayne University Press, 1952), 46–47.

21. DUL, Vocational Services Department, Monthly Report, September 1952, FK, Box 6, Folder 184; for a discussion of these practices a decade earlier, see Sixth Civilian Defense Region, "Report on Survey on Race Relations," September 3, 1943, p. 8.

22. Interview with Hillory Weber in *End of the Line: Autoworkers and the American Dream: An Oral History*, ed. Richard Feldman and Michael Betzold (New York: Weidenfeld and Nicolson, 1988), 85. See also Dan Georgakas and Marvin Surkin, *Detroit: I Do Mind Dying: A Study in Urban Revolution* (New York: St. Martin's Press, 1975), 35.

23. George Robinson, Oral History, 1–2, Blacks in the Labor Movement Collection, ALUA.

24. "UAW is Leader of US Labor," *Color*, July 1948, 12–13. On the links between the UAW and the civil rights movement in the postwar era, see Meier and Rudwick, *Black Detroit*, 207–22; Robert Korstad and Nelson Lichtenstein, "Opportunities Found and Lost: Labor Radicals and the Early Civil Rights Movement," *Journal of American History* 75 (1988): 786–811; Kevin Boyle, "Politics and Principle: The United Automobile Workers and American Labor-Liberalism, 1948–1968" (Ph.D. diss., University of Michigan, 1991).

25. Meier and Rudwick, *Black Detroit*, 162–74; Clive, *State of War*, 141–43; Kevin Boyle, "'There Are No Union Sorrows That the Union Can't Heal': The Struggle for Racial Equality in the United Automobile Workers, 1940–1960," *Labor History* 36 (Winter 1995): 5–23.

26. The Detroit Transmission Division of General Motors had separate seniority lines for black-dominated jobs as late as 1955. See William Oliver to Frederick Bibber, UAW-FP, Box 17, Folder 17–51. A superb discussion of UAW localism and its role in discrimination is Boyle, "'There Are No Union Sorrows,'" esp. 8–12. On the UAW's reluctance to challenge skilled trades, see Korstad and Lichtenstein, "Opportunities Found and Lost," 809. For similar patterns in another CIO-unionized northern industry, see Bruce Nelson, "Race Relations in the Mill: Steelworkers and Civil Rights, 1950–1965," paper presented to the conference "Toward a History of the 1960s," Madison, Wis., April 1993.

27. The tremendous resistance of corporations to the enactment of a state Fair Employment Practices Commission testifies to the unpopularity of measures to control hiring practice. Walter Reuther, testifying to the Civil Rights Commission, noted that implementation of fair employment policies "have been most successful in every area except hiring, where management's prerogative has been a stumbling block." Walter P. Reuther, testimony, in *Hearings*, 57. The Trade Union Leadership Council, composed of black UAW members, on the other hand, criticized the UAW for inaction on antidiscrimination policy.

28. George Crockett, Oral History, 28–29, Blacks in the Labor Movement Collection, ALUA; see also interview with George Crockett in *Detroit Lives*, ed. Robert H. Mast (Philadelphia: Temple University Press, 1994), 167.

29. Walter P. Reuther, testimony, *Hearings*, 42.

30. Walter P. Reuther, "The Negro Worker's Future," *Opportunity* 23 (Fall 1945): 205–6; Denby, *Indignant Heart*, 97; see also Robert Zeiger, *The CIO, 1935–1955* (Chapel Hill: University of North Carolina Press, 1995), 347; Nelson Lichtenstein, *The Most Dangerous Man in Detroit: Walter Reuther and the Fate of American Labor* (New York: Basic Books, 1995), 210.

31. Apprenticeship Standards, Ford Motor Company, December 10, 1941, in UAW-RD, Box 80, Folder: Ford Motor Company: Apprenticeship Programs, 1941–1967; Apprenticeship Standards, Joint Apprenticeship Committee of Ford Motor Company, 1943, in VF, Box 18, Folder: Industrial Education, 1940s.

32. Steve Babson, *Building the Union: Skilled Workers and Anglo-Gaelic Immigrants in the Rise of the UAW* (New Brunswick, N.J.: Rutgers University Press, 1991), 53–54. For an illuminating discussion of unions, management, and apprenticeship programs in another city, see Licht, *Getting Work*, 98–121.

33. International Union Apprenticeship Committee, UAW-CIO, "Apprenticeship Standards, UAW-CIO," September 30, 1947, in UAW-RD, Box 13, Folder 13–32.

34. National Apprentice Agreement, Chrysler Corporation Apprentice Standards, 1955, ibid., Box 78, Folder: Chrysler Contracts, 1937–1955 (1); General Motors Corporation Standard Apprentice Plan, October 19, 1942, VF, Box 18, Folder: Industrial Education, 1940s.

35. Apprenticeship Standards, Ford Motor Company, July 1, 1955, in UAW-RD, Box 82, Folder: Ford Industrial Relations, 1950–59 (2); see also Apprenticeship Standards, Ford Motor Company, October 20, 1961, ibid., Box 80, Folder: Ford Motor Company—Apprenticeship Programs, 1941–1967.

36. These are Walter Reuther's words, in *Hearings*, 57; representatives of the top automobile companies declined the commission's invitation to testify at the Detroit hearings. In fact, in the case of apprenticeship positions in the auto industry, the

UAW played an important role in the hiring process (see below). On the importance of management hiring practices in perpetuating discrimination, see Milkman, *Gender at Work*, 99–127.

37. See for example, Ford-UAW Agreement, February 26, 1946, Article VIII, 43–59, UAW-RD, Box 80, Folder: Ford Contract 1946. On seniority in the auto industry, see Lloyd H. Bailer, "Automobile Unions and Negro Labor," *Political Science Quarterly* 59 (1944): 562–66 and Carl Gersuny and Gladis Kaufman, "Seniority and the Moral Economy of U.S. Automobile Workers, 1934–1946," *Journal of Social History* 18 (1985): 463–75. Eli Chinoy, *The Automobile Worker and the American Dream* (New York: Random House, 1955), 39–40, offers a useful summary of seniority rules in the automobile industry in the 1940s and early 1950s. For a comparison with other industries, see the comprehensive discussion of seniority rules in the electrical industry in Ronald Schatz, *The Electrical Workers: A History of Labor at General Electric and Westinghouse, 1923–1960* (Urbana: University of Illinois Press, 1983), 105–32. On seniority generally, see the excellent discussion by David Montgomery and Ronald Schatz, "Facing Layoffs," in David Montgomery, *Workers' Control in America,* (New York: Cambridge University Press, 1979), 140–43.

38. Martin Glaberman, *Wartime Strikes: The Struggle Against the No-Strike Pledge During World War II* (Detroit: Bewick Editions, 1980), 31–32.

39. On separate seniority lists for women, see "Problems of Women Workers in the Auto Industry," January 21, 1963, UAW-RD, Box 64, Folder: Youth. See also Steve Babson, *Working Detroit: The Making of a Union Town* (Detroit: Wayne State University Press, 1986), 144–45; Milkman, *Gender at Work*, 104–12, 130–44.

40. Fair Practices Seniority Statement, July 14, 1947, and correction, July 30, 1947, in UAW-FP, Box 3, Folder 3–3. On "flexible" seniority, see *Daily Worker*, October 8, 1944. See also Marshall Stevenson, "Points of Departure, Acts of Resolve: Black-Jewish Relations in Detroit, 1937–1962" (Ph.D. diss., University of Michigan, 1988), 287–88. Others, including the NAACP and left-led unions, called for the adoption of plantwide seniority measures. See Leslie S. Perry to Roy Wilkins, December 27, 1944, in NAACP, Group II, Box A257, Folder: FEPC 1942–55; *Ford Facts*, December 22, 1951.

41. "Survey: Salaried Employment of Negroes in the Automobile Industry," November 1963, DUL, Box 52, Folder A16–1; *Hearings*, 63–65; Francis Kornegay to Rev. Louis Johnson, December 30, 1963, DUL, Box 45, Folder A9–14.

42. Interview with Clyde Cleveland, in Mast, *Detroit Lives*, 203.

43. Richard L. Rowan, *The Negro in the Steel Industry*, The Racial Policies of American Industry, Report No. 3 (Philadelphia: Industrial Research Unit, Department of Industry, Wharton School, University of Pennsylvania, 1968), 18, 40–44.

44. Oral history interview with Charles Younglove, conducted by Donald Kennedy, May 1975, pp. 6–7, Oral History Collection, PL; see also Notes, United Steel Workers of America Conference, District 29 Conference on Civil Rights, January 27, 1951, USWA-CRD, Box 2, Folder 17.

45. Walter Zyngier, Local 3232, to USWA, March 14, 1950; A. J. Euabska, Local 1297, to USWA, February 23, 1950, both ibid., Box 3, Folder 21. See also Rowan, *Negro in the Steel Industry*, 54–73. Compare with Bruce Nelson, "Race Relations in the Mill" (on Youngstown, Ohio); Judith Stein, "Southern Workers and National

Unions: Birmingham Steel Workers, 1936–1951," in *Organized Labor in the Twenti-eth-Century South*, ed. Robert Zeiger (Knoxville: University of Tennessee Press, 1991), 135–57; Robert J. Norrell, "Caste in Steel: Jim Crow Careers in Birmingham," *Journal of American History* 73 (1986) 669–94; Dennis C. Dickerson, *Out of the Crucible: Black Steel Workers in Western Pennsylvania, 1875–1980* (Albany: State University of New York Press, 1986).

46. Testimony of Joseph Kanthack, *Hearings*, 114–19, quotes 115; William How-ard Quay, Jr., *The Negro in the Chemical Industry*, The Racial Policies of American Industry, Report No. 7 (Philadelphia: Industrial Research Unit, The Wharton School of Finance and Commerce, University of Pennsylvania, 1969), 27.

47. "Vocational Services Monthly Report," August 1950, NUL, Part I, Series 7, Box 55, Folder: Detroit Reports, 1950; Vocational Services Department, DUL, "Em-ployment of Negroes in Brewing Industry Fact Sheet," September 24, 1955, FK, Box 4, Folder 4–22; *The Cotillion News*, June 15, 1955, copy in UAW-FP, Box 26, Folder 26–28; *Michigan Chronicle*, July 30, 1955, August 27, 1955; William Brown, Confer-ence Notes: Pfeiffer's Beer, March 14, 1957, National Bohemian Beer, March 21, 1957, E and B Brewery, March 6, 1957 in DUL, Box 48, Folder A12–10.

48. *Pittsburgh Courier* (Detroit edition), July 16, 1955; Vocational Services De-partment, DUL, "Employment of Negroes in Brewing Industry Fact Sheet," Sep-tember 24, 1955; and Francis Kornegay to August Scholle, September 22, 1955, in FK, Box 4, Folder 122. See also William J. Brown, Conference Notes: Mr. Harold Wagoner, VP Sales, Stroh's Brewery Company, March 7, 1957, DUL, Box 48, Folder A12–10, and Brewery Union Confrence, October 29, 1958, ibid., Folder A12–11; letter from Frank R. Owens to Arthur S. Johnson, May 8, 1962, DNAACP, Part I, Box 15, Folder: Fifteenth District Democrats—1962; "Detroit Metropolitan Area Em-ployment and Income by Age, Sex, Color and Residence, 1960," ibid., Part II, Box 10, Folder 10–11. It was not until the summer of 1963 that the first black driver-salesmen were hired; see *Detroit Free Press*, August 25, 1963.

49. Richard Hagemeyer, "Apprenticeship Selection Practices in Michigan's Man-ufacturing Companies" (Dearborn: Henry Ford Community College, 1961), 3, in DUL, Box 47, Folder A11–26.

50. "Detroit Metropolitan Area Employment and Income by Age, Sex, Color and Residence, 1960," DNAACP, Part II, Box 10, Folder 10–11.

51. James A. Oliver to William T. Patrick, June 18, 1962, DUL, Box 46, Folder A10–21. David M. Gordon, Richard Edwards, and Michael Reich, *Segmented Work, Divided Workers: The Historical Transformation of Labor in the United States* (Cam-bridge: Cambridge University Press, 1982) note that the machine tool industry is the classic example of a "peripheral" firm: it is a "weak" and "poorly financed" industry, subject to violent cyclical fluctuations. Workers in these firms are not subject to the same bureaucratic organization as workers in multinational "core" industries like automobile production. For an illuminating discussion of work relations in the ma-chine tool industry, see Max Holland, *When the Machine Stopped* (Cambridge, Mass.: Harvard Business School Press, 1990).

52. Francis Kornegay to Chester Cahn, January 15, 1951, in FK, Box 5, Folder 145; Detroit Urban League, Industrial Relations Committee, Minutes, January 26, 1951, FK, Box 6, Folder 146.

53. Ibid., March 27, 1951, in FK, Box 6, Folder 146; Francis Kornegay to Russell

Leach, June 11, 1951, ibid., Folder 145. A year after first attempts to negotiate with Local 155 over the placement of blacks in apprenticeship programs, the Urban League found discussion "dragging." See DUL Vocational Services Department, "Employer Relations—Worker-Union Relations—Community Relations," n.d. [1952], FK, Box 6, Folder 184; Local 155 units, April 7, 1953, and William Oliver to Russell Leach, April 6, 1954, both in UAW-FP, Box 14, Folder 14–10.

54. Memorandum to Paul Sifton from William Oliver, November 30, 1951; "Now is the Time for FEPC in Defense Employment," December 1951; Letter from Charlie Bates and David Elliott to Walter P. Reuther, January 27, 1953; Memorandum to Walter P. Reuther from William Oliver, February 2, 1953, all in UAW-FP, Box 16, Folder 16–7.

55. Local 49 Shop Committee to Brother Oliver, n.d. [c. March–April 1950], and Malcolm Evans to William Oliver, April 10, 1950, UAW-49; "EXCELLO—Local 49 UAW-CIO," Report of H. Ross, July 27, 1951; and letter [unidentified], July 9, 1956, all UAW-FP, Box 16, Folder 16–23; Executive Secretary's Report to the Executive Board of Directors, Detroit Branch NAACP, September 8, 1952, 2, NAACP, Group II, Box C90, File: Detroit, Mich., July–December 1952; Complaint Against Excello Corporation, 1962, DUL, Box 48, Folder A12–25.

56. "Negro Detroit, What Now?: Food For Thought and Cause for Action, Painful Facts," Educational Lesson No. 6, Detroit Civic Rights Committee, n.d. [1936] and "Detroit Civic Rights Committee Calls Negro Organizations to Arms," Educational Lesson No. 22, n.d. [1941], DUL, Box 70. For a glimpse at black employment in 1940, see "Observations on Conditions Among Negroes in the Fields of Education, Recreation, and Employment," June 1941, pp. 16–18, 41, ibid., Box 74, Folder: History. On the shortage of whites for city jobs, see *Pittsburgh Courier* (Detroit Edition), December 12, 1942. On Grigsby's efforts to open the public sector, see interview with Snow Grigsby, in Blacks in the Labor Movement Collection, ALUA; see also Richard W. Thomas, *Life for Us Is What We Make It: Building Black Community in Detroit, 1915–1945* (Bloomington: Indiana University Press, 1992), 150–56, 235–43. For an example of a black firefighter hired because of Grigsby's efforts, see interview with Marcena W. Taylor, in *Untold Tales, Unsung Heroes: An Oral History of Detroit's African American Community, 1918–1967*, ed. Elaine Latzman Moon (Detroit: Wayne State University Press, 1994), 193–94; on Reading, see Robert Conot, *American Odyssey* (New York: Bantam, 1975), 468–69. Reading was a Republican who largely ignored black Detroiters. On the black shift to the Democratic party in Detroit, see Nancy J. Weiss, *Farewell to the Party of Lincoln: Black Politics in the Age of FDR* (Princeton, N.J.: Princeton University Press, 1983), 205–7. On Jeffries and black employment, see Dominic J. Capeci, Jr., *Race Relations in Wartime Detroit: The Sojourner Truth Housing Controversy of 1942* (Philadelphia: Temple University Press, 1984), 16–20, 22, 29.

57. *Pittsburgh Courier* (Detroit edition), December 12, 1942; Francis Kornegay, "Employment of Negroes in City Departments as of February 15, 1946," NUL, Part I, Series 6, Box D41, Folder: Detroit, Mich., Employment; Capeci, *Race Relations*, 29; "Report of the Subcommittee to Study the Practices of the Public Schools," Appendix II, March 25, 1949, in CCR, Part I, Series 1, Box 11, Folder 1/49–12/49; Clive, *State of War*, 114; Detroit Police Department, Office of Director of Personnel, "Tabulation of Non-White Personnel," March 24, 1953, in DSL, Box 21, Folder:

Racial—Cotillion Club. In addition, only one black served as a lieutenant, only four as sergeants, and only eight as detectives.

58. "Highlights of Commission Meeting," FK, Box 9; Memorandum of Ernest L. Brown, Jr. to Francis Kornegay, July 15, 1963, DUL, Box 51, Folder A15–4; Conot, *American Odyssey*, 751; Research Department, Detroit Urban League, "A Profile of the Detroit Negro, 1959–1964" (June 1965), 8, in author's possession; Jeffrey Mirel, *The Rise and Fall of an Urban School System: Detroit, 1907–1981* (Ann Arbor: University of Michigan Press, 1993), 224–25; on the slow desegregation of the Detroit Police Department, see Sidney Fine, *Violence in the Model City: The Cavanagh Administration, Race Relations, and the Detroit Riot of 1967* (Ann Arbor: University of Michigan Press, 1988), 11–14, 105, 410–12. Thomas J. Anton, *Federal Aid to Detroit* (Washington, D.C.: The Brookings Institution, 1983), 32–36, notes that high levels of federal government aid to Detroit in the 1970s meant that wages remained high and the loss of city jobs was not as great as it could have been. On the role of government employment as a niche for blacks in New York, see Suzanne Model, "The Ethnic Niche and the Structure of Opportunity: Immigrants and Minorities in New York City," in *The "Underclass" Debate: Views from History*, ed. Michael B. Katz (Princeton, N.J.: Princeton University Press, 1993), 183–85; Harvey Kantor and Barbara Brenzel, "Urban Education and the 'Truly Disadvantaged': The Historical Roots of the Contemporary Crisis, 1945–1990," ibid., 386, 399.

59. Conference Notes, Kilgore and Hurd, October 9, 1956, DUL, Box 48, Folder A12–26. *Detroit News*, April 18, 1963. In 1950 and 1960, 12 percent of men in metropolitan Detroit were employed in retail work; in 1950, 23.8 percent of women worked in the retail sector; in 1960, 21.5 percent of women worked in retail. See *1950 Census*, Part 22, Table 77; *1960 Census*, Table 122. On the intricate connections between race, gender, and marketing strategies in the downtown shopping district, see Alison Ellen Isenberg, "Downtown Democracy: Rebuilding Main Street Ideals in the Twentieth-Century American City," (Ph.D. diss., University of Pennsylvania, 1995), 391–476; on retail employers' racial fears, see Troy Duster, "Postindustrialism and Youth Employment: African Americans as Harbingers," in *Poverty, Inequality, and the Future of Social Policy: Western States in the New World Order*, ed. Katherine McFate, Roger Lawson, and William Julius Wilson (New York: Russell Sage Foundation, 1995), 466–73.

60. Conference Notes, Kilgore and Hurd, October 9, 1956, DUL, Box 48, Folder A12–26; "Vocational Services Department Annual Report," 1956, ibid.. Box 45, Folder A9–2; "Number of Negroes Employed in Selected Retail Stores," FK, Box 6, Folder 188; Detroit Urban League, Annual Report, 1954, WS, Box 3, Folder 3–10; Detroit Urban League, Vocational Services Department, Men's Clothing Stores Survey, 1959, DUL, Box 46, Folder A10–7.

61. Data from "Employment Survey in Supermarkets, 1954–1955" and "Detroit Area Supermarkets Survey, 1954–1955" both in FK, Box 6, Folder 187. In 1955, two supermarkets that catered to a largely black clientele in the Conant Gardens, Sojourner Truth, and Grixdale Park area of northeast Detroit hired blacks. See *The Community Herald* 1, no. 3 (August 1955), reproduced in "The History of Grixdale Park, 1953–1958: Site Commemoration and Dedication of Grixdale's Historic Preservation Park Ceremonial—Unveiling Observance," June 9, 1988, 21, copy in Detroit Public Library, Detroit, Michigan.

62. "Teenage Job Availability Surveys," FK, Box 4, Folder 119; see also Vocational Services Department, Monthly Report, May 1960, DUL, Box 45, Folder A9–9. On the looting of groceries and other stores, see Fine, *Violence in the Model City*, 40–42, 343–47. There were, to be sure, other reasons for the resentment of neighborhood groceries, particularly accusations of price gouging.

63. Advisory Committee on Housing, Minutes, March 18, 1946, CHPC, Box 16, Folder: Advisory Committee.

64. U.S. Congress, Joint Committee on Housing, *Study and Investigation of Housing, Hearings, Proceedings at Detroit, Michigan, October 22, 1947*, 80th Congress, First Session 1948, 421.

65. Burneice Avery, "Never All (Detroit) 1941–1953," 20, in BA, Box 1, Folder: Literary Works 2.

66. Detroit Urban League, Industrial Relations Committee Minutes, April 24, 1951, in FK, Box 5, Folder 144; Detroit Urban League, Vocational Services Department Monthly Report, March 1950, NUL, Part I, Series 7, Box 55, Folder: Detroit Reports, 1950; *Detroit Tribune*, August 11, 1951; George Strauss and Sidney Ingerman, "Public Policy and Discrimination in Apprenticeship," in *Negroes and Jobs: A Book of Readings*, ed. Louis A. Ferman, Joyce L. Kornbluh, and J. A. Miller (Ann Arbor: University of Michigan Press, 1968), 300, citing Richard R. Myers, "The Building Workers: A Study of Industrial Sub-Culture" (Ph.D. diss., University of Michigan, 1946), 118–19.

67. On the proportion of black male craftsmen, see Appendix B, Table B.1. City of Detroit, Mayor's Interracial Committee, "Racial Discrimination in Employment and Proposed Fair Employment Measures: A Report to the Common Council," December 7, 1951, 2, CCR, Part I, Series 1, Box 11, Minutes Binder 1/51–12/51.

68. Francis Kornegay to J. A. Thomas, April 4, 1946, NUL, Series IV, Box 20, Folder: Veterans Building Trades. Ernest L. Brown to Julius Thomas, January 29, 1961, in DUL, Box 47, Folder A11–27; Department of Industrial Relations, National Urban League, "Summary Report: Apprenticeship and Training Opportunities for Negro Youths in Selected Urban League Cities," February 15, 1961, ibid., Box 46, Folder A10–17; "NAACP Study Concerning Apprenticeship," 19–22.

69. Joint Committee on Housing, *Study and Investigation*, 410, 412–13; Detroit Carpentry Apprenticeship Standards, Detroit Carpentry Joint Apprenticeship Committee, 1946, and Sheet Metal Workers Apprenticeship Standards, 1946, both in VF—Pre 1960s, Box 18, Folder: Industrial Education, 1940s.

70. Board of Education, City of Detroit, "Apprentice Training School General Information," n.d. [c. late 1950s], DUL, Box 20, Folder 20–17.

71. Testimony of Ernest L. Brown, Jr., director, Vocational Services Department, Detroit Urban League, *Hearings*, 124; for a variation on this analysis that stresses union power over the joint hiring process, see "Concerning NAACP Study Apprenticeship", 57.

72. A. L. Zwerdling to Irving Bluestone, April 28, 1966, in UAW-WPR, Box 428, Folder 428–11.

73. See Michael Kazin, "A People Not a Class: Rethinking the Political Language of the Modern U.S. Labor Movement," and David Roediger, "'Labor in White Skin: Race and Working-Class History," both in *Reshaping the U.S. Left: Popular Struggles in the 1980s*, ed. Mike Davis and Michael Sprinker (London: Verso, 1988), chaps. 11

and 12. Michael Kazin, *Barons of Labor: The San Francisco Building Trades and Union Power in the Progressive Era* (Urbana: University of Illinois Press, 1987), esp. 162–71, discusses racism in the building trades as a manifestation of what Hofstadter identified as the "paranoid style in American history." Other influential works that take this perspective include Herbert Hill, "Race, Ethnicity, and Organized Labor: The Opposition to Affirmative Action," *New Politics* 1 (1987): 32–82.

74. A particularly perceptive article on the masculine culture of the building trades is Joshua Freeman, "Hardhats: Construction Workers, Manliness, and the 1970 Pro-War Demonstrations," *Journal of Social History* 26 (1993): 725–44. On employers' reliance on word of mouth, see "NAACP Study Concerning Apprenticeship," 34–38. On nepotism more generally, see F. Ray Marshall and Vernon M. Briggs, Jr., *The Negro and Apprenticeship* (Baltimore: Johns Hopkins University Press, 1967), 36; and Strauss and Ingerman, "Public Policy and Discrimination in Apprenticeship," 310–11. For a structural discussion of the differential impact of job networks on the employment opportunities of different ethnic groups, see Model, "The Ethnic Niche and the Structure of Opportunity," 161–93. An influential discussion of brotherhood and fraternal organizations, with relevance for Detroit's building trades, is Mary Ann Clawson, *Constructing Brotherhood: Class, Gender, and Fraternalism* (Princeton, N.J.: Princeton University Press, 1989).

75. Joint Committee on Housing, *Study and Investigation*, 426–27; "Door Shut to Apprentices," *Architectural Forum*, January 1946, 20, 24, 28, 32; *Detroit News*, July 1, 1963.

76. Memo from Ernest L. Brown to Francis Kornegay, June 17, 1963, DUL, Box 51, Folder A15–4.

77. Jones, *The Dispossessed*, chap. 8.

78. Research Division, Detroit Commission on Community Relations, "Earnings of the Experienced Labor Force By Sex, Color, and Industry, Detroit Metropolitan Area," February 1963, in DNAACP, Part I, Box 24, Folder: Commission on Community Relations.

79. *Michigan Chronicle*, September 21, 1946; *Detroit Free Press*, November 10, 1961.

80. *Michigan Chronicle*, September 21, 1946; Incident Report, CCR, Part I, Series 1, Box 4, Folder 47–57a; Monthly Report, Northwest Branch, Detroit Urban League, October 1951, DUL, Box 44, Folder A8–9.

81. The classic study remains Elliot Liebow, *Tally's Corner: A Study of Negro Streetcorner Men* (Boston: Little Brown, 1967), see especially 29–71. Descriptions of street corner life, like Liebow's, were deeply humanistic and offered liberal policy prescriptions for the alleviation of poverty. Beginning in the late 1960s, however, cultural descriptions of poverty became the basis of conservative arguments about the fecklessness of black men. For a particularly influential conservative application of this model, see Lawrence Mead, *The New Politics of Poverty* (New York: Basic Books, 1992); and a critique, see Thomas J. Sugrue, "The Impoverished Politics of Poverty," *Yale Journal of Law and the Humanities* 6 (1994): 163–79.

82. It should be noted that many of the urban riots of the 1960s were sparked by arrests and harassment of young men hanging out on street corners. See, for example, *Report of the National Advisory Commission on Civil Disorders* (New York: Bantam Books, 1968), 303.

83. My thinking on these matters has been shaped by the work of urban geographers. On the "constitutive role" of urban space in shaping and reinforcing racial identity, see Robert W. Lake, "Recent Geographic Perspectives on the Social Construction of Race and Place," Paper presented to the American Historical Association Annual Meeting, New York, December 29, 1990; and the seminal article by Kay J. Anderson, "The Idea of Chinatown: The Power of Place and Institutional Practice in the Making of a Racial Category," *Annals of the Association of American Geographers* 77 (1987): 580–98.

84. The resilience of racial distinctions in hiring is explored most provocatively in Neckerman and Kirschenmann, "'We'd Love to Hire Them, But . . . ,'" 203–34.

85. Michael B. Katz, *The Undeserving Poor: From the War on Poverty to the War on Welfare* (New York: Pantheon, 1989); see also Katz, "The Urban 'Underclass' as Metaphor for Social Transformation," in *The "Underclass" Debate*, 3–23.

86. For an overview of employment opportunities for blacks at the beginning of World War II, see National Urban League, Department of Research, "Observations on Conditions Among Negroes in the Fields of Education, Recreation, and Employment in Selected Areas of the City of Detroit, Michigan," June 1941, in DUL, Box 74, Folder: History. Quote from "Study Reveals Little Change in Hiring Patterns Since Riot," *Michigan Chronicle*, March 7, 1953. Reprinted in Charles Wartman, *Detroit— Ten Years After* (Detroit: Michigan Chronicle, 1953), 8.

87. Seabron quoted in *Detroit News*, May 11, 1953. For similar patterns in other cities, see Arthur Butler, Henry Louis Taylor, Jr., and Doo-Ha Ryu, "Work and Black Neighborhood Life in Buffalo, 1930–1980," in *African Americans and the Rise of Buffalo's Post-Industrial City, 1940 to Present*, ed. Henry Louis Taylor, Jr., vol. 2 (Buffalo, N.Y.: Buffalo Urban League, 1990), 129–56; Julie Boatright Wilson and Virginia W. Knox, "Cleveland: The Expansion of a Metropolitan Area and Its Ghettos," Malcolm Wiener Center for Social Policy, John F. Kennedy School of Government, Harvard University, Working Paper Series, No. H-91–8, July 1991, 46–50; Julie Boatright Wilson, "Milwaukee: Industrial Metropolis on the Lake," John F. Kennedy School of Government, Harvard University, Faculty Research Working Paper Series, No. R95–19, April 1995, Section III, 12–17.

Chapter 5
"The Damning Mark of False Prosperities":
The Deindustrialization of Detroit

Parts of chapters 5 and 6 appeared "'Forget about Your Inalienable Right to Work': Deindustrialization and Its Discontents at Ford, 1950–1953," *International Labor and Working-Class History* 48 (Fall 1995): 112–30. Reprinted with the permission of International Labor and Working-Class History, Inc.

1. For descriptions of plants, see *Michigan: A Guide to the Wolverine State*, Work Projects Administration American Guide Series (New York: Oxford University Press, 1941), 234, 277–78, 286–87. Seventy-six tons of soot and ash per square mile fell each year in the inner-city section of Detroit bounded by Grand Boulevard and the Detroit River. James Sweinhart, "What Detroit's Slums Cost Its Taxpayers," (Detroit: Detroit News Reprints, 1946), 9, CHPC, Box 73, Folder: Racial Relations. Quotes from Gloria Whelan, "The First City," *Michigan Quarterly Review* 25 (1986): 184.

2. On fluctuations in the Detroit economy, see G. Walter Woodworth, *The Detroit Money Market, 1934–1955*, Michigan Business Studies, vol. 12, no. 4 (Ann Arbor: Bureau of Business Research, School of Business Administration, University of Michigan, 1956), 14–17.

3. Mary West Jorgensen, "A Profile of Detroit," January 1952, DUL, Box 21, Folder 21–17. On job loss in other major industrial cities, see Appendix A. For a snapshot of industrial problems in other cities in the 1950s, see Irving Bernstein, *Promises Kept: John F. Kennedy's New Frontier* (New York: Oxford University Press, 1991), 160–67. The history of deindustrialization after World War II has yet to be written. But glimpses of the overall pattern in other cities can be found in: "Deindustrialization: A Panel Discussion," *Pennsylvania History* 58 (1991): 181–211; John T. Cumbler, *A Social History of Economic Decline: Business, Politics, and Work in Trenton* (New Brunswick, N.J., Rutgers University Press, 1989); Irwin Marcus, "The Deindustrialization of Homestead: A Case Study, 1959–1984," *Pennsylvania History* 52 (1985) 162–82; Gary Gerstle, *Working-Class Americanism: A History of Labor in a Textile City, 1920–1960* (Cambridge: Cambridge University Press, 1989), 320–28; Ronald Schatz, *The Electrical Workers: A History of Labor at General Electric and Westinghouse* (Urbana: University of Illinois Press, 1983), 232–36. Not all northern cities experienced economic decline in the postwar years. Indianapolis, for example, grew during the postwar years. See Robert G. Barrows, "Indianapolis: Silver Buckle on the Rustbelt," in *Snowbelt Cities: Metropolitan Politics in the Northeast and Midwest since World War II*, ed. Richard M. Bernard (Bloomington: Indiana University Press, 1990), 137–57.

4. For an overview see Bruce Schulman, *From Cotton Belt to Sunbelt: Federal Policy, Economic Development and the Transformation of the South, 1938–1980* (New York: Oxford University Press, 1991). See also Ann Markusen, Peter Hall, Scott Campbell, and Sabina Deitrick, *The Rise of the Gunbelt: The Military Remapping of Industrial America* (New York: Oxford University Press, 1991); Roger Lotchin, *Fortress California 1910–1961: From Warfare to Welfare* (New York: Oxford University Press, 1992); Roger Lotchin, ed., *The Martial Metropolis: U.S. Cities in Peace and War* (New York: Praeger, 1984).

5. For a general overview, see Thomas J. Sugrue, "The Structures of Urban Poverty: The Reorganization of Space and Work in Three Periods of American History," in *The "Underclass" Debate: Views from History*, ed. Michael B. Katz (Princeton, N.J.: Princeton University Press, 1993), 85–117; David M. Gordon, "Capitalist Development and the History of American Cities," in *Marxism and the Metropolis: New Perspectives in Urban Political Economy*, ed. William K. Tabb and Larry Sawers (New York: Oxford University Press, 1978), 25–63. For a discussion of these processes, see Eva Mueller, Arnold Wilken, and Margaret Wood, *Location Decisions and Industrial Mobility in Michigan, 1961* (Ann Arbor: Institute for Social Research, University of Michigan, 1961), 5–6.

6. Douglas Reynolds, "Engines of Struggle: Technology, Skill, and Unionization at General Motors, 1930–1940," *Michigan Historical Review* 15 (1989): 79–81, 91–92.

7. Detroit Metropolitan Area Regional Planning Commission, "Location of Industrial Plants," 16, SEMCOG, Box 9.

8. On plant deconcentration in the 1940s and 1950s, see Detroit Metropolitan Area Regional Planning Commission, "Location of Automotive Plants," Michigan

P-1 (G) Project Completion Report, 1955–56, 18, SEMCOG, Box 9. For a general survey of Detroit's industrial patterns, see Robert Sinclair, *The Face of Detroit: A Spatial Synthesis* (Detroit: Department of Geography, Wayne State University, 1972), 36–41.

9. "Location of Automotive Plants," 17; untitled memo with list of auto plants constructed since 1949, in UAW-RD, Box 76, Folder 5; for a discussion of similar patterns in the 1970s and 1980s, see Barry Bluestone and Bennett Harrison, *The Deindustrialization of America: Plant Closings, Community Abandonment, and the Dismantling of Basic Industry* (New York: Basic Books, 1982), 166–68, 170–78.

10. Mueller et al., *Location Decisions*, 53.

11. "Available Industrial Properties Adjacent to Railroads, City of Detroit," February 1, 1951, in Mayor's Papers (1951), Box 2; on commuting patterns, see Detroit Metropolitan Area Regional Planning Commission, "Home Location Patterns of Industrial Workers in the Detroit Region," December 1955, copy in Department of Labor Library, Washington, D.C. Harold Black, "Detroit: A Case Study in Industrial Problems of a Central City," *Land Economics* 34 (1958): 218–26; "Report of a Survey by a Special Committee of the Michigan Chapter of the Society of Industrial Realtors on Trends in Industrial Location," 1956, p. 2, copy in VF—Pre 1960s, Box 18, Folder: Industries, location of, 1950s.

12. Detroit Metropolitan Area Regional Planning Commission, *The Manufacturing Economy of the Detroit Region*, Part I Revised, (March 1950), 15; Detroit Metropolitan Area Regional Planning Commission, *Recent Growth and Trends in Manufacturing in the Detroit Region* (1956), 2–3, 10 (both in Department of Labor Library, Washington, D.C.)

13. See for example, Paul E. Peterson, "Introduction: Technology, Race, and Urban Policy," in *The New Urban Reality*, ed. Paul E. Peterson (Washington, D.C.: The Brookings Institution, 1985), 1–29. A powerful rejoinder is David F. Noble, *Forces of Production: A Social History of Industrial Automation* (New York: Knopf, 1984). For a general discussion of regional industrial decline, see George Sternlieb and James W. Hughes, eds., *Post-Industrial America: Metropolitan Decline and Inter-Regional Job Shifts* (New Brunswick, N.J.: Rutgers University, Center for Urban Policy Research, 1975); John Kasarda, "Urban Industrial Transition and the Underclass," *Annals of the American Academy of Political and Social Science* 501 (January 1989): 26–47.

14. See statement of D. J. Davis, Ford vice president for Manufacturing, U.S. Congress, Joint Committee on the Economic Report, Subcommittee on Economic Stabilization, *Hearings on Automation and Technological Change*, 84th Congress, 1st Session, October 1955, 53 (hereafter referred to as *Automation Hearings*). On the roots of automation, see Stephen Meyer, "The Persistence of Fordism: Workers and Technology in the American Automobile Industry," in *On the Line: Essays in the History of Autowork*, ed. Nelson Lichtenstein and Stephen Meyer (Urbana: University of Illinois Press, 1989), esp. 86–93.

15. Quoted in James C. Keebler, "Working Automation," *Automation* 3 (January 1957): 29.

16. Harder quoted in Floyd G. Lawrence, "Union Belabors Automation," ibid., 2 (May 1955): 22; For further discussion of employers' defense of automation, see Ronald Edsforth, "Why Automation Didn't Shorten the Work Week: The Politics of

Work Time in the Automobile Industry," in *Autowork*, ed. Robert Asher and Ronald Edsforth (Albany: State University of New York Press, 1995), 165–67.

17. James C. Keebler, "Another Milestone Passed," ibid., 5 (February 1959): 26.

18. Floyd G. Lawrence, "Progress With Ideas," ibid., 2 (July 1955): 23. For a discussion of automation and workers' control in other industries, see Noble, *Forces of Production*.

19. Reuther testimony, *Automation Hearings*, 124. For a variation on this quote, see John Barnard, *Walter Reuther and the Rise of the Auto Workers* (Boston: Little, Brown, 1983), 154. In Barnard's version, Reuther offered the acerbic response: "And not one of them buys new Ford cars either."

20. Davis statement in *Automation Hearings*, 56–57, 63; Ford Press Releases, January 18, 1950, February 26, 1950, March 30, 1952, July 7, 1954, all in UAW-RD, Box 82, Folder: Ford Motor Company Plants and Equipment. See also Nelson Lichtenstein, "Life at the Rouge: A Cycle of Workers' Control," in *Life and Labor: Dimensions of American Working-Class History*, ed. Charles Stephenson and Robert Asher (Albany: State University of New York Press, 1986), 251–53. The most comprehensive lists of Ford expansion projects are Ford Press Release, August 20, 1957, and Memo from George Marrelli to Nelson Samp, June 13, 1957 (which includes number of employees in each plant), both in UAW-RD, Box 76, Folder 5.

21. Allan Nevins and Frank Ernest Hill, *Ford: Decline and Rebirth, 1933–1962* (New York: Scribner, 1963), 340–41; U.S. Congress, House of Representatives, *Hearings Before the Committee on Unemployment and the Impact of Automation of the Committee on Education and Labor*, 87th Congress, First Session 1961, 512; Memo, Carrol Colburn to Woody Ginsburg, "Material for NBC," March 26, 1959, UAW-RD, Box 50, Folder 13.

22. Ford press releases, August 18, 1949, July 7, 1954, June 20, 1955; Nevins and Hill, *Ford: Decline and Rebirth*, 364–65; Stephen Amberg, *The Union Inspiration in American Politics: The Autoworkers and the Making of a Liberal Industrial Order* (Philadelphia: Temple University Press, 1994), 190.

23. Ford press releases, September 3, 1953, June 14, 1955. In both, Ford stated that these new plants "will not replace any existing facilities," but merely "add to our present engine capacity." Nevins and Hill, *Ford: Decline and Rebirth*, 340, 364–65; Lichtenstein, "Life at the Rouge," 252; Memo on Automation in Ford Plants, from Jim O'Rourke to Ken Bannon, January 31, 1957, in UAW-RD, Box 65; Edward B. Shils, *Automation and Industrial Relations* (New York: Holt, Rinehart and Winston, 1963), 231.

24. John Bugas to Carl Stellato, June 7, 1950, and Manton Cummins to Carl Stellato, July 18, 1950, copies in UAW-WPR, Box 249, Folder 249–19.

25. James C. Keebler, "More Automatic Operation," *Automation* 6 (February 1960): 46.

26. *Detroit Free Press*, April 29, 1955.

27. Louis Seaton, "Expanding Employment: The Answer to Unemployment," General Motors pamphlet (c. 1959), 4, 12, in VF, Pre-1960, Box 4, Folder: Employment-Unemployment 1950s.

28. See Reuther testimony, *Automation Hearings*, 97–149; Shils, *Automation and Industrial Relations*, 127–72; an optimistic view on automation, by the Dean of the University of Chicago Business School and an Eisenhower administration adviser, is W. Allen Wallis, "Some Economic Considerations," in *Automation and Technological*

Change, ed. John Dunlop (Englewood Cliffs, N.J.: Prentice-Hall, 1962), 103–13. For greater detail on union responses to automation, see Chapter 6 below.

29. I borrow the term "silent firing" from Julius Rezler, *Automation and Industrial Labor* (New York: Random House, 1969), 30.

30. "Displacement of Workers Increasing in Michigan," *Michigan CIO News*, June 13, 1957; Keebler, "More Automatic Operation," 44.

31. Steve Jefferys, *Management and Managed: Fifty Years of Crisis at Chrysler* (Cambridge: Cambridge University Press, 1986), 127–45.

32. Memo from Frank Winn to Harry Chester, Re: Preferential Hiring, September 11, 1956, 2, UAW-RD, Box 72, Folder 36.

33. Studebaker and Packard's combined market share fell from 6.8 percent in 1948 to 2.1 percent in 1955; ibid., 1, 3; *Michigan CIO News*, August 18, 1956; Stephen Amberg, "Triumph of Industrial Orthodoxy: The Collapse of Studebaker-Packard Corporation," in Lichtenstein and Meyer, *On the Line*, 190–218; on the effects of the Packard closing, see Michael Aiken, Louis A. Ferman, and Harold L. Sheppard, *Economic Failure, Alienation, and Extremism* (Ann Arbor: University of Michigan Press, 1968). Ninety-five percent of Packard workers at the time of closing were over forty; nearly a quarter were over sixty. The average worker had twenty-three years of seniority.

34. *Detroit Times*, June 6, 1957; Memo from Frank Winn to Harry Chester, 2; Herbert Northrup, *The Negro in the Automobile Industry*, Report No. 1, The Racial Policies of American Industry (Philadelphia: Industrial Research Unit, The Wharton School of Finance and Commerce, University of Pennsylvania, 1968), 30; *Detroit News*, July 23, 1959.

35. *Detroit Free Press*, June 4, 1954; "Summary of Changes of Chrysler Corporation," July 8, 1960, UAW-RD, Box 76, Folder 5; Steve Babson et al., *Working Detroit: The Making of a Union Town* (Detroit: Wayne State University Press, 1986), 162.

36. Harold L. Sheppard and James L. Stern, "Impact of Automation on Workers in Supplier Plants: A Case Study," (c. 1956), typescript in VF, Box 4, Folder: Employment-Unemployment 1950s; James Stern, "Facts, Fallacy, and Fantasy of Automation," in *IRRA Proceedings, 1958* (Madison, Wis.: Industrial Relations Research Association, 1959), 54.

37. "Homes and Industry" (1945), 3, UAW-RD, Box 9, Folder 9–19.

38. Detroit Metropolitan Area Regional Planning Commission, "The Changing Pattern of Manufacturing Plants and Employment, 1950–1960, in the Detroit Region," 2, SEMCOG, Box 9; Nevins and Hill, *Ford: Decline and Rebirth*, 340, 352.

39. "The Change in the Michigan Share of the UAW Membership, 1947–49 to 1955–56," 1, in UAW-RD, Box 76, Folder 5.

40. *Michigan CIO News*, November 4, 1954, June 13, 1957; *Northeast Detroiter*, February 27, 1957; Memo from Frank Winn to Henry Chester, 3.

41. H. G. Bixby, "How Shall We Produce a More Favorable Climate for Business, Industry, and Payrolls in Detroit and Michigan" (hereafter referred to as "Favorable Climate"), speech before the Economic Club of Detroit, April 18, 1960, copy in FK, Box 8, Folder 265. For an attempt to refute rationales like Bixby's, see Edward D. Wickersham, "Labor as a Factor in Plant Location in Michigan" (Ann Arbor: School of Business Administration, University of Michigan, 1957), copy in VF, Box 18, Folder: Industries, location of, 1950s.

42. Mueller et al., *Location Decisions*, 30–31.

43. Mueller et al., *Location Decisions*, 40–41.

44. "Why They Are Shifting Plants out of Detroit," *Militant*, March 27, 1950.

45. *The Detroiter*, November 15, 1954.

46. *Detroit Free Press*, April 28, 1957; Bixby, "Favorable Climate"; *Detroit Free Press*, n.d. [c. 1959], clipping in UAW-PAC, Box 60, Folder 60–35.

47. Mueller et al., *Location Decisions*, 38–39.

48. *Detroit Free Press*, November 9, 1954; *Detroit News*, June 5, 1957; *Community News*, February 28, 1957; Jon C. Teaford, *The Rough Road to Renaissance: Urban Revitalization in America, 1940–1985* (Baltimore: Johns Hopkins University Press, 1990), 75–76, 140, 143–44.

49. Mueller et al., *Location Decisions*, 23–24; *Detroit Times*, June 16, 1957; Bixby, "Favorable Climate," 9. In a 1972 survey, taxes ranked second after wages on a list of reasons why Detroit firms planned to relocate outside the city. See Lewis Mandell, *Industrial Location Decisions: Detroit Compared with Atlanta and Chicago* (New York: Praeger Publishers, 1975).

50. Detroit Metropolitan Area Regional Planning Commission, "Location of Automotive Plants," 13, SEMCOG, Box 9.

51. Detroit Metropolitan Area Regional Planning Commission, "Industrial Land Use in the Detroit Region," February 1952, 2, ibid.

52. *Detroit Free Press*, July 15, 1951.

53. "Tank Output Lags Six Months," *New York Times*, January 7, 1952.

54. *Military Procurement Hearings before a Subcommittee of the Committee on Armed Services of the United States Senate*, 86th Congress, 1st Session, July 1959, 25. On the rise of the sunbelt, see also Schulman, *From Cotton Belt to Sunbelt*, 135–73. For comparisons with Detroit, see Kenneth T. Jackson, "The City Loses the Sword: The Decline of Major Military Activity in the New York Metropolitan Region," in Lotchin, *The Martial Metropolis*, 151–62; Geoffrey Rossano, "Suburbia Armed: Nassau County Development and the Rise of the Aerospace Industry," ibid., 61–87; and Martin J. Schiesl, "Airplanes to Aerospace: Defense Spending and Economic Growth in the Los Angeles Region, 1945–1960," ibid., 135–49.

55. William Haber, Eugene C. McKean, and Harold C. Taylor, *The Michigan Economy: Its Potentials and Its Problems* (Kalamazoo, Mich.: The W. E. Upjohn Institute for Employment Research, 1959) 14, 17, 66. For a concise summary of the causes for the decline of Detroit as a military production center, see Markusen et al., *The Rise of the Gunbelt*, 62–68.

56. Guy Nunn, "Detroit: Ghost Arsenal?" *New Republic*, February 4, 1952, 16–17.

57. Haber, McKean, and Taylor, *Michigan Economy*, 90–91; statewide defense manufacturing employment peaked at 220,758 in March 1953, and fell to 28,857 in January 1959. See Memo from Carrol Colburn to Woody Ginsburg, "Material for NBC," March 26, 1959, UAW-RD, Box 50, Folder 13.

58. The classic article on job mismatch (a case study of Detroit) is John F. Kain, "Housing Segregation, Negro Employment, and Metropolitan Decentralization," *Quarterly Journal of Economics* 82 (1968): 175–97. "NAACP Study Concerning Trade Union Apprenticeship," (prepared by Herbert Hill), 1960, pp. 41–42, NAACP, Group III, Box A180, Folder: Labor: Apprenticeship Training; on discrimination in new General Motors plants in small-towns and suburbs in Ohio, the South and the West, see "Report of the Labor Secretary," April 1957, NAACP, Group III, Box A309, Folder: Staff: Herbert Hill Reports, 1957–63; *Wall Street Journal*, October 24,

1957; Kevin Boyle, "'There Are No Union Sorrows that the Union Can't Heal': The Struggle for Racial Equality in the United Automobile Workers, 1940–1960," *Labor History* 35 (1995): 5–23.

59. *Detroit News*, January 1, 1954; Tom Kleene, "Ford Opposes Reuther Again, Sees No Cause for Gloom," *Detroit Times*, January 18, 1954.

60. *Detroit News*, October 25, 1955; *Michigan's Labor Market* 11, no. 2 (February 1956), 11; "Production Worker Overtime Hours in Manufacturing (1958–1962)," and "Overtime in Manufacturing and in the Motor Vehicle Industry, 1965," both in UAW-RD, Box 65, Folder: Auto Industry—Big Three—Workforce, Salaries, and Benefits, 1950–67.

61. Statement of Leonard Woodcock Before the General and Select Subcommittee on Labor, House Committee on Education and Labor, on H.R. 9802, March 11, 1964, 20–23, in UAW-RD, Box 65, Folder: Auto Industry—Output, 1947–64.

62. Testimony by Theodore Yntema, vice president of Ford, Statement of Automobile Manufacturers Association before the Joint Committee of General Subcommittee on Labor and Select Subcommittee on Labor of the Committee on Education and Labor, on H.R. 9802, "The Overtime Penalty Pay Act of 1964," February 28, 1964, 7, in UAW-RD, Box 65, Folder: Auto Industry-Output 1947–64. Emphasis in original.

63. Galbraith quoted in William Serrin, *The Company and the Union: The Civilized Relationship of the General Motors Company and the United Automobile Workers* (New York: Knopf, 1973), 237.

64. *Detroit News*, April 4, 1955.

65. Auto industry leaders recognized that workers usually found overtime appealing. See Testimony by Theodore Yntema, 14–17, 19. On the barriers to occupational advancement within plants, see Eli Chinoy, *Automobile Workers and the American Dream* (New York: Random House, 1955); on the difficulties of mandatory overtime, see Dan Georgakas and Marvin Surkin, *Detroit: I Do Mind Dying: A Study in Urban Revolution* (New York: St. Martin's Press, 1975), 31, 33; for a perceptive discussion of contemporary workers' attitudes toward overtime, see Richard Feldman and Michael Betzold, eds., *End of the Line: Autoworkers and the American Dream: An Oral History* (New York: Weidenfeld and Nicolson, 1988), 283.

66. Harold L. Sheppard, Louis Ferman, and Seymour Faber, "Too Old To Work—Too Young to Retire: A Case Study of a Permanent Plant Shutdown," Report to United States Senate, Special Committee on Employment Problems, December 21, 1959 (Washington, D.C.: U.S. Government Printing Office, 1960), quote on 8; pamphlet copy in VF—Pre-1960, Box 4, File: Employment—Unemployment 1950s. For a further discussion of the impact of unemployment on Packard workers, see Aiken, Ferman, and Sheppard, *Economic Failure*, esp. 30–151.

67. Figures from U.S. Department of Commerce, Bureau of the Census, *Census of Population, 1960*, PC(1)-24C (Washington, D.C.: U.S. Government Printing Office, 1962), Table 77.

68. *Michigan Labor Market Letter*, November 1962, 14, 15.

69. See Sheppard, Ferman, and Faber, Report to the U.S. Senate, Special Committee on Employment Problems; Michael Aiken and Louis A. Ferman, "The Social and Political Reactions of Older Negroes to Unemployment," *Phylon* 17 (1966): 333–46.

70. Sheppard and Stern, "Impact of Automation," typescript, 3, 6, VF—Pre-1960, Box 4.

71. "Youth and Automation," n.d. [c. 1960], UAW-RD, Box 64, Folder: Youth.

72. Manton Cummins to Carl Stellato, July 18, 1950, in UAW-WPR, Box 249, Folder 249–19.

73. *Detroit News*, July 15, 1959; Vocational Services Monthly Report, April 1959, DUL, Box 45, Folder A9–7; see also Vocational Services Annual Report, 1959, ibid., Folder A9–8.

74. Vocational Services Department Monthly Report, April 1959, ibid., Folder A9–7.

75. Detroit City Plan Commission, *Industrial Study: A Survey of Existing Conditions and Attitudes of Detroit's Industry* (Master Plan Technical Report, Second Series), July 1956, 46; *Detroit Times*, June 2, 1957.

76. "When People Move," DUL, Box 46, Folder A10–13; *East Side Shopper*, June 6, 1957. The case of Pittsburgh's Hazelwood neighborhood offers an interesting point of comparison. Between 1950 and 1970, the area, centered around the Jones and Loughlin steel plant, with sizable railyards and a thriving business district, lost half of its workers and 28.4 percent of its residents, and witnessed a dramatic decline in its commercial district. See Joel A. Tarr and Denise DiPasquale, "The Mill Town in the Industrial City: Pittsburgh's Hazelwood," in *Urbanism Past and Present* 13 (Winter/Spring 1982): 9–11.

77. *East Side Shopper*, April 18, 1957; *Detroit News*, May 5, 1957; *Detroit Free Press*, January 18, 1961.

78. Ibid., February 29, 1961. It is not clear from the article whether or not Haines's wife worked. The average unemployed worker in Detroit in early 1961 shared much in common with Haines: male, age thirty-seven, married with one child.

79. Jacqueline Jones, "Southern Diaspora: Origins of the Northern Underclass," paper presented to the 106th Annual Meeting of the American Historical Association, Chicago, December 30, 1991, noted that small towns in Ohio and Indiana, many of which attracted auto factories and suppliers, had minuscule black populations, and remained hotbeds of hostility to blacks.

80. *Ford Facts*, December 1, 1951.

Chapter 6
"Forget about Your Inalienable Right to Work": Responses
to Industrial Decline and Discrimination

1. *Ford Facts*, September 8, 1951; *Michigan CIO News*, September 6, 1951; *Detroit Labor News*, September 7, 1951.

2. UAW-CIO Radio and TV Department, Press Release: "Senator Douglas Predicts 'Rough Times' for Detroit," November 10, 1953, copy in NAACP, Group II, Box A350, Folder: UAW, 1949–1955. On economists, industry, and employment policy in the period, see James L. Sundquist, *Politics and Policy: The Eisenhower, Kennedy, and Johnson Years* (Washington, D.C.: The Brookings Institution, 1968), 57–83; Irving Bernstein, *Promises Kept: John F. Kennedy's New Frontier* (New York: Oxford University Press, 1991), 160–91; Gary Mucciaroni, *The Political Failure of Employment Policy, 1945–1982* (Pittsburgh: University of Pittsburgh Press, 1990), 17–53;

Margaret Weir, *Politics and Jobs: The Boundaries of Employment Policy in the United States* (Princeton, N.J.: Princeton University Press, 1992), 54–58, 63–67.

3. Sundquist, *Politics and Policy*, 114–21, 125–34; Weir, *Politics and Jobs*, 67–75; Mucciaroni, *Political Failure*, 46–62; Alice O'Connor, "Community Action, Urban Reform, and the Fight Against Poverty: The Ford Foundation's Gray Areas Program," *Journal of Urban History* (forthcoming).

4. Elizabeth Fones-Wolf, *Selling Free Enterprise: The Business Assault on Labor and Liberalism, 1945–1960* (Urbana: University of Illinois Press, 1994); see also Robert Griffith, "Forging America's Postwar Order: Domestic Politics and Political Economy in the Age of Truman," in *The Truman Presidency*, ed. Michael J. Lacey (New York: Cambridge University Press, 1989), 57–88.

5. William Chafe, "Postwar American Society: Dissent and Social Reform," ibid., 156–73.

6. Martin Halpern, *UAW Politics in the Cold War Era* (Albany: State University of New York Press, 1988), 257–59; Robert Asher, "The 1949 Speed Up Strike and the Post War Social Compact, 1946–1961," in *Autowork*, ed. Robert Asher and Ronald Edsforth (Albany: State University of New York Press, 1995), 127–54.

7. *Ford Facts*, February 18, 1950

8. Letter from John Bebenhoff, Stanley Adamczyk, Allen Baker, and Earl Filban, ibid., April 22, 1950.

9. Ibid., February 18, 1950, April 22, 1950, May 6, 1950, May 12, 1951, May 19, 1951, June 2, 1951, July 7, 1951.

10. *Detroit News*, August 6, 1951; anonymous letter in *Ford Facts*, September 22, 1951.

11. Ibid., May 6, 1950, July 8, 1950.

12. In the fall of 1950, Local 600 threatened a strike to force Ford to guarantee seniority rights to Rouge workers transferred to new plants. See *Michigan CIO News*, August 10, 1950; on early antidecentralization efforts, see also ibid., August 24, 1950.

13. On wildcat strikes between 1950 and 1954, see "Study on Work Stoppages," UAW-WPR, Box 97, Folder 97–6. The study, prepared by Ford, reported 185 "unauthorized work stoppages" at the Rouge plant between 1950 and 1954, out of 408 wildcat strikes at Ford nationwide; see also *Ford Facts*, April 9, 1955; on the suggestion box, see ibid., October 13, 1951. For a discussion of the context and prevalence of wildcat strikes in the postwar years, see George Lipsitz, *Rainbow at Midnight: Labor and Culture in the 1940s* (Urbana: University of Illinois Press, 1994), 229–52.

14. "Detroit Negro Labor Council," [n.d.], UAW-PAC, Box 64, Folder 64–6; "Rough Draft for Article on National Negro Labor Council," NAACP, Group II, Box A336, Folder: Labor: General, 1950–1952; News Release, National Negro Labor Council, ibid., Folder: Labor, General, 1953.

15. "Give Us This Day Our Daily Bread," pamphlet, ibid. It is possible that the NNLC (and other union and civil rights groups) used the phrase "right to work" in another sense: as a double entendre reference to the "right-to-work" laws that enjoyed strong support among Republicans, southern Democrats, and their corporate allies.

16. *Ford Facts*, January 28, 1950. I have rephrased Thompson's statements as questions.

17. "Decentralization Means Economic Ruin," ibid., September 15, 1951.

18. Ibid., October 13, 1951; *Detroit News*, November 19, 1951; *Ford Facts*, November 24, 1951. On previous attempts to shorten the work week, see David R. Roediger and Philip S. Foner, *Our Own Time: A History of American Labor and the Working Day* (Westport, Conn.: Greenwood Press, 1989), esp. 261–71, and Benjamin Kline Hunnicut, *Work Without End: Abandoning Shorter Hours for the Right to Work* (Philadelphia: Temple University Press, 1988); Ronald Edsforth, "Why Automation Didn't Shorten the Work Week: The Politics of Work Time in the Automobile Industry," in Asher and Edsforth, *Autowork*, 155–79.

19. *Ford Facts*, February 4, 1950.

20. Copy of Dearborn Resolution in UAW-WPR, Box 97, Folder 97–4, ALUA; *Ford Facts*, September 15, 1951, November 17, 1951.

21. *Local Union No. 600 v. Ford Motor Company*, U.S. District Court for the Eastern District of Michigan, Southern Division, complaint copy in UAW-WPR, Box 249, Folder 249–23, ALUA. A general description of the suit is in "Plant Transfers Irk Unions," *Business Week*, December 1, 1951, 36, 40.

22. Letter from Carl Stellato to Walter P. Reuther, October 31, 1951, UAW-WPR, Box 249, Folder 249–23.

23. *Ford Facts*, September 22, 1951.

24. *Local Union No. 600 v. Ford Motor Company*, 3.

25. Ibid. The Local 600 argument foreshadows arguments deployed by lawyers fighting plant shutdowns in the 1970s and 1980s in cases such as *Local 1330 v. U.S. Steel*. See Staughton Lynd, *The Fight Against Shutdowns: Youngstown's Steel Mill Closings* (San Pedro, Calif.: Singlejack Books, 1983), 141–48, 160–89.

26. *Local Union No. 600 v. Ford Motor Company*, 4, 5.

27. UAW Inter-Office Communication to Walter P. Reuther from Harold A. Cranefield, November 8, 1951, UAW-WPR, Box 249, Folder 249–23.

28. David Brody, *Workers in Industrial America: Essays on the 20th Century Struggle* (New York: Oxford University Press, 1980), 173–214; 61 *NLRB* 792, at 802, quoted in Christopher L. Tomlins, *The State and the Unions: Labor Relations, Law, and the Organized Labor Movement in America, 1880–1960* (Cambridge: Cambridge University Press, 1985), 263. See also James Atleson, *Values and Assumptions in American Labor Law* (Amherst: University of Massachusetts Press, 1983), esp. 111–35; Katherine Stone, "The Post-War Paradigm in American Labor Law," *Yale Law Review* 90 (1981): 1509–80.

29. Lawrence Friedman, *A History of American Law*, 2d ed. (New York; Simon and Schuster, 1985), 514.

30. Carl Stellato to Walter P. Reuther, November 12, 1951, *Ford Facts*, November 3, 1951.

31. UAW Inter-Office Communication to Reuther from Cranefield.

32. *Ford Facts*, March 12, 1952; *Detroit Free Press*, March 18, 1952; *Detroit Times*, March 18, 1952; see also William D. Andrew, "Factionalism and Anti-Communism: Ford Local 600," *Labor History* 20 (1979): 227–55.

33. *Ford Facts*, April 19, 1952. This statewide agreement had earlier precedents. In January 1951, laid-off gear and axle workers at the Rouge could move to the new Mound Road plant or use their seniority against junior employees in the axle building at the Rouge (ibid., January 20, 1951). Later in 1951, the UAW announced

a seniority agreement with Ford that protected the seniority of laid-off workers at the Rouge, Highland Park, Lincoln, Mound Road, and Dearborn Engineering plants. Workers laid off from any of these five Detroit-area plants "will be rehired into one of the others, if work is available, before any new employees are hired" (ibid., February 24, 1951).

34. In fact, UAW membership at Ford rose by 12.6 percent nationwide between 1947–48 and 1957–58, while UAW Local 600 membership fell by 24.5 percent in the same period. See "Ford Motor Company—UAW Membership," UAW-RD, Box 76, Folder 5.

35. 113 *Federal Supplement* 834; *Michigan CIO News*, June 11, 1953. The outcome of the suit warranted only one column-inch of coverage on a back page of the *Michigan CIO News*.

36. Nelson Lichtenstein, "Auto Worker Militancy and the Structure of Factory Life, 1937–1955," *Journal of American History* 67 (1980): 335–53; Lichtenstein, "Life at the Rouge: A Cycle of Workers' Control," in *Life and Labor: Dimensions of American Working-Class History*, ed. Charles Stephenson and Robert Asher (Albany: State University of New York Press, 1986), 256–59. Other left-led unions and locals around the country also challenged deindustrialization, but like Local 600, they were largely silenced in the anticommunist and antiradical fervor of the late 1940s and early 1950s. See Steve Rosswurm, "An Overview and Assessment of the CIO's Expelled Unions," in *The CIO's Left-Led Unions* (New Brunswick, N.J.: Rutgers University Press, 1992), 1–17.

37. *Michigan CIO News*, June 21, 1956; for other expressions of ambivalence toward automation, see ibid., January 27, 1955, March 11, 1955, April 14, 1955, September 1, 1955.

38. Ibid., January 27, 1955, October 20, 1955; *Detroit Labor News*, October 4, 1956, November 1, 1956; Walter P. Reuther statement to the Special Senate Committee on Unemployment Problems, Detroit, Michigan, November 12, 1959, copy in NAACP, Group III, Box A194, Folder: Labor—UAW; "Youth and Automation," n.d. [c. 1960], in UAW-RD, Box 64, Folder: Youth; Edsforth, "Why Automation Didn't Shorten the Work Week," 173–77.

39. On the background, see Bernstein, *Promises Kept*, 181–91.

40. *Michigan CIO News*, January 26, 1956, June 21, 1956, September 6, 1956, May 9, 1957; *Detroit Labor News*, October 11, 1956.

41. The City Plan Commission was especially concerned with the lack of available land in the city for plant expansion, with the large number of multistory factories in the city, and with the lack of parking. See Detroit City Plan Commission, *Industrial Study: A Survey of Existing Conditions and Attitudes of Detroit Industry*, Master Plan Technical Report, Second Series, July 1956 (quote, 6).

42. *Master Plan for the City of Detroit* (Detroit: City of Detroit, 1946); Detroit City Plan Commission, *Industrial Study*, 5, 50–52. The history of industrial renewal in postwar American cities is still largely unwritten, but brief discussions may be found in John T. Cumbler, *A Social History of Economic Decline: Business, Politics, and Work in Trenton* (New Brunswick, N.J.: Rutgers University Press, 1989), 169–70; Jon C. Teaford, *Rough Road to Renaissance: Urban Revitalization in America, 1940–1985* (Bloomington: Indiana University Press, 1990), 149–50; Julie Boatright Wilson and Virginia W. Knox, "Cleveland: The Expansion of a Metropolitan Area and Its

Ghettos," Malcolm Wiener Center for Social Policy, John F. Kennedy School of Government, Harvard University, Working Paper Series, No. H-91–8 (July 1991), 44–45.

43. *Detroit Free Press*, January 22, 1951, April 21, 1951; Interoffice Communication from Ralph Showalter, Subject: Corktown Property Owners' Association, April 23, 1951, UAW-PAC, Box 64, Folder 64–15. UAW leaders supported the principle of industrial renewal. See "Notes on Stabilizing Employment and Output," March 13, 1957, UAW-RD, Box 65, Folder: Auto Industry Employment Stability. For a history of the West Side Industrial Project, see Robert J. Mowitz and Deil S. Wright, *Profile of a Metropolis: A Case Book* (Detroit: Wayne State University Press, 1962), 81–139; June Manning Thomas, "Neighborhood Response to Redevelopment in Detroit," *Community Development Journal* 20 (April 1985): 89–98.

44. Compare the fate of the West Side project with those of celebrated redevelopment projects in the 1970s and 1980s. See for example: David Fasenfest, "Community Politics and Urban Redevelopment: Poletown, Detroit, and General Motors," *Urban Affairs Quarterly* 22 (1986): 101–23; Jeanie Wylie, *Poletown: Community Betrayed* (Urbana: University of Illinois Press, 1989); "Detroit Journal: Jobs Oasis Is Created But Price Was High," *New York Times*, April 25, 1992 (on the Chrysler Jefferson North Assembly Plant).

45. "Detroit Urban League Chronology, 1916–1967," in DUL, Box 74, Folder: History. See also John C. Dancy, *Sand Against the Wind: The Memoirs of John C. Dancy* (Detroit: Wayne State University Press, 1966). On the early history of the DUL, see Richard W. Thomas, "The Detroit Urban League: 1916–1923," *Michigan History* 60 (1976): 315–38; Bradley H. Pollock, "John C. Dancy, the Depression and the New Deal," *UCLA Historical Journal* 5 (1984): 5–23, esp. 9.

46. See for example, Memorandum, Francis Kornegay to Executive Board Members, DUL, June 4, 1951, FK, Box 5, Folder 153.

47. Recommendations, DUL-MSES Committee, January 17, 1951, FK, Box 5, Folder 145; Michigan Employment Security Commission, Statement, July 30, 1952, ibid., Folder 154.

48. Recommendations, DUL-MSES Committee, January 17, 1951, ibid., Folder 145; Michigan Employment Security Commission, Statement, July 30, 1952, ibid., Folder 154; Interview with Francis A. Kornegay, in *Untold Tales, Unsung Heroes: An Oral History of Detroit's African American Community, 1918–1967*, ed. Elaine Latzman Moon (Detroit: Wayne State University Press, 1994), 212.

49. For a similar pattern in Birmingham, Alabama, see Robin D. G. Kelley, "The Black Poor and the Politics of Opposition in a New South City, 1929–1970," in *The "Underclass" Debate: Views from History*, ed. Michael B. Katz (Princeton, N.J.: Princeton University Press, 1993): 316–17; on Cincinnati, see Nina Mjagkij, "Behind the Scenes: The Cincinnati Urban League, 1948–1963," in *Race and the City: Work, Community, and Protest in Cincinnati, 1820–1970*, ed. Henry Louis Taylor (Urbana: University of Illinois Press, 1993), 280–94. Mjagkij argues that the CUL was more successful than the DUL in opening jobs for blacks.

50. Background Statement for Airlines Management Conference, September 10, 1957, DUL, Box 47, Folder A11–13; William J. Brown to Trudy Haynes, February 13, 1957, DUL, Folder A11–15. For examples of the difficulty in negotiating with employers, see Interview with Francis Kornegay, 213–14.

51. Vocational Services Department, Annual Report, 1957, DUL, Box 45, Folder A9–4.

52. Vocational Services Department, Quarterly Report, April–June 1963, 6, ibid., Folder A9–14.

53. *Windsor Daily Star*, January 13, 1956.

54. Vocational Services Department, Annual Report, 1959, DUL, Box 45, Folder A9–8; see also Vocational Services Department, Monthly Report, April 1959, ibid., Folder A9–7.

55. "Training and Guidance," n.d. [c. 1956], ibid., Box 50, Folder A14–7.

56. Vocational Services Department, Guidance Advisory Committee, Minutes, February 8, 1956, ibid., Folder A14–7; Francis Kornegay, "Stay in School Campaign," ibid., Box 46, Folder A10–17. The DUL's youth programs paralleled the work of foundations and social service professionals in the 1950s. DUL staff members like Francis Kornegay were trained and read widely in the social work and social-scientific literature of the era. For a lucid discussion of foundation-sponsored youth programs, see O'Connor, "Community Action, Urban Reform, and the Fight Against Poverty."

57. *Michigan Chronicle*, July 5, 1958. See materials in DUL, Box 51, Folder A15–7.

58. Roy Levy Williams, untitled plays, June 24, 1966, June 28, 1966, and July 5, 1966, ibid., Box 53, Folder A17–15.

59. Vocational Services Department, Quarterly Report, October–December 1963, ibid., Box 45, Folder A9–14. On the number of black female clerical workers, see Appendix B, Table B.2. Despite the DUL's efforts, the number of black men and women in managerial and sales positions fell in the 1950s and barely rose in the 1960s. See Appendix B, Tables B.1 and B.2. My findings diverge slightly from those of Mjagkij, "Behind the Scenes," 281–82, 288–90.

60. August Meier and Elliot Rudwick, *Black Detroit and the Rise of the UAW* (New York: Oxford University Press, 1979); Robert Korstad and Nelson Lichtenstein, "Opportunities Found and Lost: Labor Radicals and the Early Civil Rights Movement," *Journal of American History* 75 (1988): 800–801, 806–8.

61. Detroit Branch NAACP Annual Report, 1952, p. 12, NAACP, Group II, Box A90, Folder: Detroit, Michigan, July–December 1952; Arthur L. Johnson, "A Brief Account of the Detroit Branch NAACP," (1958), ibid., Group III, Box C64, Folder: Michigan—Detroit, 1958; Gloster Current, Oral History (interviewed by John Britton, March 7, 1968), 42, in Civil Rights Documentation Project, MSRC; for a general overview, see Korstad and Lichtenstein, "Opportunities Found and Lost."

62. The NAACP denounced the NNLC for its role in mustering black support for left-led unions, and passed a resolution prohibiting members from joining what it viewed as a "completely Communist-dominated" organization. See "Rough Draft for Article on National Negro Labor Council," NAACP, Group II, Box A336, Folder: Labor—General; Marshall Field Stevenson, "Points of Departure, Acts of Resolve: Black-Jewish Relations in Detroit, 1937–1962" (Ph.D. diss., University of Michigan, 1988), 272; Wilson Record, *Race and Radicalism: The Communist Party versus the NAACP* (Ithaca, N.Y.: Cornell University Press, 1964).

63. Memorandum to Roy Wilkins from Herbert Hill, April 12, 1949, in NAACP, Group II, Box A585, Folder: Staff: Herbert Hill, March–July 1949. My overview

of Hill's activities in Detroit is based on a thorough examination of the NAACP Labor Department records, and Hill's travel reports. Hill's lack of attention to Detroit may have been in large part a consequence of persistent problems with Jim Crow in other cities. Also, Detroit NAACP officials, particularly those without close ties to the labor movement, tended to downplay the problem of racial discrimination in the city. See, for example, Telegram, James J. McClendon to Walter White, April 29, 1953, copy in NAACP, Group II, Box A337, Folder: Labor: Government Contracts, 1953–55. In response to a letter to local leaders, White received detailed reports of the number of black workers in plants under government contracts all over the country. The brevity and lack of detail in McClendon's telegram stands in striking contrast to the lengthy letters and statistics sent by other branch offices around the country.

64. On the NAACP's role in the creation of the Michigan Fair Employment Practices Commission, see Stevenson, "Points of Departure," 399–427; *Michigan Chronicle*, October 19, 1946. For a succinct overview of the UAW Fair Practices Department, see William Oliver, "Summer School Course in Workers' Education on Fair Practices and Anti-Discrimination," UAW-RD, Box 11, Folder 20; see also Meier and Rudwick, *Black Detroit*, 165–74, 211–13.

65. U.S. Congress, House of Representatives, 82d Congress, 2d Session, Committee on Un-American Activities, *Hearings on Communism in the Detroit Area*, 1952. The activities of these leaders are described in detail in Stevenson, "Points of Departure," 246–327; see also Halpern, *UAW Politics in the Cold War Era*, 211–22, 245.

66. Arthur McPhaul Oral History, 8, Blacks in the Labor Movement Collection, ALUA; interview with George Crockett, in *Detroit Lives*, ed. Robert H. Mast (Philadelphia: Temple University Press, 1994), 167–69; "Dear Friends" from Michigan Committee on Civil Rights, June 22, 1951, CRC, Box 49, Folder: FEPC 1951; "Red Relations Peril FEPC," and Interoffice Communication to Walter P. Reuther from William H. Oliver, Subject: The Detroit Negro Labor Council and its initiative petition campaign, June 15, 1951, both in UAW-PAC, Box 64, Folder 64–1; William R. Hood to Olive Beasley, July 11, 1951 and Nat Ganley, Michigan State Committee Communist Party to Detroit Council of Churches, July 20, 1951, both in NAACP, Group II, Box A257, Folder FEPC-Michigan, 1942–1955.

67. Olive Beasley to Roy Wilkins, July 27, 1951, ibid.; Walter Reuther et al. to Presidents, Recording Secretaries, Executive Boards, and Fair Practices Committees in Regions 1 and 1A, July 3, 1951, UAW-PAC, Box 64, Folder 64–2; "Detroit Negro Labor Council," UAW-RD, Box 62, Folder 62–26; DUL Industrial Relations Committee Minutes, June 12, 1951, FK, Box 5, Folder 144.

68. Facts on Detroit FEPC Ordinance Drive, n.d. [1951], UAW-PAC, Box 64, Folder 64–6; Memos from William Oliver to Walter P. Reuther, July 13, 16, 17, 1951, UAW-PAC, Box 64, Folder 64–2; Father John F. Finnegan to City Council, July 24, 1951, and Detroit Council of Churches, "God's Design in the Social Order: Fact Sheet with Action Recommendation," both in NAACP, Group II, Box A257, Folder FEPC—Michigan, 1942–55; Memo: Francis Kornegay to John Dancy and William Seabron, October 2, 1951, Re: FEP Ordinance Hearing, FK, Box 5, Folder 153.

69. Press release, August 2, 1951, "TV Program Urges Detroit Enact FEPC"; Detroit Citizens Committee for Equal Employment Opportunities, to the Honorable

Common Council of the City of Detroit, July 26, 1951 and Special Bulletin, September 11, 1951 all in NAACP, Group II, Box A257, Folder FEPC—Michigan, 1942–1955; *UAW Fair Practices Fact Sheet* 5, no. 4 (July–August 1951): 1, 4; Special FEPC Bulletin, July 28, 1951, CRC, Box 49, Folder: FEPC 1951.

70. "Dear Friend," from Arthur McPhaul, Gerald Boyd, and Harold Shapiro, September 14, 1951, ibid.; *Detroit News*, November 1, 1951; *UAW Fair Practices Fact Sheet* 5, no. 5 (September–October 1951): 1–2. The Common Council, as a palliative, commissioned the Mayor's Interracial Committee to prepare a report on job bias, released as "Racial Discrimination in Employment and Proposed Fair Employment Measures," December 7, 1951, copy in CCR, Part I, Series 1, Box 12, Binder: Minutes, 1/51–12/51.

71. Executive Secretary's Report, October 13, 1952, NAACP, Group II, Box C90, File: Detroit, Mich., July–Dec. 1952; press release, Washington Bureau NAACP, February 25, 1953, ibid., Box A257, Folder: FEPC Michigan, 1942–55.

72. George Fulton to Albert Cobo, October 27, 1951, Mayor's Papers (1951), Box 4, Folder: FEPC; Benson Ford to Walter P. Reuther, in *United Automobile Worker*, May 1953; *UAW-CIO Fair Practices Fact Sheet* 6[7], no. 2 (March–April 1953): 2; ibid., 8, no. 2 (March–April 1954): 1, 5.

73. Ibid., 9, no. 1 (January–February 1955): 1; ibid. 9, no. 2 (April–May 1955): 1–6; ibid. 9, no. 3 (June–July [1955]): 1, 6; ibid. 9, no. 4 (July–August 1955): 3; *Detroit News*, June 30, 1955.

74. *UAW Fair Practices Fact Sheet*, 9, no. 3 (June–July [1955]): 1. Statement of Frederick Routh, *Hearings Before the United States Commission on Civil Rights Held in Detroit, Michigan, December 14–15, 1960* (Washington, D.C.: U.S. Government Printing Office, 1961), 105–6. Hereafter referred to as *Civil Rights Hearings*.

75. *UAW Fair Practices Fact Sheet* 9, no. 12 (November–December 1956): 1; John C. Feild, Oral History (interviewed by Katherine Shannon, December 28, 1967), 22, in Civil Rights Documentation Project, MSRC. Feild, the first director of the Michigan FEPC, is incorrectly identified as Fields in the typescript. Statistics calculated from Michigan Fair Employment Practices Commission, *Four Years on the Job in Michigan*, January 23, 1960, copy in NUL, Part I, Series III, Box A18, Folder: Michigan. For a more favorable, but still mixed evaluation of the FEPC's first five years, see Testimony of Frederick B. Routh, *Civil Rights Hearings*, 95–104. See also George Schermer, "Effectiveness of Equal Opportunity Legislation," in *The Negro and Employment Opportunity: Problems and Practices*, ed. Herbert R. Northrup and Richard L. Rowan (Ann Arbor: Bureau of Industrial Relations, Graduate School of Business Administration, University of Michigan, 1965), 74–75, 79–81. Schermer argues that state FEPC laws across the country were largely ineffective.

76. *Cotillion News*, June 15, 1955, copy in UAW-FP, Box 26, Folder 26–28; *Michigan Chronicle*, July 30, 1955, August 27, 1955. On the Cotillion Club's efforts to desegregate the police force, see DSL, Box 21, Folder: Racial—Cotillion Club. For a discussion of the formation of the Cotillion Club, see interview with Kermit G. Bailer, in Moon, *Untold Tales, Unsung Heroes*, 180.

77. On the role of the TULC, see Testimony of Horace L. Sheffield, *Civil Rights Hearings*, 77–94; *Michigan Chronicle*, May 28, 1960. The history of the TULC has yet to be written. For a brief overview, see B. J. Widick, *Detroit: City of Race and Class Violence* (Chicago: Quadrangle, 1972), 149–50; Meier and Rudwick, *Black Detroit*,

219–21; Korstad and Lichtenstein, "Opportunities Found and Lost," 809–11; and Nelson Lichtenstein, *The Most Dangerous Man in Detroit: Walter Reuther and the Fate of American Labor* (New York: Basic Books, 1995), 375–81.

78. Executive Secretary's Report, Detroit Branch NAACP Board of Directors Meeting, September 10, 1962, in NAACP, Group III, Box C66, Folder: Detroit, Michigan, 1962, January–September.

79. Request for Employees from the Negro Ministers of the City of Detroit to the Tip Top Bread Company, n.d. [late 1961–early 1962]; "To All Pastors Cooperating With Selective Patronage Program," January 4, 1962; William Coughlin to Rev. William Ardrey, January 18, 1962; "News Release From the Negro Ministers of Detroit," n.d. [1962]; and "Negro Ministers of Metropolitan Detroit to Local Pastors," March 18, 1962; all in SP-AME, Box 3.

80. On the First Federal protests, see the letters from the NAACP to individual members of the Board of Directors of First Federal Savings and Loan Association, March 4–6, 1963, and other material in DNAACP, Part I, Box 15, Folders: First Federal Savings and Loan. Roy Wilkins and Gloster Current of the national office of the NAACP were concerned that GM would manipulate a "very, very friendly press" to its advantage and mount "serious counteroffensives" against the NAACP. See Memo from Roy Wilkins to Herbert Hill, April 14, 1964, and Memo from Gloster Current to Roy Wilkins, April 21, 1964, in NAACP, Group III, Box A186, Folder: Labor—General Motors, 1956–1965. When the NAACP announced a picket of General Motors, Urban League president Whitney Young wrote a disapproving letter and noted "progress already made" with GM. See Young to Roy Wilkins, April 30, 1964, ibid. See also Press Release: "More NAACP Protests Set Against General Motors," April 24, 1964, ibid.; and "March on GM," ibid., Box A189, Folder: Labor—Michigan; Joe T. Darden, et al., *Detroit: Race and Uneven Development* (Philadelphia: Temple University Press, 1987), 71.

81. Evelyn Brooks Higginbotham, "African-American Women's History and the Metalanguage of Race," *Signs* 17 (1992): 255–56.

82. Ibid., 273–74.

83. See Robert Halpern, *Rebuilding the Inner City: A History of Neighborhood Initiatives to Address Poverty in the United States* (New York: Columbia University Press, 1995), 83–126; Thomas F. Jackson, "The State, the Movement, and the Urban Poor: The War on Poverty and Political Mobilization in the 1960s," in Katz, *The "Underclass" Debate*, 403–39.

Chapter 7
Class, Status, and Residence: The Changing
Geography of Black Detroit

1. Materials on *Sipes v. McGhee* can be found in NAACP, Group II, Boxes B135–137. Quotes from *Benjamin J. Sipes and Anna C. Sipes, James A. Coon, and Addie A. Coon, et al. v. Orsel McGhee and Minnie S. McGhee*, January 7, 1947. On other restrictive covenant cases, see Gloster Current to Shirley Adelson, July 12, 1946, ibid., Box B135, Folder: Sipes v. McGhee, 1946; Memorandum to Mr [Thurgood] Marshall from Marian Wynn Perry, May 1, 1946, ibid., Box B74, Folder: Legal, Detroit, Mich., General 1946, 1947; *Michigan Chronicle*, October 26, 1946; John C.

Dancy, *Sand Against the Wind: The Memoirs of John C. Dancy* (Detroit: Wayne State University Press, 1966), 215–16; Marshall Field Stevenson, "Points of Departure, Acts of Resolve: Black-Jewish Relations in Detroit, 1937–1962," (Ph.D. diss., University of Michigan, 1988), 346–49; Clement Vose, *Caucasians Only: The Supreme Court, the NAACP, and Restrictive Covenant Cases* (Berkeley: University of California Press, 1959), 125–27.

2. See especially ibid.; also Charles Abrams, *Forbidden Neighbors: A Study of Prejudice in Housing* (New York: Harper, 1955).

3. *Shelley v. Kraemer*, 334 U.S. 1 (1948); *Pittsburgh Courier* (Detroit edition), May 8, 1948; for similar articles, see *Michigan Chronicle*, May 8, 1948; for an overview of the NAACP's strategy, see Mark V. Tushnet, *Making Civil Rights Law: Thurgood Marshall and the Supreme Court, 1936–1961* (New York: Oxford University Press, 1994), 81–98.

4. On wartime racial liberalism, see Philip Gleason, "Americans All: World War II and the Shaping of American Identity," *Review of Politics* 43 (1981): 483–518; and Gary Gerstle, "The Working Class Goes to War," *Mid-America: An Historical Review* 75 (October 1993): 303–22. Civil rights organizations and observers of race relations in the city retained a remarkable confidence in the possibility of integration. See George Schermer, "The Transitional Housing Area" (A Statement Prepared for the Housing Workshop Session of the 1952 NAIRO Conference, Washington, D.C.), November 10, 1952, DUL, Box 38, Folder A2–8; *Michigan Chronicle*, February 28, 1953; this and other interesting articles on black Detroit in the 1950s are reprinted in Charles J. Wartman, *Detroit—Ten Years After* (Detroit: Michigan Chronicle, 1953). As late as 1964, the *Detroit News* ran an article, "Housing Bias Crumbling in Detroit, Expert Finds," which cited city race relations official Richard Marks criticizing the cynicism of those who argued that "integration is the period between the arrival of the first Negro and the departure of the last white" (*Detroit News*, March 22, 1964).

5. Bernard J. Frieden, *The Future of Old Neighborhoods: Rebuilding for a Changing Population* (Cambridge: MIT Press, 1964), 24, 26, Tables 2.4 and 2.5.

6. For a general discussion of the social geography of cities, see Thomas J. Sugrue, "The Structures of Urban Poverty: The Reorganization of Space and Work in Three Periods of American History," in *The "Underclass" Debate: Views from History*, ed. Michael B. Katz (Princeton, N.J.: Princeton University Press, 1993), 85–117.

7. Henry Lee Moon, "Danger in Detroit," *Crisis* 53 (January 1946) 28.

8. Alfred McClung Lee and Norman D. Humphrey, *Race Riot* (New York: Dryden Press, 1943), 93.

9. For a thorough discussion of Detroit's black-owned businesses, see Richard W. Thomas, *Life for Us Is What We Make It: Building Black Community in Detroit* (Bloomington: Indiana University Press, 1992), 201–23. On the growing number of black women professionals (most of whom were schoolteachers), see Appendix B, Table B. 2.

10. *Detroit Free Press*, March 3, 1953, June 20, 1957; "Detroit's Top 100 Negro Leaders: Aces Who Help Build World's Motor City," *Color*, August 1948, 24–25; "Detroit's Top 100 Negro Leaders, Second Installment," ibid., October 1948, 38–39. Ed Davis, *One Man's Way* (Detroit: Edward Davis Associates, 1979); "Why Detroit is the Money City for Negroes," *Color*, December 1955, 16–21 (thanks to Eric

Arnesen for this reference). On the rise of Motown, see Suzanne Smith, "Dancing in the Street: Motown and the Cultural Politics of Detroit" (Ph.D. diss., Yale University, 1996). The proportion of black men who were professionals, managers, proprietors, and officials did not rise until the 1960s, but it grew in absolute numbers as Detroit's black population rose. The number of black women managers, proprietors, and officials remained very small. See Appendix B, Tables B.1 and B.2.

11. "Why Detroit is the Money City," 16.

12. City of Detroit Interracial Committee, "Demonstrations Protesting Negro Occupancy of Houses (Area Bounded by Buchanan Street, Grand River Avenue, Brooklyn Avenue, Michigan Avenue, and Maybury Grand), September 1, 1945 to September 1, 1946," 2, 4, in CCR, Part I, Series 1, Box 3.

13. Mayor's Committee—Community Action for Detroit Youth Report, "A General Introduction to the Target Area," n.d. [c. 1963], DNAACP, Part I, Box 23.

14. For an overview of the MIC's history, see Tyrone Tillery, *The Conscience of a City: A Commemorative History of the Detroit Human Rights Commission and Department, 1943–1983* (Detroit: Detroit Human Rights Department, 1983). Cincinnati (and a number of other cities) had similar organizations. See Robert A. Burnham, "The Mayor's Friendly Relations Committee: Cultural Pluralism and the Struggle for Black Advancement," in *Race and the City: Work, Community, and Protest in Cincinnati, 1820–1970*, ed. Henry Louis Taylor, Jr. (Urbana: University of Illinois Press, 1993), 258–79. The notion that integration was a solution to America's racial "dilemma" was most forcefully articulated by Gunnar Myrdal, *American Dilemma* (New York: Harper, 1944).

15. Schermer, "The Transitional Housing Area," 5–6.

16. Walter White, "How Detroit Fights Race Hatred," *Saturday Evening Post*, July 18, 1953, 26–27; "Buyer Beware," *Time*, April 16, 1956, 24; "Prejudice is Not Sectional," *Christian Century*, April 18, 1956, 477; "A Northern City Sitting on the Lid of Racial Trouble," *U.S. News and World Report*, May 11, 1956, 34–40; "New Carpetbaggers," *The New Republic*, July 30, 1956, 6; "Detroit Collision," *Ebony*, August 1961, 77–80; *New York Times*, April 22, 1962 (reprinted in "The Bagley Community: A Good Place to Live in Near-Northwest Detroit," copy in DUL, Box 53, Folder A17–2). On the open housing movement in Chicago, see James R. Ralph, Jr., *Northern Protest: Martin Luther King, Jr., Chicago, and the Civil Rights Movement* (Cambridge, Mass.: Harvard University Press, 1993).

17. In southwest Detroit, for example, a Methodist Church fled from a racially changing neighborhood, while members of the Catholic parish held fast. See Mayor's Interracial Committee, Minutes, April 17, 1950, CCR, Part III, Box 25, Folder 25–114; "Joint Statement," March 8, 1957, MDCC, Part I, Box 8, Folder: Press Releases—Civil Rights, 1952–64; G. Merill Lenox to Dorothy L. Tyler, April 19, 1956, ibid., Box 9, Folder: Civil Rights Activity Feedback; *Michigan Chronicle*, March 14, 1953; *Detroit Free Press*, June 24, 1957. On Jewish civil rights efforts, see Sidney Bolkosky, *Harmony and Dissonance: Voices of Jewish Identity in Detroit, 1914–1967* (Detroit: Wayne State University Press, 1991), 368–71.

18. "Activities Report, February 1–March 1, 1957, Cherrylawn Case," DUL, Box 38, Folder: A2–23; Detroit Urban League Board of Directors, Annual Meeting Minutes, February 28, 1957, CCR, Part III, Box 11, Folder 11–19; Interview with Mel Ravitz, in *Untold Tales, Unsung Heroes: An Oral History of Detroit's African Ameri-*

can Community, 1918–1967, ed. Elaine Latzmann Moon, (Detroit: Wayne State University Press, 1994), 334–35; Gerhard Lenski, *The Religious Factor: A Sociological Study of Religion's Impact on Politics, Economics, and Family Life* (Garden City, N.Y.: Doubleday, 1961), 65, 148, 190. Lenski's study was primarily based on Detroit research. See also John T. McGreevy, "American Catholics and the African-American Migration" (Ph.D. diss., Stanford University, 1992), 61, 159–62; Leslie Woodcock Tentler, *Seasons of Grace: A History of the Catholic Archdiocese of Detroit* (Detroit: Wayne State University Press, 1990), 308–9. For more on Catholics and racial change, see Chapters 8 and 9 below.

19. William H. Boone, "Major Unmet Goals that Suggest Continuing Attention," March 9, 1956, DUL, Box 38, Folder A2–16; Draft of Letter from UAW Legal Department to Thomas Kavanagh, Michigan Attorney General, July 18, 1956, ibid., Folder A2–17, "Election Warning" [1958], CCR, Part III, Box 13, Folder 13–28; *DREB News*, April 24, 1959, copy ibid., Box 14, Folder 14–5; "Your Cooperation Asked" [1959], flyer attached to letter from Robert Hutton to Merrill Lenox, March 31, 1959; Merrill Lenox to Robert Hutton, April 8, 1959, MDCC, Part I, Box 10, Folder: Housing-Detroit Real Estate Board; Detroit Branch NAACP, Board of Directors Meeting, September 14, 1959, NAACP, Group III, Box C65, Folder: Detroit, Michigan, Sept.–Dec. 1959.

20. *Detroit Free Press*, April 21, 1960, June 22, 1960; *New York Times*, June 5, 1960; *Detroit News*, August 5, 1960, October 19, 1960, November 28, 1960; "Memorandum in Opposition to Proposal 1007," December 6, 1961, in DNAACP, Part I, Box 14; Kathy Cosseboom, *Grosse Pointe, Michigan: Race Against Race* (East Lansing: Michigan State University Press, 1972).

21. Detroit Urban League, Department of Housing, Second Quarterly Report, April–June 1964, in DUL, Box 53, Folder A27–2; Eloise Whitten, "Open Occupancy: A Challenge," ibid., Folder A17–7; *Detroit News*, January 3, 1963, July 28, 1963, September 19, 1963; Citizens for a United Detroit, "Why We Oppose the Proposed Home Onwer's Ordinance," MDCC, Part I, Box 10, Folder: Housing—Home Owners' Ordinance, Citizens for a United Detroit; Leonard Gordon, "Attempts to Bridge the Racial Gap: The Religious Establishment," in *City in Racial Crisis: The Case of Detroit Pre- and Post- the 1967 Riot* (n.p.: William C. Brown Publishers, 1971), 18–24, quotes 23–24; see also Mayor Jerome Cavanagh, Richard Marks, and Charles Butler, "Messages to the Open Occupancy Conference," ibid., 29–33; materials on "Operation Open Door," March 1965, RK, Box 5, Folder 5–24. For resistance to open housing efforts in the wealthy suburb of Birmingham, see *Brightmoor Journal*, March 17, 1966.

22. James Del Rio, résumé, MDCC, Part I, Box 10, Folder: Housing—James Del Rio; Del Rio also pioneered the sales of FHA- and VA-repossessed homes to African Americans and worked with supporters of housing integration. See *Michigan Chronicle*, April 14, 1962; *Detroit Free Press*, February 3, 1963.

23. William L. Price, "Scare Selling in a Bi-Racial Housing Market," June 11, 1957, DUL, Box 44, Folder A8–1. As of 1959, there were no black members of the Detroit Board of Real Estate Brokers. See "Major Areas of Civil Rights Violations in Detroit," September 23, 1955, ibid., Box 38, Folder A2–15. In 1960, the Detroit Real Estate Board accepted two black members. See Testimony of William R. Luedders, President Detroit Real Estate Board, *Hearings Before the United States Commission*

on Civil Rights Held in Detroit, Michigan, December 14–15, 1960 (Washington, D.C.: U.S. Government Printing Office, 1961), 243. For examples of black and Jewish brokers working in racially changing neighborhoods, see "Report on the Formation of Area B Improvement Association," February 14, 1957: 3, DUL, Box 38, Folder A2–22; Commission on Community Relations, Case Reports, October 23, 1961, RK, Box 2, Folder 4. When the first black family moved onto Dartmouth Street, black real estate agent O. H. Smith sent cards to residents asking them to sell, stating, in the paraphrase of a race relations investigator, that "he had buyers (negro implied) for their property." Incident Report, 3175 Dartmouth, May 15, 1955, DUL, Box 38, File A2–14; C. W. Smith, another black realtor, was first to offer homes for sale on all-white American Street. See Memo, n.d., ibid., Box 43, File A7–13.

24. This process is described in Mel Ravitz, "Preparing Neighborhoods for Change," July 13, 1956, ibid., Box 44, Folder A8–1; Price, "Scare Selling in a Bi-Racial Housing Market," 2; CCR Field Division Case Reports, October 23, 1961, RK, Box 2, Folder 4. For a richly detailed discussion of similar practices in Baltimore, see W. Edward Orser, *Blockbusting in Baltimore: The Edmondson Village Story* (Lexington: University Press of Kentucky, 1994).

25. Incident Report, July 6, 1950, CCR, Part I, Series 1, Box 6, Folder 50–23.

26. Mary Czechowski to Mayor Albert Cobo, October 8, 1950, ibid., Box 7, Folder 50–57.

27. CCR Minutes, November 29, 1962, ibid., Series 4, Box 4.

28. *Michigan Chronicle*, July 16, 1955.

29. William L. Price, "The Housing Situation in Detroit as it Affects Minorities," June 6, 1951, DUL, Box 38, Folder A2–4; *Detroit News*, September 14, 1962.

30. Speech, n.d., 6–7, DUL, Box 44, Folder A8–1.

31. "The City Administration's Housing Program: An Analysis," in CCR, Part I, Series 1, Box 11. For an excellent discussion of land contracts and speculation in Chicago, see Arnold Hirsch, *Making the Second Ghetto: Race and Housing in Chicago, 1940–1960* (New York: Cambridge University Press, 1983), 31–33.

32. "Fair Neighborhood Practices Ordinance," copy in DNAACP, Part I, Box 21, Folder: Commission on Community Relations; *Detroit News*, September 14, 1962; *Detroit Free Press*, September 12, 1962, September 13, 1962, September 21, 1962; *Detroit News*, October 17, 1962; November 29, 1962; "A Joint Statement on Behalf of the Detroit Branch NAACP by Edward M. Turner and Arthur L. Johnson, on the Question of the Brickley Proposal," September 25, 1962, DNAACP, Part I, Box 16, Folder: Block Busting 1962; Sidney Fine, *Violence in the Model City: The Cavanagh Administration, Race Relations, and the Detroit Riot of 1967* (Ann Arbor: University of Michigan Press, 1989), 59; for a similar effort in Cincinnati, see Charles F. Casey-Leininger, "Making the Second Ghetto in Cincinnati: Avondale, 1925–70," in Taylor, *Race and the City*, 246.

33. "Report on Meeting," 5–6, CCR, Part I, Series 1, Box 5, Folder 48–124H; Detroit Urban League, "A Profile of the Detroit Negro," June 1965, 18 (in author's possession).

34. William Julius Wilson, *The Truly Disadvantaged: The Inner City, the Underclass, and Public Policy* (Chicago: University of Chicago Press, 1987), esp. 55–62; Reynolds Farley, "Residential Segregation of Social and Economic Groups Among Blacks, 1970–1980," in *The Urban Underclass*, ed. Christopher Jencks and Paul E.

Peterson (Washington, D.C.: The Brookings Institution, 1991), 274–98, challenges Wilson's assumption of the novelty of class segregation within urban black populations. Historians have recently paid greater attention to class divisions among African Americans in the urban North. The work of Henry Louis Taylor, Jr., is particularly instructive. Taylor found that in Buffalo, "the black middle class and higher paid workers led the ghetto expansion process," moving to "the best and most expensive" housing. In contrast, poor blacks "tended to remain behind in the oldest sections of the ghetto, where housing and neighborhood conditions were the worst." Taylor challenges Wilson's argument that middle-class-led institutions fled the inner city with middle-class residents, and offers the only detailed empirical study of institutions in African American neighborhoods. For a summary, see Henry Louis Taylor, Jr., "Social Transformation Theory, African Americans, and the Rise of Buffalo's Post-Industrial City," *Buffalo Law Review* 39 (1991): 587, 594–600. On class divisions generally, see Joe William Trotter, Jr., "Blacks in the Urban North: The 'Underclass Question' in Historical Perspective," in Katz, *The "Underclass" Debate*, 55–81; Joe William Trotter, Jr., *Black Milwaukee: The Making of an Industrial Proletariat, 1915–1945* (Urbana: University of Illinois Press, 1985), 80–144; Kenneth L. Kusmer, *A Ghetto Takes Shape: Black Cleveland, 1870–1930* (Urbana: University of Illinois Press, 1976), 209–14; Laurence Glasco, "Internally Divided: Class and Neighborhood in Black Pittsburgh." *Amerikastudien* 34 (1989): 223–30; Casey-Leininger, "Making the Second Ghetto in Cincinnati," 250–51.

35. To further test this data, I conducted a cross-tabulation of median household income per tract in 1950 by the percentage black population in the tract in 1940. It also reveals a pattern of segregation by class. In 1950, of the fifteen "transitional" tracts, only one had a median income below that of the average income for all blacks in tracts containing more than five hundred blacks in 1950. "Ghetto" tracts, in contrast, were poorer—only five out of twenty-six tracts with a majority-black population in 1940 had incomes above the average for all blacks. "Infill" tracts (containing second-wave black newcomers) were split evenly between above- and below-average income. To offer a more precise statistical measure of impressionistic evidence about black residential stratification, the correlation coefficient (Pearson) was calculated for tract of percentage black population in 1940 and percentage change of black population with income in 1950. The results demonstrate a clear negative correlation between the income and percentage black in 1940 and income and increase in black population. Both correlations underscore the fact that transitional tracts—those that had smaller black populations in 1940 than in 1950, and those that gained a large number of blacks between 1940 and 1950—were those tracts that had the highest median incomes.

Correlation of Income with Percentage Black
Population and Change in Black Population in
Black Tracts, 1950

Percent Black 1940 with Income 1950	−.6129
Significance .000	
Change 1940–1950 with Income 1950	−.6563
Significance .000	
N = 65 Sig. is one-tailed.	

36. Ernest W. Burgess, "The Growth of the City: An Introduction to a Research Project," in *The City*, ed. Robert E. Park, Ernest W. Burgess, and Roderick D. McKenzie (Chicago: University of Chicago Press, 1925).

37. "The History of Grixdale Park, 1953–1958: Site Commemoration and Dedication of Grixdale's Historic Preservation Park Ceremonial-Unveiling Observance," (June 9, 1988), 11–12, copy in Detroit Public Library, Detroit, Michigan.

38. "Carver and Curtis," *Color*, July 1948; "Why Detroit is Money City," 19.

39. Ibid., 16; Schermer, "The Transitional Housing Area," 7–8. By 1960, more than one-third of the area's black families had incomes over $10,000, compared to the median citywide family income of $6,597. See U.S. Department of Commerce, Bureau of the Census, *U.S. Census of Population and Housing: 1960, Census Tracts, Detroit, Michigan Standard Metropolitan Statistical Area*, Final Report PHC(1)-40 (Washington, D.C.: U.S. Government Printing Office, 1962), Table P-4, data for tract 190. For a discussion of housing prices in the Boston-Edison area, which fell between 1940 and 1948, but rose in 1949 and 1950 when the first black pioneers moved in, see Richard S. Wander, "The Influence of Negro Infiltration upon Real Estate Values" (M.A. thesis, Wayne State University, 1953); and Luigi Laurenti, *Property Values and Race: Studies in Seven Cities* (Berkeley: University of California Press, 1961), 206–9.

40. "Races Learn to Live Together in Area of Expensive Homes," *Detroit News*, May 13, 1956; "Boston Boulevard: Signpost of the Future," *Detroit Free Press*, May 15, 1956. See also "Some of Our Distinguished Residents," BEP, Box 10, Folder 2; Davis, *One Man's Way*; interview with Kermit G. Bailer, in Moon, *Untold Tales, Unsung Heroes*, 178–79.

41. Real Estate Research Corporation, "An Analysis of the Market for New Housing Proposed for Construction in the Gratiot Redevelopment Area," November 1954, 23, in Mayor's Papers (1954), Box 4, Folder: Housing Commission.

42. Wilson J. Moses, "Ambivalent Maybe," in *Lure and Loathing: Essays on Race, Identity, and the Ambivalence of Assimilation*, ed. Gerald Early (New York: Allen Lane, 1993), 277–78.

43. "Report on the Findings of the 12th Street Survey"(1947), 20, 24, CCR, Part I, Series 1, Box 4, Folder 47–57H.

44. Mayor's Committee—Community Action for Detroit Youth Report, "A General Introduction to the Target Area," n.d. [c. 1963], DNAACP, Part I, Box 23.

45. On Boston-Edison, see materials in BEP. On Grixdale Park, see *The Grixdale Parker* 1, no. 1 (January 24, 1959), reprinted in "The History of Grixdale Park," 28; *Michigan Chronicle*, September 5, 1961; *Detroit Free Press*, July 31, 1961.

46. Richard K. Kerckhoff, "A Study of Racially Changing Neighborhoods," *Merrill-Palmer Quarterly* 4 (Fall 1957): 22–24, 33.

47. "The Bagley Community: A Good Place to Live," brochure in DUL, Box 53, Folder A17–2; Eleanor Paperno Wolf and Charles Lebeaux, *Change and Renewal in an Urban Community: Five Case Studies of Detroit* (New York: Praeger, 1969), 52–58.

48. For similar findings in Baltimore, see W. Edward Orser, "Secondhand Suburbs: Black Pioneers in Baltimore's Edmondson Village," *Journal of Urban History* 16 (1990): esp. 243–46.

49. The history of African American urban institutions in this period remains to be written; it is beyond the scope of this study. But evidence from black churches indicates that these institutions usually remained concentrated in the oldest and poorest

sections of the city. They did not move, as did many white Protestant churches or Jewish synagogues, to outer sections of the city with their congregants. See *1964 Directory of Churches and Other Religious Organizations of the Detroit Metropolian Area* (Detroit: Metropolitan Detroit Council of Churches, 1964). The African American YMCA was destroyed in 1959 to make way for the Chrysler Freeway. For a suggestive discussion of the importance of black institutions in the inner city, see Henry Louis Taylor, Jr., "The Theories of William Julius Wilson and the Black Experience in Buffalo, New York," in *African Americans and the Rise of Buffalo's Post-Industrial City, 1940 to Present* (Buffalo: Buffalo Urban League, 1990), 78–80; Mark Naison, "In Quest of Community: The Organizational Structure of Black Buffalo," in ibid., 207–16; and Kenneth L. Kusmer, "African Americans in the City Since World War II: From the Industrial to the Post-Industrial Era," *Journal of Urban History* 21 (1995): 487–89. The importance of memory in shaping perceptions of African American places may play a role in the persistence of institutions in inner-city neighborhoods, even when many of their members have left. See Earl Lewis, "Connecting Memory, Self, and the Power of Place in African American Urban History," ibid., 347–71.

Chapter 8
"Homeowners' Rights": White Resistance and the Rise of Antiliberalism

1. *Ford Facts*, July 10, 1954; *Detroit News*, August 5, 1954, November 7, 1955, February 4, 1956; *Detroit Free Press*, November 3, 1963; *Detroit Daily Press*, November 11, 1964.

2. *Detroit News*, January 8, 1962, May 19, 1962; *Detroit Free Press*, November 3, 1963. Birchers had begun to work with white homeowners' organizations in Detroit in the early 1960s. See *Detroit News*, February 13, 1962.

3. *Detroit Free Press*, November 3, 1963, November 27, 1964.

4. U.S. Congress, Senate, Committee on Commerce, *Civil Rights—Public Accommodations Hearings*, 88th Congress, August 1, 1963, part 2, esp. 1085, 1088.

5. *Detroit Daily Press*, September 3, 1964; *Brightmoor Journal*, October 29, 1964. Some of Thomas Poindexter's votes undoubtedly went to an unknown candidate, Charley Poindexter, who did not campaign and picked up 8,082 votes in the primary election. See also *Detroit Daily Press*, November 11, 1964. The abrasive Poindexter only served one term on the Common Council. In 1967, he won a seat on the Detroit Court of Common Pleas, where he served until his retirement.

6. I borrow the term "defensive localism" from Margaret Weir, "Urban Poverty and Defensive Localism," *Dissent*, Summer 1994, 337–42. She uses it in the context of city-suburban relations.

7. Joseph Coles, a prominent Democratic activist and an appointee to the Detroit Mayor's Interracial Committee (MIC), stated that 155 homeowners' associations existed in Detroit during the Cobo administration. Joseph Coles, Oral History, 15, Blacks in the Labor Movement Collection, ALUA. Coles slightly underestimated the number of associations. At least 171 organizations existed during the Cobo administration and at least 191 organizations thrived in Detroit from the end of World War II to 1965. This figure undoubtedly understates the number of such associations, for

many were ephemeral and kept no records. The most important source is: "Improvement Associations of Detroit, List From Zoning Board of Appeals," July 12, 1955, DUL, Box 43, Folder A7–13, which includes names and addresses of 88 improvement associations. Through a detailed survey of letters and petitions on matters of housing and expressway construction sent to Mayor Albert Cobo, and especially through careful examination of letters in Cobo's separate files of correspondence from "civic associations," I was able to identify another 83 neighborhood groups not included in the 1955 list. See Mayor's Papers (1950) Boxes 2, 3, 5; (1951) Boxes 2, 3; (1953) Box 1, 3, 4; (1954) Box 2; (1955) Boxes 2, 4. The remaining associations were identified in a number of sources: a list of property owners' associations that joined the amicus curiae brief for the plaintiff in *Sipes v. McGhee* before the Michigan Supreme Court in Clement Vose, *Caucasians Only: The Supreme Court, the NAACP, and the Restrictive Covenant Cases* (Berkeley: University of California Press, 1959), 272, n. 41; Richard J. Peck, Community Services Department, Detroit Urban League, "Summary of Known Improvement Association Activities in Past Two Years 1955–1957," 6, in VF, Pre-1960, Folder: Community Organization 1950s; *Michigan Chronicle*, December 4, 1948, August 6, 1955, September 9, 1961; *Detroit News*, July 21, 1962; *Brightmoor Journal*, May 3, 1956, October 29, 1964, June 2, 1966, October 19, 1967, November 16, 1967; letters and brochures in SLAA; MIC, Incident Reports 1949, CCR, Part I, Series 1, Box 6, Folder 49–37; "A Study of Interracial Housing Incidents," January 20, 1949, ibid., Folder 49–3; CCR, Field Reports December 18, 1961, in RK, Box 2, Folder 4.

8. In 1955, housing activist Charles Abrams noted the importance of improvement associations in major cities and the dearth of studies of their activities. See Charles Abrams, *Forbidden Neighbors: A Study of Prejudice in Housing* (New York: Harper, 1955), 181–90. Abrams's call for research has remained largely unheeded, with the important exception of the brilliant discussion of Los Angeles' powerful grassroots homeowners' association movement in Mike Davis, *City of Quartz: Excavating the Future in Los Angeles* (London: Verso, 1990), 153–219.

9. Quotes from *Action!* the Newsletter of the Courville District Improvement Association, vol. 1 (February 15, 1948), attached to Mayor's Interracial Committee Minutes, April 4, 1948, CCR, Part I, Series 1, Box 10; *The Civic Voice*, the newsletter of the Plymouth Manor Property Owners Association, vol. 2, no. 9 (September 1962), in CCR, Part III, Box 25, Folder 25–128. For examples of ethnic diversity in Detroit, letters to Mayor Edward Jeffries, regarding the Algonquin Street and Oakwood defense housing projects, in Mayor's Papers (1945), Box 3, Folder: Housing Commission. See also Exhibit A, October 22, 1948, 1–2, attached to Memorandum to Charles S. Johnson et al. from Charles H. Houston, NAACP, Group II, Box B133, Folder: Michigan: *Swanson v. Hayden*; *Neighborhood Informer*, Greater Detroit Neighbors Association—Unit No. 2 (December 1949), 2, UAW-CAP, Box 4, Folder 4–19. The editor of the *Informer*, it should be mentioned, was a James Sugrue, a first cousin once removed of the author. For derogatory references to Jews, see "Demonstrations Protesting Negro Occupancy of Homes, September 1, 1945–September 1, 1946: Memorandum J," 31, CCR, Part I, Series 1, Box 3; and "Activities of the East Outer Drive Improvement Association," February 8, 1947, ibid., Part III, Box 25, Folder 25–49. For a reference to "niggers, chinamen, and russians," see William K. Anderson to Herbert Schultz, October 17, 1958, SLAA. For housing

incidents involving an Indian family, a Chinese family, and a Filipino family moving into white neighborhoods, see Chronological Index of Cases, 1951 (51–31) and (51–58), CCR, Part I, Series 1, Box 13; Detroit Police Department Special Investigation Bureau, Summary of Racial Activities, April 30, 1956–May 17, 1956, DUL, Box 38, Folder A2–26. On the ethnic heterogeneity of Detroit neighborhoods, see Olivier Zunz, *The Changing Face of Inequality: Urbanization, Industrial Development, and Immigrants in Detroit, 1880–1920* (Chicago, 1982), 340–51. In his examination of arrest records for whites arrested in anti–public housing riots in Chicago, Arnold Hirsch also found great diversity in ethnic affiliations. See Hirsch, *Making the Second Ghetto: Race and Housing in Chicago, 1940–1960* (New York: Cambridge University Press, 1983), 81–84.

10. See Dominic J. Capeci, Jr. and Martha Wilkerson, *Layered Violence: The Detroit Rioters of 1943* (Jackson: The University Press of Mississippi, 1991); on Briggs, see John M. Hartigan, Jr., "Cultural Constructions of Whiteness: Racial and Class Formations in Detroit" (Ph.D. diss., University of California, Santa Cruz, 1995); Arthur Kornhauser, *Detroit as the People See It: A Survey of Attitudes in an Industrial City* (Detroit: Wayne University Press, 1952), 104. On Southern whites and their organizational affiliations, see Cleo Y. Boyd, "Detroit's Southern Whites and the Store-Front Churches," Department of Research and Church Planning, Detroit Council of Churches, 1958, in DUL, Box 44, Folder A8–25; on their voting patterns, see Handwritten Vote Counts [1949], UAW-PAC, Box 63, Folder 63–2; "Degree of Voting in Detroit Primary," September 11, 1951, and "Indexes of Group Voting for Selected Councilmanic Candidates," September 11, 1951, ibid., Box 62, Folder 62–25. In 1956, Mrs. Cledah Sundwall, a Northwest Side resident and possibly a southern white migrant, called for the creation of a White Citizens Council in Detroit, calling it a "modern version of the old-time town meeting called to meet any crisis by expressing the will of the people. The primary aim of the council is to combat the NAACP and to preserve the upkeep of neighborhoods" (*Brightmoor Journal*, May 3, 1956). There is no evidence that the organization attracted any significant number of adherents in the city, perhaps because of the strength and ubiquity of improvement associations.

11. The South Lakewood Area Association had its humble origins in a protest against a proposal to expand off-street parking for stores on Jefferson Avenue: *East Side Shopper*, April 28, 1955. The SLAA papers offer evidence of the role of the homeowners' association in matters of zoning, traffic control, and parking. The South Lakewood area, on the Southeast Side of the city, was far enough removed from Detroit's black population that race seldom became an issue for the organization. The neighborhood association was concerned about what appeared to be a boarding house at 670 Lakewood, and noted "One colored" among the many boys who played in front of the house. ("Report—July 14, 1958," SLAA, Folder: 1957–1960). For a group concerned with city services, zoning enforcement, and streets and traffic, as well as racial transition, see Interoffice Correspondence, Subject: Meeting of the Burns Civic Association, April 1, 1963, CCR, Part III, Box 25, Folder 25–40. For concern about recreation, garbage pickup, and city services, see "Report on Puritan Park Civic Association Meeting," September 20, 1956, ibid., Folder 25–101. On the role of neighborhood associations in zoning enforcement, planning, and cleanups, see Detroit City Plan Commission, *Planner*, January 1945, 3–4, in the author's pos-

session. Robert J. Mowitz and Deil S. Wright, *Profile of a Metropolis: A Case Book* (Detroit: Wayne State University Press, 1962), 426–29, describe the role of Northwest Side civic associations in battling the construction of the Lodge Freeway extension. For an excellent discussion of civic associations in Queens, New York (which, because of its distance from black populations, did not organize around racial issues in the 1950s), see Sylvie Murray, "Suburban Citizens: Domesticity and Community Politics in Queens, New York, 1945–1960" (Ph.D. diss., Yale University, 1994), esp. 78–131, 181–261.

For an example of the combination of civic uplift and racist rhetoric, see *Action!* vol. 1 (February 15, 1948). The Northwest Home Owners, Inc., met to discuss threats to the community including a city incinerator and "possible Negro residence in the neighborhood." Richard J. Peck, Community Services Department, Detroit Urban League, "Summary of Known Improvement Association Activities in Past Two Years 1955–1957," 6, VF, Pre-1960, Box 2, Folder: Community Organization 1950s. For a discussion of the role that improvement associations played in upholding restrictive covenants, see Herman H. Long and Charles S. Johnson, *People vs. Property: Race Restrictive Covenants in Housing* (Nashville, Tenn.: Fisk University Press, 1947), 39–55; for examples of similar associations in Chicago, Baltimore, Washington, D.C., Los Angeles, Houston, Miami, and San Francisco, see Abrams, *Forbidden Neighbors*, 181–90.

12. U.S. Department of Commerce, Bureau of the Census, *U.S. Census of Population and Housing, 1940, Census Tracts Statistics for Detroit, Michigan and Adjacent Area* (Washington, D.C.: U.S. Government Printing Office, 1942), Table 4; U.S. Department of Commerce, Bureau of the Census, *U.S. Census of Population and Housing: 1960, Census Tracts, Detroit, Michigan Standard Metropolitan Statistical Area* (Washington, D.C.: U.S. Government Printing Office, 1962), Table H-1.

13. Kornhauser, *Detroit as the People See It*, 68–69, 75, 77–82. Kornhauser's team interviewed 593 adult men and women randomly selected from all sections of the city. For an elaborate discussion of the survey's methodology, see ibid., Appendix B, pp. 189–96.

14. Kenneth T. Jackson, *Crabgrass Frontier: The Suburbanization of the United States* (New York: Oxford University Press, 1985), 49–52, 117–18; on the desire of immigrants to own their own homes, see John Bodnar, Roger Simon, and Michael P. Weber, *Lives of Their Own: Blacks, Italians, and Poles in Pittsburgh, 1900–1960* (Urbana: University of Illinois Press, 1982), 153–83; a succinct synthesis of literature on homeownership and mobility can be found in Eric H. Monkkonen, *America Becomes Urban: The Development of U.S. Cities and Towns* (Berkeley: University of California Press, 1989), 182–205. On high rates of homeownership among ethnic Detroiters, see Zunz, *The Changing Face of Inequality*, 152–61.

15. The National Council of Churches conducted a census of church membership by county in the mid-1950s. It estimated that 65.9 percent of residents of Wayne County, Michigan, were Roman Catholics. Because so few African Americans were Catholic, the percentage of Wayne County whites who were Catholic was probably significantly higher. See National Council of Churches, Bureau of Research and Survey, "Churches and Church Membership in the United States: An Enumeration and Analysis by Counties, States, and Regions," series C, no. 17 (1957), Table 46; Paul Wrobel, "Becoming a Polish-American: A Personal Point of View," in *Immigrants and*

Migrants: The Detroit Ethnic Experience: Ethnic Studies Reader, ed. David W. Hartman (Detroit: New University Thought Publishing Company, 1974), 187. "Survey of Racial and Religious Conflict Forces," Interviews with Father Constantine Djuik, Bishop Stephen Wozniak, Father Edward Hickey, in CRC, Box 70; Dominic J. Capeci, Jr., *Race Relations in Wartime Detroit: The Sojourner Truth Housing Controversy of 1942* (Philadelphia: Temple University Press, 1984), 77–78, 89–90; Memorandum Dictated by Major Jack Tierney, October 17, 1945, in NAACP, Group II, Box A505, Folder: Racial Tension, Detroit, Mich., 1944–46; Edward J. Hickey to Edward Connor, May 9, 1944, CHPC, Box 41. In April 1948, the pastors of Saint Louis the King Catholic Church and Saint Bartholomew's Catholic Church reportedly urged parishioners to attend City Council meetings to opposed the construction of houses for blacks on a Northeast Side site: See CCR, Part I, Series 1, Box 4, Folder 48–80. Quote on Polish parishes from Mayor's Interracial Committee Minutes, February 19, 1947, 3, ibid., Box 10. On Saints Andrew and Benedict Parish, see Mayor's Interracial Committee Minutes, April 17, 1950, ibid., Part III, Box 25, Folder 25–114. John T. McGreevy, "American Catholics and the African-American Migration, 1919–1970" (Ph.D. diss., Stanford University, 1992) 56–58, 119–20, 159–160; also on the importance of Catholicism in Detroit, see Gerhard Lenski, *The Religious Factor: A Sociological Study of Religion's Impact on Politics, Economics, and Family Life* (Garden City, N.Y.:Doubleday, 1961).

16. See Report on Meeting, Temple Baptist Church, October 25, 1956, and States-Lawn Civic Association, February 14, 1957, DUL, Box 43, Folder A7–13; Metropolitan Tabernacle pamphlets, MDCC, Part I, Box 9, Folder: Civil Rights Activity Feedback and Box 10, Folder: Housing—Homeowners' Ordinance, Friendly; Jim Wallis, "By Accident of Birth: Growing Up White in Detroit," *Sojourners*, June–July 1983, 12–16.

17. Poster, "OPEN MEETING . . . for Owners and Tenants," n.d. [c. 1945], CRC, Box 66, Folder: Property Owners Association; *Action!*, vol. 1 (Feb. 15, 1948), 2; Guyton Home Owners' Association and Connor-East Home Owners Association, leaflets, in SLAA, Folder: 1957–1960; Peck, "Summary of Known Improvement Association Activity;" *Southwest Detroiter*, May 11, 1950, copy in Mayor's Papers (1950), Box 5, Folder: Housing Commission.

18. Kornhauser, *Detroit as the People See It*, 62; "Integration Statement," anonymous letter, n.d., in MDCC, Part I, Box 9. For another example of economically vulnerable workers' insecurity about homeownership, see Bill Collett, "Open Letter to Henry Ford II," *Ford Facts*, September 15, 1951.

19. Kornhauser, *Detroit as the People See It*, 95; quotations from Kornhauser's analysis of survey response patterns.

20. The term "colored problem" was used most frequently by whites to describe black movement into their neighborhoods. See, for example, Property Owners Association flyer, 1945, in CRC, Box 66; *Action!*, vol. 1 (Feb. 15, 1948).

21. Kornhauser, *Detroit as the People See It*, 85, 185.

22. Ibid., 100. It should be recalled that there was already virtually complete residential segregation in Detroit when Kornhauser conducted his survey. In 1950, the index of dissimilarity between blacks and whites (a measure of segregation calculated on the percentage of whites who would have to move to achieve complete racial integration) was 88.8; the index of dissimilarity in 1940 had been 89.9. Respondents

to the survey then supported even stricter racial segregation than already existed. Figures from Karl E. Taeuber and Alma F. Taeuber, *Negroes in Cities: Residential Segregation and Neighborhood Change* (Chicago: Aldine, 1965), 39.

23. Kornhauser, *Detroit as the People See It*, 87, 90, 91. For findings on the racial conservatism of Detroit Catholics that confirm Kornhauser's data, see Lenski, *The Religious Factor*, 65. On the importance of Catholic parish boundaries in preserving the racial homogeneity of a neighborhood and in shaping Catholic attitudes toward blacks, see McGreevy, "American Catholics and African-American Migration" and Gerald Gamm, "Neighborhood Roots: Institutions and Neighborhood Change in Boston 1870–1994," (Ph.D. diss., Harvard University, 1994).

24. Detroit Housing Commission and Work Projects Administration, *Real Property Survey of Detroit, Michigan*, vol. 3 (Detroit: Bureau of Government Research, 1939), maps and data for Area K. As Northwest Side resident Alan MacNichol complained: "I have watched the area within the Boulevard deteriorate into slums as the character of the neighborhood changed, restrictions were broken, and multiple flats came in." *Brightmoor Journal*, December 22, 1949.

25. Outer–Van Dyke Home Owners' Association, "Dear Neighbor," [1948], CCR, Part III, Box 25, Folder 25–94; Interview with Six Mile Road–Riopelle area neighbors in Incident Report, August 30, 1954, DUL, Box 43, Folder A7–13; William Price, "Factors Which Militate against the Stabilization of Neighborhoods," July 3, 1956, ibid., Box 38, Folder A2–17; woman quoted in Lenski, *The Religious Factor*, 66.

26. Longview Home Owners Association poster, n.d., MDCC, Part I, Box 10, Folder: Housing—Homeowners Ordinance—Friendly. Ellipsis in original.

27. For statistics on crime in Detroit, see Robert Conot, *American Odyssey* (New York: William Morrow, 1974), Statistical Appendix.

28. Alex Csanyi and family to Mayor Jeffries, February 20, 1945, Mayor's Papers (1945), Box 3, Folder: Housing Commission 1945. Ellipsis in original. *Home Gazette*, October 25, 1945: copy in CAH; Gloster Current, "The Detroit Elections: A Problem in Reconversion," *Crisis* 52 (November 1945): 319–21; "Program: General Meeting Courville District Improvement Association," April 2, 1948, CCR, Part III, Box 26, Folder 26–4; *Action!* vol. 1 (February 15, 1948); "Report on Formation of Area B Improvement Association," DUL, Box 38, Folder A2–22; Detroit Urban League Housing Committee, Quarterly Report, April–June 1966, ibid., Box 53, Folder A17–1. For other examples of fears of racial mixing, see John Bublevsky, Tom Gates, Lola Gibson, Victor Harbay, and Sally Stretch, "A Spatial Study of Racial Tension or 'The Walls Come Tumbling Down,'" CCR, Part III, Box 13, Folder 13–20; "Report on the Improvement Association Meeting at Vernor School," September 13, 1955, DUL, Box 43, Folder A7–13; Kornhauser, *Detroit as the People See It*, 28, 37, 101–2.

29. The original essays and a complete typescript are in "Compositions—6B Grade—Van Dyke School," CCR, Part I, Series 1, Box 3, Folder: Community Reports—Supplementing. Accompanying the essays cited were drawings and responses to another assignment, intended to foster racial harmony, on "Why Little Brown Ko-Ko is My Friend," based on a short story about a black child. The name Mary Conk is a pseudonym.

30. Henry Lee Moon, "Danger in Detroit," *Crisis* (January 1946): 28. On the expansion of rights language in the New Deal, see Sidney M. Milkis, *The President and the Parties: The Transformation of the American Party System Since the New Deal* (New York: Oxford University Press, 1993), esp. 41–43, 48–50; Alan Brinkley, *The End of Reform: New Deal Liberalism in Recession and War* (New York: Knopf, 1995), 10–11, 164–70. More generally, see Rogers M. Smith, "Rights," in *A Companion to American Thought*, ed. Richard Wightman Fox and James Kloppenberg (Oxford: Blackwell, 1995); and Mary Ann Glendon, *Rights Talk: The Impoverishment of Political Discourse* (New York: The Free Press, 1991).

31. Report of Meeting of the National Association of Community Councils, September 24, 1945, CCR, Part III, Box 20, Folder 20–37; *Michigan Chronicle*, December 4, 1948; *Neighborhood Informer*, December 1949, 1; flyer: "Join the Fight," (November 1945) in CCR, Part III, Box 20, Folder 20–37.

32. *Action!* vol. 2 (March 15, 1948), copy in CCR, Part III, Box 18, Folder 18–29; William Leuffen to Edward Jeffries, March 6, 1945, Mayor's Papers, Box 3, Folder: Housing/Bi-Racial Letters; John Watson to Mayor Jeffries, March 6, 1945, ibid.; William Louks to Edward Connor, CHPC, Box 60, Folder: DREB; Ruritan Park Civic Association, "Dear Neighbor," n.d. [c. 1955], copy in CCR, Part III, Box 25, Folder 25–101.

33. "Survey of Racial and Religious Conflict Forces in Detroit," September 30, 1943, CRC, Box 71.

34. For an early example of collaboration between real estate brokers and neighborhood associations, see *Detroit Tribune*, August 10, 1940; John Feild, "A Study of Interracial Housing Incidents," January 20, 1949, 3, CCR, Part I, Series 1, Box 6, Folder 49–3; on Elsea's affiliation to the Southwest organization, see Zoltan Irshay and Staunton Elsea to Mayor Albert Cobo, February 20, 1951, Mayor's Papers (1951), Box 2, Folder: Civic Associations. Elsea was the owner of Elsea Realty and Investment Company and a regular contributor of a column about the northwest Detroit real estate market in Floyd McGriff's Suburban Newspapers. See for example, *Brightmoor Journal*, May 3, 1956. On Seven Mile–Fenelon, see Capeci, *Race Relations*, 77, 150. For other examples of cooperation between real estate agents and neighborhood groups, see Report on De Witt Clinton Improvement Association, January 28, 1957, DUL, Box 43, Folder A7–13; Clyde V. Fenner, Fenner Real Estate to "Dear Neighbor," April 21, 1959, copy in CCR, Part I, Series 4, Box 3, Folder: Minutes, May–July 1959.

35. "Survey of Racial and Religious Conflict Forces in Detroit," September 30, 1943, CRC, Box 71.

36. In December 1944, the MIC had received reports on six neighborhood improvement associations, only two active in the city. Because the MIC was interested in identifying areas of active racial tension, it overlooked a great number of improvement associations in other parts of the city that were not directly involved in interracial controversies. See "An Analysis of Reports to Date on Housing," December 11, 1944, CCR, Part I, Series 1, Box 1, Folder: Reports 1944–45. Long and Johnson, *People vs. Property*, 41, stated that in 1946 Detroit had fifty registered improvement associations. Quote from Memorandum to the Interracial Committee from George Schermer, Subject: Interracial Trends in Detroit, February 25, 1950, CCR, Part I,

Series 1, Box 11. In 1945, the NAACP cited a *Detroit Free Press* article which claimed that 150 "protective associations" were active in Detroit; see Vose, *Caucasians Only*, 138.

37. Ralph Smith, president of the Michigan Council of Civic Associations, to Mayor Albert Cobo, March 23, 1950, Mayor's Papers (1950), Box 2; Allan MacNichol, Federated Civic Associations of Northwest Detroit, to Mayor Albert Cobo, ibid.; Albert Blewett, secretary, Northeast Council of Home Owners Associations, to Mayor Albert Cobo, December 9, 1950, ibid.; quote, *Brightmoor Journal*, May 3, 1956.

38. *Michigan Chronicle*, December 4, 1948.

39. Annual Dinner Meeting Minutes, May 3, 1948, BEP, Box 1, Folder 1–7; Board Meeting Minutes, May 24, 1948, ibid.

40. Shelley Laffrey to Henry R. Bishop, July 6, 1949, ibid., Box 8, Folder 8–4.

41. *Detroit News*, May 13, 1956.

42. Copy of announcement of Eastside Civic Council Meeting, May 24, 1948, in CRC, Box 66, Folder: Restrictive Covenants.

43. Letter to Fellow Association Member from Palmyra Home Owners' Protective Association, December 3, 1948, ibid.; Southwest Homeowners Association, "Agreement Relating to Sales and Maintenance of Real Property," 1949, in CCR, Part III, Box 25, Folder 25–114; "Meeting of C.O.M.P. (Chicago-Ohio-Meyers-Plymouth)," May 7, 1957, ibid., Folder 25–98; Ruritan Park Civic Association, "Dear Neighbor," 2.

44. "Constitution of Plymouth-Manor Association," CCR, Part III, Box 25, Folder 25–98; see also Richard J. Peck, Community Services Department, Detroit Urban League, "Summary of Known Improvement Association Activities in Past Two Years 1955–1957," 4–5, in VF, Pre-1960, Folder: Community Organization 1950s.

45. Frank Day Smith to Mayor Albert Cobo, January 4, 1951, Mayor's Papers (1951), Box 2, Folder: Complimentary Letters; see also material in ibid., Folder: Civic Associations; *Brightmoor Journal*, January 4, 1951. On Cobo's background see Melvin G. Holli and Peter d'A. Jones, *Biographical Dictionary of American Mayors, 1820–1980* (Westport, Conn.: Greenwood Press, 1981), 69–70.

46. Quote from *Brightmoor Journal*, April 20, 1950. "Some Questions and Answers About Schoolcraft Gardens Cooperative, Inc.," and "History of Schoolcraft Gardens Housing Cooperative," CCR, Part I, Series 1, Box 7, Folder 50–7H; Leonard Farber to Cobo, April 11, 1950, Mayor's Papers (1950), Box 5, Folder: Schoolcraft Gardens. The most complete collection of material on Schoolcraft Gardens, including site plans, promotional literature, and architectural renderings, can be found in RH.

47. Louks to John Kronk, March 14, 1950, and Louks to Cobo, March 23, 1950, in Mayor's Papers (1950), Box 5, Folder: Schoolcraft Gardens.

48. See articles in *Brightmoor Journal*, December 22, 1949, December 29, 1949, January 5, 1950, February 2, 1950, February 9, 1950; *Detroit News*, December 22, 1949.

49. *Brightmoor Journal*, February 9, 1950; *Redford Record*, March 16, 1950. The postcard bombardment, coordinated by the Tel-Craft Improvement Association, was part of the northwest Detroit improvement associations' successful campaign against the construction of the union-supported Schoolcraft Gardens Cooperative.

50. *Detroit Free Press*, March 11, 1950; *Pittsburgh Courier* (Detroit edition), April 1, 1950; Cobo letter to Common Council, March 17, 1950, Mayor's Papers (1950), Box 5, Folder: Housing—Schoolcraft Gardens.

51. John Feild, "Information, Subject: Courville District Improvement Association," May 19, 1950, CCR, Part I, Series 1, Box 7, Folder 50–18. The black family clearly decided to take advantage of the racism and desperation of the Courville residents: they wanted ten thousand dollars for a house that LaVigne claimed was worth only six thousand dollars.

52. Mayor's Interracial Committee, Work Sheet, Case No. 52–16, Opened 6/30/52, Closed 9/23/52, and George Schermer, "Re: Case 52–16, Petition—Courville Improvement Association Members," July 25, 1952, 2, both in CCR, Part I, Series 1, Box 9, Folder 52–16CP. The Marx Street residents were uncertain that city officials would take their petition seriously because they "would not want to alienate the votes of the Negroes." For other examples of petitions, see Memo, Norman Hill to John Laub, August 1, 1955, in Mayor's Papers (1955), Box 4, Folder: CCR; Commission on Community Relations, Minutes, September 19, 1955, ibid.; *Michigan Chronicle*, September 17, 1955.

53. *Brightmoor Journal*, April 5, 1951.

54. Home-Owner Civic and Improvement Associations, Memorandum to Home-Owner Presidents, March 13, 1953, and C. Katherine Rentschler, "Request to Abolish the Present Mayor's Interracial Committee and to Refrain from Authorizing the Proposed 'Commission on Community Relations,' " April 7, 1953, both in Mayor's Papers (1953), Box 1, Folder: Civic Associations; Edgar Frobe to Cobo, July 12, 1951, ibid. (1951), Box 2, Folder: Civic Associations.

55. C. Katherine Rentschler to Common Council, August 17, 1953, ibid. (1953), Box 1, Folder: Civic Associations.

56. *The Detroit Focus*, March–April 1954, DUL, Box 8, Folder 8–1. Interestingly, *The Detroit Focus*, the official newsletter of the Commission on Community Relations, did not mention Laub's civic association background. See also Ed Davis, *One Man's Way* (Detroit: Edward Davis Associates, 1979), 71.

57. In a letter to Father John E. Coogan, a member of the Commission on Community Relations, Cobo stated that Whitby "seems to have been very close to organizations in the past that are not in keeping with our thinking." Albert Cobo to Father John E. Coogan, January 18, 1954, CHPC, Box 71, Folder: Freedom Agenda. Statement of the Detroit Branch NAACP Board of Directors Regarding the City of Detroit Commission on Community Relations, February 22, 1954, DUL, Box 8, Folder 8–1; Minutes, Special Meeting of the Board of Directors, Detroit Urban League, January 27, 1954, ibid., Box 11, Folder 11–18. Wieterson remained a staunch anti–civil rights activist through the 1960s. See Sol P. Baltimore, "Report of Attendance at Meeting of Ruritan Park Neighborhood Association," February 7, 1961, CCR, Part III, Box 25, Folder 25–101.

58. *Michigan Chronicle*, August 13, 1955. See also Detroit Branch NAACP Board of Directors Meeting, Minutes, March 8, 1954, NAACP, Group II, Box C90, Folder: Detroit, 1954.

59. *Michigan Chronicle*, August 27, 1955, November 5, 1955; Davis, *One Man's Way*, 76–77. Davis was ousted from membership in the Detroit Branch NAACP for

refusing to resign from the CCR. See *Detroit Free Press*, October 26, 1955; *Michigan Chronicle*, October 29, 1955.

60. Ibid., September 3, 1955; Davis, *One Man's Way*, 71–74.

61. *Brightmoor Journal*, January 12, 1950, April 21, 1966. See also *Action!* vol. 2 (March 15, 1948).

62. "Your Cooperation Asked" [1959], flyer attached to letter from Robert Hutton to Merrill Lenox, March 31, 1959, MDCC, Part I, Box 10, Folder: Housing—Detroit Real Estate Board; "THIS IS YOUR PERSONAL WAR," and "It's Up to You! HELP CRUSH DICTATOR RULE," RK, Box 6, Folder 6–18.

63. *Detroit News*, July 14, 1963; Statement by Mayor Jerome P. Cavanagh, September 26, 1963, DUL, Box 54, Folder A18–11; Detroit Commission on Community Relations, Annual Report, 1963, RK, Box 2.

64. "Annual Meeting of the Butzel-Guest Property Owners' Association," NAACP, Group III, Box A160, Folder: Housing—Michigan, Detroit, 1956–1964.

65. Glenna Stalcup to *Detroit News*, January 11, 1965; for a discussion of class resentment in other cities, see Ronald P. Formisano, *Boston Against Busing: Race, Class, and Ethnicity in the 1960s and 1970s* (Chapel Hill: University of North Carolina Press, 1991); and James R. Ralph, Jr., *Northern Protest: Martin Luther King, Jr., Chicago, and the Civil Rights Movement* (Cambridge: Harvard University Press, 1993), 114–30.

66. Anonymous letter, n.d., MDCC, Part I, Box 9, Folder: Civil Rights Activity; Albert Nahat to *Detroit News*, May 28, 1964.

67. Exhibit of Petition, Ordinance, and Ballot Proposed By Greater Detroit Homeowner's Council, MDCC, Part I, Box 10, Folder: Housing—Homeowners' Ordinance—Friendly Statements; *Detroit News*, July 1, 1963, July 14, 1963.

68. "Home Owners Ordinance," transcript of WBTM radio discussion with Thomas Poindexter and Leonard Gordon [n.d., c. Summer 1964], in NAACP, Group III (Legal Department Cases), Box 59, Folder *NAACP v. Detroit*—Background Material.

69. *Michigan Chronicle*, September 12, 1964; *East Side Shopper*, September 12, 1964; *Detroit Daily Press*, September 3, 1964; *Brightmoor Journal*, September 24, 1964. (The *Detroit Daily Press* was published in fall 1964 while workers at the *Detroit News* and *Detroit Free Press* were on strike.) "Primary Election Results, City of Detroit, September 1, 1964," NAACP, Group III, Box 59, Folder: *NAACP v. Detroit*—Background Material; *Detroit News*, December 20, 1964.

70. On other anti–open housing laws, see Bruce A. Miller, "Anti–Open Occupancy Legislation: An Historical Anomaly," *University of Detroit Law Review* 43 (December 1965): 165–72; for a summary of legal arguments challenging the constitutionality of the ordinance, see Russell E. Van Hooser, "Subtle, Sophisticated or Simple Minded: Detroit's Home Owners' Ordinance," ibid., 173–202; on Wallace's appeal to white Milwaukee voters, see *New York Times*, April 7, 1964, April 8, 1964. Wallace also won a majority of white voters in Lake County, Indiana, in the 1964 primary, drawing votes from open housing opponents. See ibid., September 17, 1964; Marshall Frady, "Gary, Indiana," *Harpers*, August 1969, 35–45; Jody Carlson, *George C. Wallace and the Politics of Powerlessness: The Wallace Campaigns for the Presidency, 1964–1976* (New Brunswick, N.J.: Transaction Books, 1981), 27–38. On opposition to open housing in Chicago, see Ralph, *Northern Protest*, esp. 92–130.

71. "This is Our Community," n.d. [c. 1945], CHPC, Box 73, Folder: Special Committee on Housing Metropolitan Detroit.

72. On the "constitutive role" of urban space in shaping and reinforcing racial identity, see Robert W. Lake, "Recent Geographic Perspectives on the Social Construction of Race and Place," Paper presented to the American Historical Association Annual Meeting, December 29, 1990, New York; and the seminal article by Kay J. Anderson, "The Idea of Chinatown: The Power of Place and Institutional Practice in the Making of a Racial Category," *Annals of the Association of American Geographers* 77 (1987): 580–98.

Chapter 9
"United Communities Are Impregnable": Violence and the Color Line

1. All quotes and details regarding the Easby Wilson case are drawn from the following sources (unless otherwise noted): "Summary of Facts of Case Involving Mr. Easby Wilson;" UAW Press Release, July 25, 1955; and "Interview: Housing Discrimination" (Mrs. Easby Wilson and Harry Ross), all in UAW-FP, Box 14, Folder 14–8; *Pittsburgh Courier*, June 18, 1955; *Michigan Chronicle*, July 30, 1955; report on racial incident, in DUL, Box 43, Folder A7–13.

2. See, for example, George Schermer, "Re: Case 52–16, Petition—Courville Improvement Association Members," July 25, 1952, 1, CCR, Part I, Series 1, Box 9, Folder 52–16CP. When a white neighbor on the same section of Riopelle Street had offered his house for sale in the fall of 1953, a crowd of five hundred had gathered on the street to protest. See Incident Report, 18176 Riopelle, October 31, 1953, ibid., Folder 53–38; *Pittsburgh Courier*, October 31, 1953; Incident Report, November 7, 1954, DUL, Box 43, Folder A7-13.

3. U.S. Department of Commerce, Bureau of the Census, *U.S. Census of Population and Housing: 1960, Census Tracts, Detroit, Michigan Standard Metropolitan Statistical Area*, Final Report PHC(1)-40 (Washington: U.S. Government Printing Office, 1962) (hereafter cited as *1960 Census*), data for tract 606.

4. "A lot of firefighting": John G. Feild, oral history, December 28, 1967 (Katherine Shannon, interviewer), 11, Civil Rights Documentation Project, MSRC. The finding guide and interview transcript mistakenly spell Feild as Fields. John Feild, "A Study of Interracial Housing Incidents," January 20, 1949, 4, CCR, Part I, Series 1, Box 6, Folder 49–3, identified five "techniques employed" by improvement associations in the 1940s: warnings, street demonstrations, anonymous threats, picketing, and property damage. I have calculated the number of racial incidents through a comprehensive survey of records in CCR, DNAACP, DUL, and Detroit's African American newspapers, *Michigan Chronicle, Detroit Tribune*, and *Pittsburgh Courier* (Detroit edition). The number of reported incidents ranged from seven in 1953 to sixty-five in 1963. Unfortunately the Commission on Community Relations only kept complete data for a limited number of years.

5. An important discussion of territoriality is Gerald D. Suttles, *The Social Construction of Communities* (Chicago: University of Chicago Press, 1972). Suttles's discussion of defended neighborhoods is rich in its theoretical implications for studies of neighborhood change. But by building on the ecological model of Chicago School

sociology, Suttles offers too deterministic a model of "invasion" and "succession," ignoring the political and economic determinants of urban transformation. An important revision that has strongly influenced my own work is Gerald Gamm, "City Walls: Neighborhoods, Suburbs, and the American City" (paper presented to the American Political Science Association, New York, September 1994).

6. Arnold Hirsch, *Making the Second Ghetto: Race and Housing in Chicago, 1940–1960* (Cambridge: Cambridge University Press, 1983), 40, calls the 1940s and 1950s in Chicago "an era of hidden violence." The history of racial violence in Detroit is strikingly similar.

7. In a discussion of tactics to mitigate racial tension in the city, the Mayor's Interracial Committee stated that "The Metropolitan Press gives only the briefest and most objective coverage so as to avoid community excitement." See "Report on Meeting," 7, CCR, Part I, Series 1, Box 5, Folder 48–124H.

8. Pioneers Club, Minutes of Meeting, October 21, 1955, William Seabron Papers, Box 4, Folder 4–20, ALUA. The Pioneers Club was an elite black organization founded in the 1950s, bringing together about twenty community leaders to discuss issues of concern to black Detroit, including politics, police-community relations, and housing incidents. The number of racial incidents in 1955 can be found in Detroit Commission on Community Relations, Annual Report, 1957, DUL, Box 8, Folder 8–1. On the Robson case, see *Detroit Free Press*, April 7, 1956. The Robson case gained national attention. See "Buyer Beware," *Time*, April 16, 1956, 24; and "Prejudice is Not Sectional," *Christian Century*, April 18, 1956, 477. In the aftermath of the Robson case, the white dailies began to report racial incidents. For an example of later coverage, see *Detroit Free Press*, June 17, 1957.

9. For one of many examples of growing black skepticism toward city officials, see the cartoon of a club-wielding white "vandal and hoodlum" whom white city officials call "just playful" in *Michigan Chronicle*, September 17, 1955.

10. On the history of the area during the Sojourner Truth controversy, see Dominic J. Capeci, Jr., *Race Relations in Wartime Detroit: The Sojourner Truth Housing Controversy of 1942* (Philadelphia: Temple University Press, 1984); and Chapter 3 above. For a definition of the area, see John Feild, "Special Report, Subject: Opposition to Negro Occupancy in Northeast Detroit," April 28, 1950, CCR, Part I, Series 1, Box 7, Folder 50–18.

11. Detroit Housing Commission and Work Projects Administration, *Real Property Survey of Detroit, Michigan* (Detroit: Detroit Bureau of Governmental Research, 1939), hereafter referred to as *Real Property Survey*, vol. 2, Table P, tracts 603 and 606; John T. McGreevy, "American Catholics and the African-American Migration, 1919–1970" (Ph.D. diss. Stanford University, 1992), 56–58; Archdiocese of Detroit, 1958 Survey of Catholic Population, Summary, Deanery Code 1, AAD; Saint Louis the King, Saint Rita, and Saint Bartholomew Parish Boundary Files, AAD. The Saint Louis the King Parish School more than doubled in size between 1945, when it had only 392 students, and 1957, when it had 856 students. See *Official Catholic Directory, 1945* (Kansas City: Sheed and Ward, 1945) 93; ibid., *1957*, 71, 72, 73.

12. See "Chronological Summary of Incidents in the Seven Mile–Fenelon Area," attached to John Feild, "A Study of Interracial Housing Incidents," January 20, 1949, CCR, Part I, Series 1, Box 6, Folder 49–3, "Chronological Summary of Incidents in the Courville Area," ibid.; Protest of Negro Occupancy at 18087 Shields, ibid., Folder

49–33; John Feild, "Special Report, Subject: Opposition to Negro Occupancy in Northeast Detroit," April 28, 1950, 3–4, ibid., Box 7, Folder 50–18; John Feild, "Special Report, Subject: Negro Occupancy in Northeast Detroit," April 28, 1950, ibid.; "The History of Grixdale Park, 1953–1958: Site Commemoration and Dedication of Grixdale's Historic Preservation Park Ceremonial-Unveiling Observance" (June 9, 1988), 11, copy in Detroit Public Library.

13. Saint Bartholomew's parish boundary, which ran along Seven Mile Road, and Saint Rita's parish boundary, which ran along Dequindre, served as effective racial dividing lines until the mid-1960s, despite the presence of a large black area in Conant Gardens and Grixdale Park, only several blocks away; see Saint Bartholomew's and Saint Rita's Parish Boundary Files, AAD. Saint Rita's was one of the largest and most vital parishes in the city of Detroit, registering 430 marriages, 146 baptisms, and 461 religious instructions. Its parish school had over one thousand children enrolled in 1945 and over eleven hundred in 1957. See *Official Catholic Directory, 1945*, 91, 92, 94; ibid., *1957*, 71, 73. For racial incidents in the area, see MIC Work Sheet, Case No. 52–16, Opened 6/30/52, closed 9/23/52, and George Schermer, "Re: Case 52–16, Petition—Courville Improvement Association Members," July 25, 1952, both in CCR, Part I, Series 1, Box 9, Folder 52–16CP; Incident Report, 960 East Nevada, October 20, 1953; ibid., Folder 53–34; Incident Report, 18176 Riopelle, October 31, 1953, ibid., Folder 53–38; *Pittsburgh Courier* (Detroit edition), October 31, 1953; Incident Report, November 7, 1954, DUL, Box 43, File A7–13; "Summary of Facts of Case Involving Mr. Easby Wilson," UAW Press Release, July 25, 1955; and "Interview: Housing Discrimination" (Mrs. Easby Wilson and Harry Ross), all in UAW-FP, Box 14, Folder 14–8; *Pittsburgh Courier* (Detroit edition), June 18, 1955; *Michigan Chronicle*, July 30, 1955, September 17, 1955; Commission on Community Relations Minutes, May 20, 1957 and June 17, 1957, CCR, Part I, Series 4, Box 2; Case Reports for the Period Oct. 21–Nov. 18, 1957, ibid.; Commission on Community Relations Minutes, September 21, 1959, ibid., Box 3; Commission on Community Relations, Field Division Case Reports, April 22, 1963, ibid., Box 4; Field Division Case Reports, Attached to Commission on Community Relations Minutes, December 16, 1963, ibid.

14. Richard J. Peck, "Summary of Known Improvement Association Activities in Past Two Years, 1955–1957," 3, VF—Pre-1960, Box 2, Folder: Community Organization 1950s; Saint Gregory the Great, Saint Francis de Sales, Saint Brigid, Saint Cecilia, and Saint Luke Parish Boundary Files, AAD; *Real Property Survey* and U.S. Department of Commerce, Bureau of the Census, *U.S. Census of Population, 1950, Census Tract Statistics for Detroit, Michigan and Adjacent Area* (Washington, D.C.: U.S. Government Printing Office, 1952) (hereafter referred to as *1950 Census*), data for tracts 201–3, 261, 263.

15. Peck, "Summary of Known Improvement Association Activities," 1–3; "Report on Ruritan Park Civic Association Meeting," 3, September 20, 1956, DUL, Box 43, Folder A7–13.

16. *Michigan Chronicle*, September 10, 1955; DUL, Box 38, Folder A2–15; for other incidents in the De Witt–Clinton area, see Commission on Community Relations Minutes, November 21, 1960, and February 20, 1961, both in CCR, Part I, Series 4, Box 3; Commission on Community Relations, Field Division, Case Reports, October 15, 1962, in DNAACP, Part I, Box 14, Folder: Commission on Community

Relations; Commission on Community Relations Minutes, May 15, 1963, April 16, 1962, January 21, 1963, April 22, 1963, May 15, 1963, October 15, 1965; all in CCR, Part I, Series 4, Box 4.

17. Ruritan Park residents did not abide by their pledge to stay within the bounds of the law. Peck, "Summary of Known Improvement Association Activities," 3; *Detroit Free Press*, April 7, 1956; "Buyer Beware," *Time*, April 16, 1956, 24. Commission on Community Relations Minutes, July 20, 1959, August 15, 1960, December 19, 1960, February 20, 1961, in CCR, Part I, Series 4, Box 3; CCR Field Division, Case Reports, November 14, 1963, ibid.; Commission on Community Relations, Field Division, Case Reports, June 19, 1961, July 17, 1961, August 11, 1961, August 14, 1961, August 18, 1961, September 18, 1961, October 23, 1961, all in RK, Box 2, Folder 4; *Michigan Chronicle*, June 12, 1961; *Detroit News*, April 6, 1962.

18. Richard J. Peck, "Report on Formation of Area E Improvement Association," 9, DUL, Box 38, Folder A2–22; "Activities Report, February 1–March 1, 1957, Current Status of Property, Cherrylawn Case," 4, ibid.; *Detroit News*, February 25, 1957, March 8, 1957; Saint Cecilia and Saint Luke Parish Boundary Files, AAD; Detroit Urban League Board of Directors, Annual Meeting Minutes, February 28, 1957, Box 11, Folder 11–19; *Michigan Chronicle*, July 22, 1961. Commission on Community Relations Minutes, June 18, 1962, September 16, 1962, CCR, Part I, Series 4, Box 3.

19. *Real Property Survey*, vol. 2, Table P, census tracts 9, 10, 35, 36, 37, 38, 39, 41.

20. My analysis draws from data for all census tracts bounded by Buchanan Street, Grand River Avenue, Brooklyn Avenue, Michigan Avenue, and Maybury Grand. For these boundaries see City of Detroit Interracial Committee, "Demonstrations Protesting Negro Occupancy of Homes, September 1, 1945 to September 1, 1946," (hereafter referred to as "Demonstrations, 1945–1946"), CCR, Part I, Series 1, Box 3. Violent resistance to black movement into the area continued through the late 1940s.

21. Ibid.; John Feild, "Information, Subject: Community Unrest in the Area Surrounding Brooklyn and Spruce Streets," July 28, 1947, CCR, Part I, Series 1, Box 4, Folder 47–56H; George Schermer to Jas. N. McNally, Wayne County Prosecutor, September 16, 1948, ibid., Box 5, Folder 48–125A; John Feild and Joseph Coles, "Report of Incident, Subject: Protest to Negro Occupancy at 3414 and 3420 Harrison Street, August 23, 1948," ibid., Folder 48–124; *Edward R. Brock and Josephine Brock v. Gertrude A. Murphy, Linda Snider, George Alton, et al.*, Opinion 437,575, State of Michigan in the Circuit Court for the County of Wayne in Chancery, NAACP, Group II, Box B133, Folder: Restrictive Covenants, General, Michigan, 1940–1950; John Feild and Joseph Coles, "Report of Incident, Subject: Continuation of Community Opposition to Negro Occupancy at 3103 National and 3414 Harrison," October 20, 1949, CCR, Part I, Series 1, Box 6, Folder 49–41H.

22. On the weakness of institutional affiliations among southern whites, see Cleo Y. Boyd, "Detroit's Southern Whites and the Store-Front Churches," Department of Research and Church Planning, Detroit Council of Churches, 1958, in DUL, Box 44, Folder A8–25. My thinking about the Lower West Side has been influenced by an extremely important historical and ethnographic study of the area, John M. Hartigan, Jr., "Cultural Constructions of Whiteness: Racial and Class Formations in Detroit" (Ph.D. diss., University of California, Santa Cruz, 1995). Hartigan lived in the still racially mixed area and interviewed old-time residents as well as relative newcomers

to the community. On the importance of ethnic affiliation and white identity, see David Roediger, *Towards the Abolition of Whiteness* (London: Verso, 1994), esp. 181–98.

23. Hirsch, *Making the Second Ghetto*, 99; Arnold R. Hirsch, "Massive Resistance in the Urban North: Chicago's Trumbull Park, 1953–1966," *Journal of American History* 82 (1995): 522–50; Gerald Gamm, "Neighborhood Roots: Institutions and Neighborhood Change in Boston, 1870–1994" (Ph.D. diss., Harvard University, 1994); McGreevy, "American Catholics and the African-American Migration"; Kenneth L. Kusmer, *A Ghetto Takes Shape: Black Cleveland, 1870–1930* (Urbana: University of Illinois Press, 1976), 71; Ronald Formisano, *Boston Against Busing: Race, Class, and Ethnicity in the 1960s and 1970s* (Chapel Hill: University of North Carolina Press, 1991), 108–37; Theodore Hershberg, Alan N. Burstein, Eugene P. Ericksen, Stephanie W. Greenberg, and William L. Yancey, "A Tale of Three Cities: Blacks, Immigrants, and Opportunity in Philadelphia, 1850–1880, 1930, 1970," in *Philadelphia: Work, Family, and Group Experience in the Nineteenth Century, Essays Toward an Interdisciplinary History of the City*, ed. Theodore Hershberg (New York: Oxford University Press, 1981), 482; John T. Cumbler, *A Social History of Economic Decline: Business, Politics, and Work in Trenton* (New Brunswick, N.J.: Rutgers University Press, 1989), 153; John F. Bauman, *Public Housing, Race, and Renewal: Urban Planning in Philadelphia, 1920–1974* (Philadelphia: Temple University Press, 1987), 160–64; Kenneth S. Baer, "Whitman: A Study of Race, Class, and Postwar Public Housing Opposition" (Senior honors thesis, University of Pennsylvania, 1994); Charles F. Casey-Leininger, "Making the Second Ghetto in Cincinnati: Avondale, 1925–1970," in *Race and the City: Work, Community, and Protest in Cincinnati, 1820–1970*, ed. Henry Louis Taylor, Jr. (Urbana: University of Illinois Press, 1993), 239–40, 247–48.

24. Incident Report, "Opposition to Negro Occupancy at 15010 Quincy and 15532 Baylis," September 15, 1948, CCR, Part I, Series 1, Box 5, Folder 48–122; NAACP news release, February 20, 1950, enclosed with letter from George Schermer to Mayor Albert E. Cobo, February 22, 1950, Mayor's Papers (1950) Box 5; Incident Report: 15781 Princeton, CCR, Part I, Series 1, Box 7, Folder 50–6; *Pittsburgh Courier* (Detroit edition), February 18, 1950.

25. See data for tracts 170 and 171, and the nearby predominantly black tracts 172 and 173, in U.S. Department of Commerce, Bureau of the Census, *U.S. Census of Population and Housing, 1940, Census Tract Statistics for Detroit, Michigan and Adjacent Area* (Washington, D.C.: U.S. Government Printing Office, 1942); *1950 Census*; *1960 Census*. The FHA made it a policy not to make loans in areas where expressways were to be built, or within three hundred feet of expressway rights-of-way. Hence, the construction of the Lodge further depreciated housing values in the area. See Robert J. Mowitz and Deil S. Wright, *Profile of a Metropolis: A Case Book* (Detroit: Wayne State University Press, 1962), 436.

26. *Real Property Survey*, vol. 2, Table P, tracts 187–88; Sidney Bolkosky, *Harmony and Dissonance: Voices of Jewish Identity in Detroit, 1914–1967* (Detroit: Wayne State University Press, 1991), 185–87, 191.

27. John Feild and Joseph Coles, Report of Incident, Subject: Opposition to Negro Occupancy at 1608 Clairmount, August 15, 1947; Memo to Acting Commanding Officer, Arson Squad, from Sgt. Hobart C. Harris and Det. Josef Van Wie, Arson

Squad, Subject: Incendiary Fire at 1608 Clairmount Ave., August 15, 1947, 9:49 P.M., August 18, 1947; and Memo to Acting Commanding Officer, Arson Squad, from Sgt. Hobart C. Harris and Det. Josef Van Wie, Arson Squad, Subject: Final Progress Report Regarding Incendiary Fire at 1608 Clairmount Ave., August 25, 1947, all in CCR, Part I, Series 1, Box 4, Folder: 47–60H.

28. Feild and Coles, Report of Incident, Subject: Opposition to Negro Occupancy at 1608 Clairmount.

29. Memo to Acting Commanding Officer, Arson Squad, from Sgt. Hobart C. Harris and Det. Josef Van Wie, Arson Squad, Subject: Incendiary Fire at 1608 Clairmount Ave., August 15, 1947, 9:49 P.M., August 18, 1947.

30. "Report on the Findings of the Twelfth Street Survey" (hereafter referred to as "Twelfth Street Survey"), 10, 27, CCR, Part I, Series 1, Box 4, Folder 47–57H.

31. Marshall Field Stevenson, "Points of Departure, Acts of Resolve: Black-Jewish Relations in Detroit, 1937–1962" (Ph.D. diss., University of Michigan, 1988), 61, 66; Gilbert Osofsky, *Harlem: The Making of a Ghetto* (New York: Harper and Row, 1968), 128–31; Hirsch, *Making the Second Ghetto*, 193–94; Kusmer, *A Ghetto Takes Shape*, 163, 170; Gamm, "Neighborhood Roots."

32. "Twelfth Street Survey," 5.

33. David Goldberg and Harry Sharp, "Some Characteristics of Detroit Area Jewish and Non-Jewish Adults," in *The Jews: Social Patterns of an American Group*, ed. Marshall Sklare (Glencoe, Ill.: The Free Press, 1958), 115.

34. Bolkosky, *Harmony and Dissonance*, 97–100, 104, 185–87, 191, 297–310; Mel Ravitz, "Consequences of Discrimination and Exclusion in Housing," February 29, 1960, p. 12, DUL, Box 70, File: General Housing (1).

35. "Let's Think Clearly! A Statement About the Twelfth Street Area by the Jewish Community Council of Detroit" [in English and Yiddish], copy in CCR, Part I, Series 1, Box 4, Folder 47–57H; for an illuminating discussion of black-Jewish relations in Detroit, see Dominic J. Capeci, Jr., "Black-Jewish Relations in Wartime Detroit: The Marsh, Loving, Wolf Surveys and the Race Riot of 1943," *Jewish Social Studies* 47 (1985): 221–42; Bolkosky, *Harmony and Dissonance*, 368–71; for the Twelfth Street area specifically, see Stevenson, "Points of Departure, Acts of Resolve," 335–38; on Detroit Jews' liberal attitudes about civil rights in the 1950s, see Gerhard Lenski, *The Religious Factor: A Sociological Study of Religion's Impact on Politics, Economics, and Family Life* (Garden City, N.Y.: Doubleday, 1961), 65–66, 148.

36. Statistics from *1950 Census*, tracts 187, 188; *1960 Census*, tracts 187, 188.

37. *1950 Census*, tracts 153, 154, 155, 156, 159, 160, 161, 162, 163, 164, 165, 166, 167, 168, 169, 175, 176, 177, 178, 179, 180, 181, 182, 183, 184, 190, 191, 201; *1960 Census*, same tracts, except 176 divided into 176A, 176B, 176C, 176D; *Real Property Survey*, vol. 2, Table P, same tracts as 1950.

38. Miller Homes brochure for Beverly Hills, CHPC, Box 16, Folder: Statements of Availability; on the development of Detroit's suburbs, see *Detroit News*, March 30, 1962; Joe T. Darden, Richard Child Hill, June Thomas, and Richard Thomas, *Detroit: Race and Uneven Development* (Philadelphia: Temple University Press, 1987), 16–21, 29–44, 77–86, 96–106. In 1949, an attempt by an African American to build a home in Lincoln Park led to protests and a City Council hearing over the provision of utilities to the house. See material in CCR, Part I, Series 1, Box 6, Folder 49–27.

For an example of resistance to blacks in Livonia, see *Michigan Chronicle*, October 28, 1961. On subterfuges to avoid restrictive covenants, see Kathy Cosseboom, *Grosse Pointe, Michigan: Race Against Race* (East Lansing: Michigan State University Press, 1972); Rose Kleinman to Edward Rutledge, November 25, 1966, and Pulte Subdivision material, December 7, 1966, RK, Box 1, Folder 1–9.

39. For examples of barriers to black movement into the suburbs, see Paul R. Dimond, *Beyond Busing: Inside the Challenge to Urban Segregation* (Ann Arbor: University of Michigan Press, 1985), 51–56.

40. *Brightmoor Journal*, October 11, 1945; *Neighborhood Informer*, December 1949, 1, 3, copy in UAW-CAP, Box 4, Folder 4–19; Handbill, "Emergency Meeting, March 11, 1950," CCR, Part III, Box 25, Folder 25–107; Ruritan Park Civic Association, "Dear Neighbor," ibid., Folder 25–101.

41. Detroit race relations official Richard Marks used the term "containment" (to describe white resistance to housing integration) in his testimony in the school desegregation case, *Milliken v. Bradley*. See Dimond, *Beyond Busing*, 43–44. For a development of the notion of "domestic containment" (though not applied to race), see Elaine Tyler May, "Cold War, Warm Hearth: Politics and the Family in Postwar America," in *The Rise and Fall of the New Deal Order, 1930–1980*, ed. Steve Fraser and Gary Gerstle (Princeton, N.J.: Princeton University Press, 1988), 153–81.

42. "Demonstrations, 1945–1946," 4.

43. National Association of Community Councils, "To Make a Long Story Short," CCR, Part III, Box 20, Folder 20–37.

44. *Action! The Newsletter of the Courville District Improvement Association*, vol. 1, February 15, 1948, 5–6, CCR, Part I, Series 1, Box 10.; *Michigan Chronicle*, March 6, 1948.

45. *Neighborhood Informer*, December 1949, March 1951, copies in UAW-CAP, Box 4, Folder 4–19; *Brightmoor Journal*, February 10, 1955, March 24, 1955; Richard J. Peck, "Summary of Known Improvement Association Activities in Past Two Years, 1955–1957," 1–2, VF—Pre-1960, Box 2, Folder: Community Organization 1950s; "Report on Ruritan Park Civic Association Meeting," 3, September 20, 1956, DUL, Box 43, Folder A7–13; Richard J. Peck, "Report on Formation of Area E Improvement Association," 9, ibid., Box 38, Folder A2–22; "Activities Report, February 1–March 1, 1957, Current Status of Property, Cherrylawn Case," 4, ibid., Folder A2–23.

46. Detroit Police Department, Special Investigation Squad, Memo from Detective Sergeant Leo Mack and Detective Bert Berry to Commanding Officer, Special Investigation Squad, November 7, 1945, CCR, Part I, Series 1, Box 3, Folder: Incidents Housing 1945.

47. *Michigan Chronicle*, November 6, 1948.

48. Memo, n.d. [c. 1955], DUL, Box 43, Folder A7–13.

49. John Feild, "Special Report, Subject: Opposition to Negro Occupancy in Northeast Detroit," April 28, 1950, 3–4, CCR, Part I, Series 1, Box 7, Folder 50–18.

50. Commission on Community Relations, Field Division, Case Reports, January 21, 1963, CCR, Part I, Series 4, Box 4; see also Memo, Classification: Housing, September 27, 1954, DUL, Box 38, Folder A2–13.

51. *Southwest Detroiter*, May 11, 1950, copy in Mayor's Papers (1950), Box 5, Folder: Housing Commission (2); *Michigan Chronicle*, July 16, 1955; Commission on

Community Relations, Minutes, June 17, 1957, CCR, Part I, Series 4, Box 2; Commission on Community Relations, Field Division Report, February 20, 1961, ibid., Box 3; McGreevy, "American Catholics and the African American Migration," 122.

52. See "Chronological Summary of Incidents in the Seven Mile–Fenelon Area," attached to John Feild, "A Study of Interracial Housing Incidents," January 20, 1949, CCR, Part I, Series 1, Box 6, Folder 49–3, ALUA.

53. Commission on Community Relations, Minutes, September 21, 1959, ibid., Part I, Series 4, Box 3. Nevada marked the boundary of Saint Rita's parish. See Saint Rita's Parish Boundary File, AAD.

54. *Michigan Chronicle*, December 4, 1948; "Demonstrations, 1945–1946": Memorandum J, 31. John Feild, "Special Report, Subject: Opposition to Negro Occupancy in Northeast Detroit," April 28, 1950, 3–4, CCR, Part I, Series 1, Box 7, Folder 50–18.

55. Thomas H. Kleene, "Report of Incident, Subject: Opposition to Negro Occupancy of Dwelling at 4227 Seventeenth Street (Continued)," ibid., Box 5, Folder 48–124H. On Courville, see Incident Report, November 7, 1954, DUL, Box 43, Folder A7–13. James Morris, the real estate broker who had originally called the police to the scene on Woodingham Street, was charged with driving with an expired license. The police, who did nothing to disperse the crowd, responded with remarkable efficiency to a neighbor's complaint that Morris's car was obstructing a driveway, the offense that gave occasion to ask Morris for his license. Another black realtist, John Humphrey, testified in the Detroit school desegregation case *Milliken v. Bradley* that he had suffered harassment by the police when he showed houses in predominantly white neighborhoods. See Dimond, *Beyond Busing*, 50–51. CCR Field Division, Case Reports, September 18, 1961, in RK, Box 2, Folder 4; on Tuller and Cherrylawn, see CCR Field Division, Case Reports, August 11, 1961, October 23, 1961, ibid. See also *East Side Shopper* clipping, n.d. [September 1952], in CCR, Part I, Series 1, Box 9, Folder 52–30; *Michigan Chronicle*, December 4, 1948; "9423 Meyers," Case Reports for Period August 27–September 23, 1957, CCR, Part I, Series 4, Box 2.

56. John Feild and Joseph Coles, "Report of Incident, Subject: Protest to Negro Occupancy at 3414 and 3420 Harrison Street, August 23, 1948," in CCR, Part I, Series 1, Box 5, Folder 48–124; included in the file are Brock's card and the attached notice; see also "Buyer Beware," *Time*, April 16, 1956, 24.

57. Richard J. Peck, "Summary of Known Improvement Association Activity in Past Two Years 1955–1957," 3, in VF—Pre-1960, Box 2, Folder: Community Organization 1950s; see also Report of Second Meeting of Ruritan Park Civic Association, Fitzgerald School, November 29, 1956, DUL, Box 43, Folder A7–13; Commission on Community Relations Minutes, February 18, 1957, CCR, Part I, Series 4, Box 2.

58. Successful purchases include Yorkshire and Evanston (1948), ibid., Series 1, Box 5, Folder 48–120; 7745 Chalfonte and Tracy and Chippewa in 1955, DUL, Box 38, File A2–15; 15550 Robson, *Detroit Free Press*, May 7, 1956; Richard J. Peck, "Summary of Known Improvement Association Activities in the Past Two Years, 1955–1957," pp. 1, 4, in VF—Pre-1960, Box 2, Folder: Community Organization 1950s. Attempts include "Report of Incident: Intimidation of Henry Lyons (Negro) by a White Group at 18680 Caldwell," September 22, 1947, CCR, Part I, Series 1, Box 4, Folder 47–59H; "Protest of Negro Occupancy at 18087 Shields," 1949, ibid.,

Box 6, Folder 49–33; Detroit Police Department Interoffice Memorandum, Subject: Racial Disturbance at 2966 Greyfriars, August 31, 1953, DSL, Box 20, Folder: Racial—Gang Activities and Complaints (2).

59. "Demonstrations, 1945–1946": Memorandum J, 31.

60. Attachment to letter, Miss James, Detroit Branch NAACP, to George Schermer, August 23, 1948, CCR, Part I, Series 1, Box 5, Folder 48–125A; *Michigan Chronicle*, August 21, 1948, August 28, 1948; *Detroit Tribune*, August 28, 1948. On baby carriage protests in New York, see Sylvie Murray, "Suburban Citizens: Domesticity and Community Politics in Queens, New York, 1945–1960" (Ph.D. diss., Yale University, 1994), 317–26. Murray points out that baby buggy parades were not singular events, as the sensational press sometimes portrayed them, but were "part of larger neighborhood protests" (326).

61. *Action!* vol. 1, February 15, 1948; 2–3; *The Civic Voice*, newsletter of the Schaefer-Meyers Property Owners Association, Inc., vol. 2, no. 9 (September 1962), copy in CCR, Part III, Box 25, Folder 25–108. On Catholic women, gender, and family ideology in the postwar era, see Kathryn Johnson, "Creating an American Catholic Identity: The Politics of Family Life in Postwar American Culture" (paper presented to the American Studies Association Annual Meeting, Pittsburgh, November 1995), and Johnson's important dissertation in progress at the University of Pennsylvania. On the family wage, see Martha May, "The Historical Problem of the Family Wage: The Ford Motor Company and the Five Dollar Day," *Feminist Studies* 8 (1982): 399–424; Elizabeth Faue, *Community of Suffering and Struggle* (Chapel Hill: University of North Carolina Press, 1991). On female labor force participation and changing ideas about women and work, see the important article by Susan M. Hartmann, "Women's Work and the Domestic Ideal in the Early Cold War Years," in *Not June Cleaver: Women and Gender in Postwar America*, ed. Joanne Meyerowitz (Philadelphia: Temple University Press, 1994), 84–100.

62. On female labor force participation in Detroit, see Table 9.1 above. There is an enormous literature on female networks in urban America. The work of John R. Logan and Harvey Molotch, *Urban Fortunes: The Political Economy of Place* (Berkeley and Los Angeles: University of California Press, 1987), 106–7, cites recent sociological literature on women's networks in recent America; for a longer-term historical view, see Christine Stansell, *City of Women: Sex and Class in New York, 1780–1860* (New York: Knopf, 1986).

63. Arthur Kornhauser, *Detroit as the People See It: A Survey of Attitudes in an Industrial City* (Detroit: Wayne University Press, 1952), 47, 74; National Association of Community Councils, "All Out, America! United Communities are Impregnable," in CCR, Part III, Box 20, Folder 20–37.

64. Case Report, No. 54, Neighborhood Protest to Sale of House on 13933 Maine Street, ibid., Part I, Series 1, Box 4, Folder 47–54H; "Summary of Facts of Case Involving Mr. Easby Wilson," UAW-FP, Box 14, Folder 14–8; *Detroit News*, February 25, 1957, April 12, 1957. The postwar domestic ideology is best described in Elaine Tyler May, *Homeward Bound: American Families in the Postwar Era* (New York: Basic Books, 1988) and Barbara Ehrenreich, *The Hearts of Men: American Dreams and the Flight from Commitment* (Garden City, N.Y.: Anchor Books, 1982). Women also played an important role in Chicago housing protests: see Hirsch, *Making the Second Ghetto*, 76–78.

65. *Action!*, vol. 1, February 15, 1948, 2. The paucity of names of men involved in protests makes it impossible to determine occupational patterns of protesters. It should be noted that neighborhood associations sometimes used craft union halls for their meetings, but it is unclear from the sources whether or not unions knew of or approved of the nature of the meetings. On the networks that tied together skilled workers, see Chapter 4 above. On the role of masculinity in vigilantism more generally, see Nancy MacLean, *Behind the Mask of Chivalry: The Making of the Second Ku Klux Klan* (New York: Oxford University Press, 1994), 162–65.

66. The window breaking cases are too numerous to list here. On paint bombs, see CCR, Field Division, Case Report, July 17, 1961, RK, Box 2, Folder 4; on painting, see also the discussion of the Easby Wilson case above. On garden trampling, see *Pittsburgh Courier* (Detroit edition), June 28, 1947; Commission on Community Relations, Minutes, May 20, 1957, CCR, Part I, Series 4, Box 2. On the porch incident, see "Demonstrations, 1945–1946," Memoranda A–C, 10–14.

67. John Feild, "Special Report, Subject: Opposition to Negro Occupancy in Northeast Detroit," April 28, 1950, 3–4, CCR, Part I, Series 1, Box 7, Folder 50–18; Incident Report, 5060, 5061, and 5066 Burns, ibid., Box 8, Folder 51–25; *Michigan Chronicle*, April 21, 1951; "Chronology of Incidents in the Joy Road–Cloverlawn Area," July 17, 1961, attached to CCR Meeting Minutes, July 17, 1961, FK, Box 9, Folder 308; CCR, Field Division, Case Reports, October 15, 1962, 3–4, in DNAACP, Part I, Box 14, Folder: CCR; CCR Meeting Minutes, September 16, 1962, CCR, Part I, Series 4, Box 2.

68. In a thorough examination of cases found in the city files, the papers of black organizations, and black newspapers, I have uncovered only three incidents involving attacks on individuals in a housing case. Homer Garr, a resident of 4433 33rd Street, suffered the usual window breaking and vandalism, including the destruction of his garage door. On July 14, 1950, a group of five men attacked Garr while he was taking out his garbage. See "Report on Incident at 4433 33rd Street," CCR, Part I, Series 1, Box 7, Folder 50–21. The NAACP protested to police about the Garr incident: see Edward Turner, president Detroit Branch NAACP, to Mayor Albert Cobo (telegram), May 24, 1950; Edward Turner to Police Commissioner George F. Boos, July 17, 1950; both in Mayor's Papers (1951), Box 6, Folder: NAACP. The second case involved a James Fludd, who assaulted the white owner of a house for sale on Cloverlawn, and attacked a prospective black buyer with a club. See Commission on Community Relations, Field Division, Case Reports, May 15, 1961, CCR, Part I, Series 4, Box 3. The third case involved white neighbors attacking a white man whose mother had listed her home on the 19000 block of Buffalo with a black real estate firm. See Commission on Community Relations, Field Division, Case Reports, October 23, 1961, RK, Box 2, Folder 4. For examples of youth involved in physical violence, none of it clearly related to housing, but much occurring in or near racially changing neighborhoods, see "Summary of Gang and Racial Activities," August 14, 1953, and other materials, in DSL, Box 20, Folder: Racial-Gang Activities (1) and (2). It should be noted that physical violence between blacks and whites occurred in many other settings in the postwar city, mainly brawls outside bars, struggles between white police officers and black civilians, and youth fights in parks and playgrounds. Often, as the reports in the Leonard Papers show, youth brawls were initiated by black youths.

69. "Courville Area—Problems and Needs," October 1946, p. 5, in CCR, Part III, Box 26, Folder 26–4; Commission on Community Relations, Field Division, Case Reports, 8320 Greenlawn, July 17, 1961, RK, Box 2, Folder 4; Commission on Community Relations Minutes, October 15, 1965, CCR, Part I, Series 4, Box 4.

70. *Pittsburgh Courier* (Detroit edition), June 28, 1947.

71. Commission on Community Relations Minutes, April 16, 1962; January 21, 1963; April 22, 1963; October 10, 1965, CCR, Part I, Series 4, Box 4.

72. Commission on Community Relations, Field Division, Case Reports, August 14, 1961, RK, Box 4, Folder 2; *Michigan Chronicle*, August 12, 1961. For other incidents of teenagers singing and chanting, see "Activities Report, February 1–March 1, 1957, Cherrylawn Case," DUL, Box 38, Folder A2–23.

73. "Prejudice is Not Sectional," *Christian Century*, April 18, 1956, 477; Commission on Community Relations, Field Division, Case Reports, August 14, 1961, RK, Box 2, Folder 4.

74. Commission on Community Relations Minutes, January 21, 1963, DNAACP, Part I, Box 21. After an attack on a black family moving onto Nevada Street, white neighbors blamed "children of people from other neighborhoods," despite evidence to the contrary. See *Michigan Chronicle*, September 17, 1955.

75. On fears of juvenile delinquency in the 1950s, see James Gilbert, *A Cycle of Outrage: America's Reaction to the Juvenile Delinquent of the 1950s* (New York: Oxford University Press, 1985); William Graebner, *Coming of Age in Buffalo: Youth and Authority in the Postwar Era* (Philadelphia: Temple University Press, 1990). On the role of teenagers in Chicago antiblack riots, see Hirsch, *Making the Second Ghetto*, 74–75.

76. On the Overton move-in, see John Feild and Joseph Coles, "Report of Incident, Subject: Protest to Negro Occupancy at 3414 and 3420 Harrison Street, August 23, 1948," in CCR, Part I, Series 1, Box 5, Folder 48–124. Jennie Overton's memories of the events are recorded and analyzed in Hartigan, "Cultural Constructions of Whiteness," 98–103. On infrapolitics, see Robin D. G. Kelley, "The Black Poor and the Politics of Opposition in a New South City, 1929–1970," in *The "Underclass" Debate: Views from History*, ed. Michael B. Katz (Princeton, N.J.: Princeton University Press, 1993), 293–333.

77. John Feild, "Information, Subject: Courville District Improvement Association," May 19, 1950, CCR, Part I, Series 1, Box 7, Folder 50–18; Commission on Community Relations, Minutes, November 21, 1960, ibid., Series 4, Box 3; Sol Baltimore, "Report of Attendance at Meeting of Ruritan Park Neighborhood Association," February 7, 1961, ibid., Part III, Box 25, Folder 25–101. In 1962, Mitcham recounted his experience with a blockbusting real estate broker. The hapless agent approached Mitcham's house, and did not recognize him as black through the screen door. He informed the minister that "I ought to sell to him because 'they' are moving in." When Mitcham stepped out onto the porch, "the man blinked and said, 'Oh, you wouldn't be interested.'" *Detroit News*, November 1, 1962.

78. Commission on Community Relations, Minutes, July 17, 1961, FK, Box 9, Folder 308.

79. *1950 Census*, tract 603; *1960 Census*, tracts 603A, 603B.

80. Ibid., data for tracts 604, 605, 606.

81. *Michigan Chronicle*, September 10, 1955; Incident Report, DUL, Box 38, Folder A2–15. *1960 Census*, tract 261; tracts to the east, 170, 171, 172, 173.

82. *1950 Census* and *1960 Census*, tracts 9, 10, 35, 36, 37, 38, 39, 41.

83. *Detroit News*, October 4, 1961.

84. Hirsch, *Making the Second Ghetto*, 40–99.

85. Kenneth T. Jackson, *Crabgrass Frontier: The Suburbanization of the United States* (New York, 1985), esp. 190–218; Patricia Burgess Stach, "Deed Restrictions and Subdivision Development in Columbus Ohio, 1900–1970," *Journal of Urban History* 15 (November 1988): 42–68.

86. Albert Mayer and Thomas F. Hoult, *Race and Residence in Detroit* (Detroit: Urban Research Laboratory, Institute for Urban Studies, Wayne State University, 1962), 2.

87. A superb overview of patterns of racial segregation in Detroit is Donald R. Deskins, Jr., *Residential Mobility of Negroes in Detroit, 1837–1965* (Ann Arbor: Department of Geography, University of Michigan, 1972). For a perceptive discussion of similar patterns nationwide, see Douglas S. Massey and Nancy A. Denton, *American Apartheid: Segregation and the Making of the Underclass* (Cambridge: Harvard University Press, 1993).

88. Reverend Charles W. Butler, "Message to the Open Occupancy Conference," in *A City in Racial Crisis: The Case of Detroit Pre– and Post– the 1967 Riot*, ed. Leonard Gordon (n.p.: William C. Brown Publishers, 1971), 33. For an earlier statement of black suspicion of white homeowners, vandals, and the police, see *Michigan Chronicle*, September 24, 1955.

Conclusion
Crisis: Detroit and the Fate of Postindustrial America

1. The most complete narrative of the Detroit riot is Sidney Fine, *Violence in the Model City: The Cavanagh Administration, Race Relations and the Detroit Riot of 1967* (Ann Arbor: University of Michigan Press, 1988); his bibliography offers a comprehensive overview of journalistic accounts, sociological studies, and other sources on the riot. Detroit was the subject of numerous post-riot studies. See especially *Report of the National Advisory Commission on Civil Disorders* (New York: Bantam, 1968), 84–108. Data from the Detroit riot served as the basis for many of the Kerner Commission's conclusions.

2. John C. Leggett, *Class, Race, and Labor: Working-Class Consciousness in Detroit* (New York: Oxford University Press, 1968), 4–5.

3. Mayor's Committee—Community Action for Youth Reports, Chapter 2: "Target Area Youth: Their Life Style," in DNAACP, Part I, Box 23; on youth unemployment generally, see Fine, *Violence in the Model City*, 72–73, 92.

4. For a detailed development of this argument, see Thomas J. Sugrue, "The Structures of Urban Poverty: The Reorganization of Space and Work in Three Periods of American History," in *The "Underclass" Debate: Views from History*, ed. Michael B. Katz (Princeton, N.J.: Princeton University Press, 1993), 85–117. For figures on joblessness nationwide, see William Julius Wilson, *The Truly Disadvantaged: The Inner City, the Underclass, and Public Policy* (Chicago: University of Chicago Press, 1987), 42; for various cities, see Loic J. D. Wacquant and William Julius Wilson, "The Cost of Racial and Class Exclusion in the Inner City," *Annals of the American Academy of Political and Social Science* 501 (January 1989): 11–14 (on

Chicago); Julie Boatright Wilson and Virginia W. Knox, "Cleveland: The Expansion of a Metropolitan Area and Its Ghettos," Malcolm Wiener Center for Social Policy, John F. Kennedy School of Government, Harvard University, Working Paper Series, No. H-91–8, July 1991, 67–68; Julie Boatright Wilson, "Milwaukee: Industrial Metropolis on the Lake," John F. Kennedy School of Government, Harvard University, Faculty Research Working Paper Series, No. R95–19, April 1995, Section IV, p. 14.

5. *Detroit Free Press*, March 19, 1961.

6. See "Plans for Operation Open Door," RK, Box 5, Folder 5–24; Reports from testers, ibid., Box 8, Folder 8–2.

7. James A. Geschwender, *Class, Race, and Worker Insurgency: The League of Revolutionary Black Workers* (Cambridge: Cambridge University Press, 1977); Dan Georgakas and Marvin Surkin, *Detroit: I Do Mind Dying: A Study in Urban Revolution* (New York: St. Martin's Press, 1975); Heather Ann Thompson, "Auto Workers, Dissent and the UAW: Detroit and Lordstown," in *Autowork*, ed. Robert Asher and Ronald Edsforth (Albany: State University of New York Press, 1995), 181–208.

8. On the changing balance of power in Detroit politics, see J. David Greenstone, "A Report on the Politics of Detroit," unpublished paper, Harvard University, 1961 (in possession of Kresge-Purdy Library, Wayne State University Library, Detroit, Michigan); Dudley Buffa, *Union Power and American Democracy: The UAW and the Democratic Party, 1935–1972* (Ann Arbor: University of Michigan Press, 1984), 140–41; James Q. Wilson, *Negro Politics: The Search for Leadership* (New York: Macmillan, 1960); Fine, *Violence in the Model City*, 3, 6, 16; on Miriani's relationship to white neighborhood groups, see *Small Property Owner*, November 1949, UAW-CAP, Box 5, Folder 5–2.

9. Fine, *Violence in the Model City*, 71–93. *Michigan Labor Market Letter*, December 1964, 14; Ira Katznelson, "Was the Great Society a Lost Opportunity?" in *The Rise and Fall of the New Deal Order, 1930–1980*, ed. Steve Fraser and Gary Gerstle (Princeton, N.J.: Princeton University Press, 1989), 185–211; Thomas F. Jackson, "The State, the Movement, and the Urban Poor: The War on Poverty and Political Mobilization in the 1960s," in Katz, *The "Underclass" Debate* 403–39; Allen Matusow, *The Unraveling of America: A History of Liberalism in the 1960s* (New York: Harper, 1984).

10. Fine, *Violence in the Model City*, especially 95–125, offers an overview of tensions between police and blacks; police brutality was an area of especially great tension in Detroit in the 1960s. On the youthfulness and employment status of rioters, see ibid., 330–34. A sophisticated discussion of the oppositional culture of urban blacks, especially with regard to the police, is Robin D. G. Kelley, "The Black Poor and the Politics of Opposition in a New South City, 1929–1970," in Katz, *The "Underclass" Debate*, 293–333.

11. Not all of the cross burnings were housing related. One cross, for example, was burned in front of the home of Anthony Liuzzo, husband of slain civil rights activist Viola Liuzzo. Other crosses were burned at an Islamic center, in front of a hospital, at the City County building, and at a Catholic convent. Commission on Community Relations Minutes, April 19, 1965, October 15, 1965, in CCR, Part I, Series 4, Box 4; Fine, *Violence in the Model City*, 133.

12. *New York Times*, October 6, 1968, May 18, 1972, June 12, 1972; United Automobile Workers, Straw Poll Returns, UAW-WPR, Box 436, Folder 7; County of Wayne, Board of Election Canvassers, "Statement of Election Returns, General

Election, November 3, 1968," and County of Wayne, Board of County Canvassers, "Statement of Election Returns, Presidential Primary Election, May 16, 1972," microfilm in Office of the Wayne County Clerk, City County Building, Detroit, Michigan. There are no histories of Wallace supporters in the north. The best overview, drawing from survey data, is Jody Carlson, *George C. Wallace and the Politics of Powerlessness: The Wallace Campaigns for the Presidency, 1964–1976* (New Brunswick, N.J.: Transaction Books, 1981); for local case studies, see Jefrey Ian Pollock, "The Appeal of George Corley Wallace in the Election of 1968: A Case Study of Philadelphia" (Senior honors thesis, University of Pennsylvania, 1993); C. T. Husbands, "The Campaign Organizations and Patterns of Popular Support of George C. Wallace in Wisconsin and Indiana in 1964 and 1968" (Ph.D. diss., University of Chicago, 1972).

13. Fine, *Violence in the Model City*, 133, 456; Jeffrey Mirel, *The Rise and Fall of an Urban School System: Detroit, 1907–1981* (Ann Arbor: University of Michigan Press, 1993); Paul R. Dimond, *Beyond Busing: Inside the Challenge to Urban Desegregation* (Ann Arbor: University of Michigan Press, 1985), 21–118; Eleanor P. Wolf, *Trial and Error* (Detroit: Wayne State University Press, 1981).

14. June Tony Zimeski and Michael Kenyon, "Where the Racism Really Is—In the Suburbs," *Detroit Scope*, August 31, 1968; Thomas J. Anton, *Federal Aid to Detroit* (Washington, D.C.: The Brookings Institution, 1983), 11; "HUD's Failure in Warren, Michigan," in *Suburbia in Transition*, ed. Louis H. Masotti and Jeffrey K. Hadden (New York: New Viewpoints, 1974), 154–57; Joe T. Darden, Richard Child Hill, June Thomas, and Richard Thomas, *Detroit: Race and Uneven Development* (Philadelphia: Temple University Press, 1987), 137–46; Fine, *Violence in the Model City*, 148–49.

15. Jody Carlson, *George C. Wallace and the Politics of Powerlessness* (New Brunswick, N.J.: Transaction Books, 1981); Thomas Byrne Edsall and Mary D. Edsall, *Chain Reaction: The Impact of Race, Rights, and Taxes on American Politics* (New York: Norton, 1991), 27–28, 181–84, 191; Stanley Greenberg, *Middle Class Dreams: The Politics and Power of the New American Majority* (New York: Times Books, 1995), esp. 23–54, 215–30.

16. Matusow, *The Unraveling of America*, 438.

17. Jonathan Rieder, "The Rise of the 'Silent Majority,'" in Fraser and Gerstle, *The Rise and Fall of the New Deal Order*, 254.

18. Edsall and Edsall, *Chain Reaction*, 77. Similar views pervade the scholarly and popular literature on the 1960s. See also Frederick F. Siegel, *The Troubled Journey: From Pearl Harbor to Ronald Reagan* (New York: Hill and Wang, 1983), esp. 152–215; Jim Sleeper, *The Closest of Strangers: Liberalism and the Politics of Race in New York City* (New York: Norton, 1990); Jonathan Rieder, *Canarsie: The Jews and Italians of Brooklyn Against Liberalism* (Cambridge: Harvard University Press, 1985); Edward G. Carmines and James A. Stimson, *Issue Evolution: Race and the Transformation of American Politics* (Princeton, N.J.: Princeton University Press, 1989). Important critical reviews of this literature include James R. Grossman, "Traditional Politics or the Politics of Tradition?" *Reviews in American History* 21 (1993): 533–38; Adolph Reed and Julian Bond, "Equality: Why We Can't Wait," *The Nation*, December 9, 1991, 723–37; and Adolph Reed, "Review: Race and the Disruption of the New Deal Coalition," *Urban Affairs Quarterly* 27 (1991): 326–33.

19. See Arnold R. Hirsch, "Chicago: The Cook County Democratic Organization and the Dilemma of Race, 1931–1987," in *Snowbelt Cities: Metropolitan Politics in the Northeast and Midwest since World War II*, ed. Richard M. Bernard (Bloomington: Indiana University Press, 1988), 63–90; Richard M. Bernard, "Milwaukee: The Death and Life of a Midwestern Metropolis," ibid., esp. 173–75. Especially perceptive on the rhetoric of Wallace, Nixon, Agnew, and Reagan is Michael Kazin, *The Populist Persuasion: An American History* (New York: Basic Books, 1995), 221–66.

20. On the growing influence of suburbs in American politics, see Margaret Weir, "Urban Poverty and Defensive Localism," *Dissent* (Summer 1994), 337–42; and William Schneider, "The Suburban Century Begins," *Atlantic*, July 1992, 33–44; Raymond A. Mohl, "Shifting Patterns of American Urban Policy Since 1900," in *Urban Policy in Twentieth-Century America*, ed. Arnold R. Hirsch and Raymond A. Mohl (New Brunswick, N.J.: Rutgers University Press, 1993), 1–45; Loic J. D. Wacquant, "Urban Outcasts: Stigma and Division in the Black American Ghetto and the French Urban Periphery," *International Journal of Urban and Regional Research* 17 (1993): 366–83.

21. On the continuing deindustrialization of Detroit, see Darden et al., *Detroit*, 11–65; Sharon Zukin, *Landscapes of Power: From Detroit to Disney World* (Berkeley: University of California Press, 1991), 103–33; Richard Child Hill, "Transnational Capitalism and Urban Crisis: The Case of the Auto Industry and Detroit," in *Cities in Recession*, ed. Ivan Szeleyni (Beverly Hills, Calif.: Sage Publishers, 1984). For similar patterns elsewhere, see John A. Kasarda, "Urban Industrial Transition and the Underclass," *Annals of the American Academy of Political and Social Science* 501 (January 1989): 26–47; William Julius Wilson, *The Truly Disadvantaged: The Inner City, the Underclass, and Public Policy* (Chicago: University of Chicago Press, 1987); David Bensman and Roberta Lynch, *Rusted Dreams: Hard Times in a Steel Community* (New York: McGraw-Hill, 1987). On the growth of contingent work, see Chris Tilly, *Short Hours, Short Shrift: Causes and Consequences of Part-Time Work* (Washington, D.C.: Economic Policy Institute, 1990); Polly Callaghan and Heidi Hartmann, *Contingent Work: A Chart Book on Part-Time and Temporary Employment* (Washington, D.C.: Economic Policy Institute, 1991).

22. For similar residential patterns in Washington, D.C., see Dennis E. Gale, *Washington, D.C.: Inner-City Revitalization and Minority Suburbanization* (Philadelphia: Temple University Press, 1987), 111–21; Roger Waldinger and Thomas Bailey, "The Continuing Significance of Race: Racial Conflict and Racial Discrimination in Construction," *Politics and Society* 19 (1991): 291–323. A superb overview is Philip Moss and Chris Tilly, *Why Black Men Are Doing Worse in the Labor Market: A Review of Supply-Side and Demand-Side Explanations* (New York: Social Science Research Council, 1991).

23. Diana Pearce, "Gatekeepers and Homeseekers: Institutionalized Patterns in Racial Steering," *Social Problems* 26 (1979): 325–42, is a comprehensive study of real estate practices in metropolitan Detroit. Reynolds Farley, Charlotte Steeh, Tara Jackson, Maria Krysan, and Keith Reeves, "Continued Racial Residential Segregation in Detroit: 'Chocolate City, Vanilla Suburbs' Revisited," *Journal of Housing Research* 4, no. 1 (1993): 1–38, discuss white attitudes about racial integration and note the importance of memories of racial hostility in shaping black residential choices. On patterns of segregation nationwide, see Douglas S. Massey and Nancy A. Denton,

American Apartheid: Segregation and the Making of the Underclass (Cambridge, Mass.: Harvard University Press, 1993); Arnold R. Hirsch, "With or Without Jim Crow: Black Residential Segregation in the United States," in Hirsch and Mohl, *Urban Policy*, 65–99; Gary Orfield, "Ghettoization and Its Alternatives," in *The New Urban Reality*, ed. Paul E. Peterson (Washington, D.C.: The Brookings Institution, 1985), 161–93. On class segregation, see Wilson, *The Truly Disadvantaged*, 46–62; and Kenneth L. Kusmer, "African Americans in the City Since World War II: From the Industrial to the Post-Industrial Era," *Journal of Urban History* 21 (1995): 479–81. In an important article on Buffalo, Henry Louis Taylor, Jr. suggests that class divisions grew deeper within Buffalo's East Side, but that there was not a middle-class exodus comparable to that of cities like Chicago and Detroit. See Henry Louis Taylor, Jr., "Social Transformation Theory, African Americans, and the Rise of Buffalo's Post-Industrial City," *Buffalo Law Review* 39 (1991): 594–600.

24. For an overview of patterns in Detroit and other cities, see Paul Jargowsky and Mary Jo Bane, "Neighborhood Poverty: Basic Questions," in *Inner City Poverty in the United States*, ed. Laurence E. Lynn, Jr., and Michael G. H. McGeary (Washington, D.C.: National Academy Press, 1990), 16–67.

25. Ze'ev Chafets, *Devil's Night and Other True Tales of Detroit* (New York: Random House, 1990), 177. Chafets, like most recent commentators on the urban crisis in Detroit, sees 1967 as the turning point in the city's history. For a much richer journalistic account, see Robert Conot, *American Odyssey* (New York: William Morrow, 1974). On redevelopment plans in Detroit since the riot, see Darden et al., *Detroit*, 44–65, 175–200; Anton, *Federal Aid to Detroit*, 44–49; Jeanie Wylie, *Poletown: Community Betrayed* (Urbana: University of Illinois Press, 1989); David Fasenfest, "Community Politics and Urban Redevelopment: Poletown, Detroit, and General Motors," *Urban Affairs Quarterly* 22 (1986): 101–23; John Bukowczyk, "The Decline and Fall of a Detroit Neighborhood: Poletown v. General Motors and the City of Detroit," *Washington and Lee University Law Review* 41 (1984): 49–76; Dan Luria and Jack Russell, *Rational Reindustrialization: An Economic Redevelopment Plan for Detroit* (Detroit: Widgetripper Press, 1981); Richard Child Hill, "Economic Crisis and Political Response in the Motor City," in *Sunbelt/Snowbelt: Urban Development and Regional Restructuring*, ed. Larry Sawers and William K. Tabb (New York: Oxford University Press, 1984), 313–38. On current responses to Detroit's economic and social problems, see the interviews in Robert M. Mast, ed., *Detroit Lives* (Philadelphia: Temple University Press, 1996); "Hope for Motown," *Utne Reader*, May/June 1994, 16–17, 20.

Index

A&P stores, 113
Adler, Rabbi Morris, 192
African Americans: businesses owned by, 47,
    188–89, 195, 269; class divisions among,
    12, 41, 176, 180, 188–89, 198–207, 269,
    336–37; discrimination against (see em-
    ployment discrimination); housing
    discrimination; disproportionate impact
    on, of industrial decline, 144–52, 155, 176–
    77; migration of, to Detroit, 19, 23, 29–30,
    37 (see also migrants, black); neighbor-
    hoods of (see black enclaves; black inner-
    city neighborhoods); proportion of, in
    Detroit population, 23, 265–66; stereotypes
    of, 8–9, 93, 100, 113, 120–21, 216–18, 229;
    types of jobs held by, 25–26, 28, 95–119,
    275–78; young, 146–47, 168–69, 261, 264
affirmative action, 4, 267–69
"affluent society," 6, 143
Agnew, Spiro, 266–67
Akron, 13, 227–28
Allan, Finlay C., 85
American Civil Liberties Union, 171
American Federation of Labor (AFL), 85, 117
Americanism, 7, 9, 79, 212, 220
American Motors, 136, 163
anticommunism: impact of, on civil rights
    groups, 80–82, 156, 170–73, 225–26; and
    stifling of dissent, 7, 156
antiradicalism. See anticommunism
anti-Semitism, 193, 248
apartment buildings, 21, 51–52, 54–55. See
    also public housing
apprenticeship programs, 102–3, 116–17; ex-
    clusion of most black workers from, 102–3,
    109, 116–17
Archdiocesan Council for Catholic Women,
    192
Arden Park neighborhood, 203–4
Area Redevelopment Acts, 155
arson, 253
Asian Americans, 13, 212
Association of Catholic Trade Unionists, 171
Austin, Richard, 266
automation, 130–38, 163–64; and black work-
    ers, 165, 167–68, 275; and job loss, 132–35;

unions' responses to, 134–35, 158, 163–64;
    as weapon against labor, 130–33
automobile industry, 17–19, 126, 136, 163;
    automation in, 130–38, 158, 163; black
    workers in, 25–27, 90–92, 95–105; decen-
    tralization of, 128–29, 135–38, 140, 157–
    62; declining employment in, in Detroit,
    125–26, 128–29, 132–38, 142, 144, 146;
    increased overtime in, 141–43. See
    also American Motors; Chrysler Corpora-
    tion; Ford Motor Company; General
    Motors Corporation; Hudson Motors;
    Packard Motors
Avery, Burneice, 39, 66, 115

Bagley neighborhood, 204, 206
Baltimore, 3, 29, 127–28, 228
banks, 34, 36, 46–47, 196
Barthwell, Sidney, 189, 204
Belle Isle, 29
Bentley, Harry R., 130
Berge, Frank, 79
Big Bear supermarkets, 113
Birmingham, Michigan, 203, 245
Bixby, H. G., 138–40
Black, Harold, 44
Black Bottom area, 23, 36, 49
black bourgeoisie, 188–89, 204
black enclaves, 37–41, 198–99; on the West
    Side, 35, 38, 47, 198–99. See also Conant
    Gardens; Eight Mile–Wyoming area
black inner-city neighborhoods, 36–37;
    destruction of, in urban redevelopment,
    36, 47–51, 294–95; deterioration of
    housing in, 9, 35–37, 55, 183, 216–17; flight
    of better-off blacks from, 37–38, 188–90;
    high rents in, 34, 37, 50, 53–54; high turn-
    over in, 54–55, 198; institutions in, 36–37,
    47, 206–7, 338–39; overcrowding in, 33,
    38–39, 42–43, 53–54, 72, 188; public hous-
    ing in, 50, 86
Bledsoe, Geraldine, 25
"blockbusting," 46, 194–97
Bloomfield Hills, 203, 245
Boggs, James, 27, 190
Borden Dairies, 175

PRINCETON STUDIES IN AMERICAN POLITICS:
HISTORICAL, INTERNATIONAL, AND COMPARATIVE PERSPECTIVES